Moral Issues
in Global Perspective

Moral Issues in Global Perspective

second edition

Volume III: Moral Issues

edited by

Christine M. Koggel

broadview press

Library and Archives Canada Cataloguing in Publication

Moral issues in global perspective / edited by Christine M. Koggel. — 2nd ed.

Includes bibliographical references.
Contents: v. 1. Moral and political theory — v. 2. Human diversity and equality — v. 3. Moral issues.
ISBN 1-55111-747-9 (v. 1).—ISBN 1-55111-748-7 (v. 2).—ISBN 1-55111-749-5 (v. 3)

1. Social ethics—Textbooks.   I. Koggel, Christine M.

HM665.M67 2006   170   C2005-907079-X

Broadview Press is an independent, international publishing house, incorporated in 1985. Broadview believes in shared ownership, both with its employees and with the general public; since the year 2000 Broadview shares have traded publicly on the Toronto Venture Exchange under the symbol BDP.

We welcome comments and suggestions regarding any aspect of our publications—
please feel free to contact us at the addresses below or at broadview@broadviewpress.com.

North America
Post Office Box 1243, Peterborough, Ontario, Canada K9J 7H5
Post Office Box 1015, 3576 California Road, Orchard Park, NY, USA 14127
Tel: (705) 743-8990; Fax: (705) 743-8353;
email: customerservice@broadviewpress.com

UK, Ireland, and continental Europe
NBN International, Estover Road, Plymouth PL6 7PY UK
Tel: 44 (0) 1752 202300   Fax: 44 (0) 1752 202330
email: enquiries@nbninternational.com

Australia and New Zealand
UNIREPS, University of New South Wales
Sydney, NSW, 2052 Australia
Tel: 61 2 9664 0999; Fax: 61 2 9664 5420
email: info.press@unsw.edu.au

www.broadviewpress.com

Broadview Press gratefully acknowledges the financial support of the Government of Canada through the Book Publishing Industry Development Program for our publishing activities.

Copy-edited by Betsy Struthers.

Typesetting and assembly: True to Type Inc., Mississauga, Canada.

PRINTED IN CANADA

For Kyle, Dillon, and Molly

Contents

PREFACE

A central question in ethics is: how should we live our lives and interact with others? Exploring answers to this question in the context of the international community or "global village" in which we live was the prime motivation for putting out the First Edition of this anthology. This motivation persists into the production of this Second Edition, now expanded into three volumes.

The collection works with the idea that we live in an increasingly interdependent world, one in which features and factors of globalization shape the lives and experiences of people no matter who they are or where they live. "Globalization" is a concept used increasingly in a variety of contexts and in ways that are both positive and negative: in discussions of markets, international relations, economic development, human rights, education, health care, the environment, labor, media, and information technology. Globalization can be characterized as increased flows — of people, information, technology, consumer goods, and trade — across ever more permeable borders. Globalization in the form of increased flows of information, for example, has broadened our exposure to beliefs and values very different from our own and allowed us to communicate instantaneously with people from faraway places. The almost limitless access to information through television and the Internet not only makes it possible for us to learn about others, but it also makes it easy to praise or condemn people, policies, practices, values, beliefs, and political structures in other places. Globalization has universalized human rights discourse from its roots in liberal theory and has given a prominent place to international organizations that monitor human rights violations. An important effect of globalization has been to intensify our awareness of the devastating ways in which policies and practices in one area may affect not only the livelihood and choices of people in other areas, but the world as a whole.

Increased globalization not only means that no community is isolated from the world's gaze and influence, but also that virtually no communities remain unaffected by the influx of people from other places. The latter describes the phenomenon of multiculturalism: difference and diversity within a community of people who have various beliefs. Multiculturalism means that we need not look across borders to find instances of discrimination against and unequal treatment of people identified as different. It calls on us to examine the ways in which our embeddedness in particular contexts and practices shapes our perceptions of and interactions with those different from ourselves. Multiculturalism opens the door to examining relationships and to thinking critically about our interactions with others. In making it possible to scrutinize beliefs and practices different from our own, globalization and multiculturalism ask us to critically examine the judgments we render about others both across and within borders.

These facts and effects of globalization and the related phenomenon of multiculturalism raise questions that have become increasingly pressing to moral inquiry. This anthology assumes that these questions are relevant to the central question of how we live our lives and interact with others. Does our situatedness in a Western liberal democratic society generate problematic assumptions about what human beings are like; what we need to flourish; and what rights and responsibilities we hold? Might our commitment to the notion of the primacy of individual liberty rights change if we learned about commitments to rights different from these in contexts, including liberal societies, outside the U.S.? Would our understanding of what constitutes just social and political structures change if we became aware of theories that defend alternative structures, particularly by authors from societies with structures different from our own? Can social relations and policies in other contexts give us insights into ways to approach moral issues of inequality and discrimination in our own context? Does our understanding of the right way to live and of how to determine morally right action reflect the biases of Western liberal beliefs and values? Does the impact of policies in one society on the welfare and well-being of members of another society hinder us from acquiring an adequate understanding of moral, social, and political issues and of how to resolve them? In general, does our view of moral issues change when we turn our attention to the global context?

Most contemporary collections on moral issues make it difficult to raise these questions. They tend to feature the narrow band of agreements and disagreements within Western liberal theory and practice. As with the First Edition, this Second Edition of *Moral Issues in Global Perspective* seeks to challenge our thinking about morality and moral issues as it has been shaped by the Western liberal tradition and to extend the inquiry beyond the context of North America and specifically that of the U.S. It includes analyses of moral issues by both liberal and non-liberal theorists from around the world, many of whom question predominant understandings of human rights, justice, democracy, social welfare, and development. It includes critiques of traditional accounts of moral theory, rights, justice, and democracy, critiques that examine whether these accounts ignore or fail to address the discriminatory treatment of disadvantaged groups inside and outside the borders of countries. It incorporates work by race, class, feminist, and disability theorists that challenges traditional moral and political theory and opens up new perspectives on issues such as reproduction, euthanasia, censorship, animal rights, and environmental ethics.

This collection incorporates these kinds of perspectives into each chapter, more so than is the case with many of the textbooks on practical ethics that are currently available in North America. So, for example, we are asked to confront challenges by non-Western writers that liberal beliefs about the importance of individual rights to free speech and property may reflect a discourse about rights that has little or no application in places with traditions that uphold community values, or with pasts they want to change, or in countries struggling to achieve stability, let alone economic viability. We may need to question our assumptions about gender when we examine the role and activities of women in places like Indonesia. We are asked to think about how issues of reproductive health may be shaped differently in a context like Argentina where a strong tradition of Catholicism pulls against the interests and aspirations of women. This expanded Second Edition gives testimony to the importance of these issues and to the approach to ethics that it adopts.

Even greater efforts were made with this new edition than with the previous to represent the range of theories and the work of theorists from around the world. In its current three volumes, this anthology collects the work of more than 80 authors, thus presenting a broad range of views from all over the world. In doing so, it attempts to show the complexity of moral issues when examined in a global context and the richness and diversity of writing on these issues by authors outside American and Western thought more generally. Of course, one cannot move in new directions without a base in the familiar. Many of the readings are intended to reflect not only the wide spectrum of views among liberal theorists, but also the discussion of moral issues as it takes place in North America. With this background, we can then take up the two challenges of globalization and multiculturalism. A global context of increased awareness of the impact of globalization on the environment, levels of poverty, prospects for human flourishing, and indigenous cultures challenges the notion that answers to complex moral issues can be found by focusing only on Western liberal values in a North American context. *Moral Issues in Global Perspective* stands as an illustration of how the field of moral inquiry is greatly enriched when we turn our attention to disenfranchised voices within particular societies and to contexts outside North America.

This expanded Second Edition is divided into three separate volumes, each of which corresponds roughly with the three parts of the single volume First Edition. Volume I covers kinds of moral and political theory and topics related to these. The first four chapters in Volume I present traditional and contemporary theories of morality and of concepts such as human rights, justice, and democracy. These concepts have been central to Western liberal theory. The fundamental teaching of classical liberal theory that each human being has equal moral value and deserves equal concern and respect has become the foundation for theories about how societies ought to be structured to ensure equal treatment, for accounts of what human beings need in order to flourish, and for attempts to formulate universal human rights. Yet, liberal theory has been criticized for its excessive individualism, an individualism that critics take to be apparent in the policies, structures, and kinds of human rights that liberals tend to defend. This criticism moves to center stage when we turn to a global context and examine theorists who challenge the very framework of individual freedom that dominates accounts of human rights and theories of justice and democracy in Western liberal societies. The final two chapters in Volume I apply insights from these theories to concrete contexts, ones in which awareness of histories and social conditions in specific parts of the world sometimes support and sometimes challenge understandings of justice, human rights, and democracy. Chapter Six applies these insights to the specific and timely issue of war and terrorism.

Volume II continues the exploration of the relevance of globalization and multiculturalism to moral inquiry by zeroing in on accounts of human nature and the moral questions raised by issues of diversity and difference among human beings. Are we all the same? Can we provide a list of essential human functions and capabilities that generates moral imperatives for what it is for human beings to flourish no matter who they are or where they live? Do we operate with a set of assumptions about human beings that result in stereotypes about difference and critical judgments about other people's beliefs and practices? Do facts of discrimination and inequality both across and within borders shape perceptions, self-perceptions, and opportunities in ways that call for international policies to eliminate the resulting injustices? Is it possible to understand the perspectives and life experiences of members of disadvantaged groups from a vantage point of privilege or to speak for them when making judgments about them? Answers to these sorts of questions in the theory chapter that opens Volume II are then followed by several chapters in which discrimination on the grounds of race and ethnicity, gender, sexual orientation, disability, and poverty are examined. These chapters explore moral issues raised by relationships that are shaped by the different histories, identities, and levels of power of people within and across societies. The issues in this volume cut to the heart of the central question of how to interact with others in morally responsible ways.

The relationship of the individual to society tends to be central to most collections about moral issues. Volume III explores the relationship between the individual and society by surveying some of the practical issues that have acquired particular prominence in Western liberal contexts: individual choice and social responsibility at the beginning and end of human life, the value of liberty and its connection to pornography and hate speech, and how we live and interact with animals and the environment. Liberal theory has tended to examine these issues in terms of the conflict between the individual and society: what, if any, restrictions to individual freedom are permissible and what sorts of moral justifications can be provided for using the power of the state to limit individual freedom? The readings in the chapters of Volume III represent both defenses and critiques of this characterization of how practical moral issues need to be resolved, and they open up inquiry into how moral issues are impacted by a global context. Do debates about issues such as reproduction, euthanasia, health care, pornography, hate speech, animals, and the environment change when we learn about concrete practices in non-Western contexts or in places outside North America? Do the policies in place for dealing with these issues in particular contexts have a differential impact on members of traditionally disadvantaged groups?

The three volumes can be used separately or as a whole. Various threads related to globalization and multiculturalism weave their way through all the volumes and allow issues to cross over from one volume to the next. For example, issues of discrimination on the basis of gender and race are covered explicitly in Volume II but can be found in the examination of reproductive issues, pornography, and hate speech in Volume III. Tendencies of ethnocentrism that result in judgments by developed countries about practices and beliefs in developing countries are explored in the conceptions of human rights, justice, and democracy discussed in Volume I and also in the discussions of health care, the environment, and pornography in Volume III. Discussions in Volume I of the significance of historical and cultural contexts in the shaping of beliefs, practices, and values are revisited in Volume II in the examination of discrimination and unequal relations of power between peoples within a country and across the borders of countries. And arguments by theorists in Volume I that defend particular accounts of morally right action or conceptions of justice are applied to specific moral issues in Volume III. While the volumes may have distinctive topics and titles, the issues and themes intersect and are interconnected.

The revision and expansion of the First Edition would not have been possible without the help and support of many people along the way. I want to begin by thanking all the authors who granted permission to print their work in the collection, including both the authors who were first time contributors to the First Edition and whose work reappears in this Second Edition and the authors whose work appears for the first time in this Second Edition. Don LePan, the long time President of Broadview Press who stepped down in 2004, was committed to the project from its earliest stages and has provided encouragement and support throughout and into the preparation of this Second Edition. The torch has been passed to Michael Harrison, someone as committed to supporting authors and their work. Broadview people are wonderful to work with and their competence and care are greatly appreciated. The Production Editors, Barbara Conolly, Jennifer Bingham, and Judith Earnshaw handled this large and complex project with professionalism and enthusiasm throughout. Tania Terrien, Jennifer Findlay, Tammy Roberts, and Joelle Dunne dealt with the many details of permissions and my questions of process and procedures along the way. Betsy Struthers edited each of the volumes in a way that made my job easier and the production process smoother. I would like to thank several anonymous reviewers of early versions of the Second Edition for their helpful suggestions concerning the organization, topics, and readings. A special thanks goes to Keith Burgess-Jackson, whose advice and impressive knowledge of the extensive literature in moral theory and practical issues was as important to the Second Edition as it was to the First.

Countless people took an interest in this project and discussions with them sometimes provided valuable advice and sometimes unearthed readings that have turned out to be key pieces in both the First and Second Editions. In this respect, I would like to thank Susan Babbitt, Nathan Brett, Cheshire Calhoun, David Crocker, Jay Drydyk, Marvin Glass, Jennifer Llewellyn, and Janice Newberry. In doing revisions for the Second Edition, I was fortunate to be in the right places at the right times to discover important and innovative work being done at conferences and colloquia. Working with these people on their contributions to the Second Edition has been a pleasure. In particular, I would like to thank Frank Cunningham, Sally Haslanger, Alison Minea, Roland Pierik, Ingrid Robeyns, Asuncion Lera St. Clair, and Kok-Chor Tan.

I could not have completed the painstaking work of preparing the manuscript if it were not for the competence and dedication of two fabulous Bryn Mawr students: Valori Jankowski and Risa Rice. I cannot say enough about how important they were to the completion of this project. Jessica Moss, Erin McCartney, Erin LaFarge, and Lilian Bürgler are just some of the many students who offered valuable advice as I worked my way through the structure of and selections for the Second Edition. Sue Campbell, Lorraine Code, Lorraine Kirschner, Michael Krausz, Ralph Kuncl, Christine Overall, and Susan Sherwin influenced the project and ensured its completion in ways that only they can know. This is not the first project that Andrew Brook has been there to help me through. His help was, as always, matched by his unwavering confidence in my work and his encouragement and support throughout. Finally, I would like to express my gratitude to the many students with inquiring minds and diverse backgrounds who made this exploration possible and to the young people in my life, to whom I dedicate these volumes. It is they who keep me optimistic about the future.

CHAPTER ONE: REPRODUCTIVE ISSUES

INTRODUCTION

The central liberal tenet that human beings have inherent worth has generated moral imperatives about how human beings ought to be treated. A fairly uncontroversial principle that emerges from the idea of the intrinsic value of human beings is that it is wrong to end the life of a human being or, in positive terms, that human beings have a right to life. This principle has played a central role in the debates on abortion and reproductive technologies in traditional Western moral theory.

A question that has dominated the debate on abortion in Western liberal contexts is the issue of the moral status of the fetus. Kant, for example, intended his account of inherent worth to cover entities with a will; that is, human beings who could reason, act to fulfill or reject particular inclinations and desires, and perform the moral duties dictated by reason. None of these characteristics appear to be possessed by human beings who are not yet born or, some would argue, even by human beings in the early years of their lives. Some theorists have captured this distinction between human beings with developed capacities and those who lack them by referring to the first as "persons" and to the second as "human beings" and reserving the right to life for persons. Some theorists grant that the fetus is not a person, but argue that its potential to be one makes abortion morally wrong. Yet others argue that the question of the status of the fetus and its right to life is neither the only issue nor the most important one in the debate on abortion and that there are competing rights that carry moral weight and need to be taken into account.

The value accorded individual autonomy generates an account of the right to make choices about one's own life and one's own body that some take to provide a moral justification for abortion. Some defend the right to choose as absolute, arguing that a woman should be able to evaluate her own goals and aspirations and make decisions that affect her life. Some argue that the right to choose is outweighed by the interests of the state in protecting fetuses who are sufficiently like persons in the later stages of pregnancy. Others argue that only certain cases, such as rape or a woman's life at risk, justify exercising the right to choose in the case of abortion.

The issues and arguments have become even more complex in the contemporary context. Advances in reproductive technology have created possibilities for terminating, correcting, and extending human life at the very earliest stages of development and for expanding choices with respect to when, where, and how life begins. These advances have expanded the debates from the issue of the moral justifiability of abortion to a complex set of issues raised by technologies that provide new methods for creating human life and new choices for women. Questions about the status of entities in labs and about the choices now open to women with respect to reproduction are now being raised.

The debates on these issues in North America are taken by some theorists to reflect what has been identified in numerous readings in Volumes I and II as a justice approach to moral theory and issues: the identification of competing values, the prioritizing and universalizing of rules, the abstraction of the individual from the concrete details of contexts and lives, and the application of general principles to all cases. In recent years, this approach to reproductive issues has been challenged by feminists, some of whom defend an ethic of care approach to morality. We will examine these challenges as well as policies on reproductive issues in other countries and thereby raise questions about how the debates are framed in Western societies.

In the first reading, Don Marquis develops the argument that abortion is in the same moral category as killing an innocent adult human being and is, therefore, seriously immoral. He bases his argument on what he takes to be a central premise in the debate on abortion: the question of whether abortion is morally permissible stands or falls on the issue of whether the fetus is the sort of entity whose life it is seriously wrong to end. Marquis argues that this question has resulted in a standoff between anti-abortionists and pro-choice advocates. The anti-abortionist defends a moral principle about the wrongness of killing that is broad in scope and covers fetuses even at the earliest stages, but this embraces too much and cannot explain why it is not wrong to destroy a living human cancer cell or why mere possession of the human genetic code is morally relevant. The pro-choicer finds a moral principle about the wrongness of killing that is narrow in scope so that fetuses do not fall under it, but this does not embrace enough and cannot explain why it is wrong to kill infants or the severely disabled.

Marquis holds that a way out of the standoff is to provide a more complete account of the wrongness of killing. What makes killing wrong, he argues, is that "the loss of one's life deprives one of all the experiences, activities, projects, and enjoyments that would otherwise have constituted one's future." Killing infants and fetuses is wrong because they have futures that include a set of experiences, projects, and activities that are identical to the futures of adult human beings. Because the category is "future-like-ours" and not person-hood, Marquis claims that his argument avoids equivocations on concepts like human life, human being, or person as well as difficulties encountered in moves by anti-abortionists that the fetus has the *potential* to become a person. Marquis ends by raising several possible objections to his own account and reaffirming his argument that the property of a "future like ours" is one that can settle the central question about the moral status of the fetus.

Ann Cudd provides a short critique of Marquis's essay in the second reading. Her goal is to rebut what she takes as Marquis's initial assumption that the central question for settling the issue of abortion is that of the moral status of the fetus. Cudd charges that Marquis conflates two questions: 1) is

the fetus the sort of thing that could have any rights and toward which we could have obligations? and 2) are these rights or obligations absolute? She maintains that whatever we decide about the status of the fetus, there remain important questions about the bundle of rights held by the woman carrying the fetus. Cudd argues that taking this bundle of rights seriously is precisely what many of the authors that Marquis wrongly depicts as focusing on the question of the status of the fetus do. Some of these authors argue that the fetus's lack of personhood is a sufficient but not a necessary condition for abortion to be morally permissible, and others argue that the woman's right to life or her serious loss of well-being overrides the rights of the fetus. Cudd argues that even if we agree that the fetus is the sort of thing whose killing is so morally wrong as to overwhelm completely a woman's rights to privacy, health, medical care, and even life, the point needs argument and not assertion.

Susan Sherwin questions the framework assumed in the arguments about the right to life and the right to choose exemplified in the first two readings, a framework that illustrates a justice approach to issues of reproduction. She argues that the contemporary context of rapid technological advances and economic pressures to develop them calls for core insights from feminist ethics. Morally adequate policy-making requires an ontological shift from the dominant political framework of liberal individualism to an explicitly feminist understanding of persons as relational beings. Sherwin grounds her argument by applying it to issues introduced by the specific technologies of *in vitro* fertilization (IVF) and pre-implantation genetic diagnosis (PGD). She argues that debates in Western democracies on these technologies mirror the old arguments on abortion and contraception — religious commitments to the sanctity of human life versus liberalism's commitment to individual liberty. Because the language of freedom of personal choice is central to calls for the unrestricted development of biotechnology, those asking for limits to the development or use of technologies are forced to use this framework of analysis or turn to religious values.

While Sherwin grants that "freedom of choice" has been important in feminist struggles to obtain and retain rights to abortion and contraception, she also claims that these arguments are problematic when it comes to evaluating the technologies of assisted conception and reproductive genetics. With respect to these issues, an account of autonomy as relational challenges simplistic interpretations of freedom as reducible to enhancing consumer choice. Sherwin argues that adopting an ontological framework of feminist relational understandings of personhood will allow policy-makers to appreciate the force of feminist and moral concerns, to explore a wider range of morally relevant questions about how *groups* may be affected by the policies under review, and to formulate ethically adequate policies in the expanding area of biotechnology.

Sherwin calls for a radical shift from the liberal individualist framework within which issues of reproductive technologies are currently debated to a relational account that pays attention to the social and political context within which women make choices. Amy Harmon turns us back to the individual in her survey of women undergoing prenatal testing and needing to make decisions about whether to abort fetuses diagnosed with "abnormalities." Prenatal testing presents women with difficult choices about whether to continue a pregnancy, choices that involve evaluating the severity of the "defect" and weighing the advice given by medical practitioners, genetic counselors, partners, and family members. Because developments in prenatal testing methods allow women to have this information early in the pregnancy, many women undergo early abortions that they need not reveal to anyone. Harmon notes that women with objections to abortion find themselves overwhelmed by personal feelings of being unable to cope with the difficulties of having a disabled child. She also notes that many disability theorists protest what they view as a eugenics movement that will result in greater intolerance of disabilities and fewer medical resources for and accommodation of disabled people. Disability theorists also raise concerns about decisions that some women may make to abort fetuses with relatively minor defects or of a specific sex. Harmon ends by presenting examples in which the women themselves discuss their cases, the decisions they made, and the effects these decisions have had on their lives.

The issue of eugenics touched on in the reading by Harmon is revisited in a different context in the fourth reading by Michael DeFine. DeFine traces the development of the eugenics movement from the nineteenth century on in the theories used by governments, scientists, and doctors to justify the regulation of reproduction. More specifically, he describes the government-funded procedures that resulted in the sterilization of Native American women because of beliefs about their inferiority. He reports, for example, that between 1970 and 1982, 15 per cent of white women, 24 per cent of African-American women, 35 per cent of Puerto Rican women, and 42 per cent of Native American women were sterilized. DeFine then turns to the effects of sterilization practices on Native American women today by discussing federal relationships with American Indian tribes, personal accounts from Native American women who were sterilized and the effects of this on their attitudes about family planning, state and federal policies regarding informed consent and sterilization, and the role of the Indian Health Service.

In the final reading, Florencia Luna turns to the issues of reproductive health and research ethics in Argentina. Argentina has a history of good public health care, education, and medical research. Yet, it is a developing country with high poverty rates and wide gaps in social classes, both of which increased dramatically with the 2001 economic crisis. Against this backdrop, notes Luna, is the strong social and political power of the Catholic Church which, she argues, has established strong barriers to reproductive policy that have resulted in high levels of hypocrisy and some absurd practices. She examines the issues of contraception, abortion and the anencephalic fetus, and embryos and assisted reproductive technologies to argue that there is a conflict between what the Catholic Church permits and what women and researchers do.

The lack of sexual and reproductive rights in Argentina results in illegal abortions, post-abortion health problems, and high rates of teenage pregnancy. Restrictive abortion laws force women to deliver fetuses with serious genetic problems only to have them die. Laws specify that embryos are considered persons, but these laws ignore the creation of embryos in medical research centers. Luna highlights these and other contradictions and problems that emerge from laws and policies that are in tension with the health and welfare of women and with the practices of doctors and researchers. She ends by examining research ethics in Argentina in the broader context of Latin America and international debates and agreements.

WHY ABORTION IS IMMORAL

Don Marquis

🍂

Don Marquis is Professor of Philosophy at the University of Kansas, Lawrence. He has published a number of journal articles in the areas of ethics and medical ethics. "Why Abortion is Immoral" has been reprinted in numerous ethics collections.

Marquis accepts that the question of whether abortion is morally permissible stands or falls on the issue of the status of the fetus. He argues that we can best answer questions about the status of the fetus by asking what makes killing adult human beings wrong. His answer is that killing is wrong because one is deprived of "the experiences, activities, projects, and enjoyments that would otherwise have constituted one's future." Because the fetus possesses this valuable property of having a "future-like-ours," abortion is immoral and in the same moral category as killing an innocent human being or wantonly killing innocent animals. He concludes that abortion is seriously immoral in the great majority of cases.

The view that abortion is, with rare exceptions, seriously immoral has received little support in the recent philosophical literature. No doubt most philosophers affiliated with secular institutions of higher education believe that the anti-abortion position is either a symptom of irrational religious dogma or a conclusion generated by seriously confused philosophical argument. The purpose of this essay is to undermine this general belief. The essay sets out an argument that purports to show, as well as any argument in ethics can show, that abortion is, except possibly in rare cases, seriously immoral, that it is in the same moral category as killing an innocent adult human being.

The argument is based on a major assumption. Many of the most insightful and careful writers on the ethics of abortion — such as Joel Feinberg, Michael Tooley, Mary Anne Warren, H. Tristram Engelhardt, Jr., L.W. Sumner, John T. Noonan, Jr., and Philip Devine[1] — believe that whether or not abortion is morally permissible stands or falls on whether or not a fetus is the sort of being whose life it is seriously wrong to end. The argument of this essay will assume, but not argue, that they are correct.

Also, this essay will neglect issues of great importance to a complete ethics of abortion. Some anti-abortionists will allow that certain abortions, such as abortion before implantation or abortion when the life of a woman is threatened by a pregnancy or abortion after rape, may be morally permissible. This essay will not explore the casuistry of these hard cases. The purpose of this essay is to develop a general argument for the claim that the overwhelming majority of deliberate abortions are seriously immoral.

I

A sketch of standard anti-abortion and pro-choice arguments exhibits how those arguments possess certain symmetries that explain why partisans of those positions are so convinced of the correctness of their own positions, why they are not successful in convincing their opponents, and why, to others, this issue seems to be unresolvable. An analysis of the nature of this standoff suggests a strategy for surmounting it.

Consider the way a typical anti-abortionist argues. She will argue or assert that life is present from the moment of conception or that fetuses look like babies or that fetuses possess a characteristic such as a genetic code that is both necessary and sufficient for being human. Anti-abortionists seem to believe that (1) the truth of all of these claims is quite obvious, and (2) establishing any of these claims is sufficient to show that abortion is morally akin to murder.

A standard pro-choice strategy exhibits similarities. The pro-choicer will argue or assert that fetuses are not persons or that fetuses are not rational agents or that fetuses are not social beings. Pro-choicers seem to believe that (1) the truth of any of these claims is quite obvious, and (2) establishing any of these claims is sufficient to show that an abortion is not a wrongful killing.

In fact, both the pro-choice and the anti-abortion claims do seem to be true, although the "it looks like a baby" claim is more difficult to establish the earlier the pregnancy. We seem to have a standoff. How can it be resolved?

As everyone who has taken a bit of logic knows, if any of these arguments concerning abortion is a good argument, it requires not only some claim characterizing fetuses, but also some general moral principle that ties a characteristic of fetuses to having or not having the right to life or to some other moral characteristic that will generate the obligation or the lack of obligation not to end the life of a fetus. Accordingly, the arguments of the anti-abortionist and the pro-choicer need a bit of filling in to be regarded as adequate.

Note what each partisan will say. The anti-abortionist will claim that her position is supported by such generally accepted moral principles as "It is always prima facie seriously wrong to end the life of a baby." Since these are generally accepted moral principles her position is certainly not obviously wrong. The pro-choicer will claim that her position is supported by such plausible moral principles as "Being a person is what gives an individual intrinsic moral worth" or "It is only seriously prima facie wrong to take the life of a member of the human community." Since these are generally accepted moral principles, the pro-choice position is certainly not obviously wrong. Unfortunately, we have again arrived at a standoff.

Now, how might one deal with this standoff? The standard approach is to try to show how the moral principles of one's opponent lose their plausibility under analysis. It is easy to see how this is possible. On the one hand, the anti-abortionist will defend a moral principle concerning the wrongness of killing which tends to be broad in scope in order that even fetuses at an early stage of pregnancy will fall under it. The problem with broad principles is that they often embrace too much. In this particular instance, the principle "It is always prima facie wrong to take a human life" sees to entail that it is wrong to end the existence of a living human cancer-cell culture, on the grounds that the culture is both living and human. Therefore, it seems that the anti-abortionist's favored principle is too broad.

On the other hand, the pro-choicer wants to find a moral principle concerning the wrongness of killing which tends to be narrow in scope in order that fetuses will *not* fall under it. The problem with narrow principles is that they often do not embrace enough. Hence, the needed principles such as "It is prima facie seriously wrong to kill only persons" or "It is prima facie wrong to kill only rational agents" do not explain why it is wrong to kill infants or young children or the severely retarded or even perhaps the severely mentally ill. Therefore, we seem again to have a standoff. The anti-abortionist charges, not unreasonably, that pro-choice principles concerning killing are too narrow to be acceptable; the pro-choicer charges, not unreasonably, that anti-abortionist principles concerning killing are too broad to be acceptable.

Attempts by both sides to patch up the difficulties in their positions run into further difficulties. The anti-abortionist will try to remove that problem in her position by reformulating her principle concerning killing in terms of human beings. Now we end up with: "It is always prima facie seriously wrong to end the life of a human being." This principle has the advantage of avoiding the problem of the human cancer-cell culture counterexample. But this advantage is purchased at a high price. For although it is clear that a fetus is both human and alive, it is not at all clear that a fetus is a human *being*. There is at least something to be said for the view that something becomes a human being only after a process of development, and that therefore first trimester fetuses and perhaps all fetuses are not yet human beings. Hence, the anti-abortionist, by this move has merely exchanged one problem for another.[2]

The pro-choicer fares no better. She may attempt to find reasons why killing infants, young children, and the severely retarded is wrong which are independent of her major principle that is supposed to explain the wrongness of taking human life, but which will not also make abortion immoral. This is no easy task. Appeals to social utility will seem satisfactory only to those who resolve not to think of the enormous difficulties with a utilitarian account of the wrongness of killing and the significant social costs of preserving the lives of the unproductive.[3] A pro-choice strategy that extends the definition of "person" to infants or even to young children seems just as arbitrary as an anti-abortion strategy that extends the definition of "human being" to fetuses. Again, we find symmetries in the two positions and we arrive at a standoff.

There are even further problems that reflect symmetries in the two positions. In addition to counterexample problems, or the arbitrary application problems that can be exchanged for them, the standard anti-abortionist principle "It is prima facie seriously wrong to kill a human being," or one of its variants, can be objected to on the grounds of ambiguity. If "human being" is taken to be a *biological* category, the anti-abortionist is left with the problem of explaining why a merely biological category should make a moral difference. Why, it is asked, is it any more reasonable to base a moral conclusion on the number of chromosomes in one's cells than on the color of one's skin?[4] If "human being," on the other hand, is taken to be a *moral* category, then the claim that a fetus is a human being cannot be taken to be a premise in the anti-abortion argument, for it is precisely what needs to be established. Hence,

either the anti-abortionist's main category is a morally irrelevant, merely biological category, or it is of no use to the anti-abortionist in establishing (noncircularly, of course) that abortion is wrong.

Although this problem with the anti-abortionist position is often noticed, it is less often noticed that the pro-choice position suffers from an analogous problem. The principle "Only persons have the right to life" also suffers from an ambiguity. The term "person" is typically defined in terms of psychological characteristics, although there will certainly be disagreement concerning which characteristics are most important. Supposing that this matter can be settled, the pro-choicer is left with the problem of explaining why *psychological* characteristics should make a *moral* difference. If the pro-choicer should attempt to deal with this problem by claiming that an explanation is not necessary, that in fact we do treat such a cluster of psychological properties as having moral significance, the sharp-witted anti-abortionist should have a ready response. We do treat being both living and human as having moral significance. If it is legitimate for the pro-choicer to demand that the anti-abortionist provide an explanation of the connection between the biological character of being a human being and the wrongness of being killed (even though people accept this connection), then it is legitimate for the anti-abortionist to demand that the pro-choicer provide an explanation of the connection between psychological criteria for being a person and the wrongness of being killed (even though that connection is accepted).[5]

Feinberg has attempted to meet this objection (he calls psychological personhood "commonsense personhood"):

The characteristics that confer commonsense personhood are not arbitrary bases for rights and duties, such as race, sex or species membership; rather they are traits that make sense out of rights and duties and without which those moral attributes would have no point or function. It is because people are conscious; have a sense out of their personal identities;

have plans, goals, and projects; experience emotions; are liable to pains, anxieties, and frustrations; can reason and bargain, and so on — it is because of these attributes that people have values and interests, desires and expectations of their own, including a stake in their own futures. And a personal well-being of a sort we cannot ascribe to unconscious or non-rational beings. Because of their developed capacities they can assume duties and responsibilities and can have and make claims on one another. Only because of their sense of self, their life plans, their value hierarchies, and their stakes in their own futures can they be ascribed fundamental rights. There is nothing arbitrary about these linkages (*op.cit.,* p. 270).

The plausible aspects of this attempt should not be taken to obscure its implausible features. There is a great deal to be said for the view that being a psychological person under some description is a necessary condition for having duties. One cannot have a duty unless on is capable of behaving morally, and a being's capability of behaving morally will require having a certain psychology. It is far from obvious, however, that having rights entails consciousness or rationality as Feinberg suggests. We speak of the rights of the severely retarded or the severely mentally ill, yet some of these persons are not rational. We speak of the rights of the temporarily unconscious. The New Jersey Supreme Court based their decision in the Quinlan case on Karen Ann Quinlan's right to privacy, and she was known to be permanently unconscious at that time. Hence, Feinberg's claim that having rights entails being conscious is, on its face, obviously false.

Of course, it might not make sense to attribute rights to a being that would never in its natural history have certain psychological traits. This modest connection between psychological personhood and moral personhood will create a place for Karen Ann Quinlan and the temporarily unconscious. But then it makes a place for fetuses also. Hence, it does not serve Feinberg's pro-choice purposes. Accordingly, it seems that the pro-

choicer will have as much difficulty bridging the gap between psychological personhood and personhood in the moral sense as the anti-abortionist has bridging the gap between being a biological human being and being a human being in the moral sense.

Furthermore, the pro-choicer cannot any more escape her problem by making person a purely moral category that the anti-abortionist could escape by the analogous move. For if person is a moral category, the pro-choicer is left without the resources for establishing (noncircularly, of course) the claim that a fetus is not a person, which is an essential premise in her argument. Again, we have both a symmetry and a standoff between pro-choice and anti-abortion views.

Passions in the abortion debate run high. There are both plausibilities and difficulties with the standard positions. Accordingly, it is hardly surprising that partisans of either side embrace with fervor the moral generalizations that support the conclusions they preanalytically favor, and reject with disdain the moral generalizations of their opponents as being subject to inescapable difficulties. It is easy to believe that the counterexamples to one's own moral principles are merely temporary difficulties that will dissolve in the wake of further philosophical research, and that the counterexamples to the principles of one's opponents are as straightforward as the contradiction between A and O propositions in traditional logic. This might suggest to an impartial observer (if there are any) that the abortion issue is unresolvable.

There is a way out of this apparent dialectible quandary. The moral generalizations of both sides are not quite correct. The generalizations hold for the most part, for the usual cases. This suggests that they are all *accidental* generalizations, that the moral claims made by those on both sides of the dispute do not touch on the *essence* of the matter.

This use of the distinction between essence and accident is not meant to invoke obscure metaphysical categories. Rather, it is intended to reflect the rather atheoretical nature of the abortion discussion. If the generalization a partisan in the abortion dispute adopts were derived from the reason why ending the life of a human being is wrong, then there could not be exceptions to that generalization unless some special case obtains in which there are even more powerful countervailing reasons. Such generalizations would not be merely accidental generalizations; they would point to, or be based upon, the essence of the wrongness of killing, what it is that makes killing wrong. All this suggests that a necessary condition of resolving the abortion controversy is a more theoretical account of the wrongness of killing. After all, if we merely believe, but do not understand, why killing adult human beings such as ourselves is wrong how could we conceivably show that abortion is either immoral or permissible?

II

In order to develop such an account, we can start from the following unproblematic assumption concerning our own case: it is wrong to kill *us*. Why is it wrong? Some answers can be easily eliminated. It might be said that what makes killing us wrong is that a killing brutalizes the one who kills. But the brutalization consists of being inured to the performance of an act that is hideously immoral; hence, the brutalization does not explain the immorality. It might be said that what makes killing us wrong is the great loss others would experience due to our absence. Although such hubris is understandable, such an explanation does not account for the wrongness of killing hermits, or those whose lives are relatively independent and whose friends find it easy to make new friends.

A more obvious answer is better. What primarily makes killing wrong is neither its effect on the murderer nor its effect on the victim's friends and relative, but its effect on the victim. The loss of one's life is one of the greatest losses one can suffer. The loss of one's life deprives one of all the experiences, activities, projects, and enjoyments that would otherwise have constituted one's future. Therefore, killing someone is wrong, primarily because the killing inflicts (one of) the greatest possible losses on the victim. To describe this as the loss of life can be misleading, however. The change

in my biological state does not by itself make killing me wrong. The effect of the loss of my biological life is the loss to me of all those activities, projects, experiences, and enjoyments which would otherwise have constituted my future personal life. These activities, projects, experiences, and enjoyments are either valuable for their own sakes or are means to something else that is valuable for its own sake. Some parts of my future are not valued by me now, but will come to be valued by me as I grow older and as my values and capacities change. When I am killed, I am deprived both of what I now value which would have been part of my future personal life, but also what I would come to value. Therefore, when I die, I am deprived of all of the value of my future. Inflicting this loss on me is ultimately what makes killing me wrong. This being the case, it would seem that what makes killing *any* adult human being prima facie seriously wrong is the loss of his or her future.[6]

How should this rudimentary theory of the wrongness of killing be evaluated? It cannot be faulted for deriving an "ought" from an "is" for it does not. The analysis assumes that killing me (or you, reader) is prima facie seriously wrong. The point of the analysis is to establish which natural property ultimately explains the wrongness of the killing, given that it is wrong. The point of the analysis is to establish which natural property ultimately explains the wrongness of the killing, given that it is wrong. A natural property will ultimately explain the wrongness of killing, only if (1) the explanation fits with our intuitions about the matter and (2) there is not other natural property that provides the basis for a better explanation of the wrongness of killing. This analysis rests on the intuition that what makes killing a particular human or animal wrong is what it does to that particular human or animal. What makes killing wrong is some natural effect or other of the killing. Some would deny this. For instance, a divine-command theorist in ethics would deny it. Surely this denial is, however, one of those features of divine-command theory which renders it so implausible.

The claim that what makes killing wrong is the loss of the victim's future is directly supported by two considerations. In the first place this theory explains why we regard killing as one of the worst of crimes. Killing is especially wrong, because it deprives the victim of more that perhaps any other crime. In the second place, people with AIDS or cancer who know they are dying believe, of course, that dying is a very bad thing for them. They believe that the loss of a future to them that they would otherwise have experienced is what makes their premature death a very bad thing for them. A better theory of the wrongness of killing would require a different natural property associated with killing which better fits with the attitudes of the dying. What could it be?

The view that what makes killing wrong is the loss to the victim of the value of the victim's future gains additional support when some of its implications are examined. In the first place, it is incompatible with the view that it is wrong to kill only beings who are biologically human. It is possible that there exists a different species from another planet whose members have a future like ours. Since having a future like that is what makes killing someone wrong, this theory entails that it would be wrong to kill members of such a species. Hence, this theory is opposed to the claim that only life that is biologically human has great moral worth, a claim which many anti-abortionists have seemed to adopt. This opposition, which this theory has in common with personhood theories, seems to be a merit of the theory.

In the second place, the claim that the loss of one's future is the wrong-making feature of one's being killed entails the possibility that the futures of some actual nonhuman mammals on our own planet are sufficiently like ours that it is seriously wrong to kill them also. Whether some animals do have the same right to life as human beings depends on adding to the account of the wrongness of killing some additional account of just what it is about my future or the futures of other adult human beings which makes it wrong to kill us. No such additional account will be offered in this essay. Undoubtedly, the provision of such an account would be a very difficult matter. Undoubtedly, any such account would be quite controversial. Hence, it surely should not reflect badly on this sketch of an elementary theory of the wrongness of killing that it is indeterminate with respect to some very difficult issues regarding animal rights.

In the third place, the claim that the loss of one's future is the wrong-making feature of one's being killed does not entail, as sanctity of human life theories do, that active euthanasia is wrong. Persons who are severely and incurably ill, who face future of pain and despair, and who wish to die will not have suffered a loss if they are killed. It is, strictly speaking, the value of a human's future which makes killing wrong in this theory. This being so, killing does not necessarily wrong some persons who are sick and dying. Of course there may be other reasons for a prohibition of active euthanasia, but this is another matter. Sanctity-of-human-life theories seem to hold that active euthanasia is seriously wrong even in an individual case where there seems to be good reason for it independently of public policy considerations. This consequence is most implausible, and it is a plus for the claim that the loss of a future of value is what makes killing wrong that it does not share this consequence.

In the fourth place, the account of the wrongness of killing defended in this essay does straightforwardly entail that it is prima facie seriously wrong to kill children and infants, for we do presume that they have futures of value. Since we do believe that it is wrong to kill defenseless little babies, it is important that a theory of the wrongness of killing easily account for this. Personhood theories of the wrongness of killing, on the other hand, cannot straightforwardly account for the wrongness of killing infants and young children.[7] Hence, such theories must add special ad hoc accounts of the wrongness of killing the young. The plausibility of such ad hoc theories seems to be a function of how desperately one wants such theories to work. The claim that the primary wrong-making feature of a killing is the loss to the victim of the value of its future accounts for the wrongness of killing young children and infants directly; it makes the wrongness of such acts as obvious as we actually think it is. This is a further merit of this theory. Accordingly, it seems that this value of a future-like-ours theory of the wrongness of killing shares strengths of both sanctity-of-life and personhood accounts while avoiding weaknesses of both. In addition, it meshes with a central intuition concerning what makes killing wrong.

The claim that the primary wrong-making feature of a killing is the loss to the victim of the value of its future has obvious consequences for the ethics of abortion. The future of a standard fetus includes a set of experiences, projects, activities, and such which are identical with the futures of adult human beings and are identical with the futures of young children. Since the reason that is sufficient to explain why it is wrong to kill human beings after the time of birth is a reason that also applies to fetuses, it follows that abortion is prima facie seriously morally wrong.

This argument does not rely on the invalid inference that, since it is wrong to kill persons, it is wrong to kill potential persons also. The category that is morally central to this analysis is the category of having a valuable future like ours; it is not the category of personhood. The argument to the conclusion that abortion is prima facie seriously morally wrong proceeded independently of the notion of person or potential person or any equivalent. Someone may wish to start with this analysis in terms of the value of a human future, conclude that abortion is, except perhaps in rare circumstances, seriously morally wrong, infer that fetuses have the right to life, and then call fetuses "persons" as a result of their having the right to life. Clearly, in this case, the category of person is being used to state the *conclusion* of the analysis rather than to generate the *argument* of the analysis.

The structure of this anti-abortion argument can be both illuminated and defended by comparing it to what appears to be the best argument for the wrongness of the wanton infliction of pain on animals. This latter argument is based on the assumption that it is prima facie wrong to inflict pain on me (or you, reader). What is the natural property associated with the infliction of pain which makes such infliction wrong? The obvious answer sees to be that the infliction of pain causes suffering and that suffering is a misfortune. The suffering caused by the infliction of pain is what makes the wanton infliction of pain on other adult humans causes suffering. The wanton infliction of pain on animals causes suffering. Since causing suffering is what makes the wanton infliction of pain wrong and since the wanton infliction of pain on animals causes suffering, it follows that the wanton infliction of pain on animals is wrong.

This argument for the wrongness of the wanton infliction of pain on animals shares a number of structural features with the argument for the serious prima facie wrongness of abortion. Both arguments start with an obvious assumption concerning what it is wrong to do to me (or you, reader). Both then look for the characteristic or the consequence of the wrong action which makes the action wrong. Both recognize that the wrong-making feature of these immoral actions is a property of actions sometimes directed at individuals other than postnatal human beings. If the structure of the argument for the wrongness of the wanton infliction of pain on animals is sound, then the structure of the argument for the prima facie serious wrongness of abortion is also sound, for the structure of the two arguments is the same. The structure common to both is the key to the explanation of how the wrongness of abortion can be demonstrated without recourse to the category of person. In neither argument is that category crucial.

This defense of an argument for the wrongness of abortion in terms of a structurally similar argument for the wrongness of the wanton infliction of pain on animals succeeds only if the account regarding animals is the correct account. Is it? In the first place, it seems plausible. In the second place, its major competition is Kant's account. Kant believed that we do not have direct duties to animals at all, because they are not persons. Hence, Kant had to explain and justify the wrongness of inflicting pain on animals on the grounds that "he who is hard in his dealings with animals becomes hard also in his dealing with men."[8] The problem with Kant's account is that there seems to be no reason for accepting this latter claim unless Kant's account is rejected. If the alternative to Kant's account is accepted, then it is easy to understand why someone who is indifferent to inflicting pain on animals is also indifferent to inflicting pain on humans, for one is indifferent to what makes inflicting pain wrong in both cases. But, if Kant's account is accepted, there is not intelligible reason why one who is hard in his dealings with animals (or crabgrass or stones) should also be hard in his dealings with men. After all, men are persons: animals are no more persons than crabgrass or stones. Persons are Kant's crucial moral category. Why, in short, should a Kantian accept the basic claim in Kant's argument?

Hence, Kant's argument for the wrongness of inflicting pain on animals rests on a claim that, in a world of Kantian moral agents, is demonstrably false. Therefore, the alternative analysis, being more plausible anyway, should be accepted. Since this alternative analysis has the same structure as the anti-abortion argument being defended here, we have further support for the argument for the immorality of abortion being defended in this essay.

Of course, this value of a future-like-ours argument, if sound, shows only that abortion is prima facie wrong, not that it is wrong in any and all circumstances. Since the loss of the future to a standard fetus, if killed, is, however, at least as great a loss as the loss of the future to a standard adult human being who is killed, abortion, like ordinary killing, could be justified only by the most compelling reasons. The loss of one's life is almost the greatest misfortune that can happen to one. Presumably abortion could be justified in some circumstances, only if the loss consequent on failing to abort would be at least as great. Accordingly, morally permissible abortions will be rare indeed unless, perhaps, they occur so early in pregnancy that a fetus is not yet definitely an individual. Hence, this argument should be taken as showing that abortion is presumptively very seriously wrong, where the presumption is very strong — as strong as the presumption that killing another adult human being is wrong.

III

How complete an account of the wrongness of killing does the value of a future-like-ours

account have to be in order that the wrongness of abortion is a consequence? This account does not have to be an account of the necessary conditions for the wrongness of killing. Some persons in nursing homes may lack valuable human futures, yet it may be wrong to kill them for other reasons. Furthermore, this account does not obviously have to be the sole reason killing is wrong where the victim did have a valuable future. This analysis claims only that, for any killing where the victim did have a valuable future like ours, having that future by itself is sufficient to create the strong presumption that the killing is seriously wrong....

V

In this essay, it has been argued that the correct ethic of the wrongness of killing can be extended to fetal life and used to show that there is a strong presumption that any abortion is morally impermissible. If the ethic of killing adopted here entails, however, that contraception is also seriously immoral, then there would appear to be a difficulty with the analysis of this essay.

But this analysis does not entail that contraception is wrong. Of course, contraception prevents the actualization of a possible future of value. Hence, it follows from the claim that futures of value should be maximized that contraception is prima facie immoral. This obligation to maximize does not exist, however; furthermore, nothing in the ethics of killing in this paper entails that it does. The ethics of killing in this essay would entail that contraception is wrong only if something were denied a human future of value by contraception. Nothing at all is denied such a future by contraception, however.

Candidates for a subject of harm by contraception fall into four categories: (1) some sperm or other, (2) some ovum or other, (3) a sperm and an ovum separately, and (4) a sperm and an ovum together. Assigning the harm to some sperm is utterly arbitrary, for no reason can be given for making a sperm the subject of harm rather than an ovum. Assigning the harm to some ovum is utterly arbitrary, for no reason can be given for making an ovum the subject of harm rather than a sperm. One might attempt to avoid these problems by insisting that contraception deprives both the sperm and the ovum separately of a valuable future like ours. On this alternative, too many futures are lost. Contraception was supposed to be wrong, because it deprived us of one future of value, not two. One might attempt to avoid this problem by holding that contraception deprives the combination of sperm and ovum of a valuable future like ours. But here the definite article misleads. At the time of contraception, there are hundreds of millions of sperm, one (released) ovum and millions of possible combinations of all of these. There is no actual combination at all. Is the subject of the loss to be a merely possible combination? Which one? This alternative does not yield an actual subject of harm either. Accordingly, the immorality of contraception is not entailed by the loss of a future-like-ours argument simply because there is no nonarbitrarily identifiable subject of the loss in the case of contraception.

VI

The purpose of this essay has been to set out an argument for the serious presumptive wrongness of abortion subject to the assumption that the moral permissibility of abortion stands of falls on the moral status of the fetus. Since a fetus possesses a property, the possession of which in adult human beings is sufficient to make killing an adult human being wrong, abortion is wrong. This way of dealing with the problem of abortion seems superior to other approaches to the ethics of abortion, because it rests on an ethics of killing which is close to self-evident, because the crucial morally relevant property clearly applies to fetuses, and because the argument avoids the usual equivocations on "human life," "human being," or "person." The argument rests neither on religious claims nor on Papal dogma. It is not subject to the objection of "speciesism." Its soundness is compatible with the moral permissibility of euthanasia and contraception. It deals with our intuitions concerning young children.

Finally, this analysis can be viewed as resolving a standard problem — indeed, *the* standard problem — concerning the ethics of abortion. Clearly, it is wrong to kill adult human beings. Clearly, it is not wrong to end the life of some arbitrarily chosen single human cell. Fetuses seem to be like arbitrarily chosen human cells in some respects and like adult humans in other respects. The problem of the ethics of abortion is the problem of determining the fetal property that settles this moral controversy. The thesis of this essay is that the problem of the ethics of abortion, so understood, is solvable.

NOTES

1. Feinberg, "Abortion," in *Matters of Life and Death: New Introductory Essays in Moral Philosophy*, Tom Regan, ed. (New York: Random House, 1986), pp. 256-293; Tooley, "Abortion and Infanticide," *Philosophy and Public Affairs*, II, 1 (1972): 37-65; Tooley, *Abortion and Infanticide* (New York: Oxford, 1984); Warren, "On the Moral and Legal Status of Abortion," *The Monist*, I.VII, 1 (1973): 43-61; Engelhardt, "The Ontology of Abortion," *Ethics*, I. XXXIV, 3 (1974): 217-234; Sumner, *Abortion and Moral Theory* (Princeton: University Press, 1981); Noonan, "An Almost Absolute Value in History," in *The Morality of Abortion: Legal and Historical Perspective*, Noonan, ed. (Cambridge: Harvard, 1970); and Devine, *The Ethics of Homicide* (Ithaca: Cornell, 1978).
2. For interesting discussions of this issue, see Warren Quinn, "Abortion: Identity and Loss," *Philosophy and Public Affairs*, XIII. 1 (1984): 24-54; and Lawrence C. Becker, "Human Being: the Boundaries of the Concept," *Philosophy and Public Affairs*, IV, 4 (1975): 334-359.
3. For example, see my "Ethics and The Elderly: Some Problems," in Stuart Spicker, Kathleen Woodwark and David Van Tassel, eds., *Aging and the Elderly: Humanistic Perspectives in Gerontology* (Atlantic Highlands, NJ: Humanities, 1978), pp. 341-355.
4. See Warren, *op.cit.*, and Tooley, "Abortion and Infanticide."

5. This seems to be the fatal flaw in Warren's treatment of this issue.

6. I have been most influenced on this matter by Jonathan Glover, *Causing Death and Saving Lives* (New York: Penguin, 1977), ch. 3; and Robert Young, "What is So Wrong with Killing People?" *Philosophy*, LIV, 210 (1979): 515-528.

7. Feinberg, Tooley, Warren, and Engelhardt have all dealt with this problem.

8. "Duties to Animals and Spirits," in *Lectures on Ethics*, Louis Infeld, trans. (New York: Harper, 1963), p. 239.

SENSATIONALIZED PHILOSOPHY:
A REPLY TO MARQUIS'S "WHY ABORTION IS IMMORAL"

Ann E. Cudd

Ann E. Cudd teaches philosophy at the University of Kansas, Lawrence. She is the author of Analyzing Oppression *(forthcoming 2006) and co-editor of* Feminist Theory: A Philosophical Anthology *(2005, with Robin O. Andreason) and* Theorizing Backlash: Philosophical Reflections on the Resistance to Feminism *(2002, with Anita M. Superson).*

Cudd identifies what she takes to be a fundamental flaw in Marquis's argument against abortion. She rejects his claim that the moral justifiability of abortion stands or falls on the issue of the moral status of the fetus as well as his claim that philosophers on both sides of the debate accept this claim. She argues that even if we grant that the fetus has moral status, there are other values and rights that justifiably enter the debate on abortion.

In a recent article, Don Marquis[1] claims to show "Why Abortion is Immoral." The title is, as I shall show, much bolder than what is warranted by his argument. This essay simply rebuts Marquis's initial assumption: that the only important question for settling the abortion issue is the moral status of the fetus, and the corroboration for this claim which he alleges to exist in the abortion literature. I mean this as only a partial reply,[2] and I do not claim to add to the positive argument here. In fact, I would not add to the thousands of pages written on this topic if I did not feel morally compelled to rebut what I see as a sensationalized and erroneous treatment of an issue of utmost current political importance.

In the beginning of his article, Marquis explicitly makes the assumption that "whether or not abortion is morally permissible stands or falls on whether or not a fetus is the sort of being whose life it is seriously wrong to end." There are two issues that arise in assessing this claim: (1) Is the fetus the sort of thing that could have any rights or toward which we could have obligations? (2) Are these rights or obligations prima facie or absolute?

Marquis's claim seems to conflate the two issues, assuming that whatever rights of, or obligations to, fetuses there are, they must be absolute.

The assumption that any obligations we have to fetuses are absolute, presented without argument, is philosophically (and politically) irresponsible. It is as if fetuses were things growing out in the garden, and the question of abortion were whether one may decide to till them under rather than let them come to fruition. The question of abortion inextricably involves (at least) two lives and a compelling bundle of rights on the side of the woman carrying the fetus, whatever we decide about the status of the fetus. Ignoring these rights makes about as much sense as considering the issue of the moral permissibility of killing adult, fully-conscious humans without considering the justification of self-defense. If no countervailing rights or other moral considerations were to be allowed to figure into the judgment, the criterion on which Marquis claims that abortion is impermissible, having a "future-like-ours," would also rule out killing in self-defense. He makes no exceptions to his claims that abortion is immoral.

Thus, it seems that to be consistent he would also have to reject any self-defense plea in killing any human being.

The only justification Marquis provides for the dubious assumption that a fetus's right to its future is absolute and overriding is an appeal to his favorite authors on abortion. He writes:

> Many of the most insightful and careful writers on the ethics of abortion ... believe that whether or not abortion is morally permissible *stands or falls* on whether or not the fetus is the sort of being whose life it is seriously wrong to end (emphasis mine).

The list of authors Marquis provides is quite impressive. The claim he makes about their arguments here is false, however. They all contain rights (and other moral concerns) of the pregnant woman, and find cases in which her rights or concerns override any considerations in favor of the fetus.[3] The authors cited can be divided into two categories: those who argue that abortions are permissible because the fetus is not the sort of being whose life it is seriously wrong to end,[4] and those who argue that abortions are impermissible in most (but not all) cases because the fetus is such a being.[5]

With regard to the first group, it is an obvious logical mistake to infer from:

> (A) Since the fetus is not the sort of being whose life it is seriously wrong to end, it is morally permissible to abort.

That therefore,

> (B) If it were the case that the fetus is the sort of being whose life it is seriously wrong to end, then it would be morally impermissible to abort.

The writers in the first group hold (A), but they make no claims like (B). That is, these writers merely claim that the fetus's lack of personhood is a sufficient, though not necessary, condition on the permissibility of abortion.

In the second group, both authors deny (A), but allow that, in cases in which the mother's life is in danger, or, perhaps, the woman was a victim of rape, abortion is morally permissible, thus denying (B) as well. In these cases, they reason, the woman's right to life or her serious loss of well-being overrides the rights of the fetus. Thus, they regard the woman's rights as a relevant issue in deciding the moral permissibility of abortion, and so could hardly be said to argue that the moral permissibility of abortion stands or falls with the issue of whether it is wrong to kill fetuses.

Even if we might ultimately agree that the fetus is the sort of thing whose killing is so morally wrong as to overwhelm completely a woman's rights to privacy, health, medical care, and even life, the point surely needs argument. Nothing that has been said in the abortion debate to date has come close to settling this issue against the woman. So *at most* Marquis can claim to have shown "Why Abortion is Killing a Being Like Us." When one recalls that persons may legitimately be killed for many reasons, this title has not the same moral urgency of Marquis's.

Author's Note

I would like to thank Neal Becker, Jack Bricke, Tony Genova, Leslie Jones and JoAnn Reckling for helpful comments. I, alone, am responsible for any remaining errors.

NOTES

1. [*The Journal of Philosophy*] LXXXVI, 4 (April 1989): 183-202.
2. This is only part of what was originally a longer reply, which is available on request from the author.
3. Mary Anne Warren, "On the Moral and Legal Status of Abortion," *The Monist*, LVII, 1 (1973): 43-61: "The immorality of abortion is no more demonstrated by the humanity of the fetus, in itself, than the immorality of killing in self-defense is demonstrated by the fact that the assailant is a human being" (p. 46). H.T. Engelhardt, Jr., "The Ontology of Abortion," *Ethics*, LXXXIV, 3

(1974): 217-234: "The rights of the mother regarding abortion are paramount. After all, she is the only actual person involved. Consequently, it is to her that one owes overriding obligations" (p. 233). Michael Tooley, "Abortion and Infanticide," *Philosophy and Public Affairs*, II, 1 (1972): 37-65. Tooley claims that the argument is settled by the fact that the fetus is not a person, and endorses Judith Jarvis Thomson's general claims about what would be the case if the fetus were a person, namely, that the woman's rights override. Joel Feinberg, "Abortion," in *Matters of Life and Death: New Introductory Essays in Moral Philosophy*, Tom Reagan, ed. (New York: Random, 1986), pp. 256-293: "Even if we grant that the fetus is a moral person and thus has a valid claim to life, it does not follow that abortion is always wrong" (p.233). J.T. Noonan, *Private Choice* (New York:

Free Press, 1979). Noonan urges the reversal of Roe v. Wade, but on many grounds, including the rights of the family and the poor, as well as his view that fetuses are the sorts of beings that it is seriously wrong to kill. Philip Devine, *The Ethics of Homicide* (Ithaca: Cornell 1978). Devine allows that there are cases when abortion is not morally impermissible, see esp. Ch. III. It also seems that one cannot legitimately ignore Thomson, "A Defense of Abortion," *Philosophy and Public Affairs*, I, 1 (1971): 47-66, as being among the most insightful writers on abortion. Her view is quite clearly opposed to Marquis's: the legal, if not in each case moral, permissibility of abortion stands on the rights of women to refuse to donate their bodies to others.

4. Warren, Engelhardt, Tooley, and Feinberg.
5. Noonan and Devine.

THE IMPORTANCE OF ONTOLOGY FOR FEMINIST POLICY-MAKING IN THE REALM OF REPRODUCTIVE TECHNOLOGY

Susan Sherwin

Susan Sherwin is University Research Professor of Philosophy and Women's Studies with a cross-appointment to the Department of Bioethics at Dalhousie University in Halifax. She is co-editor with Barbara Parish of Women, Medicine, Ethics, and the Law *(2001) and the author of* The Politics of Women's Health: Exploring Agency and Autonomy *(1998) and* No Longer Patient: Feminist Ethics and Health Care *(1992).*

Sherwin argues that rapid technological advances in biotechnologies and economic pressures to develop them call for a shift from the dominant political framework of liberal individualism to an explicitly feminist understanding of persons as relational beings. While she grants that "freedom of choice" has been important in feminist struggles to obtain and retain rights to abortion and contraception, she claims that these arguments are problematic when it comes to evaluating the technologies of assisted conception and reproductive genetics. An account of autonomy as relational challenges simplistic interpretations of freedom as reducible to enhancing consumer choice. Sherwin argues that adopting an ontological framework of relational understandings of personhood will allow policy-makers to appreciate the force of feminist and moral concerns, to explore a wider range of morally relevant questions about how groups may be affected by the policies under review, and to formulate ethically adequate policies in the expanding area of biotechnology.

1. Introduction

In the face of rapid technological developments and growing economic pressures, governments around the world are being called upon to regulate activities in the realm of biotechnology. My aim in this paper is to argue that core conceptual insights of feminist ethics are essential to ethically adequate policy making in this area. Specifically, I shall argue that development of ethical biotechnology require that policy-makers undergo an ontological shift from the currently widespread assumptions of the dominant political framework of liberal individualism to an explicitly feminist understanding of subjects as relational beings. To ground my discussion, I shall explore the field of reproductive technologies, especially as they are

(or may soon be) used for genetic "improvements." I shall pay particular attention to the use of *in vitro* fertilization (IVF) in conjunction with pre-implantation genetic diagnosis (PGD) and related variations.

Briefly, IVF, the core technology of so-called new reproductive technologies, is a platform technology that facilitates many other practices through affording access to oocytes (eggs) and embryos. The first step of IVF involves collection of multiple mature eggs from a woman's body through invasive methods, including "controlled" ovarian hyperstimulation through the use of various types of artificial hormones, followed by multiple transvaginal needle insertions in the ovarian follicles. Generally, the laboratory technicians involved in this treatment will expose all collected eggs to sperm (collected by masturbation from the intended biological father) in order to achieve the maximum number of embryos (fertilized eggs) — frequently more than ten. In traditional IVF, two or three of the embryos are transferred to the woman's uterus at the two to four cell stage, three days after fertilization. Those not used in the current fertility cycle can be frozen for later use or "donated" to other women or to research.[1]

It is also possible to keep the embryos in culture media longer. When an embryo reaches the eight cell stage, it is possible to remove one or two cells for genetic testing (pre-implantation genetic diagnosis, or PGD) and then transfer only the desired embryo(s) into the womb of the woman.[2] Because there are frequently more fertilized eggs present than can be responsibly transferred within a given cycle, there is a temptation to try to choose the "best" among them: those free of diagnosable anomalies, perhaps eventually those with genetic tendencies toward desirable characteristics such as high intelligence, musical or athletic abilities, or the preferred sex (and sexuality). For most women who undergo IVF, disposal of "inferior" embryos at this stage is far simpler psychologically and physically than it is at twelve or twenty weeks into a pregnancy, as is necessitated by standard current means of prenatal diagnosis. Hence, the range of conditions considered appropriate for termination will almost surely expand as PGD becomes commonplace. Moreover, as some of the unused embryos are donated for research, we can anticipate growing efforts to manipulate the genetic makeup of early embryos in efforts to "correct" problematic genes and to enhance or add supposedly desirable ones. Already, this technology is being used by some couples who are not infertile but choose IVF as a means to increase their sense of control over the genetic makeup of their offspring.[3]

At present, policy debates in Western democracies in the area of human reproduction and genetics ("reprogenetics") tend to center around two conflicting worldviews: religious commitments to the sanctity of human life as it occurs "naturally" on the one hand, and liberalism's commitment to the fundamental political value of personal freedom on the other. In other words, the policies addressing new reproductive and genetic technologies tend to mirror those that govern "old" reproductive technologies (abortion and contraception): they are either restrictive in deference to religious or social conservatism or they are permissive in response to the ideals of individual liberty. As reproductive and genetic services move steadily closer to a consumer model, we are also increasingly hearing arguments structured around the (il)legitimacy of restricting corporate and consumer activities for social purposes — i.e., does the state have the power and authority to intervene in the "private" exchanges of the marketplace? The usual answer is that the state can (and should) intervene to the extent necessary to ensure safety for "consumers" (i.e., to regulate adequate health and safety standards and, when necessary, to monitor the accuracy of advertising claims), but no further.

In most public debates regarding reproductive and other forms of biotechnology, the language of freedom of personal choice — the core value of liberal individualism — is central. Its importance is generally accepted without question and it functions in such a way as to make acceptance of each form of biotechnology the default position. The burden of proof falls to those who propose limiting the development or deployment of a specific type of biotechnology precisely because such positions are framed as limiting individual freedom. Moreover, and significantly, opponents of permissive biotechnology policies are expected to build their arguments from the conceptual tools inherent to liberal individualism — or else to appeal to the "higher" values of religious conservatism.[4]

This is an untenable position for feminists. To be sure, many feminists have found comfort and political strength in the protections provided by commitments to individual liberty in the area of the "old" reproductive technologies: "freedom of choice" has been the principal slogan for campaigns to support permissive policies with respect to contraception and abortion. Nevertheless, for reasons I shall explain, many feminists find this perspective problematic when it comes to evaluating the technologies of assisted conception and reproductive genetics. Ultimately, appeals to unconstrained freedom fail to provide the full range of safeguards feminists seek. As well, feminists concerned about the industrialization of reproductive and genetic technologies are generally reluctant to couch their challenges in the very language of capitalism (e.g., informed consumer choice will guide the market towards appropriate products). In addition to these political concerns, feminist research reveals theoretical reasons to oppose reliance on the conceptual framework at the heart of most public policy debates on these matters. Specifically, feminist discussions of relational autonomy have revealed serious difficulties with simplistic interpretations of freedom as reducible to an ideal of consumer choice. Therefore, it is necessary for feminists to part ways with the assumptions of liberal individualism if we are to capture the concerns of an explicitly feminist political, moral, and social view and be in a position to promote a morally adequate social policy governing these areas.

Canada, like many other countries, has spent many years trying to determine the appropriate legislative policy to regulate existing and emerging genetic technologies associated with the use of reproductive technology.[5] My aim is to show that development of appropriate policies in this area will require adoption of feminist relational understandings of personhood. Specifically, I shall argue that a key step in promoting feminist policies in the area of biotechnology is to alter the ontological framework of the policy-makers with respect to the fundamental concept of personhood as it functions with respect to autonomy and justice. Only when this ontological change is established will policy-makers be in a position to appreciate the force of feminist moral and political concerns.

My motivation is both pragmatic and theoretical. Pragmatically, I believe that the proposed conceptual shift is essential in order to achieve the types of policies I seek. My interest in these policies is not merely strategic, however. Elsewhere, I and other feminists have argued that feminist relational understandings of personhood are conceptually superior to liberal individualistic notions.[6] I shall draw on these arguments to make the moral case that feminist relational conceptions of personhood are *required* for an adequate ethics for public policy-making.

2. The Liberal Framework

Discussions of the ethics of policies concerned with reproductive and genetic interventions are primarily situated within the field of bioethics, where commitment to liberal individualist perspectives is pervasive.[7] Most of the issues that helped to generate the field of bioethics have been interpreted as consequences of a failure to respect individual autonomy. For example, the research scandals of the Nazi regime and of Tuskegee are widely perceived as arising from a failure to respect the autonomous right of research subjects to refuse participation in research trials. The remedy has been to develop codes of ethics for research involving humans that insist on individual informed consent from each research participant. Similarly, documented abuses of physician authority in clinical encounters with patients have been addressed by a widely recognized commitment to legally enforceable standards of voluntary informed consent — i.e., a mechanism for ensuring respect for individual patient authority over their clinical care because of the importance of the outcome to their lives. Thus, the concepts and values of liberal individualism, especially respect for individual autonomy, provide the backdrop for most debates about ethical policies governing particular forms of biotechnology policy.[8]

Maximum personal freedom is also considered a cornerstone of liberal political theories that inform the workings of modern democratic states. Within these theories, it is assumed that individual citizens have a wide range of ends and objectives. In light of such diversity, it is futile to try to specify any single, common conception of the good life. Rather, individuals are best served by being granted the most extensive liberty possible ("the greatest equal liberty compatible with a like liberty for all") to pursue their particular ends. Indeed, it is a common presupposition of liberal individualist theories that the primary motivation agents have for cooperating in social and political arrangements is to protect their own liberty to pursue their particular interests. According to this familiar view, the state has an obligation to support all citizens' pursuit of their particular conceptions of the good so far as possible; the best means of accomplishing this end is assumed to be extending the sphere of personal liberty as far as possible. The major difficulty faced by the state is that the interests and projects of individuals inevitably conflict. Hence, legislators and bureaucrats must develop and enforce fair procedures to regulate interpersonal conflicts. Individual freedom can be assured only to a level compatible with a like liberty for all. Personal freedom may be restricted when — and only when — its exercise will interfere with a more basic level of freedom for others, e.g., by causing serious harm to other individual persons.

Of course, protection of individual freedom is not the only value of liberal individualist moral and political theories. Justice is also a fundamental consideration. Most liberal individualist theories treat justice as involving the fair distribution of benefits and burdens within a society; that is, they understand justice as a distributive matter, concerned with appropriate assignments of commensurable (quantifiable) benefits and burdens. Liberal theories differ in their analyses of what constitutes fair rules of distribution and in the weighting they assign to the potentially conflicting values of respect for individual freedom and fair distribution of benefits, but all liberal theories treat the values of autonomy and justice as central. And all interpret these values as captured by examining the situation of individuals relative to that of their fellow citizens.

At the core of the various moral and political theories of liberal individualism is a particular metaphysical understanding of persons as the basic unit of social arrangements. Families, communities, states, and other significant types of social groups are composed of individual persons who are, by definition, ontologically prior to all social structures. It is assumed that each person has a well-defined set of interests, and, frequently, it is also assumed that these interests are transparent to the agent. Thus, on most accounts, persons are thought to be (at least ideally) rational deliberators who know their own interests and desires and make choices that fall within their own interests (broadly defined). As citizens, then, persons are primarily viewed as possessors of rights and goods. For moral and political purposes, each person is considered to be independent of others; i.e., they play their social and political roles as individuals.[9] The state's responsibility is to ensure that every person's respective interests are treated with equal concern and respect.

Therefore, when policy-makers approach worrisome forms of reproductive technology from within the conceptual framework of liberal individualist theories, they are expected to determine the impact of various policy options on all the individuals who will be affected. This injunction supports a particular line of questions. For example, when setting policy to govern contractual pregnancies (popularly known as surrogacy contracts), they will seek to ensure that all parties enter these contracts voluntarily. Hence, they will insist on full disclosure of the terms of the contract. Typically, they will also want assurance that conditions are in place to protect all parties from exploitation, by, for example, seeking to establish fair rates of pay for impoverished women with few alternative sources of income.

Similarly, when policy-makers reflect on appropriate policies regarding prenatal testing for fetal anomalies that might be associated with various sorts of disability after birth, they will insist on practices that provide pregnant women with the necessary information to make informed choices about the use of these technologies and subsequent decisions about the possible termination of their pregnancies in the face of problematic results. Welfare liberals will also be concerned to ensure that these services are equitably available so that poor women do not face unreasonable barriers to access to these technologies. Here, too, the focus of their deliberations will be on ensuring that women's choices are fully informed and truly voluntary.

Consider how this framework plays out in the area of reproductive technologies used for genetic purposes (i.e., IVF used for the purpose of PGD).

Society has already become accustomed to the routine use of blood tests, ultrasounds, and, in particular circumstances, more invasive prenatal tests to determine whether the fetus possesses certain types of genetic, chromosomal, or developmental anomalies that will result in some degree of disability after birth. The language supporting this practice is that it provides pregnant women with information and increases their "choices." In practice, most women who learn that their fetus possesses such an anomaly decide to terminate the pregnancy. Within a liberal individualist conception, the important questions to ask — besides those dealing with the moral legitimacy of abortion — are largely those of informed consent and fair access to the technology. The principle of autonomy may direct us to ask whether or not pregnant women have sufficient counseling before undergoing prenatal testing to appreciate the range of possible outcomes and the decisions they will be called upon to make in the event of a positive result.[10] It calls for conditions that ensure fully voluntary, informed consent to both the testing and any subsequent decision regarding selective abortion. In these cases and most others in the realm of reproductive and genetic technologies, liberal individualist theories tend to agree on the fundamental importance of what John Robertson calls "reproductive autonomy": a negative right against interference with personal projects to pursue one's own interests in reproducing or avoiding reproduction.[11]

More left-leaning liberals might also want to ensure that the opportunities to participate in these various forms of reproductive and genetic technology are justly distributed and not restricted to members of privileged groups. For example, many insist that contractual pregnancy arrangements not be limited to traditional family units but also be available to single and gay people. Prenatal screening has become such a routine aspect of pregnancy that most liberal individualist accounts stress the importance of ensuring that all pregnant women have access to it and that none are excluded from testing, or from subsequent selective abortion, on financial grounds. These are morally important concerns.

3. Feminist Concerns

Thus, the liberal framework presents us with a wide range of important ethical questions regarding the policies under consideration. All demand careful attention. There are, however, many additional questions that feminist ethics directs us to ask about these types of technology. In particular, feminist ethics requires us to move beyond questions of information and access and ask how the product or service under review will affect existing barriers to equality.[12] Hence, we must ask how the availability of a particular product or service will affect others besides the direct consumers. For example, in deciding whether to regulate or prohibit commercial surrogacy arrangements, legislators should consider how a practice of surrogacy, legitimised by state regulations, would be likely to affect prevailing social attitudes towards reproduction and offspring.

When evaluating IVF and other reproductive technologies we need to investigate how the technology in question supports other technologies such as PGD (and, probably, in time, genetic modifications of embryos), and how the resulting array of technologies is likely to alter social attitudes towards children and towards women as the bearers of children. Since PGD will undoubtedly expand the conditions considered appropriate for disposal of viable embryos, we must ask whether it is possible to pursue such options without encouraging views of children as products (which may be valued instrumentally such that they can be discarded if they do not meet minimum standards) rather than persons (to be valued intrinsically). Psychologically, is it even possible to try to screen out a wide range of "unacceptable" conditions in an embryo without viewing the resulting child as a commodity at least to some degree? Is it socially likely that we could introduce such "preventative" technologies and not hold women blameworthy if their refusal to participate in these practices results in children born with foreseeable disabilities? How have the various practices aimed at creating the "best possible" child already altered the experience of pregnancy and of parenting?[13] What is the impact of such practices on the lives of people who are now disabled? (Does putting so many resources into efforts to prevent the birth of others like them convey a social message that it would be better if those who are disabled had not been born?) How do these practices affect existing patterns of inequality when they enact practices that place radically different values on different genetic backgrounds? In what sense can we call women's choices autonomous when social circumstances make it virtually impossible for many to refuse offers of contractual pregnancies or prenatal testing?

The types of questions feminists add to the moral agenda cannot be captured from within the moral and political resources of liberal individualism; they require a different type of moral and political framework. Liberal individualism asks us to consider the impact of practices, policies, and products on individuals qua individuals. It directs us to consider whether any particular person will face reduced autonomy if they use these products and services and whether using these products and services will directly interfere with the autonomy of other individuals. Under some interpretations (welfare liberalism), it also directs us to ensure that each individual is comparably placed with respect to opportunities for access to desired technologies. In both cases, the focus of analysis is the individual as in independent unit and the criterion of evaluation involves the rights of individuals.

The questions that feminists raise involve more than violations of individual autonomy or failures of distributive justice among individuals in isolation, however. Feminists ask how different social *groups* are likely to be affected by the technologies in question. These are different questions, not alternative variations of the existing ones. Social groups are not mere conglomerations of existing individuals, such that impacts on groups can be calculated by summing the impact of practices and policies on the individuals that make up the group. Nor can the harms (or benefits) associated with patterns of systemic differences between groups be wholly reduced to the effects on particular individuals. It is not possible to capture all of the harms of pervasive patterns such as sexism and racism by identifying the degree of harm experienced by individual

women or people of African or Asian descent; rather, it is essential to consider the effect of policy options on groups as well as on individuals.

There are two reasons for the claim that the effect on groups cannot be reduced to the specific harms experienced by individuals. First, there is the pragmatic concern: group harms, such as racism and sexism, cannot even be perceived, let alone identified, examined, or evaluated, without seeing their impact on social groups. So long as we look only at the level of the individual, we will miss many of the dimensions that constitute oppression. For example, the psychological discomfort that I, personally, may feel about my failure to live up to cultural standards of youth and beauty for women, or the diminished happiness I may experience because I do not feel safe traveling alone to cultural or entertainment venues will not figure very high on any community-wide utility calculation. But I would not even think to identify these feelings as worthy of consideration without familiarity with feminist analyses about the collective impact of cultural norms of feminine beauty on the expectations and attitudes of women and men or the systemic way in which gender-based violence limits most women's freedom of movement in their own communities. The harms to individuals only appear significant *after* we identify the group-based harms associated with different practices.

Similarly, the benefits that accrue to members of privileged groups by virtue of their being free of the damage experienced by members of oppressed groups also remains invisible if we restrict our focus only to the level of individuals. For example, most men enjoy the relative advantage of feeling safe in (some) streets; this is significant, not only for the ways it expands their range of possible leisure activities, but also for affecting their freedom to participate in educational or social programs that might enhance their job opportunities. As well, men are the primary beneficiaries of the widespread tendency for women to take on a greater share of the unpaid labour required in the domestic sphere, yet when considered on a case-by-case basis, the patterns of work distribution are usually either invisible or easily explained away.

We can only begin to explore strategies for eliminating the injustice represented by these group-based harms and benefits if we understand the fact that they are essentially group-based in their construction. Thus, we need a moral and political ontology that recognizes the possibility of group-based harms and benefits even if we remain committed to the view that all harms ultimately attach to individuals.

Once these group-based harms have been identified and analyzed, however, it might appear that we could then translate the impact of these harms to a sum of their impact on the individual members of the group. Such a reduction is not possible because there is a second, deeper, reason for resisting the view that group based harms are reducible to the sum of individual harms. To understand this reason, I shall appeal to Iris Marion Young's efforts to explain oppression in terms of five "faces" that represent the range of effects oppression may have on different social groups: exploitation, marginalization, cultural imperialism, violence, and powerlessness.[14] Some of these harms, such as cultural imperialism, can only be calculated at the level of groups. (Cultural imperialism occurs when the dominant group controls most tools of culture formation and dissemination and its members either ignore the experiences of oppressed minorities or misleadingly represent them through pejorative stereotypes.) It is a phenomenon that does not make sense at the level of the individual since it involves ways in which one group represents another *as a group* and it is central to the formation of cultural beliefs about the character, activities, and value of members of both groups.

Other types of group harms, such as violence, exploitation, or powerlessness, assume a different meaning when they occur in the context of group oppression. Any person can experience violence at the hands of another and this would represent a significant harm to that person. But members of oppressed groups tend to be subject to additional reasons for violent attack: their membership in a socially vulnerable group. Thus, their gender is a causal factor in many attacks against women (especially, but not solely, sexual assaults), as race often is in attacks against blacks, and sexuality is in attacks against gay men. Moreover, violence based on the victim's group identity, whereby a principal contributing factor is the race, gender, or sexuality of the victim, represents a harm not only to the specific victim but to the group itself which is increasingly viewed as a routine target of such violence. ("Gay-bashing" is a particular form of violence that is viewed by both perpetrators and victims as involving a social message as well as a personal affront.) In the face of repeated attacks on members of an oppressed social group, the entire group may experience a diminished sense of safety, self-esteem, community acceptance, and social value. Conversely, members of privileged social groups may experience an inflated sense of their own safety and importance that might encourage them to participate in future events of bullying, or at least to refrain from efforts to improve public safety. If we look only at the particular harms of a series of attacks on individuals, we may record the suffering of the victims and their loved ones, but we will not see how each one connects with other gender or race-based violence to diminish the opportunities and social status of women and racial minorities. That is why hate crimes are particularly insidious, even though the impact on the individual victims may be quite analogous to the impact of a comparable attack precipitated by "personal" reasons.

Note that focus on the ways in which oppression affects social groups still leaves room for concern about the harms suffered by individuals. The harms Young identifies as the five faces of oppression are harms at *both* the level of the group and the level of the individual. Violence based on group membership is still painful to the individual; it is just that the damage done by such violence cannot be fully calculated by looking only at the victim's personal pain. Similarly, exploitation, marginalization, powerlessness, and cultural imperialism are the result of, and contributory to, power differentials between social groups. They reflect, and they reinforce, differences in power between social groups. The notion of power differences is a relational concept that characterizes the relative status of groups; insofar as it also describes the (typical) relative status of individual members of those groups, that status is a function of — and secondary to — their group-based power.[15] Of course, these various practices or "faces" of oppression take a toll on individual members of these groups. Hence, for most feminists, the costs of oppression must be measured in both group and individual effects. Neither category can be fully reduced to the other.

When they enter the realm of policy-making, feminists seek to translate their understanding of the importance of considering the effect of policy options on social groups into a revised moral agenda. In particular, in seeking to determine the likely effect of different policies on vulnerable groups, feminists expand the list of morally relevant dimensions for policy-making well beyond the agenda that is typically discussed. Indeed, they identify and make explicit morally important questions that are invariably overlooked within traditional individualistic frameworks.

The difficulty that feminists face is that in order to make many of these additional moral questions meaningful to policy-makers, they must shift the focus of concern from the restrictive orientation of liberal individualism towards a relational approach to ethics and politics. Specifically, they require us to redefine the terms of autonomy and justice in ways that make clear the moral significance of considering the impact of policies on social groups as well as on individuals.[16] Thus, there is a clear strategic interest in persuading policy-makers to abandon the framework of liberal individualism in favour of a relational understanding of core moral categories. There are, also, good theoretical reasons for making this shift: relational interpretations of personhood, autonomy, and justice are conceptually more adequate than narrowly individualistic accounts.

4. A Feminist Relational Alternative

Let us turn, then, to a brief review of a feminist relational framework in order to explore its conceptual advantages over traditional accounts. At its core, feminist relational theory challenges the reigning conception of persons. Specifically, relational theory requires us to supplant the familiar ideal of the independent, rational, self-interested deliberator of liberal individualism with a relational subject who is (at least partially) constituted by social interactions. Rather than understanding persons as ontologically prior to society, a relational account envisions persons as beings who are created — in large part — through their social relations. As Annette Baier explained, persons are always "second persons," created through social processes; we become persons through learning from other persons how to be persons ourselves.[17]

As a result, relational persons are more complex and less transparent than are the persons of most liberal individualist theories. Where liberal theories favour views of selfhood as a unified state with well-ordered, rational preferences clearly known by the agent, relational accounts understand it to be a rather messy, on-going project in which different aspects of the self may be in tension with one another. Where traditional theories act as if people either always know their own values or else can discover them best by introspection, relational theorists believe that most people discover many of their values in the process of dialogue and action. In other words, values are formed through social engagement, not prior to such interaction. Thus, it is not sufficient to provide processes that allow agents the freedom to act on their objectives (the focus of liberal accounts). It is also essential to establish processes that support opportunities for agents to determine where their interests lie.

According to most feminist accounts, persons are essentially embodied beings and their bodily characteristics carry important social meanings. Within contemporary Western society, social and political significance is attached to such features as sex, race, disability, sexuality, class, and age. These features are the basis of social groups that exist in relations of oppression or dominance with other social groups. Individuals derive their identity in part from their membership in these social groups, in that their sense of themselves is affected by the meanings assigned to their sex, race, class, and so on. Thus, identity is not just a reflection of their rational interests and conscious choices, but also a response to their classification within a complex array of social groups. In other words, relational persons are deeply embedded in their particular historical, social, and political circumstances; they cannot be properly understood in abstraction from these contexts.

This means that moral and political discussions about persons must be attentive to ways in which these social differences can produce morally relevant differences in the circumstances of individuals affected by generic principles and policies. As relational beings, persons develop their values and abilities to act on these values through processes shaped by their interpersonal interactions and by those produced by their broadly political social status. It is necessary to pay attention to the effects of both levels of interaction when exploring ways of respecting individual autonomy. Yet, traditional liberal theories reduce personhood to an abstract conception that erases differences between persons that are based on group differences. It is deliberately inattentive to morally and politically important relational features.

It is worth mentioning that feminists are not the only ones to reject liberal individualist moral and political theories and the over-simplified metaphysical view of the person that underlies these approaches. Communitarians are also critical of the presuppositions of liberal individualism. They, too, see persons as essentially social beings and they demand a moral and political vision that recognizes this relational status and assigns value to the relationships that constitute persons. What distinguishes feminist from other relational accounts, such as communitarian theories, is that feminists are concerned with the ways in which power operates between different social groups. Feminists look beyond the macro level of the state and the micro level of family life to investigate the relationships that exist between and among social groups. Specifically, they see moral and political significance in relationships of oppression and privilege between groups.

If we accept the need to understand persons, the focus of liberal concern, as relational rather than self-contained beings, then we must also modify the ways we understand our principal moral and political obligations to them. In particular, we need to revise the ways in which we understand the tra-

ditional liberal concerns of autonomy and justice to reflect the fact that persons are now conceived as being a different type of entity. Feminism, on my view, does not require us to abandon commitment to these values at the heart of liberal theories, but it does demand significant reinterpretation of each. Because social group membership is a principal component of a feminist relational account of personhood, efforts to promote the core liberal values of freedom and justice must consider ways in which autonomy and justice can be addressed at the level of social groups as well as the level of individuals.

A significant amount of recent feminist work has gone into examining ways in which feminist relational theory transforms traditional understandings of autonomy. While some feminist theorists have proposed abandoning the concept of autonomy altogether, many others recommend reframing it in relational terms to take account of the social context within which individuals make choices.[18] Accounts of relational autonomy make explicit the fact that autonomy is both defined and pursued in social contexts; as well, social conditions significantly affect an individual's very ability to exercise autonomy. Hence, where liberal individualist theories either look at the generic conditions required for any individual to exercise autonomy (in political theory) or they focus on the quality of decision-making by individuals as they are presently constituted (in practical ethics), feminist relational accounts explore the social conditions that support — or inhibit — each person's ability to identify and pursue her own concerns. Feminist accounts are particularly sensitive to the ways in which oppressive structures limit the types of choices available to members of particular social groups and interfere with the opportunities members of oppressed groups have for developing the skills necessary for exercising autonomy.[19]

In practice, this interpretation demands consideration of the social, as well as the physical and psychological, impacts of proposed new technologies. It greatly expands the range of questions that need to be addressed regarding the degree of autonomy required for introduction of various biotechnologies. And it alters the types of answers appropriate even to the original set of questions. For example, it demands that we consider the ways in which normalization and widespread availability of PGD may increase pressure on women to make use of this technology even if they have no history of infertility problems. It asks us to reflect on ways in which this technology extends the widespread tendency, already present with extensive use of other forms of prenatal testing and a growing list of behavioural recommendations for pregnant women, to expect women to do everything in their power to create the "healthiest" possible baby. Currently available reproductive and genetic technologies are altering cultural norms about what is morally required of pregnant women with respect to the health of their subsequent offspring. In the face of such changes in cultural expectations and demands, women are finding that their freedom to refuse genetic tests and technological interventions in their pregnancies have, for all practical purposes, virtually disappeared.[20]

These practical limitations on women's freedom to set the terms of their own pregnancies and to refuse the imposition of cultural values they may personally oppose involves a constraint on autonomy that can only be captured through relational understandings. As we have seen, traditional liberal conceptions of autonomy encourage opportunities for women to obtain the information necessary for rational deliberation and a freedom from explicit coercion; they require careful procedures for informed consent. But they do not provide relief from the social pressures women experience to produce babies of "acceptable quality" nor from the expectation that refusal of prenatal genetic selection can only be justified in the face of rational, coherent individual arguments. It is only when we consider the social conditions associated with prenatal — and, ultimately, pre-pregnancy — testing and selection affecting women collectively that we see how individual women's autonomy may be reduced by the availability of additional options for control over their pregnancies.

Similarly, justice needs to be redefined in feminist relational terms. This requires supplementing considerations of distributive justice with questions of social justice. Traditional liberal individu-

alist accounts tend to focus narrowly on questions of distributive (and retributive) justice.[21] Distributive justice is designed to address allocations of quantifiable, finite, material things and does not capture the conditions necessary for proper access to social goods such as rights, opportunity, power, and self-respect. In contrast, feminist accounts of social justice provide tools for investigating the ways in which sexism, racism, and other forms of oppression support unjust arrangements of social goods.[22] They encourage us to look at effects of policies, procedures, and practices at the level of social groups and to pay particular attention to ways in which oppression structures relationships among different groups.

Feminist relational accounts of social justice ask us to investigate ways in which different policies governing the use of reproductive technologies for genetic purposes will affect the status of oppressed groups. For example, widespread use of PGD has the potential to change cultural norms of health and acceptability for children born with conditions subject to detection through this technology. Such shifts may increase the significant marginalization and social discrimination experienced by people with disabilities. (Already, existing forms of prenatal testing have caused serious anxiety within the community of disability activists and extensions of the technology that expand the range of choices available will likely exacerbate social prejudices against "preventable disabilities.") The very use of these technologies increases the tendency to treat reproduction as just another form of production, subject to the same demands for quality control as consumers expect in other spheres of their lives. Such habits of thought view women as producers and hold them to standards of accountability for the "quality" of their offspring in ways that may reduce their already precarious social standing and may seriously undermine the possibility of treating children as full members of the moral community.

All of these questions suggest reasons to be wary of these new technologies. I do not want to imply, however, that feminist relational accounts inevitably lead to conservative policy options regarding innovative forms of biotechnology. There are many types of technology that have served to reduce the oppression of vulnerable groups. Certainly, contraceptive technologies that have allowed women to avoid unwanted pregnancies have played a major role in increasing most women's social and economic equality. Technologies that allow people with mobility impairments to move about or allow those with visual impairments to read have increased the social and economic participation of many people with disabilities. Feminist relational theory asks us to consider if there are ways in which genetic technologies might be deployed to lessen rather than increase the oppression of vulnerable groups.

My point is that the additional questions feminists ask are different from (and, hence, additional to) liberal concerns about the fair distribution of opportunities for access to these technologies. Attention to social justice moves our investigations beyond questions of fair payment and access to reproductive and genetic services to consideration of how new practices and products will affect current barriers to equality of respect, status, and influence in society. They require us to consider how the policies in question affect social groups as well as individual persons.

5. Feminist Relational Theory and Policy

As we have seen, relational views of personhood, along with the implications of this view for autonomy and justice expand the agenda of policy deliberations beyond the familiar questions of liberal individualism to the broader concerns of feminist ethics. Currently, most policy-makers work within the conceptual framework of liberal individualism. This framework limits their vision of both questions and answers. When a narrow, individualistic conception of autonomy and justice is assumed, policy-makers cannot explore in any meaningful way the question of how existing patterns of oppression will be affected by the policy options under review. The familiar liberal framework renders invisible important questions dealing with the impact of policies on social groups by addressing only those effects captured by summing apparent effects on the individual members of social

groups. It is only when we perceive people as members of social groups that can be collectively harmed (or benefited) by products or policies that we are able to recognize some types of effects they may each experience. When policy-makers restrict their focus to individuals as the fundamental units of social policy, they fail to see ways in which the practices under review contribute to patterns of oppression.

The case I have made here is a largely a pragmatic one. I have not proven that it is logically impossible for policy-makers to appreciate the significance of questions about the impact of their decisions on oppressed social groups from within the framework of liberal individualism. Many liberals will continue to argue that their theory can accommodate such concerns. I do not believe that it can, and I have tried to show why it is virtually impossible to capture all relevant moral dimensions of the subject without shifting to a group-based analysis. Thus, there is reason for concern that most policy-makers approach their work within the conceptual scheme provided by liberal individualism, narrowly construed. It is possible that they can learn to ask the types of questions feminists wish within this current framework, but as a matter of fact, few actually do.

If, however, policy-makers can be persuaded to shift their moral and political framework from liberal individualist accounts of autonomy and justice to richer relational interpretations, they will be compelled to address a much broader range of moral questions. This requires them to reject conceptions of persons as pre-social in favour of relational accounts that view persons as products of society, inseparable from the complex social interactions in which they engage. The preferred account would make clear that the interests and identities of persons are not independent of their social circumstances but are actually framed by them. If policy-makers accomplish the ontological shift to a feminist relational understanding of persons, their moral and political agendas will almost certainly become sensitive to relational concerns. At that point, feminists will be in a position to more effectively communicate important concerns about biotechnologies that are now not heard because they do not fit within dominant conceptual structures.

Moreover, as I have tried to indicate, however briefly, relational accounts of personhood, autonomy, and justice, are not merely convenient strategic devices; they are conceptually preferable to narrowly individualistic interpretations. Persons actually are inextricably socially embedded beings and their membership in certain types of social groups shapes their moral and political experiences in significant ways. Theories that erase these differences from our moral and political landscape are poor reflectors of important dimensions of moral personhood and agency. Relational accounts reframe traditional liberal worries about autonomy and justice and place them within a richer context; in so-doing, they allow us to explore a wider range of morally relevant considerations than is revealed by traditional conceptions of autonomy. Within a relational framework, all of the familiar moral and political questions about the impact of policies on individuals remain, but they are now supplemented with other morally significant questions that have to do with how groups are likely to be affected by the policies under review.

It is my contention that these richer, more adequate accounts of moral and political considerations *require* a different understanding of what it means to be a person in the morally relevant sense. In other words, they require a shift in the ontological framework of all those engaged in policy deliberations from narrow abstractions to complex relational understandings. Feminist epistemologists and philosophers of science have demonstrated the many ways in which social and political assumptions lie at the core of even the most abstract, apparently objective theories. The same can be said of metaphysics: here, too, we need to reflect on the moral and political dimensions of our core concepts and assumptions. My argument in this paper is not with liberalism's concern with autonomy and justice, but with its metaphysical construction of persons as subjects of meaningful moral and political deliberations in the absence of attention to important relational dimensions of persons as socially constituted beings.

Author's Note

I wish to thank all those who generously commented on earlier drafts of this paper, particularly Richmond Campbell, Sue Campbell, Jeffrey Nisker, and Jason Scott Robert.

NOTES

1. In practice, women are often allowed some relief on the high costs of the treatment if they agree to "donate" their eggs to other women or to science. These financial incentives call into question the voluntariness of their "donations."

2. J. Nisker and R.E. Gore-Layton, "Pre-Implantation Genetic Diagnosis: A Model of Progress and Concern." *Journal of the Society of Obstetricians and Gynecologists of Canada* 17(1995): 247-61.

3. R.J. Boyle and J. Savulescu, "Ethics of using preimplantation genetic diagnosis to select a stem cell donor for an existing person." *British Medical Journal* 323(7323) (2001): 1240-43. G. Pennings, R. Schots and I. Liebars, "Ethical considerations on preimplantation genetic diagnosis for HLA typing to match a future child as a donor of haematopietic stem cells to a sibling." *Human Reproduction* 17(3) (2002): 534-38.

4. Religious arguments tend to become marginalized in the secularized context of Canadian policy-making. While they are respected as sincere and important to individuals, the logic of liberal individualism relegates religious conviction to the "private sphere" to be celebrated as part of the diverse cultural mosaic of the nation but an inappropriate basis for social policy. Given the conservative nature of most traditional religions and their tendency to embrace policies oppressive to women, I have no interest in challenging this response to policy arguments based solely on religious beliefs.

5. After more than ten years of reflection, including a four year long, multi-million dollar Royal Commission investigation, the Canadian government is currently poised (fall 2002) to introduce legislation that will regulate reproductive technologies (Bill C-13). [In March 2004, the government passed Bill C-6, *Assisted Human Reproduction Act.*]

6. S. Sherwin, Coordinator, *Feminist Health Care Ethics Research Network. The Politics of Women's Health: Exploring Agency and Autonomy* (Philadelphia, PA: Temple University Press, 1998). C. Mackenzie and N. Stoljar, eds., *Relational Autonomy: Feminist Perspectives on Autonomy, Agency, and the Social Self* (New York, NY: Oxford University Press, 2000).

7. S.M. Wolf, "Erasing Difference: Race, Ethnicity, and Gender in Bioethics" In *Embodying Bioethics: Recent Feminist Advances*, ed. A. Donchin and L.M. Purdy (Lanham, MD: Rowman and Littlefield, 1999).

8. While moral theorists differ on many important matters, most of the reigning moral theories of the West treat respect for individual autonomy as foundational. For example, protection of the freedom of individual persons to pursue their own conception of the good is a core value of Kantian, rights-based, and social contract moral theories. Even utilitarians believe that respect for individual autonomy is extremely important, if only for extrinsic reasons. (John Stuart Mill was the author of *On Liberty* as well as *Utilitarianism*.)

9. Some theorists, e.g., Rawls, treat families or households as the basic unit of analysis at certain levels. See John Rawls, *A Theory of Justice* (Cambridge, MA: Harvard University Press, 1971). This practice carries with it a host of other concerns for feminists as has been articulated by Okin. See S.M. Okin, *Justice, Gender, and the Family* (New York, NY: Basic Books, 1989).

10. This is a significant demand. It appears that at present few women actually receive the level of counseling a genuine commitment to informed consent would require, and that there are nowhere near the number of trained counselors available to meet the need associated with such a commitment. For a sense of the scope of the problem regarding a single genetic disease, see B. Wilfond and N.C. Fost, "The Introduction of Cystic Fibrosis Carrier Screening into Clinical Practices: Policy Considerations." *The Millbank Quarterly* 70(4) (1992): 629.

11. J.A. Robertson, *Children of Choice: Freedom and the New Reproductive Technologies* (Princeton, NJ: Princeton University Press, 1994).

12. S. Sherwin, *No Longer Patient: Feminist Ethics and Health Care* (Philadelphia, PA: Temple University Press, 1992).

13. B.K. Rothman, *The Tentative Pregnancy: Prenatal Diagnosis and the Future of Motherhood* (New York, NY: Viking, 1986).

14. I.M. Young, *Justice and the Politics of Difference* (Princeton, NJ: Princeton University Press, 1990).

15. This does not mean that every member of an oppressed group has less power than every member of a dominant group, of course. Obviously, there are some very powerful women in society. It is that women, collectively, have less power than men collectively (and similarly, people of colour have less power than white people, people with disabilities have less power than those without disabilities, and so on). Indeed, it is the relative power of groups — rather than of each individual member — that is at issue here.

16. S. Sherwin, *No Longer Patient.*

17. A. Baier, *Postures of the Mind: Essays on Mind and Morals* (Minneapolis, MN: University of Minnesota Press, 1985).

18. S. Sherwin, Coordinator. *Feminist Health Care Ethics Research Network*; Mackenzie and Stoljar, *Relational Autonomy.*

19. D.T. Meyers, *Self, Society, and Personal Choice* (New York, NY: Columbia University Press, 1989).

20. B.K. Rothman, *The Tentative Pregnancy.* A. Lippman, "Prenatal Genetic Testing and Screening: Constructing Needs and Reinforcing Inequalities." *American Journal of Law and Medicine* 17 (1991): 15-50. S. Sherwin, "Normalizing Reproductive Technologies and the Implications for Autonomy" in *Globalizing Feminist Bioethics*, ed. G. Anderson, A. Santos and R. Tong (Boulder, CO: Westview Press, 2001).

21. I.M. Young, *Justice and the Politics of Difference* (Princeton, NJ: Princeton University Press, 1990).

22. Ibid.

IN NEW TESTS FOR FETAL DEFECTS, AGONIZING CHOICES FOR PARENTS

Amy Harmon

Amy Harmon is a reporter who covers issues of technology for The New York Times.

Harmon talks to women undergoing prenatal testing and deciding about whether to abort fetuses diagnosed with "abnormalities." Prenatal testing presents women with difficult choices about whether to continue a pregnancy, choices that involve evaluating the severity of the "defect" and weighing the advice given by medical practitioners, genetic counselors, partners, and family members. Harmon discusses objections by disability theorists who view prenatal testing as a eugenics movement and argue that it will result in greater intolerance of disabled persons and fewer medical resources and accommodation for disabled people. Disability theorists also raise concerns about increased pressure on women by doctors, health care providers, or family members to abort fetuses with relatively minor defects or of a specific sex. Harmon ends by presenting examples in which the women themselves discuss their cases, the decisions they made, and the effects these decisions have had on their lives.

Lying in the darkened doctor's office, Kate Hoffman stared at the image of the 11-week-old fetus inside her on the ultrasound screen, a tiny ghost with a big head. It would have been so sweet, Ms. Hoffman said, if something had not been so clearly wrong.

Ms. Hoffman's first three children had been healthy, and she was sure this one would be, too. She was not planning to have the amniocentesis procedure often used to test for fetal health problems, preferring to avoid even the slightest risk that the insertion of a needle into her uterus would cause her to miscarry.

But when her doctor told her there was a new way to assess the chance of certain abnormalities with no risk of miscarriage — a blood test and special sonogram — she happily made an appointment.

The result, signaling that the child had a high chance of having Down syndrome, thrust Ms. Hoffman and her husband into a growing group of prospective parents who have learned far more about the health of their fetus than was possible even three years ago.

Fetal genetic tests are now routinely used to diagnose diseases as well known as cystic fibrosis and as obscure as fragile X, a form of mental retardation. High-resolution sonograms can detect life-threatening defects like brain cysts as well as treatable conditions like a small hole in the heart or a cleft palate sooner and more reliably than previous generations of the technology. And the risk of Down syndrome, one of the most common birth defects, can be assessed in the first trimester rather than waiting for a second-trimester blood test or amniocentesis.

Most couples say they are both profoundly grateful for the new information and hugely burdened by the choices it forces them to make. The availability of tests earlier in pregnancy mean that if they opt for an abortion it can be safer and less public.

But first they must decide: What defect, if any, is reason enough to end a pregnancy that was very much wanted? Shortened limbs that could be partly treated with growth hormones? What about a life expectancy of only a few months? What about 30 years? Or a 20 percent chance of mental retardation?

Striving to be neutral, doctors and genetic counselors flood patients with scientific data, leaving them alone for the hard conversations about the ethics of abortion, and how having a child with a particular disease or disability would affect them and their families. There are few traditions to turn to, and rarely anyone around who has confronted a similar dilemma.

Against the backdrop of a bitter national divide on abortion, couples are devising their own very private scales for weighing whether to continue their pregnancies. Often, political or religious beliefs end up being put aside, trumped by personal feelings. And even many of those who have no doubts about their decision to terminate say the grief is lasting.

"It was never even anything I had considered until I had the bad results," said Ms. Hoffman, who ended her pregnancy last year after a follow-up test confirmed that her child, if it survived, would have Down syndrome. "It was the hardest decision I ever had to make."

She and her husband, Drew, of Marblehead, Mass., decided that the quality of the child's life, and that of the rest of their family, would be too severely compromised. "I don't look at it as though I had an abortion, even though that is technically what it is," she added. "There's a difference. I wanted this baby."

Whatever they choose, couples find themselves exposed to judgments from all sides. Several of those interviewed asked that personal details be withheld because they had let friends and family believe that their abortion was a miscarriage. Others say they have been surprised that even conservative parents, who never faced such decisions themselves, have counseled them to abort rather than face too hard a life.

Activists for the rights of the disabled say that a kind of grass-roots eugenics is evolving that will ultimately lead to greater intolerance of disabilities and less money for cures or treatments. And even some doctors who perform abortions are uncomfortable as some patients choose to quietly abort fetuses with relatively minor defects.

No one tracks the number of abortions performed for medical reasons, but obstetricians say several factors are most likely contributing to a growth in their frequency, including broader availability of new screening technologies and more pregnancies among women over 35, who are at greater risk of carrying a fetus with chromosomal abnormalities.

About a dozen tests for genetic mutations that could cause diseases or disabilities in a child are now regularly offered to pregnant women and their partners, depending on their ethnicity and conditions that run in their families.

More than 450 conditions, including deafness, dwarfism and skin disease, can be diagnosed by testing fetal cells, with more than 100 tests added in the last year alone. African-Americans are widely screened for sickle-cell anemia, and a panel that now includes nine tests for diseases common to Ashkenazi Jews has virtually eliminated the birth of children in the United States with Tay-Sachs, a fatal early childhood genetic disorder.

Next month, the Baylor College of Medicine plans to introduce a pilot program with perhaps the largest panel of prenatal tests ever offered. For $2,000, a pregnant woman will be able to have her fetus tested for some 50 conditions that cause mental retardation.

Quest Diagnostics, a leading provider of medical tests, said prenatal and genetic mutation tests were one of the fastest-growing parts of its business.

"People are going to the doctor and saying, 'I don't want to have a handicapped child, what can you do for me?'" said Charles Strom, medical director of Quest's genetic testing center.

A Couple's Choice

The new screening tests provide reassuring news for the vast majority of pregnant women. But

Amy D., a preschool teacher in Livingston, N.J., who terminated a pregnancy after finding out the child would have cystic fibrosis, remembers falling to her knees in the schoolyard when her genetic counselor called her with the test results.

She and her husband did not know what cystic fibrosis was and had no known family history of the disease, which causes progressive lung failure and carries an average life expectancy of 35 years. But in the fall of 2001, the American College of Obstetricians and Gynecologists recommended that a blood test for the gene mutations that cause the disease be offered in all pregnancies when either the man or woman is Caucasian.

Amy D. screened positive as a carrier in August 2002, shortly after she found out she was pregnant with her first child. When her husband also turned out to be a carrier, there was a one-in-four chance that their fetus would have the disease. An amniocentesis showed that it would. Having watched her husband shrink from scenes of suffering, whether in movies or during his own father's illness, she said she knew her marriage would not survive having a severely ill child. "My life would have been caring for my child, which would have been fine if she would be O.K.," said Amy D., who asked that her last name be withheld for fear that anti-abortion activists would harass her. "But she wasn't going to be O.K."

After months of depression, she said she is thrilled to be adopting an infant boy from Asia. Still, when she watches the 20-something woman with cystic fibrosis on MTV's "Real World" dating and getting body piercings, Amy D. says she cannot help wondering if her daughter, who would have been named Sydney Frances, would have been like that — at least for a while.

With the number of American couples being tested to determine if they carry cystic fibrosis soaring from a few thousand in 2000 to several hundred thousand last year, more people are tackling similar decisions. Sometimes, the gene tests can even distinguish between a mutation that causes a mild form of cystic fibrosis and one that is more severe.

Kaiser Permanente, a large managed health care organization, said that when both members of a couple among its patients in Northern California tested positive, 80 percent opted for the follow-up test of their fetus. Of those whose fetus was affected, 95 percent terminated the pregnancy.

"It's a crummy disease, the treatments are far from what we would like, and we have a reliable test," said Dr. David R. Witt, director of Kaiser's Northern California prenatal screening program. "Based on the response, people are grateful they had an opportunity to take advantage of it."

A Slippery Slope

The wider range and earlier timing of prenatal tests are raising concern among some bioethicists and advocates for disability rights who argue that the medical establishment is sending a message to patients that the goal is to guard against the birth of children with disabilities.

"By putting them out there as something everyone must do, the profession communicates that these are conditions that everyone must avoid," said Adrienne Asch, a bioethicist at Wellesley College. "And the earlier you can get it done the more you can get away with because you never have to tell anybody."

Some doctors, too, say they are troubled by what sometimes seems like a slippery slope from prenatal science to eugenics. The problem, though, is where to draw the line.

Dr. Jonathan Lanzkowsky, an obstetrician affiliated with Mount Sinai Hospital in Manhattan, described one woman who had been born with an extra finger, which was surgically removed when she was a child. Her children have a 50-50 chance of inheriting the condition, but she is determined not to let that happen. Detecting the extra digit through early ultrasounds, she has terminated two pregnancies so far, despite doctors' efforts to persuade her to do otherwise, Dr. Lanzkowsky said.

Other doctors said that they had seen couples terminate pregnancies for poor vision, whose effect they had witnessed on a family member, or a cleft palate, which they worried would affect the quality of their child's life.

In an extreme case, Dr. Mark Engelbert, an obstetrician and gynecologist on the Upper East Side of Manhattan, said he had performed an abortion for a woman who had three girls and wanted a boy.

"She was much more comfortable with it than I was," Dr. Engelbert said. "I told her if it was a new patient I wouldn't have done it. But my feeling as a physician was that I've accepted the responsibility of being her health care provider. She's not doing anything illegal, and it's not for me to decide."

Perhaps the hardest cases for both doctors and patients come when technology provides enough information to raise concerns about the health of a fetus but not enough to make a conclusive diagnosis. When Tom Horan and his wife learned in April that their fetus's legs were bowed and shortened, they were told that the condition could be healed through braces, growth hormones and surgical procedures in childhood.

But before they decided what to do, a closer examination by a specialist with a 3-D ultrasound machine revealed other deformities: the left arm was missing below the elbow, and the right hand was only partially developed. Moreover, sometimes such features are a sign of a neurological impairment, the doctors told them, but in this case it was impossible to tell.

"Our main concern was the quality of life that the child would have growing up with such extensive limb deformities, even in the absence of cognitive problems," Mr. Horan said. He and his wife, who have three other children, were reared Roman Catholic and had never considered terminating a pregnancy. Yet even his father, Mr. Horan said, who had long been opposed to abortion, supported their decision to end the pregnancy.

"Confronted with this question and knowing what we knew, it changed his mind," Mr. Horan said. "It's not just a question of right and wrong; it introduces all sorts of other questions that one has to consider, whether it is the survivability of the child, quality of life of parents, quality of life of siblings, social needs. And it becomes much

more real when you're confronted with an actual situation."

After the termination, an examination showed that if he survived, Mr. Horan's son would have had an extremely rare condition, Cornelia de Lange syndrome. He would have been severely mentally and physically disabled.

The news was a relief to Mr. Horan, who said he felt sadness and grief, but no regrets about the decision. But before the diagnosis, he said, he felt guilt and uncertainty. At 21 weeks, the fetus was not viable when his wife underwent induced labor and delivery but survived briefly.

"Our son lived for three hours, and I spent almost all that time holding him," Mr. Horan said. "I worried that I had decided to rob him of his life simply based on limb deformities. I wondered about the ethical implications of taking a life simply on that basis. What did that say about me?"

Contradicting Beliefs

That is just one of many questions that couples ask themselves as they confront the ethics of whether to abort a fetus with disabilities. But because it is such a charged subject, many are loath to discuss it with others. They say there is often no outlet for their grief.

"I cannot turn on the computer any day without getting an e-mail from someone who needs help," said the woman who runs A Heartbreaking Choice, an Internet support group for people who have terminated pregnancies because of their fetus's health. "But nobody's talking about it. Certainly not here in southeastern Virginia," where anti-abortion groups are so vocal.

A nurse practitioner in New Jersey said her parents, in-laws and best friends all believed she had a miscarriage. In reality, after having an amniocentesis because she was 39, she discovered that the male fetus had two X chromosomes in addition to a Y chromosome. Men with the condition, Klinefelter's syndrome, have little body hair and feminine features. Some lead normal lives, but others have learning difficulties and virtually all are sterile.

"We didn't want to put ourselves in the position to be judged, because it was difficult enough as it was," she said, though she said she wished she had told her family about the diagnosis. "I was thinking about Klinefelter's constantly, but I couldn't mention it to anyone."

Dr. John Larsen, chairman of the department of obstetrics and gynecology at George Washington University Medical Center, said the sense of taboo was amplified by how often people's choices contradict their previously held beliefs.

"People will come into my office in tears and say they've been against abortion their whole lives," he said, "but they'll make an exception for themselves."

Parents of children with Down syndrome, Dr. Larsen said, also come to him for a test called chorionic villus sampling, or C.V.S. Similar to an amniocentesis, the procedure is less widely used because it carries a slightly higher risk of miscarriage, but it can be performed as early as nine weeks — for many women, well before their pregnancies are apparent.

"They want it kept a secret," Dr. Larsen added. "They don't want their friends in the Down Syndrome Society to know that they got tested and would abort or did abort if it was positive. They'll say, 'I love my child with special needs, but I can't handle two.'"

Some parents are trying to avoid both abortion and disease by opting for in-vitro fertilization, even if they do not need it to conceive. A new procedure can test embryos in the petri dish for chromosomal abnormalities or a genetic condition known to run in a family.

That is how Sara and Benjamin Porush of Chicago came to have their 21-month-old triplets. After their first son was born with familial dysautonomia, which causes difficulty breathing and swallowing and a shortened life, the couple, who are Orthodox Jews, had 16 embryos tested for the disease, 9 of which had the gene mutations for it. Ms. Porush was implanted with three of the others.

But some couples who terminate pregnancies for fetal health conditions say no one has a right to judge them. A child psychologist in Atlanta who terminated a Down syndrome fetus earlier this year said she was outraged by people who told her, "If you have to have a perfect baby, you shouldn't be a parent."

"I was like, 'What!?'" said the psychologist, who is 35. "I've always been pro-choice, but now I'm pro-choice with a vengeance. Don't tell me I have to have a baby with Down syndrome just because you say so."

And Cristy Hollin of Gladwyne, Pa., is unapologetic about having invasive procedures to test fetal cells early in the two pregnancies that followed the diagnosis of her first son's condition as fragile X mental retardation. Neither fetus tested positive for the condition, but if they had, she said, she and her husband had planned to have an abortion.

"You love your child," said Ms. Hollin, who was told that the best she could ever hope for her fragile X son, who is now 11, was that he could one day read well enough to take a bus on his own. "But the fact is it's really, really hard. When we went to have our other kids we said we'd be fools not to know everything we can."

Factors in Decisions

Doctors and genetic counselors say the new reproductive decisions hinge on a complex equation that includes patients' perception of disabilities, their financial situation, their ethical beliefs and their desire for a baby.

A recent study of the first-trimester screen for Down syndrome found that only 6 percent of women in Utah who tested positive for a high risk of having a fetus with the condition went on to find out definitively with an amniocentesis, said Dr. Mary D'Alton, chairwoman of obstetrics and gynecology at Columbia University Medical Center, who led the study. By contrast, at Mount Sinai in Manhattan, more than 90 percent chose to have the follow-up test.

Age can also play a role. A 44-year-old woman with her first pregnancy may look differently at an imperfection than a 23-year-old who has two children, said Dr. Ilan E. Timor, director of the ultrasound division of the obstetrics and gynecology department at New York University Hospital.

"I have seen patients with relatively minor anomalies as far as I'm concerned who don't care and terminate the pregnancy," Dr. Timor said. "Then you see the other end of it, patients that have pretty major anomalies and don't want to terminate. Every patient has a dilemma that is measured by personal needs."

When Dondakay DeMaria, 27, and her husband, Andrew, of Campbell, Calif., who work at the same Silicon Valley technology company, both tested positive as cystic fibrosis carriers, Ms. DeMaria was sure she wanted to have an amniocentesis, and perhaps terminate the pregnancy. But after much soul-searching, the couple, who describe themselves as pro-choice, decided not to take the risk of miscarrying in order to find out the status of their fetus.

"There's a lot of kids born into the world that have severe problems and that doesn't stop them from having a life or having a lot of love to give," said Mr. DeMaria, citing his adult cousin with Down syndrome as an example. "If my aunt and uncle would have terminated that pregnancy we would never have known Suzie."

Some critics of the new culture of prenatal testing argue that it is causing needless anxiety for the vast majority of couples whose babies will be perfectly healthy. But some women say the new tests actually make them less anxious. Ms. Hoffman, who terminated her pregnancy last year after the first-trimester screening test alerted her to the risk of Down syndrome, is now pregnant again. She was sure she would have an amniocentesis this time, despite her fears of miscarriage. But when she went for her screening the doctor said her risk of an abnormality had fallen from one in 43 to one in 351, odds that were good enough for her.

"It took me a long time before I was ready to risk getting pregnant again," Ms. Hoffman said. "And that time period couldn't have gone fast enough before I could have my test."

A HISTORY OF GOVERNMENTALLY COERCED STERILIZATION: THE PLIGHT OF THE NATIVE AMERICAN WOMAN

Michael Sullivan DeFine

Michael Sullivan DeFine is in the School of Law at the University of Maine.

DeFine traces the development of the eugenics movement beginning in the nineteenth century in the theories used by governments, scientists, and doctors to justify the regulation of reproduction. He then describes the government-funded sterilization of Native American women and links this to beliefs about their inferiority. He examines the effects of sterilization practices on Native American women today by discussing federal relationships with American Indian tribes, personal accounts by women who were sterilized and the effects of this on their attitudes about family planning, state and federal policies regarding informed consent and sterilization, and the current role of the Indian Health Service.

I. Introduction

The purpose of this article is to trace the historical influence of governmentally funded sterilization from the beginning of the eugenics movement in the 19th century to see how this effects Native American women today. This topic will investigate the social prejudices and rationalizations for sterilization of the "less-talented" members of society advocated by the most influential social and biological scientists in American history.

These "science"-based eugenic influences break through the lines of science into the world of politics, promulgating anti-humanistic views of poor women of color in the form of legislation fraught with bigotry and baseless generalizations. This political view flows through the judicial system, as courts apply eugenic philosophies in determining who should be sterilized and for what reasons.

Turning specifically to the sterilization of Native American women, this article concludes with a discussion of the federal relationship with American Indian tribes, personal accounts from Native American women who were sterilized and their attitudes toward family planning, state and federal policies regarding informed consent and sterilization, an examination of the contractual relationship between the Indian Health Service and private practices, the United States General Accounting Office investigation of Indian Health Service sterilization procedures, and the meaning behind the statistics of population growth.

II. History of Eugenics

A. Pre-Eugenic Thinking

In the early 19th century, before Darwinism entered the lexicon of science, racist as well as sexist attitudes led scientists to become preoccupied with ranking human beings according to purportedly neutral scientific criteria.[1] Some believed in monogenism, a notion that all humans descended from the common ancestor Eve, but that the races degenerated in various degrees from an original state of perfection.[2] This theory, therefore, assumed that the white race had degenerated the least, and people of color were developmentally further away from the original divine plan.

Anthropometry (skull measuring) was also a serious scientific endeavor. The physician Samuel George Morton gathered more than 1,000 skulls to prove that intelligence is related to brain size and that there are innate racial differences in mental capacities.[3] Morton's studies on the sizing of human skulls were used throughout the 19th century as scientific proof of a racial hierarchy in intelligence.[4] After the Civil War, scientists were still engaged in anthropometry. In 1870, Dr. Sanford B. Hunt claimed that the average African American brain weighs five ounces less than the average white individual's brain, and the average mulatto's brain is smaller than the brain of an average African American.[5] From this, Hunt concluded intermarriage between the races would produce inferior offspring.[6] His studies played a role in justifying the need for segregated school systems.[7]

As Darwinism began to entrench itself into popular scientific thought, it brought with it distinct racist and sexist overtones. The writings of E.D. Cope popularized what was known as recapitulation, the notion that modern human beings pass through a succession of evolutionary stages, repeating the progression of the species.[8] Cope identified four groups that displayed characteristics evidencing lower evolutionary status: the non-white races, all women, southern European whites (Jewish people and Italians included), and the lower classes within the superior races (Cope was particularly contemptuous of "the lower classes of the Irish").[9] The adults of inferior groups were considered throwbacks who remained in an arrested evolutionary stage, more like the children of superior white males.[10] Women's essential nature was characterized as similar to what men exhibit at a younger age. America's premier psychologist, G. Stanley Hall, interpreted the higher suicide rate in women as a sign of their stunted evolutionary development.[11]

B. The Early Eugenics Movement

The pre-eugenics evolutionary theories noted above germinated the seeds of the eugenics movement. The term eugenics, which means literally "wellborn", originated in 1883 with Sir Francis Galton, a cousin of Charles Darwin.[12] Galton advocated the scientific regulation of human breeding to ensure the more talented (primarily those of the upper-class and the industrious members of the middle-class) have a better chance of predominating in the propagation of the species.[13] By the 1920's, when eugenics became a required course in many universities,[14] a typical textbook published by Bobbs-Merrill stated:

> For our own protection we must face the question of what types of races should be ruled out … many students of heredity feel that there is great hazard in the mongrelizing of distinctly unrelated races … However, it is certain that under existing social conditions in our own country only the most worthless and vicious of the white race will tend in any considerable way to mate with the negro and the result cannot but mean deterioration on the whole for either race.[15]

This academic agenda of fear found its way into the political ranks when Congress passed the Immigration Act of 1924, which limited immigration to two percent of those of the same national origin that lived in the United States in 1890.[16] This Act was passed by Congress in large measure because of information supplied by the intelligentsia of the eugenics movement, namely Carl Brigham. He interpreted army data on immigrant intelligence and concluded that as the proportion of those with "superior" Nordic blood decreased, and "inferior" Alpine and Mediterranean blood increased, the intelligence of the immigrants declined.[17] Other "scientific" studies characterized the inferior races as "human parasites"[18] and "filthy, un-American and often dangerous in their habits".[19]

The eugenics movement promoted the elimination of so-called inferior immigrants from entering the United States and spreading their inferiority "upon the stock of the nation". [20] The primary goal of the movement, however, was to promote the sterilization of the "unfit". With success in influencing Congress established, Harry Laughlin, a eugenics movement supporter, drafted a model eugenics sterilization law that was adopted in various versions by many states in this country.[21] The laws were typically aimed at epileptics, the mentally impaired, alcoholics, drug addicts, and criminals.[22]Approximately 50,000 sterilizations were performed in the United States by the end of World War II.[23] This number pales in comparison, however, with the number of women sterilized in more recent years.[24]

C. Eugenics in the Modern Age

Since the 1970's, sterilization has become the most common form of birth control for women over the age of twenty-five in the United States.[25] Between 1970 and 1980, sterilization rates tripled, and in 1987, twenty-four percent of the entire population of women of childbearing age were sterilized. Part of this increase in surgical procedure is due to the liberalization of indications for sterilization recommended by the American College of Obstetricians and Gynecologists.[26] More significantly, as in the past, societal prejudices and a class-based racist ideology determine the selection process, although on the surface women voluntarily consent to the procedure.[27] Sterilization might not be the choice of many women if they were better informed and able to receive higher quality medical care.

As of 1982, fifteen percent of white women had been sterilized, compared with twenty-four percent of African-American women, thirty-five percent of Puerto Rican women, and forty-two percent of Native American women.[28] In the early 1970's, an estimated 100,000 to 150,000 low-income individuals were annually subjected to sterilization under federally funded programs.[29]

Turning now to the resultant effects on Native American women, a class traditionally oppressed by economic, social, and financial hardship, one can see just how influential the philosophies of the eugenics movement have been in recent years.

III. Native American Sterilization, 1972-1976

A. The Federal Relationship with American Indian Tribes

The federal trust relationship with American Indian tribes is based on numerous treaty rights and agreements that include availability of medical services and physicians for Indians. However, there are very few statements that mention medical services specifically; instead there is an implicit understanding of the trust responsibility that includes the health of the American Indians.[30] As stated in the American Indian Policy Review Commission's report on Indian health, "the federal responsibility to provide health services to Indians has its roots in the unique moral, historical, and treaty obligations of the federal government, no court has ever ruled on the precise nature of that legal basis nor defined the specific legal rights for Indians created by those obligations."[31] The implied meaning of health care responsibilities is somewhat vague, but the treaties and agreements were supposedly intended to favor Indians.

In 1955, The Indian Health Service was transferred from the Bureau of Indian Affairs to the Public Health Service.[32] This move was made with the expectation that the Public Health Service could improve health care for Indians living on reservations.[33] Even after the transfer took place, however, the health needs for Indians were still not adequately met.[34] This was due to the ambiguous nature of the federal government's responsibility to provide health care.[35] In turn, the Indian Health Service had no concrete goals or objectives and operated day to day with only a faint clue as how it should render services.[36]

Even today, an Indian client will be given services that may well vary each time that patient enters an Indian Health Service facility. "The specific services available to [the patient] will vary from day to day and year to year, depending on unpublished discretionary decisions made by

Indian Health Service officials and commitments and conditions contained in often voluminous appropriation hearings."[37] This quote suggests that the Indian Health Service system is ripe for mismanagement of policies, funding, and staff supervision.[38] It also comes as no surprise to find that the Indian Health Service has been the subject of a number of investigations.[39]

B. Personal Accounts from Sterilized Native American Women and Their Attitude Toward Family Planning

One of the people who initiated the government investigation into the Indian Health Service's sterilization policy was Dr. Connie Uri, a Choctaw Indian Physician working at the Claremore, Oklahoma Indian Health Service facility.[40] Dr. Uri noticed in the hospital records that a large number of sterilization surgeries had been performed. This prompted her to conduct her own interviews with the women involved and she found that many had received the operation only a day or two after childbirth.[41] In the month of July, 1974 alone there were forty-eight sterilizations performed and several hundred had been conducted in the previous two years.[42] The hospital records showed that both tubal ligation and hysterectomies were used in sterilization. Dr. Uri commented that "in normal medical practice, hysterectomies are rare in women of child bearing age unless there is cancer or other medical problems".[43]

Besides the questionable surgery techniques taking place, there was also the charge of harassment in obtaining consent forms.[44] In an incident of harassment at the Claremore facility, one woman was told by social workers and other hospital personnel that she was a bad mother, and they threatened to place her children in foster homes if she would not agree to the surgery.[45]

In one study conducted on the Navajo Reservation and sponsored by the Public Health Service, researchers reported:

From 1972 to 1978 we observe a 130 per cent increase in the number of induced abortions performed. During this time the ratio of abor-

tions per 1,000 deliveries has increased from approximately 34 to 77 (an increase of 126 per cent).[46] While not exactly within the confines of sterilization, the numbers indicate that the family planning program on the Navajo Reservation was definitely acquiring federal funds to carry on such a massive project.[47]

The statistics concerning Navajo sterilization were also addressed by a Public Health Service sponsored study, which found that "between 1972 and 1978, the percentage of interval sterilization has more than doubled from 15.1 per cent in 1972 to 30.7 per cent in 1978."[48]

Although the report itself was conducted in a clinical and methodical manner, the researchers did comment slightly about the relationship between patient and physician, stating that "[o]lder women who become pregnant may be much less concerned about reducing their childbearing and may do so primarily when they are influenced by health care providers."[49] In light of previously mentioned tactics promoting the sterilization of Native American women, one can only speculate regarding the nature of the "advice" or "influence" provided by these health care providers.

Once the word of sterilization spread throughout Indian Country, some tribal leaders carried on their own investigations. Marie Sanchez, a tribal judge of the Northern Cheyenne Reservation, interviewed fifty women, twenty-six of whom reported that they were sterilized.[50] One doctor told several women that they each had enough children and it was time they stopped having children.[51] Others were even told that they could have children after the operation.[52]

The attitudes of some members of the health care profession regarding the appropriateness of the number of children these Native American women "should" bear underlines the differing value structure between "white" America and Native American culture. The idea of such population control measures leaves many Native Americans understandably concerned. They believe that the federal government has done enough throughout history to limit the number of

Indians living on this continent, and the idea of limiting the number of Indian children is based on what whites feel is an appropriate amount.[53]

Other researchers have found these general feelings to be true, regarding the limitation of Indian family members. One group of researchers gathered data on urban and rural Omaha Indians in Nebraska to determine if either group had different opinions on family planning. The team found that "the family economic situation, the ability to care for the children now and later, family happiness, and the feeling that the couple had enough children were valid considerations in a decision to delay or prevent further pregnancies."[54] The team also noted that the "freedom for the mother to work, and the belief that a small population was good for the country, were generally not sufficient cause [for birth control]."[55]

C. State and Federal Policies Regarding Informed Consent and Sterilization

Dr. Louis Hellman, the Deputy Assistant Secretary for Population Affairs in the Public Health Service, presented statistics confirming that 150,000 low income people were sterilized in the United States by means of federal grant money.[56] These funds allowed the states to be reimbursed for up to 90 percent of the cost of sterilizing indigent women. A report from the Department of Health, Education, and Welfare stated:

> Voluntary sterilization is legal in all states. Although most states have no statute regulating voluntary sterilization, over half authorize the procedure either explicitly by statute, attorney general's opinion, judicial decision, or policies of [the] Health and Welfare department or implicitly through consent requirements....[57]

Since the states themselves are not following any set policies, it would be reasonable to assume that the Indian Health Service does not either. Thus, there is a valid suspicion regarding the effective management of resources and people at the Indian Health Service.

D. An Examination of the Contractual Relationship between the Indian Health Service and Private Practices

Researchers on the Navajo Reservation observed that the trend toward increased female sterilizations had to do with the health care providers, who were found to be responsible for the huge increase (almost 300% since 1970)[58] of patients "agreeing" to surgery. The team further stated that the pattern of childbearing on the Navajo Reservation was very similar to those in developing countries.[59] The following statement further illustrates the paternalistic and authoritative attitude that many physicians have toward women: "persons in the lower educational classes rely more on such operations [hysterectomies]; they have been least likely to control their fertility in other ways, and doctors may finally suggest this method."[60]

Contract Care entails formal agreements with private vendors and is used when the Indian Health Service cannot equip its staff or facilities for emergency or specialty care or if there is an overload of patients.[61] Contract physicians associated with the Indian Health Service are reimbursed for each sterilization.[62] The reimbursements that the physicians receive come from federal funds, but are not federally accountable: "thirty percent of the sterilizations were performed at 'contract' facilities. [Indian Health Service] officials in the Albuquerque and Aberdeen areas said they do not monitor the consent procedures in contract care, nor are doctors required to follow federal regulations."[63]

Normally, agencies which receive funding from the federal government must follow federal guidelines. The Indian Health Service, however, shows a lack of concern and accountability with the patients they treat and the money they handle.[64]

E. The United States General Accounting Office Investigation of the Indian Health Service Sterilization Procedures and the Meaning behind Statistics of Population Growth

Complaints of these unethical sterilization practices continued, but little was done until the matter was brought to the attention of Senator

James Abourezk (D-SD). Finally, affirmative steps were taken — specifically the commissioning of the General Accounting Office — to investigate the affair and to determine if the complaints of Indian women were true — that they were undergoing sterilization as a means of birth control, without consent.[65] The problem with the investigation was that it was initially limited to only four area Indian Health Service hospitals (later twelve); therefore, the total number of Indian women sterilized remains unknown.[66] The General Accounting Office came up with a figure of 3,400 women who had been sterilized; but others speculate that at least that many had been sterilized each year from 1972 through 1976.[67]

The General Accounting Office confined its investigation to Indian Health Service records and failed to probe case histories, to observe patient-doctor relationships, or to interview women who had been sterilized.[68] This deplorable lack of thorough investigation only served as an attempt to placate the concerns of Indian people.

The General Accounting Office investigators concluded that Indian Health Service consent procedures lacked the basic elements of informed consent, particularly in informing a patient orally of the advantages and disadvantages of sterilization.[69] Furthermore, the consent form had only a summary of the oral presentation, and the form lacked the information usually located at the top of the page notifying the patient that no federal benefits would be taken away if she did not accept sterilization.[70] The General Accounting Office notified the Indian Health Service that it should implement better consent procedures. Some Indian Health Service Area Directors were pressured by local Indians and by Indian physicians and staff to suspend certain nurses and to move the hospital administrators to another post. Other than that, however, there was little else done by government officials.[71]

Outraged by the level of governmental inaction, Indian people accused the Indian Health Service of making genocide a part of its policy. For the Indian Health Service, this was a serious accusation, as the purpose of this agency was to somehow alleviate the terrible health conditions in Indian communities. The Indian Health Service defended itself by relying on the inaccurate sterilization figures provided by the General Accounting Office.[72] In reality, however, the accusation of genocide was not far off base. As Thomas Littlewood stated in his book on the politics of population control, "non-white Americans are not unaware of how the American Indian came to be called the vanishing American ... [t]his country's starkest example of genocide in practice."[73]

From a statistical point of view, the reality of the devastation of Native American women victimized by sterilization can be observed through the comments of Senator Abourezk himself: "given the small American Indian population, the 3,400 Indian sterilization figure [out of 55,000 Indian women of childbearing age] would be compared to sterilizing 452,000 non-Indian women."[74]

IV. Conclusion

Science has provided a means of categorizing and victimizing those in society deemed unworthy of continued existence. Its influence in academic and political circles has created a pervasive social bigotry that rewards extermination over reform. The failure to embrace the racial and cultural diversity of this country has left a wake of destruction and oppression in minority populations. It is time for the pundits of social change to rearrange their thinking and give back to the people the power to choose what is right for themselves.

NOTES

1. Beverly Horsburgh, *Schrödinger's Cat, Eugenics, and the Compulsory Sterilization of Welfare Mothers: Deconstructing an Old/New Rhetoric and Constructing the Reproductive Right to Natality for Low-Income Women of Color*, 17 Cardozo Law Review 536 (1996).
2. Id. at 538.
3. Id. at 539.
4. Id.

5. Herbert Hovenkamp, *Social Science and Segregation before Brown*, 1985 Duke L.J. 624, 625.

6. Id.

7. Id. at 630-632 (citing Berea College v. Kentucky, 211 U.S. 45 (1908) (upholding a Kentucky statute prohibiting integrated schools)).

8. Beverly Horsburgh, *Schrödinger's Cat, Eugenics, and the Compulsory Sterilization of Welfare Mothers: Deconstructing an Old/New Rhetoric and Constructing the Reproductive Right to Natality for Low-Income Women of Color*, 17 Cardozo Law Review 536 (1996) (citing Stephen J. Gould, *The Mismeasure of Man* (1981) at 114-115).

9. Id. at 115.

10. Id.

11. Id. at 118.

12. Ruth Hubbard and Elijah Wald, *Exploding the Gene Myth: How Genetic Information is Produced and Manipulated by Scientists, Physicians, Employers, Insurance Companies, Educators, and Law Enforcers* (1993), at 14.

13. Beverly Horsburgh, *Schrödinger's Cat, Eugenics, and the Compulsory Sterilization of Welfare Mothers: Deconstructing an Old/New Rhetoric and Constructing the Reproductive Right to Natality for Low-Income Women of Color*, 17 Cardozo Law Review 536 (1996) (citing Francis Galton, *Hereditary Talent and Character,* in *Adam Miller, Professors of Hate,* in *The Bell Curve Debate: History, Documents, Opinions* (Russell Jacoby and Naomi Glauberman eds., 1995) at 393, 396, 406-442).

14. Linda Gordon, *Woman's Body, Woman's Right: A Societal History of Birth Control in America* (rev. ed. 1990), at 276.

15. Id. at 277-278 (quoting Michael F. Guyer, *Being Well-Born* (1916), at 296-298).

16. The Immigration Act of 1924, ch.190, §11(a), 43 Stat. 153, 159, amended by The Immigration and Nationality Act, ch. 477, §201, 66 Stat. 175 (1952), amended by Pub. L. No. 89-236, §1, 79 Stat. 911 (1965).

17. Leon J. Kamin, *The Pioneers of IQ Testing,* in *The Bell Curve Debate* (1995), at 494.

18. Howard M. Sachar, *A History of Jews in America* (1992), at 321.

19. Id.

20. Id.

21. Adam Miller, *Professors of Hate,* in *The Bell Curve Debate: History, Documents, Opinions* (Russell Jacoby and Naomi Glauberman eds., 1995) at 172.

22. Ruth Hubbard and Elijah Wald, *Exploding the Gene Myth: How Genetic Information is Produced and Manipulated by Scientists, Physicians, Employers, Insurance Companies, Educators, and Law Enforcers* (1993), at 21.

23. Robert N. Proctor, *Genomics and Eugenics: How Fair is the Comparison?* in Gene Mapping: Using Law and Ethics as Guides, at 61.

24. Beverly Horsburgh, *Schrödinger's Cat, Eugenics, and the Compulsory Sterilization of Welfare Mothers: Deconstructing an Old/New Rhetoric and Constructing the Reproductive Right to Natality for Low-Income Women of Color*, 17 Cardozo Law Review 554 (1996).

25. Linda Gordon, *Woman's Body, Woman's Right: A Societal History of Birth Control in America* (rev. ed. 1990), at 437.

26. Id.

27. Id. at 432-433.

28. Charles Rutherford, *Reproductive Freedoms and African American Women*, 4 Yale J.L. & Feminism 255, 273-74 (1992).

29. Relf v. Weinberger, 372 F. Supp. 1196, 1199 (D.D.C. 1974).

30. Charles R. England, *A Look at the Indian Health Service Policy of Sterilization*, 1972-1976, at 1 (available on-line at http://www.dickshovel.com/IHSSterPol.html).

31. American Indian Journal of the Institute for the Development of Indian Law, Feb., 1977, at 22-23.

32. England, at 1.

33. Id.

34. Id.

35. Id.

36. Id.

37. American Indian Journal of the Institute for the Development of Indian Law, Feb., 1977, at 23.

38. England, at 1.

39. Id.

40. Id., at 2.

41. Id.

42. Akwesasne Notes, *Sterilization of Young Native Women Alleged at Indian Hospital* (July, 1974), at 22.

43. Id.

44. England, at 2.

45. Akwesasne Notes, *Sterilization of Young Native Women Alleged at Indian Hospital* (July, 1974), at 22.

46. Helen Temkin-Greener, *Surgical Fertility Regulation Among Women on the Navajo Indian Reservation*, American Journal of Public Health, (April, 1981), at 405.

47. Id.

48. Id., at 406.

49. Id.

50. England, at 2.

51. Brint Dillingham, *American Indian Women and I.H.S. Sterilization Practices*, American Indian Journal (January, 1977), at 28.

52. Id.

53. England, at 2.

54. Margot Liberty, *Rural and Urban Omaha Indian Fertility*, Human Biology (February, 1976), at 63-64.

55. Id., at 64.

56. Gayle Mark Jarvis, *The Theft of Life*, Akwesasne Notes (1977), at 22.

57. U.S. Department of Health, Education, and Welfare, Indian Health Trends and Services [report] (GPO, 1978), at 89.

58. Gayle Mark Jarvis, *The Theft of Life*, Akwesasne Notes (1977), at 31.

59. Temkin-Greener, at 406.

60. Leslie A. Westoff and Charles F. Westoff, *From Now to Zero*, Little, Brown & Co. (1971), at 56.

61. U.S. Department of Health, Education, and Welfare, *Family Planning, Contraception, Voluntary Sterilization and Abortion* (GPO, 1978), at 2.

62. Mark Miller, *Native American Peoples on the Trail of Tears Once More*, America (December 1978), at 424.

63. *Killing Our Future: Sterilization and Experiments*, Akwesasne Notes (Autumn, 1977), at 4.

64. England, at 4.

65. Dillingham, at 27.

66. Id., at 27-28.

67. England, at 4.

68. Jarvis, Akwesasne Notes (Autumn, 1977), at 30.

69. England, at 5.

70. Bill Wagner, *Lo the Poor and Sterilized Indian*, America (January 29, 1977), at 75.

71. Akwesasne Notes, *Sterilization of Young Native Women Alleged at Indian Hospital* (July, 1974), at 22.

72. Janet Karstan Larson, *And Then There Were None: Is Federal Policy Endangering the American Indian Species?*, Christian Century (January 26, 1977), at 63.

73. Thomas B. Littlewood, *The Politics of Population Control*, The University of Notre Dame Press (1977), at 82.

74. Wagner, at 75.

REPRODUCTIVE HEALTH AND RESEARCH ETHICS:
HOT ISSUES IN ARGENTINA

Florencia Luna

Florencia Luna teaches bioethics at the University of Buenos Aires (UBA) and FLASCO (Latinamerican University of Social Sciences), where she also directs a research program. She is editor of Prespectivas Bioéticas. *Presently she is working on issues related to research in developing countries, international codes of ethics, and genetics and ethics. She is the current President of the International Association of Bioethics.*

Luna discusses issues of reproductive health and research ethics in Argentina, which has a history of good public health care, education, and medical research, but high poverty rates and wide gaps in social classes that increased dramatically with the 2001 economic crisis. Against this backdrop is the strong social and political power of the Catholic Church, which, Luna argues, has established strong barriers to reproductive policy that have resulted in high levels of hypocrisy and some absurd practices. Luna describes the laws and policies that are in tension with the health and welfare of women and with the practices of doctors and researchers. She ends by examining research ethics in Argentina in the broader context of Latin America and international debates and agreements.

In this article I focus on two issues concerning bioethics in Argentina: reproductive health and ethics in research. Although these topics are quite dissimilar, they share a particular feature: their special relationship with context.

Argentina is a multifaceted and paradoxical South American country whose population is basically of European descent. It has a history of good public healthcare and education, and it can boast several Nobel Prize winners in science. Laboratories are working on new trends in genetic research and have managed to clone cows with special milk. Sophisticated medical technologies — from organ transplantations and assisted reproductive technologies (ART) to genetic and preimplantatory testing — are quick to be adopted. The 2002 Human Development Index ranked Argentina thirty-fourth among the countries with the highest levels of human development. The same report points out that the 2000 survey shows a life expectancy of 73.4 years and a literacy rate of 96.8.

However, Argentina is a developing country. The report also reveals that the percentage of the population with ameliorated water is 79%, and the percent age of the population with access to essential drugs is between 50% and 79% (prior to the 2001 economic crisis). Hence, there are and had been wide gaps in and between the social classes, and the 2001 economic crisis deepened these gaps even further. According to a new United Nations report, indicators from 1999 to 2002 in Argentina's urban areas show that poverty rates almost doubled, going from 23.7% to 45.4%, and indigence grew threefold, from 6.7% to 20.9%.[1] The economic crisis devastated our traditionally large middle class and left the country poorer. Malnutrition and poverty are now part of our everyday life. Against this backdrop we face another factor: the Catholic Church and its strong political power. It shapes nearly all regulations and laws regarding sexual and reproductive rights, which institute a highly conservative legal framework with dramatic consequences on public health.

In this report I focus on these contextual factors and related bioethical concerns. Reproductive issues are associated with a lack of respect for women's rights and the broad political influence of the Roman Catholic Church. Many of the concerns over research ethics are related to the environment within which research is conducted: poverty and the possibility of exploitation.

Reproductive issues and ethics in research are hot topics in Argentina, though their impacts and the areas of discussion are quite different. Whereas the first — reproductive rights — implies legislation, public policies, and a public debate, the second — research ethics — has had a narrower discussion, mainly within academic and scientific circles. Both topics have generated literature, workshops, and training. In this brief report I present some of the issues under discussion, their link to the context, and the activities that have ensued.

Reproductive Issues

I first consider some of the relevant problems concerning reproductive health, illustrating the strong barriers established by the Catholic Church and how embryo protection has restricted basic reproductive rights and led to high levels of hypocrisy and some absurd practices. I will focus on three points: (1) the lack of respect for reproductive rights and the first attempt to reverse some of these omissions; (2) the restrictive abortion laws and their consequences on pregnancies, for example, with the anencephalic fetus; and, (3) the incoherence of adopting techniques like preimplantatory genetic diagnosis or ART and of maintaining specific conceptions of embryos.

Contraception

The teachings of the Catholic Church are present throughout most of the legal framework. However, there is also the practice of a "double

moral standard." One thing is what religion says; another is what people do. The great majority of the population have had a Catholic upbringing (84.4% claim to be Catholic) but do not follow Catholic teachings. Nor are they truly devout. Abortion laws are highly restrictive. However, illegal abortions are carried out continuously. In Argentina, between 450,000 to 500,000 illegal abortions are performed every year. The problem with this double moral standard is how it impacts the vulnerable population, especially poor women and teenagers.

Forty-five percent of the beds in obstetric wards in public hospitals are occupied by women with postabortion problems. In fact, complications due to illegal abortions are the main cause of maternal death. The WHO indicates that Argentina has 38 maternal deaths per 100,000 live births, whereas Canada, for instance, has 4 per 100,000. Argentina does not fare well even when compared to Chile, 21/100,000, or Uruguay, 23/100,000. In some provinces of northern Argentina, the situation is even worse: Formosa shows 177/100,000.

Another pressing issue is the matter of teenage pregnancies. They are on the rise at a rate of 20% of all live births. In the city of Rosario, 30% of the deliveries occur with girls under age 19, and a high percentage are single mothers. Additionally, babies born to mothers under 15 years of age suffered double the average mortality rate.[2]

With respect to this dramatic public health situation, this is the first time that a political power such as the Ministry of Health has explicitly acknowledged the lack of reproductive rights as a problem. Consider that until 2003 no national law existed concerning sexual and reproductive rights. Law 25,673 created a national program that stipulated the provision of contraceptives in public hospitals, as well as the provision of information about sexual education, and the diagnosis and treatment of sexually transmitted diseases and ovarian and breast cancers. However, the proposal of the program generated strong criticisms from the Catholic Church. A prolife nongovernmental organization (NGO) interfered legally and obtained a judge's support. Her extreme position reached the point that she tried to forbid all use and sale of contraceptives, even in cases of medical use for gynecological and fertility problems. Although the case underwent various legal steps, it nevertheless could not stop the program.

Note that this is a program for reproductive health and responsible procreation — basic issues for a healthy reproductive life. It is one of the paths toward preventing abortions. It offers choices regarding when to have a child and helps prevent sexually transmitted diseases that in many cases cause secondary infertility. One concern to the Church was the possibility of its providing information to teenagers, so they opposed it on grounds of *patria potestas* or parental authority. What this legal battle did achieve was to foster a discussion in the media and bring about an awareness of the problems involved. However, this was merely the tip of the iceberg, and the polemic and legal barriers that arose illustrate how difficult it is to legislate this area in Argentina.

Abortion and the Anencephalic Fetus

If we consider abortion and its impact on certain problematic cases, here too we find problems concerning the position of the Catholic Church. The restrictive abortion laws have consequences on pregnancies, for example, with anencephalic fetuses.

In Argentina, Article 86 of the Penal Code bans abortion. Exceptions are considered ambiguous by many judges. There are three exceptions: (1) when the mother's health and life are in danger, (2) when the pregnancy is the consequence of rape, and (3) when the pregnancy is the result of a dishonest act on a demented woman. However, the current interpretation reads the exceptions as only two: the first rarely considers the mother's health and only a life-threatening condition is grounds for abortion; the second conflates the second and third exceptions and accepts abortion only when a demented woman is the victim of rape.

However, not even these extreme exceptions are respected. What is worse, physicians at public hospitals choose not to perform these accepted abortions[3] and petition a judicial authorization even when the law does not require it. While judges and physicians deny their responsibility and refuse to perform the requested abortion, the pregnancy continues.

Cases of fetuses with serious genetic problems or illnesses that will result in the death of the newborn are ignored. During the past few years, some cases of anencephalic-fetus pregnancies have been taken up by the media. Women or couples wanting to end such pregnancies face endless legal battles. Because of these cases, legislation was passed for the City of Buenos Aires (the most "progressive" part of Argentina). This law sanctions an "early delivery" in cases of anencephalic fetuses or any analogous condition that is incompatible with life, only if viable after 24 gestational weeks.[4]

Note that the law does not speak of "abortion" but of "early deliveries." In no way does this legislation open the door to "eugenic/genetic abortions." Moreover, consider that this law is not a fitting solution: a woman may be diagnosed at week 16 or even earlier. Under this law, however, she has to wait two painful months with the physical, psychological, and emotional costs this may imply.

However, the worst aspect of this law is that it impedes a better solution. If the three exceptions of the penal code are to be seriously and correctly interpreted, this is a case of nonpunitive abortion. It is implicit in the first exception. If we consider health not only as merely biological functions but also psychological ones, a woman who does not wish to carry out the pregnancy of a deformed fetus that will die immediately upon delivery may have to endure great psychological suffering. This embraces the correct application of the first exception, owing to the psychological harm such a pregnancy can inflict on the woman. According to this interpretation, there is no need to wait until week 24. In fact, this was the position of the Ombudsman of the City of Buenos Aires, who participated in the legal resolution of several of these cases. Hence, even if the law was an attempt at a first step with the best of intentions, it fell short.

Embryos and Assisted Reproductive Technologies

The same pattern occurs in a related arena, ART. Religious background appears to play a role in the provision of treatment, as well as in treatment-seeking behavior. Embryos are considered "persons," which, in turn, leads to problems with their manipulation. However, Argentina counts with quite sophisticated centers. These centers manipulate embryos — creating, selecting, and cryopreserving them. As no law regulates these practices, these centers face no legal impediments. However, because they do not wish to alter the status quo, or the approval and perception of their activities, they may ultimately prioritize embryos over the well-being of the woman and may limit the options a woman or a couple is offered.

Even if the importance and beneficial aspects of cryopreservation are recognized,[5] Argentine ART centers limit the number of embryos that can be frozen. Hence, women may have to submit more frequently to hormones and medication, with their associated inconveniences and harms. There is an ongoing trend by which centers are cryopreserving fewer embryos.[6] No option for discarding embryos is offered, and the *only* alternative available — when a person does not choose to transfer the remaining embryos to herself — is to donate the embryos to another couple. This "compulsive donation" is quite a strong obligation and can also have disturbing psychological effects. It may prove to be especially painful when the donor cannot achieve pregnancy.

A second consideration arises with the practice of "embryo donation" and its current denotation. Terminology carries weight; it implies a particular way of understanding facts. The term "prenatal adoption" is deceptive and conveys the idea of an "actual adoption." It is not a neutral term, much less so in a region where embryos are sometimes more protected than women. I will not enter here into the controversy regarding the ontological or ethical status of embryos. However, with the current denotation, embryos are treated as "orphans," an analogy that leads to

paradoxes. If we were to grant embryos the condition of persons, the whole process of cryopreservation would, at least, be odd — how could we freeze persons? Moreover, in vitro fertilization could be seen as a massacre, owing to the losses of embryos when transferring them to the woman's uterus. Additionally, the same practice of giving them up for adoption (with the obvious intention of protecting them) may imply their death and destruction.[7]

Another problem relates to the embryo's health status and the prohibition against discarding embryos. Whereas the International Federation of Fertility Societies encourages screening for serious diseases that would be a potential threat to the potential child's health,[8] the majority of Argentine ART centers reject the discarding of embryos. However, genetic testing is offered.

This poses a paradox. Even if embryos are tested and proven to be genetically abnormal or to have severe genetic problems, they "must" be transferred (because they cannot be discarded). This transfer leads to the nightmare of a woman who has to accept the transference of an embryo and pregnancy with the knowledge that her future offspring will carry a serious or even fatal illness.[9]

Hence, if this conservative framework is to be followed, preimplantatory prenatal diagnosis should be banned, and this might be harmful to the couple and the future offspring, especially if they are undergoing these procedures to avoid transmitting a genetic disease. Or, conversely, a preimplantatory prenatal diagnosis could be made and embryos with genetic problems discarded. However, this is an option the majority of fertility centers deny doing — another example of hypocrisy and double standards, not to mention possible harm to the couple or the offspring, because of the embryo's status in the culture. The practical solution that many centers are finding is simply to avoid the problem and freeze the genetically disabled embryos. Instead of confronting the problems and paradoxes that an extreme respect for the embryos poses, ART centers and physicians ignore the issue and conceal the problem. The pattern of hypocrisy and double moral standards is once again replicated.

Latin America, Argentina, and Research Ethics

Research ethics is another heated topic in Argentina and Latin America. I focus here on the recent debates about the Helsinki Declaration and the proposal of amendments.

After the 2001 economic crisis, Argentina's health situation deteriorated dramatically. Public hospitals were in higher demand, and drugs and basic items were practically nonexistent. For many people, participation in a research protocol was their only chance to acquire a needed drug.

Meanwhile, since 1997, strong debates have arisen in the international research setting. Controversial clinical cases, such as Zidovudine (AZT) trials with pregnant women in Africa, have triggered different initiatives to change ethical codes. Since then, important ethical documents have come under scrutiny. For example, the Helsinki Declaration was updated after a series of discussions and disputes.

The two main points in the controversy over ethical codes, at that time, were the standard of care during the trial and the use of placebos. That is, what are research subjects entitled to during research, and what is the adequate comparator in a clinical research trial? The first issue considered (1) a single- versus double-standard discussion and (2) the level of treatment to be offered in a research trial (e.g., best proven, highest attainable and sustainable, standard of care, proven effective).

This discussion took place mainly during the redrafting of the Helsinki Declaration. At that time, different proposals were presented.[10] The final version (Helsinki, 2000) in its "renowned" paragraph 29 refers to "the *best current* prophylactic, diagnostic, or therapeutic methods" endorsing a single standard.[11]

Details about this controversy, which have been examined thoroughly, go beyond this article.[12] What I would like to point out is how various developing countries reacted to this proposal and how Argentina participates in this context. When this discussion arose, UNAIDS conducted workshops regarding ethical issues of the human in virus (HJV) vaccine in Thailand, Uganda, and Brazil, and UNAIDS regional groups discussed the issues with great dissidence and controversy. For example, Thailand considered it acceptable not to offer antiretroviral treatment. The country said that the treatment of research subjects who became infected during the research (but not as a result of the research) was to be consistent with that of the rest of the country. There was no healthcare requirement like the one proposed by the sponsoring country. Uganda indicated difficulties in establishing the level of treatment to be given to their research subjects, but ultimately decided not to give antiretroviral treatment. It claimed that some treatment should be offered but the sponsoring country should decide on the appropriate kind and level of the treatment. It could include immune monitoring, physicians' visits, prevention and treatment of infections, and palliative treatment but not necessarily antiretroviral therapy.

In contrast, Brazil claimed it was unacceptable to not offer antiretroviral treatment and rejected not treating research subjects. It stated that infected participants should be treated like those in the sponsoring country. This was later backed by a resolution of Brazil's National Council of Health.[13]

UNAIDS reveals significant differences in the way the developing countries are trying to resolve the issue. Brazil strongly resisted and prioritized the condition of the research subjects. Thailand or Uganda privileged the urgency of the researchers and sponsors. Leaving the decision in the hands of the individual countries can also prove problematic. Social pressure and the lack of resources may force countries to accept disadvantaged positions, as Thailand and Uganda did.

At that time, Brazil took the lead in the region with the Resolution of their National Council. Argentina, as a country, did not take a stance. The standard of care and the placebo debate, at that time, was of personal concern to the author (having been invited to some of the international forums such as the CIOMS redrafting) rather than being a public or even academic debate. Even if justified exceptions might exist, I endorsed the region's position. I considered that, given the commercialization of drug research and socioeconomic problems, a double standard might be very dangerous. It could and can open the door to abusive research.[14]

The second point — use of placebo — was explicit, for the first time, in the latest version of the Helsinki Declaration (section 29). So strong were the debates and criticisms over the use of placebos in the Helsinki Declaration that the World Medical Association (WMA) issued a Note of Clarification in October 2001.

Months earlier, in February 2001, the Food and Drug Administration (FDA) had seriously been considering endorsing the design of a Surfaxin trial in Ecuador, Bolivia, Peru, and Mexico. This study proposed a control group of 325 premature newborn infants with potentially fatal respiratory distress syndrome (RDS) to be treated with placebos instead of a lifesaving and already FDA-approved surfactant drug.[15] This study would have meant accepting the preventable death of 17 infants.[16] Even more questionable was the fact that the same manufacturer was seeking approval for this drug in Europe, where infants would not be under placebo but would receive an FDA-approved surfactant drug.

The Surfaxin proposal was viewed as completely unethical by the majority of Latin America. It was considered to repeat a well-known pattern in the region: exploitative and abusive behavior.

The Note of Clarification of section 29 of the Helsinki Declaration has two clauses. If we require and consider only "compelling sound methodological reasons" (the first clause), the flexible use of placebos might be very dangerous mainly in resource poor countries. The main and truly relevant clause is the second one: It considers the use of placebos "*for a minor condition* and where the patients who receive placebo will not be subject to any *additional risk or serious or irreversible harm*."[17] This allows placebo use in studies with some analgesics, hypnotics, antihistamines, antiemetics, *provided that the condition is minor and will not entail additional risk or*

serious or irreversible harm, for example, a temporary discomfort. However, no placebo is acceptable in the case of anti-emetic drugs in a chemotherapy treatment. The second clause's flexibility will allow for cases that are often deemed important,[18] such as mild hypertension. It accepts the use of add-on treatments because it does not deny the research subject's treatment. It implies close monitoring, adequate end points, rescue treatments, and so on.

The first and second clauses should be respected simultaneously — an issue that the Note of Clarification, unfortunately, does not require. In this sense, it was widely felt in Latin America that the Note of Clarification was problematic for developing countries and that it would not preclude abusive research like the proposed surfactant study.

As the international debate increased, Argentina's awareness also grew. In contrast to other debates such as the standard of care and even the placebo debate, the latest attempt to amend the Helsinki Declaration raised concern in the academic and medical communities. In this case the discussion focused on the 2003 attempt to amend section 30. It covered new issues such as the posttrial obligations (though some people confused this with the double-standard debate). Argentina's position, and the region's, called for caution and a wider presence of developing countries. It was felt that they should have a voice in this international discussion.

This interest in and impetus on research ethics has had many manifestations in Argentina. Since 2000, a Fogarty Training Program has begun. It was originally intended as a collaborative effort to be conducted six months in New York and six months in Buenos Aires. It is now being fully conducted in Buenos Aires and has had its second year of trainees. There has also been networking, not only in the region, but also within Argentina, and this has led to the creation of an Argentine chapter of FLACEIS (a Latin American network of research ethics committees created in Mexico in 2000). Additionally, *Perspectivas Bioéticas*, the first Argentine journal wholly devoted to bioethics is preparing a special monographic issue on research ethics and on the recent debates. There have also been governmental initiatives, such as the creation of a Central Research Ethics Committee of the City of Buenos Aires that will have a voice in all public hospitals of the City of Buenos Aires (where most research in Argentina is conducted). The Ombudsman Agency of the City of Buenos Aires has made a survey regarding the situation of research ethics committees and is counseling the Ministry of Health about these organizations. The National Regulatory Agency, ANMAT, is preparing a new regulation with stringent ethical requirements. They are also trying to implement inspections of the research ethics committees. Also, multiple seminars and workshops are being held (e.g., FLENI, University of Buenos Aires School of Medicine). Undoubtedly, research ethics is one of the relevant topics and one of the main concerns in Argentina today.

NOTES

1. Economic Commission for Latin America and the Caribbean (ECLAC). Social Panorama of Latin America. Available at: http://www.eclac.cl

2. Reporte Sombra on the Third Report by Argentina before the Human Rights Committee.

3. An example of the lack of respect of the accepted exceptions even within the more conservative framework is the dramatic case of a demented girl of 13 who had been raped but was denied an abortion in a public hospital.

4. Law 1,044.

5. Latin American Network for Assisted Reproduction. *Consenso Latinoamericano en aspectos ético-legales relativos a las técnicas en reproducción asistida*. Reñaca, Chile: 1996:13-7.

6. Personal conversations with directors of Argentine fertility centers.

7. Luna F. Assisted reproductive technology in Latin America: some ethical and socio-cultural issues. In: Vayena E, Rowe P, Griffin D, ed. *Current Practices and Controversies in Assisted Reproduction*. Geneva: World Health Organization; 2002: 31-41.

8. Jones H, Cohen J. Surveillance 1998. *Fertility and Sterility* 1999;71(6): 518.

9. Also at stake here is the physician's responsibility and the couple or woman who is denied rights. A number of thorny questions arise: Can we knowingly seek a pregnancy resulting in a handicapped or severely ill offspring? What are our responsibilities toward this future human being? Should we avoid bringing "evitable suffering" into the world?

10. For details, see: Luna F. Is "best proven" a useless criterion? *Bioethics* 2001;15(4): 273-88.

11. World Medical Association. *Declaration of Helsinki*. Edinburgh, Scotland. Oct 2000: section 29 (emphasis added).

12. See note 10, Luna 2001.

13. Conselho Nacional de Saúde (Brazil). Resolucao N 301 (16 Mar 2000).

14. See note 10, Luna 2001.

15. Lurie P, Wolfe S. Request to the Department of Health and Human Services to halt plans for unethical placebo-controlled study of drug for respiratory distress syndrome in Latin America unless it is redesigned to treat all patients: HRG publication 1558. 22 Feb 2001. Available at: http://www.citizen.org/publications/release.cfm

16. This drug is shown to reduce neonatal mortality by 34%. See note 15, Lurie, Wolfe 2001.

17. World Medical Association. *Declaration of Helsinki: Note of clarification on placebo-controlled trials*. Edinburgh, Scotland. October 2000 (emphasis added).

18. Levine R. The need to revise the Declaration of Helsinki. *New England Journal of Medicine* 99; 341(7): 531-4.

STUDY QUESTIONS

1 According to Don Marquis, what features of the anti-abortionist and pro-choice positions result in a standoff on the question of the status of the fetus? How does he propose to resolve this standoff?

2 Do you think Marquis succeeds in defending the moral impermissibility of abortion by arguing that the fetus has a "future-like-ours"? Does he succeed in his claim that his argument avoids the usual equivocations on "human life," "human being," or "person"? Provide reasons for your answers.

3 What does Marquis mean when he claims that his argument can show "that abortion is, except possibly in rare cases, seriously immoral"? Would he allow exceptions? If so, what sort? Would exceptions undermine his argument? Provide reasons for your answers.

4 Why does Ann Cudd raise objections to Marquis's identification of the status of the fetus as the only issue in the abortion debate? What other considerations should be given weight and why?

5 What characterizes the dominant political framework of liberal individualism identified by Susan Sherwin? Why does Sherwin advocate an ontological shift from this framework to an explicitly feminist understanding of persons as relational beings?

6 Sherwin grants that freedom of choice has been important to feminists in obtaining rights to abortion and contraception, but she argues that this argument is problematic when it comes to evaluating the technologies of assisted conception and reproductive genetics. Why is freedom of choice problematic in the context of new technologies? Do you agree? Why or why not?

7 According to Sherwin, what are the benefits of adopting an ontological framework of feminist relational understandings of personhood? What sorts of policies regarding biotechnology might emerge from this feminist relational framework?

8 What does Amy Harmon's examination of prenatal testing reveal about women's decision-making processes regarding abortion?

9 Outline and evaluate the concerns raised by disability theorists about prenatal testing as reported by Harmon. Do you think disability theorists are right to view prenatal testing as a form of eugenics? Defend your answer.

10 Should women's decisions to abort fetuses be evaluated in the context of showing how such choices are often the result of misinformation about and stereotypes of disability and of pressure by family members, doctors, genetic counselors, and institutions? Defend your answer.

11 Michael DeFine describes the development of the eugenics movement that allowed governments, scientists, and doctors to justify the sterilization of women. What was this movement about? Who was sterilized and why?

12 According to DeFine, what effects did sterilization procedures have on Native American women? What effects did it have on federal relationships with American Indian tribes? Are there ongoing effects with respect to policies regarding consent and sterilization?

13 Given what you have learned from Sherwin, Harmon, and DeFine, do you think that eugenics still plays a role in the development and practice of reproductive procedures and technologies? Defend your answer.

14 Florencia Luna describes the background conditions that shape issues of reproductive rights and research ethics in Argentina. What are these conditions and is an account of them relevant to an analysis of reproductive rights more generally?

15 Luna argues that the conflict between what the Catholic Church permits with respect to reproductive policy and what women and researchers in Argentina do results in hypocrisy and absurd practices. What does she mean by the conflict and what are the absurd practices that result?

16 Do you think that women's liberation requires the full implementation of reproductive rights? Should an answer to this question depend on an analysis of social and political conditions? Should it depend on the values and beliefs in particular contexts? Formulate your answer by evaluating how Sherwin, DeFine, and Luna would respond to these questions.

SUGGESTED READINGS

Beutelspacher, Austreberta Nazar, *et al.* "Does Contraception Benefit Women? Structure, Agency, and Well-Being in Rural Mexico." *Feminist Economics*, v. 9, nos. 2-3 (2003): 213-38.

Callahan, Daniel. "How Technology is Reframing the Abortion Debate." *Hastings Center Report*, v. 16, no. 1 (1986): 33-42.

Callahan, Joan (editor). *Reproduction, Ethics, and the Law: Feminist Perspectives*. Bloomington, IN: Indiana University Press, 1995.

Cook, Rebecca, Bernard Dickens, and Mahmoud Fathalla. *Reproductive Health and Human Rights: Integrating Medicine, Ethics, and Law*. Oxford: Oxford University Press, 2003.

Daniels, Cynthia R. "Between Fathers and Fetuses: The Social Construction of Male Reproduction and the Politics of Fetal Harm." *Signs*, v. 22, no. 3 (1997): 579-616.

Donchin, Anne. "The Future of Mothering: Reproductive Technology and Feminist Theory." *Hypatia*, v. 1, no. 2 (Fall 1986): 121-37.

English, Jane. "Abortion and the Concept of a Person." *Canadian Journal of Philosophy*, v. 5, no. 2 (October 1975): 233-43.

Greenhalgh, Susan, and Jiali Li. "Engendering Reproductive Policy and Practice in Peasant China: For a Feminist Demography of Reproduction." *Signs*, v. 20, no. 3 (1995): 601-41.

Kymlicka, Will. "Moral Philosophy and Public Policy: The Case of NRTs." *Bioethics*, v. 7, no. 1 (1993): 1-26.

Li, Xiaorong. "Two Concepts of Reproductive Rights." *Report from the Institute for Philosophy & Public Policy*, v. 13, no. 4 (Fall 1993): 22-23.

Lichtenberg, Judith. "Population Policy and the Clash of Cultures." *Report from the Institute for Philosophy & Public Policy*, v. 13, no. 4 (Fall 1993): 23-27.

Mahowald, Mary B. "Self-Preservation: An Argument for Therapeutic Cloning, and a Strategy for Fostering Respect for Moral Integrity." *The American Journal of Bioethics*, v. 4, no. 2 (Spring 2004): 56-66.

Molyneux, Maxine. "The Politics of Abortion in Nicaragua: Revolutionary Pragmatism — or Feminism in the Realm of Necessity?" *The Feminist Review*, v. 29 (May 1988): 114-32.

Morgan, Lynn M. "Fetal Relationality in Feminist Philosophy: An Anthropological Approach." *Hypatia*, v. 11, no. 3 (Summer 1996): 47-70.

Nedelsky, Jennifer. "Property in Potential Life? A Relational Approach to Choosing Legal Categories." *Canadian Journal of Law and Jurisprudence*, v. 7, no. 2 (1994): 343-65.

Overall, Christine. *Ethics and Human Reproduction: A Feminist Analysis*. Boston, MA: Unwin Hyman, 1987.

Palmer-Fernandez, Gabriel, and James E. Reagan. "Human Fetal Tissues Transplantation Research and Elective Abortion." *Journal of Social Philosophy*, v. 29, no. 1 (Spring 1998): 5-19.

Parens, Erik, and Adrienne Asch (editors). *Prenatal Testing and Disability Rights*. Washington, DC: Georgetown University Press, 2000.

Porter, Elisabeth. "Abortion Ethics: Rights and Responsibilities." *Hypatia*, v. 9, no. 3 (Summer 1994): 66-87.

Roberts, Dorothy. "Race and the New Reproduction." *Hastings Law Journal*, v. 47, no. 4 (April 1996): 25-39.

Robinson, Bambi E.S. "Birds Do it, Bees Do it: So Why Not Single Women and Lesbians?" *Bioethics*, v. 11, nos. 3-4 (1997): 217-27.

Sherwin, Susan. "Abortion Through a Feminist Ethics Lens." In *No Longer Patient: Feminist Ethics and Health Care*. Philadelphia, PA: Temple University Press, 1992.

— . "Moral Perception and Global Visions." *Bioethics*, v. 15, no. 3 (2001): 175-88.

Thomson, Judith Jarvis. "A Defense of Abortion." *Philosophy & Public Affairs*, v. 1, no. 1 (Fall 1971): 47-66.

Tooley, Michael. "Abortion and Infanticide." *Philosophy & Public Affairs*, v. 2, no. 1 (1972): 37-65.

Tong, Rosemarie (editor). *Globalizing Feminist Bioethics: Crosscultural Perspectives*. Boulder, CO: Westview Press, 2001.

Warren, Mary Anne. "On the Moral and Legal Status of Abortion." *The Monist*, v. 57, no. 1 (1973): 43-61.

Wasserman, David. "Population Programs and Individual Autonomy." *Report from the Institute for Philosophy & Public Policy*, v. 13, no. 4 (Fall 1993): 16-21.

CHAPTER TWO:
EUTHANASIA, ASSISTED SUICIDE, AND HEALTH CARE

INTRODUCTION

The right to life, the right to choose, and the weighing of these rights have been as central to debates about euthanasia and health care as they are to reproductive issues. Euthanasia, sometimes referred to as mercy killing, asks us to consider whether it is ever morally justified to end the life of someone who is incurably ill and suffering. It is important to begin by laying out a number of distinctions. *Active* and *passive* euthanasia marks the distinction between actively or directly taking measures to end the life of a patient by administering a drug, for example, and letting or allowing the patient to die by withholding or withdrawing treatment. Some argue that the distinction between these cannot be upheld or justified. *Voluntary* and *involuntary* euthanasia marks the difference between cases in which patients voluntarily express a desire to have their lives ended and those in which patients are unable to do so, either because they are infants or because they have lost the capacity to express desires or make decisions. Lastly, there is the distinction between suicide, the taking of one's own life, and being assisted to die by another, such as a doctor or agency. Theorists make use of these distinctions in their arguments about whether euthanasia can be morally justified and in what cases.

When the issue of euthanasia is placed in a broader social and political context, complex issues of the significance of health care policies are raised. Is autonomy enhanced or diminished in contexts where health care is taken to be a matter of individual choice rather than provided by the state? If autonomy is diminished, what does this mean for the right to make decisions about health care or treatment? Are decisions about resources, the availability of medical technologies, and terminating treatment affected by factors such as disability, age, gender, and race? If so, what does this tell us about conceptions of

equality and arguments for universal health care? Should facts about the vast disparities in wealth between countries that are rich and poor affect our thinking about the right to health care or our obligations to provide care to those in less fortunate circumstances? Do discriminatory perceptions and stereotypes of disability affect policies regarding euthanasia and health care?

In the first reading, Michael Stingl examines the general issue of health care in Canada. The provision of health care, publicly funded through taxation and available to everyone, is valued highly by Canadians, but public discussions about changes to the system to reduce costs continue to take place. Stingl discusses the two social values of equality and efficiency at issue in the debate and the ways in which they coincide and collide in discussions about health care. He begins by applying the two liberal conceptions of equality to the different approaches to health care in Canada and in the U.S. For formal equality theorists, or what Stingl refers to as libertarianism, state authority exists to enforce rules of non-interference between individuals, each of whom is then free to pursue the goals that give meaning and structure to their lives, enter into relationships of exchange of goods or services, and acquire material and social goods. Stingl takes the health care system of the U.S. to be closely aligned with libertarianism in that it gives individuals freedom to purchase private insurance plans in the free market and extends public insurance only to those who fall below a certain economic baseline. Liberal egalitarians, or substantive equality theorists, also value individual liberty, but recognize how it is limited for some people in ways that result in diminished life prospects and unequal opportunities.

Stingl argues that something like liberal egalitarianism is behind the single-tiered structure of the current Canadian health care system, the justification being that because health is a good important to each person's ability to pursue projects and goals, justice demands equal health care benefits for everyone. Stingl applies this discussion of equality to proposals for reforming Canada's health care system, arguing that a two-tiered system based on a distinction between basic and non-basic medical services undermines equality because it cannot ensure that decisions about what counts as medically necessary are not based on factors such as age, gender, and race. Reforms, he argues, need to take place in the areas of reconceiving efficiency so that unequal access for some is eliminated, preventative rather then curative health services are put in place, and social programs are strengthened rather than undermined.

The debate about public versus privately funded health care takes on added complexity when we examine how practices and policies regarding euthanasia and assisted suicide vary from country to country. In the second reading, Margaret Battin examines the issues of active euthanasia and assisted suicide by discussing end-of-life dilemmas in the Netherlands, Germany, and the U.S. — three advanced industrial democracies that share features of sophisticated medical technology, high life expectancy, and a higher percentage of deaths by cancer and organ disease than by parasitic or infectious diseases. She uses this examination to reveal the background assumptions underlying each society's set of practices, to explore the moral justifiability of euthanasia, and to shed light on whether the comparisons have implications for policy in the U.S.

The U.S. has developed a body of case law and state statute that permits a framework of passive euthanasia, the determination to withhold or withdraw treatment when there is no medical or moral point in going on. Voluntary active euthanasia was prohibited by law in the Netherlands, but was legally tolerated and defended in court decisions that protected physicians who performed euthanasia (euthanasia was legalized in 2001). The protection covers doctors who follow specific guidelines, the most important of which is that the patient's request be voluntary.

Germany's history of Nazism has resulted in an understandable distrust of doctors by the German public and has generated opposition to active euthanasia. However, assisted suicide is not a violation of the law and a private organization, the German Society for Humane Dying (DGHS), helps those who choose suicide as an alternative to terminal illness by providing the means for ending one's life. Battin raises objections to each of these practices and considers the similarities and differences between the three countries, including the lack of universal health care in the U.S. She cites advances with respect to women's rights, a confrontational public, a tendency for personal self-analysis, and a resistance to authority as differences that can justify a policy of physician-assisted suicide in the U.S.

The description of Americans as "independent, confrontational, self-analyzing, do-it-yourself, authority-resisting" would seem to clinch the case for voluntary euthanasia as respectful of autonomous capacities so valued in liberal theory. It would also seem to clinch the case that Battin presents for physician-assisted suicide in the U.S. In the third reading, Thomas Cavanaugh argues that the two justifications of respecting a patient's wanting to die and the patient's having a medically established good reason for suicide are in tension with one another. Cavanaugh explores these two justifications to argue against the standard belief that good reasons connect easily or naturally with complying with a patient's wanting to kill him or herself. A patient must not only have a good reason *and* want to kill him or herself, but he or she must want to die for the good reason. Cavanaugh argues that this subordinates autonomy to the good reason as is evident in safeguards that prevent patients from killing themselves for bad reasons.

Cavanaugh cites excerpts from the *Oregon Act* to illustrate how it collapses the motive requirement (*wanting* to die for the good reason) with the good reason requirement. The *Oregon Act* does not justify a patient pursuing physician-assisted suicide if the reason is to ease the burden of family members caring for him or her. Cavanaugh examines the soft-paternalist position that disconnects the motive from the good reason by arguing that a patient's wanting to die is a sufficient reason for a physician to assist. Because those who defend the standard justification do not accept autonomy as sufficient, they have a difficult time supporting those cases in which someone has a medically established good reason but does not want to die. Cavanaugh identifies this as an asymmetry in the standard justification and rejects various answers that could be given to it. He concludes by arguing that given the independent character of the two-part justification, there is no sound basis for the legalization of physician-assisted suicide.

In the fourth reading, Harriet McBryde Johnson tells her story of living with serious disabilities in order to raise objections to involuntary euthanasia, the putting to death or letting die of those who are or are perceived to be unable to make this decision for themselves. Johnson focuses her critique on the work of Peter Singer, someone, she claims, who would argue that the disabled person that she is should have been killed at birth. She records her ambivalence about accepting Singer's invitation to two speaking engagements by juxtaposing conversations she had with people from the disability rights movement, who objected to her having anything to do with Singer, and with those she had with him. Interwoven in Johnson's descriptions of her interactions with Singer, speaking to his classes, and answering questions from him and his students are descriptions of the details of her daily routine that complicate assumptions about who she is and what it means for her to travel, eat, sleep, and get around. Johnson finds herself realizing that Singer's arguments, while too theoretical and ideal, are not as simple as she and disability theorists believe and that taking him to be a monster is not a solution in a world that thinks it would be better if she and others like her did not exist.

Some of the concerns raised by Cavanaugh about autonomy and by Johnson about disability are explored from a slightly different angle in the final reading by Nathan Brett. Brett begins with the story of Margo, an Alzheimer's patient and a citizen of the Netherlands who has signed a living will giving advance directives to her caretakers to end her life in the event that she suffers substantial loss of memory and other mental capacities. Margo is now in that condition, but appears to be happy, giving no indication of wanting to die and every indication of being fearful that her caretakers will harm her. Brett asks, is there a case for saying that her life should be ended anyway? If so, how good is the case? Brett explores answers to these questions through a discussion of Ronald Dworkin's account of critical interests.

Critical interests describe the structure, consistency, coherence, and meaning given to whole lives. To respect Margo as an autonomous agent is to respect her competent decisions about her life and the way she makes sense of it. If we assume that Margo's reflection before the onset of Alzheimer's about her life and prospects was not based on misinformation and that her decision is not out of character, then it would seem to be in her critical interests to end her life sooner rather than after years of dementia. While Brett finds these arguments plausible, he thinks that ending Margo's life is problematic. He argues that the demented Margo is not the same person as the one who wrote the advance directive and she cannot use a living will to end the life of someone different from herself. Margo has a simple, childlike perspective on the world and lacks any connection with the author of the orders for her death. Margo's life has ended and been replaced by someone who can experience pain and pleasure and has needs and desires. Brett argues that the satisfaction of these interests is a source of value and makes demands on our compassion in the same way that human beings who are infants or infantile demand our compassion.

EQUALITY AND EFFICIENCY AS BASIC SOCIAL VALUES

Michael Stingl

Michael Stingl teaches in the Department of Philosophy at the University of Lethbridge, Alberta. He is co-editor with Donna Wilson of Efficiency vs. Equality: Health Reform in Canada *(1996). He has written articles on euthanasia and the fair distribution of health resources, as well as on more general topics in philosophical ethics.*

Stingl frames the ongoing discussion of health care reform in Canada in terms of an examination of the two conceptions of equality in the liberal tradition: libertarianism and liberal egalitarianism. Canada's health care system can be said to fit the liberal egalitarianism found in Rawls. Because health is a good each of us needs to pursue life plans at all, we are treated as moral equals only if each is given an equal amount of health insurance. Stingl argues that the current health system of the U.S. reflects the libertarian rejection of state interference and the defense of an individual's freedom to purchase private insurance plans. However, health care raises particularly complex issues of efficiency, ones that tend to push away from a strict liberal egalitarian justification for equal health care. Stingl argues that introducing additional inequalities into Canada's health system is neither reasonable nor fair.

Social Values and Political Choices

Equality and efficiency are two key terms in the growing national debate over reforming the Canadian health system. Both are widely understood to refer to values basic in the structure and identity of Canadian society. But this is true only on a loose understanding of both terms; in the debate over health reform, both terms mean different things to different people. As long as equality and efficiency remain widely but only loosely understood, the likelihood increases that this debate will become politically intractable and socially divisive.

In this paper, I examine some of the different things that those participating in the debate often mean by equality and efficiency. Taking stock of these different meanings, I distinguish several points of potential reform where we can expect the two values to coincide, as well as several

where we can expect them to collide. It is this latter possibility, of course, that is the more ethically interesting and troubling: the fact that in reforming the health system, having more of the one value will sometimes mean having less of the other.

Basic social values guide public policy, and more generally, determine the conditions and limits of social interaction between individuals, groups, and institutions within Canada. They provide the shared social framework within which each of us defines his or her own life. When such values collide, we are individually and collectively faced with a social choice. On the one hand, we might allow our social values to shift in ways that, at least on the surface, avoid conflict; on the other hand, we might simply accept the fact that social values will sometimes collide, and when this happens, face the difficult choice of which value ought to give way to which. In either case, we need to be clear about who the "we" is that is determining the course of social change. Choices regarding basic social values must not be hidden away within governmental bureaucracies, but debated publicly and openly within the larger political context of Canadian society as a whole. In a modern liberal society, determining the basic conditions of our social network with one another is an important right and an important responsibility, for again, basic social values not only determine the structure and identity of Canadian society, but as well, the structure and identity of our lives as individual Canadians.

Determining which basic social value should give way to which is thus a political choice in the broadest sense of the term. What is required to make such choices is public debate and government action. And this is what we are now seeing in varying degrees across Canada: public debate about the importance and possible limits of the Canadian health system and Canadian social services more generally, and government initiatives to make these services more responsive to deficit and debt as well as the needs of all Canadians. To evaluate these initiatives, and to make the social choices they represent wisely, we need a clear public understanding of what terms equality and efficiency really mean.

Two Different Meanings of Equality

In the debate over health reform it is necessary to distinguish between two very different ways of thinking about human society. On the one hand, we might see society as providing nothing more than the institutional framework necessary for humans to organize the individual pursuit of their own separate ends, as they personally choose to define them. On this picture of society, it is the individual who is of fundamental value; society exists only as a set of formalized arrangements to better enable each individual to pursue his or her own personal good. This is the libertarian view of society.

On the other hand, we might see society as a joint, cooperative venture, participation in which creates the sense of a greater, social good that grounds and gives context to everyone's own personal good. On this second picture of human society individuals will still be fundamentally important, but so too will society. Personal goods may be pursued, but only as part of a larger, cooperative enterprise that works fairly and equally for the good of everyone. This second sort of view might be called liberal egalitarianism, "liberal" because it values the liberty to pursue one's own personal good, but "egalitarian" because it is prepared to limit such liberty for the good of others.[1]

Each of the two different ways of thinking about human society leads to its own idea of what it means to treat persons equally. To understand these two different meanings of equality, we need to examine more fully the views of society on which they are based.[2]

Let us start with what is common between the two views: the value of individual liberty. What makes human beings the interesting, valuable creatures that they are is the fact that they are able to think about and choose the ends towards which they will act. At the most general level, these ends may include such diverse things as material wealth, love and friendship, knowledge, or social power and prestige. Whatever particular mix of such ends a person might choose to pursue, the important thing about people is that they are able to make such choices; they are able, that is, to determine the goals and aims that give structure and meaning to their individual lives.

Acting alone, however, no one individual is likely to get very far towards any of the more interesting or complex ends that make our lives richly of fully human. For the goods that matter most to us, like having children or embarking on a career, we need the help of other people, or at the very least, their non-interference. This, then, is one minimal role that society might play in human life: to insure that no one individual unfairly interferes with the independent choices of another.

This libertarian view of society is developed at length by the philosopher Robert Nozick in his book *Anarchy, State and Utopia*.[3] According to

Nozick, legitimate state authority exists only to enforce rules of non-interference between individual citizens, rules that outlaw things like lying, cheating, stealing, or reneging on promises. Regulating such actions allows a free market to develop between individuals that enables them to trade goods and service in ways that are mutually beneficial. On this free market view of human society, any trade that is consented to is fair, as long as the consent is not the result of coercion; as long, that is, as it is not the result of anything like lying, cheating, or any of the other forms of illicit interference in the life of another. The function of the state is not to create a market of exchanges, but rather to create the social conditions that freely allow such markets to develop and flourish. The markets themselves are nothing more than the separately motivated choices of individuals to enter into trading arrangements with one another.

According to this first view of society, people are ultimately separate from one another, and relationships of interchange and benefit require mutual agreement. Beyond non-interference, no one owes anyone anything. Each may enter into a free market of exchanges to derive whatever goods or services others agree to trade, but no one is obliged to participate in whatever markets might otherwise develop between others, nor to benefit in any way those who are for some reason unable to participate in such markets. Out of charity one might choose to help such a person, but no one is in any way morally obliged to render aid. The motto of this view is that I have my life, and you have yours: and just as I might choose to enter freely into an exchange of goods or services with you, I might just as freely choose not to.

The second way of thinking about human society and human life is not a simple reversal of libertarianism. It does not move to the opposite extreme of declaring that it is society that is of fundamental or primary importance, and individuals of mere derivative value. Liberal egalitarianism, like libertarianism, values individual choice. But unlike libertarianism, it gives independent value to the ongoing social relationships that link the choices of one person to those of the next. It recognized that although each of us may choose the course of our own life, none of us chooses the background of ongoing social cooperation that makes such a choice possible. Where libertarianism sees society as nothing more than a series of individual agreements, the second conception sees society as having an independent existence and value of its own.

This second view of society is developed at length by the philosopher John Rawls in his book *A Theory of Justice*.[4] According to Rawls, a society is fairly arranged only when it is reasonable for any and all its members to consent to being part of it. Because the rich, full lives that matter most to humans require the shared cooperation of others, some social arrangement will be preferable to no social arrangement in all but the most dire circumstances. The problem is that different arrangements will offer different benefits to different people. A social arrangement that benefits some individuals more will benefit others less, depending on whose natural talents are in greater demand and generate greater social and individual rewards. Moreover, just as some individuals will suffer accidents that diminish whatever opportunities they would have had for developing their talents or lives in ways they might otherwise have chosen, some individuals will be born in ways that similarly limit the range of opportunities available to them.

So the question is, what sort of social arrangement would it be reasonable to enter into, regardless of one's plans, talents, or infirmities? According to Rawls, the only society it would be reasonable for each of us to enter into is one that guarantees every individual the same equal chance to pursue whatever life plan he or she might choose. People being people, such plans will of course vary greatly, some plans requiring more social resources, some fewer. But Rawls' idea is that whatever sort of life we might choose to lead, two basic sorts of goods will be important to us: civil liberties, like freedom of speech, association, and conscience, and material resources, like income and wealth. Since there is no way that those with fewer civil liberties could ever be advantaged by a social system that distributed such liberties unequally, the first principle of a just society is equal liberty for all. But with regard to material resources, Rawls claims that the situation is markedly different: if more productive individuals are allowed economic incentives, the social pie as a whole will be greater, and so those with lower incomes will have more material resources than they would under a system which distributed income and wealth in a strictly egalitarian fashion. To the extent that those with less material wealth are more advantaged than they otherwise would be, unequal levels of material wealth will be reasonable in a fair and just society.

We will return to Rawls' two principles in the next section, the first governing the fair distribution of basic liberties, and the second governing the fair distribution of material wealth. The question there will be whether health care, or health more generally, is a good more like liberty or more like wealth.

The point here is that just as there are two different ideals of modern society, there are also two different conceptions of equality. For the libertarian, each individual is treated equally by a state that guarantees no more than non-interference between individuals. The state itself treats individuals unequally when it interferes in the lives of its citizens to transfer between them material resources that were initially acquired through free exchange. Enforced charity, by means of a taxation scheme, for example, that transfers resources from those with more to those with less, is not fair or just according to the libertarian view of human life and society. Again, those with more may freely choose to help those with less, but they may just as freely choose not to.

For Rawls, on the other hand, transfers between individuals are required to ensure that each has an equal opportunity to lead whatever life he or she might choose. Since more productive individuals are allowed greater material resources only so far as this is required as an economic incentive to produce more goods and services overall, taxation is just up to the point that the social product as a whole would begin to diminish. Taxation is fair, that is, up to the point that the economic incentives for the better off would cease to motivate them to be more productive.

Something like this second notion of equality is arguably behind the single-tiered structure of the current Canadian health system.[5] The general form of the argument would be that because our health is equally important to all of us regardless of what sort of life we might choose to pursue, taxation schemes that provide equal health benefits to everyone represent a fair and just social arrangement, one that it would be reasonable for all individuals to enter into no matter what their talents of infirmities. Because of the kind of good that health is, each of us is treated as a moral equal only if we are each given an equal amount of health insurance.

In contrast, the current health system of the United States is more nearly libertarian, since individuals are guaranteed only as much health insurance as they are able to purchase in the free market of private insurance plans. This system is not perfectly libertarian, however, because public insurance is provided for people falling below a certain economic baseline or over a certain age limit. Even so, public insurance plans in the U.S. are extremely limited in their coverage, and there are a significant number of Americans above the economic baseline for public insurance who can nevertheless afford little or no private insurance.[6] It is thus unclear to what extent public insurance plans in the U.S. represent charity or justice for those unable to afford adequate private insurance.

More interesting than the U.S. system, and more conceptually problematic, is the sort of hybrid, two-tiered system of health insurance advocated by some Canadian health reformers.[7] Unlike public insurance plans in the United States, all medically necessary services would be covered for all Canadians, but for services deemed not necessary, or for faster or better quality service, access would be available only to people able to afford additional insurance or direct payment. As we shall see in the next section, it is hard to determine whether the idea of equality presupposed by this sort of two-tiered health system is a coherent one.

Health as a Basic Social Good

Just as there are two importantly different ways in which we might think about society, and hence equality, there are two importantly different ways in which we might think about the value of health services.

On the one hand, we might think of health services as services like any other: just as we might avail ourselves of the services of a travel agent or hair dresser, we might also avail ourselves of the services of a doctor, nurse, or any other health professional. On the other hand we might think of health services as having a direct tie to health, which alongside political liberty and material wealth we might consider a basic social good.[8]

If we follow Rawls in defining basic goods as those things that are likely to matter to us whatever our life plan might be, health seems an obvious addition to the list. Some people, however, seem entirely prepared to trade off at least portions of their health for other goods, such as the pleasures of smoking or high cholesterol diets. Although this does not change the fact that certain levels of health are needed to lead human lives however they might be defined by the individuals leading them, it does raise the possibility of a mixed understanding of the good of health, and hence, of health services. Perhaps only some health services, but not all, need to be understood as integral to the basic good of health. The health services that are not tied directly to the level of health needed to lead a good life, however one might define it, might then be understood as service like any other, commodities to be sought out and paid for by those who desire them.

Let us return here to Rawls' two principles for distributing basic goods. The first principle, the one regarding liberty, is strictly egalitarian. Because of the kind of basic good civil liberties represent, people are treated equally only if they receive equal amounts of this particular good. Here we need to remember the leading idea of Rawls' two principles, that it is equally reasonable for all to participate in a given social arrangement only if that arrangement gives everyone an equal opportunity to pursue their life plans however they might choose to define them. In general, this conception of society requires basic social goods to be distributed equally; the only exception is when distributing a good unequally means more of that same good for all. This is the situation, Rawls says, with material wealth: all do better than they otherwise would if some are given economic incentives to be more productive.

Considered alongside the basic goods of liberty and material wealth, health would seem to be a good more like the former than the latter. Allowing different levels of health does not in any immediate sort of way make those with less health better off than they would otherwise be, and so in this important respect, health seems to have more in common with political liberty than material wealth. If there are no other important differences between them, then it would seem that health ought to be distributed like liberty: in a strictly egalitarian way.

But there are a number of important differences between health services and the sorts of social arrangements needed to guarantee our civil liberties. First, health services can increase in number, kind, and cost. Civil liberties, on the other hand, are limited in number, and tend to be all or nothing. Were a state, for example, to guarantee political but not religious freedom, we would not think it a state that guaranteed freedom of speech, association, and conscience. But it does not seem in principle wrong that a state might provide antibiotics for everyone who needed them but not artificial hearts. Moreover, certain choices of what sort of a life one is going to lead seem legitimately to require or to allow trade-offs involving increased health risks. So while a state can guarantee through its laws and political institutions equal liberty, it cannot through its health services guarantee anything approaching equal health, whatever technologies might be available to it.

Finally, it may be that by allowing a second tier of health services to develop, those with only publicly provided, first-tier services available to them will do better than they otherwise might.

There are several ways this might happen, such as less waiting time or innovative treatment options that are developed at and filter down from the more expensive privately purchased second tier of services. But there are also reasons for supposing that things will not be better for those who find themselves limited to first-tier services, as resources, personnel, and finally funding are increasingly drawn away from the first tier to the second. What would in fact happen were the Canadian system to go from one tier to two is far from clear.

Taken together, these differences between liberty and health suggest that health services might be more appropriately distributed in accord with something like Rawls' second principle of justice, the one regarding material wealth. The most straightforward way of doing this would be to incorporate their distribution directly into the second principle's distribution of material wealth. Assume, that is, that income and wealth were distributed in such a way that whatever inequalities existed made those with less as well off as they could be. To give those with less any more would be to decrease the incentives to the more productive members society below the level at which they will continue to be as productive as they are.[9] It might then seem to be fair to allow people to purchase as much or as little as they wanted. What rankles about this suggestion given the current free market method of distributing health services in the U.S. is that material wealth is clearly not distributed in accord with Rawls' second principle in either the U.S. or Canada; one result in the U.S., of course, is that a significant number of Americans are unable to purchase health insurance that would be considered in any way adequate or affordable by Canadian standards. But suppose wealth were distributed in a more equal fashion; why not let people spend their money on as much or as little as they wanted?

One practical problem with this market approach to the distribution of health services is that it would seem to require private insurance schemes, which are economically inefficient.[10] A second problem is that preventative services are in some ways more efficient than curative services, and it is not immediately clear how or why people would choose to insure themselves in ways that might allow full realization of the advantages of preventative medicine.[11]

These sorts of practical problems might be resolved with the right sort of public insurance plan, and the right sort of political will to establish and maintain such a plan. But this suggests an even more insurmountable problem for any proposal tying the distribution of health services to a more equal distribution of material wealth: to the extent that the struggle in both Canada and the U.S. for more egalitarian health systems has been uphill, the struggle for greater economic equality has faced a more nearly vertical climb.

This being so, we might wonder whether Rawls' theory of justice has any relevance for the current debate over Canadian health reform. Whatever we might want to say about the overall distribution of material wealth in Canada, all health services are currently available to all Canadians, at least in principle. But this very principle is itself one significant aspect of the Canadian health system that is now being threatened by governmental responses to increasing deficits and debts. Thinking about universality in the context of Rawls' two principles of justice may yet help clarify some of the larger social issues that are at stake in initiatives to trim deficits by trimming health services.

For example, one direct response to the problems involved in tying health services to the principle for distributing material wealth is to insist that health is ultimately more like liberty than not; despite the differences listed above, health services, like liberty, ought to be distributed in a strictly equal fashion. This would respond well to the idea that like liberty, having a certain level of health is central to our having any life plans at all. But we must still recognize at least this one important difference between the two goods: health services can escalate in cost and number in a way that the institutional arrangements guaranteeing equal liberty cannot. This difference could be met, however, by limiting the comprehensiveness of services provided rather than their universal provision. That cost containment should be focused on comprehensiveness rather than universality is suggested by the idea that health is more like liberty than material wealth.

Limiting the comprehensiveness of the public health plan raises a second interesting question regarding current proposals for reforming the health system. Would it be fair to all Canadians to tie basic, medically necessary services to the strictly egalitarian sort of principle appropriate to liberty, and then, in addition, piggyback the accessibility of all other services onto something like Rawls' second principle? This would preserve universal medical coverage for those services determined to be medially necessary, and allow people with more income or wealth to purchase whatever additional services they wanted to. The underlying idea would be that it is only basic health services that are like liberty; whatever life a person might choose to lead, certain basic health services, like liberty, are equally important to everyone. Additional health services, though, are like material wealth: some people will want to pursue more, some people less, depending on the different kinds of lives they choose to lead. Unequal access to additional health services, like unequal levels of material wealth, will be a fair social arrangement just so long as those who have less benefit more than they otherwise would have given a completely equal arrangement.

Arguments of precisely this kind were aired at the 1995 annual general meeting of the Canadian Medical Association.[12] Some doctors, agreeing that equality requires all basic health services be provided to all Canadians, suggested that there was nothing wrong with providing additional services to those who were willing to pay for them. They argued that in allowing this second tier of services to develop, the first tier of basic services would in fact be strengthened.

Again, it is an open question whether this last claim is true. But even ignoring the question of how a second tier of health services might in fact impact on the quality of the first tier of publicly funded services, and ignoring, as well, the question of whether material wealth is itself fairly distributed in Canadian society, there is a deeper conceptual problem with this two-tiered sort of approach to reforming the health system. How are we to distinguish between basic and non-basic services? In some few cases, the distinction may appear to be quite clear: face lifts are not a medical necessity, however much one might plan one's life around the availability of such a service. But this is hardly the sort of service that is causing any cost problems for the health system, especially since it is not now included in any public health insurance plan. More relevant in this regard are newly developing life-saving technologies, many of which are costly and publicly available. For the individuals directly affected by them, such technologies will certainly appear to be medically necessary. The problem facing a publicly funded health system, however, is what happens when services of this kind begin to overreach the public's ability to pay for them? What happens when we can't afford to provide life-saving technologies to all those whose lives could thus be saved? Talking about basic versus non-basic services does nothing to resolve this problem.

We might, of course, try to avoid the problem by reinterpreting basic to refer only the those services that could be provided to all who need them, given the limitations of an antecedently determined budget, one that balanced the costs of the health against those of other public goods, such as defense, education, social assistance, and economic development. But what this means is that some individuals with the life-threatening conditions will be saved, while other individuals, with other life-threatening conditions, will not. Are those who are not saved treated equally to those who are? Even in a single-tiered system, one which accepts the economic necessity of limitations on comprehensiveness, this is a question that would have to faced. But it is an even more difficult question if we allow those who can afford it to purchase life-saving treatments privately. The problem of what it means to call some services but not others part of the basic package of health insurance owed equally to every member of Canadian society is exacerbated by the fact that in a two-tiered system, those who would find themselves unable to purchase the additional treatments available to the economically advantaged would be even more disadvantaged by the advent of their ill health than they already are. Worse yet, those individuals least able to afford to purchase additional services would be the same ones most likely to need to.[13]

It is thus far from clear whether any proposal for two-tiered health reform based on a distinction between basic and non-basic services is workable or coherent. What this suggests, from the perspective of a liberal egalitarian theory of justice, is that the only fair health system is one that is single-tiered.

Conflicts Between Equality and Efficiency

Complicating questions about equality is the ambiguity of its companion term in the health reform debate, efficiency. Everyone seems to agree, in a vague, general sort of way, that the health system can and should be more efficiently organized and operated. The differences of opinion are over what exactly this means.

In its simplest use, pursuing greater efficiency means doing what we now do better. Better utilization of the services now available, it is claimed, will cost governments less and at the same time respond more fully to the actual health needs of all Canadians. The argument is that many tests, treatments, and services are currently being provided to those who do not need them or in ways that have not been proven to be generally effective and that may be even harmful.[14]

Regardless of the extent to which this is in fact true, problems regarding equality arise on even this simplest understanding of efficiency. For example, while the current system overtreats individuals consulting their doctors with nothing more than a common cold, other individuals, such as pregnant women who are economically or otherwise disadvantaged, go without appropriate medical care. Merely eliminating the waste in the health system as it currently exists will do nothing by itself to respond to this second sort of problem, which bears directly on the question of the extent to which the current system is responding equally to the health needs of all Canadians. Achieving better treatment for disadvantaged individuals is, however, one important area of health reform where equality and efficiency might coincide, were the right sorts of reforms to be pursued. Current data suggests that a great many costly medical conditions arise out of early deficiencies in prenatal and childhood nutrition and care. Thus, ensuring that all Canadian fetuses and children receive sufficient nutrition and care is not just a question of greater social equality, but greater economic efficiency as well.

This leads us to a second meaning of efficiency, one that emphasizes preventative over curative health services. The argument here is that it is cheaper to prevent illness rather than to treat it once it has arisen. So far as those who are the most economically disadvantaged are also among the sickest, this is a second important area of health reform where considerations of equality and efficiency might coincide. The extent to which this is so, however, will depend on the extent to which the health statuses of those who are economically less advantaged are tied to social conditions that go beyond the purview of the health system. If a low income job, for example, is bad for your health, it is not clear what the health system can or should do about this fact.

Equality and efficiency are also less clearly connected in a third sense of efficiency, the one at issue in the discussion of the preceding sections. Given the ever expanding horizon of medical possibility, we will soon be at that point, if we are not indeed already there, of not being able to afford to provide every possible medical service to every Canadian who might benefit from it. If we can't provide every service to everyone who might need it, what might it mean to provide as many services to as many people as we can? How are we to measure the efficiency of responding to the health needs of some Canadians, but not others?[15] Even supposing we felt able to answer such questions about efficiency, there is no reason to assume that the most efficient use of services would necessarily be the most equal.

Suppose, for example, that considerations regarding the most efficient use of health services led us to offer hip surgery to those younger than seventy-five but not to those over seventy-five. Would such a policy represent equal treatment for younger and older people, or is it in some sense ageist? Or suppose we were to treat less serious but more prevalent conditions at the expense of more serious but less prevalent conditions; are those affected by the more serious conditions and those affected by the less serious conditions treated as true equals? These sorts of questions are again exacerbated by the data that suggest that those individuals with less advantaged economic backgrounds are likely to experience more, and more serious, medical conditions.

A fourth and final meaning of efficiency involves reforms to the health system that reduce the cost to governments of providing, but increase the cost to consumers of these in either time or money. One example of such a reform is shortened hospital stays, which cost the hospital and hence the government less, but cost the consumer more in paying for home care or in relying on the time and energy of family members of friends. Assuming the current tax system to be more or less equal, the question is whether transferring such costs from the citizen as taxpayer to the citizen as consumer of health services introduces more or less equality into Canadian society. Looking back to the discussion of the second section of this paper, we might say, if we were libertarians, that those who are healthy have no social obligation to pay for those who are not. If some people get sick, this is their problem, those of us who are healthy might choose to help those of us who are sick out of charity, but the state should not compel such help by transferring money from the healthy to the sick through taxation.

On the liberal egalitarian conception of society, however, we must ask ourselves whether it would be reasonable to enter into a society that does not provide equal care for its sick and injured, regardless of their individual ability to pay for health services. For just as any one of us might find ourselves sick or injured, any one of us

might experience a dramatic change in our ability to pay for whatever health we might need. This sort of situation is prevalent in the United States, where for many people, losing either their jobs or their health means losing their health insurance.[16]

One way of responding to this problem is the health system adopted by Canada, universally available to all and publicly funded through taxation. Compared to the European Union, taxes in both Canada and the U.S. are low; yet in the U.S., and increasingly in Canada, there is much concern that taxes are too high. There is also concern in the European Union over high taxes, but it exists alongside concern for preserving the basic structure of the egalitarian sort of society that these taxes support. One German, a corporate manager facing a tax rate of nearly 60 percent, put the point this way:

> The European knows that if he gets sick he can go to a good hospital and it won't bankrupt him ... he knows that if his old parents get sick ... they're protected. To Americans, these can be financially disastrous. But we don't fear them. That is why we keep paying. That is why we say we don't like it but the taxes are necessary.[17]

This point returns us the idea that the current health reform debate in Canada is not just about the kind of health system we want for ourselves and our family members. At a deeper and more far-reaching level, it is about the kind of society we want to live in, one that feels an obligation to care for its sick and injured or one that does not. Economic inequalities may be part of a fair and reasonable society, as both libertarians and liberal egalitarians seem to agree. But unless we are willing to adopt the libertarian view of what a modern, liberal society should be, introducing additional inequalities into our health system does not appear to be either reasonable or fair.

NOTES

1. This is the term used, for example, by Will Kymlicka in *Contemporary Political Philosophy: An Introduction* (Oxford University Press, 1990).

Some commentators on the health reform debate call the second view of society communitarianism, but this term has quite a different meaning in contemporary political debate. For a thorough discussion of the main differences between communitarianism and liberal egalitarianism, see Kymlicka, Chapter 6.

2. For further discussion of these different approaches to equality, as well as some of their implications for the just distribution of health care services, see Allen Buchanan, "Justice: A Philosophical Review" in *Justice and Health Care*, ed. Earl Shelp (Dordrecth: Reidel, 1981), 3-21.

3. Robert Nozick, *Anarchy, State, and Utopia* (New York: Basic Books, 1974).

4. John Rawls, *A Theory of Justice* (Cambridge: Harvard University Press, 1971).

5. For such an argument see Kai Nielsen, "Autonomy, Equality and a Just Health Care System," *The International Journal of Applied Philosophy* 4 (Spring 1989): 39-44.

6. Robert G. Evans, "Less is More: Contrasting Styles in Health Care," in *Canada and the United States: Differences that Count*, ed. David Thomas (Peterborough: Broadview, 1993), 21-41. For a glimpse into what the statistics mean for the everyday lives of affected Americans, see Eleanor D. Kinney and Suzanne K. Steinmetz, "Note from the Insurance Underground: How the Chronically Ill Cope," *Journal of Health Politics, Policy and Law* 19, 3 (1994): 633-642.

7. Patrick Sullivan, "Private Health Care Dominates Meeting as General Council Calls for National Debate on Issue," *Canadian Medical Association Journal* 153, 6 (1995): 801-803.

8. For a more extended effort to include health in Rawls' theory of justice, see Norman Daniels, *Just Health Care* (Cambridge: Cambridge University Press, 1985). An interesting alternative to Daniels approach, closer to the one suggested here, is provided in Ronald M. Green, "The Priority of Health Care," *Journal of Medicine and Philosophy* 9 (1983): 373-379. Recent work on the social determinants of health (see note 13) suggests, however, that we might regard health itself, and not just health care services or health more

generally, as a primary social good; this is the view I begin to develop here.

9. Again, the idea here is that if the general level of productivity in a society goes down there is less for everybody, those who are less advantaged together with those who are more advantaged. The underlying assumption is that financial incentives, and hence inequalities in the distribution of wealth, are necessary for high levels of productivity in any modern, industrial society. Social programs whose costs cut too deeply into these incentives will thus have less funding available to them that they otherwise might due to a diminished GDP in the society in question. True or not, the underlying assumption of this line of thought is generally accepted among liberal egalitarians.

10. Evans.

11. One important option here is the idea of health maintenance organizations. For the preventative and health promotional potential of this sort of insurance and delivery arrangement, see Michael Rachlis and Carl Kushner, *Strong Medicine: How to Save Canada's Health Care System* (Toronto: Harper Collins, 1994), 248-252, and H.H. Schauffler and T. Rodriguez, "The Availability and Utilization of Health Promotion Programs and Satisfaction with health Plan," *Medical Care* 32, 12 (1994): 1182-1196. But for concomitant problems relating to equal access to all provided services, see H.B. Fox, L.B. Wicks, and P.W. Newacheck, "Health Maintenance Organizations and Children with Special Health Needs: A Suitable Match?" *American Journal of Diseases of Children* 147, 5 (1993): 546-552.

12. Sullivan.

13. There is a fast-growing literature on the linkages between health and social position. An early work is Michael Marmot and Tores Theorell, "Social Class and Cardiovascular Disease: The Contribution of Work," *International Journal of Health Science* 18, 4 (1988): 659-674. Recent collections are Robert G. Evans, M.L. Barer, and T.R. Marmor, eds., *Why are Some People Healthy and Others Not? The Determinants of Health of Populations* (New York: Aldine de Gruyter, 1994) together with the fall 1994 issue of *Daedalus*. Especially interesting with regard to the version

of liberal egalitarianism explored above is Richard G. Wilkinson, "National Mortality Rates: the Impact of Inequality?" *American Journal of Public Health* 82, 8 (1992): 1082-1084, and Richard G. Wilkinson, "Income Distribution and Life Expectancy," *British Medial Journal* 304, 6820 (1992): 165-168.

14. Rachlis and Kushner.

15. Health economists have, of course, developed an extensive literature devoted to the question of how we might measure the efficiency of different treatment or service options. But whether such precise, technical definitions of efficiency capture what we really ought to mean by the term remains an open question, depending, in part, on how acceptable we find the simplifying assumptions that are necessary to produce precise, technical definitions of such a multifaceted and complex idea. In the debate over health reform, efficiency is in many ways a much more slippery term than equality. For a recent challenge to economic notions of efficiency as they relate to health reform, see Erik Nord, Jeff Richardson, Andrew Street, Helga Kuhse, and Peter Singer, "Who Cares about Cost? Does Economic Analysis Impose or Reflect Social Values?" *Health Policy* 34, 2 (1995): 79-94, and Alastair V. Campbell, "Defining Core Health Services: The New Zealand Experience," *Bioethics* 9, 3/4 (1995): 252-258.

16. Evans.

17. Nathaniel C. Nash, "Europeans Brace Themselves for Higher Taxes," *Globe and Mail*, 25 February 1995, 4 (D).

EUTHANASIA: THE WAY WE DO IT, THE WAY THEY DO IT

Margaret Battin

🍃

Margaret Battin is Professor of Philosophy and Adjunct Professor of Internal Medicine, Division of Medical Ethics, University of Utah. She is the author of Ethical Issues in Suicide (1995) and Least Worst Death: Essays in Bioethics on the End of Life (1994) and co-editor with Rosemond Rhodes and Anita Silvers of Physician Assisted Suicide: Expanding the Debate (1998) and of Medicine and Social Justice: Essays on the Distribution of Health Care (2002).

   Battin discusses the morality of euthanasia by providing a critical examination of euthanasia practices in three different societies: the Netherlands, which allows active euthanasia; Germany, which allows assisted suicide but not active euthanasia; and the U.S., which allows neither active euthanasia nor assisted suicide. Based on her analysis of these practices situated in their particular contexts of beliefs, values, and social conditions, she concludes that the U.S. should allow physician-assisted suicide.

Introduction

Because we tend to be rather myopic in our discussions of death and dying, especially about the issues of active euthanasia and assisted suicide, it is valuable to place the question of how we go about dying in an international context. We do not always see that our own cultural norms may be quite different from those of other nations, and that our background assumptions, and actual practices, differ dramatically. Thus, I would like to examine the perspectives on end-of-life dilemmas in three countries, the Netherlands, Germany, and the USA.

The Netherlands, Germany, and the United States are all advanced industrial democracies. They all have sophisticated medical establishments and life expectancies over 70 years of age; their populations are all characterized by an increasing proportion of older persons. They are all in what has been called the fourth stage of the epidemiologic transition[1] — that stage of societal development in which it is no longer the case that

most people die of acute parasitic or infectious diseases. In this stage, most people do not die of diseases with rapid, unpredictable onsets and sharp fatality curves; rather, the majority of the population — as much as perhaps 70%-80% — dies of degenerative diseases, especially delayed degenerative diseases, that are characterized by late, slow onset and extended decline. Most people in highly industrialized countries die from cancer, atherosclerosis, heart disease (by no means always suddenly fatal), chronic obstructive pulmonary disease, liver, kidney or other organ disease, or degenerative neurological disorders. Thus, all three of these countries are alike in facing a common problem: how to deal with the characteristic new ways in which we die.

Dealing with Dying in the United States

In the United States, we have come to recognize that the maximal extension of life-prolonging treatment in these late-life degenerative conditions is often inappropriate. Although we could keep the machines and tubes — the respirators, intravenous lines, feeding tubes — hooked up for extended periods, we recognize that this is inhumane, pointless, and financially impossible. Instead as a society we have developed a number of mechanisms for dealing with these hopeless situations, all of which involve withholding or withdrawing various forms of treatment.

Some mechanisms for withholding or withdrawing treatment are exercised by the patient who is confronted by such a situation or who anticipates it; these include refusal of treatment, the patient-executed DNR order, the Living Will, and the Durable Power of Attorney. Others are mechanisms for decision by second parties about a patient who is no longer competent or never was competent. The latter are reflected in a long series of court cases, including *Quinlan, Saikewicz, Spring, Eichner, Barber, Barling, Conroy, Brophy,* the trio *Farrell, Peter* and *Jobes,* and *Cruzan.* These are cases that attempt to delineate the precise circumstances under which it is appropriate to withhold or withdraw various forms of therapy, including respiratory support, chemotherapy, antibiotics in intercurrent infections, and artificial nutrition and hydration. Thus, during the past 15 years or so, roughly since *Quinlan* (1976), we have developed an impressive body of case law and state statute that protects, permits, and facilitates our characteristic American strategy of dealing with end-of-life situations. These cases provide a framework for withholding or withdrawing treatment when we believe there is no medical or moral point in going on. This is sometimes termed *passive euthanasia*; more often, it is simply called *allowing to die*, and is ubiquitous in the United States.

For example, a recent study by Miles and Gomez indicates that some 85% of deaths in the United States occur in health-care institutions, including hospitals, nursing homes, and other facilities, and of these, about 70% involve electively withholding some form of life-sustaining treatment.[2] A 1989 study cited in the *Journal of the American Medical Association* claims that 85%-90% of critical care professionals state that they are withholding and withdrawing life-sus-

taining treatments from patients who are "deemed to have irreversible disease and are terminally ill."[3] Still another study identified some 115 patients in two intensive-care units from whom care was withheld or withdrawn; 110 were already incompetent by the time the decision to limit care was made. The 89 who died while still in the intensive care unit accounted for 45% of all deaths there.[4] It is estimated that 1.3 million American deaths a year follow decisions to withhold life support,[5] this is a majority of the just over 2 million American deaths per year. Withholding and withdrawing treatment is the way we in the USA go about dealing with dying, and indeed "allowing to die" is the only legally protected alternative to maximal treatment recognized in the United States. We do not legally permit ourselves to actively cause death.

Dealing with Dying in the Netherlands

In the Netherlands, voluntary active euthanasia is also an available response to end-of-life situations. Although active euthanasia remains prohibited by statutory law, it is protected by a series of lower and supreme court decisions and is widely regarded as legal, or, more precisely, *gedoeken*, legally "tolerated." These court decisions have the effect of protecting the physician who performs euthanasia from prosecution, provided the physician meets a rigorous set of guidelines.

These guidelines, variously stated, contain five central provisions:

1. that the patient's request be voluntary;
2. that the patient be undergoing intolerable suffering;
3. that all alternatives acceptable to the patient for relieving the suffering have been tried;
4. that the patient have full information;
5. that the patient consult with a second physician whose judgment can be expected to be independent.

Of these criteria, it is the first which is central: euthanasia may be performed only at the voluntary request of the patient. This criterion is also understood to require that the patient's request be a stable, enduring, reflective one — not the product of a transitory impulse. Every attempt is to be made to rule out depression, psychopathology, pressures from family members, unrealistic fears, and other factors compromising voluntariness.

Putting an end to years of inflammatory discussion in which speculation about the frequency of euthanasia had ranged from 2,000 (close to correct) to 20,000 cases a year, a comprehensive study requested by the Dutch government was published in late 1991; an English version appeared in *The Lancet*.[6] Popularly known as the Remmelink Commission report, this study provided the first objective data about the incidence of euthanasia as well as a wider range of medical practices at the end of life: the withholding or withdrawal of treatment, the use of life-shortening doses of opioids for the control of pain, and direct termination, including active euthanasia, physician-assisted suicide, and life-ending procedures not termed euthanasia. This study was supplemented by a second empirical examination, focusing particularly carefully on the characteristics of patients and the nature of their euthanasia requests.[7]

About 130,000 people die in the Netherlands every year, and of these deaths, about 30% are acute and unexpected; 70% are predictable and foreseen, usually the result of degenerative illnesses comparatively late in life. Of the total deaths in the Netherlands, the Remmelink Commission's study found, about 17.5% involved decisions to withhold or withdraw treatment although continuing treatment would probably have prolonged life; another 17.5 % involved the use of opioids to relieve pain but in dosages probably sufficient to shorten life. A total of 2.9% of all deaths involved euthanasia and related practices.

About 2,300 people, 1.8% of the total deaths in the Netherlands, died by euthanasia, understood as the termination of the life of the patient at the patient's explicit and persistent request. Another 400 people, 0.03% of the total, chose physician-assisted suicide. About 1,000 additional patients died as the result of "life-termi-nating procedures," not technically called euthanasia, in virtually all of which euthanasia had either been previously discussed with the patient or the patient had expressed in a previous phase of the disease a wish for euthanasia if his or her suffering became unbearable, or the patient was near death and clearly suffering grievously, yet verbal contact had become impossible.

Although euthanasia is thus not frequent — a small fraction of the total annual mortality — it is nevertheless a conspicuous option in terminal illness, well known to both physicians and the general public. There has been *very* widespread public discussion of the issues in euthanasia during the last several years, especially as the pros and cons of full legalization have been debated, and surveys of public opinion show that the public support for a liberal euthanasia policy has been growing: from 40% in 1966 to 81% in 1988.[8] Doctors too support this practice, and although there is a vocal opposition group, the opposition is in the clear minority. Some 54% of Dutch physicians said that they performed euthanasia or provided assistance in suicide; including 62% of *huisarts* or general practitioners, and an additional 34% said that although they had not actually done so, they could conceive of situations in which they would be prepared to do so. Thus, although many who had practiced euthanasia mentioned that they would be most reluctant to do so again and that "only in the face of unbearable suffering and with no alternatives would they be prepared to take such action,"[9] some 88% of Dutch physicians appear to accept the practice in some cases. As the Remmelink Commission commented, "... a large majority of physicians in the Netherlands see euthanasia as an accepted element of medical practice under certain circumstances."[10]

In general, pain alone is not the basis for euthanasia, since pain can, in most cases, be effectively treated. Rather, "intolerable suffering," among the criteria for euthanasia, is understood to mean suffering that is intolerable in the patient's (rather than the physician's) view, and can include a fear of or unwillingness to endure *entluisterung*, that gradual effacement and loss of personal identity that characterizes the end stages of many terminal illnesses. In a year, about 25,000 patients seek reassurance from their physicians that they will be granted euthanasia if their suffering becomes severe; there are about 9,000 explicit requests, and more than two-thirds of these are turned down, usually on the grounds that there is some other way of treating the patient's suffering, and in just 14% on the grounds of psychiatric illness.

In Holland, many hospitals now have protocols for the performance of euthanasia; these serve to ensure that the court-established guidelines have been met. However, euthanasia is often practiced in the patient's home, typically by the *huisarts* or general practitioner who is the patient's long-term family physician. Euthanasia is usually performed after aggressive hospital treatment has failed to arrest the patient's terminal illness; the patient has come home to die, and the family physician is prepared to ease this passing. Whether practiced at home or in the hospital, it is believed that euthanasia usually takes place in the presence of the family members, perhaps the visiting nurse, and often the patient's pastor or priest. Many doctors say that performing euthanasia is never easy, but that it is something they believe a doctor ought to do for his or her patient, when nothing else can help.

Thus, in Holland a patient facing the end of life has an option not openly practiced in the United States: to ask the physician to bring his or her life to an end. Although not everyone does so — indeed, about 97% of people who die in a given year do not — it is a choice widely understood as available.

Facing Death in Germany

In part because of its very painful history of Nazism, Germany appears to believe that doctors should have no role in causing death. Although societal generalizations are always risky, it is fair, I think, to say that there is vigorous and nearly universal opposition in Germany to the notion of active euthanasia. Euthanasia is viewed as always wrong, and the Germans view the Dutch as stepping out on a dangerously slippery slope.

However, it is an artifact of German law that, whereas killing on request (including voluntary euthanasia) is prohibited, assisting suicide is not a violation of the law, provided the person is *tatherrshaftsfähig*, capable of exercising control over his or her actions, and also acting out of *freiverantworliche Wille*, freely responsible choice. Responding to this situation, there has developed a private organization, the *Deutsche Gesellschaft für Humanes Sterben (DGHS)*, or German Society for Humane Dying, which provides support to its very extensive membership (over 50,000 persons) in choosing suicide as an alternative to terminal illness.

After a person has been a member of the DGHS for at least a year, and provided that he or she has not received medical or psychotherapeutic treatment for depression or other psychiatric illness during the last two years, he or she may request a copy of DGHS's booklet *Menschenwürdiges und selbstverantworliches Sterben*, or "Dignified and Responsible Death." This booklet provides a list of about ten drugs available by prescription in Germany, together with the specific dosages necessary for producing a certain, painless death. (The DGHS no longer officially recommends cyanide, though its president, Hans Henning Atrott, was recently charged with selling it.) DGHS recommends that the members approach a physician for a prescription for the drug desired, asking, for example, for a barbiturate to help with sleep, or chloroquine for protection against malaria on a trip to India. If necessary, the DGHS may also arrange for someone to obtain drugs from neighboring countries, including France, Italy, Spain, Portugal, and Greece, where they may be available without prescription. In unusual cases, the DGHS will also provide what it calls *Sterbebegleitung* or "accompaniment in dying," providing a companion to remain with the person during the often extended period that is required for the lethal drug to take full effect. However, the *Sterbebegleiter* is typically a layperson, not someone medically trained, and physicians play no role in assisting in these cases of suicide. To preclude suspicion by providing evidence of the person's intentions, the DGHS also provides a form — printed on a single sheet of distinctive pink paper — to be signed once when joining the organization, expressing the intention to determine the time of one's own death, and to be signed again at the time of the suicide and left beside the body.

Because assisting suicide is not illegal in Germany, provided the person is competent and in control of his or her own will, there is no legal risk for family members, *Sterbebegleiter*, or others in reporting information about the methods and effectiveness of suicide attempts, and the DGHS encourages its network of regional bureaus (five, in major cities throughout the country) to facilitate feedback. On this basis, it regularly updates and revises the drug information it provides. It claims some 2,000-3,000 suicides per year among its members.

To be sure, assisted suicide is not the only option open to the terminally ill patient in Germany, nor is there clear evidence concerning its frequency either within the DGHS or in non-reported cases outside it. There is increasing emphasis on help in dying that does not involve direct termination, and organizations like Ormega, offering hospice-style care and an extensive program of companionship, are attracting increasing attention. Furthermore, there has been recent scandal directed towards the founder and president of the DGHS, Hans Henning Attrott, accused in late 1991 of selling cyanide to an attorney hospitalized for mental illness; in May 1992 police raided his office, finding capsules of cyanide, barbiturates, and a large amount of cash. What the outcome of this event will be remains at this writing to be seen, though it is clear that the scandal focuses on Attrott's alleged profiteering and assisting a mentally ill person, rather than with the DGHS's regular practice of assisting competent terminally ill individuals in suicide. Furthermore, the DGHS is a conspicuous, widely know organization, and many Germans appear to be aware that assisted suicide is available even if they do not use the services of the DGHS.

Objections to the Three Models of Dying

In response to the dilemmas raised by the new circumstances of death, in which the majority of the population in each of the advanced industrial nations dies of degenerative diseases after an extended period of terminal deterioration, different countries develop different practices. The United States legally permits only withholding and withdrawal of treatment, though of course active euthanasia and assisted suicide do occur. Holland also permits voluntary active euthanasia, and although Germany rejects euthanasia, it tolerates assisted suicide. But these are serious moral objections to be made to each of these practices, objections to be considered before resolving the issue of which practice our own culture ought to adopt.

Objections to the German Practice

German law does not prohibit assisting suicide, but postwar German culture discourages physicians from taking any active role in death. This gives rise to distinctive moral problems. For one thing, it appears that there is little professional help or review provided for patients' choices about suicide; because the patient makes this choice essentially outside the medical establishment, medical professionals are not in a position to detect or treat impaired judgment on the part of the patient, especially judgment impaired by depression. Similarly, if the patient must commit suicide assisted only by persons outside the medical profession, there are risks that the patient's diagnosis and prognosis are inadequately confirmed, that the means chosen for suicide will be unreliable or inappropriately used, that the means used for suicide will fall into the hands of other persons, and that the patient will fail to recognize or be able to resist intrafamilial pressures and manipulation. The DGHS policy for providing assistance requires that the patient be terminally ill and have been a member of the DGHS for at least one year in order to make use of its services, the latter requirement is intended to provide evidence of the stability of such a choice. However, these minimal requirements are hardly sufficient to answer the charge that suicide decisions, which are made for medical reasons but must be made without medical help, may be rendered under less than ideally informed and voluntary conditions.

Objections to the Dutch Practice

The Dutch practice of physician-performed active voluntary euthanasia also raises a number of ethical issues, many of which have been discussed vigorously both in the Dutch press and in commentary on the Dutch practices from abroad. For one thing, it is sometimes said that the availability of physician-performed euthanasia creates a disincentive for providing good terminal care. I have seen no evidence that this is the case; on the contrary, Peter Admiraal, the anesthesiologist who is perhaps Holland's most vocal proponent of voluntary active euthanasia, insists that pain should rarely or never be the occasion for euthanasia, as pain (in contrast to suffering) is comparatively easily treated.[11] Instead, it is a refusal to endure the final stages of deterioration, both mental and physical, that motivates requests.

It is also sometimes said that active euthanasia violates the Hippocratic Oath. Indeed, it is true that the original Greek version of the Oath prohibits the physician from giving a deadly drug, even when asked for it; but the original version also prohibits performing surgery and taking fees for teaching medicine, neither of which prohibitions has survived into contemporary medical practice. Dutch physicians often say that they see performing euthanasia — where it is genuinely requested by the patient and nothing else can be done to relieve the patient's condition — as part of their duty to the patient, not as a violation of it.

The Dutch are also often said to be at risk of starting down the slippery slope, that is, that the practice of voluntary active euthanasia for patients who meet the criteria will erode into practicing less-than-voluntary euthanasia on patients whose problems are not irremediable, and perhaps by gradual degrees develop into terminating the lives of people who are elderly, chronically ill, handicapped, mentally retarded,

or otherwise regarded as undesirable. This risk is often expressed in vivid claims of widespread fear and wholesale slaughter, claims that are repeated in the right-to-life press in both the Netherlands, and the USA, though there is no evidence for these claims. However, the Dutch are now beginning to agonize over the problems of the incompetent patient, the mentally ill patient, the newborn with serious deficits, and other patients who cannot make voluntary choices, though these are largely understood as issues about withholding or withdrawing treatment, not about direct termination.[12]

What is not often understood is that this new and acutely painful area of reflection for the Dutch — withholding and withdrawing treatment from incompetent patients — has already led in the United States to the development of a vast, highly developed body of law: namely that series of cases just cited, beginning with *Quinlan* and culminating in *Cruzan*. Americans have been discussing these issues for a long time, and have developed a broad set of practices that are regarded as routine in withholding and withdrawing treatment. The Dutch see Americans as much further out on the slippery slope than they are, because Americans have already become accustomed to second-party choices about other people. Issues involving second-party choices are painful to the Dutch in a way they are not to us precisely because *voluntariness* is so central in the Dutch understanding of choices about dying. Concomitantly, the Dutch see the Americans' squeamishness about first-party choices — voluntary euthanasia, assisted suicide — as evidence that we are not genuinely committed to recognizing *voluntary* choice after all. For this reason, many Dutch commentators believe that the Americans are at a much greater risk of sliding down the slippery slope into involuntary killing than they are. I fear, I must add, that they are right about this.

Objections to the American Practice

There may be moral problems raised by the German and the Dutch practices, but there are also moral problems raised by the American practice of relying on withholding and withdrawal of treatment in end-of-life situations. The German, Dutch, and American practices all occur within similar conditions — in industrialized nations with highly developed medical systems, where a majority of the population dies of illnesses exhibiting characteristically extended downhill courses — but the issues raised by our own response to this situation may be even more disturbing than those of the Dutch or the Germans. We often assume that our approach is "safer" because it involves only letting someone die, not killing him or her; but it too raises very troubling questions.

The first of these is a function of the fact that withdrawing and especially withholding treatment are typically less conspicuous, less pronounced, less evident kinds of actions than direct killing, even though they can equally well lead to death. Decisions about nontreatment have an invisibility that decisions about directly causing death do not have, even though they may have the same result, and hence there is a much wider range of occasions in which such decisions can be made. One can decline to treat a patient in many different ways, at many different times — by not providing oxygen, by not instituting dialysis, by not correcting electrolyte imbalances, and so on — all of which will cause the patient's death; open medical killing also brings about death, but is a much more overt, conspicuous procedure. Consequently, letting die also invites many fewer protections. In contrast to the standard slippery slope argument which sees killing as riskier than letting die, the more realistic slippery slope argument warns that because our culture relies primarily on decisions about nontreatment, grave decisions about living or dying are not as open to scrutiny as they are under more direct life-terminating practices, and hence, are more open to abuse.

Second, and closely related, reliance on withholding and withdrawing treatment invites rationing in an extremely strong way, in part because of the comparative invisibility of these decisions. When a health care provider does not offer a specific sort of care, it is not always possible to discern the motivation; the line between believing that it would not provide benefit to the patient and that it would not provide benefit worth the investment of resources in the patient can be very thin. This is a particular problem where health care financing is highly decentralized, as in the United States, and where rationing decisions without benefit of principle are not always available for easy review.

Third, relying on withholding and withdrawal of treatment can often be cruel. It requires that the patient who is dying from one of the diseases that exhibits a characteristic extended, downhill course (as majority of patients in the Netherlands, Germany and the U.S. do) must in effect wait to die until the absence of a certain treatment will cause death. For instance, the cancer patient who foregoes chemotherapy or surgery does not simply die from this choice; he or she continues to endure the downhill course of cancer until the tumor finally destroys some crucial bodily function or organ. The patient with amyotrophic lateral sclerosis who decides in advance to decline respiratory support does not die at the time the choice is made, but continues to endure increasing paralysis until breathing is impaired and suffocation occurs. We often try to ameliorate these situations by administering pain medication or symptom control at the same time we are withholding treatment, but these are all ways of disguising the fact that we are letting the disease kill the patient rather than directly bringing about death. But the ways diseases kill people are far more cruel than the ways physicians kill patients when performing euthanasia or assisting in suicide.

The Problem: A Choice of Cultures

Thus we see three similar cultures and countries and three similar sets of circumstances, but three different basic practices in approaching death. All three of these practices generate moral problems; none of them, nor any others we might devise, is free of moral difficulty. But the question that faces us is this: which of these practices is best?

It is not possible to answer this question in a less-than-ideal world without some attention to the specific characteristics and deficiencies of the society in question. In asking which of these practices is best, we must ask which is best *for us*. That we currently employ one set of these practices rather than others does not prove that it is best for us; the question is, would practices developed in other cultures of those not yet widespread in any be better for our own culture than that which has developed here? Thus, it is necessary to consider the differences between our society and these European cultures that have real bearing on which model of approach to dying we ought to adopt.

First, notice that different cultures exhibit different degrees of closeness between physicians and patients — different patterns of contact and involvement. The German physician is sometimes said to be more distant and more authoritarian than the American physician; on the other hand, the Dutch physician is sometimes said to be closer to his or her patients than either the American or the German is. In the Netherlands, basic primary care is provided by the *huisarts*, the general practitioner or family physician, who typically lives in the neighborhood, makes house calls frequently, and maintains an office in his or her own home. The *huisarts* is usually the physician for other members of the patient's family, and will remain the family's physician throughout his or her practice. Thus, the patient for whom euthanasia becomes an issue — say, the terminal cancer patient who has been hospitalized in the past but who has returned home to die — will be cared for by the trusted family physician on a regular basis. Indeed, for a patient in severe distress, the physician, supported by the visiting nurse, may make house calls as often as once a day, twice a day, or more (after all, it is right in the neighborhood), and is in continuous contact with the family. In contrast the traditional American institution of the family doctor who makes house calls is rapidly becoming a thing of the past, and although some patients who die at home have access to hospice services and housecalls from their long-term physician, many have no such long-term care and receive most of it from staff at a clinic or housestaff rotating

through the services of a hospital. The degree of continuing contact the patient can have with a familiar, trusted physician clearly influences the nature of his or her dying, and also plays a role in whether physician-performed active euthanasia, assisted suicide, and/or withholding and withdrawing treatment is appropriate.

Second, the United States has a much more volatile legal climate than either the Netherlands or Germany; our medical system is increasingly litigious, much more so than that of any other country in the world. Fears of malpractice action or criminal prosecution color much of what physicians do in managing the dying of their patients. We also tend to evolve public policy through court decisions, and to assume that the existence of a policy puts an end to any moral issue. A delicate legal and moral balance over the issue of euthanasia, as is the case in the Netherlands, would not be possible here.

Third, we in the United States have a very different financial climate in which to do our dying. Both the Netherlands and Germany, as well as every other industrialized nation except South Africa, have systems of national health insurance or national health care. Thus the patient is not directly responsible for the costs of treatment, and consequently the patient's choices about terminal care and/or euthanasia need not take personal financial considerations into account. Even for the patient who does have health insurance in the United States, many kinds of services are not covered, whereas the national health care or health insurance programs of many other countries variously provide many sorts of relevant services, including at-home physician care, home nursing care, home respite care, care in a nursing-home or other long-term facility, dietitian care, rehabilitation care, physical therapy, psychological counseling, and so on. The patient in the United States needs to attend to the financial aspects of dying in a way patients in many other countries do not, and in this country both the patient's choices and the recommendations of the physician are very often shaped by financial consideration.

There are many other differences between the USA on the one hand and the Netherlands and

Germany, with their different models of dying, on the other. There are differences in degrees of paternalism in the medical establishment and in racism, sexism, and ageism in the general cultures, as well as awareness of a problematic historical past, especially Nazism. All of these and the previous factors influence the appropriateness or inappropriateness of practices such as active euthanasia and assisted suicide. For instance, the Netherlands' tradition of close physician/patient contact, its absence of malpractice-motivated medicine, and its provision of comprehensive health insurance, together with its comparative lack of racism and ageism and its experience in resistance to Nazism, suggest that this culture is able to permit the practice of voluntary active euthanasia, performed by physicians, without risking abuse. On the other hand, it is sometimes said that Germany still does not trust its physicians, remembering the example of Nazi experimentation, and given a comparatively authoritarian medical climate in which contact between physician and patient is quite distanced, the population could not be comfortable with the practice of active euthanasia. There, only a wholly patient-controlled response to terminal situations, as in non-physician-assisted suicide, is a reasonable and prudent practice.

But what about the United States? This is a country where (1) sustained contact with the personal physician is decreasing, (2) the risk of malpractice action is increasing, (3) much medical care is not insured, (4) many medical decisions are financial decisions as well, (5) racism is on the rise, and (6) the public is naive about direct contact with Nazism or similar totalitarian movements. Thus, the United States is in many respects an untrustworthy candidate for practicing active euthanasia. Given the pressures on individuals in an often atomized society, encouraging solo suicide, assisted if at all only by nonprofessionals, might well be open to considerable abuse too.

However, there are several additional differences between the United States and both Holland and Germany that seem relevant here.

So far, the differences cited between the U.S. and both the Netherlands and Germany are nega-

tive ones, ones in which the U.S. falls far short. But there are positive differences as well, differences in which distinctive aspects of American culture are more favorable than those of Holland or Germany to the practice of euthanasia and assisted suicide. For example:

First although the U.S. is indeed afflicted by a great deal of racism and sexism, it is also developing an increasingly strong tradition of independence in women. In many other countries, especially the Far East and the Islamic countries, the role of women still involves much greater disempowerment and expectations of subservience; in contrast, the U.S. is particularly advanced — though, of course, it has a long way to go. The U.S. may even be ahead of the Netherlands and perhaps Germany in this respect. Whatever the case, this issue is of particular importance with respect to euthanasia, especially among elderly persons, because it is women whose life expectancies are longer than those of men and hence are more likely to be confronted with late-life degenerative terminal conditions.

Second, American culture is more confrontational than many others, including Dutch culture. While the Netherlands prides itself rightly on a long tradition of rational discussion of public issues and on toleration of others' views and practices, the U.S. (and to some degree, also Germany) tends to develop highly partisan, moralizing oppositional groups. In general, this is a disadvantage; but in the case of euthanasia it may serve to alert a public to issues and possibilities it might not otherwise consider, and especially to the risks of abuse.

Third, though this may at first seem to be a trivial difference, it is Americans who are particularly given to personal self-analysis. This tendency is evident not only in America's high rate of utilization of counseling services, including religious counseling, psychological counseling, and psychiatry, but is even more clearly evident in its popular culture: its diet of soap operas, situation comedies, and pop psychology books. It is here that the ordinary American absorbs models for analyzing his or her own personal relationships and individual psychological characteristics.

While of course things are changing and our cultural tastes are widely exported, the fact remains that the ordinary American's cultural diet contains more in the way of both professional and do-it-yourself amateur psychology and self-analysis than anyone else's. This long tradition of self-analysis may put us in a better position for certain kinds of end-of-life practices than many other cultures — despite whatever other deficiencies we have, just because we live in a culture that encourages us to inspect our own motives, anticipate the impact of our actions on others and scrutinize our own relationships with others, including our physicians. This disposition is of importance in euthanasia contexts because euthanasia is the kind of fundamental choice about which one may have somewhat mixed motives, be subject to various interpersonal and situational pressures, and so on. If the voluntary character of these choices is to be protected, it may be a good thing to inhabit a culture in which self-inspection of one's own mental habits and motives is encouraged.

Finally, the U.S. is also characterized by a kind of "do-it-yourself" ethic, an ethic that does not rely on others to direct you or provide for you, but encourages individual initiative and responsibility. (To be sure this feature has been somewhat eclipsed in recent years, and is little in evidence in the series of court cases cited earlier, but it is still part, I think, of the American character.) This is coupled with a sort of resistance to authority that is sometimes also said to be basic to the American temperament. If these things are the case, it would seem to suggest that Americans would seek a style of end-of-life practices which would emphasize these characteristics rather than others.

These, of course, are all mere conjectures about features of American culture which would have a positive effect on the practice of euthanasia, or assisted suicide. These are the features that one would want to reinforce, should these practices become general, in part to minimize the effects of the negative features. But, of course, these positive features will differ from one country and culture to another, just as negative features do. In each country, a different architecture of antecedent assumptions and cultural features develops around the issues of the end of life, and in each country the practice of euthanasia, if it is to be free from abuse at all, must be adapted to the culture in which it takes place.

What, then, is appropriate for our own cultural situation? Physician-performed euthanasia, though not in itself morally wrong, is morally jeopardized where the legal, time, and especially financial pressures on both patients and physicians are severe; thus it is morally problematic in our culture in a way that it is not in the Netherlands. Solo suicide outside the institution of medicine (as in Germany) may be problematic in a culture (like the United States) that is increasingly alienated, offers deteriorating and uneven social services, is increasingly racist, and in other ways imposes unusual pressures on individuals despite opportunities for self-analysis. Reliance only on withholding and withdrawing treatment (as in the United States) can be, as we've seen, cruel, and its comparative invisibility invites erosion under cost containment and other pressures. These are the three principal alternatives we've considered; but none of them seems wholly suited to our actual situation for dealing with the new fact that most of us die of extended-decline, deteriorative diseases. However, permitting physicians to supply patients with the means for ending their own lives grants physicians some control over the circumstances in which this can happen — only, for example, when the prognosis is genuinely grim and the alternatives for symptom control are poor — but leaves the fundamental decision about whether to use these means to the patient alone. It is up to the patient then — the independent, confrontational self-analyzing, do-it-yourself, authority-resisting patient — and his or her advisors, including family, clergy, physician, other health-care providers, and a raft of pop-psychology books, to be clear about whether he or she really wants to use these means or not. Thus, the physician is involved, but not directly; and it is the patient's choice, but the patient is not alone in making it. We live in a quite imperfect world, but, of the alternatives for facing death — which we all eventually must — I think the practice of permitting physician-assisted suicide is the one most nearly suited to the current state of our own somewhat flawed society. This is a model not yet central in any of the three countries examined here — the Netherlands, Germany, or the United States — but it is the one I think suits us best.

NOTES

1. Olshansky S.J., Ault A.B. "The fourth stage of the epidemiological transition: the age of delayed degenerative diseases." *Milbank Memorial Fund Quarterly/Health and Society* 1986; 64:355-391.
2. Miles S., Gomez C. *Protocols for elective use of life-sustaining treatment.* New York: Springer-Verlag, 1988.
3. Sprung C.L. "Changing attitudes and practices in foregoing life-sustaining treatments." *JAMA* 1990; 263: 2213.
4. Smedira N.G. *et al.* "Withholding and withdrawal of life support from the critically ill." *N.Engl J Med* 1990; 322: 309-315.
5. *New York Times*, July 23, 1990, p. A13.
6. Paul J. Van der Maas, Johannes J.M. vanDelden, Loes Pijnenborg, and Casper W.N. Looman, "Euthanasia and Other Medical Decisions Concerning the End of Life," *The Lancet* 338 (Sept. 14 1991): 669-674.
7. G. Van der Wal, J.The. M. Van Eijk, H.J.J. Leenen and C. Spreeuwenberg, "Euthanasie en hulp bij selfdoding door artsen in de thuissituatie. I. Diagnosen, leeftijd en geslacht van de patienten." *Nederlands Tijdschrift voor Geneesekunde* 135 (1991): 1593-1598: and II. "Lijden van de patienten," 1500-1603.
8. Else Borst-Eilers, paper delivered at the conference "Controversies in the Care of Dying Patients," University of Florida, Orlando, Feb. 14-16, 1991.
9. Van der Maas, p. 673.
10. Van der Maas, p. 671.
11. Admiraal P. *Euthanasia in a general hospital.* Address to the Eighth World Congress of the International Federation of Right-To-Die Societies, Maastricht. Holland. June 8, 1990.
12. Ten Have, H. "Coma: controversy and consensus." *Newsletter of the European Society for Philosophy of Medicine and Health Care* (May 1990) 8: 19-20.

THE INSTABILITY OF THE STANDARD JUSTIFICATION FOR PHYSICIAN-ASSISTED SUICIDE

Thomas A. Cavanaugh

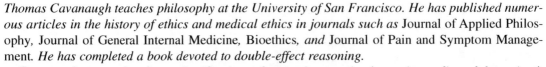

Thomas Cavanaugh teaches philosophy at the University of San Francisco. He has published numerous articles in the history of ethics and medical ethics in journals such as Journal of Applied Philosophy, Journal of General Internal Medicine, Bioethics, *and* Journal of Pain and Symptom Management. *He has completed a book devoted to double-effect reasoning.*

Cavanaugh argues that the two justifications of respecting a patient's wanting to die and the patient's having a medically established good reason for suicide are in tension with one another. A patient must not only have a good reason and want to kill him or herself, but he or she must want to die for the good reason. Because those who defend the standard justification do not accept autonomy as sufficient, they have a difficult time supporting those cases in which someone has a medically established good reason but does not want to die. Cavanaugh argues that given the independent character of the two-part justification, there is no sound basis for the legalization of physician-assisted suicide.

Proponents commonly justify the legalization of physician-assisted suicide (PAS) in terms of a patient's wanting to die (autonomy) and the patient's having a medically established good reason for suicide.[1234] These are the common elements of the standard justification offered for the legalization of PAS. In what follows, I argue that these two conditions exist in significant tension with one another, operating according to distinct dynamics that render the justification for PAS an unstable "let it be so" basis for public policy. Moreover, no natural connection keeps these two criteria united. Indeed — as I argue — the two elements of the justification oppose and threaten to exclude one another. Thus, the PAS justification is too labile a basis for sound public policy.

The PAS Justification: The Simple Version

Those who justify PAS distinguish between good and bad reasons for PAS. The proposed good reasons are either an imminently terminal illness or an incurable progressively debilitating disease, such as multiple sclerosis.[5] Other reasons, for example, clinically treatable depression[6] or pain resulting from inadequate palliative measures[7] are regarded as unacceptable. The proposed good reasons are medical and objective. Thus, a physician could establish that the patient actually does have a good reason. The good reason, however, is not proposed as the only condition that must be met. In accordance with the principle of autonomy, a patient must also really — clearheadedly, consistently, and persistently — want to kill himself.[8] If a patient wants to kill himself and he has a good reason to kill himself, then, according to the standard justification, his physician legally ought to be able to assist him by providing him with a lethal drug.

The Complex Version: The Motive Requirement

The standard justification is, however, slightly more complicated. For, according to the standard justification, it is not sufficient that the patient have a good reason to kill himself and that he want to kill himself, he must also want to kill himself *for the good reason*. Thus, his autonomy is subordinated to the good reason. This may be called the "motive requirement." The standard justification clearly incorporates the motive requirement. The standard justification has safeguards to prevent patients from killing themselves for bad reasons.[9]

For example, the following passage from the Oregon Act illustrates the presence of the motive requirement:

If in the opinion of the attending physician or the consulting physician a patient may be suffering from a psychiatric or psychological disorder, or depression causing impaired judgment, either physician shall refer the patient for counseling. No medication to end a patient's life in a humane and dignified manner shall be prescribed until the person performing the counseling determines that the person is not suffering from a psychiatric or psychological disorder, or depression.[10]

Clearly, the Oregon Act rules out depression as an acceptable basis for PAS. Again, in the Oregon Act, witnesses attest that:

[T]he person signing this request [the patient requesting PAS]: appears to be of sound mind and not under duress, fraud, or undue influence.[11]

The Oregon Act would not justify a patient's pursuing PAS if her reason for doing so was to mollify a husband or child tired of caring for her, or because she understood herself to be a burden to her loved ones.

The BANEC guidelines also incorporate the motive requirement:

The primary physician has ascertained the following.... 2.... the patient is mentally competent and not suffering from a depression that impairs decision-making capability .... 4. To the best of

the physician's knowledge, the patient's choice to hasten death has been freely made, independent of finances, family, health care workers, health insurance, or other coercion.[12]

Another proposed justification mandates that:

[T]he physician must ensure that the patient's suffering and the request are not the result of inadequate comfort care.... The presence of depression is relevant if it is distorting rational decision making and is reversible in a way that would substantially alter the situation. Expert psychiatric evaluation should be sought when the primary physician is inexperienced in the diagnosis and treatment of depression, or when there is uncertainty about the rationality of the request or the presence of a reversible mental disorder the treatment of which would substantially change the patient's perception of his or her condition.[13]

With varying degrees of precision and detail, the proposed justifications for PAS each incorporate the motive requirement by ruling out certain motives as unacceptable, leaving an imminently terminal illness or an intractable chronically debilitating disease as the sole acceptable motives for PAS.

What difference does the motive requirement make? Examples illustrate its import. If some patient had terminal cancer and wanted to die for some other, unacceptable reason — for example, because he was clinically depressed, or because his family wanted him to die — then the standard justification justifies neither his suicide nor others' assistance. For, although he wants to kill himself and he has a good reason to kill himself, he does not want to kill himself *for the right reason*. Of course, advocates of PAS could tutor him to want to kill himself for the right reason. Nonetheless, that they would have so to instruct him indicates that they could not justify assisting him, at least not according to the standard justification.

Thus, the justifications propose that PAS is justified if and only if the patient wants to die for a medically substantiated good reason.

The Problem of Asymmetry

In what follows, I reflect on the elements of the standard justification in order to determine what unites them. To do this, I contrast the standard justification with the justification offered by soft-paternalists, who maintain that a patient's really wanting to die is a sufficient reason for him to kill himself and a sufficient reason for a physician to assist him. Thus, the soft-paternalist proposes autonomy as sufficient to justify PAS.[14]

Those employing the standard justification do not accept autonomy as sufficient to justify PAS. Yet, by rejecting the soft-paternalist's account, those who rely on the standard justification have difficulty justifying their position concerning those who have medically established good reasons for killing themselves but who do not want to kill themselves. By examining such cases, it becomes clear that the two elements of the standard justification do not have any intrinsic link uniting them.

Consider the justification the soft-paternalist would offer for a patient who does not pursue PAS because he does not want to die. The soft-paternalist's position would be that the patient's really not wanting to die itself justifies him in not killing himself and justifies others in not convincing him to kill himself. This position is exactly symmetrical with the soft-paternalist's justification for PAS: autonomy is itself a justification for pursuing what the patient really wants, regardless of his reasons for wanting it. Indeed, the exactness of the symmetry between the soft-paternalist's justification for a patient's killing or not killing himself — and for a physician's assisting or not assisting — indicates a strength of the soft-paternalist's position. Moreover, the soft-paternalist's response concerning why we ought not to assist or convince a patient to kill himself who does not want to kill himself — "he really does not want to kill himself" — would be enough for most to justify not assisting or convincing him to kill himself. (Of course, this is not to argue for PAS justified in terms of soft-paternalism; it is only to note that soft-paternalism does not suffer, as the standard justification does, from the problem of asymmetry.)

Those who propose the standard justification hold, along with the soft-paternalist, that a patient's not wanting to kill himself justifies both his not killing himself and others' not assisting him. This response, however, indicates a problematic asymmetry in the standard justification. The standard justification requires a medically established reason for killing oneself and for assisting another to kill himself; it thereby subordinates the patient's self-determination to a medically established good reason. Other reasons, for example, being lonely or depressed, are not acceptable. Yet, if the patient who wants to kill himself is not to kill himself nor to be assisted either because he lacks a good reason, or because, although he has a good reason, he wants to kill himself for an unacceptable reason, then what about those who have medically established good reasons for killing themselves but who do not want to kill themselves? According to the standard justification, if a patient has a good reason to die but does not want to die, he is not to be assisted nor instructed that he ought to kill himself. Why is his autonomy not subordinated to his good reason for killing himself? How does the standard justification justify his not killing himself and others' not instructing him of the good reason he has for killing himself?

Of course, most will agree that such a patient ought not to kill himself if he does not want to and that others ought not to assist him or to instruct him to kill himself. Nonetheless, in terms of the standard justification, what grounds one's response to such a case? For, if the autonomy of a patient who wants to kill himself but lacks a good reason is not sufficient to justify his suicide or a physician's assistance, why is it sufficient to justify not assisting or instructing those who have good reasons to kill themselves but who do not want to kill themselves? Moreover, if the autonomy of a patient who wants to die and who has a good reason to die must be subordinated to his good reason such that he must want to kill himself for the good reason that he has — and not for an unacceptable reason — then why is autonomy not subordinated to a good reason when a patient has a good reason? What accounts for this asymmetry in the standard justification?

Responses to the Asymmetry Problem

In response to the asymmetry objection, the advocate of the standard justification could argue that such patients must have good countervailing reasons for wanting to live that outweigh the good reasons they have for wanting to die. Yet, if one concedes — as advocates of the standard justification do — that some people who want to kill themselves do not have good reasons, then why think that there are not also people who do not want to kill themselves but who do not have good reasons for not killing themselves? It is reasonable to think that there must be patients who, according to the standard justification, have overall good reasons for killing themselves but who do not want to kill themselves. What about these patients?

The proponent of the standard justification could argue that more is required for a patient to justify killing himself than is required for a patient to justify not killing himself. This is the argument that one ought to err, as it were, on the side of life, rather than on the side of death. It is better, or so this argument proposes, to have more unjustified lives than unjustified deaths. This line of argument, however, inclines away from legalizing PAS. Following this line of reasoning, one would erect legal barriers against homicide, such as current laws outlawing suicide-assistance, the very laws that advocates of PAS wish to change.

The advocate of the standard justification could refer to what is generally agreed to: it is wrong to kill another against his will. Yet, homicidal self-defense, surely the most widely accepted and least controversial case of legally and ethically justified homicide, almost always involves killing an assailant against his will. Moreover, even if an assailant did want to be killed, that fact would not be relied on in a legal or moral justification for killing him. Homicide in self-defense is justified without reliance on — indeed, usually in opposition to — the autonomy of the one killed. Such homicides are justified entirely in terms of the killer having a good reason for killing: in order to preserve harmless human life. Thus, the advocates of the standard justification must explain how they can assert both that a person has what they consider a good reason for killing himself (e.g., an imminently terminal illness) and that it would be wrong to assist him or to instruct him to commit suicide because he does not want to. For, as seen in the justification of homicidal self-defense, a justification that incorporates good reasons inclines away — even entirely away — from regard for what the one killed wants, relying on the good reasons as sufficient to justify killing.

In response to the charge of asymmetry, the advocate of the standard justification could simply stipulate that in order for a patient to kill himself — and for a physician to assist him — it is necessary, but not sufficient, that he want to kill himself. Thus, a patient's not wanting to kill himself would suffice to justify his not killing himself and others' not assisting or instructing him, just as his not having a good reason for suicide, or his having a good reason but wanting to kill himself for a bad reason, suffices for rejecting his request for assistance. The proponent of the standard justification could maintain that such a stipulation is enough given that we are considering public policy; that is, something that often is nothing but a "let it be so." For example, we drive on one side of the road rather than another by mere fiat. The decision is entirely arbitrary. Nonetheless, it works. Traffic laws are broken, but they are not broken because they are arbitrary. The same holds true for many other matters of public policy that repose ultimately on a publicly agreed upon "let it be so." Why would the case of PAS differ? Why can it not rest ultimately on public fiat or merely on the fact that sometimes we do not accept autonomy as a sufficient reason for honoring a patient's request and sometimes we do?

Perhaps the laws and public policy regarding PAS could repose on a practice that holds that autonomy and a medically established good reason are not sufficient to justify PAS independently of one another. Yet, there are good reasons for thinking that the dynamics of these criteria will separate them in practice. That is, as I argue in what follows, given the independent character of these two elements taken separately, neither fiat nor custom offer a sound basis for the legalization of PAS.

The Directions of Pull of Autonomy and Good Reasons

Autonomy and a medically established good reason pull in different directions. The soft-paternalist illustrates the dynamic of autonomy: as long as the patient really wants to kill herself and does not harm others by killing herself, then her suicide and others' assistance of her suicide are justified, regardless of her objective medical reasons or lack of reasons altogether. The pull of autonomy would have suicide and suicide-assistance grounded entirely in the will unfettered by reason, to be furthered as long as no one else is harmed.

In opposition to the pull of autonomy, the dynamic of a good reason — illustrated in the justification of homicidal self-defense — is indifferent to what the one killed wants, focusing entirely on the good reason for homicide. This latter justification attends to what is objective and serves as a good reason for anyone, regardless of what they want. A good reason for me to kill an assailant will be a good reason for you or anyone to kill that or any other relevantly similar assailant. Although it is fanciful, the good reason for killing the assailant will be a good reason for the assailant to kill himself. For example, if a Dr. Jekyll/Mr. Hyde personality were to exist and as Dr. Jekyll knew that he would become a homicidal Mr. Hyde, then, following the logic of a good reason, Dr. Jekyll ought to kill himself in order to prevent himself as Mr. Hyde from killing harmless human life. Because of their objective character, good reasons subordinate an individual's wants and desires to themselves. Moreover, there is nothing in the logic of a good-reason-based justification that prohibits taking life without the consent of the one whose life is taken.

That the most widely accepted legal and moral justification for homicide — self-defense — has no regard for the wishes of the one killed ought to make society hesitant to establish medical conditions as good reasons for killing oneself and as good reasons for assisting another's suicide. For, following the dynamic of a good-reason-based justification, the medical good reason offered by the advocates of PAS is inclined toward functioning independently of a patient's autonomy as a sufficient justification for suicide and suicide-assistance.

In the arena of PAS, specifically how would the dynamic of a good reason operate independently of and in opposition to autonomy? Take, for example, the distinction, offered by those who rely on the standard justification, between a good and a bad reason. As noted, this distinction partially undermines the autonomy of a patient who may want to kill himself for a reason that is not accepted as good. Moreover, by maintaining that a patient must have a good reason for killing himself in order to be assisted, by assisting some to kill themselves, physicians publicly state that certain patients have good reasons for killing themselves. Physicians thereby imply that patients relevantly similar to those other patients also have good reasons for killing themselves. Thus, the autonomy of patients who are similar but for their not wanting to kill themselves to those who have been assisted is jeopardized. In fact, the better the reason that those who were assisted had for killing themselves — and, thereby, the better the reason physicians had for assisting them — the more unreasonable relevantly similar individuals who do not want to kill themselves would be if they persist in not wanting to kill themselves. Thus, the objective character of a good-reason-based justification threatens autonomy by either rejecting the reasons that a patient has for killing himself or by implying that, although they do not want to kill themselves, some patients have good reasons for killing themselves and, to that extent, *ought* to kill themselves.

In conclusion, I have presented the opposed dynamics of the two elements of the standard justification. I have sought the nexus between these two elements that unites them to form a functioning unit with its own dynamic. I find no link other than the assertion that they are to be kept together. Given the lack of a significant internal connection and the intrinsic energies of these two elements as they operate independently of and in opposition to one another, I find the standard justification highly labile and an unsound basis for sound public policy.

NOTES

1. The Oregon Death with Dignity Act, or Measure 16.
2. Heilig S, Brody R, Marcus F, Shavelson L, Sussman P. Physician-hastened death: Advisory guidelines for the San Francisco Bay area from the Bay Area Network of Ethics Committees. *Western Journal of Medicine* 1997;166: 370-8.
3. Baron C, Bergstresser C, Brock D, et al. A model state act to authorize and regulate physician-assisted suicide. *Harvard Journal on Legislation* 1996;33: 1-34.
4. Quill T, Cassel C, Meier D. Care of the hopelessly ill: potential clinical criteria for physician-assisted suicide. *New England Journal of Medicine* 1992;327: 1380-4.
5. In the Oregon Death with Dignity Act (note 1) and the Bay Area Network's advisory guidelines (note 2), the patient must have a terminal illness with a prognosis of death within six months. In the model state act proposed by Baron et al. (note 3) and the clinical criteria proposed by Quill et al. (note 4), the patient may have either a terminal illness or an incurable progressively debilitating disease such as multiple sclerosis.
6. That clinical depression is excluded as a bad reason for resorting to PAS can be seen from, for example, the Oregon Death with Dignity Act, (note 1): "If in the opinion of the attending physician or the consulting physician a patient may be suffering from a psychiatric or psychological disorder, or depression causing impaired judgment, either physician shall refer the patient for counseling. No medication to end a patient's life in a humane and dignified manner shall be prescribed until the person performing the counseling determines that the person is not suffering from a psychiatric or psychological disorder, or depression causing impaired judgment" (from section 3.03 on Counseling Referral). A similar exclusion can be found in Baron et al. (note 3), Section 3.(a)(3): "The patient has made a request of the responsible physician to provide medical means of suicide, which request (A) is not the result of a distortion of the patient's judgment due to clinical depression or any other mental illness."
7. See, for example, note 4, Quill et al 1992: 1382: "[T]he physician must ensure that the patient's suffering and the request are not the result of inadequate comfort care."
8. See, for example, note 4, Quill et al. 1992: 1382; note 3, Baron et al. 1996: section 3.(a)(3)(D); and note 1, the Oregon Act, section 3.06.
9. The justifications also have safeguards to prevent others from assisting the patient for bad reasons, but I will not attend to this aspect of the standard justification.
10. See note 1, Oregon Act, section 3.03.
11. See note 1, Oregon Act, section 6.01.
12. See note 2, Heilig et al., 1997: 372, V. A. 1-4.
13. See note 4, Quill et al., 1992: 1382.
14. Feinberg, J. *Harm to Self.* London/New York: Oxford University Press, 1986:351-62. Soft-paternalism is the position that one may temporarily prevent another from harming himself in order to determine that he knows what he is doing and desires to do it. Once one has made this determination, then one allows him to pursue his goal unimpeded.

UNSPEAKABLE CONVERSATIONS

Harriet McBryde Johnson

🍃

Harriet McBryde Johnson practices law in Charleston, South Carolina, specializing in Social Security Disability, the Americans with Disabilities Act, *and other disability issues. She has been involved locally and nationally with the disability rights movement for about 25 years and is the author of a number of articles on law and disability. She also writes short stories and is currently working on a short novel tentatively titled* Accidents of Nature.

Johnson records her ambivalence about accepting Peter Singer's invitation to two speaking engagements by juxtaposing conversations she had with people from the disability rights movement, who objected to her having anything to do with Singer, with those she had with him. Singer, she claims, would argue that the disabled person that she is should have been killed at birth. Interwoven in Johnson's descriptions of her interactions with Singer, speaking to his classes, and answering questions from him and his students are descriptions of the details of her daily routine that complicate assumptions about who she is and what it means for her to travel, eat, sleep, and get around. Johnson finds herself realizing that Singer's arguments, while too theoretical and ideal, are not as simple as she and disability theorists believe and that taking him to be a monster is not a solution in a world that thinks it would be better if she and others like her did not exist.

He insists he doesn't want to kill me. He simply thinks it would have been better, all things considered, to have given my parents the option of killing the baby I once was, and to let other parents kill similar babies as they come along and thereby avoid the suffering that comes with lives like mine and satisfy the reasonable preferences of parents for a different kind of child. It has nothing to do with me. I should not feel threatened.

Whenever I try to wrap my head around his tight string of syllogisms, my brain gets so fried it's ... almost fun. Mercy! It's like "Alice in Wonderland."

It is a chilly Monday in late March, just less than a year ago. I am at Princeton University. My host is Prof. Peter Singer, often called — and not just by his book publicist — the most influential philosopher of our time. He is the man who wants me dead. No, that's not at all fair. He wants to legalize the killing of certain babies who might come to be like me if allowed to live. He also says he believes that it should be lawful under some circumstances to kill, at any age, individuals with cognitive impairments so severe that he doesn't consider them "persons." What does it take to be a person? Awareness of your own existence in time. The capacity to harbor preferences as to the future, including the preference for continuing to live.

At this stage of my life, he says, I am a person. However, as an infant, I wasn't. I, like all humans, was born without self-awareness. And eventually, assuming my brain finally gets so fried that I fall into that wonderland where self and other and present and past and future blur into one boundless, formless all or nothing, then I'll lose my personhood and therefore my right to life. Then, he says, my family and doctors might put me out of my misery, or out of my bliss or oblivion, and no one count it murder.

I have agreed to two speaking engagements. In the morning, I talk to 150 undergraduates on selective infanticide. In the evening, it is a convivial discussion, over dinner, of assisted suicide. I am the token cripple with an opposing view.

I had several reasons for accepting Singer's invitation, some grounded in my involvement in the disability rights movement, others entirely personal. For the movement, it seemed an unusual opportunity to experiment with modes of discourse that might work with very tough audiences and bridge the divide between our perceptions and theirs. I didn't expect to straighten out Singer's head, but maybe I could reach a student or two. Among the personal reasons: I was sure it would make a great story, first for telling and then for writing down.

By now I've told it to family and friends and colleagues, over lunches and dinners, on long car trips, in scads of e-mail messages and a couple of formal speeches. But it seems to be a story that just won't settle down. After all these tellings, it still lacks a coherent structure; I'm miles away from a rational argument. I keep getting interrupted by questions — like these:

Q: Was he totally grossed out by your physical appearance?

A: He gave no sign of it. None whatsoever.

Q: How did he handle having to interact with someone like you?

A: He behaved in every way appropriately, treated me as a respected professional acquaintance and was a gracious and accommodating host.

Q: Was it emotionally difficult for you to take part in a public discussion of whether your life should have happened?

A: It was very difficult. And horribly easy.

Q: Did he get that job at Princeton because they like his ideas on killing disabled babies?

A: It apparently didn't hurt, but he's most famous for animal rights. He's the author of "Animal Liberation."

Q: How can he put so much value on animal life and so little value on human life?

That last question is the only one I avoid. I used to say I don't know; it doesn't make sense. But now I've read some of Singer's writing, and I admit it does make sense — within the conceptual world of Peter Singer. But I don't want to go there. Or at least not for long.

So I will start from those other questions and see where the story goes this time.

That first question, about my physical appearance, needs some explaining.

It's not that I'm ugly. It's more that most people don't know how to look at me. The sight of me is routinely discombobulating. The power wheelchair is enough to inspire gawking, but that's the least of it. Much more impressive is the impact on my body of more than four decades of a muscle-wasting disease. At this stage of my life, I'm Karen Carpenter thin, flesh mostly vanished, a jumble of bones in a floppy bag of skin. When, in childhood, my muscles got too weak to hold up my spine, I tried a brace for a while, but fortunately a skittish anesthesiologist said no to fusion, plates and pins — all the apparatus that might have kept me straight. At 15, I threw away the back brace and let my spine reshape itself into a deep twisty S-curve. Now my right side is two deep canyons. To keep myself upright, I lean forward, rest my rib cage on my lap, plant my elbows beside my knees. Since my backbone found its own natural shape, I've been entirely comfortable in my skin.

I am in the first generation to survive to such decrepitude. Because antibiotics were available, we didn't die from the childhood pneumonias that often come with weakened respiratory systems. I guess it is natural enough that most people don't know what to make of us.

Two or three times in my life — I recall particularly one largely crip, largely lesbian cookout halfway across the continent — I have been looked at as a rare kind of beauty. There is also the bizarre fact that where I live, Charleston, S.C., some people call me Good Luck Lady: they consider it propitious to cross my path when a hurricane is coming and to kiss my head just before voting day. But most often the reactions are decidedly negative. Strangers on the street are moved to comment:

> I admire you for being out; most people would give up.
> God bless you! I'll pray for you.
> You don't let the pain hold you back, do you?
> If I had to live like you, I think I'd kill myself.

I used to try to explain that in fact I enjoy my life, that it's a great sensual pleasure to zoom by power chair on these delicious muggy streets, that I have no more reason to kill myself than most people. But it gets tedious. God didn't put me on this street to provide disability awareness training to the likes of them. In fact, no god put anyone anywhere for any reason, if you want to know.

But they don't want to know. They think they know everything there is to know, just by looking at me. That's how stereotypes work. They don't know that they're confused, that they're really expressing the discombobulation that comes in my wake.

So. What stands out when I recall first meeting Peter Singer in the spring of 2001 is his apparent immunity to my looks, his apparent lack of discombobulation, his immediate ability to deal with me as a person with a particular point of view.

Then, 2001. Singer has been invited to the College of Charleston, not two blocks from my house. He is to lecture on "Rethinking Life and Death." I have been dispatched by Not Dead Yet, the national organization leading the disability-rights opposition to legalized assisted suicide and disability-based killing. I am to put out a leaflet and do something during the Q. and A.

On arriving almost an hour early to reconnoiter, I find the scene almost entirely peaceful; even the boisterous display of South Carolina spring is muted by gray wisps of Spanish moss and mottled oak bark.

I roll around the corner of the building and am confronted with the unnerving sight of two people I know sitting on a park bench eating veggie pitas with Singer. Sharon is a veteran activist for human rights. Herb is South Carolina's most famous atheist. Good people, I've always thought — now sharing veggie pitas and conversation with a proponent of genocide. I try to beat a retreat, but Herb and Sharon have seen me. Sharon tosses her trash and comes over. After we exchange the usual courtesies, she asks, "Would you like to meet Professor Singer?"

She doesn't have a clue. She probably likes his book on animal rights. "I'll just talk to him in the Q. and A."

But Herb, with Singer at his side, is fast approaching. They are looking at me, and Herb is talking, no doubt saying nice things about me. He'll be saying that I'm a disability rights lawyer and that I gave a talk against assisted suicide at his secular humanist group a while back. He didn't agree with everything I said, he'll say, but I was brilliant. Singer appears interested, engaged. I sit where I'm parked. Herb makes an introduction. Singer extends his hand.

I hesitate. I shouldn't shake hands with the Evil One. But he is Herb's guest, and I simply can't snub Herb's guest at the college where Herb teaches. Hereabouts, the rule is that if you're not prepared to shoot on sight, you have to be prepared to shake hands. I give Singer the three fingers on my right hand that still work. "Good afternoon, Mr. Singer. I'm here for Not Dead Yet." I want to think he flinches just a little. Not Dead Yet did everything possible to disrupt his first week at Princeton. I sent a check to the fund for the 14 arrestees, who included comrades in power chairs. But if Singer flinches, he instantly recovers. He answers my questions about the lecture format. When he says he looks forward to an interesting exchange, he seems entirely sincere.

It is an interesting exchange. In the lecture hall that afternoon, Singer lays it all out. The "illogic" of allowing abortion but not infanticide, of allowing withdrawal of life support but not active killing. Applying the basic assumptions of preference utilitarianism, he spins out his bone-chilling argument for letting parents kill disabled babies and replace them with nondisabled babies who have a greater chance at happiness. It is all about allowing as many individuals as possible to fulfill as many of their preferences as possible.

As soon as he's done, I get the microphone and say I'd like to discuss selective infanticide. As a lawyer, I disagree with his jurisprudential assumptions. Logical inconsistency is not a sufficient reason to change the law. As an atheist, I object to his using religious terms ("the doctrine of the sanctity of human life") to characterize his critics. Singer takes a note pad out of his pocket and jots down my points, apparently eager to take them on, and I proceed to the heart of my argument: that the presence or absence of a disability doesn't predict quality of life. I question his replacement-baby theory, with its assumption of "other things equal," arguing that people are not fungible. I draw out a comparison of myself and my nondisabled brother Mac (the next-born after me), each of us with a combination of gifts and flaws so peculiar that we can't be measured on the same scale.

He responds to each point with clear and lucid counterarguments. He proceeds with the assumption that I am one of the people who might rightly have been killed at birth. He sticks to his guns, conceding just enough to show himself open-minded and flexible. We go back and forth for 10 long minutes. Even as I am horrified by what he says, and by the fact that I have been sucked into a civil discussion of whether I ought to exist, I can't help being dazzled by his verbal facility. He is so respectful, so free of condescension, so focused on the argument, that by the time the show is over, I'm not exactly angry with him. Yes, I am shaking, furious, enraged — but it's for the big room, 200 of my fellow Charlestonians who have listened with polite interest, when in decency they should have run him out of town on a rail.

My encounter with Peter Singer merits a mention in my annual canned letter that December. I decide to send Singer a copy. In response, he sends me the nicest possible e-mail message. Dear Harriet (if he may) . . . Just back from Australia, where he's from. Agrees with my comments on the world situation. Supports my work against institutionalization. And then some pointed questions to clarify my views on selective infanticide.

I reply. Fine, call me Harriet, and I'll reciprocate in the interest of equality, though I'm accustomed to more formality. Skipping agreeable preambles, I answer his questions on disability-based infanticide and pose some of my own. Answers and more questions come back. Back and forth over several weeks it proceeds, an engaging discussion of baby killing, disability prejudice and related points of law and philosophy. Dear Harriet. Dear Peter.

Singer seems curious to learn how someone who is as good an atheist as he is could disagree with his entirely reasonable views. At the same time, I am trying to plumb his theories. What has him so convinced it would be best to allow parents to kill babies with severe disabilities, and not other kinds of babies, if no infant is a "person" with a right to life? I learn it is partly that both biological and adoptive parents prefer healthy babies. But I have trouble with basing life-and-death decisions on market considerations when the market is structured by prejudice. I offer a hypothetical comparison: "What about mixed-race babies, especially when the combination is entirely nonwhite, who I believe are just about as unadoptable as babies with disabilities?" Wouldn't a law allowing the killing of these undervalued babies validate race prejudice? Singer agrees there is a problem. "It would be horrible," he says, "to see mixed-race babies being killed because they can't be adopted, whereas white ones could be." What's the difference? Preferences based on race are unreasonable. Preferences based on ability are not. Why? To Singer, it's pretty simple: disability makes a person "worse off."

Are we "worse off"? I don't think so. Not in any meaningful sense. There are too many variables. For those of us with congenital conditions, disability shapes all we are. Those disabled later in life adapt. We take constraints that no one would choose and build rich and satisfying lives within them. We enjoy pleasures other people enjoy, and pleasures peculiarly our own. We have something the world needs.

Pressing me to admit a negative correlation between disability and happiness, Singer presents a situation: imagine a disabled child on the beach, watching the other children play.

It's right out of the telethon. I expected something more sophisticated from a professional thinker. I respond: "As a little girl playing on the beach, I was already aware that some people felt sorry for me, that I wasn't frolicking with the same level of frenzy as other children. This annoyed me, and still does." I take the time to write a detailed description of how I, in fact, had fun playing on the beach, without the need of standing, walking or running. But, really, I've had enough. I suggest to Singer that we have exhausted our topic, and I'll be back in touch when I get around to writing about him.

He responds by inviting me to Princeton. I fire off an immediate maybe.

Of course I'm flattered. Mama will be impressed.

But there are things to consider. Not Dead Yet says — and I completely agree — that we should not legitimate Singer's views by giving them a forum. We should not make disabled lives subject to debate. Moreover, any spokesman chosen by the opposition is by definition a token. But even if I'm a token, I won't have to act like one. And anyway, I'm kind of stuck. If I decline, Singer can make some hay: "I offered them a platform, but they refuse rational discussion." It's an old trick, and I've laid myself wide open.

My invitation is to have an exchange of views with Singer during his undergraduate course. He also proposes a second "exchange," open to the whole university, later in the day. This sounds a lot like debating my life — and on my opponent's turf, with my opponent moderating, to boot. I offer a counterproposal, to which Singer proves amenable. I will open the class with some comments on infanticide and related issues and then let Singer grill me as hard as he likes before we open it up for the students. Later in the day, I might take part in a discussion of some other disability issue in a neutral forum. Singer suggests a faculty-student discussion group sponsored by his department but with cross-departmental membership. The topic I select is "Assisted Suicide, Disability Discrimination and the Illusion of Choice: A Disability Rights Perspective." I inform a few movement colleagues of this turn of events, and advice starts rolling in. I decide to go with the advisers who counsel me to do the gig, lie low and get out of Dodge.

I ask Singer to refer me to the person who arranges travel at Princeton. I imagine some capable and unflappable woman like my sister, Beth, whose varied job description at a North Carolina university includes handling visiting artists. Singer refers me to his own assistant, who certainly seems capable and unflappable enough. However, almost immediately Singer jumps back in via e-mail. It seems the nearest hotel has only one wheelchair-accessible suite, available with two rooms for $600 per night. What to do? I know I shouldn't be so accommodating, but I say I can make do with an inaccessible room if it has certain features. Other logistical issues come up. We go back and forth. Questions and answers. Do I really need a lift-equipped vehicle at the airport? Can't my assistant assist me into a conventional car? How wide is my wheelchair?

By the time we're done, Singer knows that I am 28 inches wide. I have trouble controlling my wheelchair if my hand gets cold. I am accustomed to driving on rough, irregular surfaces, but I get nervous turning on steep slopes. Even one step is too many. I can swallow purées, soft bread and grapes. I use a bedpan, not a toilet. None of this is a secret; none of it cause for angst. But I do wonder whether Singer is jotting down my specs in his little note pad as evidence of how "bad off" people like me really are.

I realize I must put one more issue on the table: etiquette. I was criticized within the movement when I confessed to shaking Singer's hand in Charleston, and some are appalled that I have agreed to break bread with him in Princeton. I think they have a very good point, but, again, I'm stuck. I'm engaged for a day of discussion, not a picket line. It is not in my power to marginalize Singer at Princeton; nothing would be accomplished by displays of personal disrespect. However, chumminess is clearly inappropriate. I tell Singer that in the lecture hall it can't be Harriet and Peter; it must be Ms. Johnson and Mr. Singer.

He seems genuinely nettled. Shouldn't it be Ms. Johnson and Professor Singer, if I want to be formal? To counter, I invoke the ceremonial low-country usage, Attorney Johnson and Professor Singer, but point out that Mr./Ms. is the custom in American political debates and might seem more normal in New Jersey. All right, he says. Ms./Mr. it will be.

I describe this awkward social situation to the lawyer in my office who has served as my default lunch partner for the past 14 years. He gives forth a full-body shudder.

"That poor, sorry son of a bitch! He has no idea what he's in for."

Being a disability rights lawyer lecturing at Princeton does confer some cachet at the Newark airport. I need all the cachet I can get. Delta Airlines has torn up my power chair. It is a fairly frequent occurrence for any air traveler on wheels.

When they inform me of the damage in Atlanta, I throw a monumental fit and tell them to have a repair person meet me in Newark with new batteries to replace the ones inexplicably destroyed. Then I am told no new batteries can be had until the morning. It's Sunday night. On arrival in Newark, I'm told of a plan to put me up there for the night and get me repaired and driven to Princeton by 10 a.m.

"That won't work. I'm lecturing at 10. I need to get there tonight, go to sleep and be in my right mind tomorrow."

"What? You're lecturing? They told us it was a conference. We need to get you fixed tonight!"

Carla, the gate agent, relieves me of the need to throw any further fits by undertaking on my behalf the fit of all fits.

Carmen, the personal assistant with whom I'm traveling, pushes me in my disabled chair around the airport in search of a place to use the bedpan. However, instead of diaper-changing tables, which are functional though far from private, we find a flip-down plastic shelf that doesn't look like it would hold my 70 pounds of body weight. It's no big deal; I've restricted my fluids. But Carmen is a little freaked. It is her first adventure in power-chair air travel. I thought I prepared her for the trip, but I guess I neglected to warn her about the probability of wheelchair destruction. I keep forgetting that even people who know me well don't know much about my world.

We reach the hotel at 10:15 p.m., four hours late.

I wake up tired. I slept better than I would have slept in Newark with an unrepaired chair, but any hotel bed is a near guarantee of morning crankiness. I tell Carmen to leave the TV off. I don't want to hear the temperature.

I do the morning stretch. Medical people call it passive movement, but it's not really passive. Carmen's hands move my limbs, following my precise instructions, her strength giving effect to my will. Carmen knows the routine, so it is in near silence that we begin easing slowly into the day. I let myself be propped up to eat oatmeal and drink tea. Then there's the bedpan and then bathing and dressing, still in bed. As the caffeine kicks in, silence gives way to conversation about practical things. Carmen lifts me into my chair and straps a rolled towel under my ribs for comfort and stability. She tugs at my clothes to remove wrinkles that could cause pressure sores. She switches on my motors and gives me the means of moving without anyone's help. They don't call it a power chair for nothing.

I drive to the mirror. I do my hair in one long braid. Even this primal hairdo requires, at this stage of my life, joint effort. I undo yesterday's braid, fix the part and comb the hair in front. Carmen combs where I can't reach. I divide the mass into three long hanks and start the braid just behind my left ear. Section by section, I hand it over to her, and her unimpaired young fingers pull tight, crisscross, until the braid is fully formed.

A big polyester scarf completes my costume. Carmen lays it over my back. I tie it the way I want it, but Carmen starts fussing with it, trying to tuck it down in the back. I tell her that it's fine, and she stops.

On top of the scarf, she wraps the two big shawls that I hope will substitute for an overcoat.

I don't own any real winter clothes. I just stay out of the cold, such cold as we get in Charleston.

We review her instructions for the day. Keep me in view and earshot. Be instantly available but not intrusive. Be polite, but don't answer any questions about me. I am glad that she has agreed to come. She's strong, smart, adaptable and very loyal. But now she is digging under the shawls, fussing with that scarf again.

"Carmen. What are you doing?"

"I thought I could hide this furry thing you sit on."

"Leave it. Singer knows lots of people eat meat. Now he'll know some crips sit on sheepskin."

The walk is cold but mercifully short. The hotel is just across the street from Princeton's wrought-iron gate and a few short blocks from the building where Singer's assistant shows us to the elevator. The elevator doubles as the janitor's closet — the cart with the big trash can and all the accouterments is rolled aside so I can get in. Evidently there aren't a lot of wheelchair people using this building.

We ride the broom closet down to the basement and are led down a long passageway to a big lecture hall. As the students drift in, I engage in light badinage with the sound technician. He is squeamish about touching me, but I insist that the cordless lavaliere is my mike of choice. I invite him to clip it to the big polyester scarf.

The students enter from the rear door, way up at ground level, and walk down stairs to their seats. I feel like an animal in the zoo. I hadn't reckoned on the architecture, those tiers of steps that separate me from a human wall of apparent physical and mental perfection, that keep me confined down here in my pit.

It is 5 before 10. Singer is loping down the stairs. I feel like signaling to Carmen to open the door, summon the broom closet and get me out of here. But Singer greets me pleasantly and hands me Princeton's check for $500, the fee he offered with apologies for its inadequacy.

So. On with the show.

My talk to the students is pretty Southern. I've decided to pound them with heart, hammer them with narrative and say "y'all" and "folks." I play with the emotional tone, giving them little peaks and valleys, modulating three times in one 45-second patch. I talk about justice. Even beauty and love. I figure they haven't been getting much of that from Singer.

Of course, I give them some argument too. I mean to honor my contractual obligations. I lead with the hypothetical about mixed-race, nonwhite babies and build the ending around the question of who should have the burden of proof as to the quality of disabled lives. And woven throughout the talk is the presentation of myself as a representative of a minority group that has been rendered invisible by prejudice and oppression, a participant in a discussion that would not occur in a just world.

I let it go a little longer than I should. Their faces show they're going where I'm leading, and I don't look forward to letting them go. But the clock on the wall reminds me of promises I mean to keep, and I stop talking and submit myself to examination and inquiry.

Singer's response is surprisingly soft. Maybe after hearing that this discussion is insulting and painful to me, he doesn't want to exacerbate my discomfort. His reframing of the issues is almost pro forma, abstract, entirely impersonal. Likewise, the students' inquiries are abstract and fairly predictable: anencephaly, permanent unconsciousness, eugenic abortion. I respond to some of them with stories, but mostly I give answers I could have e-mailed in.

I call on a young man near the top of the room.

"Do you eat meat?"

"Yes, I do."

"Then how do you justify — "

"I haven't made any study of animal rights, so anything I could say on the subject wouldn't be worth everyone's time."

The next student wants to work the comparison of disability and race, and Singer joins the discussion until he elicits a comment from me that he can characterize as racist. He scores a point, but that's all right. I've never claimed to be free of prejudice, just struggling with it.

Singer proposes taking me on a walk around campus, unless I think it would be too cold. What the hell? "It's probably warmed up some. Let's go out and see how I do."

He doesn't know how to get out of the building without using the stairs, so this time it is my assistant leading the way. Carmen has learned of another elevator, which arrives empty. When we get out of the building, she falls behind a couple of paces, like a respectful chaperone.

In the classroom there was a question about keeping alive the unconscious. In response, I told a story about a family I knew as a child, which took loving care of a nonresponsive teenage girl, acting out their unconditional commitment to each other, making all the other children, and me as their visitor, feel safe. This doesn't satisfy Singer. "Let's assume we can prove, absolutely, that the individual is totally unconscious and that we can know, absolutely, that the individual will never regain consciousness."

I see no need to state an objection, with no stenographer present to record it; I'll play the game and let him continue.

"Assuming all that," he says, "don't you think continuing to take care of that individual would be a bit — weird?"

"No. Done right, it could be profoundly beautiful."

"But what about the caregiver, a woman typically, who is forced to provide all this service to a family member, unable to work, unable to have a life of her own?"

"That's not the way it should be. Not the way it has to be. As a society, we should pay workers to provide that care, in the home. In some places, it's been done that way for years. That woman shouldn't be forced to do it, any more than my family should be forced to do my care."

Singer takes me around the architectural smorgasbord that is Princeton University by a route that includes not one step, unramped curb or turn on a slope. Within the strange limits of this strange assignment, it seems Singer is doing all he can to make me comfortable.

He asks what I thought of the students' questions.

"They were fine, about what I expected. I was a little surprised by the question about meat eating."

"I apologize for that. That was out of left field. But — I think what he wanted to know is how you can have such high respect for human life and so little respect for animal life."

"People have lately been asking me the converse, how you can have so much respect for animal life and so little respect for human life."

"And what do you answer?"

"I say I don't know. It doesn't make a lot of sense to me."

"Well, in my view — "

"Look. I have lived in blissful ignorance all these years, and I'm not prepared to give that up today."

"Fair enough," he says and proceeds to recount bits of Princeton history. He stops. "This will be of particular interest to you, I think. This is where your colleagues with Not Dead Yet set up their blockade." I'm grateful for the reminder. My brothers and sisters were here before me and behaved far more appropriately than I am doing.

A van delivers Carmen and me early for the evening forum. Singer says he hopes I had a pleasant afternoon.

Yes, indeed. I report a pleasant lunch and a very pleasant nap, and I tell him about the Christopher Reeve Suite in the hotel, which has been remodeled to accommodate Reeve, who has family in the area.

"Do you suppose that's the $600 accessible suite they told me about?"

"Without doubt. And if I'd known it was the Christopher Reeve Suite, I would have held out for it."

"Of course you would have!" Singer laughs. "And we'd have had no choice, would we?"

We talk about the disability rights critique of Reeve and various other topics. Singer is easy to talk to, good company. Too bad he sees lives like mine as avoidable mistakes.

I'm looking forward to the soft vegetarian meal that has been arranged; I'm hungry. Assisted suicide, as difficult as it is, doesn't cause the kind of agony I felt discussing disability-based infanticide. In this one, I understand, and to some degree can sympathize with, the opposing point of view — misguided though it is.

My opening sticks to the five-minute time limit. I introduce the issue as framed by academic articles Not Dead Yet recommended for my use. Andrew Batavia argues for assisted suicide based on autonomy, a principle generally held high in the disability rights movement. In general, he says, the movement fights for our right to control our own lives; when we need assistance to effect our choices, assistance should be available to us as a matter of right. If the choice is to end our lives, he says, we should have assistance then as well. But Carol Gill says that it is differential treatment — disability discrimination — to try to prevent most suicides while facilitating the suicides of ill and disabled people. The social-science literature suggests that the public in general, and physicians in particular, tend to underestimate the quality of life of disabled people, compared with our own assessments of our lives. The case for assisted suicide rests on stereotypes that our lives are inherently so bad that it is entirely rational if we want to die.

I side with Gill. What worries me most about the proposals for legalized assisted suicide is their veneer of beneficence — the medical determination that, for a given individual, suicide is reasonable or right. It is not about autonomy but about nondisabled people telling us what's good for us.

In the discussion that follows, I argue that choice is illusory in a context of pervasive inequality. Choices are structured by oppression. We shouldn't offer assistance with suicide until we all have the assistance we need to get out of bed in the morning and live a good life. Common causes of suicidality — dependence, institutional confinement, being a burden — are entirely curable. Singer, seated on my right, participates in the discussion but doesn't dominate it. During the meal, I occasionally ask him to put things within my reach, and he competently complies.

I feel as if I'm getting to a few of them, when a student asks me a question. The words are all familiar, but they're strung together in a way so meaningless that I can't even retain them — it's like a long sentence in Tagalog. I can only admit my limitations. "That question's too abstract for me to deal with. Can you rephrase it?"

He indicates that it is as clear as he can make it, so I move on.

A little while later, my right elbow slips out from under me. This is awkward. Normally I get whoever is on my right to do this sort of thing. Why not now? I gesture to Singer. He leans over, and I whisper, "Grasp this wrist and pull forward one inch, without lifting." He follows my instructions to the letter. He sees that now I can again reach my food with my fork. And he may now understand what I was saying a minute ago, that most of the assistance disabled people need does not demand medical training.

A philosophy professor says, "It appears that your objections to assisted suicide are essentially tactical."

"Excuse me?"

"By that I mean they are grounded in current conditions of political, social and economic inequality. What if we assume that such conditions do not exist?"

"Why would we want to do that?"

"I want to get to the real basis for the position you take."

I feel as if I'm losing caste. It is suddenly very clear that I'm not a philosopher. I'm like one of those old practitioners who used to visit my law school, full of bluster about life in the real world. Such a bore! A once-sharp mind gone muddy! And I'm only 44 — not all that old.

The forum is ended, and I've been able to eat very little of my puréed food. I ask Carmen to find the caterer and get me a container. Singer jumps up to take care of it. He returns with a box and obligingly packs my food to go.

When I get home, people are clamoring for the story. The lawyers want the blow-by-blow of my forensic triumph over the formidable foe; when I tell them it wasn't like that, they insist that it was. Within the disability rights community, there is less confidence. It is generally assumed that I handled the substantive discussion well, but people worry that my civility may have given Singer a new kind of legitimacy. I hear from

Laura, a beloved movement sister. She is appalled that I let Singer provide even minor physical assistance at the dinner. "Where was your assistant?" she wants to know. How could I put myself in a relationship with Singer that made him appear so human, even kind?

I struggle to explain. I didn't feel disempowered; quite the contrary, it seemed a good thing to make him do some useful work. And then, the hard part: I've come to believe that Singer actually is human, even kind in his way. There ensues a discussion of good and evil and personal assistance and power and philosophy and tactics for which I'm profoundly grateful.

I e-mail Laura again. This time I inform her that I've changed my will. She will inherit a book that Singer gave me, a collection of his writings with a weirdly appropriate inscription: "To Harriet Johnson, So that you will have a better answer to questions about animals. And thanks for coming to Princeton. Peter Singer. March 25, 2002." She responds that she is changing her will, too. I'll get the autographed photo of Jerry Lewis she received as an M.D.A. poster child. We joke that each of us has given the other a "reason to live."

I have had a nice e-mail message from Singer, hoping Carmen and I and the chair got home without injury, relaying positive feedback from my audiences — and taking me to task for a statement that isn't supported by a relevant legal authority, which he looked up. I report that we got home exhausted but unharmed and concede that he has caught me in a generalization that should have been qualified. It's clear that the conversation will continue.

I am soon sucked into the daily demands of law practice, family, community and politics. In the closing days of the state legislative session, I help get a bill passed that I hope will move us one small step toward a world in which killing won't be such an appealing solution to the "problem" of disability. It is good to focus on this kind of work. But the conversations with and about Singer continue. Unable to muster the appropriate moral judgments, I ask myself a tough question: am I in fact a silly little lady whose head is easily turned

by a man who gives her a kind of attention she enjoys? I hope not, but I confess that I've never been able to sustain righteous anger for more than about 30 minutes at a time. My view of life tends more toward tragedy.

The tragic view comes closest to describing how I now look at Peter Singer. He is a man of unusual gifts, reaching for the heights. He writes that he is trying to create a system of ethics derived from fact and reason, that largely throws off the perspectives of religion, place, family, tribe, community and maybe even species — to "take the point of view of the universe." His is a grand, heroic undertaking.

But like the protagonist in a classical drama, Singer has his flaw. It is his unexamined assumption that disabled people are inherently "worse off," that we "suffer," that we have lesser "prospects of a happy life." Because of this all-too-common prejudice, and his rare courage in taking it to its logical conclusion, catastrophe looms. Here in the midpoint of the play, I can't look at him without fellow-feeling.

I am regularly confronted by people who tell me that Singer doesn't deserve my human sympathy. I should make him an object of implacable wrath, to be cut off, silenced, destroyed absolutely. And I find myself lacking a logical argument to the contrary.

I am talking to my sister Beth on the phone. "You kind of like the monster, don't you?" she says.

I find myself unable to evade, certainly unwilling to lie. "Yeah, in a way. And he's not exactly a monster."

"You know, Harriet, there were some very pleasant Nazis. They say the SS guards went home and played on the floor with their children every night."

She can tell that I'm chastened; she changes the topic, lets me off the hook. Her harshness has come as a surprise. She isn't inclined to moralizing; in our family, I'm the one who sets people straight.

When I put the phone down, my argumentative nature feels frustrated. In my mind, I replay the conversation, but this time defend my position.

"He's not exactly a monster. He just has some strange ways of looking at things."

"He's advocating genocide."

"That's the thing. In his mind, he isn't. He's only giving parents a choice. He thinks the humans he is talking about aren't people, aren't 'persons.'"

"But that's the way it always works, isn't it? They're always animals or vermin or chattel goods. Objects, not persons. He's repackaging some old ideas. Making them acceptable."

"I think his ideas are new, in a way. It's not old-fashioned hate. It's a twisted, misinformed, warped kind of beneficence. His motive is to do good."

"What do you care about motives?" she asks. "Doesn't this beneficent killing make disabled brothers and sisters just as dead?"

"But he isn't killing anyone. It's just talk."

"Just talk? It's talk with an agenda, talk aimed at forming policy. Talk that's getting a receptive audience. You of all people know the power of that kind of talk."

"Well, sure, but — "

"If talk didn't matter, would you make it your life's work?"

"But," I say, "his talk won't matter in the end. He won't succeed in reinventing morality. He stirs the pot, brings things out into the open. But ultimately we'll make a world that's fit to live in, a society that has room for all its flawed creatures. History will remember Singer as a curious example of the bizarre things that can happen when paradigms collide."

"What if you're wrong? What if he convinces people that there's no morally significant difference between a fetus and a newborn, and just as disabled fetuses are routinely aborted now, so disabled babies are routinely killed? Might some future generation take it further than Singer wants to go? Might some say there's no morally significant line between a newborn and a 3-year-old?"

"Sure. Singer concedes that a bright line cannot be drawn. But he doesn't propose killing anyone who prefers to live."

"That overarching respect for the individual's preference for life — might some say it's a fiction, a fetish, a quasi-religious belief?"

"Yes," I say. "That's pretty close to what I think. As an atheist, I think all preferences are moot once you kill someone. The injury is entirely to the surviving community."

"So what if that view wins out, but you can't break disability prejudice? What if you wind up in a world where the disabled person's 'irrational' preference to live must yield to society's 'rational' interest in reducing the incidence of disability? Doesn't horror kick in somewhere? Maybe as you watch the door close behind whoever has wheeled you into the gas chamber?"

"That's not going to happen."

"Do you have empirical evidence?" she asks. "A logical argument?"

"Of course not. And I know it's happened before, in what was considered the most progressive medical community in the world. But it won't happen. I have to believe that."

Belief. Is that what it comes down to? Am I a person of faith after all? Or am I clinging to foolish hope that the tragic protagonist, this one time, will shift course before it's too late?

I don't think so. It's less about belief, less about hope, than about a practical need for definitions I can live with.

If I define Singer's kind of disability prejudice as an ultimate evil, and him as a monster, then I must so define all who believe disabled lives are inherently worse off or that a life without a certain kind of consciousness lacks value. That definition would make monsters of many of the people with whom I move on the sidewalks, do business, break bread, swap stories and share the grunt work of local politics. It would reach some of my family and most of my nondisabled friends, people who show me personal kindness and who sometimes manage to love me through their ignorance. I can't live with a definition of ultimate evil that encompasses all of them. I can't refuse the monster-majority basic respect and human sympathy. It's not in my heart to deny every single one of them, categorically, my affection and my love.

The peculiar drama of my life has placed me in a world that by and large thinks it would be better if people like me did not exist. My fight has been for accommodation, the world to me and me to the world.

As a disability pariah, I must struggle for a place, for kinship, for community, for connection. Because I am still seeking acceptance of my humanity, Singer's call to get past species seems a luxury way beyond my reach. My goal isn't to shed the perspective that comes from my particular experience, but to give voice to it. I want to be engaged in the tribal fury that rages when opposing perspectives are let loose.

As a shield from the terrible purity of Singer's vision, I'll look to the corruption that comes from interconnectedness. To justify my hopes that Singer's theoretical world — and its entirely logical extensions — won't become real, I'll invoke the muck and mess and undeniable reality of disabled lives well lived. That's the best I can do.

DEMENTIA, CRITICAL INTERESTS, AND EUTHANASIA

Nathan Brett

Nathan Brett teaches in and is currently Chair of the Department of Philosophy at Dalhousie University in Halifax. He is the author of a number of journal and book collection articles in legal, moral, and social philosophy.

Brett begins with the story of Margo, an Alzheimer's patient and a citizen of the Netherlands who has signed a living will giving advance directives to her caretakers to end her life in the event that she suffers substantial loss of memory and other mental capacities. Margo is now in that condition, but appears to be happy, giving no indication of wanting to die and every indication of being fearful that her caretakers will harm her. Brett asks, is there a case for saying that her life should be ended anyway? If so, how good is the case? Brett explores answers to these questions through a discussion of Ronald Dworkin's account of critical interests. He raises doubts about killing Margo by raising questions about personal identity.

The apartment had many locks to keep Margo from slipping out at night and wandering in the park in her nightgown, which she had done before.... She said she was reading mysteries, but [the psychologist who was studying her] "noticed that her place in the book jumps randomly from day to day; dozens of pages are dog-eared at any given moment. Maybe she feels good just sitting and humming to herself, rocking back and forth slowly, nodding off liberally, occasionally turning to a fresh page." Margo attended an art class for Alzheimer's victims — they all, including her, painted pretty much the same picture every time, except near the end, just before death, when they became more primitive.

[The psychologist reported that] "... Margo is undeniably one of the happiest people I have ever known." He noted particularly her pleasure at eating peanut butter and jelly sandwiches.[1]

To this account of the life of an Alzheimer's patient, I want to add a few details which do not in fact belong to Margo's case, though they could easily have been a feature of other cases involving Alzheimer's patients. Margo, a citizen of Holland, has signed a living will giving advance directives to her caretakers. If the disease has resulted in a substantial loss of memory and other mental capacities when she is evaluated on her 60th birthday, her life is to be ended through an overdose of painkillers.[2] This advance directive was written when Margo was 56, shortly after she received the diagnosis that she had Alzheimer's, and before the condition became advanced enough to undermine her powers of reason. In fact, it was precisely because she dreaded the prospect of living for some time in the condition of dementia which she is now in, that Margo had drawn up this directive.

Needless to say, the hospital committee charged with the examination of this case is troubled. Not only does Margo appear now to be generally happy, on the occasions when something does upset her, she gives every indication of being fearful that her caretakers will harm her.

Moreover, she now gives no indication of wanting to die. Is there any case for saying that her life should be ended anyway? If so, how good is the case?

My discussion of this problem is in two parts. Part I examines the case that Ronald Dworkin, who originally posed the problem, provides for ending Margo's life. Dworkin's theory of "critical interests," that is, interests considered in relation to people's lives as a whole, will be central to this argument. I will defend the view that both the principle of autonomy and the "best interests" standard provide reasons for following Margo's advance directive. But Part II raises doubts about killing Margo by raising questions about personal identity. I argue that if the living will is not based on beliefs or principles or even memories that belong to the demented Margo, then it cannot be legitimate to apply its directives to her.

Part I

1. Critical Interests

To understand the problem, at least as Dworkin sees it, we need to begin by distinguishing two sorts of interests that people can have.[3] In the first place we have interests that are "experiential." Everyone, including Margo, has preferences connected with their experience of the world. I think Gary Larson's cartoons are fun, for example, and like Margo, I like peanut butter sandwiches. I would enjoy painting under some circumstances, but would not like to paint the same picture over and over as Margo does. Margo (and just about everyone else) is eager to avoid pain; and (perhaps like Margo) nearly everyone is anxious to avoid situations that make them insecure, e.g., because they threaten harm.

Experiential interests, of course, presuppose consciousness, though not necessarily *self-consciousness* (this depends upon the object). Experiential interests presuppose the ability to react positively or negatively to what is experienced or anticipated. All sentient creatures have interests in this sense. Dworkin also refers to such interests as "volitional,"[4] presumably because they

are sources of voluntary behaviour. Interests in this sense are necessarily connected with dispositions to pursue or avoid the objects in question, though of course such dispositions need not be sufficient to yield action.

Critical interests, on the other hand, are not (at least not directly) a function of desires and aversions or preferences for certain experiences. In Dworkin's view, the best lives (in a non-moral sense) are lives characterized by the virtue of *integrity*, and critical interests must be understood in relation to this virtue. To understand this, we can exploit two analogies that Dworkin suggests in thinking about integrity and its connection to our critical interests. On the one hand, there is the old comparison between leading a good life and writing a good novel (or producing a good film — one might label this the "film critic" model of the good life). There is some structure, some constancy of theme (or themes) in a good novel. It cannot just proceed randomly and succeed. Even if a "stream of consciousness" constitutes all or part of a novel, it will not be good if it is just a random collage of reported experience. Its real success will depend upon thematic undercurrents (or overtures) which give it a "meaning" that is not a mere aggregative function of the episodes to which the reader is exposed. Anyone who has written even an essay in philosophy has probably experienced the difficulty of getting from the point at which one has a subject and some ideas to the point at which there is a line of thought that has a "trajectory" which carries one forward. Such a line of thought gives one's paper a kind of integrity. Lives can have a structure similar to this; and (arguably) meaningful lives do have something analogous to the trajectory that is established as one moves (either as reader or writer) through a written work. Judgments about integrity in the life of a person are made with reference to the sort of consistency of pursuit or motivation that gives this life coherence. On this view, the fundamental commitments in a life provide a basis for establishing the critical interests of a person, just as the lines of plot and theme provide a basis for judgments about what fits and what is "out of character" in the selection of the next moves in a novel.[5]

There is a misinterpretation of this "film critic" model of the critical interests (and the good life) that should be avoided. Dworkin does not think that the best lives are ones in which everything happens according to an elaborately worked out exercise in self-reflection. If this were a necessary condition of the intrinsic good that Dworkin is talking about, it would be missing from the lives of most persons. But the reflective articulation of a plot line is *not* a feature of most novel writing either. The connections of theme, which are actually developing as the "trajectory" of a novel, may not be articulated, or may only be spelled out later (and not necessarily by the author). The fact that lives are often led without any articulated vision — that unexamined lives are often worth living — does not undercut the claim that good lives are ones that have connections of goal and principle.[6]

A particularly Dworkinian analogue of integrity in a life is the sort of coherence which can and should exist in a legal system. Dworkin devotes hundreds of pages of *Laws Empire* to the development of an ideal of legal integrity, but the basic ideas are relatively simple. Judges must look in two directions in deciding the cases that come before them, including the hard cases which the black letter of statute and precedent *appear* to leave open. On the one hand, there is the ideal answer to the question that abstract (moral) justice demands. On the other hand, there are the facts of institutional history that have generated a specific legal system that has embedded certain normative commitments. Judges cannot ignore the latter — the commitments of these institutions — without at least creating injustice across time. Like cases will not be treated alike. But, on the other hand, even a cursory reflection on what previous decision makers — legislators and judges — were trying to do, would reveal the emptiness of a completely "black letter" approach. For, previous decision-makers cannot be assumed to be discovering *only* what other decision-makers have decided (*ad infinitum*). We must assume that they took their task to be (in part) that of doing justice in a substantive sense.

Now, integrity in the life of a person is analogous to this in having an historical as well as an ideal basis. A person cannot take seriously the question "What should I do?" and at the same time suppose that it really doesn't matter. However, if a person is to lead a *life*, if she is to have an identity as an agent, she can't be indifferent to the way in which new decisions connect with those that have come before.[7] Judgments about what is in the "critical interests" of a person are made in a way that is relative to the integrity of that person's life taken as a whole. Thus, they are not just judgments as to how best to satisfy the person's existing and predicted preferences. The concept of critical interests is normative, not only because it assumes that there are some things which we ought to care about because we are human beings and persons, but also because there are some things I should want (and thus some interests I have) because I am *this* person with *these* commitments.

2. Autonomy and Critical Interests

On the basis of serious reflections about her life and her prospects (given the Alzheimer's diagnosis) Margo has decided that she does not want to live for any considerable time in a demented state. We will suppose that her mind was not already warped, and that her decision was not based on misinformation (e.g., about the prospects for recovery of her abilities). We shall further suppose that Margo's decision is not out of character. It does fit with or flow from her basic principles, so that from the point of view established by reflections on integrity, it is in her critical interests that her life end sooner rather than after years of dementia. The film analogy might be useful here. A Harrison Ford high impact action film would not be improved, but worsened, perhaps ruined, by ending it with the addition of several hours from an Andy Warhol film of the bricks in a wall. Moreover, shifting to the legal analogy, Margo may have reasons of principle that connect with her belief in self-sufficiency for her refusal to impose a burden upon others.[8] I will consider two arguments for respecting Margo's directive to end her life, one involving the protection of autonomy, the other beneficence, or the attempt to do what is in her best interests.

In the first place, following the directive seems most consistent with the full recognition of Margo's autonomy. Note that we *do* implement such decisions, where the request is not to be sustained in a permanently vegetative state. To give Margo respect as an autonomous agent is to respect *her* competent decisions about her life and her way of making the best sense of it that she can. Margo's prior decision is a clear and decisive attempt to control the way in which this life ends. It was made prior to the demise of her capacity for critical reflection, and made on the basis of reflections on her life as a whole. It thus represents what she deems to be in her critical interests; and by hypothesis (in this argument) we are taking her to be right, not mistaken, about this. In her present state she is incapable of revising that judgment. Thus, the only decision that respects her autonomy is the one that implements her own will as to the way her life should end.[9]

But why should it be a matter of great importance to protect a person's own decisions about their lives? Dworkin considers two answers to this question. In the first place, there is the "evidentiary view," the answer given by John Stuart Mill. Individuals are generally in the best position to know what their own preferences are. Others are frequently wrong in thinking that they know better. Thus, a general rule that gives to individuals the final say in matters which relate specifically to their own lives is one that will in the long run do best in promoting human welfare. This evidentiary view is thus supported by a generalization about the access we have to knowledge of our interests, supplemented by a generalization concerning the effects of busybody paternalism. A right to autonomy is really a device that protects us from the negative effects of poorly informed interventions in our lives. Now, if this is the rationale for the right to autonomy, then that rationale itself will support some

general categories of exceptions; and these exceptions also have to be recognized. We have good reason to suppose that those in their infancy and the insane or demented are not the best judges of their own interests. There is no reason, therefore, to suppose that protection of autonomy should extend to these categories of persons.

Was Margo in a good position to know the interests of the person she will become? Did she base her decision on adequate information? It has been argued that the autonomy model produces distortions when it is applied to dementia cases precisely because we do not have adequate access to "what it is like to be" in this state.[10] It is arguable that an individual who writes an advance directive such as Margo's cannot be well informed about the condition she will enter and the interests she will have. Later caregivers who can base their answers to these questions on concrete information about the relative happiness or misery of their patient may actually be in a much better position to assess Margo's interests than she was, years ahead of time, basing her views on a prognosis which may or may not be accurate. Not only is there a relative lack of information for this early decision, there is also a radical difference between the perspective of the competent person writing the advance directive and the incompetent patient who will be subject to it. Finally, the author of the advance directive will often be working from stereotyped views of the condition she will enter, views which inadequately represent the interests of the patient she will become. It is not implausible to argue, as Rebecca Dresser does in defending paternalistic intervention,[11] that those caregivers who are in day-to-day contact with Margo have much better evidence of her interests than Margo would have had in making her judgment under very different conditions several years earlier. This judgment about one's future is, in fact, very much like a judgment about another human being — and not a human being that is very much like oneself.

There is no question that these are important considerations. But it should also be clear that the evidentiary view does not capture everything that we want to say about autonomy. There is often a conflict between prudence and autonomy. Individuals autonomously take huge risks, for example, refusing relatively safe operations because of their Christian Science or Jehovah's Witness beliefs. As these and a myriad of other cases indicate, the protection of autonomy is not simply the best strategy for maximizing the satisfaction of a person's experiential interests. We protect autonomy in the liberal state as a way of protecting the individual's capacity to choose a life for herself. Autonomy involves self-selection and self-endorsement. But to understand these conceptions we must understand what it is for a *self* to choose. It is in accounting for this that we are led back to the ideal of integrity, to an ideal which respects the goals and principles through which individuals make coherent sense of their own lives. If Margo's intent in drawing up an advance directive were simply to see that her later preferences were well served, then this is not a matter about which we can reasonably expect her to be more expert than her later caregivers. But that is not the point of the protection of autonomy. We need to return to the idea of her *critical* interests — the interests that express what her life is about — in order to understand what the protection of autonomy involves in this situation. In her advance directive, Margo has attempted to integrate the manner of her death with the way in which she has led her life. On Dworkin's view, it is precisely this type of decision that the principle of autonomy aims to protect.

3. Understanding Best Interests Critically

In the above argument, I have assumed that Margo is aware of the possibility that her directive may conflict with the preferences that she will have at a later time, when she is demented. How should we relate these later preferences to Margo's *interests*? In this section I will argue that only those preferences which are in accord with a person's critical interests can be said to be genuinely in that person's interests. If this is correct, then we can agree with Dworkin that not only autonomy, but also beneficence (or the best interests standard) support the decision to end Margo's life.

Assuming that Margo has correctly articulated what is in her *critical* interests, we are in a state of conflict of a sort that characterizes "Ulysses contracts" where, with foresight, one has bound another to constrain her from some expected temptation.[12] The demented Margo's current experiential interests provide a basis for continued care. She clearly enjoys eating peanut butter sandwiches and randomly turning pages in the book she is "reading." But if her advance directive does articulate her critical interests (as we have supposed) then it requires that these simple activities be brought to an end. Of course, not all cases will be of this sort. Some patients with her disease give evidence that their mental lives are ones of inescapable torment. But our concern is with the cases in which critical and experiential interests seem to pull us in *opposite* directions. In these cases Dworkin clearly assumes that the answer to our dilemma is obvious: the person's critical interests must dominate.

We can provide some argument for this way of interpreting the situation (as a conflict of two types of interests) by looking at other circumstances in which such conflicts occur. A person's appetite for soap operas may conflict with her desire to finish her degree — a goal that is a part of her aspiration to become a university professor. Another person with a powerful desire to drink may correctly regard the satisfaction of this desire as antithetical to his critical interests in saving his job and marriage. In such cases it seems plausible to say that critical interests should dominate. Of course, in these cases there is always the possibility that the conflicts can be translated into conflicts between the long and short run satisfaction of experiential interests. But they need not be reducible to this. Suppose that the life possible for this person as a university teacher is actually more filled with moments of tedium and dread (etc.) than an alternative life as a telephone sales clerk, a life that is compatible (we will suppose) with far more hours of (vicarious) soap opera. It *still* seems plausible (to me) that her critical interests take precedence.

But this model of conflict between critical and experiential interests (with the former taking precedence) may not be appropriate to account for what is going on in the cases described. If it were the appropriate model, it would be highly unclear as to how the utilities should be calculated. Should we suppose that *no* amount of pleasure associated with satisfying experiential interests (or no escape from pain) is sufficient to justify even the smallest degradation of one's life plans? This seems preposterous. If the tedium involved in the teaching career would be massive, or if it is a life of nearly perpetual panic, this will surely count as grounds for abandoning even the well-established and highly-prized goal of university teaching which has the support of a person's principles and fits the "narrative" structure of her life. What (if anything) is wrong with this picture of conflict between critical and experiential interests?

On the interpretation that I want to advance, there are several things wrong with it. Note, in the first place, we were talking about the conditions of good or meaningful lives when we introduced the discussion of critical interests. A life plan that ignored one's experiential interests, which paid no attention to "simple" pleasure and pain would be a "preposterous" life, as Dworkin himself says.[13] Thus, the successful life plans of human beings will not be ones that reflect a complete indifference to their experiential interests. Secondly, it is a mistake to suppose, for example, that anything that is pleasurable must *ipso facto* count as something in an individual's experiential interests, and that if it is shunned, then this can only be because it is outweighed by some other negative states. Consider a fictional case in which intense bodily pleasure is caused in the course of a sexual assault (by a mad scientist, say). On my view, this pleasure does not add something of value that is outweighed by the pain on the other side of a utility balance sheet. Lacking any endorsement, an affront to this person's integrity, the pleasure does not count as a satisfaction of any *interest* of the person. On the contrary, because it is at odds with the critical interests of the person, the experience of pleasure can itself

be taken as a *harm*. The opposite sort of case (involving pain as something in a person's interest) is also possible. Suffering from cold, from exhaustion, etc., states which nature and experience dispose us to avoid, can be aspects of *satisfying* the critical interests of persons. The goals of mountain climbing and long distance running (and a million other things) confer value on endurance in the face of suffering, and this suffering is an aspect of what makes the activities worthwhile.

These examples suggest a different model of the way in which critical and experiential interests are related in the life of a person. On this view, it is not the case that critical and experiential interests directly compete with one another. When we are talking about the interests of *persons*, the category of critical interests is always relevant. And whether or not a particular experience is really in one's interests depends upon whether it can be normatively integrated within the life of the person in question. It is normal for human beings to accommodate their lives to the experiential preferences that they happen to have. But, as the above examples indicate, it is perfectly possible that what nature and experience dispose a person to prefer is contrary to that person's interests. Thus, on this way of reading the dichotomy, the only genuine interests of persons are critical interests, and experiential interests are the interests of persons only because and to the extent that they receive endorsement in their lives.

Consider the implications of this interpretation for Margo's case. What appeared to be a conflict between Margo's critical and her experiential interests is not that. We have assumed that she was able to contemplate ahead of time (at least as one possibility) this dependent life of peanut butter sandwiches and leafing through books. She knowingly rejected it. This life of simple pleasures was deemed an affront to what her life had "stood for." So, it is not in her interest *at all* — but contrary to it — that she continue in a state in which she has lost control and is reduced to these simple pleasures. There may even be a small analogy with the assault case mentioned above:

•

the pleasure Margo derives from these things may itself be an aspect of harm which is done to her if her life is preserved. If this is the case, then *both* autonomy and the best interests standard demand that we accept her directive and end her life, for Margo's genuine interests are inseparable from the critical interests which are a function of her life taken as a whole.

Part II

4. The Identity Problem: Whose Interests?

Though I find some plausibility to these arguments for ending Margo's life I am also troubled by them. I would not do it. And I am not convinced that this is just weakness of will. In the remainder of this discussion, I will explore an objection to Dworkin's solution; it is an objection that does not depend on questioning the above theory about autonomy and critical interests.[14]

Margo is no longer endowed with the capacity to reflect on the course her life is taking. So, it might be argued, she no longer has critical interests. Margo has lost the capacity to put herself together, to make choices that belong to a life that has narrative structure. If having such a life is an aspect of what it is to be a person, the life of this person has ended. What is happening now to what used to be Margo only belongs to Margo because *we* continue to put her together, because we continue the narrative. That is to say, the preservation of her identity is a *fiction* of *ours*. But, if this is so, then it seems she no longer has a critical interest in having her life ended. And without such interest we don't have a case for ending a life that is comprised largely of pleasurable experiences. Given that she is generally happy but occasionally fearful that she will be harmed, it could hardly be said that this would be a *mercy* killing. Moreover, it is one of our virtues that we respond with compassion to such lives, just as it is a virtue to respect the pre-reflective life of a child.

To this, it could be replied, however, that the basis for supposing that Margo's critical interests are gone assumes what is not true, viz., that one can only have an interest in some outcome if one can desire this outcome and be satisfied by its achievement. But many of our interests persist even in the absence of any desire; and many are *not* such that one must be conscious of their satisfaction. The most obvious example (in the literature on interests) is the interest in the fidelity of one's spouse. It seems very implausible to suppose that this is reducible to the interest in not knowing of (or being otherwise affected by) unfaithful acts. But there are less controversial examples. My concern for the welfare of my grandchildren really aims at *their thriving*, not at my awareness of it. Thus, it seems that the interests of persons can outlive them. When a person makes a will or gives instructions as to what is to be done with his body, we do not suppose (absurdly) that we are released from the obligation that it sets up as soon as the person is dead. On the contrary, we often suppose that it is of the utmost importance that the person's will be done; and this seems to presuppose that the relevant interests persist. Moreover, respect for such decisions of living, reflective persons could hardly be genuine if it were not accompanied by an intention to carry out the person's will. Thus, there seem to be reasons for thinking that Margo's critical interests can survive her demise as a being capable of reflecting on and integrating the moments of her life.

That interests can survive the persons they belong to is a troublesome idea. But so is its denial. For it has led some to the conclusion that, if one thinks this through, one arrives at the view that death cannot be a harm (to a person) since there is no surviving person to be harmed. Here, I want to accept as plausible the claim that Margo's critical interests could survive dementia and even death. The objection I want to raise involves questioning whether the demented Margo is the same person as the author of the advance directive. The Margo who drew up the advance directive cannot have a continuing interest in having her life ended if it already *has* ended. And Margo cannot legitimately utilize a living will to take out a contract on someone different from herself.

But has Margo's life ended? By hypothesis, the demented Margo no longer exists as an autonomous agent. She lacks the capacity to generate any narrative that knits together the day-to-day experiences of her life. There is no longer any structure of norms that can provide the normative core of self-identity that we considered in Part I. In addition to this, memory loss leaves her without psychological connection to the person who drafted the advance directive. But if this is correct, then Margo's earlier decision, represented in her advance directive, was itself based on an error. She had assumed that the demented person left after Alzheimer's disease had removed her critical faculties would be continuing to lead her life. But without the capacities necessary to establish psychological and normative continuities, that life and that self are gone.

Consider a parallel case. A man may have so structured his life that the very idea of the continuation of his spouse after his demise is an affront to what he has stood for. What was *deemed to be* properly a part of his life would be outside his control. But if a man declares that his wife is to be thrown onto his funeral pyre, he demands what he should not, although for centuries some legal systems enforced (or at least tolerated) such wills. Notice that such a person need not be making a mistake about the structure of his own identity or the critical interests that relate to this identity. It could be of central importance to him that his spouse does not survive. On the other hand, he would be making a mistake if he supposed that this other person is a mere extension of himself, is *just* an aspect of his own life. He would have illegitimately extended the boundaries of his self.

Now it would be incorrect to take this example to be *fully* analogous to Margo's situation, to suppose that Margo's advance directive has called for execution of another person. For the disease may have removed not only the psychological connections necessary for identity, but also the very conditions necessary for being a person.[15] Margo's narrative has ended (except insofar as it is taken up by *others*). But even if this is the case, a conscious and child-like human

creature remains; and that human being clearly does have needs and desires. She is capable of experiencing pleasure and pain and capable of some rudimentary forms of communication. Other things being equal, the satisfaction of these interests is itself a source of value and a proper source of demands on our compassion.

5. Dworkin and the Identity Problem

In a work on the rights of those with senile dementia, Dworkin has considered the question of identity that the above objection depends upon. This condition he describes as follows:

> Someone seriously demented loses intellectual and emotional continuity with past stages of "his" life. He suffers total disintegration of personality, so that none of the beliefs, convictions and projects he may have can be seen as mainly fixed by earlier ones and he has total amnesia of prior experiences, identity and attachments.[16]

In this earlier work Dworkin defends the view that personal identity is *not* removed even by this sort of serious permanent dementia which has been the focus of our concern.[17] If this is correct, then the above objection misses the mark. We thus need to consider Dworkin's reasons for taking this view of personal identity.

There is a vast literature in which philosophers have sought amongst the properties of human beings a criterion that gives the identity conditions of persons and establishes what changes are sufficient to constitute loss of identity. The main contenders, of course, have involved the physical continuity of a (living) body, on the one hand, and on the other, some facts about psychological connection involving continuity of memory (and character) or a combination of these. But there is also (at least since Wittgenstein) a fairly standard objection to this way of proceeding. Should we suppose that there is any such criterion, e.g., that there are some necessary conditions which are jointly sufficient for the identity of a person? Dworkin sides with those who discard this analytical ideal (at least in relation to personal identity). Ascriptions of personal identity depend upon an array of characteristics that *do not* combine neatly to provide such a test. Moreover, what is central to such ascriptions can differ from one context to another. Across a wide set of judgments, bodily identity (established by fingerprints, DNA "signatures," etc., we may suppose) are sufficient for personal identity claims. Other contexts (e.g., those involving multiple personality) make personal identity depend upon continuity of memory and character. Puzzle cases — e.g., the present one about dementia — introduce problems that our classificatory systems are not completely equipped to handle. While some philosophers have supposed that there is some right answer to these questions discoverable in the criteria that we are assumed to utilize in more ordinary contexts, on the view Dworkin adopts, this assumption is false. Such cases present themselves as matters for *decision*. The best we can do in deciding these cases is, first, proceed in a way that does as little violence as possible to the clear cases that are similar; and second, we need to apply a directly normative test. Is there, for example, some reason to suppose that regarding this being as the same person will yield an avoidable injustice?

What should we say then (on Dworkin's view) about personal identity in the dementia cases? First, we ordinarily speak as if (total) dementia were a possible outcome for a person. I can contemplate the possibility of falling into dementia. And when I think (and write) about Margo, I think (and write) of the gradual demise of memory and other capacities of a single person. We *could* (guided by some theory) shed this way of thinking and conceive instead of a kind of metamorphosis that results in a *different* person (or quasi-person). However, it seems that the most intuitively plausible solution involves thinking of Margo as the same person throughout the progression into dementia.

But what should we say about the directly normative question? Dworkin's answer to this is clearly the opposite of the one I have given above. Nothing of significant value is sacrificed

by the supposition that identity is preserved all the way into dementia. Respect for the author of an advance directive gives us a basis for decisions about the borderline case — demented Margo. It is true that we must in these cases rely on bodily continuity for the assignment of personal identity; and it is true as well that this test will not always work. But that's just a matter of facing the reality that our categories must sometimes be adapted to fit the world, and adapted in ways that seem at first *ad hoc*.

6. Some Final Doubts

In this account, Dworkin seems to strike a nice balance between philosophical theory and its real world application. Nonetheless, I find myself with some remaining doubts. In the first place, even if personal identity *is* best thought through without the assumption that there is a single criterion of personal identity that is applicable in all contexts, it does not follow that there are no *necessary* conditions of personal identity. Dworkin's arguments have not convinced me to drop the view that some minimum of psychological continuity is such a condition. Secondly, doubts can be raised about the normative claim that there is nothing wrong with this way of assimilating cases.

Psychological Continuity: The human being who is subject to the advance directive we have been considering can remember nothing of it and does not organize her life in a way that makes the directive seem appropriate. It is true that I continue to refer to her as "Margo," and have no doubt as to what human being the living will was directed toward. However, we should notice that the same point about ordinary usage could be made with regard to "Margo" if she had become irreversibly comatose or were now *dead*. But though we know exactly what "person" is referred to in directives regarding the permanently vegetative or dead Margo, we do not need to make the unlikely inference that this is because personal identity has been preserved. Human remains do not constitute a person or preserve personal identity in any meaningful sense. We do not need to suppose that someone making decisions about how much to set aside from her income to cover her own funeral expenses has made a mistake or has some extravagant theory of personal identity. Likewise, we do not need to suppose that setting aside money to cover the expenses of becoming demented requires the supposition that I could "suffer total disintegration of personality" and still retain my identity as a person.

The Normative Question: There is a significant issue that remains, however. As we have seen, Dworkin is working with a conception of a person's life taken as a whole in thinking these problems through. He would claim that what happens, not only to the demented, but also to the comatose and dead *are* matters that are relevant to questions about the value of the life, considered from this perspective. The fact that Margo can't possibly be aware that her advance directive is being followed when she is demented or comatose or dead does not prevent her treatment from having an impact on her critical interests, on her life considered as a whole. There is an interest in a certain narrative reputation — an interest in being remembered in a certain way — which is at stake in this situation. However, there is an obvious shift from the first to the third person that is involved when we consider this question in terms of such critical interests. Normally, there is no conflict between the dictates of these two viewpoints. But, the question that has been central to our discussion concerns a case where there is such a conflict. The fact that there is no psychological continuity between this being and the author of the directive — that self-identity is not present from the *inside* — does become relevant in just this case.

To see this, consider for a moment the fate of a person who suffers from amnesia, but *not* from dementia, and who is otherwise in Margo's circumstances. Now imagine that this person is you. You can remember none of the details of the life which others say you have led. You learn that someone has expressed an interest in ending your life. That person, you are told, still has this interest. You are surprised to discover that others whom you have relied on for help now believe they have an obligation to assist this person by acting for her in bringing about your death. They also report that this person's interests *are* yours, because, though you don't realize it, she *is* you. From the inside none of this makes sense. From your point of view, the person with homicidal motives seems as alien as any stranger whose case you might read about in the newspaper. Her motive for wanting you dead — that this fits best the plan of her life — is unintelligible to you.

Admittedly, this is *not* the perspective from which Margo sees the world, for she has not just lost psychological continuity. She is demented. She could not understand these reports of others about her situation. Nonetheless Margo is conscious. There is something that it is like to be Margo. She has a simple, child-like perspective on the world, and from this perspective she lacks any connection with the author of the orders for her death. That connection is maintained, not by her, but by others. It is a product of the physical continuity that usually guides our ascriptions of identity.

The problem is complicated by the fact that Margo, in drawing up the directive, was making a first person projection of what it would be like to be in this demented state. We have stipulated for the purpose of this paper that she was not mistaken in her estimate of what this state would be like. But the fact that Margo would not be psychologically continuous with this child-like being makes a difference to this projection. If Margo takes proper account of this fact in drawing up her directive, then she can no longer view the problem from a purely prudential viewpoint. The directive she has drawn up demands the death of a conscious subject who is completely unaware of her own life and aspirations. To think this through properly, she must adopt a moral point of view from which concern for another human being becomes appropriate. We have thus found some reason to suppose that there is a moral "cost" involved in Dworkin's use of bodily continuity as the test of personal identity in this type of case. Inevitably, it forces us to look at the problem from the third-person perspective.

It might be replied, however, that the directive asking for death is acceptable precisely because the events that have removed first-person personal identity (with the Margo who wrote the advance directive) have also taken away the necessary conditions of being *any* person. Allen Buchanan has used this convergence — loss of identity and loss of personhood — to defend the view that we should adhere to advance directives in this type of case.[18] He agrees with the claim that it would be wrong to impose "euthanasia" on one person because this was the will of another. He agrees as well that the loss of psychological continuity brought about by dementia of the sort under discussion would, indeed, remove personal identity. But, Buchanan argues, since these psychological incapacities also remove the conditions of personhood, it is permissible to end the life that remains. Respect for the autonomy of the former person gives us an obligation to do just this.

I cannot deny that it is an important argument or respond to it fully here. Still, I am not convinced. In general we do not (and in my view *should* not) treat (biologically) human beings who are infants or infantile as if they were disposable. Why do we seriously contemplate making an exception in this type of case? Clearly, it is the belief that we are acting on behalf of the person who has asked to die that leads us to take the option seriously under these circumstances. But, if the argument I have given is right, the loss of personal identity *removes* this special justification for euthanasia. This case is not analogous to that in which we respect a person's will to allow the biological death of their permanently vegetative body. It is not analogous precisely because the demented Margo is a conscious subject. Of course, there could be good reasons to end her life.[19] But, given the description of her inner life with which we began (a simple but remarkably happy life), and given that personal identity has been lost, we can hardly say that it is in *her* interest to die.

But perhaps if Margo is no longer a person, we should not take seriously the conscious life that remains. I will end by reversing the central features of Margo's case as a way of responding to this suggestion. Let's suppose that Margo had lived a different life and drawn up a will that was the reverse of the one we have considered so far. Instead of euthanasia, she had expressed her will to be resuscitated and kept alive through aggressive therapy for as long as possible. But let's suppose that the outcome of the disease was not the happy being that we have been discussing. Instead, Margo's condition is excruciatingly painful and tormented. Should we let the present patient's experiential interests play a role in our decisions about treatment? On my view we should do so even if it had been Margo's intention to endure this suffering. This is because Margo would not have been justified in inflicting this condition on the child-like person that would remain after the dementia had taken its course. Here it is appropriate for us to act with compassion in not adding to this torment even though it means setting aside the advance directive. In the absence of psychological continuity, that directive would lack the authority to command this fate.

Author's Note

I would like to thank Sue Campbell, John Hubert, Duncan Macintosh, Susan Sherwin, Michael Milde, and Sheldon Wein for their helpful comments on earlier drafts of this paper and thank Mary Lou Ellerton and Christine Koggel for help in preparing the manuscript for publication.

NOTES

1. Margo's case is noted by Ronald Dworkin in *Life's Dominion* (Random House: N.Y., 1994). See Chapter 8, p. 220ff. He cites it from Andrew D. Ferlick, "Margo's Logo" 265 *Journal of the American Medical Association* (1991) p. 201. Dworkin utilizes his own embellishments of this case in presenting the problem addressed in this paper.

2. This version of the case is meant to present a dilemma in its starkest form by putting it in a

context where active euthanasia will not be prosecuted. But if this feature of the case is too distracting (because it gets us into the questions about killing and letting die) one can reconstruct it so that only passive euthanasia is at issue: Margo's advance directive specifies that she is not to be given treatment for quite treatable life-threatening conditions which arise. This second scenario may, of course, involve additional dilemmas as Margo's condition deteriorates and becomes painful. The problems to be raised in this paper are independent of the issues relating to possible differences between acts and omissions.

3. The distinction is first advanced in the *Tanner Lecture*: XI entitled "Foundations of Liberal Equality" (Salt Lake City: University of Utah, 1990) section V, pp. 42-7. It is then applied to the problems of euthanasia in the final chapters of *Life's Dominion*. The importance of this distinction goes well beyond the esoteric sort of case that I have just introduced, if Dworkin is right, and we cannot understand many of the judgments we make within ethics and about human lives without taking it into account.

4. In "The Foundations of Liberal Equality," *ibid.*, Dworkin uses a contrast between "volitional" and critical interests. In this discussion I will assume that this is the same distinction.

5. Dworkin would agree, of course, that this cannot be the whole of the account of meaningful lives, any more than consistency can be sufficient within epistemology. It is possible to make consistent choices in relation to what is not itself choiceworthy, possible to lead a consistent but awful life. One might spend a life or a sizable portion of it, say, adjusting the thermostat in one's room to maintain a certain level of comfort (or painting the same image over and over). The consistency of one's dedication to these pursuits could hardly be said to give real value to such a life. Thus, the coherence of a life, is (at most) a necessary condition of its meaningfulness. That something is consistent with what I have done does not entail that it is in my critical interests.

6. Christine Korsgaard has written about this under the description of "practical identity" in *The Sources of Normativity* (Cambridge: Cambridge

University Press, 1996). See especially Chapter Three.

7. The analogy between lives and legal systems is imperfect, of course. It is often true that *arbitrary* commitments, e.g., arbitrarily adopted goals are the source of worthwhile pursuits in the lives of individuals. Solving the four color problem, climbing K-2, discovering hitherto unknown properties of sub-atomic particles — each of these has provided inspiration and continuity in the lives of some people, though these are arbitrarily adopted goals. But there seems to be a contrast here. The function of legal systems in relation to justice might appear to leave little room — or none at all — for arbitrarily chosen pursuits; and good legal systems will converge upon highly similar decisions. But the contrast is not as sharp as this makes it seem. In the first place, persons leading good lives will find themselves converging upon many matters of moral principle. And, secondly, there are more or less arbitrary features of legal system, both at the level of specific conventions (how many signatures are required for wills) and the goals which end up being given legal implementation, e.g., supporting the massive infrastructure necessary to get to the moon, or subsidizing a steel company.

8. We should note that, of course, given a different background her autonomous decision might have been the opposite. After a life filled with responsibilities one might decide that one was entitled to a "retirement" freed from all this — or religious beliefs might forbid one to "play God" even with respect to oneself. Thus, either decision (for or against help in ending her life) could be a manifestation of integrity, though a given person with a particular biography may only be able to choose one of these options if she is to preserve her integrity.

9. A puzzle arises if we suppose that Margo can make a *mistake* about her critical interests. It seems obvious that a person could exercise bad judgment in making such a decision, just as a director could choose to end a film in a way that destroys it. The puzzle is this. Would we be recognizing Margo's autonomy if the advance directive were actually based on such a bad judgment?

Suppose that Margo's life has been a life of never "playing God." Everything she stood for seems to be undermined by her "last will" as to the way her life should end. What do we say then? Notice that we often do have conflicts between the autonomy of a person and the protection of interests over all. A decision to take up smoking can be an autonomous one despite the fact that it is foolish. Is there a parallel exercise of autonomy in which one's own *critical* interests are flouted? Dworkin's answer to this question seems to be negative. The point of autonomy rights he argues is to protect a person's critical interests. And, one cannot just "exercise" autonomy through any random choice, a choice that cannot be connected with one's life. Some consistency of self and hence of choice (i.e., some integrity) is necessarily involved in any autonomous decisions on this view. Now, if this is right, then there can be occasions in which the advance directive is not a genuine reflection of autonomy, and hence protection of autonomy will not support its enforcement. One of the problems for this account is that it rules out some types of radical change in the self-chosen life of a person.

10. Rebecca Dresser, "Missing Persons: Legal Perceptions of Incompetent Patients," *Rutgers Law Review* 46:2 (1994) pp. 609-719. See also "Dworkin on Dementia: Elegant Theory, Questionable Policy," *Hastings Center Report* 26:6 (1995) pp. 32-38.

11. "[I]f honoring an advance directive required others to compromise the clear welfare interests of the patient now before them, the directive should be disregarded. Our affection for autonomy should not be permitted to sanction the inhumane treatment of people who have lost the capacity to appreciate the forces that drove their earlier choices, but not the capacity to be harmed by those choices" Dresser (1994) p. 715.

12. This description begs some of the questions about capacity and identity that I will raise later.

13. "It seems plain that each of these — pleasurable experiences and the satisfaction of [critical interests] — must find some place in any acceptable overall philosophical account of well being ..." (*The Foundations of Liberal Equality*, p. 43). To be sure, there are lives that move fairly far in this direction, those of the ascetic or Puritan come to mind. Dworkin can make some sense of these lives, by stressing the way in which they (like scaling Mt. Everest) can manifest success in relation to a self-imposed challenge. But to most of us it seems plausible to say that these are not ideal human lives.

14. Rebecca Dresser (*supra*, note 10) has developed arguments against Dworkin's policy recommendations in "Dworkin on Dementia: Elegant Theory, Questionable Policy" which do involve questioning the protection of autonomy as the basis for decision in cases involving dementia.

15. See Allen Buchanan, "Advance Directives and the Problem of Personal Identity," *Philosophy and Public Affairs*: 17 (1988) pp. 277-302.

16. Ronald Dworkin, "Philosophical Issues Concerning the Rights of Patients Suffering Permanent Dementia," (Springfield, VA: US Office of Technology Assessment, 1987) Section 7, pp. 85-108.

17. *Ibid.*, p. 86.

18. See Allen Buchanan (*supra*, note 15). The argument is similar to that of Michael Tooley in "In Defense of Abortion and Infanticide," in Jan Narveson, *Moral Issues* (Oxford: Oxford University Press, 1984) pp. 215-33.

19. If Alzheimer's patients became "utility monsters" because of their drain on health resources, ending such lives *might* be justified by the need to prevent the destruction of the health care system. However, this justification raises questions that are not the subject of this paper. It depends in no way on the protection of autonomy or critical interests through the dictates of an advance directive.

STUDY QUESTIONS

1 Michael Stingl identifies two conceptions of equality within the liberal tradition. Outline these conceptions and show how Stingl applies them to an analysis of the different approaches to health care in Canada and the U.S.

2 What concerns are raised by Stingl about implementing a two-tier system of health care in Canada? Do you think that autonomy is enhanced or diminished when universal health care is provided by the state? Provide reasons for your answer.

3 According to Margaret Battin, what is gained by placing the issue of euthanasia in an international context and examining the norms and practices in other places? Why study the norms and practices in the three countries of the U.S., the Netherlands, and Germany?

4 Outline the different practices with respect to euthanasia in the Netherlands, Germany, and the U.S. and evaluate the objections that Battin raises to the policies and practices in each country.

5 What conclusions does Battin draw with respect to the question of the permissibility of assisted suicide in the U.S.? Do you agree with her analysis of the differences between the U.S. and the Netherlands and would these differences justify changing the policy in the U.S.? Provide reasons for your answers.

6 Identify the areas of agreement and disagreement between Battin and Thomas Cavanaugh with respect to their respective analyses of the importance of individual autonomy. Do context and conditions matter with respect to an assessment of autonomy? Why or why not?

7 According to Cavanaugh, what is the standard justification for physician-assisted suicide? How does the standard justification result in a tension between the two justifications of respecting a patient's wanting to die and the patient's having a medically established good reason for suicide? How does the soft-paternalist position avoid the tension?

8 What is the asymmetry in the standard justification and how does Cavanaugh defeat possible solutions to the asymmetry problem? Do you think that Cavanaugh's arguments support the conclusion that there is no sound basis for the legalization of physician-assisted suicide? Provide reasons for your answer.

9 Harriet McBryde Johnson claims that Peter Singer would argue that the disabled person that she is should have been killed at birth. What are Singer's arguments for this? (You could also read Singer's paper from Chapter Four on Animal Rights in this volume.)

10 Why is Johnson ambivalent about having accepted the invitation to speak to Singer's class, answering student questions, and engaging with someone perceived as her enemy?

11 Is Johnson's testimony about her life and experiences important to your assessment of Singer's arguments in favor of ending the lives of those with severe disabilities? Provide reasons for your answer.

12 What is the distinction between critical and experiential interests in Nathan Brett's account meant to capture? Is this distinction useful for evaluating whether Margo's life should be ended? Why or why not?

13 Should Margo's living will be carried out and the life of the person with Alzheimer's be ended? Formulate your answer by outlining and evaluating Brett's answer to this question.

SUGGESTED READINGS

Asch, Adrienne, and Gail Geller. "Feminism, Bioethics, and Genetics." In *Feminism & Bioethics: Beyond Reproduction*, edited by Susan M. Wolf. New York, NY: Oxford University Press, 1996.

Asch, Adrienne, and Michelle Fine. "Shared Dreams: A Left Perspective on Disability Rights and Reproductive Rights." *Radical America*, v. 18, no. 4 (1984): 51-58.

Bachelard, Sarah. "On Euthanasia: Blindspots in the Argument from Mercy." *Journal of Applied Philosophy*, v. 19, no. 2 (2002): 131-40.

Bayles, Michael D. "Allocation of Scarce Medical Resources." *Public Affairs Quarterly*, v. 4, no. 1 (January 1990): 1-16.

Beauchamp, Dan E. "Public Health as Social Justice." *Inquiry*, v. 13 (March 1976): 3-14.

Blank, Robert H. *The Price of Life: The Future of American Health Care.* New York, NY: Columbia University Press, 1997.

Brock, Dan. "Quality of Life Measures in Health Care and Medical Ethics." In *The Quality of Life*, edited by Martha C. Nussbaum and Amartya Sen. Oxford: Clarendon Press, 1992.

Buchanan, Allen E. "The Right to a Decent Minimum of Health Care." *Philosophy & Public Affairs* (Winter 1984): 55-78.

Callahan, Daniel. *What Kind of Life?* New York, NY: Simon & Schuster, 1990.

——. "When Self-Determination Runs Amok." *Hastings Center Report* (March-April 1992): 52-55.

Daniels, Norman. "Health Care Needs and Distributive Justice." In *In Search of Equity: Health Needs and the Health Care System*, edited by Ronald Bayer, Arthur Caplan, and Norman Daniels. New York, NY: Plenum Press, 1983.

—— . *Just Health Care.* Cambridge: Cambridge University Press, 1985.

Roberts, Dorothy E. "Reconstructing the Patient: Starting with Women of Color." In *Feminism & Bioethics: Beyond Reproduction*, edited by Susan M. Wolf. New York, NY: Oxford University Press, 1996.

Rothman, David J. "The International Organ Traffic." *New York Review of Books* (26 March 1998): 14-17.

Rumsey, Jean P. "Justice, Care, and Questionable Dichotomies." *Hypatia*, v. 12, no. 1 (Winter 1997): 99-113.

Sherwin, Susan. "Gender, Race, and Class in the Delivery of Health Care." In *No Longer Patient: Feminist Ethics and Health Care.* Philadelphia, PA: Temple University Press, 1992.

Wolf, Susan. "Gender, Feminism, and Death: Physician-Assisted Suicide and Euthanasia." In *Feminism & Bioethics: Beyond Reproduction*, edited by Susan M. Wolf. New York, NY: Oxford University Press, 1996.

CHAPTER THREE:
PORNOGRAPHY AND HATE SPEECH

INTRODUCTION

We have established that a discourse of individual rights has been central to debates on reproductive rights and euthanasia as they have taken place in liberal societies. Individual rights are also central to questions about whether the state is ever justified in censoring material or speech. John Stuart Mill provides a defense of freedom of speech that has become foundational in liberal societies. He argues that people should be free to express their views and to have access to a range of views because this freedom is essential to the free flow and discussion of ideas from which truth can emerge. On this account, an individual's right to freedom of expression should only be restricted if it causes clear and direct harm to other individuals. This position has shaped the debate in many liberal societies about pornography and hate speech, where much of the discussion has centered on the value of individual freedom and the justifications for limiting it.

As has been the case with the moral issues examined in all three volumes of this collection, the turn to factors of globalization and multiculturalism raises questions about how debates are framed in liberal theory. A particular set of questions are raised in connection with the issues of pornography and hate speech in this chapter. What does the free flow of ideas mean in a global context in which information is so readily available through the media and the Internet and accessible to people in all parts of the world? How do we analyze harm when technological advances allow people to interact and form relationships with people anywhere in the world for purposes of buying and selling images and services? Does an analysis of harm to members of traditionally disadvantaged groups challenge liberal accounts of individual freedom, freedom of speech, the free flow of ideas, and social responsibility? Should knowing about discrimination

within and across borders affect how we understand the effects of pornography and policies regarding it?

The chapter opens with an article by Ronald Dworkin, who gives a strong defense of liberal arguments against censorship by providing a critical analysis of Catharine MacKinnon's feminist defense of state regulation of pornography. Dworkin acknowledges that the feminist movement has given new form to campaigns to outlaw pornography in the U.S., campaigns that were once dominated by conservatives. He admits that pornography is the clearest expression of the message that women exist primarily to provide sexual service to men. He also admits that pornography is offensive and makes no contribution to political or intellectual debate. It would seem then that liberals should be uncomfortable about defending it and that society would lose nothing if pornography were banned. This is where Dworkin's agreement with MacKinnon ends.

Dworkin focuses his critique on a new argument of MacKinnon's: even if the publication of literature degrading to women is protected by the First Amendment, this material violates the competing constitutional value of the equal protection clause of the Fourteenth Amendment. The courts, argues MacKinnon, should resolve the conflict in favor of censorship because pornography undermines women's equality and contributes nothing of any importance to political debate. On this account, censoring pornography should be regarded like other kinds of institutional policies designed to promote equality of opportunity, policies such as prohibiting discrimination against women and blacks and university regulations regarding hate speech. Dworkin claims that this argument has broad and devastating implications because it would allow national and state governments to censor any expression that might reasonably be thought to sustain or exacerbate the unequal positions of women or racial, ethnic, and other minorities.

Dworkin argues that free speech contributes to political equality. It exposes corruption, generates new ideas, and refutes old ones through public debate. It demands that everyone have a chance to influence policies and elections, and it allows a diversity of social conventions, opinions, prejudices, life styles, and cultures to flourish. He argues that the ideals of political equality demand that no one be prevented from influencing the shared moral environment. Odious views cannot be blocked in advance by criminal law, but instead should be discredited by the disgust, outrage, and ridicule of other people. Dworkin concludes that the U.S. should not follow the lead of other countries in demoting freedom of speech as an elitist, inegalitarian ideal that has been of little value to women, blacks, and others without power. To follow that lead is to allow a majority to define some people as too corrupt, offensive, or radical to join in the informal moral life of the nation.

Dworkin criticizes many of the feminist arguments on the side of censoring pornography and/or hate speech. Like Dworkin, Marvin Glass examines feminist arguments, but he focuses on disagreements among feminists on the issue of censorship. Glass concentrates on two specific arguments by anti-censorship feminists — feminists who argue that the state cannot be trusted as a vehicle for their liberation and feminists who argue that a free market in sexual imagery is currently in women's best interest — and raises objections to each. Feminists who defend the first argument point out that a police and judiciary controlled primarily by sexist and homophobic men are more likely to suppress lesbian sexual representations or even feminist literature than material which is offensive and degrading to women. Glass agrees that feminist politics will not succeed in transforming the state into a pro-woman institution, but he argues that a realistic feminist political agenda is to add a strategy of fighting for feminist-inspired anti-pornography legislation to existing campaigns for pay equity and affirmation action and against sexual harassment and sexual violence. All of these strategies make use of state institutions to further the goals of feminism. Feminists who defend the second argument endorse a strategy of increasing funding so that there is more speech, literature, and imagery with positive and liberating portrayals of women's sexuality. Glass argues that leaving the ownership and control of pornography to market forces is unlikely to empower women or to ensure feminist sexual expression a prominent place in an increasingly concentrated and powerful global market. While civil and/or criminal laws may not succeed in censoring only that which degrades and exploits women, the losses in the arena of sexual expression are offset by the greater losses incurred in campaigning against the multi-billion dollar pornography industry in the marketplace.

In the third reading, Heather MacRae also examines debates within feminism about the issue of censorship, but does so in the context of European discussions of and policies regarding pornography and censorship. Her examination lends support to the idea that history, tradition, and culture matter with respect to the framing of debates and the formulation of policy. In other words, her account would allow that Dworkin's analysis of the primacy of freedom of speech might be specific to the history and culture of the U.S. MacRae argues that discussions about censorship in Europe have been made more complex through the impact of the European Union. There are differences in histories, values, and legislation regarding censorship in specific European countries as well as differences in the development of feminist movements and of legislation. Now comes the possibility for shaping legislation at the level of the European Union itself. MacRae examines these complexities in the context of discussing attempts by feminists in Germany to reframe the regulation of pornography at the German and European levels.

Germany's regulation of pornography was based on the perceived need to protect the moral development of minors. MacRae summarizes efforts by feminists to influence the policy-making process in Germany so that legislation would reflect a feminist position that defines pornography as discrimination against women. She uses the concept "triangle of empowerment" to suggest why some forms of feminist mobilization in Germany were better able to influence policy than others. Ultimately, however, feminists have had limited success shaping legislation at the German level. MacRae argues that feminists are finding new opportunities at the European level to reframe the pornography debate because greater cross-border flow has increased the trafficking in women, violence against women, sexism in advertising and the media, and child pornography and resulted in demands for legislation in these areas. MacRae thinks that the reframing of these issues at the European level could invigorate debate on pornography, promote the feminist conception of it as discriminatory, and make it possible to reframe legislation at the national level.

The fourth reading by Alison Minea and Christine Koggel picks up on a thread mentioned in the Glass and MacRae readings: the idea that the increased flow of trade and information across borders may require the reframing of conceptions of pornography and how to deal with it. The Internet allows individuals from anywhere in the world to access information and images that were once available only in stores and public spaces. The Internet provides a vast array of images and services that can be accessed in the privacy of one's home with little or no restrictions. Moreover, increasingly sophisticated technology makes it difficult to identify people using the Internet for these purposes. From the comfort of home, people can form relationships, virtual and real, with individuals or groups from anywhere in the world and say, be, and do whatever they desire with little or no monitoring or control. The Internet would appear to be a place where an individual's right to privacy is upheld and promoted.

Minea and Koggel use this context of changes brought by the Internet to raise objections to traditional liberal arguments that defend the right to privacy. Privacy has been defended as necessary

for protecting the individual from unwanted intrusion in his or her home and for allowing individuals the freedom to choose and develop relationships without censorship or interference. They argue that changes to relationships brought about by the Internet call for attention to the relationships that get formed and the effect that these have on individuals. They describe features of the Internet that allow anonymity and greater individual control over what one says and is exposed to. These are features, they argue, that diminish aspects of face-to-face contact that matter with respect to interacting with others, especially the moral responsibility and accountability we have for explaining and justifying our behavior and speech with others.

Minea and Koggel borrow insights from relational theory to reject the traditional liberal conception of individuals as self-determining entities who thrive when there is no interference with the pursuit of their desires, projects, and goals. They defend a relational conception of the self as necessarily in and shaped by relationships with others. When the focus is on the kinds of relationships that are formed on and through the Internet, moral issues of accountability and responsibility are raised. Minea's and Koggel's main concern is not with legal arguments for controlling and monitoring activity on the Internet, but with moral arguments about the implications of the isolated nature of Internet usage on the beliefs and values shaped at the level of the individual, communities, nations, and relations between countries.

In the final reading in this chapter, Mari Matsuda explores the tension between the stories told by victims of racist speech and the First Amendment story of free speech. Victims are restricted in their personal freedom because they may need to quit jobs, leave their homes, avoid certain public places, curtail their own speech, and modify their behavior to avoid receiving hate messages. The effect on one's self-esteem and sense of personal security of being hated and despised can be devastating. Matsuda argues that these victim stories present perspectives on what it is to live with fear and be effected by racist messages, but these stories are absent in the legal domain where judges and lawyers cannot imagine a life diminished by hate propaganda. When victims of racist speech are ignored, we burden one group, a traditionally disadvantaged one, with a disproportionate share of the costs of absolutist free speech principles.

Matsuda points out that the current trend in the international community, evident in Article 4 of the International Convention on the Elimination of All Forms of Racial Discrimination, the Race Relations Act in the United Kingdom, and Sections of the Canadian Criminal Code, is to outlaw racist hate propaganda. But the U.S. is out of step with these international developments and continues to defend the primacy of First Amendment values of free speech, values that are so entrenched as to seem irreconcilable with the values of equality and full participation asserted in the laws prohibiting racist speech in other countries. Matsuda argues that in a society that expresses moral judgments through the law and in which the use of law is a characteristic response to many other kinds of social phenomena, the absence of laws against racist speech in the U.S. is telling. She advocates that Americans draw from the international standard, adapt existing law, and create new law to limit hate propaganda.

WOMEN AND PORNOGRAPHY

Ronald Dworkin

Ronald Dworkin is Professor of Philosophy and Frank Henry Sommer Professor of Law at New York University. He is also Professor of Jurisprudence at Oxford and a Fellow of University College. Dworkin has authored many articles in journals as well in the New York Review of Books. *Among his books are* Taking Rights Seriously *(1977),* A Matter of Principle *(1985),* Life's Dominion: An Argument about Abortion, Euthanasia, and Individual Freedom *(1993), and* Freedom's Law: The Moral Reading of the American Constitution *(1996).*

Dworkin is critical of feminist arguments for censoring pornography and focuses his attention on those of Catharine MacKinnon in Only Words. *He raises objections to MacKinnon's specific argument that the constitutional guarantees of free speech and press in the First Amendment are justifiably overridden in the case of pornography, which in contributing to the general subordination of women violates the competing constitutional value of equality embedded in the equal protection clause of the Fourteenth Amendment. Dworkin argues that liberals defend pornography on the basis of the First Amendment precisely because this protects equality in all the processes through which moral and political views are shaped.*

1.

People once defended free speech to protect the rights of firebrands attacking government, or dissenters resisting an established church, or radicals campaigning for unpopular political causes. Free speech was plainly worth fighting for, and it still is in many parts of the world where these rights hardly exist. But in America now, free-speech partisans find themselves defending mainly racists shouting "nigger" or Nazis carrying swastikas or — most often — men looking at pictures of naked women with their legs spread open.

Conservatives have fought to outlaw pornography in the United States for a long time: for decades the Supreme Court has tried, though without much success, to define a limited category of "obscenity" that the Constitution allows to be banned. But the campaign for outlawing all forms of pornography has been given new and fiercer form, in recent years, by the feminist movement. It might seem odd that feminists have devoted such energy to that campaign: other issues, including abortion and the fight for women's equality in employment and politics seem so much more important. No doubt mass culture is in various ways an obstacle to sexual equality, but the most popular forms of that culture — the view of women presented in soap operas and commercials, for example — are much greater obstacles to that equality than the dirty films watched by a small minority.

But feminists' concentration on pornography nevertheless seems easy to explain. Pornographic photographs, films, and videos are the starkest possible expression of the idea feminists most loath: that women exist principally to provide sexual service to men. Advertisements, soap operas, and popular fiction may actually do more to spread that idea in our culture, but pornography is the rawest, most explicit symbol of it. Like swastikas and burning crosses, pornography is deeply offensive in itself, whether or not it causes any other injustice or harm. It is also particularly vulnerable politically: the religious right supports feminists on this issue, though on few others, so feminists have a much greater chance to win political campaigns for censorship than any of the other campaigns they fight.

And pornography seems vulnerable on principle as well. The conventional explanation of why freedom of speech is important is Mill's theory that truth is most likely to emerge from a "marketplace" of ideas freely exchanged and debated. But most pornography makes no contribution at all to political or intellectual debate: it is preposterous to think that we are more likely to reach truth about anything at all because pornographic videos are available. So liberals defending a right to pornography find themselves triply on the defensive: their view is politically weak, deeply offensive to many women, and intellectually doubtful. Why, then, should we defend pornography? Why should we care if people can no longer watch films of people copulating for the camera, or of women being whipped and enjoying it? What would we lose, except a repellent industry?

Professor Catharine MacKinnon's new book of three short essays, *Only Words*, offers a sharp answer to the last of these questions: society would lose nothing if all pornography were banned, she says, except that women would lose their chains. MacKinnon is the most prominent of the feminists against pornography. She believes that men want to subordinate women, to turn them into sexual devices, and that pornography is the weapon they use to achieve that result. In a series of highly charged articles and speeches, she has tried to talk or shock other women into that view. In 1986, she wrote that

> Pornography constructs what a woman is as what men want from sex. This is what pornography means. ... It institutionalizes the sexuality of male supremacy, fusing the eroticisation of dominance and submission with the social construction of male and female. ... Pornog-

raphy is a harm of male supremacy made difficult to see because of its pervasiveness, potency, and principally, because of its success in making the world a pornographic place.[1]

Only Words is full of language apparently intended to shock. It refers repeatedly to "penises slamming into vaginas," offers page after page of horrifying descriptions of women being whipped, tortured, and raped, and begins with this startling passage:

> You grow up with your father holding you down and covering your mouth so that another man can make a horrible, searing pain between your legs. When you are older, your husband ties you to the bed and drips hot wax on your nipples and brings in other men to watch and makes you smile through it. Your doctor will not give you drugs he has addicted you to unless you suck his penis.

The book offers arguments as well as images, however, and these are presented as a kind of appeal, to the general public, from a judicial decision MacKinnon lost. In 1983, she and a feminist colleague, Andrea Dworkin, drafted an ordinance that outlawed or attached civil penalties to all pornography, defined as the "graphic sexually explicit subordination of women through pictures and/or words" that meet one or more of a series of tests (some of which are impossibly vague) including: "women are presented dehumanized as sexual objects, things, or commodities"; or "women are presented as sexual objects experiencing sexual pleasure in rape, incest, or other sexual assaults"; or "in positions of sexual submission, servility, or display"; or "women's body parts — including but not limited to vaginas, breasts, or buttocks — are exhibited such that women are reduced to those parts."

In 1984, largely through their efforts, a similar ordinance was adopted by the Indianapolis legislature. The ordinance included no exception for literary or artistic value, and it could plausibly be interpreted to outlaw not only classic pornography like John Cleland's *Memoirs of a Woman of*

Pleasure, but a great deal else, including, for example, D.H. Lawrence's novels and Titian's *Danae*. In 1985, the Seventh Circuit Court of Appeals held the ordinance unconstitutional on the grounds that it violated the First Amendment's guarantees of free speech and press, and in 1986, the Supreme Court declined to overrule the Seventh Circuit's decision.[2]

Only Words offers several arguments in favor of the Indianapolis ordinance and against the Seventh Circuit's ruling, though some of these are run together and must be disentangled to make sense. Some of MacKinnon's arguments are old ones that I have already considered in these pages.[3] But she devotes most of the book to a different and striking claim. She argues that even if the publication of literature degrading to women is protected by the First Amendment, as the Seventh Circuit declared, such material offends another, competing constitutional value: the ideal of equality embedded in the equal protection clause of the Fourteenth Amendment, which declares that no state may deprive any person of the equal protection of the laws. If so, she says, then the courts must balance the two constitutional values, and since pornography contributes nothing of any importance to political debate, they should resolve the conflict in favor of equality and censorship.

Unlike MacKinnon's other arguments, this claim has application far beyond the issue of pornography. If her analysis is right, national and state governments have much broader constitutional powers than most lawyers think to prohibit or censor any "politically incorrect" expression that might reasonably be thought to sustain or exacerbate the unequal positions of women or of racial, ethnic, or other minorities. I shall therefore concentrate on this new argument, but I shall first comment briefly on MacKinnon's more conventional points.

2.

In *Only Words*, she repeats the now familiar claim that pornography significantly increases the number of rapes and other sexual crimes. If that claim could be shown to be even probable, through reliable research, it would provide a very strong though not necessarily decisive argument for censorship. But in spite of MacKinnon's fervent declarations, no reputable study has concluded that pornography is a significant cause of sexual crime: many of them conclude, on the contrary, that the causes of violent personality lie mainly in childhood, before exposure to pornography can have had any effect, and that desire for pornography is a symptom rather than a case of deviance.[4] MacKinnon tries to refute these studies, and it is important to see how weak her arguments are. One of them, though repeated several times, is only a metaphysical sleight-of-hand. She several times insists that pornography is not "only words" because it is a "reality." She says that because it is used to stimulate a sexual act — masturbation — it is sex, which seems to suggest that a film or description of rape is itself a kind of rape. But obviously that does not help to show that pornography causes rape in the criminal sense and it is only the latter claim that can count as a reason for outlawing it.

Sometimes MacKinnon relies on breathtaking hyperbole disguised as common sense. "Sooner or later," she declares, "in one way or another, the consumers want to live out the pornography further in three dimensions. Sooner or later, in one way or another, they do. *It* does make them want to; when they believe they can, when they feel they can get away, *they* do." (Confronted with the fact that many men who read pornography commit no rapes, she suggests that their rapes are unreported.)[5] Elsewhere she appeals to doubtful and unexamined correlations: In a recent article, for example, she declares that "pornography saturated Yugoslavia before the war," and suggests that pornography is therefore responsible for the horrifying and widely reported rapes of Croatian and Muslim women by Serbian soldiers.[6] But, as George Kennan has noted in these pages, rape was also "ubiquitous" in the Balkan wars of 1913, well before any "saturation" by pornography had begun.[7]

Her main arguments, however, are anecdotal: she cites examples of rapists and murderers who report themselves as having been consumers of pornography, like Thomas Shireo, who was sentenced to death in 1981 in Indiana for raping and then killing a young woman (and copulating with her corpse) and who pleaded that he was not responsible because he was a lifelong pornography reader. Such evidence is plainly unreliable, however, not just because it is so often self-serving, but because, as the feminists Deborah Cameron and Elizabeth Fraser have pointed out, criminals are likely to take their views about their own motives from the folklore of their community, whether it is sound or not, rather than from serious analysis of their motives. (Cameron and Fraser, who favor banning pornography on other grounds, concede that "arguments that pornography 'causes' violent acts are, indeed, inadequate.")[8]

MacKinnon's second argument for censorship is a radically different one: that pornography should be banned because it "silences" women by making it more difficult for them to speak and less likely that others will understand what they say. Because of pornography, she says,

> You learn that language does not belong to you. ... You learn that speech is not what you say but what your abusers do to you. ... You develop a self who is ingratiating and obsequious and imitative and aggressively passive and silent.[9]

In an earlier work she put the point even more graphically:

> Who listens to a woman with a penis in her mouth? ... anyone who cannot walk down the street or even lie down in her own bed without keeping her eyes cast down and her body clenched against assault is unlikely to have much to say about the issues of the day. ... Any system of freedom of expression that does not address a problem where the free speech of men silences the free speech of women.... is not serious about securing freedom of expression.[10]

On this view, which has been argued more elaborately by others,[11] it is women not pornographers

who need First Amendment protection, because pornography humiliates or frightens them into silence and conditions men to misunderstand what they say. (It conditions them to think, for example — as some stupid judges have instructed juries in rape trials — that when a woman says no she sometimes means yes.) Because this argument cites the First Amendment as a reason for banning, not for protecting, pornography, it has the appeal of paradox. But it is premised on an unacceptable proposition: that the right to free speech includes a right to circumstances that encourage one to speak, and a right that others grasp and respect what one means to say.

These are obviously not rights that any society can recognize or enforce. Creationists, flat-earthers, and bigots, for example, are ridiculed in many parts of America now; that ridicule undoubtedly dampens the enthusiasm many of them have for speaking out and limits the attention others pay to what they say. Many political and constitutional theorists, it is true, insist that if freedom of speech is to have any value, it must include some right to the opportunity to speak: they say that a society in which only the rich enjoy access to newspapers, television, or other public media does not accord a genuine right to free speech. But it goes far beyond that to insist that freedom of speech includes not only opportunity to speak to the public but a guarantee of a sympathetic or even competent understanding of what one says.

MacKinnon's third argument centers on the production rather than the distribution or consumption of pornography: she argues that women who act in pornographic films suffer actual, direct sexual subordination, compounded by the fact that their degradation is recorded for posterity. She points out that some women are coerced or tricked into making pornographic films, and mentions the notorious "snuff" films which are said to record the actual murder of women. But of course all these crimes can be prosecuted without banning pornography, and, as MacKinnon herself concedes, it would be wrong to "rely on the fact that some pornography is made through coercion as a legal basis for restricting all of it." Laws banning child pornography are indeed justified on the grounds that children may be damaged by appearing in pornographic films. But these laws, like many others that treat children differently, suppose that they are not competent to understand and consent to acts that may well be against their present and future interests.

It would plainly be a mistake to assume that women (or men) who appear in pornographic films do so unwillingly. Our economic system does, it is true, make it difficult for many women to find satisfactory, fulfilling employment, and may well encourage some of them to accept roles in pornographic films they would otherwise reject. The system, as MacKinnon grimly notes, works to the benefit of the pornographers. But it also works to the benefit of many other employers — fast-food chains, for example — who are able to employ women at low wages. There is great economic injustice in America, but that is not reason for depriving poor women of an economic opportunity some of them may prefer to the available alternatives.

I should mention a fourth consideration that MacKinnon puts forward, though it is difficult to find an argument in it. She says that much pornography is not just speech — it is not "only words" — because it produces erections in men and provides them with masturbatory fantasies. (She warns her readers never to "underestimate the power of an erection.") Her view of the psychology of sexual arousal is mechanical — she thinks men who read pornography "are sexually habituated to its kick, a process that is largely unconscious and works as primitive conditioning, with pictures and words as sexual stimuli." In any case, she thinks that pornography's physiological power deprives it of First Amendment protection: "An orgasm is not an argument," she says, "and cannot be argued with. Compared with a thought, it raises far less difficult speech issues, if it raises any at all." But that seems a plain non sequitur: a piece of music or a work of art or poetry does not lose whatever protection the First Amendment affords it when some people find it sexually arousing, even if that effect does not depend on its argumentative or aesthetic merits, or whether it has any such merits at all.

3.

The continued popularity of bad argument such as those in *Only Words* testifies to the strength of the real but hidden reason why so many people despise pornography and want to ban it. The sado-masochistic genre of pornography, particularly, is so comprehensibly degrading that we are appalled and shamed by its existence. Contrary to MacKinnon's view, almost all men, I think, are as disgusted by it as almost all women. Because those who want to forbid pornography know that offensiveness alone does not justify censorship, however, they disguise their repulsion as concern that pornography will cause rape, or silence women, or harm the women who make it.

In the most interesting parts of *Only Words*, MacKinnon offers a new argument that is also designed to transcend mere repulsion. She says that the way in which pornography is offensive — that it portrays women as submissive victims who enjoy torture and mutilation — contributes to the unequal opportunities of women in American society, and therefore contradicts the values meant to be protected by the equal protection clause. She concedes, for the sake of this argument, that in spite of its minimal contribution to intellectual or political debate, pornography is protected under the First Amendment. But that First Amendment protection must be balanced, she says, against the Fourteenth Amendment's requirement that people be treated equally. "The law of equality and the law of freedom of speech are on a collision course in this country," she says, and she argues that the balance, which has swung too far toward liberty, must now be redressed.

The censorship of pornography, she says, should be regarded as like other kinds of government action designed to create genuine equality of opportunity. It is now accepted by almost everyone that government may properly prohibit discrimination against blacks and women in employment and education, for example. But such discrimination may take the form, not merely of refusing them jobs or university places, but of subjecting those who do manage to find jobs or places to an environment of insult and prejudice that makes work or education less attractive or even impossible. Government prohibits racial or sexual harassment at work — it punishes employers who subject blacks to racial insult or women to sexual pressures, in spite of the fact that these objectionable practices are carried out through speech — and many universities have adopted "speech codes" that prohibit racial insults in classrooms or on campus.

Banning or publishing pornography, MacKinnon suggests, should be regarded as a more general remedy of the same kind. If pornography contributes to the general subordination of women by picturing them as sexual or servile objects, as she believes it does, then eliminating pornography can also be defended as serving equality of opportunity even though it restricts liberty.[12] The "egalitarian" argument for censorship is in many ways like the "silencing" argument I described earlier: it supposes not that pornography significantly increases sexual crimes of violence, but that it works more insidiously to damage the standing and power of women within the community. But the "egalitarian" argument is in two ways different and apparently more cogent.

First, it claims not a new and paradoxical conflict within the idea of liberty, as the silencing argument does, but a conflict between liberty and equality, two ideals that many political philosophers think more often in conflict. Second, it is more limited in its scope. The "silencing" argument supposes that everyone — the bigot and the creationist as well the social reformer — has a right to whatever respectful attention on the part of others is necessary to encourage him to speak his mind and to guarantee that he will be correctly understood; and that is absurd. The "egalitarian" argument, on the contrary, supposes only that certain groups — those that are victims of persisting disadvantage in our society — should not be subjected to the kind of insult, harassment, or abuse that has contributed to that disadvantage.

But the "egalitarian" argument is nevertheless much broader and more dangerous in its scope

than might first appear. The analogies MacKinnon proposes — to sexual harassment laws and university speech codes — are revealing, because though each of these forms of regulation might be said to serve a general egalitarian purpose, they are usually defended on much more limited and special grounds. Laws against sexual harassment are designed to protect women not from the diffuse effects of whatever derogatory opinions about them are part of the general culture, but from direct sexual taunts and other degrading language in the workplace.[13] University speech codes are defended on a different ground: they are said to serve an educational purpose by preserving the calm and reflective atmosphere of mutual respect and of appreciation for a diversity of cultures and opinions that is essential for effective teaching and research.

I do not mean that such regulations raise no problems about free speech. They do. Even if university speech codes, for example, are enforced fairly and scrupulously (and in the charged atmosphere of university politics they often are not) they sometimes force teachers and students to compromise or suppress their opinions by erring on the side of safety, and some speech codes may actually be unconstitutional. I mean only that constraints on speech at work and on the campus can be defended without appealing to the frightening principle that considerations of equality require that some people not be free to express their tastes or convictions or preferences anywhere. MacKinnon's argument for banning pornography from the community as a whole does presuppose this principle, however, and accepting her argument would therefore have devastating consequences.

Government could then forbid the graphic or visceral or emotionally charged expression of any opinion or conviction that might reasonably offend a disadvantaged group. It could outlaw performances of *The Merchant of Venice*, or films about professional women who neglect their children, or caricatures or parodies of homosexuals in nightclub routines. Courts would have to balance the value of such expression, as a contribution to public debate or learning, against the damage it might cause to the standing or sensibilities of its targets. MacKinnon thinks that pornography is different from other forms of discriminatory or hostile speech. But the argument she makes for banning it would apply to much else. She pointedly declares that freedom of speech is respected too much by Americans and that the Supreme Court was right in 1952 when it sustained a prosecution of anti-Semitic literature — a decision it has since abandoned[14] — and wrong in 1978 when it struck down an ordinance banning a Nazi march in Illinois.[15]

So if we must make the choice between liberty and equality that MacKinnon envisages — if the two constitutional values really are on a collision course — we should have to choose liberty because the alternative would be the despotism of thought-police.

But is she right that the two values do conflict in this way? Can we escape despotism only by cheating on the equality the constitution also guarantees? The most fundamental egalitarian command of the Constitution is for equality throughout the political process. We can imagine some compromises of political equality that would plainly aid disadvantaged groups — it would undoubtedly aid blacks and women, for example, if citizens who have repeatedly expressed racist or sexist or bigoted views were denied the vote altogether. That would be unconstitutional, of course; the Constitution demands that everyone be permitted to play an equal part in the formal process of choosing a president, a Congress, and other officials, that no one be excluded on the ground that his opinions or tastes are too offensive or unreasonable or despicable to count.

Elections are not all there is to politics, however. Citizens play a continuing part in politics between elections, because informal public debate and argument influences what responsible officials — and officials anxious for re-election — will do. So the First Amendment contributes a great deal to political equality: it insists that just as no one may be excluded from the vote because his opinions are despicable, so no one may be denied the right to speak or write or broadcast because what he will say is too offensive to be heard.

That amendment serves other goals as well, of course: free speech helps to expose official stupidity and corruption, and it allows vigorous public debate that sometimes generates new ideas and refutes old ones. But the First Amendment's egalitarian role is independent of these other goals: it forbids censoring cranks or neo-Nazis not because anyone thinks that their contributions will prevent corruption or improve public debate, but just because equality demands that everyone, no matter how eccentric or despicable, have a chance to influence politics as well as elections. Of course it does not follow that government will in the end respect everyone's opinion equally, or that official decisions will be equally congenial to all groups. Equality demands that everyone's opinion be given a chance for influence, not that anyone's opinion will triumph or even be represented in what government eventually does.

The First Amendment's egalitarian role is not confined, however, to political speech. People's lives are affected not just by their political environment — not just by what their presidents and legislators and other public officials do — but even more comprehensively by what we might call their moral environment. How others treat me — and my own sense of identity and self-respect — are determined in part by the mix of social conventions, opinions, tastes, convictions, prejudices, life styles, and cultures that flourish in the community in which I live. Liberals are sometimes accused of thinking that what people say or do or think in private has no impact on anyone except themselves, and that is plainly wrong. Someone to whom religion is of fundamental importance, for example, will obviously lead a very different and perhaps more satisfying life in a community in which most other people share his convictions than in a dominantly secular society of atheists for whom his beliefs are laughable superstitions. A woman who believes that explicit sexual material degrades her will likely lead a very different, and no doubt more satisfying, life among people who also despise pornography than in a community where others, including other women, think it liberating and fun.

Exactly because the moral environment in which we all live is in good part created by others, however, the question of who shall have the power to help shape that environment, and how, is of fundamental importance, though it is often neglected in political theory. Only one answer is consistent with the ideals of political equality: that no one may be prevented from influencing the shared moral environment, through his own private choices, tastes, opinions, and example, just because these tastes or opinions disgust those who have the power to shut him up or lock him up. Of course, the ways in which anyone may exercise that influence must be limited in order to protect the security and interests of others. People may not try to mold the moral climate by intimidating women with sexual demands or by burning a cross on a black family's lawn, or by refusing to hire women or blacks at all, or by making their working conditions so humiliating as to be intolerable.

But we cannot count, among the kinds of interests that may be protected in this way, a right not to be insulted or damaged just by the fact that others have hostile or uncongenial tastes, or that they are free to express or indulge them in private. Recognizing that right would mean denying that some people — those whose tastes these are — have any right to participate in forming the moral environment at all. Of course it should go without saying that no one has a right to *succeed* in influencing others through his own private choices and tastes. Sexists and bigots have no right to live in a community whose ideology or culture is even partially sexist or bigoted: they have no right to any proportional representation for their odious views. In a genuinely egalitarian society, however, those views cannot be locked out, in advance, by criminal or civil law: they must instead be discredited by the disgust, outrage, and ridicule of other people.

MacKinnon's "egalitarian" argument for censorship is important mainly because it reveals the most important reason for resisting her suggestions, and also because it allows us to answer her charge that liberals who oppose her are crypto-pornographers themselves. She thinks that people who defend the right to pornography are acting out of self-interest, not principle — she says she has been driven to the conclusion that "speech *will* be defined so that men can have their pornography." That charge is based on the inadequacy of the conventional explanation, deriving from John Stuart Mill, that pornography must be protected so that truth may emerge. What is actually at stake in the argument about pornography, however, is not society's chance to discover truth, but its commitment to the very ideal of equality that MacKinnon thinks underrated in the American community. Liberals defend pornography, though most of them despise it, in order to defend a conception of the First Amendment that includes, as at least one of its purposes, protecting equality in the processes through which the moral as well as the political environment is formed. First Amendment liberty is not equality's enemy, but the other side of equality's coin.

MacKinnon is right to emphasize the connection between the fight over pornography and the larger, more general and important, argument about the freedom of Americans to say and teach what others think politically incorrect. She and her followers regard freedom of speech and thought as an elitist, inegalitarian ideal that has been of almost no value to woman, blacks, and others without power; they say America would be better off if it demoted that ideal as many other nations have. But most of her constituents would be appalled if this denigration of freedom should escape from universities and other communities where their own values about political correctness are now popular and take root in the more general political culture. Local majorities may find homosexual art or feminist theater just as degrading to women as the kind of pornography MacKinnon hates, or radical or separatist black opinion just as inimical to racial justice as crude racist epithets.

That is an old liberal warning — as old as Voltaire — and many people have grown impatient with it. They are willing to take that chance, they say, to advance a program that seems overwhelmingly important now. Their impatience may prove fatal for that program rather than essential to it, however. If we abandon our traditional understanding of equality for a different one that allows a majority to define some people as too corrupt or offensive or radical to join in the informal moral life of the nation, we will have begun a process that ends, as it has in so many other parts of the world, in making equality something to be feared rather than celebrated, a mocking, "correct" euphemism for tyranny.

NOTES

1. Catharine MacKinnon, "Pornography, Civil Rights and Speech," reprinted in Catherine Itzin, editor, *Pornography: Women, Violence and Civil Liberties, A Radical View* (Oxford University Press, 1992), page 456. (Quotations are from 461-463.)
2. *American Booksellers Ass'n* v. *Hudnut*, 771 F. 2d 323 (1985), aff'd 475 US 1001 (1986). In a decision that MacKinnon discusses at length, a Canadian court upheld a similar Canadian statute as consistent with that nation's Charter of Rights and Freedoms. I discuss that decision in "The Coming Battle over Free Speech," *The New York Review*, June 11, 1992.
3. "Two Concepts of Liberty," in *Isaiah Berlin: A Celebration,* edited by Edna and Avishai Margalit (University of Chicago Press, 1991), and printed in *The New York Review of Books*, August 15, 1991.
4. Among the prestigious studies denying the causal link MacKinnon claims are the 1970 report of the National Commission on Obscenity and Pornography, appointed by Lyndon Johnson to consider the issue, the 1979 report of the Williams Commission in Britain, and a recent year-long British study which concluded that "the evidence does not point to pornography as a cause of deviant sexual orientation in offenders. Rather it seems to be used as part of that deviant sexual orientation."

MacKinnon and other feminists cite the voluminous, two-volume report of the infamous Meese Commission, which was appointed by Reagan to contradict the findings of the earlier Johnson-appointed group and was headed by people who had made a career of opposing pornography. The Meese Commission duly declared that although the scientific evidence was inconclusive, it believed that pornography (vast tracts of which were faithfully reprinted in its report) did indeed cause crime. But the scientists on whose work the report relied protested, immediately after its publication, that the commission had misunderstood and misused their work (For a thorough analysis of all these and other studies, see Marcia Pally *Sense and Censorship: The Vanity of Bonfires* [Americans for Constitutional Freedom, 1991]). MacKinnon also appeals to legal authority: she says, citing the Seventh Circuit opinion holding her antipornography statute unconstitutional, that "not even courts equivocate over [pornography's] carnage anymore." But this is disingenuous: that opinion assumed that pornography is a significant cause of sexual crime only for the sake of the argument it made, and it cited, among other material, the Williams Commission report, as support for the Court's own denial of any such demonstrated causal connection.
5. In "Pornography, Civil Rights and Speech," MacKinnon said, "It does not make sense to assume that pornography has no role in rape simply because little about its use or effects distinguishes convicted rapists from other men, when we know that a lot of those other men *do* rape women; they just never get caught" (Page 475).
6. "Turning Rape Into Pornography: Postmodern Genocide," *Ms.,* July/August 1993, p. 28.
7. "The Balkan Crisis: 1913 and 1993," *The New York Review*, July 15, 1993.
8. Catherine Itzin, editor, *Pornography: Women, Violence and Civil Liberties,* p. 359. At one point MacKinnon offers a surprisingly timid formulation of her causal thesis: she says that "there is no evidence that pornography does no harm." The same negative claim can be made, of course, about any genre of literature. Ted Bundy, the serial murderer

who said he had read pornography since his youth, and whom feminists often cite for that remark, also said that he had studied Dostoevsky's *Crime and Punishment*. Even MacKinnon's weak statement is controversial, moreover. Some psychologists have argued that pornography, by providing a harmless outlet for violent tendencies, may actually reduce the amount of such crime. See Patricia Gillian, "Therapeutic Uses of Obscenity," and other articles reprinted and cited in *Censorship and Obscenity*, edited by Rajeev Dhavan and Christie Davies (Rowman and Littlefield, 1978). And it is at least relevant that nations with the most permissive laws about pornography are among those with the least sexual crime (see Marjorie Heins, *Sex, Sin, and Blasphemy*, New Press, 1993, p. 152), though of course that fact might be explained in other ways.

9. MacKinnon's frequent rhetorical use of "you" and "your," embracing all female readers, invites every woman to see herself as a victim of the appalling sexual crimes and the abuses she describes, and reinforces an implicit suggestion that women are, in pertinent ways, all alike: all passive, innocent, and subjugated.

10. Reprinted in Catherine Itzin, editor, *Pornography: Women, Violence and Civil Liberties*, p. 483-484.

11. See Frank I. Michelman, "Conceptions of Democracy in American Constitutional Argument: The Case of Pornography Regulation," *Tennessee Law Review* Vol. 56. No. 2 (1989), pp. 303-304.

12. Not all feminists agree that pornography contributes to the economic or social subordination of women. Linda Williams, for example, in the Fall, 1993 issue of the *Threepenny Review*, claims that "the very fact that today a variety of different pornographies are now on the scene in mass market videos is good for feminism and that to return to the time of repressing pornographic sexual representations would mean the resurgence of at least some elements of an underground tradition ... of misogyny."

13. See Barbara Presley Noble, "New Reminders on Harassment," *The New York Times*, August 15, 1993, p. 25.

14. *Beauharnais* v. *Illinois*, 343 US 250 (1952), abandoned in *New York Times* v. *Sullivan*, 376 US 254 (1964) at 268-269.

15. See *Smith v. Collins*, 439 US 916 (1978).

FEMINIST ANTI-PORNOGRAPHY STRUGGLES:
NOT THE CHURCH, BUT MAYBE THE STATE

Marvin Glass

🖋

Marvin Glass teaches philosophy at Carleton University in Ottawa. His research is in the areas of ethics, social and political theory, Marxism, feminist theory, and children's rights. He is also co-ordinator of the Canadian Network on Cuba.

Glass focuses on two specific arguments by anti-censorship feminists — feminists who argue that feminists cannot trust the state to be a vehicle for their liberation and feminists who argue that a free market in sexual imagery is currently in women's best interests — and raises objections to each. On the first, Glass agrees that feminist politics will not succeed in transforming the state into a pro-woman institution, but he argues that a realistic feminist political agenda is to add a strategy of fighting for feminist-inspired anti-pornography legislation to existing policies for alleviating women's inequalities. On the second, Glass argues that leaving the ownership and control of pornography to market forces is unlikely to empower women or ensure feminist sexual expression a prominent place in an increasingly concentrated and powerful global market.

Whenever there is an ascendant class, a large portion of the morality of the country emanates from its class interests and its feelings of class superiority. The morality between Spartans and Helots, between planters and negroes, between princes and subjects, between nobles and returiers, between men and women, has been for the most part the creation of these class interests and feelings. ... (John Stuart Mill)[1]

Pornography, in the feminist view, is a form of forced sex, a practice of sexual politics, an institution of gender inequality. ... The feminist critique of pornography ... proceeds from women's point of view, meaning the standpoint of the subordination of women to men. (Catharine MacKinnon)[2]

Although this paper begins with quotations from J.S. Mill and Catharine MacKinnon, my views on pornography and the state were not always so esoteric. Like most males of my generation, I first became interested in pornography in my early teens, about the same time that we also considered initiating ourselves into the equally illicit world of smoking. Parental prohibition of these activities was usually based on implausible claims to the effect that we were still too young to look at pictures of naked women or inhale cigarette smoke, and so my sceptical friends and I set out to acquire these desiderata. Lack of age being the basis of our supply problem, it was clear what had to be done. First, contribute collectively to the 35-cent cost of a package of cigarettes or the 50 cents needed for a copy of *Playboy*; second, designate the oldest-looking boy in the bunch as procurer; and finally, find a far-sighted storekeeper. Of course, this strategy eventually worked.

These episodes in the life and times of my little group, particularly the pornography escapade, were instrumental to the development of our adolescent male-bonding and consciousness-lowering. For example, should we invite a few girls we know to our pornography and tobacco sessions? You must be kidding! Is the centerfold looking at us? She must be; we're the only ones here. Many years later, I regret to say that I still smoke, though now I often do it in mixed company. But seriously, thanks to the wisdom and inspiration of feminists I have worked with and read, particularly MacKinnon in the latter category, my interest in contemporary commercial pornography is now predominantly political.

I first thought about freedom of speech when, in 1974, I noticed posters denouncing Nobel Prize-winning physicist William Shockley as a "racist" and urging people to picket and obstruct, that is, censor, his Harvard University talk on alleged innate differences in intelligence between blacks and whites. Because I had never even entertained, let alone embraced, the idea that opposition to racism might be linked with opposition to free speech, I did not join the protesters. But, having some sabbatical time on my hands, I decided to investigate the matter. I read John Stuart Mill's *On Liberty* a few times, perused some commentaries, delved into a couple of books on racism, added a pinch or two of what I thought was historical materialism, neatly sidestepped the issue of censorship and the state and eventually produced a paper on the topic arguing for the moral permissibility of at least some such political protests.[3]

I first thought seriously about free speech in the context of modern pornography when, a year later, I read the aforementioned paper at a conference in Calgary to a group comprised mainly of leftist academics. Predictably, reaction was mixed, but there was one question for which I was totally unprepared. "If you are willing to censor racist language" a feminist in the audience asked, "are you also prepared to censor sexist images — *Playboy*, for example?" I had no idea how to respond, admitted as much, and said I would have to think about the matter. Almost twenty-five years later, I feel more-or-less ready to attempt an answer. This paper is part of that

answer and it is a rejoinder to what is perhaps one of the most compelling anti-censorship arguments, one popular both with feminists who agree that pornography harms women and with feminists who think pornography has more benign effects, and thus concede its alleged harm only for the sake of argument. The concern which motivates this anti-censorship argument is best summed up in this rhetorical question posed by Lisa Duggan, Nan Hunter, and Carole Vance: "How can feminists be entrusting the patriarchal state with the task of legally distinguishing permissible from impermissible images?"[4] That is to say, although not as sexist as its predecessors, the modern state's strong prejudice against women's interests, including their sexual interests, would surely transform any genuine anti-pornography concepts and principles from feminist drawing boards into laws whose first target would be feminist representations of sexuality, especially lesbian ones.

The purposes of this paper are twofold. First, I want to answer some of the concerns that the state cannot be entrusted to deal with pornography by critically examining a number of feminist articulations of this distrust. Second, I want to undermine the privatization alternative to state censorship: the claim that a "free market" in sexual imagery is currently in women's best interests. As regards particular pro-censorship tactics, this paper does not distinguish between criminal code sanctions against pornography and the civil rights strategy pioneered by Andrea Dworkin and Catharine MacKinnon. Elsewhere, however, I defend a feminist preference for the former approach.

Distrusting the State

At first sight, a strategy against misogynist representations of women's sexuality involving state bureaucrats and state mechanisms appears to be another misguided case of "feminism from above," that is, letting foxes stand guard over chicken coops or, as Audre Lorde might say, trying to use the master's tools to dismantle the master's house. Thus, Brants and Kok, in an article provocatively titled "Penal Sanctions as Feminist Strategy: A Contradiction in Terms?" urge women not to forget that: "by invoking the criminal justice, we are appealing to forces which are beyond our control and which, given the present political climate, may well get out of hand."[5] Erica Jong agrees: "Despite the ugliness of a lot of pornography ... I believe that censorship only springs back against the givers of culture — against authors, artists, and feminists, against anyone who wants to change society. Should censorship be imposed again, whether through the kind of legislation introduced in Minneapolis or Indianapolis, or through other means, feminists would be the first to suffer."[6] And Mariana Valverde and Lorna Weir believe that censoring pornography is not an appropriate strategy for feminists, particularly lesbian feminists, to pursue because "[l]egislation of this kind will only undermine our attempts to give birth to a lesbian culture. Under stricter pornography legislation, the sexist and anti-lesbian features in *Penthouse* might be prohibited — but such tougher laws could be applied equally to lesbian sexual representation."[7]

What political conclusions are to be drawn from the fact that all state institutions, particularly the police and the judiciary, are controlled primarily by men, many of whose attitudes are sexist (and racist and homophobic)? Is the question the choice between the wisdom of trusting the state to enact and enforce feminist-inspired, anti-pornography laws versus the willingness of anti-censorship feminists, such as ACLU president Nadine Strossen, "to trust our own voices — as well as those of our own anti-pornography sister feminists — to effectively counter misogynist expression, including misogynist sexual expression?"[8] If so, then history speaks clearly and consistently: women cannot trust this kind of state to be a vehicle for their liberation. But are there really feminists who embrace the contrary view, who explicitly or even implicitly place their *trust* in the modern state to effect progressive change for women?

Carol Smart thinks there are. At the end of her evaluation of the Catharine MacKinnon/Andrea

Dworkin civil rights, anti-pornography strategy she warns "that there are major problems in transforming any feminist analysis of women's oppression into a legal practice, as if law were merely an instrument to be utilized by feminist lawyers with the legal skills to draw up statutes."[9] And what puzzles Pratiba Parmar "is how women who define men as the enemy can ask the 'patriarchal state' to intervene on their behalf and pass laws in the interest of women. Expecting the state to behave in a benevolent manner is naive."[10] Adrienne Rich joins the chorus: "I am less sure than Dworkin and MacKinnon that this is a time when further powers of suppression should be turned over to the state."[11] Even neo-conservative pundit George Will appears to grasp the problem: "For someone who so strenuously loathes American society, MacKinnon is remarkably eager to vest in this society's representative government vast powers to regulate expression."[12]

Are MacKinnon and Dworkin political pollyannas? After all, most feminists recognize structural sexism within modern legal systems. MacKinnon herself puts it this way: "The law sees and treats women the way men see and treat women. The liberal state coercively and authoritatively constitutes the social order in the interests of men as a gender."[13] And Dworkin claims that "[t]here is not a feminist alive who could possibly look to the male legal system for real protection from the systematized sadism of men."[14] These are not the words of two women afflicted with a terminal case of feminist political naiveté, with the utopian view that the law can be entrusted, *carte blanche*, with representations of women's sexuality. Doubtless, as pro-censorship feminists they must believe that, for all its power, the patriarchal state is not omnipotent, that feminist-led coalitions are sometimes capable of pressuring it to enact and enforce some feminist-inspired laws. Are they entitled to believe this?

Not according to most of their critics. Nadine Strossen is just one of many commentators who characterize the Dworkin/MacKinnon analysis of sexism as a kind of patriarchal fatalism inconsistent with pro-censorship activism.

The fundamental premise in the pro-censorship's philosophy — that our entire societal and legal system is patriarchal, reflecting and perpetuating the subordination of women — itself conclusively refutes their conclusion that we should hand over to that state additional power. The pro-censorship feminists cannot have it both ways. If, as they contend, government power is inevitably used to the particular disadvantage of relatively disempowered groups, it follows that women's rights advocates should oppose measures that augment that power, including Dworkin/MacKinnon type laws.[15]

But no quotation or even specific reference is offered in support of Strossen's claim that MacKinnon and Dworkin are committed to government power "inevitably" being used to the detriment of women. Moreover, claiming to see a few windows of opportunity for anti-pornography feminists here is consistent with believing that even modest censorship victories will be impossible without grass roots organizing, education, lobbying, vigilance, and good luck, followed by more such organizing, additional education, extra vigilance, etc. Thus, when Andrea Dworkin says that "[w]omen fight to reform male law ... because something is better than nothing," *trust* of the state has nothing to do with her politics.[16] Nor do she and MacKinnon believe that campaigns against pornography should be restricted solely to passing civil rights ordinances: "Feminists have been fighting pornography for ... years. Pickets, demonstrations, slide shows, debates, leaflets, civil disobedience, must all continue. ... Passing the ordinance *does not mean stopping direct action, it means more of it.*"[17]

Myrna Kostash's views offer another illustration of how an anarchist approach can distort feminist political thinking about pornography.

Some feminists argue that the issue is to, as the feminist newspaper *Broadside* has expressed it, "regain control of the state's power by redefining and refining the definition of obscenity so that it meets our standards and needs." But ... the state is hardly a neutral, let alone pro-woman institution that can be captured and directed towards our projects; it is specific to the development of capitalist patriarchy; its capture and transformation require a revolution.[18]

Aside from parting company with *Broadside* over the notion of women "regaining" state control — they never had it — I want to defend the spirit of their project to redefine and refine the definition of obscenity.

For the foreseeable future, feminist politics will involve neither the capture of the modern state nor its transformation into a pro-woman institution. To claim otherwise, to say that these are reasonable short or mid-term goals for feminism, assumes a near-impotent state and a large, highly organized and militant women's movement. But neither of these presuppositions correspond to current or near-future reality. Instead, a realistic feminist political agenda would include pressuring an unsympathetic, often hostile state and to pass or retain legislation for pay equity and affirmative action and against sexual harassment, as well as to fund abortion and battered women's shelters. Why not include some feminist-inspired anti-pornography legislation on this list? To insist that this cannot be done without some kind of gender revolution flagrantly ignores the historical record of victories by oppressed groups, including women, where an increase in state control over some aspect of civil society has benefited them. With all their warts and scars, publicly funded education and health care (more on these later), minimum wage and workers' safety legislation are good examples of such victories. Did the governments which reluctantly adopted these measures miraculously shed forever their traditional race, class, and gender skins? Of course not; indeed, much of the progressive legislation adopted in the past sixty years is currently being diluted and even reversed by liberal, conservative, and social-democratic governments throughout the world. But to deny that, at the time of enactment, these were at least minor victories and thus small steps forward is to denigrate both reforms and reformers.[19]

A more compelling version of the "women-can't-trust-the-patriarchal-state" anti-censorship argument has been developed by Lynn King. After reviewing the history of the "Family Law Reform Act" and equal pay legislation in Ontario, King concludes:

> We must always distinguish between laws that protect women's right to public resources, such as funding for day care or battered women's shelters, and those over which we have no control. These have been and will continue to be used to maintain women's second class status. ... [L]aws dealing with pornography and censorship ... are subject to interpretation by people who are selected by an anti-feminist system. ... For feminists who are concerned about sexism, sexuality, and sexual representation, legal reform is a trap. Let's leave it unsprung and move on to better ways.[20]

What better ways do anti-censorship feminists have in mind for those concerned about the current state of the sexual representation of women? Elizabeth Wilson's analysis of the shifting politics of sex and censorship leads her to conclude that "a truly feminist agenda on sex, sexuality, and representation would emphasize the need for sex education for children."[21] Varda Burstyn, after bemoaning the scarcity of television material produced by Planned Parenthood, feminist, gay, or even forward looking church groups, proposes that government fund art bodies at all levels. "In the area of sexuality, this means subsidizing feminist and gay cultural workers and their projects in particular."[22] These feminists adopt a Brandeisian "more speech" response to pornography, that is, fighting "bad" words and pictures with "good" ones. Other non-censorship alternatives focus on job creation and law enforcement, with Ellis, O'Dair, and Talmar arguing that "[t]rue concern with violence against women would be expressed in demands as ... the rigorous enforcement of laws against rape,"[23] and Lynn Segal insisting that the only effective way of enabling women to avoid violence is "state funding for women refugees, anti-sexist,

anti-violence educational initiatives, and above all empowering women through improved job prospects, housing and welfare facilities."[24]

First, the Brandeis strategy. In *Whitney v. California*, U.S. Supreme Court Justice Louis Brandeis said: "if there be time to expose through discussion the falsehood and fallacies, to avert the evil by the process of education, the remedy to be applied is *more speech, not enforced silence.*"[25] Many (but not all) feminists who oppose censorship concede that there is an "evil" here, that is, they agree that the production and dissemination of pornography contribute to some extent to job discrimination, pay inequity, sexual harassment, sexual assault and rape against women. Thelma McCormack, for example, claims that "a cultural milieu in which women are always perceived as sex objects contributes to the devaluation of women."[26] And Duggan, Hunter and Vance admit that "pornography magnifies the misogyny in society."[27] Varda Burstyn is equally candid: "we would never suggest that sexually explicit, sexist images do not harm [women] when we so strongly insist that sexist imagery of all kinds is a powerful course in our culture as a whole."[28] Well, given women's economic and political resources, suppose that the Brandeisian educational/anti-censorship approach, if it ever did succeed, took a hundred and fifty years longer than the MacKinnon/Dworkin strategy to achieve a significant reduction in the impact of misogynist pornography. According to what criteria would Judge Brandeis say that there was time to wait? What is reasonable progress here for those who continually suffer the evil, that is, for *women*? Invariably, like Brandeis, those who urge this strategy as an alternative to censorship are silent on this important question.

Secondly, there is a disturbing ambivalence to the modern state exhibited in these alternatives to legal regulation. Why is it deemed reasonable to expect pressure to bring about rigor in state enforcement of rape laws, but unreasonable to expect agitation to lead to the enforcement of moderately progressive anti-pornography laws? Why would such a state ideologically and financially underwrite progressive sex education programs, but refrain from replacing anachronistic obscenity laws with some feminist inspired anti-pornography legislation? Why would it be any more inclined to subsidize feminist cultural enterprises than it would be to appoint at least some pro-feminist censors or judges? Why could feminists compete successfully against the Christian Right for government funding but not for progressive anti-pornography laws? And why would a homophobic state — inclined, we are told, to distort irredeemably any feminist attempt to censor pornography — give lesbian and gay groups substantial funding to produce symbols of non-exploitative, non-heterosexual sexuality?

When Robin Morgan (often mistakenly characterized as pro-censorship solely on the basis of her famous quip that "pornography is the theory; rape is the practice") asserts that "a phallocentric culture is more likely to begin its censorship purges with books on pelvic self-examination for women or books containing lyrical paeans to lesbianism than with *See Him Tear And Kill Her*," she is surely right.[29] But this is a tautology and therefore is of no help in comparative judgments about different strategies against pornography. Because "phallocentrism" permeates *all* major institutions of society, feminist liberation struggles face one or two strikes against them *wherever* they turn. Thus, the sexist and homophobic forces which operate at the level of the state would be involved in both censorship *and* funding decisions. With regard to the latter, it is well-known that they almost always come with strings attached and are often restrained by boards of directors and executive committees not directly controlled by users and workers.[30] Does this mean that feminists should accept only *carte blanche* government cheques for the production of erotica? However high-minded and principled this approach may appear, it is certain to maximize the marginalization of feminist culture because such pristine cheques will, for the foreseeable future, be few and far between. Of course, one could naively revert to the old saw that in any struggle between cultural opposites — here state-untainted but vastly underfunded and minimally distributed feminist erotica vs. ubiqui-

tous misogynist pornography — quality and truth always triumph. Instead, why not critically support both some less-than-perfect funding options and some equally flawed censorship legislation? That is, instead of rejecting out-of-hand the legislative approach, why not balance the chances of a particular piece of legislation being adopted and enforced, the frequency of misapplication and costs thereof, and the harm to women and girls the adoption and enforcement of such a law would prevent?

Trusting the Free Market

Anti-censorship feminism based on the distrust of the state is sometimes expounded in the name of both feminism and Marxism. I want to examine one such example to raise a second issue of trust — not of the state, but of the free market. Consider Sharon Smith's "Feminists For A Strong State?" In this review of MacKinnon's *Toward a Feminist Theory of the State*, Smith, after quoting Frederick Engels on the class nature of the state, concludes that:

> The state contributes to the oppression of women through its role as the enforcer of the prevailing level of class exploitation. Any strengthening of the state is a strengthening of the means of repression of the working class. ... The point for socialists — indeed for all those interested in women's liberation — is to weaken the hold of the state over worker's individual lives, not to strengthen it. Liberal democratic values such as freedom of speech, scorned by both MacKinnon and Brownmiller, strengthen the ability of the workers to organize against their exploitation and oppression. Lenin put this clearly in *State and Revolution*, when he wrote: "We are in favour of a democratic republic as the best form of state for the proletariat under capitalism ...."[31]

The very brief quotation from Lenin is found in the context of his defense of Marx's critique of "a free people's state," a slogan which appeared in the *Gotha Program* of the German Social

Democratic Party of the 1870's. But there is no mention of unlimited free speech, let alone endorsements of it, in either Marx's critique or Lenin's commentary, and arguably neither of them would reject legal sanctions against sexist pornography. Marx, for example, inveighed in more general terms against Sharon Smith's nineteenth century anti-statist precursors, followers of the anarchist (and extreme misogynist) Pierre Joseph Proudhon: "They scorn all ... action which can be carried through by political means (for instance, the legal shortening of the working day). Under the *pretext of freedom*, or of anti-governmentalism, or of anti-authoritarian individualism, these gentlemen ... actually preach ordinary bourgeois economy."[32] One doubts that Smith would oppose federal or state regulation of the length of the working day and instead, like their bosses, urge workers to exercise their "proletarian freedom from below" and negotiate such matters in individual labor contracts. Why then would women's interests best be served by her advice to feminists to abandon state regulation as part of an anti-pornography strategy?

Smith says the point for all those interested in women's liberation is "to weaken the state control over worker's [women's] lives." Well, we can at least agree that any such liberation means empowering women by making their lives safer. But, in the context of sexist pornography, this means weakening the *pornographer's* control over women's lives. Yet privatization of pornography, that is, leaving its ownership and control to market forces — which is what, at least in the short run, her agenda amounts to — is unlikely to empower women or ensure feminist sexual expression a prominent place in our cultural landscape. Smith's strategy implicitly accepts the economic status quo and expects women to struggle there, thus relegating decisions about appropriate representations of sexuality to a sphere of society where profit, not justice for women, or women's welfare, or women's sexual interest is the litmus test for economic choice.

Today the market is near-ubiquitous, increasingly concentrated and powerful, and dripping red in tooth and claw. Its sexual component takes thirteen year old Thai and Filipino girls and serves them up as sexual delight on prostitution tours. It breaks their tiny backs in third-world sweat shops so that sneakers and slacks, after the appropriate inducement of multi-million dollar ad campaigns, can be sold in first-world countries. The global market feminizes poverty throughout the world. One generation of affirmative action for women is too much for it to bear. In the name of increasing personal choice, it makes desperate women guinea pigs for multinational drug companies and creates a class of reproductive prostitutes (so-called "surrogate mothers"). It does this and much, much more to women, and it does it, as Smith's heroes, Marx and Engels, noted 150 years ago, "in the icy waters of egoistic calculation. It has resolved personal worth into exchange value."[33] These facts of the free market should have us question some of the feminist anti-pornography distrust of the state and the corresponding plethora of gloomy predictions of cultural losses for women should censorship be imposed.

The political relationship between feminist-inspired culture(s), the market, and the nature of the modern state may be illuminated by considering two analogies, one with health care and the other with schooling. Most feminists support publicly-funded health care over private plans where rich and poor alike are "free" to subscribe or refrain from subscribing to the medical plan of their choice. And they endorse the former over the latter knowing that universal government medicare entails setting up "a vast state medical bureaucracy." This is not particularly problematic for them because such a bureaucracy would be an integral part of a system that includes some public, democratic control over doctors and drug and insurance conglomerates. The benefits of such control, including lower costs, are so obvious that it seems ludicrous to most feminists to suggest that women would be better off if only they could keep the state out of the hospitals and community health centres of their society. Why then would things improve for women if only they could keep the state out of the publishing firms, movie companies and television networks of the nation? Few feminists would here respond that ideas about women's sexuality, but not their health, are socially constructed by the dominant gender and reflected by the policies of the modern patriarchal state.

Or consider modern education. Despite well-grounded criticisms of both its form and content, most feminists would be loathe to support the dissolution of all state-funded education or to wish that it had never come into existence. Although it has not been, nor is it now, the great liberal equalizer of opportunity for the underprivileged, it has, all things considered, been beneficial to the majority of society. Granted, it displays bias against unorthodox views, including feminism. Yes, much of its authoritarian structure is without rational justification. Nevertheless, it marks an historical advance over its predecessors, namely, church-dominated education, private education for the sons of the affluent, and little or no education for the poor. Analogously, a successful censorship strategy against pornography will entail some (temporary) losses in the arena of sexual expression. No feminist can guarantee that pristine anti-sexist legislation will govern the availability of sexual expression. To argue that civil and/or criminal laws can be framed, adopted and enforced so as to censor all and only that which degrades and exploits women is absolutely utopian. And worse, it is likely to induce cynicism when actual legislation falls short of this goal. But with all due respect for (and personal interest in) the siren call of erotica, are these losses the end of civilization as we know it? On the other hand, can anti-censorship feminists assure us that in a society in which there are no legal limits to degrading women through expressive liberty, where feminist artists fight it out only in the marketplace against the multi-billion dollar pornography industry, that there will not be significantly greater casualties for women?

A final note on the market and the effects of state censorship of pornography. Many have argued that even if some feminist-inspired anti-pornography laws are reluctantly passed by legislators, this will result only in pornography, like prostitution, being driven underground. Sarah

Diamond, for example, claims that "[t]he elimination of the image is not the solution to misogyny, but a process that will make some images move underground to meet the continuing demand."[34] And there, others say, it "will take root out of the public eye,"[35] "could become even more profitable than it is already,"[36] and will be "all the more difficult to fight."[37] But, *contra* Diamond, one can defend a law, for example, against driving while intoxicated, without naively clinging to the hope that enforcement will *eliminate* the offending behavior. Moreover, "underground," is not the name of a large chain of retail stores. Pro-censorship feminists are therefore not in the least embarrassed in wanting pornography to "take root out of the public eye" because this usually leads to diminished dissemination and therefore diminished profits. This likely consequence of state regulation of representations of sexuality, at least as much as their libertarian stance on freedom of expression, accounts for the universal opposition of pornocrats to any suggestion that content regulation should be applied to their products. Feminists, therefore, need not be as pessimistic as Sue George who, while conceding that pornography may oppress women and that censorship will reduce its availability, dismisses this tactic because it "has absolutely nothing to do with fighting women's oppression."[38] Absolutely *nothing*? Feminist anti-censorship hyperbole strikes again.

Author's Note

I would like to thank Christine Koggel for comments on earlier drafts of this paper.

NOTES

1. John Stuart Mill, *On Liberty*, edited by Elizabeth Rapaport (Indianapolis: Hackett, 1978), p. 6.

2. Catharine MacKinnon, *Toward a Feminist Theory of the State* (Cambridge: Harvard University Press, 1989), p. 197.

3. The paper was later published as "Anti-Racism and Unlimited Freedom of Speech: An Untenable Dualism?" in the *Canadian Journal of*

Philosophy, v. VIII, no. 3, Sept., 1978, pp. 559-575.

4. Lisa Duggan, Nan Hunter, and Carole S. Vance, "False Promises: Feminist Antipornography Legislation in the U.S." in Varda Burstyn, ed., *Women Against Censorship* (Vancouver: Douglas and McIntyre, 1985), p. 131.

5. C. Brants and E. Kok, "Penal Sanctions as a Feminist Strategy: a Contradiction in Terms?" in *International Journal of the Sociology of Law* v. 14, no. 3/4; pp. 269-286; quoted with approval in Carol Smart, *Feminism and the Power of Law* (London: Routledge, 1989), p. 136.

6. Erica Jong, "The Place of Pornography," *Harper's* (November, 1984), p. 33.

7. Mariana Valverde and Lorna Weir, "Thrills, Chills, and the 'Lesbian Threat,'" in Burstyn, *op. cit.*, p. 104.

8. Nadine Strossen, *Defending Pornography* (New York: Scribner, 1995), p. 48.

9. Smart, *op. cit.*, pp. 136-137. Pro-censorship feminists certainly see the law as instrumental. Are they then part of what Cossman and Bell describe as an "anti-pornography feminism which assumes the law is a simple instrument of change"? And are they ignoring the fact that "law is not an instrument, but a site of contradiction, where new discourses are superimposed on old?" No, to both questions. It is one thing to say that the law is neither a simple instrument nor simply an instrument, quite another to deny its instrumentality altogether. Why cannot pro-censorship feminism view the law as both a complex instrument and a site of contradiction? Moreover, the notion of a site of contradiction or struggle amongst various sectors of society (including gender, race, and class) for the *superimposition* of discourses makes law sound distinctly instrumental. See Brenda Cossman and Shannon Bell, "Introduction," in *Bad Attitude/s on Trial: Pornography, Feminism, and the* Butler *Decision* (Toronto: University of Toronto Press, 1997), p. 29.

10. Pratiba Parmar, "Rage and Desire: Confronting Pornography," in Gail Chester and Julienne Dickey, eds., *Feminism and Censorship: The Current Debate* (Dorset: Prism Press, 1988), p. 126.

11. Adrienne Rich, letter in *off our backs* XV: 6; quoted in Liz Kelly, "The US Ordinances: Censorship or Radical Law Reform," in Chester and Dickey, p. 60.

12. George Will, "Pornography Scare," *Washington Post*, October 28, 1993; quoted by Strossen, *op. cit.*, p. 218.

13. MacKinnon, *op. cit.*, p. 161-162.

14. Andrea Dworkin, "For Men, Freedom of Speech; for Women, Silence Please" in Laura Lederer, ed., *Take Back The Night: Women on Pornography* (New York: Bantam, 1982), p. 256.

15. Strossen, *op. cit.*, p. 217.

16. Dworkin, in Lederer, *op. cit.*

17. Andrea Dworkin and Catharine MacKinnon, *Pornography and Civil Rights* (Minneapolis: Organizing Against Pornography, 1988), p. 94.

18. Myrna Kostash, "Second Thoughts," in Burstyn, *op. cit.*, p. 37.

19. Consider, for example, Carol Smart's undocumented claim (*op. cit.*, p. 5) that "feminist 'legal theory' is immobilized in the face of the failure of feminism to affect law and the failure of law to transform the quality of women's lives." But MacKinnon's groundbreaking work on sexual harassment did affect the law and second-wave feminism struggled successfully in many countries for abortion rights and affirmative action. These changes to the law and the quality of women's lives did not bring about gender equality, but that's another matter.

20. Lynn King, "Censorship and Law Reform: Will Changing the Laws Mean a Change for the Better?" in Burstyn, *op. cit.*, p. 90.

21. Elizabeth Wilson, "Feminist Fundamentalism: The Shifting Politics of Sex and Censorship," in Lynn Segal and Mary McIntosh, eds., *Sex and Censorship: Sexuality and the Pornography Debate* (New Brunswick: Rutgers University Press, 1993), p. 28.

22. Varda Burstyn, "Positive Strategies," in Burstyn, *op. cit.*, p. 165.

23. Kate Ellis, Nan B. Hunter, and Abby Talmer, "Introduction," *Caught Looking*, Kate Ellis, Nan B. Hunter, Beth Jaker, Barbara O'Dair, and Abby Talmer (eds) (New York: Caught Looking Inc., 1986), p. 8.

24. Lynn Segal, "False Promises: Anti-Pornography Feminism," *Socialist Register*, edited by Ralph and Leo Panitch (London: Merlin Press, 1993), p. 100.

25. *Whitney v. California* (274 U.S. 357, 375-6, (1927), (Brandeis concurring); emphasis in original.

26. Thelma McCormack, "Making Sense of Research on Pornography," in Burstyn, *op. cit.*, p. 199.

27. Duggan, Hunter, and Vance, *op. cit.*, p. 145.

28. Burstyn, *op. cit.*, p. 181.

29. Robin Morgan, "Theory and Practice: Pornography and Rape," in Lederer, *op. cit.*, p. 137.

30. In an illuminating review of the women's health movement in South Australia in the 1970s and 80s, Jocelyn Auer concludes that while "there is constant tension in trying to maintain a commitment to feminist principles and goals while working within the state," and that while "[t]he acceptance of government funding entailed specific limitations on feminist goals and practices," it also "has given women some status and ability to seek reform there." See her "Encounters with the State: Co-option and Reform, A Case Study from Women's Health," in *Playing the State*, edited by Sophie Watson (London: Verso, 1990), p. 207-17.

31. Shannon Smith, "Feminists for a Strong State?" *International Socialism*, #51, Summer, 1991, p. 86.

32. Karl Marx, "Letter to Kugelman," Oct. 9, 1866, in *Marx, Engels, Lenin: Anarchism and Anarcho-Syndicalism* (Moscow: Progress Publishers, 1972), p. 43.

33. Karl Marx and Frederick Engels, *Manifesto of the Communist Party*, in *Marx-Engels, Collected Works* (New York: International Publishers, 1976), Vol. VI, p. 487.

34. Sarah Diamond, "Pornography: Image and Reality," in Burstyn, *op. cit.*, p. 49.

35. Avedon Carol, *nudes, prudes, and attitudes* (Cheltenham: New Clarion Press, 1994), p. 2.

36. Alisa L. Carse, "Pornography: An Uncivil Liberty?" *Hypatia*, v. 10, no. 1 (Winter, 1995), p. 168.

37. Wendy Moore, "There should be a law against it ... shouldn't there?" In Chester and Dickey, *op. cit.*, p. 147.

38. Sue George, "Censorship and Hypocrisy: Some Issues Surrounding Pornography That Feminism Has Ignored," in Chester and Dickey, *op. cit.*, p. 115.

MORALITY, CENSORSHIP, AND DISCRIMINATION: REFRAMING THE PORNOGRAPHY DEBATE IN GERMANY AND EUROPE

Heather MacRae

*

Heather MacRae has taught political science at Carleton University and at the University of Victoria. She has published articles in the areas of the European Union, feminist theory and movements, and issues of pornography and censorship.

MacRae discusses censorship in the context of Germany and of the impact of the European Union on policies regarding censorship. She examines the development of feminist movements in Germany, their attempt to reframe the regulation of pornography in Germany, and the possibilities for shaping legislation at the level of the European Union itself. She argues that the reframing of these issues at the European level could invigorate debate on pornography, promote the feminist conception of it as discriminatory, and make it possible to reframe legislation at the national level.

Reactions of the modern state toward sexuality and deviations from a declared sexual norm have ranged from criminalization to shutting its eyes to what happens behind closed doors. In this latter case, the implication of state inaction is that sexuality falls within the private realm and, as such, is not subject to state intervention. However, when sexuality takes the form of pornography, it is not only a private matter. Pornography occupies a unique position between the public and the private spheres. By representing a particular form of sexuality in words and/or pictures, pornography removes sexuality from the private mind or home and brings it into the public realm. The subsequent commodification of these representations, which in effect presents the (female) body for consumption by the general population, embeds pornography firmly in the public sphere. As the artificial division between public and private has come under increasing scrutiny from feminists, the regulation of pornography is gradually finding its way onto the political agenda. Systems of governance, both national and supranational must now act on issues once "deemed so

private they were precluded from the purview of public policy" (Elman 1996, 8). The nature of the regulation remains problematic. In general, "pornography [and its regulation in the European states] remains a moral issue. It is recognized as harmful and a violation of dignity when it constitutes part of sexual harassment in employment. At the same time, it is untouched as long as it is used in private" (Baer 1996, 57).

With a focus on the German case, this article discusses how different policy actors have framed the issue of pornography and assesses the legislation derived from these various frames. I am particularly interested in asking how women's involvement in the policy-making process may result in legislation that reflects a "feminist" position or frame. Framing here is understood as "a way of selecting, organizing, interpreting, and making sense of a complex reality so as to provide guideposts for knowing, analyzing, persuading, and acting" (Rein and Schön 1991, 264). Hence, the manner in which a group perceives an issue will influence and structure its discourse on the issue. The particular frame will restrict some policy choices and make certain outcomes more likely than others (Kohler-Koch 2000; Mazey and Richardson 1997).

It is important to clarify several assumptions that underlie this analysis. From the outset it must be recognized that the term *feminist* is somewhat problematic. There is no single German feminist movement. Nor can it be argued that German women's organizations share a common perspective on what is good for women. Any attempt to generalize *the* feminist or *the* women's movement runs the risk of homogenizing and misrepresenting the wealth of positions held by feminist women's organizations. This article focuses largely on the antipornography stance of one portion of the women's movement. I do not wish to suggest that all women's organizations oppose pornography or even that all forms of pornography are necessarily violence against all women in all circumstances. Nor do I wish to give the impression that the antipornography stance is the only or even dominant position emanating from the feminist movements. Nonetheless, for simplicity's sake, I do frequently use *feminist* to refer specifically to this position. Furthermore, this article focuses on the legal regulation of pornography and the attempts to acquire formal recognition of pornography as discrimination against women. As a result, I assume that legislation is one goal of the feminist fight. This focus has the effect of limiting the actors discussed to those who engage with the state. The position and potential impact of the large number of autonomous women's movements in Germany that consciously reject legislation and engagement with the state as a viable means of action is addressed only insofar as it is relevant to the overall policy-making process and the success of the antipornography feminist position.

The relative success of actors in pursuing a particular framework may depend on a number of factors. In the case of the regulation of pornography in Germany and Europe, I explore three factors that may have contributed to the degree of success of various women's organizations in reframing the issue. Specifically, I address (1) the degree of consensus among civil society actors on the new frame, (2) the impact of preexisting frames that the new frame must overcome, and (3) the degree to which political actors are involved in the formation and dissemination of the new frame. I draw on the concept of the triangle of empowerment (Wieringa and Vargas 1998) to suggest why some forms of feminist mobilization were better able to influence policy than others. Finally, I begin to explore possible conditions that might lead to a spiraling of ideas from the European to the national level such that the successful reframing of an issue at the European level could lead to reframing at the national level.

This article evaluates different frames put forth by various actors and suggests that efforts in Germany to define pornography as discrimination against women have been largely unsuccessful at the national level. In contrast, recent shifts in policy direction in the European Union institutions indicate potential new opportunities to redefine pornography in this way. I begin this article with a brief discussion of the issue of pornography and how, according to some feminists, it harms women. In the second section, I outline the regulation of pornography at the national level. From here, I turn my attention to the European level and two competing frameworks existing therein. On one hand, the representation of the female body is treated as a commodity, free to be traded and moved throughout the Union. On the other hand, an emergent framework structured around issues, such as trafficking in women, violence against women, the elimination of sexism in advertising and the media, and the eradication of child pornography, have contributed to a new perception of the discriminatory basis of pornography. I conclude with the observation that although the issue of pornography and its regulation has been brought to the European table in a number of ways, any real change initiated from the European level must still be accepted and passed at the national level. European regulation might increase the chances of national level acceptance of this new framework, yet it remains an uphill battle.

The choice of Germany as a single case study is deliberate. The extensive ties between Germany and the European Union as well as the political strength and international influence of the country add important dimensions to this study. Germany has been a driving force behind the European project since the early 1950s. There are consequently a number of established channels, interactions and networks of both governing bodies and civil society existing between the national and the European levels. Furthermore, the German state is clearly dominated by a conservative welfare regime and a corresponding gender regime that supports different roles for women and men. The discussion of the construction of the image of women through pornography must be understood within this framework. Finally, the existence of a variety of different women's organizations, many of which were at odds over the issue of pornography, allows me to explore how various groups competed to shape the discourse surrounding the question of pornography. Although the German response to pornography does not represent that of all the member states, the dialogue surrounding the framing of the problem of pornography may offer some important insight into the issue of framing at the European level. The position of Germany relative to the EU, the steadfastness of assumptions about men's and women's roles, and the internal disagreement within the German women's movements make Germany an interesting and relevant country study for this project.

As mentioned, the antipornography position was certainly not the only feminist position discussed in Germany. However, feminists opposing the legislation, namely the so-called autonomous women's movement, tended to avoid confronting the state directly, preferring to work through channels in civil society rather than through the state. As a result, this position was poorly represented in the formal public hearings to be discussed.[1] The focus in the following piece is primarily on antipornography feminists and their struggle to create legislation that in their view was more women-friendly.

Women and Pornography

It is helpful to begin with a definition of *pornography*, although as the article proceeds it will become clear that it is precisely the lack of agreement on a definition that lies at the heart of the issue of its regulation. For the purpose of this article, pornography shall be understood as the representation of the (female) body in a sexually explicit manner that has the effect of reducing women to sexual objects. Pornography may be overtly violent, or it may imply violence through its portrayal of women and their subordination to men.[2] In fact, a common stumbling block in the definition of pornography is the violent/nonviolent distinction (Dines et al. 1998). As we shall see, German lawmakers have focused a good deal of attention on this distinction. For the purposes of this article, violent pornography shall refer to pornographic depiction that includes elements of overt physical violence. Moreover, sexual explicitness remains a central concept to both the legal and the academic understanding of pornography.

It is the sexism and often racism that pornography represents and perpetuates that has been at the core of the antipornography feminist critique (Dines et al. 1998). Pornographic videos frequently show men forcing sex on a woman. They show women refusing sex, yet subsequently enjoying what can only be termed rape. Another common theme in porno films uses sex (often oral and often forced) to "punish" women for not immediately submitting to a man's wishes (Dines et al. 1998; Traudisch 1990). In more extreme videos and photos, women are portrayed in various levels of sexual torture, including painful restraint, physical abuse, penetration with objects, and even mutilation. These representations may take the form of acclaimed "art,"[3] glossy magazines, peep shows in the red light district, or videos.

A less overtly violent but still harmful form of pornography permeates everyday society in the form of sexist advertising. Recently, poster-sized advertisements for German public-interest magazine *Bild* depicting a 20-year-old woman wearing only a G-string were prominently displayed in bus shelters throughout Germany. The caption above her proclaimed, "My record is 8 hours" (*EMMA* On-line, 2002).[4] The text below the photo promised more such stories in the magazine. Overtly sexist advertising and photos are not restricted to adult magazines. Even weekly television guides are known to use women's sexuality to sell their product. *TV Spielfilm*, one of the leading television guides, pictured a nearly naked woman on almost every issue in 2002. These images are not clearly pornographic, given the absence of overt or implied violence. However, by consistently portraying women as sex symbols, these advertisements contribute to the overall objectification of women. This is where sexist advertising coincides with traditional pornography. The line between the two becomes somewhat blurred at this point. As subsequent sections of this article will demonstrate, the prominence of sexist advertising in German society is especially relevant given the recent campaigns at the European level to combat sexism in the media.

The central question facing policy makers requires them to capture where society defines the parameters of acceptable and unacceptable in pornographic and sexual representations. To be of value, political and legal definitions must be clear and concise. Neither German nor European law can claim to fulfill these criteria because lawmakers at both levels have consciously avoided supplying any concrete definition of the term *pornography*. Not surprisingly, this has led to variations in interpretation and difficulty prosecuting those who create and distribute even violent pornography.

Although pornography as such is not defined, German law makes a distinction between so-called *harte Pornographie* (hard pornography) depicting violence, the sexual abuse of children, or sexual acts between people and animals and other forms of pornography, usually referred to as soft or simple pornography.[5] Simple pornography is not defined. In German legal tradition, where a law is not clearly outlined, the system relies on formal commentaries to expand on and explain the intentions of the lawmaker. These commen-

taries summarize competing views, discuss existing case law, and attempt to provide a nonbinding framework within which the court can act. The discussions in legal commentaries seeking to clarify the boundaries of simple pornography frequently rely on moral criteria that are difficult to interpret and subject to different interpretations at different times and by different individuals.[6] As I will demonstrate, relying on vague measures to define pornography is indicative of the tendency in the German case to frame the issue as a moral ill rather than as a reflection of structural power relations in society.

In contrast, feminist legal scholars in both Germany and the United States have offered a precise definition of pornography that includes measures to allow for a (nearly) universal understanding of the term.[7] Rather than setting the parameters of pornography at that which society currently deems "acceptable," feminist legal scholars use concrete measures to clearly discern the pornographic from the erotic and to draw attention to the fact that "classic pornography" is in fact, a graphic representation of the subjugation and degradation of women. The feminist definition clearly establishes "pornography [as] sexual violence perpetrated against women through realistic and clearly sexually degrading representations, in print media or photos, which contain one or more of the following elements" (Baer and Slupik 1988, 172). For an image to be pornographic by this definition it must be (a) violent (explicitly or implicitly) and (b) realistic and (c) degrading and (d) contain one or more of six subsequent elements. These include the representation of women as sex objects who enjoy painful or humiliating experiences; the representation of women as enjoying rape or sexual assault; women represented in degrading scenes or scenes that depict bodily harm, torture, or humiliation or in which women are shown as dirty, to be of less value than men, bleeding, or mutilated in a context that makes this appear sexual (Baer and Slupik 1988, 172). By focusing on the precise form of pornographic depiction, this definition leaves little room for subjective interpretation.

Differently located women are affected by pornography in different ways. Those directly involved in the production of pornography are most likely to be physically and mentally abused, held against their will, and threatened.[8] There is substantial evidence of women having been killed or murdered during a shoot (Baer 1996; Itzin 1996; Schwarzer 1994a). While these women are the obvious victims, from an antipornography feminist stance, even those not directly involved in the industry are objectified and thus harmed by pornography. Pornographic depictions reduce a woman to her sexual organs, depersonalizing and objectifying her More important, pornography portrays violence against women as acceptable behavior. As such, there are indications that pornography can be both directly and indirectly linked to actual acts of violence against women in society as a whole. Though "scientific evidence" linking pornography to sexual violence, rape, and abuse is inconclusive, it is difficult to refute the many personal accounts and women's narratives that demonstrate a relationship between the two. In a study carried out in 1980 by Diane Russell, 10 percent of women reported that they had experienced a situation in which they were "upset" by someone trying to get them to act out something seen in pornographic pictures, movies or books (see Dines et al. 1998; Steinem 1993). Another study of 200 street prostitutes found that 73 percent reported having been raped; of these, 24 percent reported that the rapists had made reference to pornography. This is particularly significant given that the study did not directly address pornography, so this information emerged unsolicited (Dines et al. 1998, 109).

Personal accounts also reveal that pornography and violence are related to racism. The portrayal of race in pornography generally builds on sexual and racist stereotypes of exoticism; consequently, women of color are doubly objectified and degraded through pornography. Feminists argue that regardless of race, age, ethnicity, and nationality, women everywhere are objectified and harmed by pornography. Though women may experience this harm in different ways, the central characteristic is the objectification and degradation of women. As one German feminist put it,

> Pornography as discrimination on the basis of sex violates women everywhere. Marketed throughout the world, pornography is not limited to the countries of its production, nor is the abuse of women through it limited to such locations. In some places, women are raped and tortured and killed for pictures; everywhere, women are silenced (Baer 1996, 52).

For the antipornography feminists, it is not only the individual women used in the production of pornography who are harmed; rather, these women become symbols of Everywoman.

National (De-)Regulation: Moral Issue or Censorship?

The production, possession, distribution, and sale of pornography in Germany is currently regulated through Section 184 of the Strafgesetzbuch (Penal Code).[9] Paragraphs 1 and 2 of Section 184 make it an offense to sell or otherwise make pornographic materials available to minors under the age of 18. Individuals over the age of 18 have full access to pornography, except as limited by Section 3. It is therein illegal for anyone to possess, produce, or otherwise handle pornographic images that contain violence, depict the sexual abuse of children, or show sexual acts between humans and animals (harte Pornographie). However, the legal ban on certain types of pornography does not mean that individuals cannot usually get what they want, whether violent or not. It is generally possible for an adult to get violent pornography in any of the porn shops and most of the video stores in the country (Baer 1996, 2003). Anton-Andreas Guha, political editor of the *Frankfurter Rundschau*, one of Germany's major newspapers, notes in his analysis of the social implications of pornography that "[the law] is fairly lax and barely plays a roll in legal reality. Nobody seems to take it seriously" (1988, 100).

The difficulty with existing legislation is not only the lack of clarity of definition and the resulting inconsistency of interpretation but also a lack of implementation and execution of the legislation. This stems from at least two sources. First, the legislation is embedded in the Penal Code, rather than the Civil Code (public rather than private law). Consequently, individuals who violate that legislation can only be prosecuted by the state. Women who claim to have been harmed by pornography in any way may not press charges independent of the state. In other words, the production of pornography is not considered a crime against women (including those portrayed) but against the state. Thus, only the state may take legal action against a pornographer. This denies women any real agency and leaves an already overburdened state legal system with the task of prosecuting. As this section will demonstrate, the reality that only the state can prosecute pornography underscores the framing of the issue as one of morality rather than discrimination.

Second, the social context in Germany does not encourage censorship or the regulation of private sexuality. Freedom of expression and freedom of the press are both granted through Section 5 of the Grundgesetz (Basic Law). The crimes of the National Socialist regime, and the conviction that this form of censorship must never happen again, elevates freedom of expression and freedom of the press to a very high status within German legal tradition. This certainly has a bearing on any attempts by the state to regulate individual sexuality through measures that might be interpreted as censorship....

Women Fight Back (1976-1988)

Perhaps not surprisingly, the years immediately following the liberalization of the laws saw a dramatic increase in pornographic images with producers often admitting to pushing the limits of the acceptable (Uhse 1990). These images were not confined to the red-light district, skin magazines in the kiosks, or dark sex shops far from the center of town. Rather, the images were everywhere—billboard advertisements, television ads, mainstream news magazines, and public interest magazines. As long as the material did not actually show violence or sexual acts with children or animals, it was legally acceptable. However, even this line was crossed, in particular with reference to children. According to one report on the child sex industry in the early 1980s, children as young as eight years old were victims of child pornography (Schwarzer 1994a). It was clear that the laws were not being enforced.

At least one particular branch of the women's movement reacted against the "pornographication of society" with an open campaign against the depiction of women in sexist advertising and pornographic "art." Under the leadership of Alice Schwarzer, editor of feminist magazine *EMMA*, ten women launched a lawsuit against *Stern* magazine, charging that the sexist representation of women on the covers was an affront to their dignity. This was the first public attempt to reframe the question of pornography to address its impact on women everywhere. *EMMA* argued that the objectification of a single woman and the commodification of this woman as a sex object was degrading to all women. Though the women lost their court battle, they did celebrate two small victories. First, the judge found the women to be in the "moral right," although the law required him to find them legally "in the wrong" (Schwarzer 1994b). Moreover, he stated that he hoped that in 20 years a court would be able to rule otherwise. This moral victory was accompanied by the success of bringing pornography as discrimination into public debate. The ensuing PorNO campaign culminated in 1987 with a draft legislation proposal that declared pornography a form of violence and discrimination against women. Most important, following the example of Dworkin and MacKinnon's law in the United States, the legislation sought to move pornography from the criminal to the civil branch of law. If successful, this would give women a direct means to fight pornography. The proposed legislation reignited debate on pornography begun in the parliament in 1970....

Although the feminist framing was, in the end, unsuccessful (i.e., there is no German legislation that empowers women to seek judicial retribution if they have been harmed by pornographic images, nor is there a widely accepted understanding of pornography as discrimination and hence as one structural barrier to women's equality), the temporary prominence of the debate was largely the result of the feminist reframing attempts. Putting the pornography debate on the table was facilitated through public support and partially propagated through the widely circulated *EMMA*. It was also assisted by an increase in the number of women in the decision-making process, which gave feminists access to the political arena. To return to Vargas and Wieringa's triangle of empowerment, it is clear that all three points (the women's movement, feminist politicians, and femocrats) as well as the links between them were more developed than in the early 1970s. However, the legislation failed and the issue quickly dropped from sight. Why?

In the beginning of this article, I suggested that to be successful, a new frame must enjoy some degree of consensus among civil society actors. Given the disagreement among the various branches of the women's movement, this condition was not fulfilled. This lack of consensus gives the government an escape hatch for avoiding addressing the issue. Moreover, at least two competing frames already existed. On one hand, the 1975 legislation was based on the assumption that pornography is immoral and therefore harmful to young people. On the other hand, it was based on the premise that to ban pornography would be to restrict freedom of the press. Both of these frames (protection of the youth and freedom of the press) enjoyed very prominent positions in the collective German consciousness. The attempt to reframe pornography as discriminatory and violence against women could not compete with these existing frames. Finally, there was little support from the official political channels. Although some of the female politicians supported the legislation, they faced strong opposition from within the parties. Because Baer and Slupik were not operating from within the party structures, their access to the political arena was still limited. In addition, the issue fell from the

table as in 1989 Germany was suddenly thrown into upheaval by the fall of communism and the reunification of East and West. Pornography and women's dignity took a back seat to more pressing issues. In Europe however, the debate was only just beginning.

European Regulations: Commodity or Discrimination?

Whereas in Germany pornography is officially treated as a criminal matter and its regulation is viewed as a question of protecting youth and morality, at the supranational level pornography enters the sphere of public debate only insofar as it is considered a commercial good. The European institutions officially see regulations of pornography only as potential barriers to the free market. However, as this section demonstrates, recent years have seen a shift in these policies toward pornography as discrimination in a manner that surpasses any steps taken at the German level.

The proliferation of pornographic materials in the European Union is regulated through the Broadcasting Directive (89/552/EEC; Council of the European Communities 1989), also referred to as the Television without Frontiers Directive. This legislation aims to strengthen competition in broadcasting among the member states and to remove barriers to broadcasts between them. It places responsibility for screening the appropriateness of broadcasts with the member state in which they originate. If a transmission is deemed suitable in one member state, and it conforms to the regulations on content, advertising, and so on, then the receiving member state may not subject these transmissions to further review. In other words, what one member state deems appropriate is considered appropriate in all member states. Specific provisions do allow member states with stricter national regulation of media transmissions to maintain these standards, at least to a degree. However, in the absence of a clear definition of acceptability and pornography, this legislation suffers from many of the same problems as the German legislation.

Under Article 22 of the Television without Frontiers Directive, member states may subject transmissions that "seriously impair the physical, mental or moral development of minors" to additional review and/or barriers. Specifically, the directive mentions programs that "involve pornography or gratuitous violence" under this category. Again, without a common definition of pornography, or common guidelines to determine what might "seriously impair" the development of a child, this article is open to a great deal of interpretation. Moreover, one must consider that terms such as *gratuitous* and *moral* are as difficult to define as pornography itself. As such, this legislation alone can do little to counter the subordination of women through pornography. In fact, European law, which assumes responsibility on the part of the transmitting states, may even result in more relaxed controls (Weigend 1994) as member states assume that the transmissions are being adequately controlled in the country of origin.

In 1997 the directive was amended and expanded in light of the rapidly changing broadcast technology (97/36/EC; Council of the European Union 1997). These amendments included some minor changes to the regulation of pornographic imagery, but nothing that would represent a change in the perception of regulation of pornography as simply a barrier to the free exchange of commodities. Article 22(2) was added to distinguish between programs that might seriously impair the development of minors (as regulated by the original Article 22) from those that impair their well-being and development. Broadcasts that only impair the development of youth may be broadcast throughout the Union with certain restrictions. For example, the broadcast must be transmitted late at night when children are unlikely to be watching television or must be sent in scrambled form. If the program is broadcast in unscrambled form, an audio warning must proceed the broadcast or a visual warning must appear on screen throughout the program. Certainly, the distinction between "serious impairment" and only "impairment" is a normative question. Given the different national legis-

lation of the various member states (Weigend 1994), regulation is quite complicated. If a member state finds a broadcast to be unacceptable, it may initiate a complicated process in order to ban the station from future transmissions (European Court of First Instance 2000, case T-69/99). Clearly, the intention of the directive is to safeguard broadcasters and ensure competition in the European broadcasting system rather than limit the proliferation of pornographic materials. In contrast to the German framework, which regulates pornography based on the need to protect family values, morality, and freedom of the individual, the European framework protects the free market. This not only prevents the institutions from seeing the effects of pornographic transmissions on women but also contributes to the commodification of the human body and the objectification of women. As will be evidenced, this is perpetuated through rulings of the European Court of Justice.

The European Court has consistently reinforced pornography as a good or commodity open for trade throughout the market (European Court 1979, case 34/79; European court 1986, case 121/85). In a 1979 case, the Court permitted member states to limit the importation of pornographic materials, but in so doing formally defined pornography as a commodity. It is thus subject to the same regulatory framework as any other community good. In a later ruling, the Court found that the member states could not restrict the importation of sex toys (which, if interpreted broadly, could also include sex videos), given that the trade in these objects was not illegal on the domestic market. Thus, using the antipornography feminist argument, one must recognize that the Court has contributed to the discriminatory framework first by commodifying women and second by opening the national markets to imports of pornography from all member states.

Although the first incarnation of the Broadcast Directive came to fruition shortly after the national debates already addressed, there is no evidence that the alternate frame posed by feminists had any impact on European-level legislation. Moreover, there is no indication of women's organizations becoming involved in the negotiation of the Broadcast Directive at any level. At this early stage there appears to have been very little if any interaction between the national and the supranational levels. In 1997 neither civil society nor the German government appears to have pushed the alternate framing to be implemented through the European level.

One of the earliest indications of a "spiraling of ideas" from one level to the other on the issue of pornography seems to have come through Lissy Gröner, member of the European Parliament (MEP) and a highly positioned member of the *Arbeitskreis Sozialistischer Frauen* (Working Group of Socialist Women, the women's caucus of the SPD). In the early 1990s, Gröner made several statements to the German media that the European Television without Frontiers Directive made the trade in pornographic television productions easier (Deutscher Frauenrat 1993). Given the wording of the directive as discussed, there is certainly reason to believe that this might be the outcome of the new directive.

On a larger scale, there was a broad shift in European gender policy in the early 1990s, owing to several key developments, including the establishment of the European Women's Lobby (EWL) in 1990 and the formal incorporation of the principles of equality and mainstreaming into the Amsterdam Treaty (1996) (Hoskyns 2000; Rees 1998). Following the Beijing Conference in 1995, the Community implemented widespread mainstreaming practices through which a gender perspective was to be incorporated at all levels and in all policies. In theory, mainstreaming ought to have been implemented in the reform of the Television without Frontiers Directive, but this did not occur. Had it done so, it might have offered valuable opportunities for antipornography feminists in the Community to push the alternate frame. As Pollack and Hafner-Burton (2000) demonstrate, mainstreaming was quite slow to permeate some directorate generals (DGs), including DG Competition. This they attribute to the dominant neoliberal framework of the DG as well as the lack of a strong female presence

therein. With the Broadcast Directive on the table so early in the mainstreaming agenda, it is not surprising that a gender perspective was not adequately addressed. A further possible means to open the discussions to an antipornography feminist perspective might have come through the European Women's Lobby; however, it did not comment on or contribute to this legislative process (EWL 2003, personal communication). Failing a common national position and direct lobbying from the EWL, it is perhaps not surprising that the antipornography feminist position did not make great headway into the final directive.

In contrast, several indicators show that both the commission and the European Parliament are beginning to act against structural inequalities that contribute to women's discrimination. Included in this emergent framework is an understanding of pornography as discrimination. In 1993, the Parliament took the lead in providing an alternate framework by issuing a resolution on pornography (European Parliament 1993) in response to motions by a number of MEPs to adopt a common stance on pornography. These motions were introduced at least once a year beginning in 1990 and supported by a substantial majority of MEPs from a wide variety of member states.

This document marks the first formal step taken by a European institution to adopt an alternate framework on pornography. It recognizes pornography as "an affront to human dignity ... [stimulating] certain symptoms of undesirable social behaviors, particularly against women," and as "a systematic practice of exploitation and subordination based on sex that disproportionately harms women and contributes to inequality between the sexes, existing power imbalances in society, female subordination and male domination." Perhaps even more important, Parliament argues for European competency in this realm based on Article 3 of the European Convention for the Protection of Human Rights and Fundamental Freedoms, which guarantees protection from torture, inhuman, or degrading treatment and punishment. The body furthermore pushes for the "protection of the victims of the manufacture of offensive products (actual victims)." This constitutes the first formal acknowledgment at the European level that women are not always willing participants in the production of pornography.

The suggestions laid out in this document were largely ignored by the other bodies; it advances several important ideas. First, it officially defines pornography as discrimination against women and as contributing to the structural inequalities of women. Second, it argues boldly that in its collective opinion, the European Community does have the jurisdiction to address this issue. Finally, it establishes the "actors" in pornographic material as victims of the system. Clearly Parliament was moving beyond the framework of pornography as immoral or damaging to youth that was then prevalent in the legislation at the German national level in favor of one that views pornography as discrimination or even torture....

Finally, the current Framework Strategy on Equal Opportunities (2001-2005), a document outlining the central aims of the Community policies on gender equality, has targeted gender stereotyping as its main priority. This clearly demonstrates that the Community has recognized the need to deal with images that by presenting men and women in particular roles reinforce traditional gender roles. The representation of women as sex objects, always ready to please a man, could come under attack through programs developed under this Framework Strategy. Again, note that this does not open the debate immediately to defining pornography as discrimination, but it does open some possible new channels. Moreover, this new action to recognize media stereotypes as one possible structural barrier to women's equality also has implications for a broader understanding of discrimination, one that leaves room for the discussion of pornography from an antipornography feminist point of view....

The lack of influence of the women's organizations is not only a result of community policies. Women's organizations have not always been open to using the Community level to pursue goals at the national. Baer, commenting on the role of the European level on regulating pornography, remarked, "We didn't give it any thought ... at that time [1987]; the European Directives were such that the 1975 Directive on equal pay was central and the European Community focused on employment life. We consciously did not want to make this [the draft legislation] an issue of working life" (Baer 2003). Baer does suggest that it would have been possible to do so by making the issue one of discrimination at work, looking at it from the perspective of the actresses, and bringing the whole legislation through the prostitution track. But she argues the political climate in Germany, which viewed prostitution as immoral and illegal work, would have made this an extremely problematic route to pursue. Consequently, given the nature of the European institutions and their focus on employment, there appears to have been a conscious rejection of this level as a possible means of reframing the problem. Similarly, the relationship between the official German women's movement (Frauenrat) and the European institutions was quite strained; close ties between the organizations are only now beginning to develop.

There is no indication that the German women's movement is presently pursuing any action against pornography through the European channels, nor that the issue is of concern within the major German women's organizations.[10] A number are, however, focusing on violence against women and the proliferation of sexist advertising, and they are currently pursuing initiatives, though somewhat belatedly, at both the national and the European levels. Perhaps these organizations have learned from the successes at the European level and adopted a frame that prioritizes opposition to violence against women. By modifying their stance to better coincide with one that is more likely to be accepted by the broader public, the organizations have increased their chances of successfully influencing the understanding of the nature of violence against women. Indeed as both the Commission and Parliament demonstrate, this reframing is already under way. But the frame these organizations have chosen precludes attention to pornography by placing sexual exploitation at the center of a debate to protect women from violence and trafficking.

Conclusions

Although at the national level antipornography feminist framing played a prominent role, these women were largely unsuccessful in translating their position into legislative success. In contrast, there has been a degree of success in reframing pornography at the European level, despite no clear articulation of the antipornography feminist position. How were the conditions different at the European level than at the national level? In contrast to the German case, at the European level there seems to have been some degree of consensus among civil society actors. There has been widespread support for a frame that emphasizes the need to fight violence against women and trafficking. Though not explicitly mentioned, there is room within this frame to pick up on the issue of pornography. Moreover, the additional focus on sexist advertising also allows some room to discuss pornography as a structural barrier to women's equality. Though not as radical or as empowering as the framework put forth by German antipornography feminists, this open-ended framework allows for the incorporation of a number of issues, including that of pornography as discrimination. Perhaps these small steps may in the end prove to be more productive than radical ones.

The preexisting framework and gender regime in the European Union institutions are not as strong as at the national level. As the EU began to address trafficking in women as a problem of illegal immigration and hence necessary to the internal security of the Community, the preexisting framework that supported the commodification of sexuality came under challenge. Addressing the issue of violence against women similarly contributed to a shift in framework away from a commodification of the female body to one in which violence against women is understood as one barrier to women's equality. Moreover, given

the lack of existing (criminal) legislation on pornography (as in Germany), cognitive inertia binding the institutions to a particular framework was less intense than at the national level. Although the neoliberal framework of DG Competition and the European Court of Justice helped perpetuate the representation of pornography as a commodity, other institutions, in particular the European Parliament, have sought to go beyond this framework. New initiatives launched through the Beijing Conference, including mainstreaming, forced a certain shift in perspectives.

In the future, mainstreaming policies will require all bodies to take gender perspectives into consideration. Hence, the dominant framework will continue to be challenged. This offers the possibility to bring new issues, such as the representation of women in the media, trafficking in women, sexual exploitation of children, and violence against women, onto the agenda. In framing each of these issues, the regulation of pornography may be addressed....

I can attribute the lack of success in reframing the issue as discrimination within the German legislation to a number of factors. First, divisions in the feminist movement prevented the presentation of a strong united front. This was similarly reflected in the split in the Green Party between those in favor of protection and those in favor of freedom of expression. Second, the existing framework of pornography as a moral issue and as a cause of concern with regard to the values and development of the youth fits well in German society. The strong male breadwinner state and emphasis on the importance of the family, particularly the value of the mother in the home, supports the existing framing of the issue. Because of the extent of the broader issues connected to this, it is unlikely that the framework will undergo a rapid shift. This was evident in both of the debates surrounding the pornography laws. Third, despite attempts in 1988, the issue remained outside the broad span of party politics. The hearings took place outside of the legislature, and there was no debate within the legislature itself. Though it might have been easier to push the issue through the party route, as Baer commented, one would have still been confronted by the male gatekeepers within the parties (Baer 2003). Even if the proposals had come from within the ranks of the parties, it is unlikely that it would have made it all the way to a parliamentary debate. Finally, there was a lack of coordination between women's movement, politicians, and femocrats. Without this triangle, the issue could not be pushed from all sides. In 1988, when there was more political support for the proposal than in the 1970s, we do see limited acceptance from the politicians. None, however, was willing to take it on as a pet issue, which might have given the legislation the boost it needed.

At the European level, the prospects were somewhat better. Here, there was no preexisting framework to first be overcome. The lack of European gender regime means that the cognitive inertia framing an issue in a particular matter is not as strong.[11] Furthermore, Parliament's interest in the issue and Europe's budding competence in both trafficking and violence against women offered a legislative home for the issue of pornography as discrimination. However, because the Union does not have competency in penal law, any changes that it might be able to influence will be limited to the contextual and the perceptual.

Questions of body politics can only be changed and reframed with the cooperation of all levels and all feminist forces. As this article has demonstrated, feminists have failed to unite around the issue of pornography in Germany and at the European level. Given the complexity of the issues, it is perhaps too simplistic to consider the issue of pornography as discrimination against all women in all cases. Indeed, the multiplicity of feminisms and the huge differences in women's situations, needs, and sexuality makes it somewhat problematic to imagine a common stance on the issue in the future. As such, it might be more fruitful for those wishing to fight the sexist representation of women to first attack the representation of women in advertising and the media more broadly. As the everyday portrayal of women shifts to better represent women's multiple roles in society, perhaps the appeal of violent, degrading pornography will also decrease. Although the EU offers some new opportunities to reframe the matter of pornography as one of discrimination against women, the member states will still need to accept this framework. The EU can go a long way in eventually forcing this shift in perspective in the member states, but it cannot succeed alone.

Author's Note

I would very much like to thank Sonya Michel for her helpful comments on this piece. My thanks also to the two anonymous reviewers for their invaluable suggestions. Naturally, any mistakes remain my own.

NOTES

1. Even within the propornography and antipornography camps, it is problematic to assume a monolithic stance. Indeed, a number of organizations (including the women's religious groups) supported regulation of pornography on the basis of morality rather than discrimination. Those feminists who supported pornography similarly differed on their reasoning. The autonomous movements that took a propornography/antilegislation feminist stance frequently avoided the debate emerging in the formal and public sphere (one exception is Gehrke n.d.). In general these organizations focused their efforts on action at the level of civil society. For more on the variety of feminist positions in the pornography debate in the United States see Vance (1984) and Duggan and Hunter (1995).

2. This article deals with pornographic representations in film and photo. It does not address the widespread proliferation of pornography on the Internet.

3. The question of where to draw the line between pornography and art is a particularly complex one. German feminists have been especially vocal against the work of "artist" Helmut Newton. For more on this campaign and Newton's photos see Schwarzer (1993, 1994b).

4. This poster campaign sparked public outrage when one man wrote to *EMMA* and other institutions describing an incident he had witnessed. The man apparently approached a bus shelter late one evening where two drunk men and a lone women were waiting. The men glanced at the poster and then at the women and jeered, "Hey doll, what's your record? We could test it right here to see!" (*EMMA* On-line 2002). (This and all subsequent translations are my own.)

5. The term *simple (einfach)* seems to be the preferred one in the German literature, where a further distinction between soft and simple pornography is occasionally made. Here, "soft pornography" refers to images in which the sexual act itself is more implied than shown. Furthermore, soft pornography does not generally include close-up photos of the female genitalia or of the erect penis. In contrast, simple pornography does show the sex act but without violence or other elements that would characterize it as hard (see Traudisch 1990; Russell 1993; Dane and Schmidt 1990). It is important for the English-speaking audience to note the distinction between this understanding and the common English usage, in which *hard-core* refers to the degree of penetration shown.

6. For a more complete discussion on defining pornography in the German context, see Gehrke (n.d.), Ostendorf (2001), Tröndle and Fischer (1999), and Weigend (1994).

7. To my knowledge, the first to put forth such a definition were American feminists Andrea Dworkin and Catherine MacKinnon in 1983. The subsequent definitions and laws proposed by German feminists drew extensively on Dworkin and MacKinnon's work but adapted them to the German legal system (Baer 2003; Dworkin and MacKinnon 1988). Although there has been a particularly active network of feminists and academics working on this issue in the United States, this article relies almost exclusively on the German literature. This is a conscious decision on my part. The portrayal of pornography is dependent on society's acceptance and collective understanding of nakedness and sexuality. Differences

in the German and American context in this respect are quite great, with German society on the whole much more open to sexuality. To avoid assumptions about sexuality within the respective societies, I focus primarily on the German academic literature and debates. Though this at times comes at the expense of a very rich American literature on the subject, I consider this to be more appropriate.

8. Women of color and migrant women are more frequently the targets of sexual exploitation. Moreover, the vulnerable status of many non-EU (illegal) migrants in the European Union makes it more difficult for them to escape abusive situations. For more on this, see Elman (2001).

9. It is, to a lesser degree, also regulated by Section 131 of the Penal Code, which restricts media productions that glorify violence, as well as Section 6 of the Jugendschutzgesetz (Youth Protection Act). Given the interconnectedness of these sections, this article will focus only on Section 184.

10. I have made inquiries to several German NGOs and women's organizations, including the Frauenrat.

11. In the member states, a gender regime is constructed and reinforced through legislation in diverse areas including social security, maternity and parental leave, the availability of day care, and the opening hours of schools. The European level, given the lack of legislation in these areas, does not perpetuate a particular understanding of men's and women's roles in this manner. Though there are underlying assumptions about gender roles, these are not nearly as developed as at the national levels. For more, see MacRae (2002).

REFERENCES

Baer, Susanne. 1996. "Pornography and Sexual Harassment in the EU." Pp. 51-65 in *Sexual Politics and the European Union*, ed. R. Amy Elman. Providence: Berghahn Books.

— . 2003. Interview by author, 10 March. Tape recording. Humboldt Universität, Berlin.

Baer, Susanne, and Vera Slupik. 1988. "Entwurf Eines Gesetzes Gegen Pornographie" [Draft for an

Antipornography Legislation]. *Kritische Justiz* [Critical Justice] 21: 171-181.

Black, Ian. 2003. "Brussels considers Ban on Raunchy TV Images." *Guardian* 25 June. Available online at www.europa.eu.int/comm/commissioners/diamantopoulou/doc/guardian25062003.pdf. Accessed 20 July 2003.

Bremme, Bettina. 1990. *Sexualität im Zerrspiegel: Die Debatte um Pornographie* [Distorted Picture of Sexuality: The Debate Surrounding Pornography]. Münster and New York: Waxman.

Council of the European Communities. 1989. Council Directive of 3 October 1989 on the coordination of certain provisions laid down by Law, Regulation and Administrative Action in Member States concerning the pursuit of television broadcasting activities. Directive 89/552/EEC. Luxembourg. Published in *Official Journal of the European Communities* L298, 17/10: 23-30.

— . 2000. Communication from the Commission to the Council and the European Parliament: Combating trafficking in human beings and combating the sexual exploitation of children and child pornography. 22 January 2001. COM (2000) 854 final/2. Brussels.

— . 2003. Justice and Home Affairs Funding Programs. Online document available at www.europa.eu.int/comm/justice_home/funding_agis/funding_agis_en.htm. Accessed August 2003.

Council of the European Union. 1997. Directive of the European Parliament and of the Council of 30 June 1997 amending Council Directive 89/552/EEC on the coordination of certain provisions laid down by Law, Regulation and Administrative Action in Member States concerning the pursuit of television broadcasting activities. Directive 97/36/EC. Luxembourg. Published in *Official Journal of the European Communities* L 202, 30/70: 60-70.

Dane, Eva, and Renate Schmidt, eds. 1990. *Frauen und Männer und Pornographie* [Men, Women and Pornography]. Frankfurt: Fischer.

Deutscher Bundestag. 1971. "Ausschuss für Jugend, Familie und Gesundheit. Ausschussdrucksache 61" [German Lower House Committee for Youth, Family and Health. Committee Printed Matter]. Bonn. 9 June.

— . 1973a. "Beigabe 2. Sonderausschuss für die Strafrechtsreform" [Special Committee on Penal Code Reform]. 13 March. Bonn.

— . 1973b. "5. Sitzung des Sonderausschusses für die Strafrechtsreform" [Meeting of the Special Committee on Penal Code Reform]. 21 March. Bonn. Pp. 60-75.

Deutscher Bundesrat. 1973. "Büro des Rechtsausschusses 2701e (1)—Nr. R 63/73. Niederschrift über die Sitzung des Unterausschusses des Rechtausschusses" [German Upper House. Office of the Legal Committee. Minutes of the meeting of the Legal Committee's Subcommittee]. Bonn. 13 June.

Deutscher Frauenrat. 1993. "EG-Fernsehrichtlinie bietet Schutz für Jugend" [EC television Directive offers protection for Youth]. *Informationen für die Frau* [Information for Women] July/Aug: 25-26.

Dines, Gail, Robert Jenson, and Ann Russo. 1998. *Pornography: The Consumption and Production of Inequality*. New York: Routledge.

Duggan, Lisa, and Nan D. Hunter. 1995. *Sex Wars: Sexual Dissent and Political Culture*. New York: Routledge.

Dworkin, Andrea, and Catherine A. MacKinnon. 1988. *Pornography and Civil Rights: A New Day for Women's Equality*. Minneapolis, MN: Organizing Against Pornography.

Elman, R. Amy, ed. 1996. *Sexual Politics and the European Union: The New Feminist Challenge*. Providence, RI: Berghahn Books.

— . 2001. "Testing the Limits of European Citizenship: Ethnic Hatred and Male Violence." *NWSA Journal* fall: 49-69.

EMMA On-line. 2002. "Wie Bild so Richtig Baden Ging!" [How Bild really messed up]. Online document available at www.emma.de.content/ccc 1042475730010.html. Accessed 3 June 2003.

European Court. 1979. *Regina v. Maurice Donald Henn and John Frederick Ernest Darby*. Judgment of the Court on 14 December 1979, case 34/79.

— . 1986. *Conegate Limited v. HM Customs & Excise*. Judgment of the Court (Fourth Chamber) of 11 March 1986, case 121/85.

European Court of First Instance. 2000. *Danish Satellite TV (DSTV) A/S (Eurotica Rendez-Vous televi-*

sion) v. Commission of the European Communities.
Judgment of the Court on 13 December 2000, case
T-69/99.

European Parliament. 1993. "Resolution on Pornography." A3-0259/93. Published in Official Journal of
the European Communities C 20, 1994, Item 5.

— . 1997. "Resolution on Discrimination against
Women in Advertising." A4-0258/1997. Minutes
of 16 September 1997. Available online at
www3.eruoparl.eu.int. Accessed 28 May 2003.

FT.Com. 2003. "Europe Is a Long Way from a Sexism
Directive." 27 June. Online document available at
www.europa.eu.int/comm/commissioners/diamantopoulou/doc/ft27062003.pdf. Accessed 20 July
2003.

Gehrke, Claudia, ed. n.d. *Frauen und Pornographie:
Konkursbuch* [Women and Pornography: A Guide to
"Going Bust"]. Tübingen: Verlag Claudia Gehrke.

Guha, Anton-Andrea. 1988. "Sexuelle Gewalt und
Gesellschaftliche Vermittlung" [Sexual Violence
and Social Perceptions]. *Vorgänge* 27(5): 99-111.

Hilson, Chris. 2002. "New Social Movements: The
Role of Legal Opportunity." *Journal of European
Public Policy* 9(2): 238-255.

Hoskyns, Catherine. 2000. "A Study of Four Action
Programs on Equal Opportunities." Pp. 43-59 in
Gender Policies in the European Union, ed. Mariagrazia Rossilli. New York: Peter Lang.

Itzin, Catherine. 1996. "Pornography, Harm and
Human Rights: The UK in European Context." Pp.
67-81 in *Sexual Politics and the European Union*,
ed. R. Amy Elman. Providence, RI: Berghahn
Books.

Kohler-Koch, Beate. 2000. "Framing: The Bottleneck
of Constructing Legitimate Institutions." *Journal
of European Public Policy* 7(4): 513-531.

Leidholdt, Dorchen. 1990. "When Women Defend
Pornography." Pp. 125-131 in *The Sexual Liberals
and the Attack on Feminism*, ed. Dorchen Leidholdt and Janice G. Raymond. New York: Pergamon Press.

Lenz, Marlene. 2003. Interview by author, March
2003. Tape recording. Bonn.

MacRae, Heather. 2002. "Gender Regimes, the
German State and the European Union." Paper presented to the European Community Studies Association conference, Toronto.

Maurer, Andreas. 2003. "The Legislative Powers and
Impact of the European Parliament." *Journal of
Common Market Studies* 41(2): 227-247.

Mazey, Sonia, and Jeremy Richardson. 1997. "Policy
Framing: Interest Groups and the Lead Up to 1996
Inter-Governmental Conference." *West European
Politics* 20(3): 111-133.

Ostendorf, Heribert. 2001. "Diskussion: Zur Forderung nach einem Neuen Pornographiebegriff oder
zum Verantwortlichen Umgang mit Pornographie
im Fernsehen" [Discussion: On the Demand for a
New Definition of Pornography or the Responsible
use of Pornography on Television]. *Monatsschrift
für Kriminologie und Strafrechtsreform* [Monthly
Publication for Criminology and Penal Code
Reform] 84(5): 372-385.

Ostner, Ilona, and Jane Lewis. 1994. "Gender and the
Evolution of European Social Policies." *ZeS-Arbeitspapier* No. 4/94. Bremen: Center for Social
Policy Research.

Pollack, Mark A., and Emilie Hafner-Burton. 2000.
"Mainstreaming Gender in the European Union."
Journal of European Public Policy 7(3): 432-456.

Rees, Teresa. 1998. *Mainstreaming Equality in the
European Union*. London: Routledge.

Rein, Martin, and Schön, Daniel. 1991. "Frame-Reflective Policy Discourse." Pp. 262-289 in
Social Sciences and Modern State: National Experiences and Theoretical Crossroads, ed. P. Wagner.
Cambridge: Cambridge University Press.

Russell, Diana E.H. 1993. "Introduction." Pp. 1-20 in
Making Violence Sexy: Feminist Views on Pornography, ed. Diana E.H. Russell. Buckingham: Open
University Press.

Schwarzer, Alice. 1993. "Newton: Kunst oder
Pornografie?" [Newton: Art or Pornography?]
EMMA 6 (October). Available online at
www.aliceschwarzer.de/textevon/c104265618032
8.html. Accessed 3 June 2003.

— . 1994a. "Ein Gesetz Gegen Pornographie?" [A Law
against Pornography?]. Pp. 31-70 in *PorNO*, ed.
Alice Schwarzer. Köln: Kiepenheuer and Witsch.

— . 1994b. "Newton Und Rheims — Kunst Oder
Faschistoide Pornographie?" [Newton and Rheims
— Art or Fascistic Pornography?]. Pp. 10-27 in
PorNO, ed. Alice Schwarzer. Köln: Kiepenheuer
and Witsch.

Steinem, Gloria. 1993. "The Real Linda Lovelace." Pp. 23-31 in *Making Violence Sexy: Feminist Views on Pornography*, ed. Diana E.H. Russell. Buckingham, UK: Open University Press.

Traudisch, Dora. 1990. "Von einer, die Auszog und das Fürchten Lernte. Beobachtungen zur weiblichen Sexualität im Pornofilm" [From a Woman Who Went Forth to Learn What Fear Was: Observations on Female Sexuality in Pornofilms]. Pp. 110-129 in *Frauen und Männer und Pornographie* [Women and Men and Pornography], ed. Eva Dane and Renate Schmidt. Frankfurt: Fischer.

Tröndle, Herbert, and Thomas Fischer. 1999. *Kommentar zum Strafgesetzbuch* [Commentary on the Penal Code], 49th ed. Munich: Verlag C.H. Beck.

Uhse, Beate. 1990. "Bedarf, Bedürfnis, Befriedigung" [Need, Allowance and Satisfaction]. Pp. 94-102 in *Frauen und Männer und Pornographie*, ed. Eva Dane and Renate Schmidt. Frankfurt: Fischer.

Vance, Carole S, ed. 1984. *Pleasure and Danger: Exploring Female Sexuality*. New York: Routledge.

Weigend, Thomas. 1994. "Strafrechtliche Pornographieverbote in Europa" [The Criminal Prohibition of Pornography in Europe]. Pp. 26-49 in *Pornographie Ohne Grenzen: Proceedings from the Herbsttagung des Instituts für Urheber-und Medienrecht in Zusammenarbeit mit MEDIENTAGE MÜNCHEN held in Munich, October 13, 1993* [Pornography without Frontiers: Proceedings from the August Meeting of the Institute for Copyright and Media Law in Cooperation with Media Days Munich], ed. Jürgen Becker. Baden-Baden: Nomos.

Wieringa, Saskia, and Virginia Vargas. 1998. "The Triangle of Empowerment: Processes and Actors in the Making of Public Policy for Women." Pp. 3-23 in *Women's Movements and Public Policy in Europe, Latin America and the Caribbean*, ed. Geertje Lycklama, Saski Wieringa, and Virginia Vargas. New York: Garland Publishing.

A RELATIONAL CRITIQUE OF THE RIGHT TO PRIVACY: THE CASE OF PORNOGRAPHY AND THE INTERNET

Alison Minea and Christine M. Koggel

Alison Minea has a degree in philosophy from Bryn Mawr College. She is currently a Juris Doctor candidate at the University of Colorado, with interests in telecommunications and technology law. She is on the board of editors for the Journal on Telecommunications and High Technology Law.

Christine Koggel teaches philosophy at Bryn Mawr College. She is the author of Perspectives on Equality: Constructing a Relational Theory *(1998), editor of* Moral Issues in Global Perspective *(first edition, 1999; and second edition, 2006), and co-editor with Wesley Cragg of* Contemporary Moral Issues *(fourth edition, 1997; and fifth edition, 2004).*

Minea and Koggel critically examine traditional liberal arguments for privacy in the context of the Internet and the availability of pornographic images and services on it. Privacy has been defended as necessary for protecting the individual from unwanted intrusion and for allowing individuals freedom to choose and develop relationships without censor or interference. Minea and Koggel argue that technological features of the Internet call for a move from focusing on individual freedom to the relationships that get formed and the effect that these have on individuals. They raise moral issues of accountability and responsibility with respect to the implications of the isolated nature of Internet usage on the beliefs and values at the level of the individual, communities, and nations, and on relations between nations and peoples.

The Internet has brought unprecedented changes to human life, in terms of how we access information, what information we make available to others, the goods and services to which we have access, and the relationships we form with others in cyberspace. The Internet's usefulness as a global network for things such as fighting crime or improving medical treatment is undeniable. But that same global network has allowed the proliferation of activities and technologies that have become increasingly beyond the control of local, national, and international law. The same features that allow easy access to other cultures, languages, and practices and thereby create opportunities for increased tolerance of difference and for the protection of human rights also allow the exploitation of people by individuals or groups using the Internet as a commercial tool to promote, buy, and sell images and services. Pornography is one area of the Internet where there is an explosion of such images and services and where the exchange of such content is facilitated by increasingly sophisticated technology designed to thwart detection of the identity of those using the Internet for these purposes. A detailed study by the Council of Europe reports that most countries have no legislation regulating the use of the Internet with respect to adult pornography, prostitution, and the trafficking of human beings for the purpose of sexual exploitation (Council of Europe, 2003: 9). From the comfort of one's home, individuals can form relationships, virtual and real, with individuals or groups from anywhere in the world and say, be, and do whatever they desire with little or no monitoring or control. The Internet would appear to be a place where privacy and freedom of expression reign supreme.

In this paper, we address *moral* questions about responsibility and accountability to ourselves and others when the Internet is promoted as a place to communicate and exchange information anonymously. We take no stand on issues of censorship and control, though we point to the ways in which technological advances allow anonymity of users and thereby make legislation difficult, if not impossible. Organizations such as the American Civil Liberties Union and the Electronic Privacy Information Center attempt to safeguard the digital rights of the public by serving as watchdogs of the government and corporations. Scholars such as Lawrence Lessig in *Code and Other Laws of Cyberspace* (1999) and Billy Zoellick in *CyberRegs: A Business Guide to Web Property, Privacy, and Patents* (2001) have taken up the task of discussing issues of the government and corporations regulating the Internet and violating the privacy of citizens. We focus on ordinary people who use the Internet through applications such as the World Wide Web, electronic mail, newsgroups, Internet Relay Chat (IRC), and Electronic Bulletin Boards (EBBs). These are areas where electronic monitoring is becoming increasingly difficult. Moreover, monitoring is illegal in many countries, where using the content of electronic messages for criminal prosecution is only acceptable if it is discovered during a house search or communicated to authorities by the addressee (Council of Europe, 2003: 78). Our concern is less with the legalities of monitoring and control than with the implications of the isolated nature of Internet usage for the behavior of ordinary people and for societies that increasingly use the Internet to interact and exchange information in a medium vastly different from any other available in the pre-Internet era.

Our argument centers on the need to critically examine traditional liberal arguments that defend privacy in terms of individual rights to show their inadequacy with respect to dealing with these

structural changes to human life. In focusing exclusively on benefits to the individual when privacy rights are protected, we fail to appreciate that the Internet also provides an environment where moral accountability and responsibility in human interactions are severely diminished. We can only come to understand the dangerous implications of decreased moral accountability on the Internet when we move privacy discourse away from a narrow focus on individual needs and desires to an examination of how relationships and society as a whole are affected by the anonymous and isolated nature of Internet-based human life. We describe what the technologies allow and their use by the pornography industry to outline and defend a relational approach, one that has been used in a number of areas in applied ethics and moral enquiry more generally.[1] A relational approach asks about the kinds of relationships, at both personal and public levels, that either promote or hinder flourishing for individuals and society as a whole. While rapidly changing technological advances present new and exciting opportunities, the increasing use of the Internet to access, buy, and sell pornographic images, virtual sex, and people themselves also presents an occasion for the reevaluation of the values that bind us together as a community locally, nationally, and globally.

1. Individualist Arguments for Protecting Privacy

In the liberal tradition that has shaped American society, the individual is viewed as the lightning rod around which values like privacy are shaped and defended. Privacy is a right that attaches fundamentally to individuals. In the classic "The right to privacy [The implicit made explicit]" of the *Harvard Law Review* of 1890, Samuel Warren and Louis Brandeis introduce the concept of an "inviolate personality" (Warren and Brandeis, 1890: 211), a concept that refers to the psychological well-being of an individual that is deserving of respect and in need of protection beyond other pre-existing explicit constitutional protections. They conclude that privacy "rights, so protected, whatever their exact nature, are not rights arising from contract or from special trust, but are rights against the world" (Warren and Brandeis, 1890: 213) and describe human beings as entities whose flourishing depends on having a private physical and mental space that is protected from external influences and interference. Such a protected realm, they argue, will allow individuals the freedom to pursue the interests, projects, and goals that matter to them.

Two prominent individualist privacy theorists, James Rachels (1975) and Charles Fried (1968), argue that individuals are entitled to privacy because they must be allowed to control the flow of information about themselves to other people and to the rest of society. Fried argues that "in developed social contexts love, friendship, and trust are only possible if persons enjoy and accord to each other a certain measure of privacy" (Fried, 1968: 482). He adds that the secret, personal details about ourselves that we would not wish to make public provide us with the "moral capital" (Fried, 1968: 484) necessary to form intimate bonds with others. Rachels argues that there is a "close connection between our ability to control who has access to us and to information about us, and our ability to create and maintain different sorts of social relationships with different people" (Rachels, 1975: 326). He claims that there are "*different* patterns of behavior associated with different relationships" (Rachels, 1975: 326; his emphasis) and argues that "we need to separate our associations, at least to some extent, if we are to maintain a system of different relationships with different people" (Rachels, 1975: 330). These privacy theorists defend the right of individuals to participate in a multitude of different relationships, each for different purposes and with different behavioral expectations, as necessary for shaping who we are and what matters to us.

Individualist privacy theorists emphasize the need to shield the individual from other people and from society as a whole. They argue that unanticipated or unwanted social influences can undermine the uniqueness of individuals and that a certain degree of social isolation is neces-

sary for individuals to flourish. On this approach, an individual has a right to experiment with unpopular or socially shunned practices without fear of being observed or prosecuted because these are activities that allow an individual to shape his or her unique personality. At first glance, then, allowing individuals to use the Internet anonymously can provide a space in which the individual is protected from unwanted social pressures and can reveal only those facts about him or herself that are deemed acceptable in the process of forming and shaping a relationship. If we remain within the framework set forth by individual-oriented privacy rights, then there is every reason to maximize privacy protections on the Internet. Indeed, examined through this framework, the Internet looks like an ideal environment in which the individual can pursue his or her interests and projects and form relationships with people all over the world. Anonymous Internet usage would appear to create a barrier between the individual and society such that one is in an ideal position to pursue interests without fear of observation and judgment; to participate in interactions and exchanges of information that are less mainstream and even unconventional; to operate within a space free from unwanted social pressures; and to pursue relationships in an environment where maximum control over one's identity and personal information is made possible.

If we side with the traditional theorists, then a defense of total privacy and anonymity on the Internet is secured. Our goal is to suggest some of the potentially negative consequences that result from understanding the Internet as a resource for the individual to pursue interests and relationships in an environment of control and isolation. At the heart of the matter is the fact that an Internet composed of anonymous users creates an environment in which there is little or no *moral accountability* or *responsibility* for one's speech and actions. But the best way to make this lack of moral accountability clear is to look at how the Internet might affect and shape *relationships* rather than *individuals*. The traditional privacy theorists understand privacy to be necessary for human relationships, but they do not distinguish between relationships that allow the individual to flourish and those that harm or negatively impact that life or the lives of other individuals. Because they treat relationships as just another interest or choice that an individual might have, there does not seem to be anything morally problematic about individuals going on the Internet and forming relationships with other people while being able to withhold details of their "real life" identities. On this understanding of relationships, the Internet ought to be a place where people are able to control information about themselves through technological protection of their privacy.

We argue that we must consider the broader social implications of a community of people all of whom are enabled to have a reduced sense of moral responsibility because they have access to Internet applications where their anonymity is facilitated. In a global context, we must also consider how technologies that can allow and virtually guarantee anonymity can also allow for the formation of relationships that exploit individuals and already disadvantaged group members within and across borders. These issues of the implications of a lack of moral responsibility and accountability will be highlighted when we apply the critique of an individual-oriented privacy rights approach to the realm of pornography on the Internet. But first, we need some details about what Internet technologies allow by way of protecting privacy.

2. The Internet and Anonymity

The Internet, as it exists now, provides a variety of opportunities for people to access information and form Internet-based relationships in an entirely anonymous fashion. In effect, all users can be anonymous in the sense that they can detach themselves from their "real life" identities, from their real names, physical bodies, geographical locations, and even from all the various persons with whom they have "real life" relationships. In fact, if we maximize anonymity on the Internet, it seems as if we can create the *ideal* environment for the flourishing of the sort of individual conceived in the more traditional liberal framework of privacy rights discourse.

The Internet is a venue in which we *can*, in certain types of online communities and mediums, exercise control over our true identity with respect to other Internet users. Individuals can use the Internet in the privacy of their own home, which is their private property, the sanctity of which is protected by laws against physical trespassing. On many websites on the Internet, one may view the information therein without needing to announce one's presence or provide any information such as one's name, address, or other data. Many websites do ask you to submit your real name and perhaps a credit card number, but the Internet user may choose not to visit such websites. When you request an email account through Hotmail, you will be asked for your first and last name, language, country, state, zip code, time zone, date of birth, gender, and occupation, and then you are asked to create a user name and password that will allow you secure access to your email account. However, Hotmail does not perform any sort of verification process to see if you, the "real life" person, have supplied accurate information. Thus, the individual has the choice to supply whatever information, accurate or inaccurate, he or she wishes, and there are no penalties for lying.

Another example is Internet chat rooms, which also provide a venue for communication in which the individual exercises a great deal of control over information about him or herself. Consider Internet Relay Chat (IRC), a type of Internet application that "gives people all over the world the ability to talk (type) to one another in real time. Each user has a nickname (handle) and converses with other users either in private or on a channel (chat room)." (NewIRCusers.com, 2004). Because participation in an IRC channel requires identifying oneself only by a nickname of one's choosing, people can communicate with each other while exercising control over information about themselves. Thus, the individual's control over personal information is maximized in the sense that he or she may share with others only the information that he or she chooses to give out. The structural and technological features of the Internet make it possible for people to communicate with each other through a minimal exchange of information — no one knows anyone else's name or what they look like (and thus their gender, ethnicity, age, and race). In virtue of our current technological capabilities, we have the ability to structure the Internet so that people operate within it anonymously, with little or no ties to their "real life" identities while in cyberspace.

If we accept the arguments made by traditional privacy theorists, then the Internet seems an ideal place for the individual to form relationships with other people, all of their own choosing and for their desired purposes. If we view the Internet only in terms of its capacity to maximize individual freedom, choice, and control over personal information, it is not immediately apparent that there could be any dangerous consequences for human interactions and the functioning of society as a whole. If the Internet is a place where our identities are concealed, then we are able to exercise rigid control over the information about ourselves that is transmitted to others. In addition, anonymity would allow an individual to keep relationships with people over the Internet completely separate from the relationships he or she has in the "real world." If anonymity is protected on the Internet, then two people can form a relationship without ever needing to use their real names or give out any information that would tie either one to their "real life" spouses, friends, and co-workers. Moreover, what one reveals or says in relationships formed with others on the Internet is subject only to rules of Netiquette, the set of manners and customs governing an online community. Unlike codified, textual laws handed down by legislatures, Netiquette grew organically out of communities of early Internet users who "realized that the customs of communications used in face-to-face, telephonic, and even electronic mail conversations did not work in" online social settings (Ohm, 1999: 1975). Bound only by an increasingly loose web of customs whose enforcement is usually limited to the shun-

ning of an obnoxious user or, at most, being blocked from specific online communities, I can be who I want and treat others on the Internet as I want with lots of control over these interactions and few consequences for behavior deemed unacceptable or immoral in real life relationships. Since the individualist privacy theorists think that relationships are strengthened when particular relationships are kept exclusive and separate, the nature of Internet communication allows individuals freedom to engage in the relationships they choose without needing to share those relationships with anyone else or ask how one relationship may negatively impact another.

The following is a good example of how the Internet allows people to treat others in disrespectful and harmful ways without suffering any real consequences. One could visit an Internet community that uses an electronic bulletin board (EBB). EBBs allow each member of the community to post his or her thoughts about a particular topic. Other members of the community may view those postings and contribute their own comments and responses, and hence a discussion ensues. In most cases, in order to join an EBB community, one must make up a user name, supply a password of one's choosing, and give an email address. Suppose that I compose posts that attack other members verbally or in some way violate the posting rules of that community. What consequences would there be for these actions? An EBB's community administrator could block my user name, but there are no barriers to creating a new user name. Suppose the administrator blocks me from registering with my current email address. There are countless other organizations on the Internet that are willing to supply me with an unlimited number of free, anonymous email addresses. Some EBBs allow the administrator to block the Internet Protocol (IP) address of the computer I am using to connect to the Internet. If my IP address remains the same every time I connect through my current Internet service provider, the administrator of the EBB might be able to prevent me from using that particular bulletin board from my computer. But if I am using public computers in different libraries or Internet cafes, the administrator blocking the IP address of the computer I am using at one moment will not prevent me from further terrorizing that community's bulletin board. Moreover, software is now available that when installed on my computer will prevent anyone from tracing my IP address.

In the global context, anonymity is further protected because the Web transcends national borders and legislation differs from country to country. As pointed out in the Council of Europe report, "even if some operations are prohibited by law in Europe (i.e., Belgium), they are allowed by American legislation: it only takes a hyperlink from the Belgian site to an American one to neutralize the legislation" (Council of Europe, 2003: 13). Moreover, in attempts to avoid being traced, individuals can send their communication through a series of different servers and Internet service providers. They can also send communication through complicated routes of a number of different countries and time zones and through a series of anonymous re-mailers who strip off identifying headers, all of which makes tracing difficult.

The point of providing this technical information is to show that if an individual wishes to join an online community via something like an EBB, the only consequences for violating the rules or behaving abusively towards other members is the inconvenience of needing to constantly create new user names and email addresses or to find different computers or Internet service providers. The type of interactions facilitated by the Internet can have potentially negative outcomes when user anonymity is permitted. A great deal of moral accountability and personal inhibition falls away on the Internet. The more anonymity we facilitate online, the less moral accountability there seems to be. As we will show in the final section, in the context of users who access, buy, and sell pornography, rules of conduct can be said to be non-existent, at least with respect to communications about those whose images are viewed, bought, and sold.

When we apply these sorts of arguments about individual choice and control over relationships to the context of the Internet, it becomes clear that the sort of relationships that are formed in an environment of anonymity and isolation from real world relationships can be morally problematic. A purely individualist approach to the Internet fails to ask questions about whether privacy rights promote healthy relationships and interactions, both person-to-person and at the level of society as a whole. A relational approach takes into account the broader social context in which relationships are formed and asks whether privacy rights on the Internet help or hinder healthy social interactions. The shortcoming in arguments that focus exclusively on the individual is that they demand only that the individual be able to have relationships of his or her own choosing and to exercise control over the information that is shared with others. But these sorts of concerns should not automatically be placed above all others. We need to expand the discourse to ask about what sorts of relationships are formed at the person-to-person, societal, and global levels.

3. Why Relationships Matter

In *On the Internet* (2001), Hubert L. Dreyfus asks, "what, if anything, is lost when human beings relate to *each other* by way of teletechnology?" (Dreyfus, 2001: 52; his emphasis). He explains that teletechnology cannot ever entirely recreate the same quality of interaction as people sharing the same physical space: "Two roboticists at Berkeley, John Canny and Eric Paulos ... point out that two human beings conversing face to face depend on a subtle combination of eye movements, head motion, gesture, and posture" (Dreyfus, 2001: 57-58). So, consider that the individual forming relationships on the Internet cannot presume that these relationships are exactly like real life relationships because the lack of physical interaction changes the dynamic. Add to this the anonymity supported by an individualist privacy rights approach and the problem of human interaction deepens. Dreyfus further argues that being in the physical world entails a certain level of risk and vulnerability: "when we are in the real world, not just as minds but as embodied vulnerable human beings, we must constantly be ready for dangerous surprises" (Dreyfus, 2001: 55). Being a disembodied anonymous presence on the Internet reduces the vulnerability we feel and also prevents us from witnessing the physical reactions that would betray how our words or actions have affected another. Anonymity allows a suspension of a sense of accountability or responsibility for one's behavior toward or treatment of another.

What we convey to the other person via the Internet are only those words and feelings we choose, and the same goes for the other's communication back to us. We have none of the resources of real world interaction that would allow us to see more fully how our words and actions affect others. And if we feel that another person over the Internet is saying things that threaten or challenge us, we need only sever our connection to the Internet to avoid further interaction. The people who hurt or confront us do not know our name, where we live, or our telephone number unless we made the choice to give out that information. They cannot contact us or convey messages unless we choose to receive them, and thus we can filter out what the other has to say to us if we do not wish to hear it. Dreyfus argues that real life relationships must have some element of vulnerability and risk, much of which the Internet allows people to neutralize.

There is more to the effects of the Internet on relationships to support Dreyfus's concern about the absence of physical contact. In a *New York Times* report, Amy Harmon provides evidence that the Internet allows teenagers, for example, to say things they would not say to the person face to face: "[t]he technology, which allows its users to inflict pain without being forced to see its effect, also seems to incite a deeper level of meanness. Psychologists say the distance between bully and victim on the Internet is leading to an unprecedented — and often unintentional — degree of brutality, especially when combined with a typical adolescent's lack of impulse control and underdeveloped empathy

skills." She goes on to report that schools are now needing to deal with this new form of bullying in cyberspace by devising strategies "to address the shift to electronic taunting." Moreover, the features of anonymity that have been emphasized thus far exacerbate the effects of a lack of accountability for this brutality as "new weapons in the teenage arsenal of social cruelty include stealing each others' screen names and sending inflammatory messages to friends or crush-objects, forwarding private material to people for whom it was never intended and anonymously posting derogatory comments about fellow students on Web journals called blogs" (Harmon, 26 August 2004).

If we increasingly rely on the Internet for forming relationships, how will this shape our own lives and impact on human interactions as a whole? Relational theory argues that the picture of human beings as isolated and separable entities, each able to flourish best on their own free from interference from others, is incoherent. We can neither avoid interference from others nor thrive without it, from the time of birth and our dependency on others for survival to times when personal and public relationships of various sorts either open or close possibilities for us and shape who we become. We cannot but be shaped by the relationships we are in, whether they are of our choosing or not and whether they are face to face or not. Dreyfus calls attention to the broader social context in which Internet relationships are formed and raises concerns about the impact on society as a whole when people are less accountable to each other. A relational approach maintains that we must be aware of the possibility that the lack of moral accountability in Internet-based relationships might pervade "real life" human interactions by shaping people who are less willing or able to trust each other in a variety of different contexts, Internet or otherwise, and more willing to interact with others in ways that discourage accountability and responsibility.

The sense of isolation and detachment we might feel in Internet-based relationships is both false and highly problematic. Perhaps the question we need to be asking is *not* what sorts of privacy rights on the Internet would allow the individual to flourish, but rather how privacy rights in this context shape relationships between Internet users and the general character of an Internet-connected society. The individualist privacy theorists' exclusive focus on the choices, desires, and goals of the individual entirely misses concerns about moral accountability and responsibility in human interactions. Because Internet users need not be truthful to others concerning facts about their "real life," the Internet makes it far more *likely* that people will be guilty of hypocrisy and deceit when anonymity is permitted and encouraged. On the Internet, there are no consequences for forming relationships where you make claims to different people that are contradictory or hypocritical or abusive of others, including members of disadvantaged groups or citizens of other countries who are treated as commodities. An individualist position on privacy with respect to an individual's chosen relationships does not allow attention to be paid to how a relationship with one person may negatively affect other people within the individual's network of relationships or to how harmful stereotypes of disadvantaged group members or people from other countries may be endorsed.

In *Republic.com* (2001), Cass Sunstein raises an additional concern about the way in which the Internet is structured around the preferences of the individual when he argues that it can undermine rather than promote freedom of expression. In a way similar to John Stuart Mill's defense of freedom of speech as beneficial for society as a whole because it exposes citizens to a marketplace of ideas, Sunstein argues that "people should be exposed to materials that they would not have chosen in advance. Unplanned, unanticipated encounters are central to democracy itself" (Sunstein, 2001: 8). He also argues that "many or most citizens should have a range of common experiences. Without shared experiences, a heterogeneous society will have a much more difficult time in addressing social problems" (Sunstein, 2001: 9).

Sunstein's specific worry is about particular websites that allow individual visitors to tailor

the site such that they receive only the types of information that interest them in future visits. For example, the *Wall Street Journal* website allows "readers to create 'personalized' electronic editions, containing exactly what they want, and excluding what they do not want" (Sunstein, 2001: 5). In other words, people can tailor websites to deliver information that pertains solely to their individual interests, problems, and desires. According to Sunstein, there has been an increase in the available options an individual may exercise by way of the ever-expanding Internet and a corresponding "decrease in the power of *general interest intermediaries*" such as "newspapers, magazines, and broadcasters" (Sunstein, 2001: 11; his emphasis). People who *do* expose themselves to such general interest intermediaries "have a range of chance encounters, involving shared experiences with diverse others, and also exposure to materials and topics that they did not seek out in advance" (Sunstein, 2001: 11-12). The Internet permits people to narrow their horizons by acquiring only those pieces of information that concern them and to use the technology to filter out everything else. Sunstein argues that a well-functioning society needs to have a sense of community that is promoted through encounters with various people and topics and to be open to listening to a variety of voices without filtering out all but what we want to hear. What is most illuminating about Sunstein's argument is his desire "to defend a conception of freedom, associated with the deliberative conception of democracy, and to oppose it to a conception that *sees consumption choices by the individuals as the very embodiment of freedom*" (Sunstein, 2001: 15; emphasis ours).

For the traditional privacy rights defenders, it is essential that individuals be protected sufficiently from social pressures so that they develop a strong sense of self as distinct from other individuals and from society as a whole. Sunstein's account points to "the risks posed by any situation in which thousands or perhaps millions or even tens of millions of people are mainly listening to louder echoes of their own voices" (Sunstein, 2001: 16). An emphasis on individual freedom and choice encourages the filtering and personalization of information sent and received by Internet users and thereby produces "a substantial decrease in unanticipated, unchosen interactions with others" (Sunstein, 2001: 23). One of Sunstein's proposed solutions to this looming problem is to "have several widely publicized deliberative domains on the Internet, ensuring opportunities for discussion among people with diverse views" (Sunstein, 2001: 170).

While we agree with Sunstein that public Internet forums where diverse people can interact and discuss various views of public interest are valuable, our account also suggests that the effectiveness of such forums is undermined when the Internet is structured such that anonymity is protected. On the one hand, the protection of freedom of speech allows people to express a plurality of views without fear of persecution. So some protection against threats that might silence dissenters is necessary for free expression. On the other hand, anonymity on the Internet reduces moral accountability for one's actions and words. If people enter into a public forum anonymously, how can we trust that they are not misrepresenting the views of a group? How do we separate genuine and urgent dissent about real problems from inflammatory remarks with no goal except to incite people to anger and conflict? A relational approach examines how we are shaped by the relationships in which we find ourselves, both positive and negative. Sunstein's approach is relational in that he is concerned about developing relationships that challenge our deeply entrenched beliefs and allow greater respect for diversity and tolerance of others. In the context of the Internet, however, maintaining the traditional individual-oriented approach to privacy and merely adding possibilities for public discussion groups undermines the creation of the very sort of relationships Sunstein advocates.

A public forum where privacy and identity are protected creates enormous risks for hypocrisy, misrepresentation, lack of trust, and the forming of flawed and even exploitative human relationships. While Sunstein is right to suggest that having the Internet structured to maximize individual choices and desires undermines values important to society because people no longer have the broader social awareness brought on by encounters with different and contrasting viewpoints, we want to add that anonymity on the Internet undermines Sunstein's ideal of the Internet as a deliberative forum because it decreases moral accountability and responsibility in human interactions. Moreover, as the Dreyfus and Harmon accounts show, the Internet promotes a lack of accountability for what one says and does and even encourages behavior considered unacceptable in "real life" relationships. Nowhere does this seem more evident than in the case of pornography and the Internet, where widespread availability within and across borders raises serious questions about the relationships we have with those different from ourselves and where questions in addition to those raised by Dreyfus, Harmon, and Sunstein about human interaction and relationships are raised.

4. The Case of Pornography

The structural features of the Internet provide the potential for a form of life radically different than any we have had before: human interaction and information exchange without the use of our physical bodies and with all the particulars of our "real life" identities concealed behind a barrier of software coding and fiber-optic cables. By claiming that the individual is entitled to certain privacy rights that *cannot* be violated, traditional theorists fail to recognize how privacy rights can undermine moral accountability and responsibility in human interactions. These issues of accountability and responsibility are highlighted in the case of pornography and the Internet.

In its report, the Council of Europe summarizes its study of legislation regarding pornography on the Internet in the following:

There appears to be no standard concerning the legality of pornography in general, and punishable offences related thereto vary considerably from country to country. Child pornography, however, as well as pornography depicting acts of violence (so-called "hard" pornography), is punishable in each of the countries examined. Only in the Netherlands the Parliament approved a bill that will also penalize virtual child pornography. Traditionally, that which was punishable in connection with pornography was the manufacture, sale and/or distribution. Mere consumption was not illegal. Most countries have recently enacted legislation prohibiting the possession of hard pornography — a major step towards the prohibition of consumption. Under such legislation, although surfing on the Internet and viewing pornographic images is not punishable, downloading the same material is deemed to be effective possession and is therefore a criminal offence. (Council of Europe, 2003: 65)

The paucity of legislation noted in this report needs to be coupled with the difficulties of detection: "the transient and intangible nature of the Internet, as well as the anonymity and secrecy that communications via the Internet permits, make the identification of the author and/or intended recipient of an illicit communication, as well as the collection of evidence, much more difficult and elusive" (Council of Europe, 2003: 66).

With respect to questions about censoring pornography, traditional liberal approaches have focused on the need to prove that pornography causes substantial or direct harm in order to justify infringing an individual's right to create or consume it. Many take the fight against the censorship of adult pornography as a "victory for the individual rights of people and an end to suppressive government enforcement of morality based laws" (Council of Europe, 2003: 74). The Council of Europe defends this stance on freedom of expression, but recommends that laws be implemented when the viewing of images are connected with criminal acts of trafficking for the purpose of sexual exploitation. As with traditional liberal approaches, harm has to be shown to be direct and substantial.

Conducting research on harm within the parameters of lack of legal control and standards makes it difficult to understand who the victims are. It also makes it difficult to identify the users or comprehend the harm they cause to themselves or others. Moreover, where legislation may apply for determining exploitation in face to face contact, the case of exploitation or harm is less clear when the relationship takes place in cyberspace and the contact is virtual. In the traditional debate on censorship, liberals have wanted proof of real harm to real persons. Pornography on the Internet changes this by making it even more difficult to establish that "people" are being harmed. Because our argument is a moral one that asks us to critically examine relationships in cyberspace and the impact they have on individuals, groups, societies, and the global community as a whole, it can make a valuable contribution to this set of issues concerning harm. A relational approach does not need the high standards set by liberal approaches to harm. Instead, it asks us to review issues of moral responsibility and accountability with respect to relationships formed with others within and across societies. Here the burden of proof with respect to harm to individuals and society is on those who hold an individualist conception of a self that flourishes in isolation and who thereby defend unbridled privacy and anonymity.

Donna Hughes has conducted multiple studies (including providing data for the Council of Europe Report) of the Internet and its use in the context of pornography, prostitution, bride trafficking, and sex tours. She catalogues information regarding the proliferation of Internet activity in these areas: "at the end of 2001, there were 300,000 pornography sites on the Web. This is a 350% increase in the number of pornography sites from January to December 2001" (Hughes, 2000: 2). At the same time as those in pornographic images are more visible and exposed, those who consume these images have more privacy and anonymity. The days of embarrassment at being "caught" purchasing a pornographic magazine at the corner store or going to a theater to view pornography have been replaced with private and easy access from the comforts of home and needing only a computer, Internet access, and a click of the mouse. Some of the most technologically advanced Internet software and capabilities are being developed and used by those in the pornography industry. For example, "[b]y late 1995, live videoconferencing was delivering live strip shows and sex shows to buyers over the Internet (Rose, 1997). By either keyboard or telephone, the buyers could communicate with the women in the sex show and make requests for what they wanted the women to do. The viewer could be in another state, or even another continent from the actual show" (Hughes, 2003: 119).

Our argument focuses on the effects of these interactions on real people in their real life relationships. We cannot but be shaped by the relationships we are in. The Web allows access to and interaction with people that cannot but influence offline attitudes. An examination of chat room discussions reveals phenomena such as the use of misogynistic and racist language; the eroticization of violence, degradation, and humiliation; and the inability to perceive harm being done to the "people" portrayed in the images. One of the women Hughes interviewed, who lived in a room with 24-hour live video cameras broadcasting all her activities, reported that one paid subscriber "said that he couldn't accept that we were real people. We were just little people who lived in the computer" (Hughes, 2003: 123). While Hughes admits that the extent to which experiences and behaviors are affected by using Internet technologies is not known, "the combined experience of using high tech computer hardware and software, finding a supportive community on the Internet, and having a sexual experience (masturbating to pornography, live sex shows, and writings about prostitution) is reinforcing and powerful" (Hughes, 2003: 123).

One study shows that pedophiles are empowered and their behavior reinforced through the use of the Internet for child pornography. Some users of these communities follow no common social norms and have a minimal chance of being held accountable:

the fact that through the Internet users can in the main go anywhere and say anything without any official governing body restricting those actions means that for some people this will be their first experience of acting outside the confines of a conventional hierarchy ... Such experiences may empower some people such as sex offenders who have otherwise felt marginalized in conventional society. Those who have never been able to function at an optimal level in the real world may feel that they have the chance to do so now that conventional structures are broken down. (Taylor *et al.*, 2001: 99)

If we use the arguments presented thus far, several points can be made about the results of this study. The privacy rights theorists we examined would have no reason not to applaud the fact that the Internet allows one to act "outside the confines of a conventional hierarchy." Even Sunstein, who is concerned about freedom to access different worldviews, would not be unhappy about "stretching" one's imagination through access to non-conventional views, though his approach might explain why pedophiles in this context of "mainly listening to louder echoes of their own voices" are empowered. The relational approach we advocate is better positioned to reveal the relationships that are at stake in the life of the individual involved and in the lives of those affected by this Internet activity.

The Internet permits easy access to information about "where to go to find prostitutes, hotel prices, telephone numbers, taxi fares, cost of alcohol, the sex acts that can be bought, the price for each act, and evaluations of women's appearances and performances" (Hughes, 1997: 3). A global network also permits such information to cross borders, where poverty in other countries is merely viewed as a way to increase access and decrease costs. Hughes says of the individuals using the Internet in these ways: "their awareness of racism, colonization, global economic inequalities, and of course, sexism, is limited to how these forces benefit them. A country's economic or political crisis and the accompanying poverty are advantages, which produce cheap women for the men. Often the men describe how desperate the women are and how little the men have to pay" (Hughes, 1997: 4). Sex tours on the Internet and the advertising of them enable men to travel imaginatively and physically to "exotic" places and to ignore community standards that may constrain them in relationships at home or in their own country. Tourism, recommended by the United Nations and the World Bank as a way for third world countries to generate income, is being used in countries like the Philippines to promote the sex tour industry in their own countries. An advertisement in *Travel Philippines* describes the country as an "exotic and interesting place to visit" and provides information on places and costs for getting kinds of sex and people. From the comfort of one's home, an Internet user can select, for virtual or real engagement, eight and nine year old virgins, brides, or serial and group sex with a variety of people. As Hughes points out, "powerful forces of racism, misogyny, 'first world' domination and economic exploitation are merged in the selling of 'exotic and erotic' sex vacations" (Hughes, 1997: 7).

A relational approach asks us to consider the impact on individuals, their relationships, communities, and the world as a whole of these aspects of pornography on the Internet. We can only come to understand the morally problematic implications of the Internet when we look beyond the flourishing of an isolated, self-interested individual. It is not that the needs, goals, and interests of the individual ought to be considered irrelevant when deciding how much privacy we ought to demand on the Internet. However, a relational approach reinterprets individual rights in terms of relationships. We must be concerned with human relationships and the functioning of society as a whole when considering privacy rights. Some might argue that the Internet could never be an environment of complete anonymity given the increasing regulation by the government and large corporations. Our inquiry is a moral and not a legal one in that it demands a reevaluation and reconception of privacy rights that pays greater attention to human relationships and social practices. When dramatic paradigm shifts in human

forms of life occur, we do not immediately dispose of all our old values and beliefs and make new ones to conform to our new way of life. Rather, into these new frontiers we bring with us these old values and beliefs and grapple with whether we should try to fit them into the new system or cast them away as too arcane to be used any longer. Our conclusion is that now, in the Internet age, we cannot cling to our traditional ideas of the flourishing of the individual in isolation from others as the sole and highest end goal of our moral arguments about privacy. Rather, discourses about privacy on the Internet, as well as privacy in general, must take into account how relationships and our society will be shaped by whatever privacy protections we choose to enact.

Authors' Note

This paper began as a senior thesis. It has been updated and gone through a number of revisions. Work on this challenging topic would not have been possible without the feedback of members of the Philosophy Department at Bryn Mawr College, the support of the seniors in the class of 2002, and the always efficient and enjoyable collaboration of the co-authors.

NOTE

1. In applying a relational approach to the issue of privacy rights on the Internet, we draw on insights from work on relational theory in Koggel, *Perspectives on Equality: Constructing a Relational Theory* (1998) and from various authors in Koggel *et al.* (editors), *Confidential Relationships: Psychoanalytic, Ethical, and Legal Contexts* (2003).

REFERENCES

Council of Europe. (2003). *Group of Specialists on the Impact of the Use of New Information Technologies on Trafficking in Human Beings for the Purpose of Sexual Exploitation: Final Report*. Strasbourg: Council of Europe EG-S-NT (2002) 9.

Dreyfus, Hubert L. (2001). *On the Internet*. New York, NY: Routledge.

Fried, Charles. (1968). "Privacy (A Moral Analysis)." *Yale Law Journal*, v. 77: 475-93.

Hughes, Donna. (2003). "Prostitution Online." *Journal of Trauma Practice*, v. 2, No. 3/4: 115-32.

— . (1997). "Sexual Exploitation and Trafficking of Women on the Internet." <http://www.uri.edu/artsci/wms/hughes/catw/dhpolice.htm>.

"Introduction to IRC for the Novice." NewIRCusers.com. <http://www.newirc users.com/ircchat.html>, retrieved 23 September 2004.

Koggel, Christine M. (1998). *Perspectives on Equality: Constructing a Relational Theory*. Lanham, MD: Rowman & Littlefield.

Koggel, Christine M., Allannah Furlong, and Charles Levin (editors). (2003). *Confidential Relationships: Psychoanalytic, Ethical, and Legal Perspectives*. Amsterdam: Rodopi Press.

Lessig, Lawrence. (1999). *Code and Other Laws of Cyberspace*. New York, NY: Basic Books.

Ohm, Paul K. (1999). "On Regulating the Internet: Usenet, A Case Study." *UCLA Law Review*, v. 46: 1941-87.

Rachels, James. (1975). "Why Privacy is Important." *Philosophy & Public Affairs*, v. 4: 323-33.

Schoeman, Ferdinand D. (editor). (1984). *Philosophical Dimensions of Privacy: An Anthology*. Cambridge: Cambridge University Press.

Sunstein, Cass. (2001). *Republic.com*. Princeton, NJ: Princeton University Press.

Taylor, M., E. Quayle, and G. Holland. (2001). "Typology of Paedophile Picture Collections." *The Police Journal*, v. 74: 97-107.

Warren, Samuel D., and Louis D. Brandeis. (1890). "The Right to Privacy [The Implicit Made Explicit]." *Harvard Law Review*, v. 4: 193-220.

Zoellick, Billy. (2001). *CyberRegs: A Business Guide to Web Property, Privacy, and Patents*. Boston, MA: Addison-Wesley.

PUBLIC RESPONSE TO RACIST SPEECH: CONSIDERING THE VICTIM'S STORY

Mari J. Matsuda

Mari J. Matsuda teaches at the School of Law at Georgetown University, Washington, DC. She is the author of Where is Your Body? And Other Essays on Race, Gender and the Law *(1996) and co-author with Charles Lawrence, Kimberle Crenshaw, and Richard Delgado of* Words that Wound: Critical Race Theory, Assaultive Speech and the First Amendment *(1993) and with Charles Lawrence of* We Won't Go Back: Making the Case for Affirmative Action *(1997).*

Matsuda tells victims' stories of the effects of racist hate messages as an entry point for defending legal sanctions against racist speech. She acknowledges the strength of arguments for First Amendment values of free speech in the U.S., but argues that this absolutist commitment to free speech conflicts with recent developments in other countries and in international law. International conventions declare a commitment to eliminating racism, and many countries outside of the U.S. as well as international bodies are moving to create laws to restrict racist hate propaganda. Matsuda defines a special, narrow class of hate speech and applies it to various problem cases to defend her argument that the American legal system needs to respond to the real harm of racist hate messages.

A Black family enters a coffee shop in a small Texas town. A white man places a card on their table. The card reads, "You have just been paid a visit by the Ku Klux Klan." The family stands and leaves.[1]

A law student goes to her dorm and finds an anonymous message posted on the door, a caricature image of her race, with a red line slashed through it.[2]

A Japanese-American professor arrives in an Australian city and finds a proliferation of posters stating "Asians Out or Racial War" displayed on telephone poles. She uses her best, educated inflection in speaking with clerks and cab drivers and decides not to complain when she is overcharged.[3]

These unheralded stories share company with the more notorious provocation of swastikas at Skokie, Illinois, and burning crosses on suburban lawns. The threat of hate groups like the Ku Klux Klan and the neo-Nazi skinheads goes beyond their repeated acts of illegal violence. Their presence and the active dissemination of racist propaganda means that citizens are denied personal security and liberty as they go about their daily lives....

[This paper] moves between two stories. The first is the victim's story of the effects of racist hate messages. The second is the first amendment story of free speech. The intent is to respect and value both stories. This bipolar discourse uses as its method what many outsider intellectuals do in silence: it mediates between different ways of knowing to determine what is true and what is just.

In calling for legal sanctions for racist speech, this chapter rejects an absolutist first amendment position. It calls for movement of the societal response to racist speech from the private to the public realm. The choice of public sanction, enforced by the state is a significant one. The kinds of injuries historically left to private individuals to absorb and resist through private means are no accident. The places where the law does not go to redress harm have tended to be the places where women, children, people of color, and poor people live. This absence of law is itself another story with a message, perhaps unintended, about the relative value of different human lives. A legal response to racist speech is a statement the victims of racism are valued members of our polity.

The call for a formal, legal-structural response to racist speech goes against the long-standing and healthy American distrust of government power. It goes against an American tradition of tolerance that is precious in the sense of being both valuable and fragile.

Lee Bollinger, dean of the University of Michigan Law School, has concluded that a primary reason for the legal protection of hate speech is to reinforce our commitment to tolerance as a value.[4] If we can shore up our commitment to free speech in the hard and public cases, like *Skokie*,[5] perhaps we will internalize the need for tolerance and spare ourselves from regrettable error in times of stress. Given the real historical costs of state intolerance of minority views, the first amendment purpose Bollinger identifies is not one lightly set aside.

Recognizing both the real harm of racist speech and the need to strengthen our dangerously fickle collective commitment to freedom of discourse, I intend to feel and to work within the first amendment tension armed with stories from human lives. This chapter suggests that outsider jurisprudence — jurisprudence derived from considering stories from the bottom — will help resolve the seemingly irresolvable conflicts of value and doctrine that characterize liberal thought. I conclude that an absolutist first amendment response to hate speech has the effect of perpetuating racism: Tolerance of hate speech is not tolerance borne by the community at large.

Rather, it is a psychic tax imposed on those least able to pay....

Racist Hate Messages: The Victim's Story

The attempt of split bias from violence has been this society's most enduring rationalization.
— Patricia Williams[6]

Who Sees What: Some Initial Stories

In writing this chapter I am forced to ask why the world looks so different to me from the way it looks to many of the civil libertarians whom I consider my allies. Classical thought labels ad hominem analysis a logical fallacy. The identity of the person doing the analysis often seems to make the difference, however, in responding to racist speech. In advocating legal restriction of hate speech, I have found my most sympathetic audience in people who identify with target groups, whereas I have often encountered incredulity, skepticism, and even hostility from others.

This split in reaction is also evident in case studies of hate speech. The typical reaction of target group members to an incident of racist propaganda is alarm and immediate calls for redress. The typical reaction of non-members is to consider the incidents isolated pranks, the product of sick but harmless minds. This is in part a defensive reaction: a refusal to believe that real people, people just like us, are racists. This disassociation leads logically to the claim that there is no institutional or state responsibility to respond to the incident. It is not the kind of real and pervasive threat that requires the state's power to quell.

Here are some true "just kidding" stories:

An African-American worker found himself repeatedly subjected to racist speech when he came to work. A noose was hanging one day in his work area; a dead animal and other threatening objects were placed in his locker. "KKK" references were directed at him, as well as other racist slurs and death threats. His employer discouraged him from calling the police, attributing the incidents to "horse-play."[7]

In San Francisco, a swastika was placed near the desks of Asian-American and African-American inspectors in the newly integrated fire department. The official explanation for the presence of the swastika at the fire department was that it was presented several years earlier as a "joke" gift to the battalion chief, and that it was unclear why or how it ended up at the work stations of the minority employees.[8]

In Jackson, Mississippi, African-American employees of Frito-Lay found their cars sprayed with "KKK" inscriptions and were the targets of racist notes and threats. Local African Americans and Jews were concerned, but officials said the incidents were attributable to children.[9]

An African-American FBI agent was subject to a campaign of racist taunts by white coworkers. A picture of an ape was pasted over his child's photograph, and racial slurs were used. Such incidents were called "healthy" by his supervisor.[10]

In Seattle, a middle-management Japanese American was disturbed by his employer's new anti-Japanese campaign. As the employer's use of slurs and racist slogans in the workplace increased, so did the employee's discomfort. His objections were viewed as overly sensitive and uncooperative. He finally quit his job, and he was denied unemployment insurance benefits because his departure was "without cause."[11]

In Contra Costa County, California, Ku Klux Klan symbols were used to turn families looking for homes away from certain neighborhoods. The local sheriff said there was "nothing ... to indicate this is Klan activity."[12]

Similarly, a Hmong family in Eureka, California, was twice victimized by four foot-high crosses burning on their lawn. Local police dismissed this as "a prank."[13]

Why might anti-Japanese racial slurs mean something different to Asian and white managers? Here is a story of mine:

As a young child I was told never to let anyone call me a J-p. My parents, normally peaceable and indulgent folk, told me this in the tone reserved for dead-serious warnings. Don't accept rides from strangers. Don't play with matches. Don't let anyone call you that name. In their tone they transmitted a message of danger, that the word was a dangerous one, tied to violence.

Just as I grew up to learn the facts about the unspoken danger my parents saw in the stranger in the car, I learned how they connected the violence of California lynch mobs and Hiroshima atom bombs to racist slurs against Japanese Americans.

This early training in vigilance was reinforced by what I later learned about violence and Asian Americans: That people with features like mine are regular victims of violence tied to a wave of anti-Asian propaganda that stretches from Boston to San Francisco, from Calveston to Detroit.

The white managers who considered Mr. O. (the Japanese-American manager) an overly sensitive troublemaker and the unemployment board that determined there was no good cause for him to quit his job came from a different experience. They probably never heard of Vincent Chin, a twenty-seven-year-old Chinese American beaten to death by thugs wielding baseball bats who yelled, "It's because of you fucking J-ps that we're out of work!" They do not know about the Southeast-Asian-American children spat upon and taunted as they walk home from school in Boston; about the vigilante patrols harassing Vietnamese shrimpers in Texas. Nor do they know that the violence in all these cases is preceded by propaganda similar to that used in Mr. O.'s workplace: that those [racist slur for Asian groups] are taking over "our" country.

Stories of anti-Asian violence are regularly reported in the Asian-American press; just as stories of synagogue vandalism are regularly reported in the Jewish-American press; and anti-African-American violence, including the all-too-common phenomenon of "move-in" violence, is regularly reported in the African-American press. Members of target-group communities tend to know that racial violence and harassment are widespread, common, and life threatening; that, as one Georgia observer put it, "The youngsters who paint a swastika today may throw a bomb tomorrow."[14]

The mainstream press often ignores these stories, giving rise to the view of racist and anti-Semitic incidents as random and isolated and the corollary that isolated incidents are inconsequential. For informed members of the victim communities, however, it is logical to link together several thousand real life stories into our tale of caution....

The Specific Negative Effects of Racist Hate Messages

  everywhere the crosses are burning,
  sharp-shooting goose-steppers around every corner,
  there are snipers in the schools ...
  (I know you don't believe this.
  You think this is nothing
  but faddish exaggeration. But they
  are not shooting at you.)
  — Lorna Dee Cervantes[15]

Racist hate messages are rapidly increasing and are widely distributed in this country through a variety of low and high technologies, including anonymous phone calls and letters, posters, books, magazines and pamphlets, cable television, recorded phone messages, computer networks, bulk mail, graffiti, and leafleting. The negative effects of hate messages are real and immediate for the victims. Victims of vicious hate propaganda experience physiological symp-

toms and emotional distress ranging from fear in the gut to rapid pulse rate and difficulty in breathing, nightmares, post-traumatic stress disorder, hypertension, psychosis, and suicide. Patricia Williams has called the blow of racist messages "spirit murder" in recognition of the psychic destruction victims experience.[16]

Victims are restricted in their personal freedom. To avoid receiving hate messages, victims have to quit jobs, forgo education, leave their homes, avoid certain public places, curtail their own exercise of speech rights, and otherwise modify their behavior and demeanor. The recipient of hate messages struggles with inner turmoil. One subconscious response is to reject one's own identity as a victim-group member. As writers portraying the African-American experience have noted, the price of disassociating from one's own race is often sanity itself.

As much as one may try to resist a piece of hate propaganda, the effect on one's self-esteem and sense of personal security is devastating. To be hated, despised, and alone is the ultimate fear of all human beings. However irrational racist speech may be, it hits right at the emotional place where we feel the most pain. The aloneness comes not only from the hate message itself, but also from the government response of tolerance. When hundreds of police officers are called out to protect racist marchers, when the courts refuse redress for racial insult, and when racist attacks are officially dismissed as pranks, the victim becomes a stateless person. Target-group members must either identify with a community that promotes racist speech or admit that the community does not include them.

The effect on non-target-group members is also of constitutional dimensions. Associational and other liberty interests of whites are curtailed in an atmosphere rife with racial hatred. Hate messages, threats, and violence are often the price for whites of hiring, marrying, adopting, socializing with, and even jogging with people of color. In addition, the process of disassociation can affect the mental health of non-targets. Dominant-group members who rightfully, and often angrily, object to hate propaganda share a guilty secret: their relief that they are not themselves the target of the racist attack. Even as they reject the Ku Klux Klan, they may feel ambivalent relief that they are not African-American, Asian, or Jewish. Thus they are drawn into unwilling complicity with the Klan, spared from being the feared and degraded thing.

Just as when we confront human tragedy — a natural disaster, a plane crash — we feel the blessing of the fortunate that distances us from the victims, the presence of racist hate propaganda distances right-thinking dominant-group members from the victims, making it harder to achieve a sense of common humanity. Similarly, racist propaganda forces victim-group members to view all dominant-group members with suspicion. It forces well-meaning dominant-group members to use kid-glove care in dealing with outsiders. This is one reason why social relations across racial lines are so rare in the United States.

Research in the psychology of racism suggests a related effect of racist hate propaganda: At some level, no matter how much both victims and well-meaning dominant-group members resist it, racial inferiority is planted in our minds as an idea that may hold some truth.[17] The idea is improbable and abhorrent, but because it is presented repeatedly, it is there before us. "Those people" are lazy, dirty, sexualized, money grubbing, dishonest, inscrutable, we are told. We reject the idea, but the next time we sit next to one of "those people," the dirt message, the sex message, is triggered. We stifle it, reject it as wrong, but it is there, interfering with our perception and interaction with the person next to us. In conducting research for this chapter, I read an unhealthy number of racist statements. A few weeks after reading about a "dot busters" campaign against immigrants from India, I passed by an Indian woman on my campus. Instead of thinking, "What a beautiful sari," the first thought that came into my mind was "dot busters." Only after setting aside the hate message could I move on to my own thoughts. The propaganda I read had taken me one step back from casually treating a fellow brown-skinned human being as that, rather than as someone distanced from myself.

For the victim, similarly, the angry rejection of the message of inferiority is coupled with absorption of the message. When a dominant-group member responds favorably, there is a moment of relief — the victims of hate messages do not always believe in their insides that they deserve decent treatment. This obsequious moment is degrading and dispiriting when the self-aware victim acknowledges it.

Psychologists and sociologists have done much to document the effects of racist messages on both victims and dominant-group members.[18] Writers of color have given us graphic portrayals of what life is like for victims of racist propaganda.[19] From the victim's perspective, racist hate messages cause real damage.

If the harm of racist hate messages is significant, and the truth value marginal, the doctrinal space for regulation of such speech becomes a possibility. An emerging international standard seizes this possibility.

International Law of Human Rights: The Emerging Acceptance of the Victim's Story

The international community has chosen to outlaw racist hate propaganda. Article 4 of the International Convention on the Elimination of All Forms of Racial Discrimination states:

State Parties condemn all propaganda and all organizations which are based on ideas or theories of superiority of one race or group of persons of one colour or ethnic origin, or which attempt to justify or promote racial hatred and discrimination in any form, and undertake to adopt immediate and positive measures designed to eradicate all incitements to, or acts of, such discrimination and, to this end, with due regard to the principles embodied in the Universal Declaration of Human Rights and the rights expressly set forth in Article 5 of this Convention, *inter alia*:

(a) Shall declare as an offence punishable by law all dissemination of ideas based on racial superiority or hatred, incitement to racial discrimination, as well as all acts of violence or incitement to such acts against any race or group of persons of another colour or ethnic origin, and also the provision of any assistance to racist activities, including the financing thereof;

(b) Shall declare illegal and prohibit organizations, and also organized and all other propaganda activities, which promote and incite racial discrimination, and shall recognize participation in such organization or activities as an offence punishable by law; [and]

(c) Shall not permit public authorities of public institutions, national or local, to promote or incite racial discrimination.[20]

Under this treaty, nation-states are required to criminalize racist hate messages. Prohibiting dissemination of ideas of racial superiority or hatred is not easily reconciled with U.S. concepts of free speech. The convention recognizes this conflict. Article 4 acknowledges the need for "due regard" for rights protected by the Universal Declaration of Human rights and by Article 5 of the convention — including the rights of freedom of speech, association, and conscience.

Recognizing these conflicting values and nonetheless concluding that the right to freedom from racist hate propaganda deserves affirmative recognition represents the evolving international view. A U.S. lawyer, trained in a tradition of liberal thought, would read Article 4 and conclude immediately that it is unworkable. Acts of violence and perhaps imminent incitement to violence are properly prohibited, but the control of ideas is doomed to failure. This position was voiced continually in the debates preceding adoption of the convention,[21] leading to the view that Article 4 is both controversial and troublesome ....

The General Assembly debates on Article 4 focused on free speech. Although the issue was never clearly resolved, it is significant that no country, not even the United States, was willing to abandon the basic premise of Article 4. The article declares that parties "condemn all propaganda ... based on ideas or theories of superiority ... or which attempt[s] to justify or promote racial hatred and discrimination in any form."[22] Simi-

larly, the preamble to the convention states explicitly that "any doctrine of superiority based on racial differentiation is scientifically false, morally condemnable, socially unjust and dangerous, and that there is no justification for racial discrimination."[23] The community of nations has thus made a commitment, with U.S. support, to eliminate racism. It has recognized that racist hate propaganda is illegitimate and is properly subject to control under the international law of human rights. The debate, then, centers around the limits of such control, not around the basic decision to control racism....

The convention is not the only expression of the emerging international view. The need to limit racist hate messages is implicit in basic human rights documents such as the UN Charter and the Universal Declaration of Human Rights. Both documents recognize the primacy of the right to equality and freedom from racism. Other human rights treaties, such as the European Convention of the Protection of Human Rights and Fundamental Freedoms[24] and the American Declaration of the Rights and Duties of Man,[25] also recognize this primacy. The United States is also a party to an international convention on genocide that forbids, *inter alia*, incitement to genocide.[26] Finally, the existing domestic law of several nations — including states that accept the Western notion of freedom of expression — has outlawed certain forms of racist speech.

The United Kingdom, for example, under the Race Relations Act, has criminalized incitement to discrimination and incitement to racial hatred.[27] The act criminalizes the publication or distribution of "threatening, abusive, or insulting" written matter or use of such language in a public place. The United Kingdom standard originally differed from the international standard in that it required proof of intent to incite to hatred. The intent requirement was later dropped.[28] The act is consistent with the international standard in that it recognizes that avoiding the spread of hatred is a legitimate object of the law and that some forms of racist expression are properly criminalized. The legislative history of the act suggests that the drafters were concerned with the spread of racist violence. Imminent violence, however, was not the only object of the act. The act recognized the inevitable connection between the general spread of race hatred and the spread of violence. Although commentators have suggested that the act is ineffective and capable of misuse,[29] the existence of the act supports the growing international movement toward outlawing racist hate propaganda.

Canada has similarly adopted a national statue governing hate propaganda. Sections 318 and 319 of the Canadian Criminal Code[30] outlaw advocacy of genocide, defined as *inter alia*, an act designed to kill a member of an identifiable group. Also outlawed are communications inciting hatred against any identifiable group where a breach of peace is likely to follow. The law further prohibits the expression of ideas inciting hatred if such expression is tied to a probable threat to order.

The new Canadian Bill of Rights incorporates strong protections for freedom of speech and association.[31] Conflict between the new Bill of Rights and the antihate legislation has not prevented actions to limit hate speech.

Australia and New Zealand also have laws restricting racist speech,[32] leaving the United States alone among the major common law jurisdictions in its complete tolerance of such speech. What the laws of these other countries and the UN conventions have in common is that they specify a particularly egregious form of expression for criminalization. All expressions concerning differences between races is not banned. The definitive elements are discrimination, connection to violence, and messages of inferiority, hatred, or persecution. Thus the entire spectrum of what could be called racist speech is not prohibited. A belief in intellectual differences between the races, for instance, is not subject to sanctions unless it is coupled with an element of hatred or persecution. What the emerging global standard prohibits is the kind of expression that most interferes with the rights of subordinated-group members to participate equally in society and maintain their basic sense of security and worth as human beings.

The failure of U.S. law to accept this emerging standard reflects a unique first amendment jurisprudence. This jurisprudence is so entrenched in U.S. law that it at first seems irreconcilable with the values given primacy in Article 4, such as the values of equality and full participation....

Narrow Application and Protection of First Amendment Values

This chapter attempts to recognize and accommodate the civil libertarian position. The victim's perspective requires respect for the idea of rights, for it is those on the bottom who are most hurt by the absence of rights, and it is those on the bottom who have sustained the struggle for rights in U.S. history. The image of book burnings should unnerve us and remind us to argue long and hard before selecting a class of speech to exclude from the public domain. I am uncomfortable in making the suggestions in this section when others fall too easily into agreement.

A definition of actionable racist speech must be narrow in order to respect first amendment values. I believe racist speech is best treated as a sui generis category, presenting an idea so historically untenable, so dangerous, and so tied to perpetuation of violence and degradation of the very classes of human beings who are least equipped to respond that it is properly treated as outside the realm of protected discourse. The courts in the *Skokie* case[33] expressed doubt that principles were available to single out racist speech for public limitation. Here I attempt to construct a doctrinal and evidentiary world in which we might begin to draw the lines the *Skokie* courts could not imagine.

The alternative to recognizing racist speech as qualitatively different because of its content is to continue to stretch existing first amendment exceptions, such as the "fighting words" doctrine and the "content/conduct" distinction. This stretching ultimately weakens the first amendment fabric, creating neutral holes that remove protection for many forms of speech. Setting aside the worst forms of racist speech for special treatment is a non-neutral, value-laden approach that will better preserve free speech.

To distinguish the worst, paradigm example of racist hate messages from other forms of racist and nonracist speech, I offer three identifying characteristics:

1. The message is of racial inferiority
2. The message is directed against a historically oppressed group
3. The message is persecutory, hateful, and degrading.

Making each element a prerequisite to prosecution prevents opening of the dreaded floodgates of censorship.

The first element is the primary identifier of racist speech: Racist speech proclaims racial inferiority and denies the personhood of target group members. All members of the target group are at once considered alike and inferior.

The second element attempts to further define racism by recognizing the connection of racism to power and subordination. Racism is more than race hatred or prejudice. It is the structural subordination of a group based on an idea of racial inferiority. Racist speech is particularly harmful because it is a mechanism of subordination, reinforcing a historical vertical relationship.

The final element is related to the "fighting words" idea. The language used in the worst form of racist speech is language that is, and is intended as, persecutory, hateful, and degrading.

The following section applies these three elements to hypothetical cases. Using these elements narrows the field of interference with speech. Under these narrowing elements, arguing that particular groups are genetically superior in a context free of hatefulness and without the endorsement of persecution is permissible. Satire and stereotyping that avoids persecutory language remains protected. Hateful verbal attacks upon dominant-group members by victims is permissible. These kinds of speech are offensive, but they are, in respect of first amendment principles, best subjected to the marketplace of ideas. This is not to suggest that we remain silent in the face of offensive speech of this type. Rather, the range of private remedies — including counterspeech,

social approbation, boycott, and persuasion — should apply.

If the most egregious, paradigmatic racial hate messages are not properly left to private remedy, it is important to explain why. One way to explain this is to consider the difference between racist hate messages and Marxist speech. Marxist speech is the kind of popular political expression the first amendment is intended to protect. Marxist speech is, according to a once-prevalent view, the advocacy of overthrow of existing governments, inevitably leading to dictatorships and persecution of dissidents and capitalists. It is thus, it was argued, dangerous speech, properly censored. The legacy of this view was McCarthyism and the shattered lives of hundreds of decent citizens.

How can one argue for censorship of racist hate messages without encouraging a revival of McCarthyism? There is an important difference that comes from human experience, our only source of collective knowledge. We know, from our collective historical knowledge, that slavery was wrong. We know white minority rule in South Africa is wrong. This knowledge is reflected in the universal acceptance of the wrongness of the doctrine of racial supremacy. There is no nation left on this planet that submits as its national self-expression the view that Hitler was right....

At the universities, at the centers of knowledge of the international community, the doctrines of racial supremacy and racial hatred are again uniformly rejected. At the United Nations the same is true. We have fought wars and spilled blood to establish the universal acceptance of this principle. The universality of the principle, in a world bereft of agreement on many things, is a mark of collective human progress. The victim's perspective, one mindful of the lessons of history thus accepts racist speech as sui generis and universally condemned.

Marxist speech, however, is not universally condemned. Marxism presents a philosophy for political organization, distribution of wealth and power, ordering of values, and promotion of social change. By its very content it is political speech going to the core of ongoing political debate. It is impossible to achieve world consensus either for or against this political view. Marxists teach in universities. Although Marxist ideas are rejected and abhorred by many, Marxist thought, like liberal thought, neoconservative economic theory, and other conflicting structures for understanding life and politics, is part of the ongoing efforts of human beings to understand their world and improve life in it.

What is argued here, then, is that we accept certain principles as the shared historical legacy of the world community. Racial supremacy is one of the ideas we have collectively and internationally considered and rejected. As an idea connected to continuing racism and degradation of minority groups, it causes real harm to its victims. We are not safe when these violent words are among us.

Treating racist speech as sui generis and universally condemned on the basis of its content and the harmful effect of its content is precisely the censorship that civil libertarians fear. I would argue, however, that explicit content-based rejection of narrowly defined racist speech is more protective of civil liberties than the competing-interests tests of the likely-to-incite-violence tests that can spill over to censor forms of political speech.

Looking to the emerging critical race theory, I derive basic principles: the need to fight racism at all levels, the value of explicit formal rules, and a fear of tyranny. These principles suggest the wisdom of legal intervention with only a narrowly defined class of racist hate propaganda.

A range of legal interventions, including the use of tort law and criminal law principles, is appropriate to combat racist hate propaganda. Although the value of free speech can guide the choice of procedure — including evidentiary rules and burdens of persuasion — it should not completely remove recourse to the institutions of law to combat racist speech. Racism as an acquired set of behaviors can be disacquired, and law is the means by which the state typically provides incentives for changes in behavior.

Hard Cases

In order to get beyond racism, we must first take account of race. There is no other way.
— Harry Blackmun[34]

Of course I emphasize different things, Doctor, because history has treated my people differently from yours.
— Richard Delgado[35]

In this section I consider stories at the edge, a tentative discussion of problem cases that may arise under the definition of actionable racist speech discussed here. The connecting thread in these examples is the need for clarity about the historical context in which racist speech arises and attention to the degree of harm experienced by targets of different kinds of racist speech.

A Case of the Angry Nationalist

Expressions of hatred, revulsion, and anger directed against members of historically dominant groups by subordinated-group members are not criminalized by the definition of racist hate messages used here. Malcom X's "white devil" statements — which he later retracted — are an example. Some would find this troublesome, arguing that any attack on any person's ethnicity is harmful. In the case of the white devil, there is harm and hurt, but it is of a different degree. Because the attack is not tied to the perpetuation of racist vertical relationships, it is not the paradigm worst example of hate propaganda. The dominant-group member hurt by conflict with the angry nationalist is more likely to have access to a safe harbor of exclusive dominant-group interactions. Retreat and reaffirmation of personhood are more easily attained for members of groups not historically subjugated.

Although white-hating nationalist expressions are condemnable both politically and personally, I would interpret an angry, hateful poem by a person from a historically subjugated group as a victim's struggle for self-identity in response to racism. It is not tied to the structural domination of another group. Part of the special harm of racist speech is that it works in concert with other racist tools to keep victim groups in an inferior position. Should history change course, placing former victim groups in a dominant or equalized position, the newly equalized group will lose the special protection suggested here for expression of nationalist anger.

Critics of this proposal ask how one knows who is oppressed and who is not. Poor whites, ethnic whites, wealthy ethnics — the confusing examples and barriers to classification abound. The larger question is how anyone knows anything in life or in law. To conceptualize a condition called subordination is a legitimate alternative to denying that such a condition exists. In law we conceptualize. We take on mammoth tasks of discovery and knowing. We can determine when subordination exists by looking at social indicators: Wealth, mobility, comfort, health, and survival — or the absence of these — tend to mark the rise to the top and the fall to the depths. The rise and fall of group status is relevant even when an individual is a counterexample, because when the group is subordinated, even the lucky counterexample feels the downward tug. Luck is not the same as privilege.

In some cases, a group's social well-being may improve even as its victimization continues. Asians who experience economic success are often under employed relative to their talents. Jews who attain equality in employment still experience anti-Semitic vilification, harassment, and exclusion. Catholics are relatively free from discrimination is some communities and subject to vile bigotry in others. Evidence of the relative subjugation of various groups is available to fact finders.

In the same way that lawyers marshal evidence in an adversarial setting to find facts in other areas of law, we can learn to know the facts about subordination and to determine when hate speech is used as an instrument of that subordination.

First Variation: Anti-Semitism and Racism Within Subordinated Communities

What of hateful racist and anti-Semitic speech by people within subordinated communities? The phenomenon of one subordinated group inflicting racist speech upon another subordinated group is a persistent and touchy problem. Similarly, members of a subordinated group sometimes direct racist language at their own group. The victim's privilege becomes problematic when it is used by one subordinated person to lash out at another. I argue here for tolerance of hateful speech that comes from an experience of oppression, but when that speech is used to attack a subordinated-group member, using language of persecution and adopting a rhetoric of racial inferiority, I am inclined to prohibit such speech.

History and context are important in this case because the custom in a particular subordinated community may tolerate racial insults as a form of wordplay. Where this is the case, community members tend to have a clear sense of what is racially degrading and what is not. The appropriate standard in determining whether language is persecutory, hateful, and degrading is the recipient's community standard. We should beware lest by misunderstanding linguistic and cultural norms we further entrench structures of subordination.

Second Variation: Zionism

I reject the sweeping charge that Zionism is racism and argue instead for a highly contextualized consideration of Zionist speech. To the extent that any racial hostility expressed within a Zionist context is a reaction to historical persecution, it is protected under the doctrinal scheme suggested in this chapter. Should Zionists ever lose this historically based privilege? If Zionist speakers are white, do hateful, race-bound expressions of theirs necessarily reinforce historical conditions of white dominance over brown and black people? The analysis must turn on the particular context. If a Zionist's expression of anger includes a statement of generic white supremacy and persecution, the speaker chooses to ally with a larger, historically dominant group, and the privilege should not apply. On the other hand, angry, survivalist expression, arising out of the Jewish experience of persecution and without resort to the rhetoric of generic white supremacy, is protected under the contextualized approach. Again, it is important to add that the various sub-ordinated communities are best equipped to analyze and condemn hate speech arising within their midst.

The Case of the Dead-Wrong Social Scientist

Another difficult case is that of the social scientist who makes a case for racial inferiority in an academic setting based on what is presented as scientific evidence. Various theories of genetic predisposition to violence, cultural lag, and a correlation between race and intelligence fall into this category. Critics note that these pseudoscientific theories are racist and ignorant.[36] This raises two separate questions. First, should such views receive an audience and a forum in an academic setting? Second, should we criminalize expressions of such views?

As to the first question, the answer may well be no. Not all views deserve the dignity of an academic forum. Poorly documented, racially biased work does not meet the professional standards required of academic writing. If a writer manages to come up with a theory of racial inferiority supported by evidence acceptable within the relevant discipline, that theory may deserve a forum. Under the principle of academic freedom, ignorant views need not be heard, but unpopular, academically tenable views should be.

As to the second question, outlawing this type of speech might be inappropriate. Assuming the dead-wrong social science theory of inferiority is free of any message of hatred and persecution, the ordinary, private solution is sufficient: Attack such theories with open public debate and with denial of a forum if the work is unsound in its documentation....

The Special Case of Universities

A marked rise of racial harassment, hate speech, and racially motivated violence marks the beginning of the 1990s. The epidemic of racist incidents on university campuses is a disturbing example of this. The application of the first amendment to racist speech, once discussed hypothetically in law schools, is now debated in classrooms where hate messages have actually appeared. The current judicial opinions tangling with hate speech and the first amendment often come from the universities.

The university case raises unique concerns. Universities are special places, charged with pedagogy and duty bound to a constituency with special vulnerabilities. Many of the new adults who come to live and study at the major universities are away from home for the first time and at a vulnerable stage of psychological development. The typical university student is emotionally vulnerable for several reasons. College is a time of emancipation from a preexisting home or community, of development of identity, of dependence-independence conflict, of major decision-making, and of formulation of future plans. The move to college often involves geographic relocation — a major life-stress event — and the forging of new peer ties to replace old ones. All of these stresses and changes render the college years critical in development of one's outlook on life. College students experiment with different passions, identities, and risks. A negative environmental response during this period of experimentation could mar for life an individual's ability to remain open, creative, and risk taking.[37] Students are particularly dependent on the university for community, for intellectual development, and for self-definition. Official tolerance of racist speech in this setting is more harmful than generalized tolerance in the community at large. It is harmful to student perpetrators in that it is a lesson in getting away with it that will have lifelong repercussions. It is harmful to targets, who perceive the university as taking sides through inaction and who are left to their own resources in coping with the damage wrought. Finally, it is a harm to the goals of inclusion, education, development of knowledge, and ethics that universities exist and stand for. Lessons of cynicism and hate replace lessons in critical thought and inquiry.

The campus free speech issues of the Vietnam era and those evoked by the antiapartheid movement pit students against university administrators, multinational corporations, the U.S. military, and established governments. In the context of that kind of power imbalance, the free speech rights of students deserve particular deference. Unfortunately, as we know from our memory of four dead in Ohio, that deference is not always forthcoming.

Racist speech on campus occurs in a vastly different power context. Campus racism targets vulnerable students and faculty. Students of color often come to the university at risk academically, socially, and psychologically. Faculty of color — if they exist at all — are typically untenured, overburdened, and isolated.[38] The marginalized position of faculty of color further marginalizes students of color.

There is legal precedent for considering the status of the target in measuring the amount of freedom verbal attackers enjoy. In the law of defamation, private figures can more easily obtain damages for harm to their reputation than can public figures. This is based on the greater ability of public figures to launch an effective rebuttal and on their voluntary choice to enter the public eye. An additional implicit justification is that wealth, power, and fame provide ego support that helps one weather verbal abuse. If nothing else, the defamed movie star can retreat to Malibu.

The student, like the private figure, has fewer avenues of retreat. Living on or near campus, studying in the library, and interacting with fellow students are integral parts of university life. When racist propaganda appears on campus, target-group students experience debilitated access to the full university experience. This is so even when hate propaganda is directed at groups rather than at individuals.

Students are analogous to the captive audience that is afforded special first amendment consideration in other contexts. Similarly, students who support universities through tuition and who are encouraged to think of the university as their home are involuntarily forced into a position of complicity with racism when their campus is offered to hate groups as a forum.

A related and literally captive group deserves mention here. The majority of prison inmates in many communities are people of color. Prisons are also fertile grounds for spreading racist hate speech. Courts have protected the rights of hate groups in prisons. The physical vulnerability and inability to escape that characterize prison life make restriction of hate speech in prisons more important than in the population at large....

The Unintended Story: The Meaning of Legal Protection of Racist Hate Messages

The legal response to racist propaganda provides an interesting context for examination of the relation between law and racism. Legal protection of racism is seen in these doctrinal elements:

1. The limits of doctrinal imagination in creating first amendment exceptions for racist hate speech
2. The refusal to recognize the competing values of liberty and equality at stake in the case of hate speech
3. The refusal to view the protection of racist speech as a form of state action

The limits of the lawmaking imagination of judges, legislators, and other legal insiders who have considered proposals to outlaw hate propaganda are symptomatic of the position of privilege from which legal doctrine develops. Legal insiders cannot imagine a life disabled in a significant way by hate propaganda.

This limited imagination has not affected lawmakers faced with other forms of offensive speech. The law of defamation and privacy recognizes that certain forms of expression are qualitatively different from the kind of speech deserving absolute protection. The legal imagination is able to contemplate what it feels like to hear lies spread about one's professional competency or to have one's likeness used for commercial gain without consent. American law has even, at times, provided a tort remedy for white plaintiffs who are "insulted" by "imputation of association with persons of a race against which there is prejudice."[39] When the legal mind understands that reputational interests, which are analogized to the preferred interest in property, must be balanced against first amendment interests, it recognizes the concrete reality of what happens to people who are defamed. Their lives are changed. Their standing in the community, their opportunities, their self-worth, their free enjoyment of life are limited. Their political capital — their ability to speak and be heard — is diminished. To see this, and yet to fail to see that the very same things happen to the victims of racist speech, is selective vision.

The selective consideration of one victim's story and not another's results in unequal application of the law. Unlike the victims of defamation and other torts, the victims of racist speech are not representative of the population at large. In making typical legal concessions to the first amendment, we burden a range of victims. In the case of flag burning, we force flag lovers of all races and class positions to tolerate flag desecration as part of the price of freedom. In contrast, when victims of racist speech are left to assuage their own wounds, we burden a limited class: the traditional victims of discrimination. This class already experiences diminished access to private remedies such as effective counterspeech, and this diminished access is exacerbated by hate messages. As the feminist scholar Catharine MacKinnon notes, debasing speech discredits targets, further reducing their ability to have their speech taken seriously.[40] The application of absolutist free speech principles to hate speech, then, is a choice to burden one group with a disproportionate share of the costs of speech promotion. Tolerance of hate speech thus creates superregressivity — those least able to pay are the only ones taxed for this tolerance. The principle of equality is violated by such allocation. The more progressive principle of rectification or reparation — the obligation to repair effects of historical wrongs — is even more grossly violated....

The constitutional commitment to equality and the promise to abolish the badges and incidents of slavery are emptied of meaning when the target-group members must alter their behavior, change their choice of neighborhood, leave their jobs, and warn their children off the streets because of hate group activity. When the presence of the Klan deters employers from hiring target-group members, prevents citizens from socializing freely, and keeps parents from sending their children to integrated schools, the goal of nondiscrimination is moved farther away from present realities. When hate propaganda spreads attitudes of racism and desensitizes potential abusers to the wrongness of violence, other more obvious goals of safety and order are sacrificed.

The third doctrinal pillar supporting racist speech is the refusal to recognize that tolerance and protection of hate group activity by the government is a form of state action. Hate groups have operated openly in prisons, in the military, in law enforcement, and in other government institutions. To allow an organization known for violence, persecution, race hatred, and commitment to racial supremacy to exist openly and to provide police protection and access to public facilities, streets, and college campuses for such a group means that the state is promoting racist speech. But for such support, hate groups would decline in efficacy. The chilling sight of avowed racists in threatening regalia marching through our neighborhoods with full police protection is a statement of state authorization. The Klan marches because marching promotes the Klan and because of the terrorizing and inciting effect of its public displays. Open display conveys legitimacy. The government advances this effect when it protects these marches. In addition, the failure to provide a legal response limiting hate propaganda elevates the liberty interests of racists over the liberty interests of their targets. A member of the Georgia Bureau of Investigation, for example, once suggested to whites targeted for hate speech because of their association with African Americans that they should avoid being seen in cars with African Americans and cease inviting African Americans to their homes.[41]

The effect of racist propaganda is to devalue the individual and to treat masses of people in a degraded way with no measure of individual merit. This is precisely what civil libertarians oppose when the state acts. Because racist speech is seen as private, the connection to loss of liberty is not made. State silence, however, is public action where the strength of the new racist groups derives from their offering legitimation and justification for otherwise socially unacceptable emotions of hate, fear, and aggression. The need for a formal group, for a patriotic cause, and for an elevation of the doubting self are part of the traditional attraction of groups like the Klan. Government protection of the right of the Klan to exist publicly and to spread a racist message promotes the role of the Klan as a legitimizer of racism.

Further, the law's failure to provide recourse to persons who are demeaned by the hate messages is an effective second injury to that person. The second injury is the pain of knowing that the government provides no remedy and offers no recognition of the dehumanizing experience that victims of hate propaganda are subjected to. The government's denial of personhood through its denial of legal recourse may be even more painful than the initial act of hatred. One can dismiss the hate group as an organization of marginal people, but the state is the official embodiment of the society we live in.

The legal realists and their progeny recognize that law formation is largely a matter of value.[42] There are no inevitable results; there is no controlling logic or doctrine that can make the hard choices for us. Reversion to discredited doctrinal absolutism carries a strong implication that racist activities are supported, albeit unintentionally, by the law. In a society that expresses its moral judgments through the law, and in which the rule of law and the use of law are characteristic responses to many social phenomena, this absence of laws against racist speech is telling.

We can defy the proposition that racism is part of law by opening our eyes to the reality of racism and making the decision to outlaw hate groups. We can draw from the international standard and acknowledge the competing interests at stake, adapting existing law and creating new law to limit hate group activities. It is not necessary to abandon first amendment values in order to do this. The analytical dexterity of legal thinkers offers many options for reconciling the U.S. posi-

tion with the international goal of elimination of all forms of racial discrimination.

This chapter suggests that the stories of those who have experienced racism are of special value in defeating racism. It further suggests that we can, and have, chosen as a primary value freedom from racial oppression. Finally, in doing the awkward work of constructing doctrine, this chapter suggests a belief in the possibility and the necessity of creating a legal response to racist speech — not because it isn't really speech, not because it falls within a hoped-for neutral exception, but because it is wrong.

There is in every constitutional doctrine we devise the danger of misuse. For fear of falling, we are warned against taking a first step. Frozen at the first amendment bulkhead, we watch the rising tide of racial hatred wash over our schools and workplaces. Students victimized by racist speech turn to university administrators for redress and are told that the first amendment forecloses institutional action. We owe those students a more thoughtful analysis than absolutism. At the least, before we abandon the task of devising a legal response to racist speech, we should consider concretely the options available to us. The legal imagination is a fruitful one. That is the one hopeful message of the postmodern critique of law. Nothing inherent in law ties our hands, and lawyers through the ages have displayed abundant skills of invention.

Conclusion

Critical race theory uses the experience of subordination to offer a phenomenology of race and law. The victims' experience reminds us that the harm of racist hate messages is a real harm to real people. When the legal system offers no redress for that real harm, it perpetuates racism.

This chapter attempts to begin a conversation about the first amendment that acknowledges both the civil libertarian's fear of tyranny and the victim's experience of loss of liberty in a society that tolerates racist speech. It suggests criminalization of a narrow, explicitly defined class of racist hate speech to provide public redress for the most serious harm, leaving many forms of racist speech to private remedies. Some may feel that this proposal does not go far enough, leaving much hurtful speech to the uneven control of the marketplace of ideas. Others will cringe at what they perceive as a call for censorship. This is not an easy legal or moral puzzle, but it is precisely in these places where we feel conflicting tugs at heart and mind that we have the most work to do and the most knowledge to gain.

Ours is a law-bound culture. If law is where racism is, then law is where we must confront it. The doctrinal reconstruction presented here is tentative and subject to change as our struggle around this issue continues. However we choose to respond to racist speech, let us present a competing ideology, one that has existed in tension with racism since the birth of our nation: There is inherent worth in each human being, and each is entitled to a life of dignity.

NOTES

1. Incidents such as this are described in P. Sims, *The Klan* 167-72 (1978).

2. At the University of California Hastings College of the Law, someone defaced a Black History Month Display in just such a manner. "Racist Caricatures Anger Students," *Recorder* (San Francisco), Feb. 11, 1989, at 1.

3. Author's personal experience, Perth, Western Australia, July 1987, recounted in "Language as Violence v. Freedom of Expression: Canadian and American Perspectives on Group Defamation," 37 *Buffalo. L. Rev.* 337 (1989) (transcript of the James McCormick Mitchell Lecture, State University of New York at Buffalo School of Law, Nov. 4, 1988) [herinafter cited as *Language as Violence*].

4. L. Bollinger, *The Tolerant Society: Free Speech and Extremist Speech in America* (1986).

5. *Collin v. Smith*, 447 F. Supp. 676 (N.D. Ill.) *Affd.*, 578 F. 2d 1197 (7th Cir.) *cert. denied*, 439 U.S. 916 (1978); *Village of Skokie v. National Socialist Party*, 51 Ill. App. 3d 279, 366 N.E. 2d 347 (1977), *modified*, 69 Ill. 2d 605, 373 N.E. 2d 21 (1978).

6. Williams, "Spirit-Murdering the Messenger: The Discourse of Fingerpointing as the Law's Response to Racism," 42 *Miami L. Rev.* 127, 139 (1987).

7. See *Critchen v. Firestone Steel Prods. Co.* Nos. 12,190 — EM & 15,389 — EM (Mich. Civ. Rts. Comm'n May 23, 1984) *reported in* 1984 Michigan Civ. Rts. Commission, Case Digest 13, 17-18.

8. "S.F. Fire Department Declared 'Out of Control,'" *Asian L. Caucus Rep.*, July/Dec. 1987, at 1, col. 1.

9. *Poverty Law Report*, Mar.-Apr. 1982, at 11, col. 2.

10. "Black F.B.I. Agent's Ordeal: Meanness That Never Let Up," *N.Y. Times*, Jan. 25, 1988, at 1, col.1.

11. Complaint at 3, *EEOC v. Hyster Co.*, Civ. No. 88-930 — DA (D. Ore., filed Aug. 15, 1988) (alleging a hostile work environment created by racially objectionable advertisement campaign and use of racial slurs by management in work place). An answer denying those allegations was filed by the defendant.

12. "Racial Violence Belies Good Life in Contra Costa County," *L.A. Times*, Dec. 7, 1980, at 3, col. 5.

13. Asian and Pacific Islander Advisory Comm., Office of Attorney Gen. Cal. Dept. Of Justice, *Final Report* 45 (1988).

14. Ga. State Advisory Comm'n to the U.S. Comm'n on Civil Rights, Perceptions of Hate Group Activity in Georgia 3 (1983) (testimony of Stuart Lowengrub, Southeastern Regional Director, Anti-Defamation League of B'nai B'rith, Atlanta).

15. Cervantes, "Poem for the Young White Man Who Asked Me How I, An Intelligent Well Read Person could Believe in the War Between Races," *Emplumada* (1981).

16. Williams, *supra* note 9, at 129.

17. Greenberg and Pyszcynski, "The Effect of an Overheard Ethnic Slur on Evaluation of the Target: How to Spread a Social Disease," 21 *J. Experimental Soc. Psychology* 61, 70 (1985).

18. G. Allport, *The Nature of Prejudice* 461-78 (1954); H. Kitano, *Race Relations* 113-14 (1974); H. Schuman, C. Steeh & L. Bobo, *Racial Attitudes in America* 137 (1985).

19. See, eg., *Afro-American Writing* (R. Long & E. Collier eds. 1985).

20. International Convention on the Elimination of All Forms of Racial Discrimination opened for signature Mar. 7, 1966, 660 U.N.T.S. 195 [hereinafter Racial Discrimination Convention].

21. See N. Lerner, *The U.N. Convention on the Elimination of All forms of Racial Discrimination* 43-53 (ed. 1980).

22. Racial Discrimination Convention, *supra* note 23, at 218.

23. *Id.* At 214.

24. Council of Europe, *European Convention on Human Rights: Collected Texts 1* (7th ed. 1971).

25. Pan American Union, *Final Act of the Ninth International Conference of American States* 38 (1948).

26. The Convention on the Prevention and Punishment of the Crime of Genocide, art,. 3(c), *adopted* Dec.9, 1948, 78 U.N.T.S. 277, 280, requires member states to prohibit "[d]irect and public incitement to commit genocide." The convention was ratified by the U.S. Senate in 1986 with reservations noting that the U.S. Constitution would override any provisions of the convention, 132 Cong. Rec. 2349 — 50 (Feb. 19, 1986).

27. *Race Relations Act*, 1965, c. 73 6 (1), amended in 1976 and 1986.

28. See *Race Relations Act*, of 1976, c. 74 70.

29. I. MacDonald, *Race Relations and Immigration Law* 8 (1969).

30. *Can. Rev. Stat*. Ch. C-46 318, 319 (1985).

31. *Constitution Act of 1982*, 2.

32. See, e.g., the proposed amendments to the New South Wales Racial Discrimination Act reported in Woomera, June/July 1987, at 1 (allowing group defamation actions for racial slurs). Violent racist groups are gaining in membership and visibility in Australia.

33. *Collin v. Smith*, 447 F. Supp. 676 (N.D. Ill.) *Affd.* 578 F. 2d 1197 (7th Cir.), *cert. denied,* 439 U.S. 916 (1978); *Village of Skokie v. National Socialist Party*, 51 Ill.App. 3d 279, 366 N.E. 2d 347 (1977), modified, 69 Ill. 2d 605, 373 N.E. 2d 21 (1978).

34. *Regents of the Univ. v. Bakke*, 438 U.S. 265, 407 (1978) (Blackmum, J., dissenting).

35. Delgado, "Derrick Bell and the Ideology of Racial Reform," 97 *Yale L.J.* 923, 937 (1988).

36. See "A Theory Goes on Trial," *Time*, Sept. 24, 1984, at 62 (Dr. Shockley, who admits to subscribing to the white supremacist publication *Thunderbolt*, is called "nearly incompetent" by trained geneticist).

37. I thank my colleague Dr. Chalsa Loo, a psychologist, college counselor, and specialist in multicultural interaction, for these insights.

38. See Delgado, "Minority Law Professors' Lives: The Bell-Delgado Survey," 24 *Harv. Civ. Rts.-Civ. Lib. L. Rev.* 407 (1989) (reporting on widespread effects of discrimination and high attrition rates among minority law teachers); Chused, "The Hiring and Retention of Minorities and Women on American Law School Faculties," 137 *U. Pa. L. Rev.* 537 (1988); Haines, "Minority Law Professors and the Myth of Sisyphus: Consciousness and Praxis Within the Special Teaching Challenges in American Law Schools," 10 *Nat'l Black L.J.* 247 (1988); McGee, "Symbol and Substance in the Minority Professoriat's Future," 3 *Harv. BlackLetter J.* 67 (1986) (special burdens and obligations of minority law professors).

39. Annotation, "Libel and Slander: Imputation of Association with Persons of Race or Nationality as to Which there Is Social Prejudice," 121 *A.L.R.* 1151, 1151 (1939) (citing *Sharp v. Bussey*, 137 Fla. 96, 187 So. 779 [1939]).

40. MacKinnon, "Not a Moral Issue," 2 *Yale L. & Pol'y. Rev.* 321 (1984).

41. Ga. State Advisory Comm'n to the U.S. Comm'n on Civil Rights, *supra* note 16, at 21.

42. Llewellyn, "Some Realism About Realism: Responding to Dean Pound," 44 *Harv. L. Rev.* 1222, 1236 (1931) ("The conception of law as a means to social ends and not an end in itself").

STUDY QUESTIONS

1 According to Ronald Dworkin's account of Catharine MacKinnon's argument for censorship, what are the two constitutional values that need balancing in the debate in the U.S. about censoring pornography? What arguments does Dworkin give for defending the primacy of the First Amendment? What arguments does he provide for rejecting Catharine MacKinnon's resolution of the conflict of values in favor of the Fourteenth Amendment?

2 Is equality enhanced or threatened by censorship? Formulate your answer to this question by outlining and evaluating the contrasting views of equality defended by Dworkin and MacKinnon.

3 Did Marvin Glass's outline of disagreements among feminists regarding censorship raise questions for you about Dworkin's analysis of the arguments used by anti-pornography feminists? Why or why not?

4 Given the feminist analysis of the patriarchal nature of the state, how does Glass answer the charge that anti-pornography feminists place too much trust that the state will only censor material that is harmful to women?

5 According to Glass, anti-censorship feminists belie their distrust in the state by defending such institutions as public education and health care. Does their trust of the state in these areas contradict their distrust of the state in the case of censorship? Defend your answer.

6 Do you agree with Glass that the state should censor pornography even with the likelihood that the legislation will be applied to lesbian representations of sexuality or to feminist theory itself? Defend your answer.

7 Heather MacRae and Glass both defend a feminist conception of pornography as discriminatory and harmful to women. What is this conception? Can pornography be defined so that legislation can succeed in targeting only that material that is morally objectionable? Defend your answer.

8 According to MacRae, what changes are happening as a result of the European Union that make reexamining feminist conceptions of pornography timely and important? What aspects of the impact of the European Union are likely to facilitate legislation in the area of pornography? What aspects might hinder the development of legislation? Do you think legislation should be facilitated or blocked and at what level? Does your answer depend on the context of European countries and the European Union? Defend your answers.

9 What does MacRae mean by "triangle of empowerment"? Why is this concept important to her analysis of legislation regarding pornography in Germany?

10 What prompts Alison Minea and Christine Koggel to reevaluate traditional liberal arguments defending privacy? What are those arguments? What objections do Minea and Koggel raise against them?

11 What features of the Internet do Minea and Koggel find particularly problematic from the point of view of relationships? Were you already aware of these features in your use of the Internet? Do you think that these changes to relationships ought to concern us? Defend your answers.

12 What are the features of a relational conception of the self that make it applicable to an assessment of pornography and the Internet? Do we have a responsibility and should we be accountable for what we say and do on the Internet? Should there be legislation to control this activity? What do Minea and Koggel argue? What would you argue?

13 What are some of the effects of racist speech on those targeted in the speech, as reported by Mari Matsuda? Does learning about victims' stories change your thinking about the regulation of hate speech? Why or why not?

14 According to Matsuda, the U.S. is out of step with moves in the international community to criminalize racist hate messages as is evident in the International Convention on the Elimination of All

Forms of Racial Discrimination and in the human rights legislation of various countries. Is being out of step relevant to the question of which policies the U.S. should adopt for dealing with racist hate speech? How does Matsuda answer this question? How does Dworkin answer this question? How would you?

15 Matsuda attempts to define racist speech in a way sufficiently narrow to preserve First Amendment values in the U.S. and yet allow legal restrictions. Is her case convincing? Formulate your answer by discussing her analysis of some of the hard cases.

SUGGESTED READINGS

Adams, Carol J. *The Pornography of Meat*. New York, NY: Continuum, 2003.

Burstyn, Varda (editor). *Women Against Censorship*. Vancouver, BC: Douglas & McIntyre, 1985.

Cohen, Cheryl H. "The Feminist Sexuality Debate: Ethics and Politics." *Hypatia*, v. 1, no. 2 (Fall 1986): 71-86.

Davies, Jacqueline MacGregor. "Pornographic Harms." In *Feminist Perspectives: Philosophical Essays on Method and Morals*, edited by L. Code, S. Mullett, and C. Overall. Toronto, ON: University of Toronto Press, 1988.

Diamond, Irene. "Reflections on a Nondogmatic Feminism: The Case of Pornography." *Humanities in Society*, v. 7 (Winter/Spring 1984): 77-86.

Duggan, Lisa, Nan Hunter, and Carole Vance. "False Promises: Feminist Antipornography Legislation." In *Women Against Censorship*, edited by Varda Burstyn. Toronto, ON: Douglas and McIntyre, 1985.

Dwyer, Susan. "Caught in the Web: Sexual Fantasizing, Character, and CyberPornography." In *Contemporary Moral Issues*, edited by Wesley Cragg and Christine Koggel. 5th edition. Toronto, ON: McGraw-Hill Ryerson, 2005.

Dwyer, Susan (editor). *The Problem of Pornography*. Belmont, CA: Wadsworth, 1995.

Dyzenhaus, David. "Pornography and Public Reason." *Canadian Journal of Law and Jurisprudence*, v. 7, no. 2 (1994): 261-81.

Fish, Stanley. "Boutique Multiculturalism, or Why Liberals are Incapable of Thinking about Hate Speech." *Critical Inquiry* 23 (Winter 1997): 378-95.

Garry, Ann. "Pornography and Respect for Women." *Social Theory and Practice*, v. 4 (1978): 395-421.

Heldke, Lisa. "Do You Mind if I Speak Freely: Reconceptualizing Freedom of Speech." *Social Theory and Practice*, v. 17, no. 3 (Fall 1991): 349-68.

Hill, Judith M. "Pornography and Degradation." *Hypatia*, v. 2 (1987): 39-54.

Kimmel, Michael (editor). *Men Confront Pornography*. New York, NY: Meridian, 1991.

Langton, Rae. "Whose Right? Ronald Dworkin, Women, and Pornographers." *Philosophy & Public Affairs*, v. 19, no. 4 (1990): 311-59.

Lederer, Laura (editor). *Take Back the Night: Women on Pornography*. New York, NY: Morrow, 1980.

Loftus, David. *Watching Sex: How Men Really Respond to Pornography*. New York, NY: Thunder's Mouth Press, 2002.

Longino, Helen. "Pornography, Oppression, and Freedom: A Closer Look." In *Take Back the Night: Women on Pornography*, edited by Laura Lederer. New York, NY: Morrow, 1980.

MacKinnon, Catharine. "Francis Biddle's Sister: Pornography, Civil Rights, and Speech." In *Feminism Unmodified: Discourses in Life and Law*. Cambridge, MA: Harvard University Press, 1987.

— . *Only Words*. Cambridge, MA: Harvard University Press, 1993.

Mahoney, Kathleen E. "Pornography and Violence Towards Women: Comparisons Between Europe, the United States and Canada." In *International Human Rights Law: Theory and Practice*, edited by Irwin Cotler and F. Pearl Eliadis. Montreal, QC: The Canadian Human Rights Foundation, 1992.

Mann, Doug. "Porn Revisited." *Journal of Social Philosophy*, v. 28, no. 1 (Spring 1997): 77-86.

Matsuda, Mari, Charles R. Lawrence III, Richard Delgado, and Kimberlè Williams Crenshaw. *Words That Wound: Critical Race Theory, Assaultive Speech, and the First Amendment*. Boulder, CO: Westview, 1993.

Scoccia, Danny. "Can Liberals Support a Ban on Violent Pornography?" *Ethics*, v. 106 (July 1996): 776-99.

Stoltenberg, John. "Gays and the Pro-Pornography Movement: Having the Hots for Sex Discrimination." In *Men Confront Pornography*, edited by Michael S. Kimmel. New York, NY: Meridian, 1991.

CHAPTER FOUR: ANIMAL RIGHTS

INTRODUCTION

Thus far, our discussion of moral theory and issues has centered on the interaction of human beings within and across societies. Volume I examines the concepts of human rights, justice, and democracy and explores answers to questions about their meaning, universalizability, and the social and political structures needed to respect them. Volume II examines various kinds of discrimination based on membership in traditionally disadvantaged groups and the historical and social conditions that sustain them. Volume III investigates answers to kinds of moral dilemmas about human life and human flourishing in various social and political contexts. Issues of non-human animals and the environment are touched on, but only by implication in liberal arguments that capacities unique to human beings give them inherent worth that justifies their privileged status over non-human entities and in the questions raised about the effects of globalization on development policies. In this and the following chapter, we deal explicitly with questions about our treatment of non-human animals and the environment and do so in a global context of differing values, practices, and policies. As well as examining responsibilities for protecting the rights of non-human entities and for maintaining resources, species, and the environment itself for future generations, we will also explore the particular challenges that these issues pose for traditional Western moral theory.

In the first reading, Peter Singer surveys the arguments underlying the principle of equality in various liberation movements. The principle of equality is not a description of an actual equality: human beings come in different sizes and shapes, with different moral and intellectual capacities, and different capacities for pleasure and pain and for communication with others. Singer defends a conception of equality as equal consideration and argues that what gives entities a right to equal consideration is the capacity for suffering, a capacity that is a prerequisite for having capacities at all. But speciesism, like racism and sexism, violates the principle of equal consideration because it is a prejudice or bias in favor of the interests of members of one's own species and against members of other species. Singer chastises philosophers for taking suffering to be morally relevant in the case of human beings, yet failing to apply this simple principle to members of other species. Proper moral decision-making involves paying attention to the consequences and choosing those actions that reduce or minimize the suffering of human beings and animals.

To avoid speciesism, argues Singer, we must allow that beings similar in relevant respects are owed similar consideration and that mere membership in a biological category is not morally relevant. Concerning the sanctity of life, Singer argues that speciesism is at work when we preserve infants who have suffered irreparable brain damage, but kill non-human animals who surpass the brain-damaged infant in capabilities. Singer does not advocate an absolute prohibition on killing non-human animals, but rather argues that consistency demands that we bring non-human animals within our sphere of moral concern and treatment and cease to treat their lives as expendable for whatever trivial purposes we have. He argues that the principle of minimizing suffering can tell us what our duties to animals are. In our reading, he applies this principle to the case for vegetarianism. Becoming a vegetarian is a practical and effective step toward ending the killing and infliction of animal suffering. Because it is not possible to rear animals for food on a large scale without inflicting suffering, vegetarianism is a form of boycott that can reduce the number of animals raised in factory farms and slaughtered for food.

Peter Singer's defense of animal rights is challenged by Tom Regan in the second reading. While Singer's is a utilitarian/consequentialist approach that has us make moral decisions regarding animals by weighing kinds and levels of suffering, Regan's is a rights-based approach that holds that what is fundamentally wrong is a system that allows us to view animals as *resources*, there for us to be eaten or used for research, sport, or money. Relieving their suffering by improving their living conditions will not eliminate the basic wrong of viewing and treating animals as our resources. Regan defends his case for animal rights by questioning utilitarianism as well as traditional moral theory that grants rights to human beings but stops at animals.

Moral theory in the liberal tradition holds that only human beings have inherent value and that animals have value only insofar as they are of value to human beings. On this sort of account, we have only indirect duties to animals. Regan highlights inconsistencies in this approach. Not all human beings have the capacities that are said to justify their privileged status. Children and the severely disabled, for example, do not have the full reasoning capacity that Kant and Rawls, for example, use to justify membership as full citizens. Utilitarians, argues Regan, fare no better. Their promotion of pleasure and pain as that which determines what is morally right means that human beings have value but only as "containers" of pleasures and pains. The utilitarian calculation can result in justifying an evil action against a minority of individuals in order to achieve greater happiness for a greater number of entities. Regan develops his case for animal rights by providing his account of inherent value: we are each "the experiencing subject of a life, a conscious creature having an individual welfare that has importance to us whatever our usefulness to others." But this description also applies to animals. Consistency demands that we accord rights to animals in the same way that we accord them to all human beings and that practices that use animals as resources be stopped. Regan calls for the total abolition of the use of animals in

science, the total dissolution of commercial agriculture, and the total elimination of commercial and sport hunting and trapping.

In the third reading, Nathan Nobis examines the issue of vegetarianism to argue that both Singer's consequentialist approach and Regan's rights-based approach are inadequate for defending the moral obligation to become a vegetarian or vegan. Nobis begins by providing facts about modern animal agriculture and human nutrition, facts that support Singer's consequentialist view of the immense suffering of animals and that provide evidence that the consumption of animals is not needed for human health or survival. The consequentialist case rests on the idea that being a vegetarian or vegan maximizes utility — the fewer animals that are raised and killed for food, the less suffering there is. Nobis argues that this argument does not work on an individual level — my becoming a vegetarian makes no difference to the overall utility of reducing animal suffering in a context of a huge industry and market unaffected by my actions.

Nobis turns to virtue theory to argue that while it can support vegetarianism by defending virtues such as care and compassion, it cannot tell us *why* we should be caring or compassionate. He merges the insights of virtue ethics with consequentialism to argue that individuals can bring about more goodness if they have the virtues of compassion, care, and sensitivity to unnecessary cruelty and suffering. Vegetarians and vegans live lives that recognize that the most effective way to promote human health is through dietary changes and that show concern for environmental problems and public health and safety. These character traits have a positive impact on one's own life and the lives of those around one. If one ought to be compassionate, sensitive to cruelty, resist injustice, and be morally integrated, then, Nobis argues, one ought to be a vegetarian or vegan.

In the fourth reading, Deborah Slicer highlights deficiencies in both the rights-based and utilitarian approaches to the issue of animal research. She defends ecofeminism, arguing that animal rights issues are also feminist issues. She argues that Singer's and Regan's arguments share a number of features in what she refers to as "the

Singer-Regan approach": they are justice approaches to morality that hold essentialist views of the moral worth of human beings and animals and thereby ignore relationships that promote attention to care and responsibility. Ecofeminists criticize the hierarchical nature of patriarchy that categorizes women, animals, and nature on the same devalued side of binaries such as reason/emotion and man/nature. Slicer uses recent ecofeminist critiques of deep ecology and the Singer-Regan approach to argue that both accounts neglect context and concrete individuals, overestimate the scope of principles, and discount affective responses in moral life. There is no reason, she argues, why animals' differences cannot ground caring relationships of respect, compassion, fellow feeling, gratitude, and wonder.

Slicer then applies insights from the ecofeminist approach that calls for attention to context and relationships to a discussion of the use of live animals in biomedical research. Researchers claim that we must choose between "us" (human beings) and "them" (animals), between our daughters and our dogs, and that medical progress is threatened if there are restrictions on the use of animals in research. Slicer argues that this and the Singer-Regan characterization of the issue are dangerously misleading. A contextual approach opens up questions about the overuse and misuse of animals in research, the dangerous reliance on the symmetries between animals and humans and between one species and another, the inadequacy of government regulations to protect laboratory animals, and the use of species with high psycho-social capabilities when those with less demanding capacities can do. Moreover, an ecofeminist approach has us pay attention to proactive and preventive measures for promoting and improving human health: cleaning the air, water, and soil and changing medical research and practices so that women and animals are not treated in discriminatory ways. Slicer holds that developing relationships with animals and rocks and trees can enhance one's capacity to empathize and act on behalf of others, including laboratory animals used in research.

J. Baird Callicott contrasts the individualistic and atomistic approach of mainstream moral theory, evident in Singer's consequentialist approach and Regan's rights-based approach, with the holistic and ecological approach that he explicates and defends through Aldo Leopold's land ethic in *A Sand County Almanac*. The precept of the land ethic is that "a thing is right when it tends to preserve the integrity, stability, and beauty of the biotic community. It is wrong when it tends otherwise." The land ethic challenges the individualism of traditional approaches to animals and the environment by presenting the biotic community as an ecological and holistic system of interdependent parts. It asks moral agents to respond in relation to that whole, a delicately complex, functioning social and organic system. It suggests that moral agents become ecologically literate by learning how relationships that bind organisms to one another and to the environment determine the very nature of organisms and the biotic communities in which they live and function.

Callicott gives examples of how the holistic ecological approach of the land ethic generates moral imperatives distinct from individualist approaches. Individualist approaches defend a right to life for individual members, whether of humans only or of non-human animals to which equal consideration or inherent value is extended. But the protection and preservation of individual non-human animals are practices that can threaten the environment and have devastating ecological consequences. The land ethic would, therefore, seem to demand removal or destruction of that which threatens the integrity of the biotic community, including human beings. Callicott rejects these inhumane and anti-humanitarian implications of the land ethic. The land ethic, he argues, neither replaces nor overrides moral sensibilities and obligations that human beings have to their families, neighborhoods, communities, nations, and the global context as a whole. This means that respect for human rights and for principles of individual moral worth and dignity are part of what it means to be a member that both shapes and is shaped by the biotic community.

ALL ANIMALS ARE EQUAL ...

or why the ethical principle on which human equality rests requires us to extend equal consideration to animals too

Peter Singer

Peter Singer is Ira W. DeCamp Professor of Bioethics, University Center for Human Values, at Princeton University. He is author and editor of many books, some of which include Practical Ethics *(editor, 1993),* Bioethics: An Anthology *(1999, co-edited with Helga Kuhse),* The Moral of the Story: An Anthology of Ethics Through Literature *(2005, co-edited with Renata Singer),* One World: Ethics and Globalization *(2002), and* How Ethical is Australia? An Examination of Australia's Record as a Global Citizen *(2004, with Tom Gregg).*

Singer defines speciesism as prejudice towards the interests of members of one's own species and against those of members of other species and argues that it is analogous to racism and sexism. Just as it is unjust to discriminate against women and African Americans by not considering their interests, so too is it unjust to ignore the interests of animals. Because avoidance of suffering is an interest that is shared by human and non-human animals, it is morally wrong to ignore the suffering of animals. Singer then applies his argument to the case for vegetarianism.

"Animal Liberation" may sound more like a parody of other liberation movements than a serious objective. The idea of "The Rights of Animals" actually was once used to parody the case for women's rights. When Mary Wollstonecraft, a forerunner of today's feminists, published her *Vindication of the Rights of Woman* in 1792, her views were widely regarded as absurd, and before long an anonymous publication appeared entitled *A Vindication of the Rights of Brutes.* The author of this satirical work (now know to have been Thomas Taylor, a distinguished Cambridge philosopher) tried to refute Mary Wollstonecraft's arguments by showing that they could be carried one stage further. If the argument for equality was sound when applied to women, why should it not be applied to dogs, cats, and horses? The reasoning seemed to hold for these "brutes" too; yet to hold that brutes had rights was manifestly absurd. Therefore the rea-

soning by which this conclusion had been reached must be unsound, and if unsound when applied to brutes, it must also be unsound when applied to women, since the very same arguments had been used in each case.

In order to explain the basis of the case for the equality of animals, it will be helpful to start with an examination of the case for the equality of women. Let us assume that we wish to defend the case for women's rights against the attack by Thomas Taylor. How should we reply?

One way in which we might reply is by saying that the case for equality between men and women cannot validly be extended to nonhuman animals. Women have a right to vote, for instance, because they are just as capable of making rational decisions about the future as men are; dogs, on the other hand, are incapable of understanding the significance of voting, so they cannot have the right to vote. There are many other obvious ways in which men and women resemble each other closely, while humans and animals differ greatly. So, it might be said, men and women are similar beings and should have similar rights, while humans and nonhumans are different and should not have equal rights.

The reasoning behind this reply to Taylor's analogy is correct up to a point, but it does not go far enough. There are obviously important differences between humans and other animals, and these differences must give rise to some differences in the rights that each have. Recognizing this evident fact, however, is no barrier to the case for extending the basic principle of equality to nonhuman animals. The differences that exist between men and women are equally undeniable, and the supporters of Women's Liberation are aware that these differences may give rise to different rights. Many feminists hold that women have the right to an abortion on request. It does not follow that since these same feminists are campaigning for equality between men and women they must support the right of men to have abortions too. Since a man cannot have an abortion, it is meaningless to talk of his right to have one. Since dogs can't vote, it is meaningless to talk of their right to vote. There is no reason why either Women's Liberation or Animal Liberation should get involved in such nonsense. The extension of the basic principle of equality from one group to another does not imply that we must treat both groups in exactly the same way, or grant exactly the same rights to both groups. Whether we should do so will depend on the nature of the members of the two groups. The basic principle of equality does not require equal or identical *treatment*; it requires equal consideration. Equal consideration for different beings may lead to different treatment and different rights.

So there is a different way of replying to Taylor's attempt to parody the case for women's rights, a way that does not deny the obvious differences between human beings and nonhumans but goes more deeply into the question of equality and concludes by finding nothing absurd in the idea that the basic principle of equality

applies to so-called brutes. At this point such a conclusion may appear odd; but if we examine more deeply the basis on which our opposition to discrimination on grounds of race or sex ultimately rests, we will see that we would be on shaky ground if we were to demand equality for blacks, women, and other groups of oppressed humans while denying equal consideration to nonhumans. To make this clear we need to see, first, exactly why racism and sexism are wrong. When we say that all human beings, whatever their race, creed, or sex, are equal, what is it that we are asserting? Those who wish to defend hierarchical, inegalitarian societies have often pointed out that by whatever test we choose it simply is not true that all humans are equal. Like it or not we must face the fact that humans come in different shapes and sizes; they come with different moral capacities, different intellectual abilities, different amounts of benevolent feeling and sensitivity to the needs of others, different abilities to communicate effectively, and different capacities to experience pleasure and pain. In short, if the demand for equality were based on the actual equality of all human beings, we would have to stop demanding equality.

Still, one might cling to the view that the demand for equality among human beings is based on the actual equality of the different races and sexes. Although, it may be said, humans differ as individuals, there are no differences between the races and sexes as such. From the mere fact that a person is black or a woman we cannot infer anything about that person's intellectual or moral capacities. This, it may be said, is why racism and sexism are wrong. The white racist claims that whites are superior to blacks, but this is false; although there are differences among individuals, some blacks are superior to some whites in all of the capacities and abilities that could conceivably be relevant. The opponent of sexism would say the same: a person's sex is no guide to his or her abilities, and this is why it is unjustifiable to discriminate on the basis of sex.

The existence of individual variations that cut across the lines of race or sex, however, provides us with no defense at all against a more sophisticated opponent of equality, one who proposes that, say, the interests of all those with IQ scores below 100 be given less consideration than the interests of those with ratings over 100. Perhaps those scoring below the mark would, in this society, be made the slaves of those scoring higher. Would a hierarchical society of this sort really be so much better than one based on race or sex? I think not. But if we tie the moral principle of equality to the factual equality of the different races or sexes, taken as a whole, our opposition to racism and sexism does not provide us with any basis for objecting to this kind of inegalitarianism.

There is a second important reason why we ought not to base our opposition to racism and sexism on any kind of factual equality, even the limited kind that asserts that variations in capacities and abilities are spread evenly among the different races and between the sexes: we can have no absolute guarantee that these capacities and abilities really are distributed evenly, without regard to race or sex, among human beings. So far as actual abilities are concerned there do seem to be certain measurable differences both among races and between sexes. These differences do not, of course, appear in every case, but only when averages are taken. More important still, we do not yet know how many of these differences are really due to the different genetic endowments of the different races and sexes, and how many are due to poor schools, poor housing, and other factors that are the result of past and continuing discrimination. Perhaps all of the important differences will eventually prove to be environmental rather than genetic. Anyone opposed to racism and sexism will certainly hope that this will be so, for it will make the task of ending discrimination a lot easier; nevertheless, it would be dangerous to rest the case against racism and sexism on the belief that all significant differences are environmental in origin. The opponent of, say, racism who takes this line will be unable to avoid conceding that if differences in ability did after all prove to have some genetic connection with race, racism would in some way be defensible.

Fortunately there is no need to pin the case for equality to one particular outcome of a scientific investigation. The appropriate response to those who claim to have found evidence of genetically based differences in ability among the races or between the sexes is not to stick to the belief that the genetic explanation must be wrong, whatever evidence to the contrary may turn up; instead we should make it quite clear that the claim to equality does not depend on intelligence, moral capacity, physical strength, or similar matters of fact. Equality is a moral idea, not an assertion of fact. There is no logically compelling reason for assuming that a factual difference in ability between two people justifies any difference in the amount of consideration we give to their needs and interests. *The principle of the equality of human beings is not a description of an alleged actual equality among humans: it is a prescription of how we should treat human beings.*

Jeremy Bentham, the founder of the reforming utilitarian school of moral philosophy, incorporated the essential basis of moral equality into his system of ethics by means of the formula: "Each to count for one and none for more than one." In other words, the interests of every being affected by an action are to be taken into account and given the same weight as the like interests of any other being. A later utilitarian, Henry Sidgwick, put the point in this way: "The good of any one individual is of no more importance, from the point of view (if I may say so) of the Universe, than the good of any other." More recently the leading figures in contemporary moral philosophy have shown a great deal of agreement in specifying as a fundamental presupposition of their moral theories some similar requirement that works to give everyone's interests equal consideration — although these writers generally cannot agree on how this requirement is best formulated.[1]

It is an implication of this principle of equality that our concern for others and our readiness to consider their interests ought not to depend on what they are like or on what abilities they may possess. Precisely what our concern or consideration requires us to do may vary according to the characteristics of those affected by what we do: concern for the well-being of children growing up in America would require that we teach them to read; concern for the well-being of pigs may require no more than that we leave them with other pigs in a place where there is adequate food and room to run freely. But the basic element — the taking into account of the interests of the being, whatever those interests may be — must, according to the principle of equality, be extended to all beings, black or white, masculine of feminine, human or nonhuman.

Thomas Jefferson, who was responsible for writing the principle of the equality of men into the American Declaration of Independence, saw this point. It led him to oppose slavery even though he was unable to free himself fully from his slaveholding background. He wrote in a letter to the author of a book that emphasized the notable intellectual achievements of Negroes in order to refute the then common view that they had limited intellectual capabilities:

> Be assured that no person living wishes more sincerely than I do, to see a complete refutation of the doubts I myself have entertained and expressed on the grade of understanding allotted to them by nature, and to find that they are on a par with ourselves ... but whatever be their degree of talent it is no measure of their rights. Because Sir Isaac Newton was superior to others in understanding, he was not therefore lord of the property or persons of others.[2]

Similarly, when in the 1850s the call for women's rights was raised in the United States, a remarkable black feminist named Sojourner Truth made the same point in more robust terms at a feminist convention:

> They talk about this thing in the head; what do they call it? ["Intellect," whispered someone nearby.] That's it. What's that got to do with women's rights or Negroes' rights? If my cup won't hold but a pint and yours holds a quart, wouldn't you be mean not to let me have my little half-measure full?[3]

It is on this basis that the case against racism and the case against sexism must both ultimately rest; and it is in accordance with this principle that the attitude that we may call "speciesism," by analogy with racism, must also be condemned. Speciesism — the word is not an attractive one, but I can think of no better term — is a prejudice or attitude of bias in favor of the interests of members of one's own species and against those of members of other species. It should be obvious that the fundamental objections to racism and sexism made by Thomas Jefferson and Sojourner Truth apply equally to speciesism. If possessing a higher degree of intelligence does not entitle one human to use another for his or her own ends, how can it entitle humans to exploit nonhumans for the same purpose?[4]

Many philosophers and other writers have proposed the principle of equal consideration of interests in some form or other, as a basic moral principle; but not many of them have recognized that this principle applies to members of other species as well as to our own. Jeremy Bentham was one of the few who did realize this. In a forward-looking passage written at a time when black slaves had been freed by the French but in the British dominions were still being treated in the way we now treat animals, Bentham wrote:

> The day *may* come when the rest of the animal creation may acquire those rights which never could have been withholden from them by the hand of tyranny. The French have already discovered that the blackness of the skin is no reason why a human being should be abandoned without redress to the caprice of a tormentor. It may one day come to be recognized that the number of the legs, the villosity of the skin, or the termination of the *os sacrum* are reasons equally insufficient for abandoning a sensitive being to the same fate. What else is it that should trace the insuperable line? Is it the faculty of reason, or perhaps the faculty of discourse? But a full-grown horse or dog is beyond comparison a more rational, as well as a more conversable animal, than an infant of a day or a week or even a month, old. But

suppose they were otherwise, what would it avail? The question is not, Can they *reason*? nor Can they *talk*? but, Can they *suffer*?[5]

In this passage Bentham points to the capacity for suffering as the vital characteristic that gives a being the right to equal consideration. The capacity for suffering — or more strictly, for suffering and/or enjoyment or happiness — is not just another characteristic like the capacity for language or higher mathematics. Bentham is not saying that those who try to mark "the insuperable line" that determines whether the interests of a being should be considered happen to have chosen the wrong characteristic. By saying that we must consider the interests of all beings with the capacity for suffering or enjoyment Bentham does not arbitrarily exclude from consideration any interests at all — as those who draw the line with reference to the possession of reason or language do. The capacity for suffering and enjoyment is *a prerequisite for having interests at all*, a condition that must be satisfied before we can speak of interests in a meaningful way. It would be nonsense to say that it was not in the interests of a stone to be kicked along the road by a schoolboy. A stone does not have interests because it cannot suffer. Nothing that we can do to it could possibly make any difference to its welfare. The capacity for suffering and enjoyment is, however, not only necessary, but also sufficient for us to say that a being has interests — at an absolute minimum, an interest in not suffering. A mouse, for example, does have an interest in not being kicked along the road, because it will suffer if it is.

Although Bentham speaks of "rights" in the passage I have quoted, the argument is really about equality rather than about rights. Indeed, in a different passage, Bentham famously described "natural rights" as "nonsense" and "natural and imprescriptible rights" as "nonsense upon stilts." He talked of moral rights as a shorthand way of referring to protections that people and animals morally ought to have; but the real weight of the moral argument does not rest on the assertion of the existence of the right, for this in turn has to be justified on the basis of the possibilities for suffering and happiness. In this way we can argue for equality for animals without getting embroiled in philosophical controversies about the ultimate nature of rights.

In misguided attempts to refute the arguments of this book, some philosophers have gone to much trouble developing arguments to show that animals do not have rights.[6] They have claimed that to have rights a being must be autonomous, or must be a member of a community, or must have the ability to respect the rights of others, or must possess a sense of justice. These claims are irrelevant to the case for Animal Liberation. The language of rights is a convenient political shorthand. It is even more valuable in the era of thirty-second TV news clips than it was in Bentham's day; but in the argument for a radical change in our attitude to animals, it is in no way necessary.

If a being suffers there can be no moral justification for refusing to take that suffering into consideration. No matter what the nature of the being, the principle of equality requires that its suffering be counted equally with the like suffering — insofar as rough comparisons can be made — of any other being. If a being is not capable of suffering, or of experiencing enjoyment or happiness, there is nothing to be taken into account. So the limit of sentience (using the term as a convenient if not strictly accurate shorthand for the capacity to suffer and/or experience enjoyment) is the only defensible boundary of concern for the interests of others. To mark this boundary by some other characteristic like intelligence or rationality would be to mark it in an arbitrary manner. Why not choose some other characteristic, like skin color?

Racists violate the principle of equality by giving greater weight to the interests of members of their own race when there is a clash between their interests and the interests of those of another race. Sexists violate the principle of equality by favoring the interests of their own sex. Similarly, speciesists allow the interests of their own species to override the greater interests of members of other species. The pattern is identical in each case....

So far I have said a lot about inflicting suffering on animals, but nothing about killing them. This omission has been deliberate. The application of the principle of equality to the infliction of suffering is, in theory at least, fairly straightforward. Pain and suffering are in themselves bad and should be prevented or minimized, irrespective of the race, sex, or species of the being that suffers. How bad a pain is depends on how intense it is and how long it lasts, but pains of the same intensity and duration are equally bad, whether felt by humans or animals.

The wrongness of killing a being is more complicated. I have kept, and shall continue to keep, the question of killing in the background because in the present state of human tyranny over other species the more simple, straightforward principle of equal consideration of pain or pleasure is a sufficient basis for identifying and protesting against all the major abuses of animals that human beings practice. Nevertheless, it is necessary to say something about killing.

Just as most human beings are speciesists in their readiness to cause pain to animals when they would not cause a similar pain to humans for the same reason, so most human beings are speciesists in their readiness to kill other animals when they would not kill human beings. We need to proceed more cautiously here, however, because people hold widely differing views about when it is legitimate to kill humans, as the continuing debates over abortion and euthanasia attest. Nor have moral philosophers been able to agree on exactly what it is that makes it wrong to kill human beings, and under what circumstances killing a human being may be justifiable.

Let us consider first the view that it is always wrong to take an innocent human life. We may call this the "sanctity of life" view. People who take this view oppose abortion and euthanasia. They do not usually, however, oppose the killing of nonhuman animals — so perhaps it would be more accurate to describe this view as the "sanctity of *human* life" view. The belief that human life, and only human life, is sacrosanct is a form of speciesism. To see this, consider the following example.

Assume that, as sometimes happens, an infant has been born with massive and irreparable brain damage. The damage is so severe that the infant can never be any more than a "human vegetable," unable to talk, recognize other people, act independently of others, or develop a sense of self-awareness. The parents of the infant, realizing that they cannot hope for any improvement in their child's condition and being in any case unwilling to spend, or ask the state to spend, the thousands of dollars that would be needed annually for proper care of the infant, ask the doctor to kill the infant painlessly.

Should the doctor do what the parents ask? Legally, the doctor should not, and in this respect the law reflects the sanctity of life view. The life of every human being is sacred. Yet people who would say this about the infant do not object to the killing of nonhuman animals. How can they justify their different judgments? Adult chimpanzees, dogs, pigs, and members of many other species far surpass the brain-damaged infant in their ability to relate to others, act independently, be self-aware, and any other capacity that could reasonably be said to give value to life. With the most intensive care possible, some severely retarded infants can never achieve the intelligence level of a dog. Nor can we appeal to the concern of the infant's parents, since they themselves, in this imaginary example (and in some actual cases) do not want the infant kept alive. The only thing that distinguishes the infant from the animal, in the eyes of those who claim it has a "right to life," is that it is, biologically, a member of the species Homo-sapiens, whereas chimpanzees, dogs, and pigs are not. But to use *this* difference as the basis for granting a right to life to the infant and not to the other animals is, of course, pure speciesism.[7] It is exactly the kind of arbitrary difference that the most crude and overt kind of racist uses in attempting to justify racial discrimination.

This does not mean that to avoid speciesism we must hold that it is as wrong to kill a dog as it is to kill a human being in full possession of his or her faculties. The only position that is irredeemably speciesist is the one that tries to make the boundary of the right to life run exactly parallel to the boundary of our own species. Those who hold the sanctity of life view do this, because while distinguishing sharply between human beings and other animals they allow no distinctions to be made within our own species, objecting to the killing of the severely retarded and the hopelessly senile as strongly as they object to the killing of normal adults.

To avoid speciesism we must allow that beings who are similar in all relevant respects have a similar right to life — and mere membership in our own biological species cannot be a morally relevant criterion for this right. Within these limits we could still hold, for instance, that it is worse to kill a normal adult human, with a capacity for self-awareness and the ability to plan for the future and have meaningful relations with others, than it is to kill a mouse, which presumably does not share all of these characteristics; or we might appeal to the close family and other personal ties that humans have but mice do not have to the same degree; or we might think that it is the consequences for other humans, who will be put in fear for their own lives, that makes the crucial difference; or we might think it is some combination of these factors, or other factors altogether.

Whatever criteria we choose, however, we will have to admit that they do not follow precisely the boundary of our own species. We may legitimately hold that there are some features of certain beings that make their lives more valuable than those of other beings; but there will surely be some nonhuman animals whose lives, by any standards, are more valuable than the lives of some humans. A chimpanzee, dog, or pig, for instance, will have a higher degree of self-awareness and a greater capacity for meaningful relations with others than a severely retarded infant or someone in a state of advanced senility. So if we base the right to life on these characteristics we must grant these animals a right to life as good as, or better than, such retarded or senile humans.

This argument cuts both ways. It could be taken as showing that chimpanzees, dogs, and pigs, along with some other species, have a right to life and we commit a grave moral offense whenever we kill them, even when they are old and suffering and our intention is to put them out of their misery. Alternatively one could take the argument as showing that the severely retarded and hopelessly senile have no right to life and may be killed for quite trivial reasons, as we now kill animals.

Since the main concern of this book is with ethical questions having to do with animals and not with the morality of euthanasia I shall not attempt to settle this issue finally.[8] I think it is reasonably clear, though, that while both of the positions just described avoid speciesism, neither is satisfactory. What we need is some middle position that would avoid speciesism but would not make the lives of the retarded and senile as cheap as the lives of pigs and dogs now are, or make the lives of pigs and dogs so sacrosanct that we think it wrong to put them out of hopeless misery. What we must do is bring nonhuman animals within our sphere of moral concern and cease to treat their lives as expendable for whatever trivial purposes we may have. At the same time, once we realize that the fact that a being is a member of our own species is not in itself enough to make it always wrong to kill that being, we may come to reconsider our policy of preserving human lives at all costs, even when there is no prospect of a meaningful life or of existence without terrible pain.

I conclude, then, that a rejection of speciesism does not imply that all lives are of equal worth. While self-awareness, the capacity to think ahead and have hopes and aspirations for the future, the capacity for meaningful relations with others and so on are not relevant to the question of inflicting pain — since pain is pain, whatever other capacities, beyond the capacity to feel pain, the being may have — these capacities are relevant to the question of taking life. It is not arbitrary to hold that the life of a self-aware being, capable of abstract thought, of planning for the future, of complex acts of communication, and so on, is more valuable than the life of a being without these capacities. To see the difference between the issues of inflicting pain and taking life, consider how we would choose within our own species. If we had to choose to save the life of a normal human being or an intellectually disabled human being, we would probably choose to save the life of a normal human being; but if we had to choose between preventing pain in the normal human being or the intellectually disabled one — imagine that both have received painful but superficial injuries, and we only have enough painkiller for one of them — it is not nearly so clear how we ought to choose. The same is true when we consider other species. The evil of pain is, in itself, unaffected by the other characteristics of the being who feels the pain; the value of life is affected by these other characteristics. To give just one reason for this difference, to take the life of a being who has been hoping, planning, and working for some future goal is to deprive that being of the fulfillment of all those efforts; to take the life of a being with a mental capacity below the level needed to grasp that one is a being with a future — much less make plans for the future — cannot involve this particular kind of loss.[9]

Normally this will mean that if we have to choose between the life of a human being and the life of another animal we should choose to save the life of the human; but there may be special cases in which the reverse holds true, because the human being in question does not have the capacities of a normal human being. So this view is not speciesist, although it may appear to be at first glance. The preference, in normal cases, for saving a human life over the life of an animal when a choice *has* to be made is a preference based on the characteristics that normal humans have, and not on the mere fact that they are members of our own species. This is why when we consider members of our own species who lack the characteristics of normal humans we can no longer say that their lives are always to be preferred to those of other animals. In general, though, the question of when it is wrong to kill (painlessly) an animal is one to which we need give no precise answer. As long as we remember that we should give the same respect to the lives of animals as we give to the lives of those humans at a similar mental level, we shall not go far wrong.[10]

In any case, the conclusions that are argued for in this book flow from the principle of minimizing suffering alone. The idea that it is also wrong to kill animals painlessly gives some of these conclusions additional support that is welcome but strictly unnecessary. Interestingly enough, this is true even of the conclusion that we ought to become vegetarians, a conclusion that in the popular mind is generally based on some kind of absolute prohibition on killing....

Becoming a Vegetarian ... *or how to produce less suffering and more food at a reduced cost to the environment*

As a matter of strict logic, perhaps, there is no contradiction in taking an interest in animals on both compassionate and gastronomic grounds. If one is opposed to inflicting suffering on animals, but not to the painless killing of animals, one could consistently eat animals who had lived free of all suffering and been instantly, painlessly slaughtered. Yet practically and psychologically it is impossible to be consistent in one's concern for nonhuman animals while continuing to dine on them. If we are prepared to take the life of another being merely in order to satisfy our taste for a particular type of food, then that being is no more than a means to our end. In time we will come to regard pigs, cattle, and chickens as things for us to use, no matter how strong our compassion may be; and when we find that to continue to obtain supplies of the bodies of these animals at a price we are able to pay it is necessary to change their living conditions a little, we will be unlikely to regard these changes too critically. The factory farm is nothing more than the application of technology to the idea that animals are means to our ends. Our eating habits are dear to us and not easily altered. We have a strong interest in convincing ourselves that our concern for other animals does not require us to stop eating them. No one in the habit of eating an animal can be completely without bias in judging whether the conditions in which that animal is reared cause suffering.

It is not practically possible to rear animals for food on a large scale without inflicting considerable suffering. Even if intensive methods are not used, traditional farming involves castration, separation of mother and young, breaking up social groups, branding, transportation to the slaughterhouse, and finally slaughter itself. It is difficult to imagine how animals could be reared for food without these forms of suffering. Possibly it could be done on a small scale, but we could never feed today's huge urban populations with meat raised in this manner. If it could be done at all, the animal flesh thus produced would be vastly more expensive than animal flesh is today — and rearing animals is already an expensive and inefficient way of producing protein. The flesh of animals reared and killed with equal consideration for the welfare of animals while they were alive would be a delicacy available only to the rich.

All this is, in any case, quite irrelevant to the immediate question of the ethics of our daily diet. Whatever the theoretical possibilities of rearing animals without suffering may be, the fact is that the meat available from butchers and supermarkets comes from animals who were not treated with any real consideration at all while being reared. So we must ask ourselves, not: Is it *ever* right to eat meat? But: Is it right to eat *this* meat? Here I think that those who are opposed to the needless killing of animals and those who oppose only the infliction of suffering must join together and give the same, negative answer.

Becoming a vegetarian is not merely a symbolic gesture. Nor is it an attempt to isolate oneself from the ugly realities of the world, to keep oneself pure and so without responsibility for the cruelty and carnage all around. Becoming a vegetarian is a highly practical and effective step one can take toward ending both the killing of nonhuman animals and the infliction of suffering upon them....

The people who profit by exploiting large numbers of animals do not need our approval. They need our money. The purchase of the corpses of the animals they rear is the main support the factory farmers ask from the public (the other, in many countries, is big government subsidies). They will use intensive methods as long as they can sell what they produce by these methods; they will have the resources needed to fight reform politically; and they will be able to defend themselves against criticism with the reply that they are only providing the public with what it wants.

Hence the need for each one of us to stop buying the products of modern animal farming — even if we are not convinced that it would be wrong to eat animals who have lived pleasantly and died painlessly. Vegetarianism is a form of boycott. For most vegetarians the boycott is a permanent one, since once they have broken away from flesh-eating habits they can no longer approve of slaughtering animals in order to satisfy the trivial desires of their palates. But the moral obligation to boycott the meat available in butcher shops and supermarkets today is just as inescapable for those who disapprove only of inflicting suffering, and not of killing. Until we boycott meat, and all other products of animal factories, we are, each one of us, contributing to the continued existence, prosperity, and growth of factory farming and all the other cruel practices used in rearing animals for food.

It is at this point that the consequences of speciesism intrude directly into our lives, and we are forced to attest personally to the sincerity of our concern for nonhuman animals. Here we have an opportunity to do something, instead of merely talking and wishing the politicians would do something. It is easy to take a stand about a remote issue, but speciesists, like racists, reveal their true nature when the issue comes nearer home. To protest about bullfighting in Spain, the eating of dogs in south Korea, or the slaughter of baby seals in Canada while continuing to eat eggs from hens who have spent their lives crammed into cages, or veal from calves who have been deprived of their mothers, their proper diet and the freedom to lie down with their legs extended, is like denouncing apartheid in South Africa while asking your neighbors not to sell their houses to blacks....

I have emphasized the boycott element of vegetarianism so much that the reader may ask whether, if the boycott does not spread and prove effective, anything has been achieved by becoming a vegetarian. But we must often venture when we cannot be certain of success, and it would be no argument against becoming a vegetarian if this were all that could be said against it, since none of the great movements against oppression and injustice would have existed if their leaders had made no efforts until they were assured of success. In the case of vegetarianism, however, I believe we do achieve something by our individual acts, even if the boycott as a whole should not succeed. George Bernard Shaw once said that he would be followed to his grave by numerous sheep, cattle, pigs, chickens, and a whole shoal of fish, all grateful at having been spared from slaughter because of his vegetarian diet. Although we cannot identify any individual animals whom we have benefited by becoming a vegetarian, we can assume that our diet, together with that of the many others who are already avoiding meat, will have some impact on the number of animals raised in factory farms and slaughtered for food. This assumption is reasonable because the number of animals raised and slaughtered depends on the profitability of this process, and this profit depends in part on the demand for the product. The smaller the demand, the lower the price and the lower the profit. The lower the profit, the fewer the animals that will be raised and slaughtered. This is elementary economics, and it can easily be observed in tables published by the poultry trade journals, for instance, that there is a direct correlation between the price of poultry and the number of chickens placed in broiler sheds to begin their joyless existence.

So vegetarianism is really on even stronger ground than most other boycotts or protests. The person who boycotts South African produce in order to bring down apartheid achieves nothing unless the boycott succeeds in forcing white South Africans to modify their policies (though the effort may have been well worth making, whatever the outcome); but vegetarians know that they do, by their actions, contribute to a reduction in the suffering and slaughter of animals, whether or not they live to see their efforts spark off a mass boycott of meat and an end to cruelty in farming.

NOTES

1. For Bentham's moral philosophy, see his *Introduction to the Principles of Morals and Legislation,* and for Sidgwick's see *The Methods of Ethics,* 1907 (the passage is quoted from the seventh edition; reprint, London: Macmillan, 1963), p. 382. As examples of leading contemporary moral philosophers who incorporate a requirement of equal consideration of interests, see R.M. Hare, *Freedom and Reason* (New York: Oxford University Press, 1963), and John Rawls, *A Theory of Justice* (Cambridge: Harvard University Press, Belknap Press, 1972). For a brief account of the essential agreement on this issue between these and other positions, see R.M. Hare, "Rules of War and Moral Reasoning," *Philosophy and Public Affairs* 1 (2) (1972).
2. Letter to Henry Gregoire, February 25, 1809.
3. Reminiscences by Francis D. Gage, from Susan B. Anthony, *The History of Woman Suffrage,* vol. 1; the passage is to be found in the extract in Leslie Tanner, ed., *Voices From Women's Liberation* (New York: Signet, 1970).
4. I owe the term "speciesism" to Richard Ryder. It has become accepted in general use since the first edition of this book, and now appears in *The Oxford English Dictionary,* second edition (Oxford: Clarendon Press, 1989).
5. *Introduction to the Principles of Morals and Legislation,* chapter 17.
6. See M. Levin, "Animal Rights Evaluated," *Humanist* 37: 14-15 (July/August 1977); M.A. Fox, "Animal Liberation: A Critique," *Ethics* 88: 134-138 (1978); C. Perry and G.E. Jones, "On Animal Rights," *International Journal of Applied Philosophy* 1: 39-57 (1982).
7. I am here putting aside religious views, for example the doctrine that all and only human beings have immortal souls, or are made in the image of God. Historically these have been very important, and no

doubt are partly responsible for the idea that human life has a special sanctity. Logically, however, these religious views are unsatisfactory, since they do not offer a reasoned explanation of why it should be that all humans and no nonhumans have immortal souls. This belief too, therefore, comes under suspicion as a form of speciesism. In any case, defenders of the "sanctity of life" view are generally reluctant to base their position on purely religious doctrines, since these doctrines are no longer as widely accepted as they once were.

8. For a general discussion of these questions, see my *Practical Ethics* (Cambridge: Cambridge University Press, 1979), and for a more detailed discussion of the treatment of handicapped infants, see Helga Kuhse and Peter Singer, *Should the Baby Live?* (Oxford: Oxford University Press, 1985).

9. For a development of this theme, see my essay, "Life's Uncertain Voyage," in P. Pettit, R. Sylvan and J. Norman, eds., *Metaphysics and Morality* (Oxford: Blackwell, 1987), pp. 154-172.

10. The preceding discussion, which has been changed only slightly since the first edition, has often been overlooked by critics of the Animal Liberation movement. It is a common tactic to seek to ridicule the Animal Liberation position by maintaining that, as an animal experimenter put it recently, "Some of these people believe that every insect, every mouse, has as much right to life as a human." (Dr. Irving Weissman, as quoted in Katherine Bishop, "From Shop to Lab to Farm, Animal Rights Battle is Felt," *The New York Times*, January 14, 1989.) It would be interesting to see Dr. Weissman name some prominent Animal Liberationists who hold this view. Certainly (assuming only that he was referring to the right to life of a human being with mental capacities very different from those of the insect and the mouse) the position described is not mine. I doubt that it is held by many — if any — in the Animal Liberation movement.

THE CASE FOR ANIMAL RIGHTS

Tom Regan

Tom Regan is Emeritus Professor of Philosophy at North Carolina State University in Raleigh. He is the author of numerous books, including The Case for Animal Rights *(1983),* The Struggle for Animal Rights *(1987),* Defending Animal Rights *(2001), and* Empty Cages: Facing the Challenge of Animal Rights *(2003).*

Regan defends the case for animal rights by questioning traditional moral theory that grants rights to human beings but stops at animals. On his account, inherent value is owed to "the experiencing subject of a life, a conscious creature having an individual welfare that has importance to us whatever our usefulness to others." But this description also applies to animals. Consistency demands that we accord rights to animals in the same way that we accord them to all human beings and that practices that use animals as resources be stopped. Regan calls for the total abolition of the use of animals in science, the total dissolution of commercial agriculture, and the total elimination of commercial and sport hunting and trapping.

I regard myself as an advocate of animal rights — as a part of the animal rights movement. That movement, as I conceive it, is committed to a number of goals, including:

- the total abolition of the use of animals in science;
- the total dissolution of commercial animal agriculture;
- the total elimination of commercial and sport hunting and trapping.

There are, I know, people who profess to believe in animal rights but do not avow these goals. Factory farming, they say, is wrong — it violates animals' rights — but traditional animal agriculture is all right. Toxicity tests of cosmetics on animals violates their rights, but important medical research — cancer research, for example — does not. The clubbing of baby seals is abhorrent, but not the harvesting of adult seals. I used to think I understood this reasoning. Not any more. You don't change unjust institutions by tidying them up.

What's wrong — fundamentally wrong — with the way animals are treated isn't the details that vary from case to case. It's the whole system. The forlornness of the veal calf is pathetic, heart wrenching; the pulsing pain of the chimp with electrodes planted deep in her brain is repulsive; the slow, torturous death of a raccoon caught in the leg-hold trap is agonizing. But what is wrong isn't the pain, isn't the suffering, isn't the deprivation. These compound what's wrong. Sometimes — often — they make it much worse. But they are not the fundamental wrong.

The fundamental wrong is the system that allows us to view animals as *our resources*, here for *us* — to be eaten, or surgically manipulated, or exploited for sport or money. Once we accept this view of animals — as our resources — the rest is as predictable as it is regrettable. Why worry about their loneliness, their pain, their death? Since animals exist for us, to benefit us in one way or another, what harms them really doesn't matter — or matters only if it starts to bother us, makes us feel a trifle uneasy when we eat our veal escalope, for example. So, yes, let us get veal calves out of solitary confinement, give them more space, a little straw, a few companions. But let us keep our veal escalope.

But a little straw, more space and a few companions won't eliminate — won't even touch — the basic wrong that attaches to our viewing and treating these animals as our resources. A veal calf killed to be eaten after living in close confinement is viewed and treated in this way: but so, too, is another who is raised (as they say) "more humanely". To right the wrong of our treatment of farm animals requires more than making rearing methods "more humane"; it requires the total dissolution of commercial animal agriculture.

How we do this, whether we do it or, as in the case of animals in science, whether and how we abolish their use — these are to a large extent political questions. People must change their beliefs before they change their habits. Enough people, especially those elected to public office, must believe in change — must want it — before we will have laws that protect the rights of animals. This process of change is very complicated, very demanding, very exhausting, calling for the efforts of many hands in education, publicity, political organization and activity, down to the licking of envelopes and stamps. As a trained and practising philosopher, the sort of contribution I can make is limited but, I like to think, important. The currency of philosophy is ideas — their meaning and rational foundation — not the nuts and bolts of the legislative process, say, or the mechanics of community organization. That's what I have been exploring over the past ten years or so in my essays and talks and, most recently, in my book *The Case for Animal Rights*. I believe the major conclusions I reach in the book are true because they are supported by the weight of the best arguments. I believe the idea of animal rights has reason, not just emotion, on its side.

In the space I have at my disposal here I can only sketch, in the barest outline, some of the main features of the book. It's main themes — and we should not be surprised by this — involve asking and answering deep, foundational moral questions about what morality is, how it should be understood and what is the best moral theory, all considered. I hope I can convey something of the shape I think this theory takes. The attempt to do so will be (to use a word a friendly critic once used to describe my work) cerebral, perhaps too cerebral. But this is misleading. My feelings about how animals are sometimes treated run just as deep and just as strong as those of my more volatile compatriots. Philosophers do — to use the jargon of the day — have a right side to their brains. If it's the left side we contribute (or mainly should), that's because what talents we have reside there.

How to proceed? We begin by asking how the moral status of animals has been understood by thinkers who deny that animals have rights. Then we test the mettle of their ideas by seeing how well they stand up under the heat of fair criticism. If we start our thinking in this way, we soon find that some people believe that we have no direct duties to animals, that we owe nothing to them, that we can do nothing that wrongs them. Rather, we can do wrong acts that involve animals, and so we have duties regarding them, though none to them. Such views may be called indirect duty views. By way of illustration: suppose your neighbor kicks your dog. Then your neighbor has done something wrong. But not to your dog. The wrong that has been done is a wrong to you. After all, it is wrong to upset people, and your neighbor's kicking your dog upsets you. So you are the one who is wronged, not your dog. Or again: by kicking your dog your neighbor damages your property. And since it is wrong to damage another person's property, your neighbor has done something wrong — to you, of course — not to your dog. Your neighbor no more wrongs your dog than your car would be wronged if the windshield were smashed. Your neighbor's duties involving your dog are indirect duties to you. More generally, all of our duties regarding animals are indirect duties to one another — to humanity.

How could someone try to justify such a view? Someone might say that your dog doesn't feel anything and so isn't hurt by your neighbor's kick, doesn't care about the pain because none is felt, is as unaware of anything as is your windshield. Someone might say this, but no rational person will, since, among other considerations, such a view will commit anyone who holds it to the position that no human being feels pain either — that human beings also don't care about what happens to them. A second possibility is that though both humans and your dog are hurt when kicked, it is only human pain that matters. But, again, no rational person can believe this. Pain is pain wherever it occurs. If your neighbor's causing you pain is wrong because of the pain that is caused, we cannot rationally ignore or dismiss the moral relevance of the pain that your dog feels.

Philosophers who hold indirect duty views — and many still do — have come to understand that they must avoid the two defects just noted: that is, both the view that animals don't feel anything as well as the idea that only human pain can be morally relevant. Among such thinkers the sort of view now favoured is one or other form of what is called *contractarianism*.

Here, very crudely, is the root idea: morality consists of a set of rules that individuals voluntarily agree to abide by, as we do when we sign a contract (hence the name contractarianism). Those who understand and accept the terms of the contract are covered directly; they have rights created and recognized by, and protected in, the contract. And these contractors can also have protection spelled out for others who, though they lack the ability to understand morality and so cannot sign the contract themselves, are loved or cherished by those who can. Thus young children, for example, are unable to sign contracts and lack rights. But they are protected by the contract nonetheless because of the sentimental interests of others, most notably their parents. So we have, then, duties involving these children, duties regarding them, but no duties to them. Our duties in this case are indirect duties to other human beings, usually their parents.

As for animals, since they cannot understand contracts, they obviously cannot sign; and since they cannot sign, they have no rights. Like children, however, some animals are the objects of the sentimental interest of others. You, for example, love your dog or cat. So those animals that enough people care about (companion animals, whales, baby seals, the American bald eagle), though they lack rights themselves, will be protected because of the sentimental interests of people. I have, then, according to contractarianism, no duty directly to your dog or any other animal, not even the duty not to cause them pain or suffering; my duty not to hurt them is a duty I have to those people who care about what happens to them. As for other animals, where no or little sentimental interest is present — in the case of farm animals, for example, or laboratory rats — what duties we have grow weaker and weaker, perhaps to the vanishing point. The pain and death they endure, though real, are not wrong if no one cares about them.

When it comes to the moral status of animals, contractarianism could be a hard view to refute if it were an adequate theoretical approach to the moral status of human beings. It is not adequate in this latter respect, however, which makes the question of its adequacy in the former case, regarding animals, utterly moot. For consider: morality, according to the (crude) contractarian position before us, consists of rules that people agree to abide by. What people? Well, enough to make a difference — enough, that is, *collectively* to have the power to enforce the rules that are drawn up in the contract. That is very well and good for the signatories but not so good for anyone who is not asked to sign. And there is nothing in contractarianism of the sort we are discussing that guarantees or requires that everyone will have a chance to participate equally in framing the rules of morality. The result is that this approach to ethics could sanction the most blatant forms of social, economic, moral and political injustice, ranging from a repressive caste system to systematic racial or sexual discrimination. Might, according to this theory, does make right. Let those who are the victims of injustice suffer as they will. It matters not so long as no one else — no contractor, or too few of them — cares about it. Such a theory takes one's moral breath away ... as if, for example, there would be nothing wrong with apartheid in South Africa if few white South Africans were upset by it. A theory with so little to recommend it at the level of the ethics of our treatment of our fellow humans cannot have anything more to recommend it when it comes to the ethics of how we treat our fellow animals.

The version of contractarianism just examined is, as I have noted, a crude variety, and in fairness to those of a contractarian persuasion it must be noted that much more refined, subtle and ingenious varieties are possible. For example, John Rawls, in his *A Theory of Justice*, sets forth a version of contractarianism that forces contractors to ignore the accidental features of being a human being — for example, whether one is white or black, male or female, a genius or of modest intellect. Only by ignoring such features, Rawls believes, can we ensure that the principles of justice that contractors would agree upon are not based on bias or prejudice. Despite the improvement of such a view over the cruder forms of contractarianism, it remains deficient; it systematically denies that we have direct duties to those human beings who do not have a sense of justice — young children, for instance, and many mentally retarded humans. And yet it seems reasonably certain that, were we to torture a young child or retarded elder, we would be doing something that wronged him or her, not something that would be wrong if (and only if) other humans with a sense of justice were upset. And since this is true in the case of these humans, we cannot rationally deny the same in the case of animals.

Indirect duty views, then, including the best among them, fail to command our rational assent. Whatever ethical theory we should accept rationally, therefore, it must at least recognize that we have some duties directly to animals, just as we have some duties directly to each other. The next two theories I'll sketch attempt to meet this requirement.

The first I call the cruelty-kindness view. Simply stated, this says that we have a direct duty to be kind to animals and a direct duty not to be cruel to them. Despite the familiar, reassuring ring of these ideas, I do not believe that this view offers an adequate theory. To make this clearer, consider kindness. A kind person acts from a certain kind of motive — compassion or concern, for example. And that is a virtue. But there is no guarantee that a kind act is a right act. If I am a generous racist, for example, I will be inclined to act kindly towards members of my own race, favouring their interests above those of others. My kindness would be real and, so far as it goes, good. But I trust it is too obvious to require argument that my kind acts may not be above moral reproach — may, in fact, be positively wrong because rooted in injustice. So kindness, notwithstanding its status as a virtue to be encouraged, simply will not carry the weight of a theory of right action.

Cruelty fares no better. People or their acts are cruel if they display either a lack of sympathy or, worse, the presence of enjoyment in another's suffering. Cruelty in all its guises is a bad thing, a tragic human failing. But just as a person's being motivated by kindness does not guarantee that he or she does what is right, so the absence of cruelty does not ensure that he or she avoids doing what is wrong. Many people who perform abortions, for example, are not cruel, sadistic people. But that fact alone does not settle the terribly difficult question of the morality of abortion. The case is no different when we examine the ethics of our treatment of animals. So, yes, let us be for kindness and against cruelty. But let us not suppose that being for the one and against the other answers questions about moral right and wrong.

Some people think that the theory we are looking for is utilitarianism. A utilitarian accepts two moral principles. The first is that of equality: everyone's interests count, and similar interests must be counted as having similar weight or importance. White or black, American or Iranian, human or animal — everyone's pain or frustration matter, and matter just as much as the equivalent pain or frustration of anyone else. The second principle a utilitarian accepts is that of utility: do the act that will bring about the best balance between satisfaction and frustration for everyone affected by the outcome.

As a utilitarian, then, here is how I am to approach the task of deciding what I morally ought to do: I must ask who will be affected if I choose to do one thing rather than another, how much each individual will be affected, and where the best results are most likely to lie — which option, in other words, is most likely to bring about the best results, the best balance between satisfaction and frustration. That option, whatever it may be, is the one I ought to choose. That is where my moral duty lies.

The great appeal of utilitarianism rests with its uncompromising *egalitarianism*: everyone's interests count and count as much as the like interests of everyone else. The kind of odious discrimination that some forms of contractarianism can justify — discrimination based on race or sex, for example — seems disallowed in principle by utilitarianism, as is speciesism, systematic discrimination based on species membership.

The equality we find in utilitarianism, however, is not the sort an advocate of animal or human rights should have in mind. Utilitarianism has no room for the equal moral rights of different individuals because it has no room for their equal inherent value or worth. What has value for the utilitarian is the satisfaction of an individual's interests, not the individual whose interests they are. A universe in which you satisfy your desire for water, food and warmth is, other things being equal, better than a universe in which these desires are frustrated. And the same is true in the case of an animal with similar desires. But neither you nor the animal have any value in your own right. Only your feelings do.

Here is an analogy to make the philosophical point clearer: a cup contains different liquids, sometimes sweet, sometimes bitter, sometimes a mix of the two. What has value are the liquids: the sweeter the better, the bitterer the worse. The cup, the container, has no value. It is what goes into it, not what they go into, that has value. For the utilitarian you and I are like the cup; we have no value as individuals and thus no equal value. What has value is what goes into us, what we serve as receptacles for; our feelings of satisfaction have positive value, our feelings of frustration negative value.

Serious problems arise for utilitarianism when we remind ourselves that it enjoins us to bring about the best consequences. What does this mean? It doesn't mean the best consequences for me alone, or for my family or friends, or any other person taken individually. No, what we must do is, roughly, as follows: we must add up (somehow!) the separate satisfactions and frustrations of everyone likely to be affected by our choice, the satisfactions in one column, the frustrations in the other. We must total each column for each of the options before us. That is what it means to say the theory is aggregative. And then we must choose that option which is most likely to bring about the best balance of totaled satisfactions over totaled frustrations. Whatever act would lead to this outcome is the one we ought morally to perform — it is where our moral duty lies. And that act quite clearly might not be the same one that would bring about the best results for me personally, or for my family or friends, or for a lab animal. The best aggregated consequences for everyone concerned are not necessarily the best for each individual.

That utilitarianism is an aggregative theory — different individuals' satisfactions or frustrations are added, or summed, or totaled — is the key objection to this theory. My Aunt Bea is old, inactive, a cranky, sour person, though not physically ill. She prefers to go on living. She is also rather rich. I could make a fortune if I could get my hands on her money, money she intends to give me in any event, after she dies, but which she refuses to give me now. In order to avoid a huge tax bite, I plan to donate a handsome sum of my profits to the local children's hospital. Many, many children will benefit from my generosity, and much joy will be brought to their parents, relatives and friends. If I don't get the money rather soon, all these ambitions will come to naught. The once-in-a-lifetime opportunity to make a real killing will be gone. Why, then, not kill my Aunt Bea? Of course, I *might* get caught. But I'm no fool and, besides, her doctor can be counted on to cooperate (he has an eye for the same investment and I happen to know a good deal about his shady past). The deed can be done ... professionally, shall we say. There is *very* little chance of getting caught. And as for my conscience being guilt-ridden, I am a resourceful sort of fellow and will take more than sufficient comfort — as I lie on the beach at Acapulco — in contemplating the joy and health I have brought to so many others.

Suppose Aunt Bea is killed and the rest of the story comes out as told. Would I have done anything wrong? Anything immoral? One would have thought that I had. Not according to utilitarianism. Since what I have done has brought about the best balance between totaled satisfaction and frustration for all those affected by the outcome, my action is not wrong. Indeed, in killing Aunt Bea the physician and I did what duty required.

This same kind of argument can be repeated in all sorts of cases, illustrating, time after time, how the utilitarian's position leads to results that impartial people find morally callous. It *is* wrong to kill my Aunt Bea in the name of bringing about the best results for others. A good end does not justify an evil means. Any adequate moral theory will have to explain why this is so. Utilitarianism fails in this respect and so cannot be the theory we seek.

What to do? Where to begin anew? The place to begin, I think, is with the utilitarian's view of the value of the individual — or, rather, lack of value. In its place, suppose we consider that you and I, for example, do have value as individuals — what we'll call *inherent value*. To say we have such value is to say that we are something more than, something different from, mere receptacles. Moreover, to ensure that we do not pave the way for such injustices as slavery or sexual discrimination, we must believe that all who have inherent value have it equally, regardless of their sex, race, religion, birthplace and so on. Similarly to be discarded as irrelevant are one's talents or skills, intelligence and wealth, personality or pathology, whether one is loved and admired or despised and loathed. The genius and the retarded child, the prince and the pauper, the brain surgeon and the fruit vendor, Mother Teresa and the most unscrupulous used-car salesman — all have inherent value, all possess it equally, and all have an equal right to be treated with respect, to be treated in ways that do not reduce them to the status of things, as if they existed as resources for others. My value as an individual is independent of my usefulness to you. Yours is not dependent on your usefulness to me. For either of us to treat the other in ways that fail to show respect for the other's independent value is to act immorally, to violate the individual's rights.

Some of the rational virtues of this view — what I call the rights view — should be evident. Unlike (crude) contractarianism, for example, the rights view *in principle* denies the moral tolerability of any and all forms of racial, sexual or social discrimination; and unlike utilitarianism, this view *in principle* denies that we can justify good results by using evil means that violate an individual's rights — denies, for example, that it could be moral to kill my Aunt Bea to harvest beneficial consequences for others. That would be to sanction the disrespectful treatment of the individual in the name of the social good, something the rights view will not — categorically will not — ever allow.

The rights view, I believe, is rationally the most satisfactory moral theory. It surpasses all other theories in the degree to which it illuminates and explains the foundations of our duties to one another — the domain of human morality. On this score it has the best reasons, the best arguments, on its side. Of course, if it were possible to show that only human beings are included within its scope, then a person like myself, who believes in animal rights, would be obliged to look elsewhere.

But attempts to limit its scope to humans only can be shown to be rationally defective. Animals, it is true, lack many of the abilities humans possess. They can't read, do higher mathematics, build a bookcase or make *baba ghanoush*. Neither can many human beings, however, and yet we don't (and shouldn't) say that they (these humans) therefore have less inherent value, less of a right to be treated with respect, than do others. It is the *similarities* between those human beings who most clearly, most non-controversially have such value (the people reading this, for example), not our differences, that matter most. And the really crucial, the basic similarity is simply this: we are each of us the experiencing subject of a life, a conscious creature having an individual welfare that has importance to us whatever our usefulness to others. We want and prefer things, believe and feel things, recall and expect things. And all these dimensions of our life, including our pleasure and pain, our enjoyment and suffering, our satisfaction and frustration, our continued existence or our untimely death — all make a difference to the quality of our life as lived, as experienced, by us as individuals. As the same is true of those animals that concern us (the ones that are eaten and trapped, for example), they too must be viewed as the experiencing subjects of a life, with inherent value of their own.

Some there are who resist the idea that animals have inherent value. "Only humans have such value", they profess. How might this narrow view be defended? Shall we say that only humans have the requisite intelligence, or autonomy, or reason? But there are many, many humans who fail to meet these standards and yet are reasonably viewed as having value above and beyond their usefulness to others. Shall we claim that only humans belong to the right species, the species *Homo sapiens?* But this is blatant speciesism. Will it be said, then, that all — and only — humans have immortal souls? Then our opponents have their work cut out for them. I am myself not ill-disposed to the proposition that there are immortal souls. Personally, I profoundly hope I have one. But I would not want to rest my position on a controversial ethical issue on the even more controversial question about who or what has an immortal soul. That is to dig one's hole deeper, not to climb out. Rationally, it is better to resolve moral issues without making more controversial assumptions than are needed. The question of who has inherent value is such a question, one that is resolved more rationally without the introduction of the idea of immortal souls than by its use.

Well, perhaps some will say that animals have some inherent value, only less than we have. Once again, however, attempts to defend this view can be shown to lack rational justification. What could be the basis of our having more inherent value than animals? Their lack of reason, or autonomy, or intellect? Only if we are willing to make the same judgement in the case of humans who are similarly deficient. But it is not true that such humans — the retarded child, for example, or the mentally deranged — have less inherent value than you or I. Neither, then, can we rationally sustain the view that animals like them in being the experiencing subjects of a life have less inherent value. *All* who have inherent value have it *equally*, whether they be human animals or not.

Inherent value, then, belongs equally to those who are the experiencing subjects of a life. Whether it belongs to others — to rocks and rivers, trees and glaciers, for example — we do not know and may never know. But neither do we need to know, if we are to make the case for animal rights. We do not need to know, for example, how many people are eligible to vote in the next presidential election before we can know whether I am. Similarly, we do not need to know how many individuals have inherent value before we can know that some do. When it comes to the case for animal rights, then, what we need to know is whether the animals that, in our culture, are routinely eaten, hunted and used in our laboratories, for example, are like us in being subjects of a life. And we do know this. We do know that many — literally, billions and billions — of these animals are the subjects of a life in the sense explained and so have inherent value if we do. And since, in order to arrive at the best theory of our duties to one another, we must recognize our equal inherent value as individuals, reason — not sentiment, not emotion — reason compels us to recognize the equal inherent value of these animals and, with this, their equal right to be treated with respect.

That, *very* roughly, is the shape and feel of the case for animal rights. Most of the details of the supporting argument are missing. They are to be found in the book to which I alluded earlier. Here, the details go begging, and I must, in closing, limit myself to four final points.

The first is how the theory that underlies the case for animal rights shows that the animal rights movement is a part of, not antagonistic to, the human rights movement. The theory that rationally grounds the rights of animals also grounds the rights of humans. Thus those involved in the animal rights movement are partners in the struggle to secure respect for human rights — the rights of women, for example, or minorities, or workers. The animal rights movement is cut from the same moral cloth as these.

Second, having set out the broad outlines of the rights view, I can now say why its implications for farming and science, among other fields, are both clear and uncompromising. In the case of the use of animals in science, the rights view is categorically abolitionist. Lab animals are not our tasters; we are not their kings. Because these animals are treated routinely, systematically as if their value were reducible to their usefulness to others, they are routinely, systematically treated with a lack of respect, and thus are their rights routinely, systematically violated. This is just as true when they are used in trivial, duplicative, unnecessary or unwise research as it is when they are used in studies that hold out real promise of human benefits. We can't justify harming or killing a human being (my Aunt Bea, for example) just for these sorts of reason. Neither can we do so even in the case of so lowly a creature as a laboratory rat. It is not just refinement or reduction that is called for, not just larger, cleaner cages, not just more generous use of anaesthetic or the elimination of multiple surgery, not just tidying up the system. It is complete replacement. The best we can do when it comes to using animals in science is — not to use them. That is where our duty lies, according to the rights view.

As for commercial animal agriculture, the rights view takes a similar abolitionist position.

The fundamental moral wrong here is not that animals are kept in stressful close confinement or in isolation, or that their pain and suffering, their needs and preferences are ignored or discounted. All these *are* wrong, of course, but they are not the fundamental wrong. They are symptoms and effects of the deeper, systematic wrong that allows these animals to be viewed as lacking independent value, as resources for us — as, indeed, a renewable resource. Giving farm animals more space, more natural environments, more companions does not right the fundamental wrong, any more than giving lab animals more anaesthesia or bigger, cleaner cages would right the fundamental wrong in their case. Nothing less than the total dissolution of commercial animal agriculture will do this, just as, for similar reasons I won't develop at length here, morality requires nothing less than the total elimination of hunting and trapping for commercial and sporting ends. The rights view's implications, then, as I have said, are clear and uncompromising.

My last two points are about philosophy, my profession. It is, most obviously, no substitute for political action. The words I have written here and in other places by themselves don't change a thing. It is what we do with the thoughts that the words express — our acts, our deeds — that changes things. All that philosophy can do, and all I have attempted, is to offer a vision of what our deeds should aim at. And the why. But not the how.

Finally, I am reminded of my thoughtful critic, the one I mentioned earlier, who chastised me for being too cerebral. Well, cerebral I have been: indirect duty views, utilitarianism, contractarianism — hardly the stuff deep passions are made of. I am also reminded, however, of the image another friend set before me — the image of the ballerina as expressive of disciplined passion. Long hours of sweat and toil, of loneliness and practice, of doubt and fatigue: those are the discipline of her craft. But the passion is there too, the fierce drive to excel, to speak through her body, to do it right, to pierce our minds. That is the image of philosophy I would leave with you, not "too cerebral" but *disciplined passion*. Of the discipline enough has been seen. As for the passion:

there are times, and these not infrequent, when tears come to my eyes when I see, or read, or hear of the wretched plight of animals in the hands of humans. Their pain, their suffering, their loneliness, their innocence, their death. Anger. Rage. Pity. Sorrow. Disgust. The whole creation groans under the weight of the evil we humans visit upon these mute, powerless creatures. It *is* our hearts, not just our heads, that call for an end to it all, that demand of us that we overcome, for them, the habits and forces behind their systematic oppression. All great movements, it is written, go through three stages: ridicule, discussion, and adoption. It is the realization of this third stage, adoption, that requires both our passion and our discipline, our hearts and our heads. The fate of animals is in our hands. God grant that we are equal to the task.

VEGETARIANISM AND VIRTUE:
DOES CONSEQUENTIALISM DEMAND TOO LITTLE?

Nathan Nobis

Nathan Nobis is Visiting Research Professor and Postdoctoral Fellow with the Science and the Public project at the Center for Inquiry in the Philosophy Department at State University of New York, Buffalo. He is the author of a number of articles on animal rights and moral theory more generally. He has also helped produce an investigative documentary film about the American egg industry, which is available at <http://www.CompassionateConsumers.org>.

Nobis argues that Singer's consequentialist approach is inadequate for defending the moral obligation to become a vegetarian or vegan. The consequentialist case rests on the idea that being a vegetarian or vegan maximizes utility — the fewer animals who are raised and killed for food, the less suffering and death there is. Nobis argues that this argument does not work on an individual level — in a context of a huge industry and market unaffected by my actions, becoming a vegetarian might make no difference to the overall utility of reducing animal suffering. He merges the insights of virtue ethics with consequentialism to argue that individuals can bring about more goodness if they have the virtues of compassion, care, and sensitivity to unnecessary cruelty and suffering. If one ought to be compassionate, sensitive to cruelty, resist injustice, and be morally integrated, then, Nobis argues, one ought to be a vegetarian or vegan, even if saving animals from suffering is not an immediate consequence of doing so.

"It's a matter of taking the side of the weak against the strong, something the best people have always done."
— Harriet Beecher Stowe

I will argue that each of us personally ought to be a vegetarian.[1]

Actually, the conclusion I will attempt to defend concerns more than one's eating habits in that I will argue that we should be "vegans." Not only should we not buy and eat meat, but we should also not purchase fur coats, stoles, and hats, or leather shoes, belts, jackets, purses and wallets, furniture, car interiors, and other traditionally animal-based products for which there are readily available plant-based or synthetic alternatives. (Usually these are cheaper and work just as well, or better, anyway.) I will argue that buying and eating most eggs and dairy products are immoral as well. (Since it's much easier to avoid fur, leather, and wool than eggs and dairy products, I mention those first.)

Many arguments defending the moral obligation to become vegetarian and, to a lesser extent, adopt a vegan lifestyle, have been given, especially in recent decades.[2] While these arguments have convinced many to become vegetarians or vegans, most are still not convinced.[3] My discussion is directed towards those who have not been convinced, especially for these reasons: first, it is often unclear what the argument is for the exact conclusion that "You, the reader, are morally obligated to be a vegetarian (or a vegan)."[4] Second, it is often unclear what moral premise is given to justify this conclusion. And, third, it is often especially unclear how this premise might be justified from a broadly consequentialist moral perspective.[5]

This final lack of clarity is somewhat surprising, since much of the contemporary vegetarian movement takes its inspiration from the work of Peter Singer, a self-professed utilitarian consequentialist.[6] He writes, "I am a utilitarian. I am also a vegetarian. I am a vegetarian because I am a utilitarian. I believe that applying the principle of utility to our present situation — especially the methods now used to rear animals for food and the variety of foods available to us — leads to the conclusion that we ought to be vegetarians."[7]

While a number of non-consequentialist ethical theories can easily justify a vegetarian or vegan conclusion, I will present some doubts that consequentialism can so easily do so.[8] I will then attempt to cast doubts on these doubts.

So my target reader is a consequentialist who denies that she ought to become a vegetarian or vegan. As a consequentialist, she believes this, presumably, because she thinks that her making these changes in her eating habits and lifestyle would result in her bringing about *less* goodness into the world than were she to maintain her current omnivorous eating and consumer habits. In effect, she thinks that, in terms of doing what she can to increase the world's overall amount of goodness, there are ways for her to spend her time and resources that are, at least, morally equivalent to — if not better than — becoming a vegetarian, and so it is not obligatory. She must also think that her becoming a vegetarian will *prevent her* from achieving these other goals that she believes yield equal or, perhaps greater, goods.

Consequentialism is often criticized as being "too demanding," since it demands that we do the best we can. For most of us this requires doing a lot more than what we're doing now. Since consequentialism implies that most of us are routinely doing wrong, many conclude that it must be a mistaken moral theory.[9]

I will turn this objection on its head and criticize a standard consequentialist perspective on the grounds that it seems to demand too little. I will argue that if consequentialism does not imply or justify a moral principle *that we should not benefit from or (even symbolically) support very bad practices when we can easily avoid doing so*, then consequentialism is mistaken. A principle like this has implications not only for ethical vegetarianism or veganism, but for many areas of personal morality that are motivated from a response to practices that essentially involve unnecessary suffering and unfairness. If consequentialism implies that we should be morally indifferent in our response to the factors that motivate people not only in the vegetarian and animal rights movements, but in civil rights and "liberation" movements in general (for example, opposing slavery, human rights and labor movements, bringing women, racial minorities, homosexuals, and other groups fully into the moral community), then consequentialism is a far too conservative morality because it demands far too little of its adherents in terms of their personal lives.

I will attempt to meet this kind of objection and try to show that a kind of consequentialism can justify the vegetarian conclusions presented above. This kind of consequentialism is unique in that it takes the instrumental value of having and acting from certain virtues and character traits seriously. Some might respond, "So much the worse for consequentialism," but this might be unwise, since, as Henry Sidgwick argued, the theory provides, "a principle of synthesis, and a method for binding the unconnected and occasionally conflicting principles of common moral reasoning into a complete and harmonious system."[10] My discussion is directed towards someone who thinks that consequentialism does this organizing and synthesizing job best, but is skeptical that her seemingly well-confirmed theory implies that she should be a vegetarian or vegan and do her best to develop and act from the virtues that are commonly said to motivate vegetarianism: compassion, caring, sensitivity to cruelty and suffering (both animal and human), resistance to injustice, and integrity, among others.[11]

Contemporary Animal Agriculture and Human Nutrition

First, I will briefly summarize some facts about modern animal agriculture and human nutrition. While this information is readily available, relatively few people are aware of it.

Many people become vegetarians or vegans when they learn about modern animal agriculture and slaughter techniques, especially "factory farming."[12] In the U.S., each year around nine billion animals live in factory farms where most lead generally miserable lives. Newborns are separated from their mothers hours or days after birth; they are then kept in small cages or crates or confined for most of their lives in extremely cramped, overcrowded pens. Male chicks at egg farms are discarded by the tens of thousands each day into trash bins because their meat is deemed unsuitable for human consumption, or they are ground alive into feed for other animals. Male calves of dairy cows are fed liquid, iron-deficient diets and raised in crates that wholly restrict movement so that their muscles remain weak and tender.

Most animals are confined indoors: very few live "happy lives" in an outdoor barnyard. This confinement results in the animals' basic instinctual urges being frustrated. Many animals become psychotic and exhibit neurotic, repetitive behaviors: many become unnaturally cannibalistic. To ward off death and disease from the stressful and unsanitary conditions, a constant regimen of antibiotics and growth hormones is maintained. On both factory and non-intensive family farms animals are subject to surgical modifications such as beak, toe, and tail removal, ear tagging and clipping, teeth removal, branding, dehorning, castration, and ovary removal. In the interest of containing costs, all these procedures are performed without anesthesia.

Many animals die from starvation and exposure to cold in transport to the slaughterhouse.[13] Those that are unable to walk to slaughter are labeled "downers" and are left to die lying in the yard. Those that remain are slaughtered in extremely painful and inhumane ways, including the few who are raised on small, "organic," "free-range" farms.[14] Pigs, cattle and sheep are hung upside down by one leg, which often breaks, and their throats slit and their hearts punctured. Most of these animals are improperly stunned and are still conscious throughout slaughter or have been brought into unconsciousness by painful electric shock. Since my thesis addresses fashion also, I note that fur-bearing animals are either trapped in the wild and typically die slow, painful deaths, or are raised in small cages, fed each others' remains, and killed by anal electrocution so their pelts are not marred.

Understanding these facts is a common motivation for ethical vegetarianism and adopting a vegan lifestyle: people learn of, especially by *seeing*, the pain, suffering, and death involved in these practices and, at least, simply do not want to be involved with or benefit from it anymore.

One might think that this suffering and death is justified because we need to eat meat and other animal products, but, clearly, nobody needs to eat meat to survive. In fact, the common diet in the U.S. and Europe, a meat-based diet, is strongly correlated with such health problems as heart disease, stroke, diabetes, obesity, and various cancers. Vegetarians are far less prone to these chronic diseases and they tend to outlive meat-eaters by seven years.[15] The American Dietetic Association, by no means a vegetarian advocacy group, summarizes the results of the medical literature in its position paper on vegetarian diets — effectively, an overview of the recent scientific research:

> This position paper reviews the current scientific data related to key nutrients for vegetarians, including protein, iron, zinc, calcium, vitamin D, riboflavin, vitamin B-12, vitamin A, n-3 fatty acids, and iodine. A vegetarian, including vegan, diet can meet current recommendations for all of these nutrients.... Well-planned vegan and other types of vegetarian diets are appropriate for all stages of the life cycle, including during pregnancy, lactation, infancy, childhood, and adolescence. Vegetarian diets offer a number of nutritional benefits,

including lower levels of saturated fat, cholesterol, and animal protein as well as higher levels of carbohydrates, fiber, magnesium, potassium, folate, and antioxidants such as vitamins C and E and phytochemicals. Vegetarians have been reported to have lower body mass indices than nonvegetarians, as well as lower rates of death from ischemic heart disease; vegetarians also show lower blood cholesterol levels; lower blood pressure; and lower rates of hypertension, type 2 diabetes, and prostate and colon cancer.[16]

Thus, there is strong medical evidence that *not* eating meat is to one's health advantage: even conservative health organizations encourage people to cut back on their consumption of meat to reduce cholesterol and saturated fat intake; more progressive health organizations encourage cutting it out completely for better health.

The same things, in fact, can be said about *all* animal products: no one needs to eat eggs or milk or cheese. Health organizations that seriously advocate preventative medicine, such as the Physicians Committee for Responsible Medicine, advise eliminating them completely and adopting a vegan diet that contains a wide variety of foods solely from the four new food groups: vegetables, fruits, legumes (beans and nuts), and whole grains.[17] There is ample evidence that people not only survive on such a diet, but that they thrive.[18] The list of world-champion vegan athletes is impressive, so no one can honestly say that vegans can't achieve optimal health or nutrition.[19] And, of course, no one needs to wear fur, leather, or wool, or use products made from these materials.[20]

Thus, no product of factory farming, nonintensive farming or animal slaughter is necessary for human health or survival. Animals' short and often miserable lives and cruel and painful deaths are not outweighed or justified by any human need. As for the *aesthetic* pleasures of taste and fashion, vegetarian cuisine and cruelty-free clothing and accessories can easily gratify those interests. But even if the pleasures of consuming animal-based dishes uniformly outweighed the pleasures of all vegan alternatives (which they don't), it is exceedingly unlikely that the difference in aesthetic pleasure for us outweighs the great pains, suffering, and death for the animals. Thus, it is quite unlikely that the status quo regarding the use and treatment of animals is justified from a consequentialist perspective, since the consequences of the *status quo* is quite bad for animals (in terms of their well being and very lives) and for humans (in terms of the consequences for health).

Singer, Regan, and The "Impotence of the Individual" Objection

I now turn to some of the philosophical literature on vegetarianism. I will discuss some recent arguments for vegetarianism and, from a consequentialist critic's perspective, identify a common difficulty for these arguments that makes it difficult for them to establish the conclusion that each of us, personally, ought to be a vegetarian or vegan.

As sketched above, Singer holds that we should be vegetarians because our being vegetarian will maximize utility: if we were all vegetarians, there would be no demand for meat and so animals would no longer be inhumanely raised and killed for products that are unnecessary and often harmful for human health and well-being.

A critic might accept that it is likely that if *everyone* became a vegetarian (perhaps gradually, so the economy is not disturbed) utility would be maximized, but object that her *personally* becoming a vegetarian won't make any difference to the overall utility. Because the meat and animal products industry is so huge — over a million animals, mostly chickens, are killed *each hour* in the United States to be eaten — and markets are too insensitive, no consequence of *her* becoming a vegetarian, or even a vegan, would be that fewer animals would be raised and killed than if she were to continue in her omnivorous ways. While these industries do exist only because people buy their products, they don't exist because *she* buys their products, and they won't come tumbling down if she divests herself

from them. If she is supposed to become a vegetarian or vegan because doing so will immediately help the plight of animals, this seems to not
be the case.

Call this the "impotence of the individual"
objection. It obviously depends on an empirical
assumption concerning the inability of an individual's consumer behavior to affect a huge
industry. This claim seems plausible; it is even
accepted by a number of philosophers who
defend vegetarianism.[21] As far as I know, nobody
has summoned the empirical data to show that it
is false. I will presume it is true and so here's the
rub: if an individual's refraining from purchasing
animal-based products does not make a difference for the animals, then this critic might think
that Singer's argument is sound, but that it just
does not imply the relevant conclusion, namely
that *she* should become a vegetarian. The conclusion seems to be that *it ought to be the case that
we are all vegetarians*, which is importantly different from the conclusion that *she ought to be
vegetarian*, irrespective of whether others do the
same (for one difference, the critic can make it
the case that she is vegetarian, but her powers
over others are quite limited). A consequentialist
case for personal vegetarianism or veganism, if it
can be made, will thereby have to be made on the
actual positive consequences of an individual's
becoming a vegetarian, and it appears that less
animals being raised and killed is, unfortunately,
not one of the actual consequences.

This problem is not unique to consequentialism, since it plagues Regan's account of animal
rights as well. Suppose animals do have moral
rights that make it, at least, wrong to cause them
to have lives full of pain and suffering and, at
most, wrong to kill them painlessly for no reason
other than many find them tasty to eat and fash-
ionable to wear. A critic might object that since
he's not killing them, he's not violating their
rights. Again, since the market is so big and his
share of the purchases so small, his refraining
from purchasing these products will not result in
any less animals' rights being violated either. And
his eating the last burger at the picnic won't result
in any more animal's rights being violated. So,

even if animals have rights, in itself this does
seem to directly support personal vegetarianism,
unless animals have an additional right not to be
purchased, eaten, worn, and so on, even after they
are dead. But this is doubtful. Additional premises are needed here, as in Singer's case, to render
personal vegetarianism obligatory....

Clear Consequences of Vegetarianism

So where are we? One route is to abandon the
idea that, in becoming a vegetarian or vegan, one
is immediately helping suffering animals and that
this is a reason to do so. If we go this route, then
the case has to be made wholly on the basis of
concerns that don't have much to do with
animals: improved personal health, appearance
and well-being, a longer lifespan, and lower costs
associated with healthcare. Since a vegan
lifestyle is cheaper, as meat and animal-products
are a luxury, one could forgo them and use that
savings to bring about greater goods, for
example, by supporting organizations that save
people who, unlike livestock, are starving to
death or are chronically malnourished. While
one's not purchasing animal products won't make
a difference to the meat industry, providing
support for smaller vegetarian-product companies might. There, even an individual's financial
contributions, as well as his or her trying a
product and telling others about it, might very
well make a difference to the fate of a product or
company. Finally, many people find great value
in the friendships they develop in the vegetarian
community: being among and working with
people who advocate healthful and compassionate living can be quite rewarding. Anecdotal evidence suggests that many people who adopt this
kind of lifestyle find their lives to have greater
meaning and purpose, compared to when they
were not vegetarians or vegans.[22]

It might be that the consequentialist argument
can run on these considerations alone and get one
very close to the vegan conclusion: it might be
that for each opportunity to buy, eat, or use an
animal product, there is nearly always something
better that one can purchase, eat, or use that does

not involve animals. Going these routes can plausibly be said to result in better consequences for one's health and finances and so better enable one to bring about more goods for others, as well as one's self.

Vegetarianism and Virtue

… The common suggestion is that one should be a vegetarian or a vegan because, given an understanding of the relevant facts about both animal and human suffering, this is just how a virtuous, good person would respond. Since people should be virtuous, and being virtuous entails being caring and compassionate (among having other traits), and these traits entail disassociation from the animal-products industry even if doing so won't result in less harm to animals, virtuous people should be vegetarian.

In exploring a virtue-based defense of vegetarianism, Russ Shafer-Landau suggests that meat-eaters may be "condemnable to the extent that they display an indifference to the cruelty that went into the 'production' of their 'goods'," and that "they demonstrate a disregard for the suffering experienced by the animals whose remains one is wearing or eating." He describes fur-wearers as "callous." He writes that "[s]eeking and deriving satisfaction from 'products' that are known to result from cruel practices diminishes one's admirability. This is so even if the practical impact of one's indulgence is nonexistent or negligible." Similar judgments are made outside of the vegetarian context: there is "something morally repugnant about a willingness to utilize or purchase soap made from the bodies of concentration camp victims," even if doing so won't prevent any future harms. Also, voicing one's support for a racist dictator or wearing a fur coat received as a gift both seem objectionable.[23]

From these intuitions, Shafer-Landau formulates a moral principle …: "One must refuse (even symbolic) support of essentially cruel practices, if a comparably costly alternative that is not tied to essentially cruel practices is readily available."[24] He suspects that something like this principle offers the best hope for those concerned to defend the existence of an obligation to refrain from animal consumption. The problem here, as he notes, is that it's not easy "to identify the sorts of considerations that can ground such a principle," or to find a general moral theory that would justify such a principle.[25]

One approach would be to go the route of a rule-based non-consequentialist or deontological ethic, and hold that this is one of the rules. However, this probably wouldn't be wise, since an ethic of rules is often thought to be "fundamentally non-explanatory" and "anti-theoretical."[26] Presumably, there is a unifying principle that makes these rules the right rules: if there is such a principle, then this is what justifies the rule and makes it the case that the rule should be followed. This fundamental principle is thereby of theoretical interest, not the mid-level rule.

Another route would be virtue ethics. Virtue ethics says, roughly, that evaluations of character and motive are primary in ethics and that other ethical evaluations — say of actions — are derivative from considerations of character and motive: for example, that an action is right if, and only if, a virtuous person would do it.[27] The morality of an action is to be explained by the character of the agent. If one is interested in defending vegetarianism or veganism (and other intuitions about concerned and responsible consumer behavior in general), and one suspects that non-virtue-based theories have a hard time generating the correct judgments about these cases, then one might have a good reason to take more interest in virtue-based ethical theory.[28] It just seems that a virtuous person would not, in response to an understanding of the facts about animal agriculture and nutrition, think that even though animals suffer greatly and die for these products that she does not need (and, in fact, are sometimes harmful to her) and thus only fulfill aesthetic preferences for her, she is nevertheless justified in consuming and using them, even though she could easily refrain from doing so. Thus, virtue theory seems to provide a ready defense for a general principle, similar to … Shafer-Landau's, that we shouldn't (even symbolically) support bad practices when good alternatives are readily available, which we might call the "vegetarian justifying principle."

Virtue theory's greatest "vice," however, is that it simply does not seem to provide much of an explanation for why it's good to be virtuous, for example, why it's good (or virtuous) to be compassionate or why a virtuous person would accept the vegetarian justifying principle. Consequentialists can plausibly argue that it's good to be compassionate because compassionate people tend to bring more happiness into the world. They see the virtues as instrumentally valuable: virtue ethics, at least in its bolder varieties (and the non-bold varieties seem to just be theories of the virtues, which don't imply anything about ethical theory), holds that the virtues are intrinsically valuable.

In taking a consequentialist view on the virtues, one attempts to give more basic reasons why someone should be compassionate (assuming compassion is a virtue), not merely asserting, as virtue ethics does, that it's just a brute, unexplained fact that compassion is good. The consequentialist critic, of course, will be more attracted to the option that it's a brute fact that, say, happiness or pleasure is good and that virtues are means to those ends. This seems more plausible than the suggestion that the virtues are ends in themselves or are intrinsically good.

If this criticism of virtue ethics is compelling, then, while virtue ethics does readily support vegetarianism, it lacks explanatory power. The theory-minded ethical vegetarian seems to be faced with a dilemma: *either* accept a generally plausible ethical theory (for example, consequentialism) that gets a broad range of cases right (and for seemingly good reasons) but doesn't seem to do as well with personal vegetarianism or veganism in that it seems to lack a place for concerns about animals to provide reasons for action, *or* adopt a virtue ethics or other non-consequentialist, rule-based perspective that readily supports vegetarianism or veganism but, unfortunately, doesn't amount to much of a general moral theory because it lacks explanatory power.

I suspect that there may be a compromise here, one that will be amenable to consequentialists and help them defend the vegetarian justifying principle. There already are reasons to believe that the locus of evaluation for consequentialism should be broadened beyond individual actions to include the "life histories" of a person.[29] One proposal is to hold that an individual action is right for a person just in case it is part of one of that person's optimal life histories, that is, a life history in which moral value is maximized over the span of the life.

And here we have a natural place to merge the plausible insights of virtue ethics with consequentialist ethical theory. Pre-theoretically, it seems that, all else equal, a person will bring about more goodness if she has the virtue of compassion, cares about and is sensitive to unnecessary cruelty and suffering (wherever it is found, in humans or animals), opposes injustice and unfairness, and, in general, attempts to have an integrated, coherent moral outlook. These seem to be virtues that we try to instill in our children, and for good reason. And earlier we saw that these virtues (and others) readily support vegetarianism and veganism, as well as a general moral outlook typically associated with them (for example, deep concerns about human health and the recognition that the easiest, most effective, and cheapest ways to promote this are through simple dietary changes and non-animal based medical research,[30] disappointments that people are starving to death while cattle are well-fed, environmental concerns, concern for public health and safety, concerns about the exploitation of slaughterhouse workers, and so on).

These virtues have deep implications for how one lives one's life and how one affects others' lives. For each person, it is unclear how their characters would not be improved and how they would fail to bring about more goodness were they to adopt the virtues that commonly motivate vegetarian or veganism. What other better character traits would preclude doing this? How would becoming more compassionate, caring, and sensitive to these issues make one a *worse* person? Becoming caring and compassionate about animals invariably seems to have "trickle down" positive effects for the rest of one's life. It seems exceedingly unlikely that anyone would, in general, come to treat other humans worse were she to become a vegetarian or vegan out of compassion or sympathy for animals. In fact, the opposite seems likely. One common motive for telling others about the plight of animals, and attempting to persuade them to be vegetarian or vegan, is that others' lives will improve and they will develop these virtues.

One could practice these virtues selectively and not have them affect one's views about animals, or allow oneself to occasionally eat, but probably not buy, meat (whatever amount won't have negative consequences for health, which is unknown). In doing so, however, it seems not unlikely that one would be taking oneself down a life history that would be, on balance, worse than the vegan one. This is because, first, a thoughtful person who does not care about animals at all should come to conclusions about how to behave that would be very similar to the vegan's (since all their prescriptions promote human well-being anyway) and, second, personal consistency, integrity and commitment typically contribute to better character anyway. It might be difficult to be selectively caring and compassionate: if this would lead one down a slippery slope, the better strategy for doing the best one can with one's life might be to consistently hold these virtues and act in accordance with them. If this is the case, this bridges the gap between the consequentialist case for near-vegetarianism or veganism articulated above and the more consistent outlook, character, and behavior that many vegetarian and vegan philosophers advocate.

Singer states that "becoming a vegetarian [or a vegan, I think he'd agree] is a way of attesting to the depth and sincerity of one's belief in the wrongness of what we are doing to animals."[31] He probably would agree that veganism also is a way to attest to the sincerity of one's belief in the wrongness of what happens to humans as a result of how animals are used. I suspect that, in general, a person who has these beliefs and attests to them by becoming a vegetarian or vegan brings more goodness into the world than her non-vegetarian counterpart: some of these

ways are more obvious (for example, health, comparative ability to make financial contributions to good causes), others are less obvious and, of course, harder to evaluate (for example, consequences of character). [If a switch to a vegetarian or vegan lifestyle and, in general becoming an advocate for animals, results in a life history] that brings about greater overall value than an omnivorous life history, then this is what consequentialism demands, and, therefore, consequentialism does not demand "too little" because it will require that one conform one's behavior to the "vegetarian justifying principle" (which has implications beyond vegetarianism).

In conclusion, my discussion can be presented as this argument:

(1) If consequentialism is true, then each individual person ought to live an optimal life history.

(2) If each individual person ought to live an optimal life history, then each individual person ought to have the virtues entailed by an optimal life history.

(3) If each individual person ought to have the virtues entailed by an optimal life history, then each individual person ought to be compassionate, sensitive to cruelty (wherever it is found), resist injustice, have moral integrity, etc.

(4) If each individual person ought to be compassionate, sensitive to cruelty (wherever it is found), resist injustice, and be morally integrated, etc., then each individual person ought to be a vegetarian or vegan.

(5) Therefore, if consequentialism is true, then each individual person ought to be a vegetarian or vegan.

(6) Therefore, if consequentialism is true, then, *you* — the reader of this paper — ought to be a vegetarian or vegan.

Consequentialists readily accept premise (1) and should accept premise (2) as well, since it explains why it's good to be virtuous. Premise (3) is defended by the informal, quasi-empirical observation that people with these and related virtues tend to, in general, bring about more goodness into the world than people who lack these virtues. Were major lifestyle changes not at stake, many would probably readily accept this premise: it is difficult to see how people who *lack* compassion, caring, and sensitivity would bring about more goods than those who have these traits, or have them to a greater degree.

Premise (4) is obviously difficult, since it concerns empirical matters. It is the claim that people who become vegetarians or vegans in order to more consistently practice virtue produce more overall good than those who dabble in virtue or practice it selectively. Admittedly, this is an exceedingly difficult premise to defend. The data regarding the positive consequences of changing one's character by becoming vegetarian are, for the most part, anecdotal, speculative, and based in personal observations. However, this is a problem in general for trying to defend any view about personal morality from a consequentialist perspective, since it is very difficult to find any hard data on the consequences of character and lifestyle. Intuitions and impressions are often all we have to go on for such matters, especially those concerning personal choice.

But that does not leave us in the dark, since one impression that most of us have is that it is better to be more compassionate and caring, compared to less, unless doing so would be emotionally draining, which being a vegetarian typically isn't (in fact, many find it quite uplifting). Furthermore, whatever other projects we have, it is unclear exactly how becoming a vegetarian could preclude our efforts with them: if our other projects are noble, it is likely that our reasons for doing them would support being a vegetarian as well, and our being vegetarian would only help us with our other projects also.

So, while (4) is not easy to defend on consequentialist grounds, it is not easy to deny either. The vegetarian consequentialist typically has some personal experience to justify her sense that her becoming a vegetarian or vegan has resulted in her bringing about better consequences, while the critic typically has little personal experience to think that her being an omnivore has had the best consequences. If this consequentialist strat-

egy for defending personal vegetarianism has promise, further research into the actual consequences of having the kind of character that is receptive to concerns about animal suffering will be necessary.

Until then, I hope that some burden has been shifted to those who hold that their becoming vegetarians or vegans would *not* maximize intrinsic value to explain why this is so and why their characters, and the consequences of their characters, would become worse for their making this change. For those who value compassion, kindness and consistency, and oppose cruelty and exploitation, I hope that I have shown that each time they sit down to eat, they have an opportunity to develop their characters in these virtuous ways. Since this is likely part of each of us doing the best we can to bring more goodness into the world, let us each make the most of these opportunities.

NOTES

1. My argument is restricted to apply only to people with nutritious and readily available alternatives to meat. I will say nothing about the morality of meat eating among the relatively few people who, due to insufficient vegetable-food sources, literally must eat meat to survive.

2. The recent literature on ethical issues concerning non-human animals is immense, but the writings of Peter Singer and Tom Regan have been most influential. See, for example, Peter Singer, *Animal Liberation*, 3rd ed. (New York, NY: Ecco Press, 2001), and *Practical Ethics*, 2nd ed. (Cambridge: Cambridge University Press, 1993); Tom Regan, *Empty Cages: Facing the Challenge of Animal Rights* (Lanham, MD: Rowman & Littlefield, 2004), and *The Case for Animal Rights*, 2nd Edition (Berkeley, CA: University of California Press, 2004).

3. It seems that for some philosophers their unwillingness to modify their dining and consumer habits is not due to their finding serious defects in the common arguments for vegetarianism. Mylan Engel reports that his "experience has been that when confronted with these arguments [for vegetarianism] meat-loving philosophers often casually

dismiss them as follows: 'Singer's ... utilitarianism is irremediably flawed, as is Regan's theory of moral rights. Since Singer's and Regan's arguments for vegetarianism are predicated on flawed ethical theories, their arguments are also flawed. Until someone can provide me with clear moral reasons for not eating meat, I will continue to eat what I please'." See Mylan Engel, "The Immorality of Eating Meat," in Louis Pojman (ed.), *The Moral Life: An Introductory Reader in Ethics and Literature* (New York, NY: Oxford University Press, 2000), pp. 856-90, at p. 857. Engel notes that "[a] moment's reflection reveals the self-serving sophistry of such a reply. Since no ethical theory to date is immune to objection, one could fashion a similar to reply to 'justify' or rationalize virtually any behavior ... [A] fictitious rape-loving philosopher could ... point out that all ... ethical theories are flawed and ipso facto so too are all the arguments against rape [and] ... then assert: 'Until someone can provide me with clear moral reasons for not committing rape, I will continue to rape whomever I please'." For a response to a similar philosophers' "rationalization [in the context of discussing ethical vegetarianism] that there are simply too many issues on which [philosophers] could be expected to have a settled opinion, especially given [their] philosophical understanding of the complexity of any issue," see Joel Marks, *Moral Moments: Very Short Essays on Ethics* (Lanham, MD: University Press of America, 2000), p. 60-61.

4. I will argue that many arguments on this topic, if sound, establish a conclusion concerning collective vegetarianism, but that this is importantly different from personal vegetarianism or veganism and that the latter might not obviously entail the former. My proposal attempts to bridge this gap within consequentialist constraints.

5. Consequentialism is, very roughly, the ethical theory that says the morality of an action is determined solely by the value of the consequences in terms of the overall balance of intrinsic goods versus evils produced by that action. The view most readily contrasts with views that hold that actions get their moral status in virtue of being of *kinds* or *types* of action that are intrinsically

(albeit perhaps prima facie) moral or immoral, for example, acts of promise-keeping, respectful treatment, torture, and so on.

One problem for the non-consequentialist is explaining what grounds their (often quite plausible) moral rules, if it isn't the consequences of following them. I will attempt to ground the rule that seems necessary for justifying personal vegetarianism (or veganism) by appeal to some, often unnoticed, consequences of following this rule. The demand that personal vegetarianism be justified from general consequentialist principles is important because if buying and eating meat, purchasing leather, and so on, are wrong actions, then they possess the essential wrong-making features that a general theory about right and wrong, like consequentialism, attempts to identify. If personal vegetarianism doesn't seem to share much in common with other, more obviously wrong acts and the moral premises used to justify the vegetarian conclusion do not seem to be entailed by a person's general theory of right and wrong, it makes sense (at least for a consequentialist) to be skeptical about the wrongness of animal-product purchasing and consumption.

6. Utilitarianism is a species of consequentialism that says, roughly, that the only morally relevant consequence is the overall balance of pleasures and pains that come about as a result of the action. Other consequentialists take a broader view on what is good and bad, in itself.

7. Peter Singer, "Utilitarianism and Vegetarianism," *Philosophy & Public Affairs* 9 (1980): 325-37, p. 325 (my emphasis).

8. In "Collective Responsibility and Moral Vegetarianism," *Journal of Social Philosophy* 24 (1993): 89-104, p. 89, Hud Hudson reports: "A colleague once pointed out to me that there seems to be a higher percentage of Kantian ethicists who are vegetarians than, say, Utilitarian ethicists who are vegetarian, although from a cursory reading of the primary texts and the popular expositions of these schools of thought, one would have expected just the opposite."

9. For a forceful reply to this objection, see Shelly Kagan, *The Limits of Morality* (Oxford: Oxford University Press, 1989).

10. Henry Sidgwick, *The Methods of Ethics*, 7th ed. (London: Macmillan, 1907), p. 422.

11. For discussion of vegetarianism and these and other virtues, see Nicholas Dixon, "A Utilitarian Argument for Vegetarianism," *Between the Species* 11 (1995): 90-97, p. 96; Steve Sapontzis, "Everyday Morality and Animal Rights," *Between the Species* 3 (1987): 107-27; Russ Shafer-Landau, "Vegetarianism, Causation and Ethical Theory," *Public Affairs Quarterly* 8 (1994): 85-100, pp. 97-98; William Stephens, "Five Arguments for Vegetarianism," *Philosophy in the Contemporary World* 1 (1994): 25-39, p. 33; and Andrew Tardiff, "Simplifying the Case for Vegetarianism," *Social Theory and Practice* 22 (1996): 299-314, pp. 307, 312.

12. Documentary films are the best ways to learn about factory farming. Some of the best include *Tribe of Heart*'s "Peaceable Kingdom" (2004) and "The Witness" (2000), *People for the Ethical Treatment of Animals*' "Meet Your Meat", *Compassion Over Killing*'s documentary on poultry industry, "45 Days" (2004) and *Compassionate Consumers*' film on the egg industry. A film that focuses on Canadian animal agribusiness is Jennifer Abbot's "A Cow at My Table" (Flying Eye Productions, Canada, 1999).

   For books, see Regan, *Empty Cages: Facing the Challenge of Animal Rights*, Peter Singer, *Animal Liberation*, Engel, "The Immorality of Eating Meat" (and his six-minute video documentary "Modern Factory Farming and Slaughter: The Cruelty Behind the Cellophane" that narrates pp. 861-67 of his article); and Gail Eisnitz, *Slaughterhouse: The Shocking Story of Greed, Neglect, and Inhumane Treatment Inside the U.S. Meat Industry* (Amherst, NY: Prometheus Books, 1997). The latter discusses the abusive, disrespectful treatment of human workers in factory farms and slaughterhouses, in addition to routine animal abuse.

13. In 1998, USDA inspectors condemned 28,500 ducks, 768,300 turkeys, and 37.6 million chickens before they entered the slaughter plant because they were either dead or severely injured upon arrival. See *Poultry Slaughter*, National Agricultural Statistics Service, USDA (Washington, D.C.: February 2, 1999): pp. 2, 4 f.

14. Gail Eisnitz, chief investigator for the Humane Farming Association, in *Slaughterhouse*, p. 71, 126-28, reports that speeds are so fast in slaughterhouses that animals frequently do not have time to bleed out and die before reaching the skinners and leggers. As a result, fully conscious animals often have their legs cut off and their skin removed while they are still alive. Pigs are often lowered into the 140F scalding tank while still conscious. See also Joby Warrick, "They Die Piece by Piece: In Overtaxed Plants, Humane Treatment of Cattle is Often a Battle Lost," *Washington Post*, April 10, 2001, p. A1.

15. Mylan Engel, in "The Immorality of Eating Meat," summarizes the extensive medical literature on the health benefits of vegan and vegetarian diets. See also Mark and Virginia Messina, *The Dietician's Guide to Vegetarian Diets: Issues and Applications*, 2nd ed. (Gaithersburg, Md.: Aspen Publications, 2001); John Robbins, *The Food Revolution* (Berkeley: Conari Press, 2001); and Brenda Davis and Vesanto Melina, *Becoming Vegan: The Complete Guide to Adopting a Healthy Plant-Based Diet* (Summertown, TN: Book Publishing Co., 2000).

16. "American Dietetic Association: Position Paper on Vegetarian Diets," *Journal of the American Dietetic Association*, 2003;103:748-765.

17. Available at http://www.pcrm.org/health/veginfo/vsk/

18. See the references to the nutrition literature above.

19. See Robbins, *The Food Revolution*, pp. 78-79.

20. In "The Mere Considerability of Animals," *Acta Analytica* 16 (2001): 89-108, Mylan Engel notes: "To be sure, sometimes being a vegetarian is inconvenient. But lots of times, eating meat is just as inconvenient (for example, it takes hours to roast a turkey, whereas it takes only a few minutes to heat up some pasta with fresh veggies), and the inconvenience of eating meat (when it is inconvenient) does not dissuade most meat-eaters from eating meat. If one can put up with the inconvenience of eating meat, one can just as easily put up with the inconvenience of eating vegetables." Similarly, buying non-animal based clothing and products is either not incon-

venient or no more inconvenient than buying animal-based items.

21. Hud Hudson, in "Collective Responsibility," writes that he "is persuaded that the [meat] industry is not fine-tuned enough to be affected at all by [his] becoming a [strict] vegetarian," much less be affected by his purchasing a "large basket of extra-hot chicken wings" every two weeks at his favorite restaurant (p. 94). James Rachels, in "The Moral Argument for Vegetarianism," in his *Can Ethics Provide Answers?* (Lanham, MD: Rowman & Littlefield, 1997), pp. 99-107, notes: "It is discouraging to realize that no animals will actually be helped simply by one person ceasing to eat meat. One consumer's behavior, by itself, cannot have a noticeable impact on an industry as vast as the meat industry" (p. 106).

Bart Gruzalki discusses this objection in his "The Case Against Raising and Killing Animals for Food," in Harlan Miller and William Williams (eds.), *Ethics and Animals* (Clifton, NJ: Humana Press, 1983), pp. 251-66, p. 265. His reply focuses on dubious estimations of the *probable* positive consequences for animals that an individual's becoming a vegetarian would have. In "Opportunistic Carnivorism," *Journal of Applied Philosophy* 17 (2000): 205-11, p. 205, Michael Almeida and Mark Bernstein argue that "insensitivity of the market notwithstanding, consistent consequentialists are morally prohibited from each additional purchase and consumption of meat" because of the very small *probability* that any individual will purchase the "threshold chicken" (or other animal) that will result in the "increased terror, slaughter, and death of more chickens" (or other animals). The argument is troubled by the dubious empirical assumption that there is such a "threshold chicken" and a wavering back and forth between a subjective or probabilistic consequentialism that judges acts by their expected or probable consequences and an "objective" consequentialism that judges acts by their actual consequences,

R.G. Frey raised this objection in his *Rights, Killing, and Suffering: Moral Vegetarianism and Applied Ethics* (Oxford: Basil Blackwell, 1983); Michael Martin raises it in "A Critique of Moral

Vegetarianism," *Reason Papers*, No. 3, Fall 1976, pp. 13-43, and his "Vegetarianism, the Right to Life and Fellow Creaturehood," *Animal Regulation Studies* 2 (1979-80): 205-14. This objection is not new. Unfortunately, it seems too little has been said to respond to it.

22. See the essay "A Meaningful Life," by Matt Ball, at http://www.veganoutreach.org/advocacy/meaningfullife.html. Ball is co-founder of the organization *Vegan Outreach*, which works to promote veganism through the widespread distribution of illustrated booklets about contemporary animal agriculture and the vegan and vegetarian response to it. Also see Peter Singer's *Ethics into Action: Henry Spira and the Animal Rights Movement* (Lanham, MD: Rowman & Littlefield, 2000).

23. Shafer-Landau, "Vegetarianism, Causation and Ethical Theory," pp. 96-98.

24. Ibid., p. 95. DeGrazia, in *Taking Animals Seriously*, pp. 262, 285, advocates the principle, "Make every reasonable effort not to provide financial support for institutions or practices that cause or support unnecessary harm." He notes: "This principle might worry some utilitarians, because it might sometimes require one to abstain, boycott, or divest without its being clear that doing so will actually lead to good results. But, if so, that is a knock against the version of utilitarianism in question, not against the principle." He goes on to argue that these kinds of worries would "doom potential social reforms from the start," but also suggests that "[a]ctually, there is probably considerable utility in the ... principle. But it need not rest on so uncertain a basis as utilitarianism." As an adherent of a "coherence model of ethical justification," DeGrazia does not think his principles need to "rest" on a theoretical foundation because "normative ethics does not need a foundation" (p. 12). So he denies the theoretical assumptions of the "concerned consequentialist critic" who is the target of this paper.

25. Shafer-Landau, "Vegetarianism, Causation and Ethical Theory," p. 96.

26. See David McNaughton, "Intuitionism," in Hugh LaFollette (ed.), *The Blackwell Guide to Ethical Theory* (Oxford: Blackwell, 2000), pp. 268-87, at pp. 270-71.

27. For presentations of virtue ethics, see Rosalind Hursthouse, *On Virtue Ethics* (Oxford: Oxford University Press, 1999), and Linda Zagzebski, *Virtues of the Mind: An Inquiry into the Nature of Virtue and the Ethical Foundations of Knowledge* (Cambridge: Cambridge University Press, 1996).

28. In personal correspondence, Linda Zagzebski noted that considerations about these kinds of moral cases are unique motivations for exploring virtue ethics because a common criticism of virtue ethics is that it is unable to provide adequate guidance for matters of "applied" ethics or moral problems. My suggestion here is that virtue ethics seems to provide the most adequate practical moral guidance concerning ethical vegetarianism and similar moral issues. However, virtue ethics unfortunately seems subject to the traditional criticisms of divine command and ideal observer theories.

29. This view is a response to a challenging problem, informally stated, that "big" actions that span over a long period of time with very good consequences can be composed of "small" actions that, in themselves, have very bad consequences, and so consequentialism might say that a "big" action is obligatory, but its "parts" forbidden. See Fred Feldman, *Utilitarianism, Hedonism, and Desert: Essays in Moral Philosophy* (Cambridge: Cambridge University Press, 1997), on this problem of formulating a coherent statement of consequentialism that deals with problems of act individuation. He develops the formulation of consequentialism that I am suggesting, although my version is very informal.

30. See Hugh LaFollette and Niall Shanks, *Brute Science: Dilemmas of Animal Experimentation* (London: Routledge, 1997), and Ray and Jean Greek, *Sacred Cows and Golden Geese: The Human Cost of Experiments on Animals* (New York, NY: Continuum, 2001).

31. Singer, "Utilitarianism and Vegetarianism," p. 337.

YOUR DAUGHTER OR YOUR DOG?
A FEMINIST ASSESSMENT OF THE ANIMAL RESEARCH ISSUE

Deborah Slicer

Deborah Slicer teaches philosophy at the University of Montana in Missoula. She is the recipient of the 2004 Autumn House Prize for Poetry for The White Calf Kicks. *She was editor of* Ethics and the Environment *special issue on environmental narrative (2003) and has published articles in* Environmental Ethics, Ethics and Agriculture, Teaching Philosophy, *and several anthologies.*

Slicer highlights deficiencies in both the rights-based and utilitarian approaches to the issue of animal research. "The Singer-Regan approach" reflects a justice approach that neglects context and detail, overestimates the scope of principles, and discounts affective responses in moral life. Slicer argues that the contextual approach of ecofeminism pays attention to issues such as the overuse and misuse of animals in research, the inadequacy of government regulations to protect laboratory animals, proactive and preventive measures for promoting and improving human health, and changing medical research and practices so that women and animals are not treated in discriminatory ways. Slicer holds that developing relationships with animals, rocks, and trees can enhance one's capacity to empathize and act on behalf of others, including with laboratory animals used in research.

John Stuart Mill said that "every great movement must experience three stages: ridicule, discussion, adoption."[1] What is popularly called the animal rights movement is a significant contemporary social movement. And while this movement continues to take its undeserved share of ridicule, it has, for the most part, advanced beyond that first stage and into the second, discussion. There is even some encouraging evidence that its recommendations are being adopted by a significant number of people who are becoming vegetarians; buying "cruelty-free" toiletries, household products and cosmetics; refusing to dissect pithed animals in biology classes or to practice surgery on dogs in medical school "dog labs"; and rethinking the status of fur.

In the academy, a busy decade or more of writing and debate has coincided with a decade of intense social activism. A vast amount of litera-ture in this area has been written by utilitarian theorist Peter Singer, rights theorist Tom Regan, and those who are responding to them.

Singer's and Regan's arguments share a number of features, and I refer to those collectively as the Singer-Regan approach.[2] I begin by outlining this approach in section I. In section II, I draw from recent ecofeminist critiques of ecological ethics, especially of deep ecology, to explain how, similarly, the Singer-Regan approach neglects context and concrete individuals, how it overestimates the scope of principles and discounts our affective responses in moral life. In section III, I discuss the use of live animals in biomedical research. Researchers constantly tell us that we must choose between "us" (human beings) and "them" (animals), between our daughters and our dogs. They tell us it is either medical progress via the current, virtually unchecked rate and standards of animal sacrifice, or else a return to the Dark Ages. I think that both this characterization *and* the Singer-Regan characterization of the issue are dangerously misleading, for reasons I explain in that section. Throughout the paper, I try to make clear why animal rights issues, including the research one, are feminist issues, and I will make clearer the connections between some recent ecofeminist work and animal rights issues.[3]

I want to say that I have the utmost respect for both Singer and Regan as committed and inspiring activists and as academicians who have worked very hard to give these issues credibility in a discipline disposed toward dismissing them either as nonissues or as "pop" philosophy. Even though our scholarship differs, what we ultimately hope to accomplish for the several billion animals who are destroyed on this planet each year by and for the sake of human beings is the same.

I.

Singer and Regan question traditional criteria that are offered as necessary and sufficient conditions for an entity's being owed moral consideration — moral personality, an ability to enjoy the "higher" pleasures — on the grounds that such criteria exclude certain human "marginal" cases, e.g., infants, the severely mentally disabled, the very senile, and the comatose. Their approach is to search for what R.G. Frey (1980) has called a "lowest common denominator," a capacity or characteristic that is common to both the "normal" and the problematic human cases. The criterion they settle on is the capacity to have "interests."

Singer and Regan give basically the same account of these interests. In *The Case for Animal Rights*, Regan argues that at least mammalian animals, one year old or older, have both "preference" and "welfare" interests, which can be either frustrated or enhanced. By "preference" interests, Regan means "those things that an individual is *interested* in, those things he likes, desires, wants or, in a word, prefers having, or, contrariwise, those things he dislikes, wants to

avoid or, in a word, prefers not having" (Regan 1983, 87). By "welfare" interests, he means those things that are in an individual's interests, something that would benefit an individual (Regan 1983, 88). Of course an individual may or may not be interested in what is in that individual's interests.

Wishing to avoid the problem of so-called marginal cases, Regan says that individuals with preference interests have inherent value and that this value is marked by certain minimal rights, the most basic of which is the right to "treatment that is respectful of the kind of value they have, and all are owed this treatment equally; in particular, individuals who have inherent value are not to be treated as if they were mere 'receptacles' of valuable experiences" (Regan 1983, 277).[4] Singer says that sentient beings have interests, much like Regan's preference interests, in, at least, avoiding painful experiences and acquiring pleasurable ones. Possessing such interests entitles an individual to have those interests given due weight in a utilitarian calculation.

As many critics have noted, a great deal hinges on the lowest common denominator argument, an argument that appeals to the rationalist's penchant for parsimony and logical consistency. It insists that we choose an essential — that is, a necessary and sufficient — criterion of moral considerableness and that we apply it consistently to bring a vast array of both human and nonhumans equally into the moral fold. Failure to give animals the moral consideration they are due is "speciesist," a moral wrong similar to racism and sexism. To paraphrase Singer, speciesism is an irrational bias toward members of one's own species and against members of other species (Singer 1977, 7).

According to Singer, a utilitarian calculation of both the animal and human pleasures and sufferings that result from such practices as flesh eating, product testing, biomedical research and education, and recreational hunting will in the vast majority of cases weigh in favor of the animals. According to Regan, these various practices violate an animal's right to respectful treatment, that is, we do not treat them in ways consistent with the recognition of their equal posses-sion of inherent value. Instead, we treat them as receptacles of intrinsic value (e.g., pleasure), lacking any value of their own.

II.

Singer's and Regan's arguments are recognizable offshoots of what some feminists, following Carol Gilligan's analysis (1982), call the "justice tradition" in moral and political philosophy.[5] Here, I will focus on how such theories misrepre-sent our moral relations with animals rather than with other human beings.

1. Essentialism

Singer and Regan, like their mentors the utilitari-ans and Kant, respectively, have an "essentialist" view of the moral worth of both human beings and animals. This means that they propose a single capacity — the possession of interests — for being owed moral consideration. It is clear that they believe this condition is a sufficient one for being owed such consideration. And while they do not say specifically that possessing such interests is *necessary*, Singer and Regan *treat* the possession of preference interests as a necessary condition. For example, the lowest common denominator argument, which is central to their respective attempts to bring animals into the moral fold equally with human beings, is sound only if possessing interests is treated as neces-sary. Both writers say that those who do not possess interests are, at best, problematic. And both Singer and Regan condone sacrificing those without interests for the sake of those who do possess them.[6]

Essentialism is objectionable for a number of reasons. First, it renders inessential and unimpor-tant certain relationships — familial relationships or friendships, for example — that do seem essential and important to many of the rest of us (Francis and Norman 1978). Second, as some feminist writers have noted, essentialism strips an individual of his or her "specific history, identity, and affective-emotional constitution" (Walker

1989, 18). Specifically, animal rights theories reduce individuals to that atomistic bundle of interests that the justice tradition recognizes as the basis for moral considerableness. In effect, animals are represented as beings with the *kind of capacity* that human beings most fully possess and deem valuable for living a full *human* life.

Several ecofeminists, including Marti Kheel (1985), Jim Cheney (1987), and Karen Warren (1990), have noted something very much like essentialism, or at least a certain arrogance underlying essentialism, in the environmental ethics literature, especially among deep ecolo-gists.[7] Both Kheel and Warren show how such arrogance leads to hierarchical and dualistic thinking. Jim Cheney agrees with Ariel Kay Salleh who claims that, as Cheney puts it, attempts by deep ecologists "to overcome human (really masculine) alienation from nature fail in the end because they are unable to overcome a masculine sense of the self and the kinds of ethical theory that go along with this sense of self" (Cheney 1987, 121). I agree with Cheney, who points out that some deep ecologists fail to recognize and respect the integrity of the "other," of animals and nonsentient nature, when they describe their relationship to nature in terms of nature being a part of *them*, when they merely expand "the self to *include* that in relationship to which it feels alienated" (Cheney 1987, 121). Cheney describes this metaphorically as a "megalomaniacal pond sucking up all the water of the world and becoming itself an ocean" (Cheney 1987, 124).

In contrast to this "megalomaniacal" view, as Karen Warren discusses her first rock-climbing experiences she compares a potentially "arro-gant" relationship with the rock — as invasive, as conqueror, as coercive — with a climber's "loving" relationship. She says of the latter:

One recognizes the rock as something very dif-ferent, something perhaps totally indifferent to one's own presence, and finds in that differ-ence joyous occasion for celebration. One knows "the boundary of the self," where the self — the "I," the climber — leaves off and the rock begins. There is no fusion of two into one, but a complement of two entities *acknowledged* as separate, different, independent, yet *in relationship*; they are in relationship *if only* because the loving eye is perceiving it, responding to it, noticing it, attending to it (Warren 1990, 137).

Singer and Regan extend the moral community to include animals on basis of sameness. They do not acknowledge, much less celebrate, differences between humans and other animals. This sort of self-centric importance, this assimilation of the other into the sameness of self, the "fusion of two into one" and the "erasure of difference," as Warren puts it, is central to the concept of arrogance that Marilyn Frye (1983) and Iris Murdoch (1970) have previously articulated.

Warren's loving attention to the rock's difference, independence, indifference did not result in her antipathy or moral apathy with regard to the rock. Instead, she says, "I felt an overwhelming sense of gratitude for what it offered me — a chance to know myself and the rock differently, to appreciate unforeseen miracles like the tiny flowers growing in the even tinier cracks in the rock's surface, and to come to know a sense of *being in relationship* with the natural environment. ... I felt myself *caring* for this rock" (Warren 1990, 135).

There is no reason why animals' differences, independence, indifference cannot be grounds for caring, for relationships characterized by such ethically significant attitudes as respect, gratitude, compassion, fellow or sisterly feeling, and wonder. Such animal ethologists as Jane Goodall (1971) have practiced for decades what Warren (1990), who is indebted to Marilyn Frye (1983), calls "loving attention." Goodall and other women (some of them feminist) scientists have suggested that such an attitude and its practice are not only appropriate moral attitudes with regard to the subjects they are studying but an epistemologically fruitful one as well (e.g., see Keller 1983).

Both Warren and Kheel note how arrogant essentialism re-creates moral hierarchies and dualistic thinking in ways that "establish inferiority and subordination" (Warren 1990, 129).[8] Marti Kheel puts the point like this: "Ironically, although many of these writers feel that they are arguing against notions of hierarchy, the vast majority simply remove one set of hierarchies only to establish another. Thus, many writers on the subject of animal liberation may raise the status of animals to a level that warrants our moral concern only to exclude other parts of nature, such as plants and trees" (Kheel 1985, 139). And there is even a pecking order among those in the upper echelons (among those who possess interests) of the hierarchy. Singer and Regan say that in dire cases, when we must choose between animal and human life, the life of the human, because it has more valuable potential experiences, takes priority.[9]

Central to an ecofeminist analysis of patriarchy is the claim that such value hierarchies, which categorize women, animals, and nonsentient nature on the same devalued side of the dualism, serve to oppress women along with nature in a vast array of similar ways.[10] Unfortunately, like many of the deep and certainly the "shallow" ecologists, Singer's and Regan's analyses do not cut deeply enough into our culture's objectionable use of these dualistic hierarchies. In fact, their "liberation" theories only perpetuate such thinking.

A second feature of the justice tradition that has received attention is the propensity among those working in that tradition to characterize moral situations generally and abstractly and at the expense of contextual detail. What is lost in this kind of characterization of moral life or of a moral dilemma are historical, social, economic, familial, and other details that seem crucial to an assessment of a situation, a decision, or a character. Singer and Regan give us such delimited descriptions, and these descriptions allow them to formulate general, prescriptive principles that are applicable to similarly and superficially described situations. The use of such principles is a third feature of the Singer-Regan approach that I discuss.

As noted in section I., for Singer and Regan the animal research issue and the vegetarian issue are described similarly as situations in which animals' interests, given the strict and impartial consideration they are due, override human interests in eating them or in using them as experimental subjects. And the reasons our desires are overridden — because animals' desires are stronger or their rights given priority by an adjudicatory principle of justice that we have all decided on — should be recognized as good reasons by anyone capable of following a logical inference.

At least since Gilligan, a central task of feminist moral criticism has been to assess the role, proper status, and nature of principles in moral life. Some ecofeminists have raised similar questions about principles in reviewing work by deep ecologists and in deciding whether there is a place for principles in their own theories.[11] It is often said that general principles are too legalistic and abstract to be helpful in resolving unique, highly context-laden, nongeneralizable situations and that a "principled morality" leaves no room for virtue and affection.[12] While these writers do not eschew the use of principles entirely, they do reject any morality that worships principles while neglecting such things as virtue or the affections. I agree with these writers, and I object to the way rights and utilitarian principles are often presented to us in classrooms, textbooks, and scholarly books and articles as our only "reasonable" options. This is objectionable because if these are our only options, then we must sometimes disregard what our imaginations or hearts or the simple facts are telling us, in order to articulate situations, some of them very uncooperative, in a way that fits these principles and their corresponding conceptual frameworks. Singer's and Regan's awkward attempts to articulate interspecies moral relations using these standard theories and conceptual frameworks exemplify this point.

What principles we articulate and ultimately choose to rely on are relevant to a very complex web of "beliefs, feelings, modes of expression, circumstances and more, arranged in characteristic ways and often spread out over time" (Walker 1989, 18). In an essay on bioregional narrative,

Jim Cheney suggests that we "extend these notions of context and narrative outward so as to include not just the human community, but also the land, one's community in a larger sense." Moreover, "for a genuinely contextualist ethic to include the land ... the land must *speak* to us; we must stand in *relation* to it; it must *define* us, and we it" (Cheney 1989, 128-29). I should think that this concept of "the land" would entail sentient nature. And because we not only are *defined by* but also *define* this relationship — not in terms of static and essentialist necessary and sufficient conditions but in contextually rich and evolving terms — we will have opportunities to evaluate and alter aspects of the relationship when certain features of it (our arrogance and our waste, for example) are brought forcefully to our attention, and we may well want to recommend some of these alternatives universally.

Recently, Karen Warren articulated eight "boundary conditions" — necessary conditions that "delimit the territory of a piece without dictating what the interior ... looks like" — of any feminist ethic and of any ecofeminist ethic. One of those conditions states that a feminist ethic or an ecofeminist ethic cannot be naturist — that is, cannot condone the oppressive domination of sentient and nonsentient nature — or contribute to any other " '-ism' which presupposes and advances a logic of domination." Warren defines a "logic of domination" as "a structure of argumentation which leads to a justification of subordination" (Warren 1990, 128). This "logic" entails a value system that designates "subordinates" and their "inferior" characteristics or capacities. A second condition holds that any theory should be fluid, in process, changing over time, and emerging out of "concrete and alternative descriptions of ethical situations." A third requires that feminist ethics must give a place to "values typically unnoticed, underplayed, or misrepresented in traditional ethics" and will do so while recognizing a role for traditional values (Warren 1990, 139-40).

These boundary conditions are also relevant to any critique of the animal rights literature and to attempts to reconceptualize our moral relationships with and obligations to the animals with whom Singer and Regan are concerned. I have already discussed how Singer and Regan retain an unfortunate "logic of domination" in their respective theories. Their atemporal, abstract, and acontextual characterizations of issues, of the values at stake, and of appropriate resolutions grossly oversimplify some of these highly complex issues, including, as I show in section III., the research one. Such characterizations also oversimplify our actual and potential relationships with and responses to animals, depriving us of opportunities to respond to and make responsible choices about the enormous cost to other sentient life of such intimate and routine practices involving, e.g., what we eat, the bath soap and shampoo that we use, and the pills that we take for a headache or to prevent a pregnancy.

3. The Affections

Peter Singer says that he does not "love" animals, that he has "argued" his case, "appealing to reason rather than to emotion or sentiment ... because reason is more universal and more compelling in its appeal" (Singer 1977, 255). Regan says that we should make "a concerted effort not to indulge our emotions or parade our sentiments. And that requires making a sustained commitment to rational inquiry" (Regan 1983, xii).

A fair number of critics, after and long before Carol Gilligan, have said that such faith in the rational and universal force of principles at the expense of our emotional responses is naive, based on an insensitivity to our actual moral psychology and a Western and perhaps masculinist contempt for our emotions, which are considered "womanish." Critics have shown how this rationalist ideal fails to account for what motivates us in many of our personal relations, where love, or friendship, or the affections, for example, often are, and should be, a (or the) predominant motive.[13] Singer and Regan follow the tradition that polarizes reason and the emotions and that privileges reason when the two conflict.

There is no pat formula for deciding when our affective responses have a place, or how much weight they should have, in resolving dilemmas affecting either personal or public relations. For the most part, deciding when and to what extent our affective responses are appropriate and helpful involves entering into a particular narrative. Probably there are situations, even involving personal relations, that call for the use of some maxim that is impartial and dispassionate. Apportioning family goods, services, or energy among rivaling children might be an example. And certainly we sometimes do and should be allowed to respond affectively to strangers. We feel what might be an empathetic sympathy and embarrassment when we witness, for example, someone else's public humiliation or a parent pleading on television for the return of a missing child.

Marti Kheel (1985) has said that the argument Singer and Regan make from "marginal cases" relies on an emotional appeal. The argument holds that we either revoke the moral standing of "defective" human beings or else grant standing to those animals that are intellectually and emotionally on par with these humans. Since we have some very strong feelings or intuitions about the humans the argument is persuasive: we are willing to accord moral status to animals rather than deny it to the humans.

What Kheel advocates, along with Mary Midgley, Sara Ruddick, and Robin Morgan, is what Morgan calls a "unified sensibility," or a recognition of the "fusion of feeling and thought" as characteristic of moral life (Kheel 1985, 144). Karen Warren (1990) is advocating something similar when she says that an ecofeminist ethic will emerge out of individuals' concrete relationships and experiences and will recognize a variety of affective responses along with formal and abstract principles, all in their appropriate contexts.

Kheel and Warren suggest that whenever possible we must *experience* the full impact of our moral decisions," especially of those decisions that we make daily and so casually and that have such an enormous impact on the rest of sentient life (Kheel 1985, 145). This implies that those individuals who believe that flesh eating is morally permissible or even morally neutral should visit chickens who are confined along with three to six other chickens in a cage the size of a record album cover in a battery shed that holds up to 10,000 other chickens. They should see bobby calves tethered in veal sheds and cows on the killing floor and witness a sow's confinement in the "iron maiden."[14] Those who condone animal research and testing should request a tour of laboratories at the nearest research university. They should see the equipment — the surgical tables, restraining chairs, "rape racks," and "guillotines" — and experience the smells and the sounds.[15]

Will these individuals still think and feel the same about such practices? I am not saying that moral disagreement will disappear when we expand the range of experiences or responses that enrich our moral lives. But I do agree with those who emphasize the importance of direct experience for making responsible choices *and* for articulating desperately needed new moral visions, particularly in animal and environmental ethics.

III.

In this section I begin to give the research issue the kind of contextual attention that Singer and Regan fail to give it. This needs to be done before we can assess the role of abstract principles, including Singer's and Regan's principles, and of the affections in resolving the issue. In the course of recontextualizing the issue, I examine it holistically and explore several related ecofeminist themes.

I limit the focus of my discussion to the use of animals in biomedical research. I do not attempt to justify the use of animals in any such studies. In fact, I am sympathetic with Singer's and Regan's repugnance over using animals as research tools, even though I disagree with their arguments. What I have to say here has some special bearing on feminist critiques of androcentric science and on recent attempts to articulate "feminine" and especially feminist alternatives.

If, as ecofeminists say, naturism is something that feminists should condemn and always avoid in their own work, then the use of 20 million research animals annually in this country deserves more attention in this feminist literature than it has received.[16]

The few ecofeminists who have written in any depth about animal research (Kheel 1985; Collard 1988; Adams 1990) insist that we examine the issues contextually and holistically. Only then can we make knowledgeable and responsible decisions, in the rich sense of weighing facts, theoretical knowledge, and our affections. In this spirit, then, we should consider the many well-documented studies that demonstrate: (1) how animals are grossly overused and misused in research that is trivial, duplicative to the point of redundancy, badly designed, or that fails to use existing nonanimal alternatives or to develop them;[17] (2) how many researchers use species with more demanding psycho-social needs when those with less demanding needs will do; (3) how animals often do not serve as reliable models for human beings and how it can be very dangerous to extrapolate from results obtained from one species to another;[18] and (4) how federal and in-house regulations that are supposed to protect laboratory animals are grossly inadequate and how regulatory agencies are extremely lax in enforcing the few regulations that do exist.

In addition, as a variety of activists and ecofeminists have said, our society, including the medical establishment, needs to insist on such *pro*active measures as cleaning our air, water, soil, and the poisons from our grocery shelves if we are serious about our physical and psychological well-being. Americans see precious little of that from the National Institutes of Health, the world's largest funder of *re*active animal research, or from the American Medical Association. And of course we are unlikely to see a preventative emphasis from these institutions, as feminists writing about science (e.g., Harding 1986), women's health care (e.g., Corea 1988), and technology (e.g., Merchant 1980; Collard 1988) have pointed out. As Collard puts it, these institutions use a strategy "typical of patriarchal control ... whereby the integrity of matter (living and nonliving) is broken, artificially restored/recombined, and marketed in such a way (cure, improvement, etc.) as to elicit gratitude" (Collard 1988, 79). Animal research is a part of the strategy, and animals are among its subjects, along with women, whose natural lives have been "enhanced" by these "helping" institutions in everything from our pregnancies to our breast size.

These mostly methodological considerations certainly are not lost on Singer and Regan, but they are superfluous to what Regan calls the "moral heart of the matter" (Regan 1983, 384): the conflict between human and animal interests and our unjustified willingness to sacrifice the latter for the former. But for many thoughtful people the question of *whether* animals should be used in research is more pertinently one of *when* they should be used and *how* they will be treated, just as, to make some very imperfect comparisons, for many people the question of whether euthanasia is morally permissible is also a question of how and when it is performed, and for some, the question of "just" war is not so much a question of whether it is justifiable but of how and when. I am not claiming here that these three practices — euthanasia, "just" war, and animal research — are analogous; they are, in fact, significantly disanalogous. Instead, my point is that many people will consider any characterization of these issues that leaves out information about methodology and other contextual features to be decontextualized to the point of being misleading, even irrelevant.

How, exactly, do Singer and Regan themselves resolve this "moral heart of the matter"? In his chapter on research Regan advocates the total abolition of the use of animals in research, even granting, as he puts it, "that we face greater prima facie harm than laboratory animals presently endure if future harmful research on these animals is stopped, and even granting that the number of humans and other animals who stand to benefit from allowing this practice to continue exceeds the number of animals used in it" (Regan 1983, 389).

But in his discussion of biomedical research, Regan also makes a distinction between "exceptional" sacrifice and "routine" or "institutionalized" sacrifice of animal life. And he says that any judgments we make about the former (lifeboat cases, for example) are not transferable to the latter (the routine and prevalent use of animals in research, for example); but he does not condemn the former, nonroutine sacrifice. This is a suggestive but much underdeveloped point. If Regan is saying that the nonroutine use of some animals might be justified in desperate times in extreme situations, then we will most certainly have to muck around in the contextual particulars to sort these cases out. Most of all, we will want to know what constitutes "nonroutine" use, that is, how many animals may be used with what frequency and for what. And I expect that there will be no pat formula for deciding this, that we will have to sort this out on a case-by-case basis.

Singer resorts to an argument that appears frequently in the literature. I call it the onus argument. His version of it follows:

So whenever an experimenter claims that his experiment is important enough to justify the use of an animal, we should ask him whether he would be prepared to use a retarded human at a similar mental level to the animal he is planning to use. (Singer 1977, 67)

Singer does not advocate using human beings as research subjects. He is making a point about consistency: an experimenter cannot consistently condone the use of an animal while condemning the use of a human being when each will suffer roughly the same. Singer is basically correct when he says that the research community bears the onus of justifying its use of animals, even when it is clear that some significant benefits could come of it. But there is also an onus on the rights community to justify their abolitionist stance, to justify not using animals, especially when we stand to lose some significant future benefits. Singer's response to that onus is to lead us into a utilitarian impasse. Arguing that there are no defensible grounds on which to base a choice does not make the problem go away. Oddly, Singer considers this impasse a kind of victory. I think that he has reached something more like a dead end, that this impasse is an indication that utilitarianism, at least in itself, is unable to resolve this problem. Utilitarianism might even *be* the problem; an impartial or misleading characterization of an issue can make it seem obdurate, unresolvable.

Recently, ecofeminist Ynestra King (1987) took to task a certain "Malthusian wing" of deep ecologists for their shallow analyses of the political and social causes of such environmental problems as global over-population and for the impracticality and bureaucratic heartlessness of their proposed solutions. I feel a similar frustration with the shallow utilitarian analysis of the research issue that leads to Singer's impasse, with the impracticality of the impasse itself as some sort of proposed resolution, and with Singer's and Regan's assumptions that our allegiance to principled demands will and should cut cleanly through any preexisting emotional or other bonds we might have to members of our own species, community, friends, family, or lovers who may suffer as a result of Singer's and Regan's recommendations.[19] My point is *not* to justify any and all of these bonds as automatic trumps against animals' sufferings. Rather than say that these bonds should count for nothing (as the animal rights literature suggests) or that they count for everything (as the research community suggests), I have been trying to show all along that there are numerous relevant issues that are neglected by both sides, including this one, and there may well be more than just two sides.

The following are among some of the more significant issues neglected by mainstream writers on animal research. I only gesture at them here and hope that they receive more attention in the future. First, can we justify sacrificing beings who are extremely vulnerable to the whims and powers of human beings? How do we justify sacrificing beings who are "innocent," that is, who are neither actually nor potentially culpable or even capable of any wrongdoing? We all seem to

recognize some fairly stringent moral prohibitions against taking advantage of the innocent and the vulnerable, *even* in cases of self-defense, even in lifeboat cases. In fact, taking such advantage is often seen as especially malign. Do animals fall outside the scope of this prohibition completely, and if so, why? If not, why not? And if sometimes, then when and why?

Andrée Collard (1988) suggests that along with the self-serving appropriation of animals for the ostensive purpose of advancing human health, there is also a familiar attitude that "might makes right" with regard to the capture, breeding, genetic engineering, use and disposal of research animals. Every feminist knows that women have been and are affected by this form of arrogance in science, in the streets, in our own bedrooms and elsewhere. To condone such an attitude and practice in any context is to perpetuate it in all. Ynestra King puts this basic ecofeminist thesis forcefully when she says that "the hatred of women and the hatred of nature are intimately connected and mutually reinforcing" (King 1989, 18).

Furthermore, one popular nineteenth-century antivivisectionist argument, advanced by George Bernard Shaw, among others, held that the appropriation of unwilling and unwitting subjects for research that is painful and deadly erodes any aspirations or pretensions we might have about living in a "civilized" society, about possessing a "civilized" character. Ecofeminists have made similar points with regard to the arrogant and violent appropriation of non-human nature and women, particularly by American and Anglo-European cultures. Collard says that we live in a society "dominated by the 'ideology of cultural sadism,'" one in which "violent acts are neutralized by virtue of being so common. In the case of animal experimentation, these acts are admired (published and replicated) and the actors honored (tenured and funded)" (Collard 1988, 68). The same culture that at best is apathetic about and at worst valorizes the deaths of 20 million research animals in U.S. laboratories annually also allowed the country's 750,000 *reported* rapes during the 1980s, the murder of 50,000 women by their male partners, and the hospitalization of more women from beatings by their male partners than from auto accidents during that decade.[20] All this seems at least prima facie evidence that acts of violence against women have been similarly neutralized.

As a final consideration, we might also examine the affective schizophrenia of a country that spends more money than any other in the world on its "pets," while spending more than any other on animal research, much of it involving the use of cats and dogs, hamsters and bunnies. How and why do we circumscribe our collective and individual imaginations in this manner? Certainly whatever is going on here is complicated and beyond the scope of this paper. But our reasons for such seemingly arbitrary circumscription must include such obvious things as consumer convenience and the research and testing industry's secrecy about and, more recently, outright denial of the violence of so-called routine testing and research. Do we want to condone whatever sophisticated emotional bracketing is at work here? I should hope not. To do so is to give up any significant account of collective and individual moral responsibility regarding, as I have said before, the impact on the rest of sentient life of some of our most routine and intimate practices (e.g., what we eat) and consumer purchases (e.g., the dish soap we buy).

Surely we will not and probably cannot have the same affections or degrees of affection for the cat or dog in the laboratory that we have for the animals in our households, nor can we have the same feeling for a stranger's lost or abused child that we would have for our own child in a similar situation. These special ties *do* bind, and I am not recommending that we bracket them for the sake of blind impartiality, at least not always. While we cannot feel or care the *same* for every human being or animal, the feeling or caring that we do have for our immediate companions should extend some, via imagination and empathy, to our feeling for, our caring about, the plight of more extended others. And for those who have a rich enough moral imagination, this regard will cross species boundaries. Someone who has cared

about a rock or a tree or a dog or a cat may well care about what happens to, and particularly about the destruction of, other rocks, trees, cats, and dogs. Such particular relationships can and should enhance one's capacity to empathize, "feel with," and act on behalf of others.

I am not saying that everyone who cares about laboratory animals will condemn experimentation. I am saying that we will at least cease to condone the practice so cavalierly. We will find that there are certain elements of moral tragedy in having to make some choices despite the daunting complexity of these situations, despite having few, if any, principles or precedents to guide us, despite having little or no assurance that we have chosen rightly. And regardless of how we choose, we may have to live with, as some have recently put it, irresolute, nagging "moral remainders."[21]

IV.

I am convinced that as feminist theorists and practitioners we must address the interconnecting dominations of women, animals, and nonsentient nature, as ecofeminists insist, along with other social dominations, in order to understand sufficiently and correct any one and all of them. Ecofeminist analyses include those facets of patriarchal domination that are often neglected by other feminists, by environmental ethicists, *and* by animal rights proponents. I realize that I have made very few recommendations about when, if ever, we may use animals in research, although I have made my general antipathy toward such use clear. Nonetheless, and this may be obvious, I still feel some ambivalence over this issue, a gut sense that my antipathy is appropriate but that its grounds are not yet well enough articulated. I hope to inspire other feminist voices to help articulate these grounds and to do so in a way that avoids simplistic characterizations in terms of daughters and dogs.

Author's Note

Many thanks to the *Hypatia* referees, Tony Crunk, and especially Karen Warren for their comments on an earlier version of this paper. I also gratefully acknowledge Cora Diamond's influence on my thinking about these issues.

NOTES

1. Tom Regan (1983, 400) cites this passage from Mill.
2. Cora Diamond (1978) also uses the term "Singer-Regan approach." My characterization of the approach shares certain features with hers, but our characterizations are not the same.
3. I use the popular term "animal rights" to refer to political and philosophical debates over the moral status of mostly domestic, agricultural, and laboratory animals. I do not argue anywhere that animals have moral or legal rights.
4. Regan includes mammalian animals, one year and older, who are not psychologically impaired under the jurisdiction of this principle because, he says, we can be assured that these animals have preference interests. He also says that his is a "minimal" case, which means that he does not rule out the possibility of nonmammals and of mammals younger than one year having preference interests.
5. See especially Kittay and Meyers (1987).
6. For example, Singer (1979) says that we may eat "humanely" raised and slaughtered chickens and ducks because, he claims, they probably have no interests in their future; in fact, they probably have no notion of a "future" whatsoever, he says. Regan (1983), who wants to give ducks and chickens and other nonmammals, as well as mammals younger than one year, the "benefit of the doubt," does say that it is permissible to sacrifice fetal mammals and nonmammals in their early stages of development because they do not possess interests.
7. Deep ecologists eschew "shallow" ecologists' anthropocentric philosophies. A major tenet of the deep ecology movement is, as Arne Naess puts it, "the well-being of nonhuman life on Earth has a value in itself. This value is independent of any instrumental usefulness for limited human purposes" (Naess 1984, 266; see also Naess 1973).

8. "The problem is not simply *that* value-hierarchical thinking and value dualisms are used, but *the way* each has been used in *oppressive conceptual frameworks* to establish inferiority and to justify subordination" (Warren 1990, 128-29).
9. Both Singer (1977, 21-22) and Regan (1983, 324) make a distinction between the value of a "normal" human life and that of an animal, and each say the human life is the more valuable.
10. See Susan Griffin (1978) and Carol Adams (1990).
11. See Jim Cheney (1987, 1989) and Karen Warren (1990).
12. See especially Murdoch (1970), Gilligan (1982), Noddings (1984), Ruddick (1980).
13. See Gilligan (1982) and Noddings (1984).
14. The "iron maiden" is used to confine a sow's movements after she delivers her litter. This is manufacturers' and breeders' slang for this device.
15. A "rape rack" immobilizes primates as they are impregnated (Benney 1983).
16. The U.S. Department of Agriculture and researchers currently say that 20 million animals are used annually for research in the United States. This figure may well be low because institutions are not required to report the use of mice and rats (80% of the animals used in research), and farm animals. Animal rights groups put the annual figure at 40-60 million.
17. Standards in the Animal Welfare Act that are supposed to define and control "trivial" experimentation and minimize redundancy are enforced by an institution's Animal Care and Use Committee, an in-house committee which generally consists of researchers and individuals friendly to animal research. Decisions about the numbers and types of animals used in an experiment and about whether to withhold pain medication are also left to the discretion of this in-house committee. I highly recommend the studies by the United Action for Animals, 205 East 42nd Street, New York, NY 10017 on duplication and redundancy.
18. Thalidomide was tested on several nonhuman animal species before being given to human beings. Insulin deforms mice and rabbits. Penicillin is toxic to guinea pigs.

19. Mary Midgley (1983) has made a very similar point.
20. These figures are cited in "Hate Crimes Bill Excludes Women," in *off our backs* 20, no. 6 (June 1990).
21. "'Moral remainders' refers to some genuine moral demands which, because their fulfillment conflicted with other genuine moral demands, are 'left over' in episodes of moral choice, and yet are not nullified" (Walker 1989, 21).

REFERENCES

Adams, Carol J. 1990. *The sexual politics of meat: A feminist vegetarian critical theory*. New York: Crossroads/Continuum.

Benney, Norma. 1983. All of one flesh: The rights of animals. In *Reclaim the earth: Women speak out for life on earth*. Léonie Caldecutt and Stephanie Leland, eds. London: The Women's Press.

Cheney, Jim. 1987. Ecofeminism and deep ecology. *Environmental Ethics* volume 9 (2): 115-45.

— . 1989. Postmodern environmental ethics: Ethics as bioregional narrative. *Environmental Ethics* 11 (2): 117-34.

Collard, Andrée, with Joyce Contrucci. 1988. *Rape of the wild: Man's violence against animals and the earth*. Bloomington: Indiana University Press.

Corea, Gena. 1988. *The mother machine: Reproductive technologies from artificial insemination to artificial wombs*. London: The Women's Press.

Diamond, Cora. 1978. Eating meat and eating people. *Philosophy* 53: 465-79.

Francis, Leslie Pickering and Richard Norman. 1978. Some animals are more equal than others. *Philosophy* 53: 507-27.

Frey, R.G. 1980. *Interests and rights*. Oxford: Clarendon Press.

Frye, Marilyn. 1983. Arrogance and love. In *The politics of reality*. Freedom, CA: The Crossing Press.

Gilligan, Carol. 1982. *In a different voice*. Cambridge: Harvard University Press.

Goodall, Jane. 1971. *In the shadow of man*. Boston: Houghton Mifflin.

Griffin, Susan. 1978. *Woman and nature: The roaring inside her*. New York: Harper and Row.

Harding, Sandra. 1986. *The science question in feminism*. Ithaca and London: Cornell University Press.

Keller, Evelyn Fox. 1983. *A feeling for the organism: The life and work of Barbara McClintock*. New York: W.H. Freeman.

Kheel, Marti. 1985. The liberation of nature: A circular affair. *Environmental Ethics* 7 (2): 135-49.

King, Ynestra. 1987. What is ecofeminism? *The Nation*, 12 December.

— . 1989. The ecology of feminism and the feminism of ecology. In *Healing the wounds: The promise of ecofeminism*. Judith Plant, ed. Santa Cruz: New Society Publishers.

Kittay, Eva Feder and Diana T. Meyers, eds. 1987. *Introduction to women and moral theory*. Totowa, NJ: Rowman and Littlefield.

Merchant, Carolyn. 1980. *The death of nature: Women, ecology and the scientific revolution*. San Francisco: Harper and Row.

Midgley, Mary. 1983. *Animals and why they matter*. Athens: University of Georgia Press.

Murdoch, Iris. 1970. *The sovereignty of good*. London: Routledge and Kegan Paul.

Naess, Arne. 1973. The shallow and the deep, long-range ecology movement: A summary. *Inquiry* 16: 95-100.

— . 1984. A defense of the deep ecology movement. *Environmental Ethics* 6(3): 265-70.

Noddings, Nell. 1984. *Caring: A feminine approach to ethics and moral education*. Berkeley and Los Angeles: University of California Press.

Regan, Tom. 1983. *The case for animal rights*. Berkeley and Los Angeles: University of California Press.

Ruddick, Sara. 1980. Maternal thinking. *Feminist Studies* 6 (2): 342-67.

Singer, Peter. 1977. *Animal liberation*. New York: Avon Books.

— . 1979. *Practical ethics*. Cambridge: Cambridge University Press.

Walker, Margaret. 1989. Moral understandings: Alternative "epistemology" for a feminist ethics. *Hypatia* 4(2): 15-28.

Warren, Karen. 1990. The power and promise of ecological feminism. *Environmental Ethics* 12(1): 125-46.

THE CONCEPTUAL FOUNDATIONS OF THE LAND ETHIC

J. Baird Callicott

J. Baird Callicott is in the Department of Philosophy and Religious Studies at the University of North Texas. He is the author of In Defense of the Land Ethic: Essays in Environmental Philosophy *(1989) and* Beyond the Land Ethic: More Essays in Environmental Philosophy *(1999), co-author with Michael Nelson of* American Indian Environmental Philosophy: An Ojibwa Case Study *(2004), and co-editor with Clare Palmer of the five-volume* Environmental Philosophy: Critical Concepts in the Environment *(2004).*

Callicott defends the often maligned and misunderstood land ethic by explaining the conceptual foundations underlying Aldo Leopold's formulation of it in A Sand County Almanac: *"a thing is right when it tends to preserve the integrity, stability, and beauty of the biotic community. It is wrong when it tends otherwise." By depicting the biotic community as an ecological and holistic system of interdependent parts, the land ethic asks moral agents to respond in relation to that whole, a delicately complex, functioning social and organic system. It thereby challenges individualist approaches that defend a right to life for individual members, whether for humans only or for non-human animals to which equal consideration or inherent value is extended. Because protecting and preserving individual members can have devastating ecological consequences, the land ethic would seem to demand removal or destruction of that which threatens the integrity of the biotic community, including human beings. Callicott rejects these inhumane and antihumanitarian implications. The land ethic, he argues, neither replaces nor overrides moral sensibilities and obligations that human beings have to their families, neighborhoods, communities, nations, and the global context as a whole. This means that respect for human rights and for principles of individual moral worth and dignity are part of what it means to be a member that both shapes and is shaped by the biotic community.*

The two great cultural advances of the past century were the Darwinian theory and the development of geology. ... Just as important, however, as the origin of plants, animals, and soil is the question of how they operate as a community. That task has fallen to the new science of ecology, which is daily uncovering a web of interdependencies so intricate as to amaze — were he here — even Darwin himself, who, of all men, should have least cause to tremble before the veil. (Aldo Leopold, fragment 6B16, no. 36, Leopold Papers, University of Wisconsin-Madison Archives)

I

As Wallace Stegner observes, *A Sand County Almanac* is considered "almost a holy book in conservation circles," and Aldo Leopold a prophet, "an American Isaiah." And as Curt Meine points out, "The Land Ethic" is the climactic essay of *Sand County*, "the upshot of 'The Upshot.'"[1] One might, therefore, fairly say that the recommendation and justification of moral obligations on the part of people to nature is what the prophetic *A Sand County Almanac* is all about.

But, with few exceptions, "The Land Ethic" has not been favorably received by contemporary academic philosophers. Most have ignored it. Of those who have not, most have been either nonplussed or hostile. Distinguished Australian philosopher John Passmore dismissed it out of hand, in the first book-length academic discussion of the new philosophical subdiscipline called "environmental ethics."[2] In a more recent and more deliberate discussion, the equally distinguished Australian philosopher H.J. McCloskey patronized Aldo Leopold and saddled "The Land Ethic" with various far-fetched "interpretations." He concludes that "there is a real problem in attributing a coherent meaning to Leopold's statements, one that exhibits his land ethic as representing a major advance in ethics rather than a retrogression to a morality of a kind held by various primitive peoples."[3] Echoing McCloskey, English philosopher Robin Attfield went out of his way to impugn the philosophical respectability of "The Land Ethic." And Canadian philosopher L.W. Sumner has called it "dangerous nonsense."[4] Among those philosophers more favorably disposed, "The Land Ethic" has usually been simply quoted, as if it were little more than a noble, but naive, moral plea, altogether lacking a supporting theoretical framework — i.e., foundational principles and premises which lead, by compelling argument, to ethical precepts.

The professional neglect, confusion, and (in some cases) contempt for "The Land Ethic" may, in my judgment, be attributed to three things: (1) Leopold's extremely condensed prose style in which an entire conceptual complex may be conveyed in a few sentences, of even in a phrase or two; (2) his departure from the assumptions and paradigms of contemporary philosophical ethics; and (3) the unsettling practical implications to which a land ethic appears to lead. "The Land Ethic," in short, is, from a philosophical point of view, abbreviated, unfamiliar, and radical.

Here I first examine and elaborate the compactly expressed abstract elements of the land ethic and expose the "logic" which binds them into a proper, but revolutionary, moral theory. I then discuss the controversial features of the land ethic and defend them against actual and potential criticism. I hope to show that the land ethic cannot be ignored as merely the groundless emotive exhortations of a moonstruck conservationist or dismissed as entailing wildly untoward practical consequences. It poses, rather, a serious intellectual challenge to business-as-usual moral philosophy.

II

"The Land Ethic" opens with a charming and poetic evocation of Homer's Greece, the point of which is to suggest that today land is just as routinely and remorsely enslaved as human beings then were. A panoramic glance backward to our most distant cultural origins, Leopold suggests, reveals a slow but steady moral development over three millennia. More of our relationships and activities ("fields of conduct") have fallen under the aegis of moral principles ("ethical criteria") as civilization has grown and matured. If moral growth, and development continue, as not only a synoptic review of history, but recent past experience suggest that it will, future generations will censure today's casual and universal environmental bondage as today we censure the casual and universal human bondage of three thousand years ago.

A cynically inclined critic might scoff at Leopold's sanguine portrayal of human history. Slavery survived as an institution in the "civilized" West, more particularly in the morally self-congratulatory United States, until a mere generation before Leopold's own birth. And Western history from imperial Athens and Rome to the Spanish Inquisition and the Third Reich has been a disgraceful series of wars, persecutions, tyrannies, pogroms, and other atrocities.

The history of moral practice, however, is not identical with the history of moral consciousness. Morality is not descriptive; it is prescriptive or normative. In light of this distinction, it is clear that today, despite rising rates of violent crime in the United States and institutional abuses of human rights in Iran, Chile, Ethiopia, Guatemala,

South Africa, and many other places, and despite persistent organized social injustice and oppression in still others, moral consciousness is expanding more rapidly now than ever before. Civil rights, human rights, women's liberation, children's liberation, animal liberation, etc., all indicate, as expressions of newly emergent moral ideals, that ethical consciousness (as distinct from practice) has if anything recently accelerated — thus confirming Leopold's historical observation.

III

Leopold next points out that "this extension of ethics, so far studied only by philosophers" — and therefore, the implication is clear, not very satisfactorily studied — "is actually a process in ecological evolution" (202). What Leopold is saying here, simply, is that we may understand the history of ethics, fancifully alluded to by means of the Odysseus vignette, in biological as well as philosophical terms. From a biological point of view, an ethic is "a limitation on freedom of action in the struggle for existence" (202).

I had this passage in mind when I remarked that Leopold manages to convey a whole network of ideas in a couple of phrases. The phrase "struggle for existence" unmistakably calls to mind Darwinian evolution as the conceptual context in which a biological account of the origin and development of ethics must ultimately be located. And at once it points up a paradox: Given the unremitting competitive "struggle for existence" how could "limitations on freedom of action" ever have been conserved and spread through a population of *Homo sapiens* or their evolutionary progenitors?

For a biological account of ethics, as Harvard social entomologist Edward O. Wilson has recently written, "the central theoretical problem ... [is] how can altruism [elaborately articulated as morality or ethics in the human species], which by definition reduces personal fitness, possibly evolve by natural selection?"[5] According to modern sociobiology, the answer lies in kinship. But according to Darwin — who had tackled this problem himself "exclusively from the side of natural history" in *The Descent of Man* — the answer lies in society.[6] And it was Darwin's classical account (and its divers variations), from the side of natural history, which informed Leopold's thinking in the late 1940s. ...

Darwin ... turned to a minority tradition of modern philosophy for a moral psychology consistent with and useful to a general evolutionary account of ethical phenomena. A century earlier, Scottish philosophers David Hume and Adam Smith had argued that ethics rest upon feelings or "sentiments" — which, to be sure, may be both amplified and informed by reason.[7] And since in the animal kingdom feelings or sentiments are arguably far more common or widespread than reason, they would be a far more likely starting point for an evolutionary account of the origin and growth of ethics.

Darwin's account, to which Leopold unmistakably (if elliptically) alludes in "The Land Ethic," begins with the parental and filial affections common, perhaps, to all mammals.[8] Bonds of affection and sympathy between parents and offspring permitted the formation of small, closely kin social groups, Darwin argued. Should the parental and filial affections bonding family members chance to extend to less closely related individuals, that would permit an enlargement of the family group. And should the newly extended community more successfully defend itself and/or more efficiently provision itself, the inclusive fitness of its members severally would be increased, Darwin reasoned. Thus, the more diffuse familial affections, which Darwin (echoing Hume and Smith) calls the "social sentiments," would be spread throughout a population.[9]

Morality, properly speaking — i.e., morality as opposed to mere altruistic instinct — requires, in Darwin's terms, "intellectual powers" sufficient to recall the past and imagine the future, "the power of language" sufficient to express "common opinion," and "habituation" to patterns of behavior deemed, by common opinion, to be socially acceptable and beneficial.[10] Even so, ethics proper, in Darwin's account, remains firmly rooted in moral feelings or social sentiments which were — no less than physical faculties, he expressly avers — naturally selected, by the advantages for survival and especially for successful reproduction, afforded by society.[11]

The protosociobiological perspective on ethical phenomena, to which Leopold as a natural historian was heir, leads him to a generalization which is remarkably explicit in his condensed and often merely resonant rendering of Darwin's more deliberate and extended paradigm: Since "the thing [ethics] has its origin in the tendency of interdependent individuals or groups to evolve modes of co-operation, ... all ethics so far evolved rest upon a single premise: that the individual is a member of a community of interdependent parts" (202-3).

Hence, we may expect to find that the scope and specific content of ethics will reflect both the perceived boundaries and actual structure or organization of a cooperative community or society. *Ethics and society or community are correlative.* This single, simple principle constitutes a powerful tool for the analysis of moral natural history, for the anticipation of future moral development (including, ultimately, the land ethic), and for systematically deriving the specific precepts, the prescriptions and proscriptions of an emergent and culturally unprecedented ethic like a land or environmental ethic. ...

IV

Today we are witnessing the painful birth of a human super-community, global in scope. Modern transportation and communication technologies, international economic interdependencies, international economic entities, and nuclear arms have brought into being a "global village." It has not yet become fully formed and it is at tension — a very dangerous tension — with its predecessor, the nation-state. Its eventual institutional structure, a global federalism or whatever it may turn out to be, is, at this point, completely unpredictable. Interestingly, however, a corresponding global human ethic — the "human rights" ethic, as it is popularly called — has been more definitely articulated.

Most educated people today pay lip service at least to the ethical precept that all members of the human species, regardless of race, creed, or national origin, are endowed with certain fundamental rights which it is wrong not to respect. According to the evolutionary scenario set out by Darwin, the contemporary moral ideal of human rights is a response to a perception — however vague and indefinite — that mankind worldwide is united into one society, one community — however indeterminate or yet institutionally unorganized. As Darwin presciently wrote:

As man advances in civilization, and small tribes are united into larger communities, the simplest reason would tell each individual that he ought to extend his social instincts and sympathies to all the members of the same nation, though personally unknown to him. This point being once reached, there is only an artificial barrier to prevent his sympathies extending to the men of all nations and races. If, indeed, such men are separated from him by great differences of appearance or habits, experience unfortunately shows us how long it is, before we look at them as our fellow-creatures.[12]

According to Leopold, the next step in this sequence beyond the still incomplete ethic of universal humanity, a step that is clearly discernible on the horizon, is the land ethic. The "community concept" has, so far, propelled the development of ethics from the savage clan to the family of man. "The land ethic simply enlarges the boundary of the community to include soils, waters, plants, and animals, or collectively: the land" (204).

As the foreword to *Sand County* makes plain, the overarching thematic principle of the book is the inculcation of the idea — through narrative description, discursive exposition, abstractive generalization, and occasional preachment — "that land is a community" (viii). The community concept is "the basic concept of ecology" (viii). Once land is popularly perceived as a biotic community — as it is professionally perceived in ecology — a correlative land ethic will emerge in the collective cultural consciousness.

V

Although anticipated as far back as the mid-eighteenth century — in the notion of an "economy of nature" — the concept of the biotic community was more fully and deliberately developed as a working model or paradigm for ecology by Charles Elton in the 1920s.[13] The natural world is organized as an intricate corporate society in which plants and animals occupy "niches," or as Elton alternatively called them, "roles" or "professions," in the economy of nature.[14] As in a feudal community, little or no socio-economic mobility (upward or otherwise) exists in the biotic community. One is born to one's trade.

Human society, Leopold argues, is founded, in large part, upon mutual security and economic interdependency and preserved only by limitations on freedom of action in the struggle for existence — that is, by ethical constraints. Since the biotic community exhibits, as modern ecology reveals, an analogous structure, it too can be preserved, given the newly amplified impact of "mechanized man," only by analogous limitations on freedom of action — that is, by a land ethic (viii). A land ethic, furthermore, is not only "an ecological necessity," but an "evolutionary possibility" because a moral response to the natural environment — Darwin's social sympathies, sentiments, and instincts translated and codified into a body of principles and precepts — would be automatically triggered in human beings by ecology's social representation of nature (203).

Therefore, the key to the emergence of a land ethic is, simply, universal ecological literacy.

VI

The land ethic rests upon three scientific cornerstones: (1) evolutionary and (2) ecological biology set in a background of (3) Copernican astronomy. Evolutionary theory provides the con-

ceptual link between ethics and social organization and development. It provides a sense of "kinship with fellow-creatures" as well, "fellow-voyagers" with us in the "odyssey of evolution" (109). It establishes a diachronic link between people and non-human nature.

Ecological theory provides a synchronic link — the community concept — a sense of social integration of human and nonhuman nature. Human beings, plants, animals, soils, and waters are "all interlocked in one humming community of cooperations and competitions, one biota."[15] The simplest reason, to paraphrase Darwin, should, therefore, tell each individual that he or she ought to extend his or her social instincts and sympathies to all the members of the biotic community though different from him or her in appearance or habits.

And although Leopold never directly mentions it in *A Sand County Almanac*, the Copernican perspective, the perception of the Earth as "a small planet" in an immense and utterly hostile universe beyond, contributes, perhaps subconsciously, but nevertheless very powerfully, to our sense of kinship, community, and interdependence with fellow denizens of the Earth household. It scales the Earth down to something like a cozy island paradise in a desert ocean.

Here in outline, then, are the conceptual and logical foundations of the land ethic: Its conceptual elements are a Copernican cosmology, a Darwinian protosociobiological natural history of ethics, Darwinian ties of kinship among all forms of life on Earth, and an Eltonian model of the structure of biocenoses all overlaid on a Humean-Smithian moral psychology. Its logic is that natural selection has endowed human beings with an affective moral response to perceived bonds of kinship and community membership and identity; that today the natural environment, the land, is represented as a community, the biotic community; and that, therefore, an environmental or land ethic is both possible — the biopsychological and cognitive conditions are in place — and necessary, since human beings collectively have acquired the power to destroy the integrity, diversity, and stability of the environing and supporting economy of nature. In the remainder of this essay I discuss special features and problems of the land ethic germane to moral philosophy.

VII

The most salient feature of Leopold's land ethic is its provision of what Kenneth Goodpaster has carefully called "moral considerability" for the biotic community per se, not just for fellow members of the biotic community:[16]

> In short, a land ethic changes the role of *Homo sapiens* from conqueror of the land-community to plain member and citizen of it. It implies respect for his fellow-members, *and also respect for the community as such.* (204, emphasis added)

The land ethic, thus, has a holistic as well as an individualistic cast.

Indeed, as "The Land Ethic" develops, the focus of moral concern shifts gradually away from plants, animals, soils, and waters severally to the biotic community collectively. Toward the middle, in the subsection called Substitutes for a Land Ethic, Leopold invokes the "biotic rights" of *species* — as the context indicates — of wildflowers, songbirds, and predators. In The Outlook, the climactic section of "The Land Ethic," nonhuman natural entities, first appearing as fellow members, then considered in profile as species, are not so much as mentioned in what might be called the "summary moral maxim" of the land ethic: "A thing is right when it tends to preserve the integrity, stability, and beauty of the biotic community. It is wrong when it tends otherwise" (224-25).

By this measure of right and wrong, not only would it be wrong for a farmer, in the interest of higher profits, to clear the woods off a 75 percent slope, turn his cows into the clearing, and dump its rainfall, rocks, and soil into the community creek, it would also be wrong for the federal fish and wildlife agency, in the interest of individual animal welfare, to permit populations of deer,

rabbits, feral burros, or whatever to increase unchecked and thus to threaten the integrity, stability, and beauty of the biotic communities of which they are members. The land ethic not only provides moral considerability for the biotic community per se, but ethical consideration of its individual members is preempted by concern for the preservation of the integrity, stability, and beauty of the biotic community. The land ethic, thus, not only has a holistic aspect; it is holistic with a vengeance.

The holism of the land ethic, more than any other feature, sets it apart from the predominant paradigm of modern moral philosophy. It is, therefore, the feature of the land ethic which requires the most patient theoretical analysis and the most sensitive practical interpretation.

VIII

As Kenneth Goodpaster pointed out, mainstream modern ethical philosophy has taken egoism as its point of departure and reached a wider circle of moral entitlement by a process of generalization:[17] I am sure that *I*, the enveloped ego, am intrinsically or inherently valuable and thus that *my* interests ought to be considered, taken into account, by "others" when their actions may substantively affect *me*. My own claim to moral consideration, according to the conventional wisdom, ultimately rests upon a psychological capacity — rationality or sentiency were the classical candidates of Kant and Bentham, respectively — which is arguably valuable in itself and which thus qualifies *me* for moral standing.[18] However, then I am forced grudgingly to grant the same moral consideration I demand from others, on this basis, to those others who can also claim to possess the same general psychological characteristic.

A *criterion* of moral value and consideration is thus identified. Goodpaster convincingly argues that mainstream modern moral theory is based, when all the learned dust has settled, on this simple paradigm of ethical justification and logic exemplified by the Benthamic and Kantian prototypes.[19] If the criterion of moral values and consideration is pitched low enough — as it is in Bentham's criterion of sentiency — a wide variety of animals are admitted to moral entitlement.[20] If the criterion of moral value and consideration is pushed lower still — as it is in Albert Schweitzer's reverence-for-life ethic — all minimally conative things (plants as well as animals) would be extended moral considerability.[21] The contemporary animal liberation/rights, and reverence-for-life/life-principle ethics are, at bottom, simply direct applications, of the modern classical paradigm of moral argument. But this standard modern model of ethical theory provides no possibility whatever for the moral consideration of wholes — of threatened *populations* of animals and plants, or of endemic, rare, or endangered *species*, or of biotic *communities*, or most expansively, of the *biosphere* in its totality — since wholes per se have no psychological experience of any kind.[22] Because mainstream modern moral theory has been "psychocentric," it has been radically and intractably individualistic or "atomistic" in its fundamental theoretical orientation.

Hume, Smith, and Darwin diverged from the prevailing theoretical model by recognizing that altruism is as fundamental and autochthonous in human nature as is egoism. According to their analysis, moral value is not identified with a natural quality objectively present in morally considerable beings — as reason and/or sentiency is objectively present in people and/or animals — it is, as it were, projected by valuing subjects.[23]

Hume and Darwin, furthermore, recognize inborn moral sentiments which have society as such as their natural object. Hume insists that "we must renounce the theory which accounts for every moral sentiment by the principle of self-love. We must adopt a more *public affection* and allow that the *interests of society* are not, *even on their own account*, entirely indifferent to us."[24] And Darwin, somewhat ironically (since "Darwinian evolution" very often means natural selection operating exclusively with respect to individuals), sometimes writes as if morality had no other object than the commonweal, the welfare of the community as a corporate entity:

We have now seen that actions are regarded by savages, and were probably so regarded by primeval man, as good or bad, solely as they obviously affect the welfare of the tribe, — not that of the species, nor that of the individual member of the tribe. This conclusion agrees well with the belief that the so-called moral sense is aboriginally derived from social instincts, for both relate at first exclusively to the community.[25]

Theoretically then, the biotic community owns what Leopold, in the lead paragraph of The Outlook, calls "value in the philosophical sense" — i.e., direct moral considerability — because it is a newly discovered proper object of a specially evolved "public affection" or "moral sense" which all psychologically normal human beings have inherited from a long line of ancestral social primates (223).[26] ...

IX

Ecological thought, historically, has tended to be holistic in outlook.[27] Ecology is the study of the *relationships* of organisms to one another and to the elemental environment. These relationships bind the *relata* — plants, animals, soils, and waters — into a seamless fabric. The ontological primacy of objects and the ontological subordination of relationships, characteristic of classical Western science, is, in fact, reversed in ecology.[28] Ecological relationships determine the nature of organisms rather than the other way around. A species is what it is because it has adapted to a niche in the ecosystem. The whole, the system itself, thus, literally and quite straightforwardly shapes and forms its component parts. ...

X

The living channels — "food chains" — through which energy courses are composed of individual plants and animals. A central, stark fact lies at the heart of ecological processes: Energy, the currency of the economy nature, passes from one organism to another, not from hand to hand, like coined money, but, so to speak, from stomach to stomach. Eating *and being eaten*, living *and dying* are what make the biotic community hum.

The precepts of the land ethic, like those of all previous accretions, reflect and reinforce the structure of the community to which it is correlative. Trophic asymmetries constitute the kernel of the biotic community. It seems unjust, unfair. But that is how the economy of nature is organized (and has been for thousands of millions of years). The land ethic, thus, affirms as good, and strives to preserve, the very inequities in nature whose social counterparts in human communities are condemned as bad and would be eradicated by familiar social ethics, especially by the more recent Christian and secular egalitarian exemplars. A "right to life" for individual members is not consistent with the structure of the biotic community and hence is not mandated by the land ethic. This disparity between the land ethic and its more familiar social precedents contributes to the apparent devaluation of individual *members* of the biotic community and augments and reinforces the tendency of the land ethic, driven by the systemic vision of ecology, toward a more holistic or community-per-se orientation.

Of the few moral philosophers who have given the land ethic a moment's serious thought, most have regarded it with horror because of its emphasis on the good of the community and its deemphasis on the welfare of individual members of the community. Not only are other sentient creatures members of the biotic community and subordinate to its integrity, beauty, and stability; so are *we*. Thus, if it is not only morally permissible, from the point of view of the land ethic, but morally required, that members of certain species be abandoned to predation and other vicissitudes of wild life or even deliberately culled (as in the case of alert and sentient white-tail deer) for the sake of the integrity, stability, and beauty of the biotic community, how can we consistently exempt ourselves from a similar draconian regime? We too are only "plain members and citizens" of the biotic community. And our global population is growing unchecked. Accord-

ing to William Aiken, from the point of view of the land ethic, therefore, "massive human diebacks would be good. It is our duty to cause them. It is our species' duty, relative to the whole, to eliminate 90 percent of our numbers." Thus, according to Tom Regan, the land ethic is a clear case of "environmental fascism."[29]

Of course Leopold never intended the land ethic to have either inhumane or antihumanitarian implications or consequences. But whether he intended them or not, a logically consistent deduction from the theoretical premises of the land ethic might force such untoward conclusions. And given their magnitude and monstrosity, these derivations would constitute a *reductio ad absurdum* of the whole land ethic enterprise and entrench and reinforce our current human chauvinism and moral alienation from nature. If this is what membership in the biotic community entails, then all but the most radical misanthropes would surely want to opt out.

XI

The land ethic, happily, implies neither inhumane nor inhuman consequences. That some philosophers think it must follows more from their own theoretical presuppositions than from the theoretical elements of the land ethic itself. Conventional modern ethical theory rests moral entitlement, as I earlier pointed out, on a criterion or qualification. If a candidate meets the criterion — rationality or sentiency are the most commonly posited — he, she, or it is entitled to equal moral standing with others who possess the same qualification in equal degree. Hence, reasoning in this philosophically orthodox way, and forcing Leopold's theory to conform: if human beings are, with other animals, plants, soils, and waters, equally members of the biotic community, and if community membership is the criterion of equal moral consideration, then not only do animals, plants, soils, and waters have equal (highly attenuated) "rights," but human beings are equally subject to the same subordination of individual welfare and rights in respect to the good of the community as a whole.

But the land ethic, as I have been at pains to point out, is heir to a line of moral analysis different from that institutionalized in contemporary moral philosophy. From the biosocial evolutionary analysis of ethics upon which Leopold builds the land ethic, it (the land ethic) neither replaces nor overrides previous accretions. Prior moral sensibilities and obligations attendant upon and correlative to prior strata of social involvement remain operative and preemptive.

Being citizens of the United States, or the United Kingdom, or the Soviet Union, or Venezuela, or some other nation-state, and therefore having national obligations and patriotic duties, does not mean that we are not also members of smaller communities or social groups — cities or townships, neighborhoods, and families — or that we are relieved of the peculiar moral responsibilities attendant upon and correlative to these memberships as well. Similarly, our recognition of the biotic community and our immersion in it does not imply that we do not also remain members of the human community — the "family of man" or "global village" — or that we are relieved of the attendant and correlative moral responsibilities of that membership, among them to respect universal human rights and uphold the principles of individual human worth and dignity. The biosocial development of morality does not grow in extent like an expanding balloon, leaving no trace of its previous boundaries, so much as like the circumference of a tree.[30] Each emergent, and larger, social unit is layered over the more primitive, and intimate, ones.

Moreover, as a general rule, the duties correlative to the inner social circles to which we belong eclipse those correlative to the rings farther from the heartwood when conflicts arise. Consider our moral revulsion when zealous ideological nationalists encourage children to turn their parents in to the authorities if their parents should dissent from the political or economic doctrines of the ruling party. A zealous environmentalist who advocated visiting war, famine, or pestilence on human populations (those existing somewhere else, of course) in the name of the integrity, beauty, and stability of the biotic community would be similarly perverse. Family obligations in general come before nationalistic duties and humanitarian obligations in general come before environmental duties. The land ethic, therefore, is not draconian or fascist. It does not cancel human morality. The land ethic may, however, as with any new accretion, demand choices which affect, in turn, the demands of the more interior social-ethical circles. Taxes and the military draft may conflict with family-level obligations. While the land ethic, certainly, does not cancel human morality, neither does it leave it unaffected.

Nor is the land ethic inhumane. Nonhuman fellow members of the biotic community have no "human rights," because they are not, by definition, members of the human community. As fellow members of the biotic community, however, they deserve respect.

How exactly to express or manifest respect, while at the same time abandoning our fellow members of the biotic community to their several fates or even actively consuming them for our own needs (and wants), or deliberately making them casualties of wildlife management for ecological integrity, is a difficult and delicate question.

Fortunately, American Indian and other traditional patterns of human-nature interaction provide rich and detailed models. Algonkian woodland peoples, for instance, represented animals, plants, birds, waters, and minerals as other-than-human persons engaged in reciprocal, mutually beneficial socioeconomic intercourse with human beings.[31] Tokens of payment, together with expressions of apology, were routinely offered to the beings whom it was necessary for these Indians to exploit. Care not to waste the usable parts, and care in the disposal of unusable animal and plant remains, were also an aspect of the respectful albeit necessarily consumptive, Algonkian relationship with fellow members of the land community. As I have more fully argued elsewhere, the Algonkian portrayal of human-nature relationships is, indeed, although certainly different in specifics, identical in abstract form to that recommended by Leopold in the land ethic.[32] …

XII

As a culture evolves toward civilization, it increasingly distances itself from the biotic community. "*Civili*zation" means "citification" — inhabitation of and participation in an artificial, humanized environment and a corresponding perception of isolation and alienation from nature. Nonhuman natural entities, thus, are divested of their status as members in good standing of the moral community as civilization develops. Today, two processes internal to civilization are bringing us to a recognition that our renunciation of our biotic citizenship was a mistaken self-deception. Evolutionary science and ecological science, which certainly are products of modern civilization now supplanting the anthropomorphic and anthropocentric myths of earlier civilized generations, have rediscovered our integration with the biotic community. And the negative feedback received from modern civilization's technological impact upon nature — pollution, biological impoverishment, etc. — forcefully reminds us that mankind never really has, despite past assumptions to the contrary, existed apart from the environing biotic community.

XIII

This reminder of our recent rediscovery of our biotic citizenship brings us face to face with the paradox posed by Peter Fritzell:[33] Either we are plain members and citizens of the biotic community, on a par with other creatures, or we are not. If we are, then we have no moral obligations to our fellow members or to the community per se because, as understood from a modern scientific perspective, nature and natural phenomena are amoral. Wolves and alligators do no wrong in killing and eating deer and dogs (respectively). Elephants cannot be blamed for bulldozing acacia trees and generally wreaking havoc in their natural habitats. If human beings are natural beings, then human behavior, however destructive, is natural behavior and is as blameless, from a natural point of view, as any other behavioral

phenomenon exhibited by other natural beings. On the other hand, we are moral beings, the implication seems clear, precisely to the extent that we are civilized, that we have removed ourselves from nature. We are more than natural beings; we are metanatural — not to say, "supernatural" — beings. But then our moral community is limited to only those beings who share our transcendence of nature, i.e., to human beings (and perhaps to pets who have joined our civilized community as surrogate persons) and to the human community. Hence, have it either way — we are members of the biotic community or we are not — a land or environmental ethic is aborted by either choice.

But nature is *not* amoral. The tacit assumption that we are deliberating, choice-making ethical beings only to the extent that we are metanatural, civilized beings, generates this dilemma. The biosocial analysis of human moral behavior, in which the land ethic is grounded, is designed precisely to show that in fact intelligent moral behavior *is* natural behavior. Hence, we are moral beings not in spite of, but in accordance with, nature. To the extent that nature has produced at least one ethical species, *Homo sapiens*, nature is not amoral.

Alligators, wolves, and elephants are not subject to reciprocal interspecies duties or land ethical obligations themselves because they are incapable of conceiving and/or assuming them. Alligators, as mostly solitary, entrepreneurial reptiles, have no apparent moral sentiments or social instincts whatever. And while wolves and elephants certainly do have social instincts and at least protomoral sentiments, as their social behavior amply indicates, their conception or imagination of community appears to be less culturally plastic than ours and less amenable to cognitive information. Thus, while we might regard them as ethical beings, they are not able, as we are, to form the concept of a universal biotic community, and hence conceive an all-inclusive, holistic land ethic.

The paradox of the land ethic, elaborately noticed by Fritzell, may be cast more generally still in more conventional philosophical terms: Is the land ethic prudential or deontological? Is the land ethic, in other words, a matter of enlightened (collective, human) self-interest, or does it genuinely admit nonhuman natural entities and nature as a whole to true moral standing?

The conceptual foundations of the land ethic, as I have here set them out, and much of Leopold's hortatory rhetoric, would certainly indicate that the land ethic is deontological (or duty oriented) rather than prudential. In the section significantly titled The Ecological Conscience, Leopold complains that the then-current conservation philosophy is inadequate because "it defines no right or wrong, assigns no obligation, calls for no sacrifice, implies no change in the current philosophy of values. In respect of land-use, it urges *only* enlightened self-interest" (207-8, emphasis added). Clearly, Leopold himself thinks that the land ethic goes beyond prudence. In this section he disparages mere "self-interest" two more times, and concludes that "obligations have no meaning without conscience, and the problem we face is the extension of the social conscience from people to land" (209).

In the next section, Substitutes for a Land Ethic, he mentions rights twice — the "biotic right" of birds to continuance and the absence of a right on the part of human special interest to exterminate predators.

Finally, the first sentences of The Outlook read: "It is inconceivable to me that an ethical relation to land can exist without love, respect, and admiration for land, and a high regard for its value. By value, I of course mean something far broader than mere economic value; I mean value in the philosophical sense" (223). By "value in the philosophical sense," Leopold can only mean what philosophers more technically call "intrinsic value" or "inherent worth."[34] Something that has intrinsic value or inherent worth is valuable in and of itself, not because of what it can do for us. "Obligation," "sacrifice," "conscience," "respect," the ascription of rights, and intrinsic value — all of these are consistently opposed to self-interest and seem to indicate decisively that the land ethic is of the deontological type. ...

XIV

From an objective, descriptive sociobiological point of view, ethics evolve because they contribute to the inclusive fitness of their carriers (or, more reductively still, to the multiplication of their carriers' genes); they are expedient. However, the path to self-interest (or to the self-interest of the selfish gene) is not discernible to the participating individuals (nor, certainly, to their genes). Hence, ethics are grounded in instinctive feeling — love, sympathy, respect — not in self-conscious calculating intelligence. Somewhat like the paradox of hedonism — the notion that one cannot achieve happiness if one directly pursues happiness per se and not other things — one can only secure self-interest by putting the interests of others on a par with one's own (in this case long-range collective human self-interest and the interest of other forms of life and of the biotic community per se).

So, is the land ethic deontological or prudential, after all? It is both — self-consistently both — depending upon point of view. From the inside, from the lived, felt point of view of the community member with evolved moral sensibilities, it is deontological. It involves an affective-cognitive posture of genuine love, respect, admiration, obligation, self-sacrifice, conscience, duty, and the ascription of intrinsic value and biotic rights. From the outside, from the objective and analytic scientific point of view, it is prudential. "There is no other way for land to survive the impact of mechanized man," nor, therefore, for mechanized man to survive his own impact upon the land (viii).

NOTES

1. Wallace Stegner, "The Legacy of Aldo Leopold"; Curt Meine, "Building 'The Land Ethic'"[in *Companion to* A Sand County Almanac: *Interpretive & Critical Essays* (Madison: University of Wisconsin Press, 1987)]. The oft-repeated characterization of Leopold as a prophet appears traceable to Roberts Mann, "Aldo Leopold: Priest and Prophet," *American Forests* 60, no. 8 (August

1954): 23, 42-43; it was picked up, apparently, by Ernest Swift, "Aldo Leopold: Wisconsin's Conservationist Prophet," *Wisconsin Tales* and Trails 2, no. 2 (September 1961): 2-5; Roderick Nash institutionalized it in his chapter, "Aldo Leopold: Prophet," in *Wilderness and the American Mind* (New Haven: Yale University Press, 1967; revised edition, 1982).

2. John Passmore, *Man's Responsibility for* [significantly not *"to"*] *Nature: Ecological Problems and Western Traditions* (New York: Charles Scribner's Sons, 1974).

3. H.J. McCloskey, *Ecological Ethics and Politics* (Totowa, N.J.: Rowman and Littlefield, 1983), 56.

4. Robin Attfield, in "Value in the Wilderness," *Metaphilosophy* 15 (1984), writes, "Leopold the philosopher is something of a disaster, and I dread the thought of the student whose concept of philosophy is modeled principally on these extracts. (Can value 'in the philosophical sense be contrasted with instrumental value? If concepts of right and wrong did not apply to slaves in Homeric Greece, how could Odysseus suspect the slavegirls of 'misbehavior'? If all ethics rest on interdependence how are obligations to infants and small children possible? And how can 'obligations have no meaning without conscience,' granted that the notion of conscience is conceptually dependent on that of obligation?)" L.W. Sumner, "Review of Robin Attfield, *The Ethics of Environmental Concern*," *Environmental Ethics* 8 (1986): 77.

5. Edward O. Wilson, *Sociobiology: The New Synthesis* (Cambridge: Harvard University Press, 1975), 3. See also W.D. Hamilton, "The Genetical Theory of Social Behavior," *Journal of Theoretical* Biology 7 (1964): 1-52.

6. Charles R. Darwin, *The Descent of Man and Selection in Relation to Sex* (New York: J.A. Hill and Company, 1904). The quoted phrase occurs on p. 97.

7. See Adam Smith, *Theory of the Moral Sentiments* (London and Edinburgh: A Millar, A. Kinkaid, and J. Bell, 1759) and David Hume, *An Enquiry Concerning the Principles of Morals* (Oxford: The Clarendon Press, 1777; first published in

1751). Darwin cites both works in the key fourth chapter of *Descent* (pp. 106 and 109, respectively).

8. Darwin, *Descent*, 98ff.

9. Ibid., 105f.

10. Ibid., 113ff.

11. Ibid., 105.

12. Ibid., 124.

13. See Donald Worster, *Nature's Economy: The Roots of Ecology* (San Francisco: Sierra Club Books, 1977).

14. Charles Elton, *Animal Ecology* (New York: Macmillan, 1927).

15. Aldo Leopold, *Round River* (New York: Oxford University Press, 1953), 148.

16. Kenneth Goodpaster, "On Being Morally Considerable," *Journal of Philosophy* 22 (1978): 308-25. Goodpaster wisely avoids the term *rights*, defined so strictly albeit so variously by philosophers, and used so loosely by nonphilosophers.

17. Kenneth Goodpaster, "From Egoism to Environmentalism" in *Ethics and Problems of the 21st Century*, ed. K.E. Goodpaster and K.M. Sayre (Notre Dame, Ind.: University of Notre Dame Press, 1979), 21-35.

18. See Immanuel Kant, *Foundations of the Metaphysics of Morals* (New York: Bobbs-Merrill, 1959; first published in 1785); and Jeremy Bentham, *An Introduction to the Principles of Morals and Legislation*, new edition (Oxford: The Clarendon Press, 1823).

19. Goodpaster, "Egoism to Environmentalism." Actually Goodpaster regards Hume and Kant as the cofountainheads of this sort of moral philosophy. But Hume does not reason in this way. For Hume, the other-oriented sentiments are as primitive as self-love.

20. See Peter Singer, *Animal Liberation: A New Ethics for Our Treatment of Animals* (New York: Avon Books, 1975) for animal liberation; and see Tom Regan, *All That Dwell Therein: Animal Rights and Environmental Ethics* (Berkeley: University of California Press, 1982) for animal rights.

21. See Albert Schweitzer, *Philosophy of Civilization: Civilization and Ethics*, trans. John Naish

(London: A. & C. Black, 1923). For a fuller discussion see J. Baird Callicott, "On the Intrinsic Value of Non-human Species," in *The Preservation of Species*, ed. Bryan Norton (Princeton: Princeton University Press, 1986), 138-72.

22. Peter Singer and Tom Regan are both proud of this circumstance and consider it a virtue. See Peter Singer, "Not for Humans Only: The Place of Nonhumans in Environmental Issues" in *Ethics and Problems of the 21st Century*, 191-206; and Tom Regan, "Ethical Vegetarianism and Commercial Animal Farming" in *Contemporary Moral Problems*, ed. James E. White (St. Paul, Minn.: West Publishing Co., 1985), 279-94.

23. See J. Baird Callicott, "Hume's Is/Ought Dichotomy and the Relation of Ecology to Leopold's Land Ethic," *Environmental Ethics 4* (1982): 163-74, and "Non-anthropocentric Value Theory and Environmental Ethics," *American Philosophical Quarterly 21* (1984): 299-309, for an elaboration.

24. Hume, *Enquiry*, 219.

25. Darwin, *Descent*, 120.

26. I have elsewhere argued that "value in the philosophical sense" means "intrinsic" or "inherent" value. See J. Baird Callicott, "The Philosophical Value of Wildlife," in *Valuing Wildlife: Economic and Social Values of Wildlife*, ed. Daniel J. Decker and Gary Goff (Boulder, Col.: Westview Press, 1986), 214-221.

27. See Worster, *Nature's Economy*.

28. See J. Baird Callicott, "The Metaphysical Implications of Ecology," *Environmental Ethics 8* (1986): 300-315, for an elaboration of this point.

29. William Aiken, "Ethical Issues in Agriculture," in *Earthbound: New Introductory Essays in Environmental Ethics*, ed. Tom Regan (New York: Random House, 1984), 269. Tom Regan, *The Case for Animal Rights* (Berkeley: University of California Press, 1983) 262, and "Ethical Vegetarianism," 291. See also Eliott Sober, "Philosophical Problems for Environmentalism," in Norton, *Preservation of Species*, 173-94.

30. I owe the tree-ring analogy to Richard and Val Routley (now Sylvan and Plumwood, respectively), "Human Chauvinism and Environmental Ethics," in *Environmental Philosophy*, ed. D. Mannison, M. McRobbie, and R. Routley (Canberra: Department of Philosophy, Research School of the Social Sciences, Australian National University, 1980), 96-189. A good illustration of the balloon analogy may be found in Peter Singer, *The Expanding Circle: Ethics and Sociobiology* (New York: Farrar, Straus and Giroux, 1983).

31. For an elaboration see Thomas W. Overholt and J. Baird Callicott, *Clothed-in-Fur and Other Tales: An Introduction to an Ojibwa World View* (Washington, D.C.: University Press of America, 1982).

32. J. Baird Callicott, "Traditional American Indian and Western European Attitudes Toward Nature: An Overview," *Environmental Ethics 4* (1982): 163-74.

33. Peter Fritzell, "The Conflicts of Ecological Conscience," [in *Companion to* A Sand County Almanac: *Interpretive & Critical Essays* (Madison: University of Wisconsin Press, 1987)].

34. See Worster, *Nature's Economy*.

STUDY QUESTIONS

1 What does Peter Singer mean when he says: "The principle of the equality of human beings is not a description of an alleged actual equality among humans: it is a prescription of how we should treat human beings"? How does Singer use this understanding of equality to argue that "all animals are equal"?

2 What arguments does Singer mount in favor of vegetarianism? Do these arguments call for an absolute prohibition on killing animals?

3 Why does Tom Regan object to Singer's approach of questioning our treatment of animals? Do you find his arguments against utilitarianism convincing?

4 Why does Regan object to the social contract theory approach to animals? According to Regan, what is it that gives value to entities? What entities should then be accorded rights? Is the criteria used by Regan too broad or too narrow? Defend your answers.

5 Is Regan's argument for the total abolition of factory farming, hunting, and animal research convincing? Why or why not?

6 Why does Nathan Nobis find Singer's argument in favor of vegetarianism inadequate and unconvincing? Are you persuaded by this critique of utilitarianism? Why or why not?

7 What is it about virtue ethics that Nobis finds of value in developing his argument in favor of vegetarianism or veganism? Why does he think that virtue ethics needs to be combined with insights from utilitarianism? Do you find his arguments convincing? Why or why not?

8 Are the arguments that Nobis uses in favor of vegetarianism sufficiently strong to support veganism over vegetarianism? Defend your answer.

9 According to Deborah Slicer, what characteristics are shared by the "Singer-Regan approach" and why is she critical of this approach to our treatment of animals? What objections does she raise against a deep ecology approach?

10 Why does Slicer hold that our treatment of animals is a feminist issue? What is ecofeminism and how does it challenge traditional approaches to animal rights?

11 What answers to the question of your daughter or your dog can be given by an ecofeminist approach? Is this approach instructive? Why or why not? What sorts of policies on animal research might emerge from this approach?

12 What similarities, if any, are there between Nobis's promotion of virtue ethics and Slicer's defense of a contextual and relational approach? Are there differences as well? Defend your answer.

13 According to J. Baird Callicott, what are the features of and problems with the kind of moral theory that Singer and Regan use to extend moral consideration to non-human animals? Outline features of the contrasting moral psychology approach that Callicott favors and from which he borrows insights.

14 Summarize the main features of Aldo Leopold's the "land ethic" as described and defended by Callicott. Why does Callicott claim that it represents a shift in the way the environment and our treatment of it is conceived? How does he defend his claim that the land ethic need not have inhumane or antihumanitarian principles?

15 On a survey of the arguments in this chapter regarding our treatment of animals, which account do you find more convincing and why? Has one particular argument convinced you to become a vegetarian if you are not already one? Have your views on animal research changed?

SUGGESTED READINGS

Burgess-Jackson, Keith. "Doing Right by Our Animal Companions." *Journal of Ethics*, v. 2 (1998): 57-83.

Cavelieri, Paola. *The Animal Question: Why Nonhuman Animals Deserve Human Rights*. New York, NY: Oxford University Press, 2001.

Cohen, Carl. "The Case for the Use of Animals in Biomedical Research." *New England Journal of Medicine*, v. 315 (1986): 865-70.

Curnutt, Jordan. "A New Argument for Vegetarianism." *Journal of Social Philosophy*, v. 28 (1997): 153-72.

Dixon, Nicholas. "A Utilitarian Argument for Vegetarianism." *Between the Species*, v. 11 (1995): 90-97.

Donovan, Josephine. "Attention to Suffering: A Feminist Caring Ethic for the Treatment of Animals." *Journal of Social Philosophy*, v. 27, no. 1 (1996): 81-102.

Fox, Michael. *Deep Vegetarianism*. Philadelphia, PA: Temple University Press, 1999.

Frey, R.G. *Interests and Rights: The Case Against Animals*. Oxford: Oxford University Press, 1980.

Garner, Robert. "Animal Rights, Political Theory and the Liberal Tradition." *Contemporary Politics*, v. 8, no. 1 (2002): 7-22.

George, Kathryn Paxton. "Discrimination and Bias in the Vegan Ideal." *Journal of Agricultural and Environmental Ethics*, v. 7, no. 2 (1994): 19-28.

— . "Should Feminists be Vegetarians?" *Signs: Journal of Women in Culture and Society*, v. 19, no. 2 (1994): 405-34.

Heeger, Robert, and Frans Brom. "Intrinsic Value and Direct Duties: From Animal Ethics towards Environmental Ethics?" *Journal of Agricultural and Environmental Ethics*, v. 14, no. 2 (2001): 241-52.

Hud, George. "Collective Responsibility and Moral Vegetarianism." *Journal of Social Philosophy*, v. 24 (1993): 89-104.

Marcus, Erik. *Vegan: The New Ethics of Eating*. Ithaca, NY: McBooks Press, 2001.

Regan, Tom. *All that Dwell Therein*. Berkeley, CA: University of California Press, 1982.

Sapontzis. Steve. "Everyday Morality and Animal Rights." *Between the Species*, v. 3 (1987): 107-27.

Shaffer-Landau, Russ. "Vegetarianism, Causation, and Ethical Theory." *Public Affairs Quarterly*, v. 8 (1994): 85-100.

Stephens, William. "Five Arguments for Vegetarianism." *Philosophy in the Contemporary World*, v. 1 (1994): 25-39.

Tardiff, Andrew. "Simplifying the Case for Vegetarianism." *Social Theory and Practice*, v. 22, no. 3 (Fall 1996): 299-314.

Taylor, Andrew. *Animals & Ethics*. Peterborough, ON: Broadview Press, 2003.

Varner, Gary E. "What's Wrong with Animal By-products?" *Journal of Agricultural and Environmental Ethics*, v. 7, no. 1 (1994): 7-17.

Walters, Kerry S., and Lisa Pormess (editors). *Ethical Vegetarianism: From Pythagoras to Peter Singer*. Albany, NY: State University of New York Press, 1999.

CHAPTER FIVE: THE ENVIRONMENT

INTRODUCTION

In the final reading of the previous chapter, J. Baird Callicott argues that the strategy of drawing an increasing number of entities into the circle of beings worthy of moral consideration is severely limited as an environmental ethic. He argues that the individualist approach in traditional moral theory cannot provide moral reasons for why rivers, mountains, or ecosystems should be respected or protected. Callicott uses Aldo Leopold's land ethic, the central principle of which is that "a thing is right when it tends to preserve the integrity, stability, and beauty of the biotic community," to argue for a holistic perspective, one more generally referred to as "deep ecology." Deep ecologists reject individualist approaches that seek to broaden the number of entities to which we have responsibility. Instead, they defend an account of the biotic community as a system of parts that are interdependent, and they ask moral agents to respond in relation to that whole, a delicately complex, functioning social and organic system.

Deep ecology has played a fundamental role in environmental ethics. It has heightened awareness of the distinction between anthropocentric and non-anthropocentric approaches to the environment. Anthropocentric approaches argue for consideration of the environment in terms of the harms to human beings and future generations of human beings if animals and the environment are not cared for. Non-anthropocentric approaches remove the focus from a calculation of benefits and harms to human beings to the environment itself. Non-anthropocentrism, sometimes referred to as biocentrism or deep ecology, has been controversial in the debates between environmentalists and development theorists, the first of whom tend to put the environment first and the second of whom place the value on human development. As we will dis-

cover in this chapter, deep ecology has had its detractors, who argue that how it is conceived and what policies are implemented has depended on where its defenders are located.

The first reading by Ramachandra Guha argues that the tenets of deep ecology cannot be assumed to be universal. Deep ecology, he argues, reflects diverse theories and movements in different countries in the world. More specifically, he argues that because of dissimilar cultural and social histories, deep ecology in the U.S. differs from environmental movements in places like Germany and India. Guha takes these differences to be relevant to a critical analysis of the American version of deep ecology, one that tends to be depicted in universalistic terms and takes itself to have policy implications for places outside the U.S. While Guha applauds the check on human arrogance demanded by deep ecology's non-anthropocentric approach, he argues that American discussions of the dichotomy between anthropocentric and biocentric perspectives are of little use in understanding such fundamental ecological problems as overconsumption by the industrialized world and by the urban elite of developing countries. He also points out that deep ecologists' invocation of Eastern philosophies fails to appreciate the complex and differentiated traditions of Hinduism, Buddhism, and Taoism and romanticizes and simplifies human relations with nature. Lastly, Guha contends that American policies of preserving wilderness and creating parks fit with rather than challenge a consumer society that is rich, urban, and sophisticated.

Guha applies his critique of the American version of deep ecology to Third World contexts. In places like India, the preservation of unspoilt wilderness is harmful. India has a long history of agrarian populations achieving a finely balanced relationship with nature. Here, the central issue is preventing the state and the industrial sector from taking control of nature and exploiting it for resources. Guha argues that these areas need to be kept in the hands of rural communities who live within and know that environment. For these communities, the issues are equity, justice, and survival itself. Rural communities make fewer demands on the environment and can draw on a reservoir of cooperative social institutions and local ecological knowledge in managing and sustaining the environment in which they live.

While Guha raises objections to the theoretical focus of non-anthropocentrism, Eric Katz and Lauren Oechsli argue that the goal of formulating effective policies needs a theory that justifies direct moral consideration of the environment. They base their argument on a narrow interpretation of anthropocentrism as values, goods, and interests that promote human welfare to the near exclusion of competing, non-human values, goods, and interests. They argue that the failure of the restrictive framework of anthropocentrism is exemplified by the dilemma of Third World development policy and point to the example of the controversy over and failure of policies for preserving the Amazon rainforest.

Anthropocentric arguments can justify preserving a particular species or animal on the grounds that they might prove useful to humans in the future. Katz and Oeschli argue that such arguments, based as they are on speculation about use and harm to humans, should not be the basis for policy. They also reject anthropocentric arguments that degradation to the natural environment threatens human survival and identify these arguments in the inadequate policies for dealing with the greenhouse effect, the ozone layer, and the plight of the Amazon rainforests. Katz and Oeschli acknowledge that these arguments have served a useful purpose in increasing awareness and motivating people to defend policies for reducing the destruction and degradation of the environment. But policies that are based on benefits and harms to humans are mired in calculating and quantifying the harm in the areas

being studied with implications for peoples living in those areas. Third World nations recently freed from colonialism take the development of indigenous resources to be important to their economic freedom and prosperity. Katz and Oeschli argue that legitimate charges of imperialism in Third World preservation policy can be avoided only by rejecting anthropocentrism and developing a framework that accords direct value to natural entities and systems. From this perspective, questions of trade-offs, comparison of human benefits, and issues of justice for specific human populations would no longer dominate the discussion. The new framework offered by non-anthropocentric approaches, they argue, is necessary for solving persistently difficult questions of public policy and needs to be adopted as the basis for policy decisions. They end by arguing that their approach can address the concerns raised by Guha's worries about non-anthropocentrism.

The tensions between concerns for development and concerns for the environment and between anthropocentric and non-anthropocentric approaches to the environment are explored further in the third reading by Robin Attfield. Advocates of Third World development often argue that concern for the environment is a luxury that only developed nations can afford, and some environmentalists oppose development at all costs. Attfield formulates an argument that attempts to reconcile these divisions, arguing that development theorists cannot ignore environmental concerns and that environmentalists cannot ignore development concerns.

Attfield defends an account of development that highlights the processes needed to promote human development: the elimination of malnutrition, high infant mortality, low levels of literacy, high morbidity, poor medical and educational facilities, and low income and productivity. Such an account of development emphasizes human flourishing and the importance of human participation in and deliberation about the goals of development. It also highlights the injustices in and across societies with respect to the oppression of groups and peoples. Attfield uses this to argue that concern for the needs and interests of all people is a matter of justice, one that some versions of deep ecology ignore or take to be subservient to the interests and needs of the environment itself. He points to an inconsistency in arguments that condemn humankind for its chauvinism regarding other species and the environment, but that do not protest economic oppression or sexism and racism. Against development theorists, Attfield argues that developmentalists also display chauvinism when their moral concern stops with a concern for human beings. To oppose human suffering and not animal suffering or to argue that only human beings have intrinsic value is to discriminate on the basis of species on no good grounds. Attfield calls on development theorists and policy-makers to broaden their critique to include a critique of anthropocentrism itself.

In the reading that opened this chapter, Guha claims that it is a mistake to understand Eastern thinking as monolithic. There is a diversity of views within Eastern accounts of human relations with the environment. In the fourth reading, John Patterson examines the context of the Maori in New Zealand. He argues that the Maori have maintained their tribal traditions of a traditional ethics that encodes environmental virtues while appropriating and adapting to technological thinking and advances introduced by Europeans. Patterson discusses aspects of these traditions as reflected in the largely oral narratives of the Maori passed on by ancestors and told today. These stories depict a Maori view of the place of humans in the natural world and describe human responsibilities and obligations in terms of specific virtues.

The concept and practice of *tapu*, for example, involve the idea that the world is not ours and that we need to be a certain sort of person in that world, one who embraces unconditional responsibilities of care and protection. *Mauri* expresses the idea that all things have a life or nature of their own that must be respected and calls for an understanding of and sympathetic attitude toward the nature or special character of each item. *Whanaungatanga* reminds Maori to seek and

implement ways of enhancing the welfare of the whole environment and all its members. It demands more than refraining from harming others and asks that all our activities contribute to making the whole environment better. *Mana* describes one's place in the world in terms of an acceptance that others have their place and that one's place is neither privileged nor exclusive of theirs. Patterson argues that Maori virtues challenge the anthropocentrism of the West and that the Maori display a successful environmental virtue ethic that is alive and working and can give us insights into what is needed in our contemporary technological world.

In the final reading, Michael Traynor picks up on the theme in the reading by Patterson that our contemporary technological world requires changes in attitudes and policies with respect to the environment. Unlike Patterson, however, Traynor sounds a pessimistic note that change is possible. He returns us to an anthropocentric approach to environmental policy by drawing our attention to the near universal recognition of a constitutional human right to a healthful environment. He points out, however, that given the restrictive trends in federal courts, an anti-environmental president, and an unsympathetic Congress, the chances are slim that such a right will be recognized by the U.S.

Traynor discusses commitments by countries at the United Nations World Summit on Sustainable Development, held in Johannesburg in 2002, to develop policies for strengthening and enforcing environmental laws, for expanding public participation in decision-making, and for sketching a role for the judiciary in connecting environmental law and human rights. Traynor notes that President Bush was one of the few leaders absent from the summit, instead sending the Secretary of State who concentrated on issues of protecting American oil interests. The U.S., he reports, refused to join most of the rest of the world in supporting many of the provisions emerging from the summit, maneuvering instead to defeat strong environmental commitments. Traynor expresses optimism about the widely held shared commitments of people throughout the world, including many Americans, to improving, sustaining, and saving the environment for future generations. But he also draws attention to the difficulty of change in a context in which a powerful country such as the U.S. defies and rejects national and international movements to coordinate and cooperate with respect to shaping policies that can address serious problems such as global warming.

RADICAL AMERICAN ENVIRONMENTALISM AND WILDERNESS PRESERVATION: A THIRD WORLD CRITIQUE

Ramachandra Guha

*

Ramachandra Guha was Professorial Fellow at the Centre for Contemporary Studies, Nehru Memorial Museum and Library, New Delhi. He is the author, co-author, and editor of a number of books, including The Unquiet Woods: Ecological Change and Peasant Resistance in the Himalaya *(1990),* An Anthropologist among the Marxists and Other Essays *(2001),* Ecology and Equity: The Use and Abuse of Nature in Contemporary India *(1995), and* Nature, Culture, Imperialism: Essays on the Environmental History of South Asia *(1995).*

Guha presents a Third World critique of the trend in American environmentalism known as deep ecology, raising objections to each of its central tenets: the distinction between anthropocentrism and biocentrism, the focus on wilderness preservation, the invocation of Eastern traditions, and the belief that it represents the most radical trend within environmentalism. He argues that the anthropocentrism/biocentrism distinction is of little use in understanding the dynamics of environmental degradation; that the implementation of the wilderness agenda is causing serious deprivation in the Third World; that the deep ecologist's interpretation of Eastern traditions is highly selective; and that in other contexts, such as West Germany and India, radical environmentalism is quite different. He concludes that despite its claims to universality, deep ecology is firmly rooted in American environmental and cultural history and is inappropriate when applied to the Third World.

Even God dare not appear to the poor man except in the form of bread.

— Mahatma Gandhi

I. Introduction

The respected radical journalist Kirkpatrick Sale recently celebrated "the passion of a new and growing movement that has become disenchanted with the environmental establishment and has in recent years mounted a serious and sweeping attack on it — style, substance, systems, sensibilities and all."[1] The vision of those whom Sale calls the "New Ecologists" — and what I refer to in this article as deep ecology — is a compelling one. Decrying the narrowly economic goals of mainstream environmentalism, this new movement aims at nothing less than a philosophical and cultural revolution in human attitudes toward nature. In contrast to the conventional lobbying efforts of environmental professionals based in Washington, it proposes a militant defence of "Mother Earth," and unflinching opposition to human attacks on undisturbed wilderness. With their goals ranging from the spiritual to the political, the adherents of deep ecology span a wide spectrum of the American environmental movement. As Sale correctly notes, this emerging strand has in a matter of a few years made its presence felt in a number of fields: from academic philosophy (as in the journal *Environmental Ethics*) to popular environmentalism (for example, the group Earth First!).

In this article I develop a critique of deep ecology from the perspective of a sympathetic outsider. I critique deep ecology not as a general (or even a foot soldier) in the continuing struggle between the ghosts of Gifford Pinchot and John Muir over control of the U.S. environmental movement, but as an outsider to these battles. I speak admittedly as a partisan, but of the environmental movement in India, a country with an ecological diversity comparable to the U.S., but with a radically dissimilar cultural and social history.

My treatment of deep ecology is primarily historical and sociological, rather than philosophical, in nature. Specifically, I examine the cultural rootedness of a philosophy that likes to present itself in universalistic terms. I make two main arguments: first, that deep ecology is uniquely American, and despite superficial similarities in rhetorical style, the social and political goals of radical environmentalism in other cultural contexts (e.g., West Germany and India) are quite different; second, that the social consequences of putting deep ecology into practice on a worldwide basis (what its practitioners are aiming for) are very grave indeed.

II. The Tenets of Deep Ecology

While I am aware that the term *deep ecology* was coined by the Norwegian philosopher Arne Naess, this article refers specifically to the American variant.[2] Adherents of the deep ecological perspective in this country, while arguing intensely among themselves over its political and philosophical implications, share some fundamental premises about human-nature interactions. As I see it, the defining characteristics of deep ecology are fourfold:

First, deep ecology argues, that the environmental movement must shift from an "anthropocentric" to a "biocentric" perspective. In many respects, an acceptance of the primacy of this distinction constitutes the litmus test of deep ecology. A considerable effort is expended by deep ecologists in showing that the dominant motif in Western philosophy has been anthro-

pocentric — i.e., the belief that man and his works are the center of the universe — and conversely, in identifying those lonely thinkers (Leopold, Thoreau, Muir, Aldous Huxley, Santayana, etc.) who, in assigning man a more humble place in the natural order, anticipated deep ecological thinking. In the political realm, meanwhile, establishment environmentalism (shallow ecology) is chided for casting its arguments in human-centered terms. Preserving nature, the deep ecologists say, has an intrinsic worth quite apart from any benefits preservation may convey to future human generations. The anthropocentric-biocentric distinction is accepted as axiomatic by deep ecologists, it structures their discourse, and much of the present discussion remains mired within it.

The second characteristic of deep ecology is its focus on the preservation of unspoilt wilderness — and the restoration of degraded areas to a more pristine condition — to the relative (and sometimes absolute) neglect of other issues on the environmental agenda. I later identify the cultural roots and portentous consequences of this obsession with wilderness. For the moment, let me indicate three distinct sources from which it springs. Historically, it represents a playing out of the preservationist (read *radical*) and utilitarian (read *reformist*) dichotomy that has plagued American environmentalism since the turn of the century. Morally, it is an imperative that follows from the biocentric perspective; other species of plants and animals, and nature itself, have an intrinsic right to exist. And finally, the preservation of wilderness also turns on a scientific argument — *viz.*, the value of biological diversity in stabilizing ecological regimes and in retaining a gene pool for future generations. Truly radical policy proposals have been put forward by deep ecologists on the basis of these arguments. The influential poet Gary Snyder, for example, would like to see a 90 percent reduction in human populations to allow a restoration of pristine environments, while others have argued forcefully that a large portion of the globe must be immediately cordoned off from human beings.[3]

Third, there is a widespread invocation of Eastern spiritual traditions as forerunners of deep ecology. Deep ecology, it is suggested, was practiced both by major religious traditions and at a more popular level by "primal" peoples in non-Western settings. This complements the search for an authentic lineage in Western thought. At one level, the task is to recover those dissenting voices within the Judeo-Christian tradition; at another, to suggest that religious traditions in other cultures are, in contrast, dominantly if not exclusively "biocentric" in their orientation. This coupling of (ancient) Eastern and (modern) ecological wisdom seemingly helps consolidate the claim that deep ecology is a philosophy of universal significance.

Fourth, deep ecologists, whatever their internal differences, share the belief that they are the "leading edge" of the environmental movement. As the polarity of the shallow/deep and anthropocentric/biocentric distinctions makes clear, they see themselves as the spiritual, philosophical, and political vanguard of American and world environmentalism.

III. Toward a Critique

Although I analyze each of these tenets independently, it is important to recognize, as deep ecologists are fond of remarking in reference to nature, the interconnectedness and unity of these individual themes.

(1) Insofar as it has begun to act as a check on man's arrogance and ecological hubris, the transition from an anthropocentric (human-centered) to a biocentric (humans as only one element in the ecosystem) view in both religious and scientific traditions is only to be welcomed.[4] What is unacceptable are the radical conclusions drawn by deep ecology, in particular, that intervention in nature should be guided primarily by the need to preserve biotic integrity rather than by the need of humans. The latter for deep ecologists is anthropocentric, the former biocentric. This dichotomy is, however, of very little use in understanding the dynamics of environmental degradation. The two fundamental ecological problems facing the globe are (i) overconsumption by the industrialized world and by urban

elites in the Third world and (ii) growing militarization, both in a short-term sense (i.e., ongoing regional wars) and in a long-term sense (i.e., the arms race and the prospect of nuclear annihilation). Neither of these problems has any tangible connection to the anthropocentric-biocentric distinction. Indeed, the agents of these processes would barely comprehend this philosophical dichotomy. The proximate causes of the ecologically wasteful characteristics of industrial society and of militarization are far more mundane: at an aggregate level, the dialectic of economic and political structures, and at a micro-level, the life style choices of individuals. These causes cannot be reduced, whatever the level of analysis, to a deeper anthropocentric attitude toward nature; on the contrary, by constituting a grave threat to human survival, the ecological degradation they cause does not even serve the best interests of human beings! If my identification of the major dangers to the integrity of the natural world is correct, invoking the bogy of anthropocentricism is at best irrelevant and at worst a dangerous obfuscation.

(2) If the above dichotomy is irrelevant, the emphasis on wilderness is positively harmful when applied to the Third World. If in the U.S. the preservationist/utilitarian division is seen as mirroring the conflict between "people" and "interest," in countries such as India the situation is very nearly the reverse. Because India is a long settled and densely populated country in which agrarian populations have a finely balanced relationship with nature, the setting aside of wilderness areas has resulted in a direct transfer of resources from the poor to the rich. Thus, Project Tiger, a network of parks hailed by the international conservation community as an outstanding success, sharply posits the interests of the tiger against those of poor peasants living in and around the reserve. The designation of tiger reserves was made possible only by the physical displacement of existing villages and their inhabitants; their management requires the continuing exclusion of peasants and livestock. The initial impetus for setting up parks for the tiger and other large mammals such as the rhinoceros and

elephant came from two social groups, first, a class of ex-hunters turned conservationists belonging mostly to the declining Indian feudal elite and second, representatives of international agencies, such as the World Wildlife Fund (WWF) and the International Union for the Conservation of Nature and Natural Resources (IUCN), seeking to transplant the American system of national parks onto Indian soil. In no case have the needs of the local population been taken into account, and as in many parts of Africa, the designated wildlands are managed primarily for the benefit of the rich tourists. Until very recently, wildlands preservation has been identified with environmentalism by the state and the conservation elite; in consequence, environmental problems that impinge far more directly on the lives of the poor — e.g., fuel, fodder, water shortages, soil erosion, and air and water pollution — have not been adequately addressed.[5]

Deep ecology provides, perhaps unwittingly, a justification for the continuation of such narrow and inequitable conservation practices under a newly acquired radical guise. Increasingly, the international conservation elite is using the philosophical, moral, and scientific arguments used by deep ecologists in advancing their wilderness crusade. A striking but by no means atypical example is the recent plea by a prominent American biologist for the takeover of large portions of the globe by the author and his scientific colleagues. Writing in a prestigious scientific forum, the *Annual Review of Ecology and Systematics,* Daniel Janzen argues that only biologists have the competence to decide how the tropical landscape should be used. As "the representatives of the natural world," biologists are "in charge of the future of tropical ecology," and only they have the expertise and mandate to "determine whether the tropical agroscape is to be populated only by humans, their mutualists, commensals, and parasites, or whether it will also contain some islands of the greater nature — the nature that spawned humans, yet has been vanquished by them." Janzen exhorts his colleagues to advance their territorial claims on the tropical world more forcefully, warning that the very

existence of these areas is at stake: "if biologists want a tropic in which to biologize, they are going to have to buy it with care, energy, effort, strategy, tactics, time, and cash."[6]

This frankly imperialist manifesto highlights the multiple dangers of the preoccupation with wilderness preservation that is characteristic of deep ecology. As I have suggested, it seriously compounds the neglect by the American movement of far more pressing environmental problems within the Third World. But perhaps more importantly, and in a more insidious fashion, it also provides an impetus to the imperialist yearning of Western biologists and their financial sponsors, organizations such as the WWF and IUCN. The wholesale transfer of a movement culturally rooted in American conservation history can only result in the social uprooting of human populations in other parts of the globe.

(3) I come now to the persistent invocation of Eastern philosophies as antecedent in point of time but convergent in their structure with deep ecology. Complex and internally differentiated religious traditions — Hinduism, Buddhism, and Taoism — are lumped together as holding a view of nature believed to be quintessentially biocentric. Individual philosophers such as the Taoist Lao Tzu are identified as being forerunners of deep ecology. Even an intensely political, pragmatic, and Christian influenced thinker such as Gandhi has been accorded a wholly undeserved place in the deep ecological pantheon. Thus the Zen teacher Robert Aitken Roshi makes the strange claim that Gandhi's thought was not human-centered and that he practiced an embryonic form of deep ecology which is "traditionally Eastern and is found, with differing emphasis in Hinduism, Taoism and in Theravada and Mahayana Buddhism."[7] Moving away from the realm of high philosophy and scriptural religion, deep ecologists make the further claim that at the level of material and spiritual practice "primal" peoples subordinated themselves to the integrity of the biotic universe they inhabited.

I have indicated that this appropriation of Eastern traditions is in part dictated by the need to construct an authentic lineage and in part a desire to present deep ecology as a universalistic philosophy. Indeed, in his substantial and quixotic biography of John Muir, Michael Cohen goes so far as to suggest that Muir was the "Taoist of the [American] West."[8] This reading of Eastern traditions is selective and does not bother to differentiate between alternate (and changing) religious and cultural traditions; as it stands, it does considerable violence to the historical record. Throughout most recorded history the characteristic form of human activity in the "East" has been a finely tuned but nonetheless conscious and dynamic manipulation of nature. Although mystics such as Lao Tzu did reflect on the spiritual essence of human relations with nature, it must be recognized that such ascetics and their reflections were supported by a society of cultivators whose relationship with nature was a far more *active* one. Many agricultural communities do have a sophisticated knowledge of the natural environment that may equal (and sometimes surpass) codified "scientific" knowledge; yet, the elaboration of such traditional ecological knowledge (in both material and spiritual contexts) can hardly be said to rest on a mystical affinity with nature of a deep ecological kind. Nor is such knowledge infallible: as the archaeological record powerfully suggests, modern Western man has no monopoly on ecological disasters.

In a brilliant article, the Chicago historian Ronald Inden points out that this romantic and essentially positive view of the East is a mirror image of the scientific and essentially pejorative view normally upheld by Western scholars of the Orient. In either case, the East constitutes the Other, a body wholly separate and alien from the West; it is defined by a uniquely spiritual and nonrational "essence," even if this essence is valorized quite differently by the two schools. Eastern man exhibits a spiritual dependence with respect to nature — on the one hand, this is symptomatic of his prescientific and backward self, on the other, of his ecological wisdom and deep ecological consciousness. Both views are monolithic, simplistic, and have the characteristic effect — intended in one case, perhaps unintended in the other — of denying agency and reason to the East and making it the privileged orbit of Western thinkers.

The two apparently opposed perspectives have then a common underlying structure of discourse in which the East merely serves as a vehicle for Western projections. Varying images of the East are raw material for political and cultural battles being played out in the West; they tell us far more about the Western commentator and his desires than about the "East." Inden's remarks apply not merely to Western scholarship on India, but to Orientalist constructions of China and Japan as well:

> Although these two views appear to be strongly opposed, they often combine together. Both have a similar interest in sustaining the Otherness of India. The holders of the dominant view, best exemplified in that past imperial administrative discourse (and today probably by that of "development economics"), would place a traditional, superstition-ridden India in a position of perpetual tutelage to a modern, rational West. The adherents of the romantic view, best exemplified academically in the discourses of Christian liberalism and analytic psychology, concede the realm of the public and impersonal to the positivist. Taking their succour not from governments and big business, but from a plethora of religious foundations and self-help institutes, and from allies in the "consciousness industry," not to mention the important industry of tourism, the romantics insist that India embodies a private realm of the imagination and the religious which modern, western man lacks but needs. They, therefore, like the positivist, but for just the opposite reason, have a vested interest in seeing that the Orientalist view of India as "spiritual," "mysterious," and "exotic" is perpetuated.[9]

(4) How radical, finally, are the deep ecologists? Notwithstanding their self-image and strident rhetoric (in which the label "shallow ecology" has an opprobrium similar to that

reserved for "social democratic" by Marxist-Leninists), even within the American contest their radicalism is limited and it manifests itself quite differently elsewhere.

To my mind, deep ecology is best viewed as a radical trend within the wilderness preservation movement. Although advancing philosophical rather than aesthetic arguments and encouraging political militancy rather than negotiation, its practical emphasis — viz., preservation of unspoilt nature — is virtually identical. For the mainstream movement, the function of wilderness is to provide temporary antidote to modern civilization. As a special institution within an industrialized society, the national park "provides an opportunity for respite, contrast, contemplation, and affirmation of values for those who live most of their lives in the workaday world."[10] Indeed, the rapid increase in visitations to the national parks in postwar America is a direct consequence of economic expansion. The emergence of a popular interest in wilderness sites, the historian Samuel Hays points out, was "not a throwback to the primitive, but an integral part of the modern standard of living as people sought to add new 'amenity' and 'aesthetic' goals and desires to the earlier preoccupation with necessities and conveniences."[11]

Here, the enjoyment of nature is an integral part of the consumer society. The private automobile (and the life style it has spawned) is in many respects the ultimate ecological villain, and an untouched wilderness the prototype of ecological harmony: yet, for most Americans it is perfectly consistent to drive a thousand miles to spend a holiday in a national park. They posses a vast, beautiful, and sparsely populated continent and are also able to draw upon the natural resources of large portions of the globe by virtue of their economic and political dominance. In consequence, America can simultaneously enjoy the material benefits of an expanding economy and the aesthetic benefits of unspoilt nature. The two poles of "wilderness" and "civilization" mutually coexist in an internally coherent whole, and philosophers of both poles are assigned a prominent place in this culture. Paradoxically as

it may seem, it is no accident that Star Wars technology and deep ecology both find their fullest expression in that leading sector of Western civilization, California.

Deep ecology runs parallel to the consumer society without seriously questioning its ecological and socio-political basis. In its celebration of American wilderness, it also displays an uncomfortable convergence with the prevailing climate of nationalism in the American wilderness movement. For spokesmen such as the historian Roderick Nash, the national park system is America's distinctive cultural contribution to the world, reflective not merely of its economic but of its philosophical and ecological maturity as well. In what Walter Lippman called the American century, the "American invention of national parks" must be exported worldwide. Betraying an economic determinism that would make even a Marxist shudder, Nash believes that environmental preservation is a "full stomach" phenomenon that is confined to the rich, urban, and sophisticated. Nonetheless, he hopes that "the less developed nations may eventually evolve economically and intellectually to the point where nature preservation is more than a business."[12]

The error which Nash makes (and which deep ecology in some respects encourages) is to equate environmental protection with the protection of wilderness. This is a distinctively American notion, borne out of a unique social and environmental history. The archetypal concerns of radical environmentalists in other cultural contexts are in fact quite different. The German Greens, for example, have elaborated a devastating critique of industrial society which turns on the acceptance of environmental limits to growth. Pointing to the intimate links between industrialization, militarization, and conquest, the Greens argue that economic growth in the West has historically rested on the economic and ecological exploitation of the Third World. Rudolf Bahro is characteristically blunt:

> The working class here [in the West] is the richest lower class in the world. And if I look at the problem from the point of view of the

whole of humanity, not just from that of Europe, then I must say that the metropolitan working class is the worst exploiting class in history.... What made poverty bearable in eighteenth or nineteenth-century Europe was the prospect of escaping it through exploitations of the periphery. But this is no longer a possibility, and continued industrialism in the Third Word will mean poverty for whole generations and hunger for millions.[13]

Here the roots of global ecological problems lie in the disproportionate share of resources consumed by the industrialized countries as a whole *and* the urban elite within the Third World. Since it is impossible to reproduce an industrial monoculture worldwide, the ecological movement in the West must begin by cleaning up its own act. The Greens advocate the creation of a "no growth" economy, to be achieved by scaling down current (and clearly unsustainable) consumption levels.[14] This radical shift in consumption and production patterns requires the creation of alternate economic and political structures — smaller in scale and more amenable to social participation — but it rests equally on a shift in cultural values. The expansionist character of modern Western man will have to give way to an ethic of renunciation and self-limitation, in which spiritual and communal values play an increasing role in sustaining social life. This revolution in cultural values, however, has as its point of departure an understanding of environmental processes quite different from deep ecology.

Many elements of the Green program find a strong resonance in countries such as India, where a history of Western colonialism and industrial development has benefited only a tiny elite while exacting tremendous social and environmental costs. The ecological battles presently being fought in India have as their epicenter the conflict over nature between the subsistence and largely rural sector and the vastly more powerful commercial-industrial sector. Perhaps the most celebrated of these battles concerns the Chipko (Hug the Tree) movement, a peasant movement against deforestation in the Himalayan foothills.

Chipko is only one of several movements that have sharply questioned the nonsustainable demand being placed on the land and vegetative base by urban centers and industry. These include opposition to large dams by displaced peasants, the conflict between small artisan fishing and large-scale trawler fishing for export, the countrywide movements against commercial forest operations, and opposition to industrial pollution among downstream agricultural and fishing communities.[15]

Two features distinguish these environmental movements from their Western counterparts. First, for the sections of society most critically affected by environmental degradation — poor and landless peasants, women, and tribals — it is a question of sheer survival, not of enhancing the quality of life. Second, and as a consequence, the environmental solutions they articulate deeply involve questions of equity as well as economic and political redistribution. Highlighting these differences, a leading Indian environmentalist stresses that "environmental protection per se is of least concern to most of these groups. Their main concern is about the use of the environment and who should benefit from it."[16] They seek to wrest control of nature away from the state and the industrial sector and place it in the hands of rural communities who live within that environment but are increasingly denied access to it. These communities have far more basic needs, their demands on the environment are far less intense, and they can draw upon a reservoir of cooperative social institutions and local ecological knowledge in managing the "commons" — forests, grasslands, and the waters — on a sustainable basis. If colonial and capitalist expansion has both accentuated social inequalities and signaled a precipitous fall in ecological wisdom, an alternate ecology must rest on an alternate society and polity as well.

This brief overview of German and Indian environmentalism has some major implications for deep ecology. Both German and Indian environmental traditions allow for a greater integration of ecological concerns with livelihood and work. They also place a greater emphasis on equity and social justice (both within individual counties and on a global scale) on the grounds that in the absence of social regeneration environmental regeneration has very little chance of succeeding. Finally, and perhaps most significantly, they have escaped the preoccupation with wilderness preservation so characteristic of American cultural and environmental history.[17]

IV. A Homily

In 1958, the economist J.K. Galbraith referred to overconsumption as the masked question of the American conservation movement. There is a marked selectivity, he wrote, "in the conservationist's approach to materials consumption. If we are concerned about our great appetite for materials, it is plausible to seek to increase the supply, to decrease waste, to make better use of the stocks available, and to develop substitutes. But what of the appetite itself? Surely this is the ultimate source of the problem. If it continues its geometric course, will it not one day have to be restrained? Yet in the literature of the resource problem this is the forbidden question. Over it hangs a nearly total silence."[18]

The consumer economy and society have expanded tremendously in the three decades since Galbraith penned these words; yet his criticisms are nearly as valid today. I have said "nearly," for there are some hopeful signs. Within the environmental movement several dispersed groups are working to develop ecologically benign technologies and to encourage less wasteful life styles. Moreover, outside the self-defined boundaries of American environmentalism, opposition to the permanent war economy is being carried on by a peace movement that has a distinguished history and impeccable moral and political credentials.

It is precisely these (to my mind, most hopeful) components of the American social scene that are missing from deep ecology. In their widely noticed book, Bill Devall and George Sessions make no mention of militarization or the movements for peace, while activists whose practical focus in on developing ecologically responsible

life styles (e.g., Wendell Berry) are derided as "falling short of deep ecological awareness."[19] A truly radical ecology in the American context ought to work toward a synthesis of the appropriate technology, alternate life style, and peace movements.[20] By making the (largely spurious) anthropocentric-biocentric distinction central to the debate, deep ecologists may have appropriated the moral high ground, but they are at the same time doing a serious disservice to American and global environmentalism.[21]

Author's Note

This essay was written while the author was a visiting lecturer at the Yale School of Forestry and Environmental Studies. He is grateful to Mike Bell, Tom Birch, Bill Burch, Bill Cronon, Diane Mayerfield, David Rothenberg, Kirkpatrick Sale, Joel Seton, Tim Weiskel, and Don Worster for helpful comments.

NOTES

1. Kirkpatrick Sale, "The Forest for the Trees: Can Today's Environmentalists Tell the Difference," *Mother Jones* 11, no. 8 (November 1986): 26.

2. One of the major criticisms I make in this essay concerns deep ecology's lack of concern with inequalities *within* human society. In the article in which he coined the term *deep ecology,* Naess himself expresses concerns about inequalities between and within nations. However, his concern with social cleavages and their impact on resource utilization patterns and ecological destruction is not very visible in the later writings of deep ecologists. See Arne Naess, "The Shallow and the Deep, Long-Range Ecology Movement: A Summary," *Inquiry* 16 (1973): 96 (I am grateful to Tom Birch for this reference).

3. Gary Snyder, quoted in Sale, "The Forest for the Trees," p. 32. See also Dave Foreman, "Modest Proposal for a Wilderness System," *Whole Earth Review*, no. 53 (Winter 1986-87): 42-45.

4. See, for example, Donald Worster, *Nature's Economy: The Roots of Ecology* (San Francisco, Sierra Club Books, 1977).

5. See Centre for Science and Environment, *India: The State of the Environment: A Citizens Report* (New Delhi: Centre for Science and Environment, 1982); R. Sukumar, "Elephant-Man Conflict in Karnataka," in Cecil Saldanha, ed., *The State of Karnataka's Environment* (Bangalore: Centre for Taxonomic Studies, 1985). For Africa, see the brilliant analysis by Helge Kjekshus, *Ecology Control and Economic Development in East African History* (Berkeley: University of California Press, 1977).

6. Daniel Janzen, "The Future of Tropical Ecology," *Annual Review of Ecology and Systematics* (1986): 305-06; emphasis added.

7. Robert Aitken Roshi, "Gandhi, Dogen, and Deep Ecology," reprinted as appendix C in Bill Devall and George Sessions, *Deep Ecology: Living as if Nature Mattered* (Salt Lake City: Peregrine Smith Books, 1985). For Gandhi's own views on social reconstruction, see the excellent three volume collection edited by Raghavan Iyer, *The Moral and Political Writings of Mahatma Gandhi* (Oxford: Clarendon Press, 1986-87).

8. Michael Cohen, *The Pathless Way* (Madison: University of Wisconsin Press, 1984), p. 120.

9. Ronald Inden, "Orientalist Constructions of India," *Modern Asian Studies* 20 (1986): 442. Inden draws inspiration from Edward Said's forceful polemic, *Orientalism* (New York: Basic Books, 1980). It must be noted, however, that there is a salient difference between Western perceptions of Middle Eastern and Far Eastern cultures respectively. Due perhaps to the long history of Christian conflict with Islam, Middle Eastern cultures (as Said documents) are consistently presented in pejorative terms. The juxtaposition of hostile and worshiping attitudes that Inden talks of applies only to Western attitudes toward Buddhist and Hindu societies.

10. Joseph Sax, *Mountains Without Handrails: Reflections on the National Parks* (Ann Arbor, University of Michigan Press, 1980), p. 42. Cf. Also Peter Schmitt, *Back to Nature: The Arcadian Myth in Urban America* (New York: Oxford University Press, 1969), and Alfred Runte, *National Parks: The American Experience* (Lincoln: University of Nebraska Press, 1979).

11. Samuel Hays, "From Conservation to Environment: Environmental Politics in the United States since World War Two," *Environmental Review* 6 (1982): 21. See also the same author's book entitled *Beauty, Health and Permanence: Environmental Politics in the United States, 1955-85* (New York: Cambridge University Press, 1987).

12. Roderick Nash, *Wilderness and the American Mind*, 3rd ed. (New Haven: Yale University Press, 1982).

13. Rudolf Bahro, *From Red to Green* (London: Verso Books, 1984).

14. From time to time, American scholars have themselves criticized these imbalances in consumption patterns. In the 1950s, William Vogt made the charge that the United States, with one-sixteenth of the world's population, was utilizing one-third of the globe's resources. (Vogt, cited in E.F. Murphy, *Nature, Bureaucracy and the Rule of Property* [Amsterdam: North Holland, 1977, p. 29]). More recently, Zero Population Growth has estimated that each American consumes thirty-nine times as many resources as an Indian. See *Christian Science Monitor*, 2 March 1987.

15. For an excellent review, see Anil Agarwal and Sunita Narain, eds., *India: The State of the Environment 1984-85: A Citizens Report* (New Delhi: Centre for Science and Environment, 1985). Cf. also Ramachandra Guha, *The Unquiet Woods: Ecological Change and a Peasant Resistance in the Indian Himalaya* (Berkeley: University of California Press, 1990).

16. Anil Agarwal, "Human-Nature Interactions in a Third World country," *The Environmentalist* 6, no.3 (1986): 167.

17. One strand in radical American environmentalism, the bioregional movement, by emphasizing a greater involvement with the bioregion people inhabit, does indirectly challenge consumerism. However, as yet bioregionalism has hardly raised the questions of equity and social justice (international, intranational, and intergenerational) which I argue must be a central plank of radical environmentalism. Moreover, its stress on (individual) *experience* as the key to involvement with nature is also somewhat at odds with the integration of nature with livelihood and work that I talk of in

this paper. Cf. Kirkpatrick Sale, *Dwellers in the Land: The Bioregional Vision* (San Francisco: Sierra Club Books, 1985).

18. John Kenneth Galbraith, "How Much Should a Country Consume?" in Henry Jarrett, ed., *Perspectives on Conservation* (Baltimore: Johns Hopkins Press, 1958), pp. 91-92.

19. Devall and Sessions, *Deep Ecology*, p. 122. For Wendell Berry's own assessment of deep ecology, see his "Amplications: Preserving Wildness," *Wilderness* 50 (Spring 1987): 39-40, 50-54.

20. See the interesting recent contribution by one of the most influential spokesmen of appropriate technology — Barry Commoner, "A Reporter at Large: The Environment," *New Yorker*, 15 June 1987. While Commoner makes a forceful plea for the convergence of the environmental movement (viewed by him primarily as the opposition to air and water pollution and to the institutions that generate such pollution) and the peace movement, he significantly does not mention consumption patterns, implying that "limits to growth" do not exist.

21. In this sense, my critique of deep ecology, although that of an outsider, may facilitate the reassertion of those elements in the American environmental tradition for which there is a profound sympathy in other parts of the globe. A global perspective may also lead to a critical reassessment of figures such as Aldo Leopold and John Muir, the two patron saints of deep ecology. As Donald Worster has pointed out, the message of Muir (and, I would argue, of Leopold as well) makes sense only in an American context; he has very little to say to other cultures. See Worster's review of Stephen Fox's *John Muir and His Legacy*, in *Environmental Ethics* 5 (1983): 277-81.

MOVING BEYOND ANTHROPOCENTRISM: ENVIRONMENTAL ETHICS, DEVELOPMENT, AND THE AMAZON

Eric Katz and Lauren Oechsli

Eric Katz is in the Graduate Program in Environmental Policy Studies at the New Jersey Institute of Technology in Newark. He is the author of Nature as Subject: Human Obligation and Natural Community *(1997), co-editor with Andrew Light and David Rothenberg of* Beneath the Surface: Critical Essays in the Philosophy of Deep Ecology *(2000), and co-editor with Andrew Light and William Thompson of* Controlling Technology: Contemporary Issues *(2003).*

Lauren Oechsli is Geographical Information Systems (GIS) Lab Manager at American Wildlands, a science-based conservation group for the northern Rockies.

Katz and Oechsli argue that to formulate effective environmental policy we need a theory that justifies direct moral consideration of the environment. They argue that the failure of the restrictive framework of anthropocentrism is exemplified by the dilemma of Third World development policy and, in particular, by the failure of policies for preserving the Amazon rainforest. A focus on calculations of harms and benefits to humans has resulted in charges of imperialism by Third World countries that can be avoided, they argue, only by rejecting anthropocentrism. From this perspective, questions of trade-offs, calculation of benefits and harms, and issues of justice for specific human populations would not dominate the discussion. They end by addressing the concerns raised by Guha's worries about nonanthropocentrism.

I. Introduction

In this paper, we consider the role of human interests in the formation of environmental policy. Are environmentalist policies justified solely because they benefit human individuals and human society? Or are there valid moral principles that transcend human concerns and justify a direct moral consideration of the natural environment?

These questions have dominated the field of environmental ethics since its inception. In general, the field has provided a critique of *instrumental* human-based arguments for environmental policies, and has attempted the development of a *nonanthropocentric* ethic or value theory which will account for a direct moral consideration of nature.[1]

We defend this rejection of anthropocentric instrumental reasoning as a basis for environmental policy. Although we do not formulate a value theory or a system of ethics that validates a nonanthropocentric regard for nature, we argue that this direction in environmental ethics is necessary for the solution of persistently difficult questions of public policy. As an example, we consider arguments about the development of the environment in the Third World, especially the destruction of the Amazon rain forests. Anthropocentric justifications concerning development — both for and against — lead to inescapable problems concerning both utility and justice. These problems can be avoided from a nonanthropocentric and non-instrumental perspective. We thus provide an *indirect* argument for the moral consideration of nature in the formation of environmental policy.

Our argument is based on a narrow, but, we believe, pervasive interpretation of the term *anthropocentric* to mean those values, goods, and interests that promote human welfare to the near exclusion of competing nonhuman values, goods, and interests. This version of anthropocentrism is closely aligned with the term *instrumentalism*, according to which the world is viewed as a resource valuable only as it promotes human good. Our purpose is to criticize *anthropocentric instrumentalism* as it is applied to developmental policies. Although we leave open the possible justification of environmental policies by *noninstrumental* forms of *anthropocentrism* (such as beauty or other intrinsic human ideals), we suggest primarily that a *nonanthropocentric instrumentalism* (based on the promotion of the goods of nonhuman nature) is a valid and necessary response to environmental problems.

II. Human Interests and Environmental Preservation

It is not surprising that anthropocentric arguments dominate discussions of policy: arguments for environmental preservation based directly on human interests are often compelling. Dumping toxic wastes into a community's reservoir of drinking water is clearly an irrational act; in such a case, a discussion of ethics or value theory is not necessary. The direct harm to humans engendered by this action is enough to disqualify it from serious ethical consideration. Nevertheless, other actions in the field of environmental policy are not so clear: there may be, for example, cases in which there are competing harms and goods to various segments of the human population that have to be balanced. The method for balancing these competing interests gives rise to issues of equity and justice. In addition, and more pertinent to our argument, are cases in which human actions threaten the existence of natural entities not usable as resources for human life. What reason do we humans have for expending vast sums of money (in positive expenditures and lost opportunities) to preserve endangered species of plants and animals that are literally nonresources?[2] In these cases, policies of environmental preservation seem to work against human interests and human good.

Anthropocentric and instrumental arguments in favor of preservationist policies can be developed in a series and arranged in order of increasing plausibility. First, it is argued that any particular species of plant or animal might prove useful in the future. Alastair Gunn calls this position the "rare herb" theory. According to this theory, the elimination of any natural entity is morally wrong because it closes down the options for any possible positive use.[3] A point frequently raised in discussions of this problem is that the endangered species we are about to eliminate might be the cure for cancer. Of course, it is also possible that it will cause cancer; the specific effects of any plant or animal species might be harmful as well as beneficial. Because we are arguing from a position of ignorance, it is ludicrous to assert either possibility as certain, or to use either alternative as a basis for policy.

A better argument is used by Paul and Anne Ehrlich: the metaphor of the airplane rivets.[4] The Ehrlichs tell a parable of an airplane passenger watching as a mechanic removes some of the rivets from the wing assembly of the plane he is boarding. When asked what he is doing, the mechanic replies that for reasons of economy, the airline is cutting down on the number of rivets used on each plane; some of the rivets are being removed and used on other planes. The procedure is not dangerous, continues the mechanic, since up to this point, no planes have been lost. The point of the parable is that although the elimination of individual species might not be directly harmful to human welfare, the aggregate elimination of many species probably will be. It is thus in the interests of humanity to remove as few "rivets" as possible, to preserve natural species even when they are "nonresources."

Without the use of a parable, Bryan Norton makes a similar point. In his discussion of the diversity-stability hypothesis in ecological theory, Norton argues that dynamically stable and mature ecosystems are important elements of that total diversity which stabilizes all ecosystems.[5] There is a danger in continually disrupting these diverse and stable ecosystems:

> Since the biological diversity of the planet has already entered an accelerating downward spiral, losses of species represent further accelerations toward local and global ecosystem breakdowns. The risks of breakdowns are so great and the contribution of species losses to them are so little understood that any rational society would exercise extreme caution in contributing to that acceleration.[6]

Diverse species populations thus contribute to stable ecosystems, which have positive impacts on human life.

Finally, this argument is broadened into a general concern for ecological function. The preservation of the natural environment insures a biosphere that supports human civilization. Degradation of the natural environment threatens human survival. Nevertheless, knowledge of ecological processes can help humans avoid damage to essential biological and physical links in the natural world. As Norton indicates, the loss of species and ecosystems is a sign that these natural connections are being "cut," lost, or damaged. The mere preservation of the natural environment halts this process of degradation. Nature thus has to be preserved because it has a value for human beings and human society: it insures the physical basis of human life.

In sum, these preservationist arguments based on "human interests" move from a narrow concern for the specific direct use of a natural entity or species, to the indirect importance of species as stabilizers of ecosystems, and finally to a general concern for the maintenance of ecosystems as the basis of human existence.

These anthropocentric instrumental arguments for environmental preservation are easily transferred to issues of environmental policy. Recent concern about the destruction of the ozone layer and the increased probability of the "greenhouse effect" reflect the fear that current environmental and economic polices are damaging the environment and threatening human life. Indeed, it is a mark of the success of the environmental movement that the public is now aware of the connections between environmental health and human survival.

A clear example of the connection between instrumental human interest arguments and concern for the preservation of an ecosystem is the current awareness of the plight of the Amazon rain forests. Although continued development of the forests and the conversion of rain forests to farmland and pasture contribute to a rapid loss of species,[7] the major problem is a threat to the overall ecosystems of the rain forests themselves. Deforestation has a significant impact on climate because of the increase of atmospheric carbon.[8] The recent increase in atmospheric carbon is a primary cause of the "greenhouse effect," which leads to global warming. Thus, the preservation of the rain forests is an important element in the maintenance of a biosphere habitable for humanity. This line of reasoning has been a clear argument and powerful motivation for environmental policies designed to preserve the Amazon rain forests. Environmentalists and ordinary citizens alike now seek a halt to the destruction of the Amazon; they now recognize that the welfare of all human life depends on the maintenance of this unique ecological region.

It thus appears that anthropocentric arguments for environmental preservation are useful in the justification and determination of environmental policy. Natural entities, species, and ecosystems are crucial, both for human survival and for the continuation of an advanced level of civilization. The important instrumental functions of the natural environment thus can be employed in debates over environmental policy throughout the Third World, and in particular, the Amazon rain forest. Should Third World nations be prevented from developing natural ecological areas in ways that would destroy the ecosystems of the region? Should policies of sustainable development, the economic use of the forest without clear-cutting or other forms of destruction, be mandatory? Should such countries as Brazil be persuaded to preserve the Amazon rain forest so that the harmful consequences of the "greenhouse effect" can be avoided? A consistent environmentalist, it seems, would be forced to condemn the Third World development of the natural environment on the grounds that the Amazon rain forests must be saved.

We believe that this anthropocentric and instrumental argument for the preservation of the Amazon rain forests (or any other Third World natural area) is seriously flawed. Even though the natural environment should be preserved, arguments based on human interest fail to provide an adequate justification for the preservation of ecosystems in the Third World. We discuss the problems with the anthropocentric perspective in the following two sections.

III. Problems of Utility

The first problem is empirical: there is uncertainty about the calculation of benefits and harms to be derived from alternative policies of development or preservation. In part, the problem is a traditional one encountered with any consequentialist analysis of normative action; however, in this particular case, Amazon rain forest development, we believe that the problem is acute. Although the benefits and harms to be determined are solely those of the affected human populations, the relevant populations are clearly distinct from one another, and the level and kinds of benefits and harms appear to be incommensurable.

If a policy of preservation is adopted, the benefits to be derived are those associated with the continued maintenance of the biosphere as the basis of human life: production of oxygen, consumption of atmospheric carbon, preservation of potentially useful species, etc. If a policy of development is adopted, the benefits to be derived are primarily local and economic: increased agricultural and livestock production, industry, and exports. The costs and harms within each policy are determined by the failure to achieve the alternative benefits. A policy of preservation limits economic gain; a policy of development limits the goods of a functioning natural ecosystem.

Although the choices appear clear, we lack the kind of data that would make the utility calculations possible. Is there a quantifiable good in the preservation of x amount of rain forest acreage that can be expressed in terms of biospherical maintenance and then compared to the loss of economic gains by indigenous local populations? Can we determine a quantifiable good in various methods of rain forest development, which then can be compared to losses in ecological function? It seems unlikely that these kinds of comparisons could ever be made; they are not being made now. In a recent survey of land use and management by indigenous peoples, Jason W. Clay warns: "Until now, few researchers have examined the ways indigenous inhabitants of tropical rain forests use and sustain their region's resources."[9] Clay is saying that we do not know what the economic benefits and costs are in alternative policies of preservation and development. If viewed in this way, utility calculations become impossible as a basis of policy.

Our complaint is not merely with the traditional difficulties of performing real-life utility calculations. The deeper issue is the anthropocentric framework that limits ethical and policy discussions. The primary concern for human interests or benefits — anthropocentrism — creates an irreconcilable conflict between two goods that are supposedly advocated by anthropocentric policies, i.e., the ecosystem which preserves the atmosphere, thus, preserving human life, and the economic use of the land by the indigenous population. We are faced with a classic case of a conflict between a long-term support system and short-term usable goods. This conflict cannot be resolved unless we expand the framework of discussion beyond the limits of anthropocentric instrumental reasoning.

IV. The Problem of Justice

The conflict between differing kinds of goods leads directly to the problem or dilemma of justice. This problem is a classic, long-standing difficulty in normative ethics. It arises in the context of environmental and economic policy decisions because of the exclusive use of narrowly defined anthropocentric and instrumental goods. Theoretical human goods and harms (the type discussed in the previous section) are not adequate as a basis for the determination of environmental policy, because global environmental policy cannot be determined in isolation from geopolitical concerns. The history and politics of power relations cannot be ignored. Third World nations, recently freed from political colonization, see the development of indigenous natural resources as a means of attaining economic freedom. The newly formed policies of nondevelopment and preservation appear to be a subtle form of the old imperialism. The wealthy industrialized nations of the world, having developed their own natural resources, and having "stolen" the natural resources of the Third World, now are planning to prevent any further development, so that the ecological basis of humanity can be preserved — a policy which clearly limits the economic and social development of the poorer, nonindustrialized nations.[10]

These complaints of "preservationist imperialism" are difficult to answer, and open-minded environmentalists must feel uneasy about the dilemma. Nevertheless, it is our contention (in this and the next section) that if the policies of nondevelopment and preservation continue to be justified by *instrumental* arguments regarding the ecological value of nature for human survival, then the charges of imperialism and domination remain unassailable. Only by *rejecting anthropocentrism* and developing a framework of direct value for natural entities and systems, can one avoid the charges of imperialism in Third World preservation policy.

Why is anthropocentrism a critical part of the problem of justice? The simple answer is that anthropocentric arguments emphasize merely human goods, which simultaneously ignore a direct concern for environmental preservation and create insurmountable problems of balance and equity. Anthropocentric and instrumental arguments result in a merely contingent connection between human satisfaction and the maintenance of the natural environment.[11] If the final goal of our policy is the maximization of human satisfaction, then the preservation of nature only occurs when there is a congruence of interests between humanity and nature. In practical terms, thus, any discussion of policy alternatives — development, preservation, resource conservation — involves a comparison and trade-off of human goods, and only human goods. Viewed in this way, the preservation of a natural ecosystem or an endangered species becomes merely one benefit in an entire array of possible human satisfactions. For an environmentalist policy to be adopted, the results of preservation have to outweigh the results of development. Broadly speaking, the cost-benefit ratio has to favor the nondevelopment of the natural environment.

It is here that the problems of the utility calculation noted above in section three lead to the dilemma of environmental justice. Third World nations can claim that the benefits of preserving, e.g., the Amazon rain forest, are spread out thinly across the entire human race, while the costs (in this case, the cost of lost economic opportunity) are borne primarily by Brazilians and other local human populations. Development of the rain forest, however, provides benefits for the local population while spreading the costs across the rest of humanity. Demanding that Brazil and other Third World countries limit development, therefore, violates basic and intuitive notions of equity and justice. The Third World is being asked to pay for the industrialized world's profligate use of natural resources. Having been denied the benefits of past development, they are now being asked to pay for the preservation of the biosphere.

This issue of justice arises because the policy discussion has been limited to a consideration of human interests. If the criterion for policy decisions is the maximization of human satisfactions or benefits, then it becomes appropriate — even mandatory — to ask questions about the distribution of these benefits. In this way, issues of justice, in general, serve to limit and complement teleological criteria for the determination of policy. In the context of Third World environmental development, however, considerations of justice override any plausible account of benefits resulting from the preservation of the natural environment. The need for economic development seems so great that the hypothetical long-term effects on global warming appear trivial. If we restrict our analysis of policy to the maximization of human welfare and to the creation of just social institutions, then we cannot escape the problem created by the Third World's need for economic development. Conceived as a problem in maximizing and balancing human goods, the scales incline toward policies of development. The demand for anthropocentric justice dooms the preservation of the natural environment.

V. Moving Beyond Anthropocentrism

Can an environmentalist defend a policy of preservation in the Amazon rain forest without violating a basic sense of justice? We believe that the mistake is not the policy of preservation itself, but the anthropocentric instrumental framework in which it is justified. Environmental policy decisions should not merely concern the trade-off and comparison of various human benefits. If environmentalists claim that the Third World must preserve its environment because of the overall benefits for humanity, then decision makers in the Third World can demand justice in the determination of preservation policy: preservationist policies unfairly damage the human interests of the local populations. If preservationist policies are to be justified without a loss of equity, there are only two possible alternatives: either we in the industrialized world must pay for the benefits we will gain from preservation or we must reject the anthropocentric and instrumental framework for policy decisions. The first alternative is an empirical political issue, and one about which we are not overly optimistic. The second alternative represents a shift in philosophical world view.

We are not providing a direct argument for a nonanthropocentric value system as the basis of environmental policy. Rather, our strategy is indirect. Let us assume that a theory of normative ethics which includes nonhuman natural value has been justified. In such a situation, the human community, in addition to its traditional human-centered obligations, would also have moral obligations to nature or to the natural environment in itself. One of these obligations would involve the urgent necessity for environmental preservation. We would be obligated, for example, to the Amazon rain forest directly. We would preserve the rain forest, not for the human benefits resulting from this preservation, but because we have an obligation of preservation to nature and its ecosystems. Our duties would be directed to nature and its inhabitants and environments, not merely to humans and human institutions.

From *this* perspective, questions of the trade-off and comparison of human benefits, and questions of justice for specific human populations, do not dominate the discussion. This change of emphasis can be illustrated by an exclusively human example. Consider two businessmen, Smith and Jones, who are arguing over the proper distribution of the benefits and costs resulting from a prior business agreement between them. If we just focus on Smith and Jones and the issues concerning them, we will want to look at the contract, the relevant legal precedents, and the actual results of the deal, before rendering a decision. But suppose we learn that the agreement involved the planned murder of a third party, Green, and the resulting distribution of his property. At that point the issues between Smith and Jones cease to be relevant; we no longer consider who has claims to Green's wallet, overcoat, or BMW to be important. The competing claims become insignificant in light of the obligations owed to Green. This case is analogous to our view of the moral obligations owed to the rain forest. As soon as we realize that the rain forest itself is relevant to the conflict of competing goods, we see that there is not a simple dilemma between Third World development, on the one hand, and preservation of rain forests, on the other; there is now, in addition, the moral obligation to nature and its ecosystems.

When the nonanthropocentric framework is introduced, it creates a more complex situation for deliberation and resolution. It complicates the already detailed discussions of human trade-offs, high-tech transfers, aid programs, debt-for-nature swaps, sustainable development, etc., with a consideration of the moral obligations to nonhuman nature. This complication may appear counterproductive, but as in the case of Smith, Jones, and Green, it actually serves to simplify the decision. Just as a concern for Green made the contract dispute between Smith and Jones irrelevant, the obligation *to the rain forest* makes many of the issues about trade-offs of human goods irrelevant.[12] It is, of course, unfortunate that this direct obligation to the rain forest can only be met with a cost in human satisfaction — some human interests will not be fulfilled. Nevertheless, the same can be said of all ethical decisions, or so Kant teaches us: we are only assuredly moral when we act against our inclinations.

To summarize, the historical forces of economic imperialism have created a harsh dilemma for environmentalists who consider nature preservation in the Third World to be necessary. Nevertheless, environmentalists can escape the dilemma, as exemplified in the debate over the development of the Amazon rain forest, if they reject the axiological and normative framework of anthropocentric instrumental rationality. A set of obligations directed to nature in its own right makes many questions of human benefits and satisfactions irrelevant. The Amazon rain forest ought to be preserved regardless of the benefits or costs to human beings. Once we move beyond the confines of human-based instrumental goods, the environmentalist position is thereby justified, and no policy dilemma is created. This conclusion serves as an indirect justification of a nonanthropocentric system of normative ethics, avoiding problems in environmental policy that a human-based ethic cannot.[13]

VI. Concluding Remarks

Policy makers and philosophers in the Third World may not be pleased with our conclusions here. Indeed, Ramachandra Guha has recently criticized the focus on biocentrism (i.e., nonan-thropocentrism) and wilderness preservation that pervades Western environmentalism. These Western concerns are at best, irrelevant to, and at worst, destructive of Third World societies. According to Guha, any justifiable environmental movement must include solutions to problems of equity, "economic and political redistribution."[14] We agree. Thus, as a final note, let us return from the abstract atmospheres of axiological theory and normative frameworks to the harsh realities of life in the non-industrialized world. If our argument is sound, then any destructive development of the natural environment in the Third World is a moral wrong, and a policy of environmental preservation is a moral requirement. Recognition of this moral obligation to preserve the natural environment should be the *starting point* for any serious discussion of developmental policy. But it is only a starting point. Once the preservationist obligation is accepted, the difficult trade-offs of goods between competing groups of humans can be debated, and questions of global equity can be addressed. Indeed, it is clear that they must be addressed, for the moral obligation to preserve the environment from destructive development creates additional human-based geopolitical obligations on the industrialized Western world. We must do more than lecture Third World nations; we must give them the economic aid that will make the development of their natural environments unnecessary. As Guha notes, we have to end the "expansionist character" of the West by developing an ethic of self-limitation. Only in this way can we begin to meet our obligation to preserve the natural environment.[15] In short, we must begin to pay the price for our centuries of environmental and developmental exploitation. We have outstanding debts, both to the nations of the Third World and to nature itself.

NOTES

1. The critique of anthropocentric instrumental reasoning in environmental policy begins with Aldo Leopold's attempt to develop an ethic of ecological community. See Aldo Leopold, "The Land

Ethic," in *A Sand County Almanac* (New York: Ballantine, 1970), pp. 237-64. Other important works that focus on the direct moral consideration of nature include: Holmes Rolston, III, *Environmental Ethics: Duties to and Values in the Natural World* (Philadelphia: Temple Univ. Press, 1987); J. Baird Callicott. *In Defense of the Land Ethic: Essays in Environmental Philosophy* (Albany: SUNY Press, 1989); Peter S. Wenz, *Environmental Justice* (Albany: SUNY Press, 1988); and Paul W. Taylor, *Respect for Nature: A Theory of Environmental Ethics* (Princeton: Princeton Univ. Press, 1986). For enlightened versions of anthropocentrism see Eugene C. Hargrove, *Foundations of Environmental Ethics* (Englewood Cliffs: Prentice Hall, 1989); Bryan G. Norton, *Why Preserve Natural Variety?* (Princeton: Princeton Univ. Press, 1987); and Mark Sagoff, *The Economy of the Earth* (Cambridge: Cambridge Univ. Press, 1988).

2. For a discussion of "nonresources," see David Ehrenfeld, *The Arrogance of Humanism* (New York: Oxford University Press, 1978), pp. 176-211.

3. Alastair Gunn, "Why Should We Care about Rare Species?" *Environmental Ethics* 2 (1980): 17-37.

4. Paul and Anne Ehrlich, *Extinction* (New York: Ballantine, 1981), pp. xi-xiv.

5. Norton, *Natural Variety*, pp. 80-84.

6. Ibid., p. 121.

7. Most sources, both popular and scientific, claim that the tropical rain forests are the source of almost half of the Earth's species. A comment by Eugene P. Odum is typical: "Species diversity of both plants and animals tends to be high in tropical rain forests; there may be more species of plants and insects in a few acres of tropical rain forests than in the entire flora and fauna of Europe." Eugene P. Odum, *Ecology and Our Endangered Life-Support Systems* (Sunderland: Sinauer, 1989), p. 244. See also Ehrlich and Ehrlich, *Extinction*, pp. 191-98; Thomas E. Lovejoy, "Species Leave the Ark One by One," in *The Preservation of Species*, ed., Bryan G. Norton (Princeton: Princeton University Press, 1986), pp. 13-27; Norman Myers, *The Sinking Ark* (New York: Pergamon Press, 1979) and *The Primary*

Source: Tropical Forests and Our Future (New York: W.W. Norton, 1984), pp. 36-67; and E.O. Wilson, "Threats to Biodiversity," *Scientific American* 261, no. 3 (September 1989): 108-16. A major source of articles on all aspects of species diversity is E.O. Wilson and Frances M. Peter, eds., *Biodiversity* (Washington, D.C.: National Academy Press, 1988).

8. Deforestation has two major effects on climate, one "positive" and one "negative." Burning forests releases the carbon stored in trees into the atmosphere; and with deforestation, there are fewer trees to absorb or consume the carbon dioxide in the atmosphere. For a basic discussion in an introductory ecology text, see R.F. Dasmann, *Environmental Conservation*, 5th ed. (New York: John Wiley, 1984), p. 168, or see Myers, *The Primary Source*, pp. 283-93. Recent discussions of the effects of Amazon deforestation on climate can be found in J. Shukla, C. Nobre, and P. Sellers, "Amazon Deforestation and Climate Change," *Science* 247 (March 1990): 1322-25; and Roger A. Sedjo, "Forests: A Tool to Moderate Global Warming?" *Environment* 31 (January/February 1989): 14-20. See also Richard A. Houghton and George M. Woodwell, "Global Climatic Change," *Scientific American* 260, no. 4 (April 1989): 36-44; and a report on the work of Charles Keeling in Fred Pearce, "Felled Trees Deal Double Blow to Global Warning," *New Scientist* 123, no. 1682 (September 1989): 25.

9. Jason W. Clay, *Indigenous Peoples and Tropical Forests* (Cambridge, Mass.: Cultural Survival, 1988), p. 3. We might want to modify this bleak picture; see the argument in favor of non-destructive development of the rain forest in Charles M. Peters, Alwyn H. Gentry, and Robert O. Mendelsohn, "Valuation of an Amazon Rainforest," *Nature* 339 (June 1989): 655-56.

10. Ramachandra Guha, "Radical American Environmentalism and Wilderness Preservation: A Third World Critique," *Environmental Ethics* 11 (1989): 75-76.

11. For a discussion of the contingency of human interests in environmental policy, see Martin Krieger, "What's Wrong with Plastic Trees?" *Science* 179 (1973): 446-55; Mark Sagoff, "On

Preserving the Natural Environment," *Yale Law Journal* 84 (1974): 205-67; and Eric Katz, "Utilitarianism and Preservation," *Environmental Ethics* 1 (1979): 357-64.

12. It makes many of the human interests irrelevant, but not all. See our concluding remarks below.

13. Again, we are not denying the possibility of an anthropocentric and noninstrumental ethic, a version of a so-called "enlightened anthropocentrism." The best treatments of this view are expressed by Hargrove, Norton, and Sagoff, in the works cited in n. 1 above. Hargrove uses a concept of beauty, Norton a concept of "transformative" human values, and Sagoff a concept of the ideals of the community or nation. It is our contention, however, that a direct appeal to the goods of the nonhuman natural world is a clearer and less problematic route to the goal of environmental preservation.

14. Guha, "Radical American Environmentalism and Wilderness Preservation," p. 81.

15. Ibid., p. 80.

DEVELOPMENT AND ENVIRONMENTALISM

Robin Attfield

Robin Attfield is Professor of Philosophy at Cardiff University in Wales. He is one of the founding members of the Cardiff Centre for Applied Ethics and the author of The Ethics of Environmental Concern *(1991) and* The Ethics of the Global Environment *(1999) and co-editor with Andrew Belsey of* Philosophy and the Natural Environment *(1994).*

Attfield attempts to reconcile the division between environmental ethicists and development theorists by arguing that each cannot ignore the other's concerns. He defends an account of development that emphasizes human development and highlights the injustices in and across societies with respect to the oppression of groups and peoples. He uses this account of development to argue that versions of deep ecology that take human interests to be subservient to the interests and needs of the environment are not justified. Attfield then argues that developmentalists also display chauvinism when their moral concern stops with concern for human beings. To oppose human suffering and not animal suffering or to argue that only human beings have intrinsic value is to discriminate on the basis of species for no good grounds. Attfield calls on development theorists and policy-makers to broaden their critique to include a critique of anthropocentrism itself.

The days are receding when advocates of Third World development maintained that concern for the environment was a luxury which only developed countries could afford. A similar view sometimes surfaces from British Conservative politicians, when they claim that conservation and preservation can only be afforded out of the proceeds of development, as if at least the early stages of development could take place in their absence. There is, however, an increasing realization that the kind of "development" which pollutes and sometimes undermines life-support systems is inimical to any development worthy of the name. In this more enlightened approach, human interests tend to be paramount, but there is concern for the protection of the natural world, if only for prudential reasons.

Environmentalists, meanwhile, frequently regard development and its advocacy as the enemy which is to be opposed at all costs, or at least as often as possible. While this is not the posture of groupings such as the Green parties of Britain and Germany, it is often encountered in British environmentalist circles, and is even more prevalent among environmentalists in North America and Australia. How deep this attitude goes depends in part on the underlying value-theory and ethic professed or taken for granted, and partly on the locally accepted understanding of the causes of ecological problems and of the social and political conditions necessary to solve them. Accordingly, the ranks of environmentalists include some who recognize poverty as one of the causes of environmental deterioration and welcome sustainable development in the Third World. Yet the advocates of development still come in for criticism for caring about nature largely in the human interest.

In this chapter I shall try to explain why even the "deeper" strain of environmentalists should support sustainable development (as opposed to undifferentiated growth), and are required to do so by their own principles, in so far as they are defensible. I shall also try to explain why developmentalists should equally support environmentalism, and support not merely its "shallower" but also some of its "deeper" versions,[1] and will do so if they are consistent. This double project will also involve comparing and relating the critiques of current evils propounded by the two camps: the developmentalist critique of underdevelopment and its economic causes, and the deep environmentalist critique of anthropocentrism. Critiques improve by taking greater ranges of factors into account, and I shall claim that each of these critiques is in danger of neglecting the factors stressed by the other.

A Way of Preserving the Indonesian Rainforest: Butterfly Ranching

Applied philosophy can contribute to issues such as these by close attention to concepts and principles, and by tracing their implications. But to prevent the intricacy and complexity of the circumstances to which the concepts and principles must be supplied being overlooked, I shall begin my discussion of what development involves by reference to an example drawn from *Orbit*, the magazine of the British organization, Voluntary Service Overseas. There a volunteer in the cause of overseas aid to the Third World, Ian Craven, who worked for three years in Indonesia as an environmental officer for the World Wide Fund for Nature, adduces his own experience in rejecting the kind of conservation which would involve "the total exclusion of any resource utilization" or "the segregation of land from the local population for nature's protection in certain over-stressed regions." Granted the poverty of the tribal people of the Arfak Mountains with whom he was working, and the risk that, without some financial return from the forest, they would succumb to external economic pressures (presumably from timber companies), the establishment of a nature reserve there required, and in Craven's view justifies, the participation of local

people in its management and in particular the collection for export of butterflies. Butterfly ranching involves the collection of "eggs, caterpillars or cocoons ... from areas enriched with the butterflies' plant foods"; they are then "shipped to butterfly zoos, collectors, taxonomists and scientists around the world." Since the butterflies are forest reliant and the local people know this, they thus have a strong interest in preventing the destruction of the forest. Craven's short article is entitled "Profit for the poor."[2] (The role of timber companies in Indonesia is explained on the next page of the same number in an article by Jasper Zjilstra entitled "Rainforest reality."[3])

Many developmentalists would be likely to applaud Craven's plan unreservedly, on the counts that the basic problems of Indonesia are poverty and exploitation, and that for the tribal people in question this plan appears to alleviate poverty in some degree without the further exploitation which would be involved in the destruction of their native habitat and thus their way of life. The plan also involves their active participation, another hallmark of development which is of value both in itself and because of the self-respect and the increased autonomy of previously disadvantaged people which it is likely to bring. And developmentalists who are not apologists of timber companies would add the pertinent point that the plan would help secure the forest for future generations of Indonesians, and may well be the only way in which that can be achieved.

Others, whether environmentalists or not, would want to ask a number of questions, for example about the extent to which the plan really does save the forest ecosystem from destruction. In particular we are not told how (if at all) it is proposed to ensure that the butterfly species in question do not become extinct, at least as far as sites in the Arfak Mountains are concerned. For if they were to become extinct the forest would have been impoverished and at the same time the benefits to local people would prove not to be sustainable;[4] in other words, they would be thrust back into the same problem as at the outset. Thus the plan could be counter-productive even from a purely developmentalist viewpoint.

Environmentalists of a quite moderate persuasion might well add a number of points. Thus we are not told what other forest species depend, whether through pollination or predation, on the presence of the butterflies, and should need to know this to discover to what extent the forest genuinely escapes destruction. This relates to a more general question: how much "resource utilization" is consistent with conservation? And even if the answer turns out to be "quite a lot in this case," very little follows about whether conservation should not sometimes exclude the consumption of resources, and sometimes exclude even the use of non-consumable resources, and thus an actual prohibition of the human use of certain habitats. Anthropocentric (i.e., human-centred) reasons could sustain all these possibilities, but they become stronger still when the interests of non-human species are taken into account, as advocated by environmentalists of "deeper" persuasions.

Some readers, particularly if they are also environmentalists, may by now be aghast at any amount of consideration at all being given to the cause of development, as opposed to none at all, especially if it can adopt such manifestations as this. But this is where the concept of development and the related moral obligations need to be brought into prominence. For I shall be arguing that there are obligations here to support and foster development which in any case cannot be disowned.

Why Environmentalists Should Support Development

In social and economic connections it is easier to define underdevelopment than development. Underdevelopment is a condition of society where several of the following factors reinforce one another: malnutrition, high infant mortality, low levels of literacy, relatively high morbidity among the young and the middle-aged, poor medical facilities, poor educational facilities, low levels of income per head and low levels of pro-

ductivity per head. Development may be taken, relatedly, as either the process or the condition resulting from the process of moving away from the cycle of underdevelopment.

But not just any departure from one of the mentioned variables amounts to development. The obvious example is productivity; for mere economic growth need not, as such, involve or indicate development of any kind. A number of other implications flow from the definition, such as the need for the active participation of the people concerned in the process of development if that process or its outcome is to be worthy of the name. But I have written about these matters elsewhere,[5] and should here move to a centrally relevant aspect of development (as just now defined), namely its necessary connection with justice. For injustice prevails where people's basic needs are avoidably unsatisfied; and except where underdevelopment is out of people's control, many people's basic needs are precisely unsatisfied, and avoidably so too, in the circumstances of underdevelopment. There is thus a strong moral obligation incumbent upon those who have the ability to help or hinder the process anywhere (whether by action or by inaction) to promote some form of development, for not to do so is to perpetuate injustice. This obligation is obviously particularly strong in the cases of the members of the society in question; but, short of stronger countervailing obligations, it is also a strong one for members of other societies who (individually or in concert) have the ability (whether by action or inaction) to help or to hinder the process.

To say this is certainly to assume that there can be relations of justice and injustice not only between members of one and the same society but also between different societies and their members. But this assumption cannot seriously be denied by anyone prepared to enter into moral discussion at all. For if the basic needs of anyone count, so do the basic needs of anyone else, in so far as an agent can make any difference to them. The fact that the one person is a member of the same society and another is not makes no difference at all in this regard. Certainly there are further moral rules requiring agents to pay special consideration to the needs e.g., of members of their family, and rules at that which make good moral sense; but the nature of these obligations in no way implies that all obligations depend on some special relationship or other.

Correspondingly there is a like obligation to help remove oppression wherever it is to be found, to the extent of one's power, and in so far as this does not conflict with stronger obligations. But where underdevelopment is avoidable, there, whether known or unknown, oppression exists. Accordingly, at least where other things are equal (and quite often when they are not), there is a strong obligation to combat oppression. But this is a further way of showing that it is a moral obligation to support development wherever avoidable underdevelopment is to be found. It would not be obligatory to support any and every form of development, as there are alternative forms, and some are arguably better than others. (Thus there is no general obligation to support schemes to develop tribal societies in ways which would undermine their inherited cultures.) But it is morally obligatory to support some form of development in each avoidably underdeveloped society.

But if so, the needs of the poor in Indonesia must be taken seriously, whatever our beliefs as environmentalists may be. It is morally unacceptable to claim, for example, that the needs of future generations for intact rainforest there justify us in disregarding these current needs. For if future people's needs count, so do the needs of our contemporaries. Nor is it satisfactory to maintain that what fundamentally matters in morality is the integrity and stability of the biosphere, and that as human beings sometimes subvert this integrity and stability their interests can be disregarded for the sake of the greater good. This kind of misanthropy is sometimes to be found among ecological writers;[6] but everyone should be clear that it involves disowning the intrinsic value and moral significance of the well-being of every individual, and the valuing of everyone and everything according to its relation to the biosphere instead. In other words, it is an attempt to disown all the requirements of justice. But it is hard to believe that even those who from time to time swallow this ethic can seriously employ it in their own interpersonal dealings, much less in their attitudes to themselves.

In any case, misanthropy of this kind is no part and no implication of what Arne Naess has called "Deep Ecology," one tenet of which concerns the equal right of all creatures to live and blossom.[7] While I should not seek to defend his "biospherical egalitarianism," I want to draw attention to some of its less problematic implications. For the creatures which are said to have the right to live and blossom certainly include non-human creatures, and thus insects such as butterflies. But they also include human beings, with their more complex possibilities for self-realization. According to this approach, then, while the different interests must sometimes be weighed up against one another, there is a strong case for upholding the interests of each and every human being, especially (as in conditions of underdevelopment) where these interests are significantly unsatisfied at present. Indeed, Naess explicitly maintains that the Deep Ecology movement takes into account the needs of the Third World, alongside the interests of future generations and of non-human species.

Some environmentalists, however, will now maintain that all this stress on the needs of human beings exhibits species discrimination, and thus reinforces the central, underlying source of oppression, namely anthropocentrism. Why, it will be asked, should the problems of people be singled out as they have been above, to the neglect of non-humans (and in particular those sentient non-humans whom human beings exploit for food and in experiments)? A failure to recognize anthropocentrism for what it is fundamentally vitiates any ethic and any social programme, it will be alleged. Later in this chapter I shall try to explain that there is a great deal to be said in favour of this appraisal of anthropocentrism. Here it is more relevant to point out that drawing attention to unsatisfied human needs is quite compatible with concern for the needs of non-human creatures, and need not involve neglect of them. Thus the humanitarian tradition has historically made a point of protesting not only at slavery, excessive working hours and the oppression of women and children, but also at the maltreatment of animals.

But no movement should allow itself to supply too one-dimensional a critique of oppression. I shall be returning to this point in a later connection, but in the present context its bearing is that those who recognize the evils of anthropocentrism have a distorted vision if they ascribe the world's evils to anthropocentrism alone. Such a critique neglects such other sources of oppression as economic exploitation, racism and sexism. Warwick Fox has some salient remarks about one-dimensional critiques of oppression, of which mention is now in place.[8]

Such simplistic critiques, according to Fox, suffer from two major weaknesses, in respect of which they are "not merely descriptively poor and logically facile" but also "morally objectionable." One of these is "scapegoating," by which all members of a particular class are targeted for criticism to an equal degree, whereas in fact some subclasses are much more responsible for oppression than others, and some subclasses of the targeted class are actively working to challenge ecological destruction or whatever form of oppression is envisaged. By targeting all members of the class which (in the short term) stands to gain from discrimination, scapegoating is objectionably "over-inclusive."

At the same time, simplistic critiques suffer from what Fox calls "inauthenticity" and at the same time "under-inclusiveness." For such analyses can lead to a denial of responsibility in cases where some responsibility should be accepted. Fox has in mind here critiques which focus in an uni-dimensional manner on capitalism or, again, on patriarchy; for such critiques can serve to exonerate e.g., trade unionists or women of all responsibility for oppression of any kind; but his point is not without relevance to any critique which focuses simply on anthropocentrism, and thus fails to ascribe responsibility for oppression to those human groups and individuals (not excluding some unionists and some women) who

have the power to act oppressively and do not hesitate to use it so.

Fox's points here are well taken; a critique of global problems should neither be so blunt as to bestrew blame indiscriminately nor be so unsubtle as to distract attention from genuine major sources of oppression, and tacitly to exonerate them accordingly. What is needed in a critique of social or of global problems is the kind of intelligent approach which takes into account a plurality of seats of power and sources of oppression, a variety of degrees of complicity and a range of would-be legitimations of unjustified hierarchies, all of which need to be challenged. Such an approach has the tactical advantage that, instead of writing off all males or all beneficiaries of capitalism or even the vast majority of human beings, it facilitates alliances between diverse subgroups which either suffer from oppression or are prepared to campaign against it. But, tactical considerations apart, it has the intellectual and moral advantages of being more appropriate to the actual distribution of power in society (international society included) and more just.

While Fox was primarily objecting to writers and movements which neglect anthropocentrism and environmental destruction (a theme to which I shall return), his general remarks apply similarly to those who focus on anthropocentrism and environmental destruction to the exclusion of all else besides. For the same anti-discriminatory principles which underlie e.g., the Deep Ecology stance of Arne Naess apply to other instances of discrimination, of the misuse of power and of oppression also. There is, indeed, a kind of inconsistency involved in excoriating the arrogance of humankind for its chauvinist treatment of all other species besides, and lifting not so much as a finger in protest at economic oppression, sexism and racism. It is not as if these latter misuses of power involved minor discriminations within the world elite, humanity; for in many cases discrimination against humans is at least as bad as the treatment accorded to non-human animals. It is certainly true that nobody can campaign about everything, and that different people may rightly focus their energies on one campaign rather than another. But that is no justification for asserting or giving the impression that the same principles do not apply to oppression of different kinds.

The point may be reinforced by citing the definition of chauvinism given by Richard Routley (now Sylvan) and Val Routley (now Plumwood). The Routleys used this designation of "substantially differential, discriminatory and inferior treatment by humans of nonhumans,"[9] and this is a perfectly proper extension of the use of "chauvinism." But if this kind of treatment by humans of non-humans is chauvinism, then equally so is such treatment by humans of humans, especially in connection with discrimination of a nationalist or a racist basis, the original context of application (after all) of the term. And if substantially differential, discriminatory and inferior treatment is oppressive and unjustified in the one kind of case, so (truistically) it must also be in the other.

Thus where an environmental philosophy (or "ecophilosophy") is partly grounded, like that of the Routleys, in opposition to unjustified discrimination, or, like that of Arne Naess, in the advocacy of egalitarianism on a global scale (at least in principle), or, like that of John Rodman, on the need for liberation,[10] the same grounds require support for opposition to injustice and oppression in inter-human relations. This remains the case even among those who maintain that the root cause of ecological problems is population growth, reluctant as the holders of this kind of theory may be to support some of the steps to development advocated by those who are not so persuaded. For even theorists of this kind would be obliged by their principles to oppose the oppression of those humans who are already alive. Their support of development programmes would, however, be more uninhibited if they came to recognize that the underlying cause of population growth is poverty, and that poverty is also one of the direct causes of ecological problems;[11] indeed, once these causal connections are granted, environmentalists have additional grounds for supporting the alleviation of poverty. But even if they are not recognized, such support is in any case obligatory on grounds of justice.

There is more of a problem, however, with environmentalists of two kinds, whose positions are prone to coincide in practice. One is the kind which regards humanity as a cancerous growth, so detrimental to other life-forms that the planet would be better off without it, or with drastically curtailed numbers. The other is the kind referred to above, which locates intrinsic value in the well-being of the biosphere as a whole, and determines the value of individuals and/or species by their contribution to this well-being, of which the leading criterion is diversity. Since most humans contribute little to the integrity of the whole, and since humanity has been diminishing planetary diversity, human beings would on this basis be either of neutral or of negative value, and should be treated accordingly. The first kind of position is sometimes supported on a consequentialist basis, in that humans are held to do more harm than good to life-forms overall; alternatively it can be harnessed to the ethical holism of the second kind. The second kind does not attach any value to the good of individual creatures or even life-forms, but derives its entire ethic from its collectivist and holist value-theory. Both kinds may fairly be described as misanthropic, and both earn the designation, coined I believe by Murray Bookchin, of "ecofascism."

The first kind of misanthropic environmentalism has been put forward by Dave Foreman, a supporter of Deep Ecology,[12] and has attracted from Bookchin the charge that Deep Ecology is essentially a misanthropic enterprise.[13] Foreman maintains that the best way to help Ethiopia is to let people starve, and that this will minimize suffering and death in the long term. Fox, however, is happy to see Bookchin taking Foreman to task for these "personal, unhistorical and abhorrently simplistic views on population control," and is quick to dissociate Deep Ecology from support for them. Indeed, he quotes Naess as writing that "faced with hungry children humanitarian action is a priority, whatever its relation to developmental plans and cultural invasion."[14] To Fox's criticisms it may be added that any kind of positive consequentialism, in which intrinsic value is attached to worthwhile life, would be inconsistent with Foreman's conclusions; while if Foreman is appealing to negative consequentialism, a theory which would also, depending on circumstances, support the elimination of all sentient life in the cause of preventing suffering, the unacceptable implications require the rejection of any normative theory of this kind, and thus of whatever negative consequentialist theory he may happen to be appealing to. Ecofascism, in short, cannot be defended by the harm to people which it is supposed to prevent. It is only fair to grant to Fox here that he well shows that Deep Ecology does not stand for any such misanthropic position.

As for the holistic version of misanthropic environmentalism, I have already published what I believe to be fatal criticisms.[15] The central problem here is that no defensible ethic can assume the form which this kind of collectivist holism assumes, for its implications conflict with almost all the central cases of agreed ethical judgements and principles. This becomes particularly clear in connection with the instrumental approach which this position requires to be taken to all individuals. Thus whatever we say about the well-being of the biosphere and the desirability of diversity, we cannot defensibly say this. (These remarks do not, of course, subvert certain other positions in which axiological holism is combined with belief in the intrinsic value of worthwhile individual life; but there is no need to argue against such positions as these in the current connection.)

The conclusion which I draw from consideration of these two versions of environmentalism is that they are indeed misanthropic, but that there are extremely strong grounds against adherence to either of them. To put matters another way, those forms of environmentalism which are essentially opposed to development are ones which intrinsically deserve to be rejected in any case, while the remainder require some degree of support for development in so far as their supporters are consistent, not to mention the regard which they ought to have for justice.

One qualification is in place before I move on. It should be stressed that grounds for supporting development are *pro tanto* grounds for supporting sustainable development, i.e., the kind of development which avoids harm and loss to future generations and can be sustained indefinitely. Supporters of Deep Ecology are sometimes suspicious of sustainable development; but Arne Naess himself would seem to be selectively in favour of it, to judge from his article "Sustainable development and the deep, long range ecological movement."[16] Indeed, this is where Naess's remark about humanitarian action sometimes being a priority is to be found.

Why Developmentalists Should Support Environmentalism

I now turn to the issue of whether supporters of development should also support environmentalism. Now there is not much of a problem about support for environmentalism in its shallower forms. Let us presume that the developmentalists in question are moderately well versed in the findings of ecological science, and also accept what is argued in *Blueprint for a Green Economy* in terms of the considerable impact of environmental factors on a country's economy as well as of the considerable impact of the latter on the former.[17] They will, if so, recognize that economic development requires not only the reduction of pollution and the conservation of natural resources, but also the preservation of a good deal of wilderness (e.g., wetlands and rainforest), all in the long-term interest of humanity. Indeed, the degradation of the natural environment would at some point make economic life unsupportable, while the loss of a species or an area of wetlands, being irreversible, involves a cost for ever to whichever humans could have benefited therefrom. Thus sustainable development calls for preservationist measures even more strongly than development does as such.

But these are just the kind of grounds which make environmentalists of the deeper persuasion suspicious, for they are compatible with an anthropocentric approach. And this may serve as a clue to the location of possible disagreement; for developmentalists are often reluctant to support campaigns conducted in the interests of non-human species or their members, particularly when so much human need remains unsatisfied. To some extent this would be a matter of priorities: non-human interests, it might be held, matter, but can wait. Others again might hold that they do not matter at all. And both schools of thought might well maintain that to focus on anthropocentrism in one's critique of the world's problems is to divert attention from significant evils such as inter-human oppression and the excesses of capitalism, and thus from the realities of power.

In practice, concern for human interests would bring such people into many a preservationist campaign. For humans have interests in preservation for the sake of scientific research as an end in itself, for the sake of its medical and agricultural applications, for recreation, contemplation and aesthetic enjoyment. Thus campaigns for the preservation of wildlife and the necessary habitats frequently have this kind of motivation. Yet in all these connections the natural world is regarded as nothing more than a resource, whether laboratory, museum, playground, temple, cathedral or art gallery. To this catalogue might be added the symbolic value of natural objects such as high mountains, cliffs (like those at Dover) and untamed rivers: nature as emblem, or perhaps as mascot. Nevertheless where human interests are paramount, other human interests will often take priority over all of these. So if preservationist campaigns are supported by some people on these grounds and by others on deeper environmentalist grounds, the alliance will be an uneasy one. Sometimes, indeed, the allies may part company, such as when preservationists urge (in Craven's words) "the segregation of land from the local population for nature's protection."[18] But this kind of segregation would be rejected not only by developmentalists, but also by the environmentalist movements of both Germany and India, to judge from Ramachandra Guha's excellent article "Radical American environmentalism and wilderness preservation: a Third World critique."[19] Indian environmentalists tend rather to support forest preservation for the sake of pre-

venting soil erosion and flooding, and generally for the sake of human beings as well as that of forest creatures.

Nevertheless to grasp the need to support environmentalism of a deeper kind than that of anthropocentric preservationists, a developmentalist, like anyone else, would need to see the force of the critique of anthropocentrism. This would in no way involve abandoning other forms of negative critique, concerning oppression or hierarchy for instance, any more than it would involve support for the kind of segregation which debars local people from their own countryside. Rather it would supplement such a critique, and broaden appreciation of the nature of social and global problems, and of what might count as solutions to them.

There are two kinds of ways to proceed. One is to point out the inconsistency (and sometimes hypocrisy) of opposition to human suffering which stops short at opposition to comparable suffering in animals, or to argue from the intrinsic value of human health, happiness and flourishing by analogy to there being intrinsic value in the health, happiness and flourishing of non-humans, despite the differences between the natures of the different species concerned. To discriminate on the basis of species for no good ground is just as arbitrary as to discriminate on the basis of race or sex for no good ground, as Peter Singer has long been arguing;[20] and to mete out treatment which is substantially differential and inferior on no better basis amounts to what Val and Richard Routley have called "human chauvinism."[21] These are good liberal arguments, and none the worse for that; they deserve a hearing both from supporters of possessive individualism and from its most resolute enemies, and they call for radical changes not only at the level of individual behaviour but also at the level of public policy in matters such as agricultural methods, fisheries and land use. But there is another route by which a negative critique of anthropocentrism can be commended, at least to developmentalists, and I shall attempt to expound it now.

The critique standardly advanced by developmentalists of the causes of persistent underdevelopment concerns systems of power relations. Both within and between societies, it is held, the terms on which economic and other transactions take place are so skewed that flows of resources pass from those in economically weaker positions to those in stronger positions, in forms such as rent, debt servicing and the relative prices of raw and processed commodities. These economic relations depend on relationships of power, and are perpetuated by them; not only do governments protect business corporations, landowners and local elites, but at international level transnational corporations and the governments which support them have enough power to dictate terms to the governments of most developing countries. This system of economic and political relations sometimes actually benefits some of the poor, in that they would be even worse off without the investment and employment which it offers. But for all that it is profoundly exploitative. It is also mirrored in the power relations which often hold within families and between the sexes and the generations, and is thus prone to uphold the least desirable aspects of patriarchy and of gerontocracy.

This critique depicts a hierarchy of power relations, which does a lot to explain the persistence of poverty, and suggests that lasting solutions to social and global problems depend on a radical redistribution of power. Not all developmentalists, of course, subscribe to this critique, but very many would subscribe to at least parts of it, and this accounts for an insistence on exposing capitalism, sexism, and the like, for what they are. As the present project is to persuade developmentalists of a further point, I will assume the essential acceptability of this critique, at least for present purposes. But if that much is accepted, is it credible that the base of the hierarchical pyramid consists of rural and urban proletariats, subsistence farmers and the unemployed? At each of the higher levels interest-groups and classes profit from the humbler classes. Thus, as Bahro has been pointing out,[22] the working class in developed countries has considerably profited from the much more wretched condition of the poor of the Third World. But, as Bahro would readily agree, the lives of the poor (and to some extent of the relatively rich as well) have also benefited economically from transactions between humanity and other living creatures. Domestic animals have been used for traction, transport and food; wild animals are often hunted for their hides, fur or flesh; and forests have been eradicated for timber and for farming.

Now I am certainly not suggesting that the domestication of wild species of plants and animals is reprehensible; much less, with deep ecologists like Rodman, that domesticated animals should be phased out.[23] Technology in the forms of agriculture and medicine has contributed a great deal to making civilized life possible, and thus the liberation and flourishing of humanity. Nevertheless much civilized life has depended on the toil of animals, who, to quote St Basil, "bear, with us, the heat and burden of the day";[24] and much has depended, and continues to depend, on animal deaths, in many cases before there has been time to develop the faculties proper to their kind, and often in unspeakable conditions. In the past, certainly, the system often gave some sort of dignity at least to some domesticated animals; and the use of wild species was sufficiently restrained as to be sustainable and to avoid too drastic damage to wilderness. But now two factors have intensified the time-honoured human use of nature: on the one hand, an increase in what the World Bank calls "absolute poverty" and, on the other, the extension, usually driven by the profit motive, of economic activity on the part of corporations and governments to the furthest fastnesses of the globe. (Of these developments both pressures from the timber companies and the project to ranch butterflies in the Arfak Mountains are but tiny manifestations.) Population growth has exacerbated the problems caused by poverty, but as it is itself plausibly a product of poverty, there is no need to supplement the inventory of underlying problems in its regard. And as, according to the usual critique of developmentalists, poverty is itself a function of the global system of power relations, all the indications are that here we have the underlying cause, at least to the extent that the critique is to be credited.

If it is now added that human actions and policies *vis-à-vis* non-human creatures are no more inevitable or indispensable than most inter-human relations are in their present form, it becomes extremely difficult to resist the conclusion that these actions and policies often also amount to exploitation, i.e., not just use but unjustified use. The power system which pervades inter-human relations extends also to inter-species relations, and does not become any the more excusable in the latter connection. (I have hitherto avoided the use of "exploitation" in connection with treatments of nature, as it has both a morally neutral and a morally pejorative sense; but I am now in a position to use the term without the need to qualify it.) And further, the processes which issue in exploitation within human relationships are identical with those which issue in unacceptable treatments of the natural world.

But if this is correct, then the critique adhered to by most developmentalists must itself be supplemented. For oppression turns out to be manifested not only in capitalism, sexism and racism, but also in anthropocentrism and human chauvinism. The iceberg of exploitation is even larger beneath the surface than is usually imagined; and, all along, it is habituating us to legitimize oppression, and to become hardened to it. Yet oppression is often a seamless whole, at least psychologically; when a callous disregard sets in towards any one class, the possibility opens up of the parallel unquestioning acceptance of oppression at any other level. And this symbolic factor is yet another reason for supplementing and developing the critique of the developmentalists.

There is, indeed, a close analogy of the case presented for environmentalists to broaden their critique of oppression beyond anthropocentrism alone; the developmentalist critique needs to be broadened similarly so as to include anthropocentrism. The reasons for this include the requirement to be consistent with one's own principles, the recognition that both underdevelopment and ecological problems have a common source and are causally interrelated, and the symbolic links between the different forms of oppression and, again, between the various campaigns which oppose it. A further reason would consist

in the requirements of justice. This reason has not till now been deployed, as there is a widespread view (held, for example, by John Rawls[25]) that non-human creatures fall outside the scope of justice. But to the extent that the concept of exploitation has been shown to be in place, the same will apply to the concept of justice; and if so, there is yet a further similarity between the reasons why environmentalists should support development and the reasons why developmentalists should support some non-anthropocentric version of environmentalism.

As the future of the forest is apparently at stake, as well as that of numerous butterflies, it would not follow outright that butterfly farming should be rejected. But if the case which I have been making stands up, then even in that instance the grounds of environmentalists for reluctance about farming butterflies should at least be taken seriously. Those grounds turn not only on the interests of human beings, but also on those of forest creatures including butterflies.

Author's Note

This chapter was presented as an address to the World Congress of Philosophy, Nairobi, in July 1991.

NOTES

1. The distinction between shallow and deep ecology movements was made by Arne Naess, in "The shallow and the deep long-range ecology movements. A summary." *Inquiry*, 16, 1973, pp. 95-100.

2. Ian Craven, "Profit for the poor", *Orbit*, 33, summer 1989, p. 15.

3. Jasper Zjilstra, "Rainforest reality," *Orbit*, 33, summer 1989, p. 16.

4. Such criticisms are made by Vandana Shiva in "Recovering the real meaning of sustainability," in David E. Cooper and Joy A. Palmer (eds), *The Environment in Question: Ethics and Global Issues*, London and New York: Routledge, 1992, pp. 187-93. But Shiva is also critical of the whole concept of sustainable development, a concept to

the defence of which both Nigel Dower and this chapter in different ways contribute.

5. Robin Attfleld, "Development: some areas of consensus," *Journal of Social Philosophy*, 17, 2, summer 1986, pp. 36-44.

6. See e.g., J. Baird Callicott, "Animal liberation: a triangular affair," *Environmental Ethics*, 2, 4, 1980, pp. 311-38. More recently Callicott's views have changed; see "Animal liberation and environmental ethics: back together again," in his *In Defense of the Land Ethic*, Albany, NY: State University of New York Press, 1989, pp. 49-59.

7. See Naess, op. cit.

8. Warwick Fox, "The Deep Ecology/ecofeminism debate and its parallels," *Environmental Ethics*, 11, 1, 1989, pp. 5-25.

9. Val Routley (now Plumwood) and Richard Routley (now Sylvan), "Human chauvinism and environmental ethics," in Don Mannison, Michael McRobbie and Richard Routley (eds), *Environmental Philosophy*, Canberra: Australian National University, 1980, pp. 96-189.

10. John Rodman, "The liberation of nature," *Inquiry*, 20, 1977, pp. 83-145.

11. See World Commission on Environment and Development, *Our Common Future* (the Brundtland Report), Oxford: Oxford University Press, 1987, ch. 4.

12. Thus Dave Foreman, interviewed by Bill Devall, "A spanner in the woods," *Simply Living*, 2, 12, n.d., p. 43.

13. Thus Murray Bookchin, "Thinking ecologically: a dialectical approach," *Our Generation*, 18, 2, 1987, pp. 3-40; Fox, op. cit., pp. 20f., reports finding similar sentiments in Bookchin, "Social ecology versus 'Deep Ecology'," *Green Perspectives: Newsletter of the Green Program Project*, summer 1987.

14. Fox, op. cit., quoting from Arne Naess, "Sustainable development and the deep long range ecological movement," published in *The Trumpeter*, 5, 4, 1988, pp. 138-42. Naess gives qualified support to sustainable development at p. 140, and stresses the priority of humanitarian action in face of the problem of hungry children on p. 141.

15. Robin Attfield, *The Ethics of Environmental Concern*, Oxford: Blackwell, and New York: Columbia University Press, 1983, pp. 179-82, also "Methods of ecological ethics," *Metaphilosophy*, 14, 3-4, 1983, pp. 195-208, and "Value in the wilderness," *Metaphilosophy*, 15, 3-4, 1984, pp. 289-304.

16. Naess, "Sustainable development and the deep long range ecological movement," op. cit.; see also Fox, op. cit., p. 6 and p. 21 n. 38.

17. David Pearce, Anil Markandya and Edward B. Barbier, *Blueprint for a Green Economy* (the Pearce Report), London: Earthscan, 1989, ch. 1.

18. Craven, op. cit.

19. Ramachandra Guha, "Radical American environmentalism and wilderness preservation: a Third World critique," *Environmental Ethics*, 11, 1, 1989, pp. 71-83.

20. E.g., in Peter Singer, *Animal Liberation: A New Ethic for Our Treatment of Animals*, London: Cape, 1976.

21. Routley and Routley, op. cit.

22. Rudolf Bahro, *From Red to Green*, London: Verso, 1984.

23. See Rodman, op. cit.

24. Cited in John Passmore, "The treatment of animals," *Journal of the History of Ideas*, 36, 1975. p. 198.

25. John Rawls, *A Theory of Justice*, Oxford: Oxford University Press, 1971, p. 512.

MAORI ENVIRONMENTAL VIRTUES

John Patterson

John Patterson has retired as senior lecturer in the School of Historical and Philosophical Studies at Massey University in New Zealand. His areas of interest are in Maori philosophy, Daoist philosophy, aesthetics, environmental ethics, and critical thinking. He is the author of Exploring Maori Values *(1992) and of* People of the Land: A Pacific Philosophy *(2000).*

Patterson uses Maori oral narratives to describe virtues in their tradition that delineate the place of humans in the natural world and their responsibilities and obligations to it. These environmental virtues are expressed in distinctively Maori concepts, all of which depict things in the environment as sharing a common ancestry and which demand virtues of respect and responsibility. The concept and practice of tapu, *for example, involve the idea that the world is not ours and that we need to be a certain sort of person in that world, one who embraces unconditional responsibilities of care and protection. Patterson argues that Maori virtues challenge the anthropocentrism of the West and that the Maori display a successful environmental virtue ethic that can give us insights into what is needed in the contemporary technological world.*

Maori Traditions and Maori Philosophy

The Maori were the first people to settle in New Zealand, arriving from the islands to the north some 1,000 years ago. They are closely related to the other Polynesian peoples of the pacific in language, culture, practices, and beliefs. Although until the fairly recent arrival of Europeans in New Zealand, Maori technology was simple, they have been quick to adapt European techniques and concepts to their needs, and now, after some two centuries of contact with Europeans, Maori manage to maintain a dynamic balance between traditional and technological living and thinking.

Despite their ability to adopt and adapt to European ways, Maori ethics is in important respects a traditional ethics. For example, the traditional narratives that encode central Maori environmental virtues are *tribal* traditions, varying significantly from tribe to tribe. In addition, they are *living* traditions — they have no

doubt changed in some respects in the last two centuries. While there is widespread interest among Europeans in the state of the Maori before they came into contact with Europeans, I want to point out that my interest is in the *living* traditions of the Maori, as found in the versions and interpretations of their traditions that are encountered *today*.

Maori traditions are also largely *oral* traditions, even today. Much has been written down, but a lot has not and may never be committed to paper.[1] What is more, the written versions have no special standing among Maori. Much no doubt will never be written down because the traditions are seen as being *tapu*. This concept is one of several distinctively Maori concepts that feature prominently in Maori environmental ethics, and which do not translate at all closely into English. Ideally, to come to understand any unfamiliar ethics we should come to understand the unfamiliar and possibly untranslatable concepts involved, and as a first step, we should try to familiarize ourselves with the typical contexts within which they are used. It is for this reason that I keep close to the narratives in exploring Maori environmental virtues. These narratives are regularly appealed to by Maori when ethical problems arise and provide living examples of the contexts in which concepts such as *tapu* are employed.

Although they are often or even typically presented in the form of historical narrative, Maori traditions also typically bear a range of *ethical* messages, and in particular as depicting the Maori *virtues*.[2] As should be expected, considering their role in expressing a living and complex environmental ethic, Maori traditional narratives can bear a range of rather different *interpretations*: they can be and are told in different ways to make different ethical points.

Finally, the historical and ethical aspects of Maori narrative are connected through the ethical importance to Maori of *ancestral precedent*. That is, the traditions relating to the deeds of the ancestors provide ethical models for behavior today.[3]

First Narrative: Rata and His Canoe

Here is the first of five brief narratives I wish to present, each of which contains elements of Maori environmental philosophy:

A man named Rata proposes to make a journey in order to avenge the death of his father, and needs a canoe in which to travel. He goes into the forest and fells a suitable tree, but neglects to recite the traditional *karakia* (incantations) to the forest god Tane-mahuta, seeking permission to take a tree. So, when he goes home after his day's work, the *kaitiaki* or spiritual guardians of the forest (in the form of birds) restore the felled tree to life, replacing all the wood-chips removed by Rata's axe. When he returns in the morning, Rata is amazed to find no sign of the log he prepared the day before. Again he fells the tree. Again at night the *kaitiaki* restore the tree. On the third day, after felling the tree yet again, Rata pretends to go

home but hides nearby. When the forest guardians start again to erect the fallen tree he comes out of hiding and upbraids them for interfering with his work. They respond by accusing him of taking a tree without obtaining permission from their master Tane-mahuta. Rata is overcome with shame. But the story has a happy ending, for Rata at least: he explains his project, and the *kaitiaki* realize that it is a worthy one. Instead of restoring the tree once more, they hollow it out and shape it into the canoe that Rata needs to avenge the death of his father.

Two distinguished Maori scholars comment on this narrative: Ranginui Walker says that the propitiatory rites ensure "that nature is not treated wantonly but with care and respect,"[4] and Te Rangi Hiroa comments that recognition of Tane's *parenthood* had to be made by Rata.[5] The forests are under the *mana* of a great god, and so are *tapu*. This *tapu* is enforced by agents appointed by Tane — the forest guardians of *kaitiaki*. In Maori tradition, Tane is ancestor of both trees and humans. Thus, the trees are (distant) cousins of the Maori. Maori are expected to respect Tane as their "godly" ancestor, and to respect trees as their kin and as children of Tane. The Rata narrative thus depicts a Maori view of the place of humans in the natural world: the environment is not simply a collection of resources to be exploited but a community of related beings, all of them linked to human beings by ties of kinship, all of them important in themselves, all of them needing protection (through *kaitiaki* or guardians) and demanding respect (through *tapu* and *karakia*).

Second Narrative: Tane Separates His Parents

In the beginning Papa the Earth Mother and Rangi the sky Father are close together in a loving embrace, so close that their children are cramped and unable to develop properly. A group of the children decide to separate their parents. After some of them have tried and failed, Tane places his head on his mother and his feet against his father and with the power of growth prizes his father up and away from his mother, admitting light into the world. This act allows Tane and his brothers to live their own lives fully, unencumbered by parental restriction. Nevertheless, Tane takes pity on his unadorned and unprotected parents, and proceeds to clothe his mother Papa the Earth with trees, plants, and birds, and to adorn his father Rangi the Sky with stars and comets, clouds and rainbows.

Here, early in the "creation" traditions, we find a tension in Maori environmental philosophy between the demands of kinship and the need for survival and growth. Although Tane breaks the intimate bonds of love that unite his parents so that he and his brothers can flourish, in return he takes responsibility for his parents' physical and aesthetic welfare by protecting and decorating them. Likewise, we are expected to take responsibility for the environment that nurtures us, to make sure that it is protected and enhanced. This concern is not only a matter of "negative" respect, of making sure that we do no harm. Indeed, as Tane discovered, we may well have to do harm to the environment in which we live, if we are to live at all well. Nonetheless, we are to interact in a positive and *creative* way, making up for the harm we do by enhancing the environment in appropriate ways, as Tane did with his parents.

Also, Tane's separation of earth and sky is not to be seen only as a historical event, over and done with. It must be constantly reenacted. That is, the very possibility of life and growth on the planet is seen as depending upon the children of Tane — the forests — continuing to separate earth and sky. Remove the forests, and the proper order of the world collapses. Here then is an up-to-date, familiar, and urgent message — that the forests must be protected — contained in the ancient traditions of the Maori.

Third Narrative: Tane and His Human Children

In order to produce the Maori people, Tane fashions a female being (Hine-ahu-one) from earth, breathes life into her, and mates first with her and later with their daughter Hine-titama. When Hine-titama discovers that her husband is also her father, she descends to the world of darkness (as Hine-nui-te-po). Tane follows her, but Hine tells him that she will dwell in the world of darkness and take care of their children after they have died, while Tane must return to the world of light and foster their living offspring.

This narrative illustrates the Maori virtues of *whanaungatanga* and *manaakitanga* — our obligations to support our kin. In particular it provides part of the traditional basis for the obligations we have toward our *environmental* kin. These obligations are, of course, one aspect of a two-way responsibility: our ancestors must foster us; we must foster them. Kinship obligations of respect and enhancement work in both directions.

Fourth Narrative: Tangaroa and His Brothers

One of the children of Rangi the sky Father, Tawhiri god of winds, becomes angry with his half-brothers who have deprived Rangi of his partner Papa. He therefore attacks them with his winds, causing great devastation (to forests, crops, etc.). One of the brothers, Tangaroa the ancestor of fishes, becomes angered when some of his children — the reptiles — desert him, seeking shelter from Tawhiri's onslaught in the forests of his brother Tane. He therefore attacks not Tawhiri, who caused his children to leave him, but Tane the god of forests.

It is appropriate in Maori thought for Tangaroa to take issue with Tane. Because the forests are under the *mana* of Tane, he is regarded as being responsible for everything that occurs in them, *whatever the cause.* This narrative points to a difference between Maori and Pakeha conceptions of responsibility. In Maori terms, we are often held to be responsible for states of affairs, that we have *not* brought about.[6] As a result, it is no use trying to evade our environmental responsibilities by claiming that we have not caused the present sorry state of the planet. In particular, if we are to claim any *mana* over our environment — and without *mana* we have no standing, no place, no access to "resources" — we must accept the associated, unconditional responsibilities of care and protection.

Fifth and Final Narrative: Tu and His Brothers

> Of the sons of Rangi and Papa, only Tu, the warlike ancestor of the Maori, succeeds in resisting the attacks of Tawhiri, and he in turn attacks his brothers for not supporting him against Tawhiri. He is described as killing and eating his brothers — the ancestors of trees, plants, and animals — thus, destroying their *tapu* and making them available for everyday use as food, timber and so on.

This narrative can be seen as licensing the Maori's use of the children of these brothers — the plants, birds, and fish — for food and other needs. Without this precedent, all of the children of the great gods, all of the animals and plants, would be highly *tapu* and therefore too dangerous to use. Because of Tu's actions, the *tapu* can now be removed by performing the ritual *karakia* laid down by Tu when he overcame the *mana* of his brothers. That is, by uttering the *karakia*, by reenacting Tu's recitation, his descendants can reenact his acts of desecration, can remove the *tapu* or godly *mana* from the food and materials they need. It was, of course, precisely this ritual reenactment that Rata omitted when he felled one of the children of Tane to make his canoe.

Respect for *Tapu* and *Mauri*

The concept and practice of *tapu* — as in the Rata narrative — involve the idea that *the world is not ours*. Although this idea is part of what some people mean when they say that the world is sacred,[7] the Maori concept is not exactly that of being "set apart" — we are *one with* the world in which we live, ultimately, on a Maori view. To respect *tapu* is thus an environmental *virtue*: rather than seeing a respect for *tapu* as a matter of

following rules, see it as *being a certain sort of person.* In Maori, the right to make use of the "resources" of the world in which one lives has to be established, and is conditional. The Tu narrative establishes the right in general terms, and kinship and *tapu* underlie those conditions.[8] We often need to be *reminded* of the need to respect the environment — that the world is not ours — both in general, and in particular cases — where part of the environment is imperiled, and where part of the world endangers us. The concept and practice of *tapu*[9] thus serve as constant reminders to the Maori that we must always respect the natural environment in which we live.

I want to emphasize the importance of *symbolism* in this exposition, and downplay the part of metaphysics. The narratives can be seen as *symbolic* statements of *ethical* messages rather than *literal* statements of *metaphysical* "truths."[10] The virtue of respect for *tapu* can thus be seen as respect for the *inherent worth* of all items in the environment, as being prepared to balance our customary *egocentric* position with an *ecocentric* one.

The environmental virtue of respect for all things is frequently expressed in terms of the concept of *mauri*. For example, the weaver Erenora Puketapu-Hetet says that she respects the material with which she weaves by giving another dimension to its *mauri* or life force, by making sure that what is produced is a thing of beauty, by trying to live in harmony with the natural world, by trying to be at one with the environment.[11] The carver Rangi Hetet says that the materials he uses are not simply materials — they have a spiritual nature, being descended from Tane. A carver should show respect for Tane by not carving in too flamboyant a manner; he should, of course, inject his own *mauri* into the work, but should do so for the sake of the work, not for his own sake. Hetet tries to use raw timber rather than milled timber, so as to be able to show respect by following the nature of character of the timber.[12]

This idea enters Maori tradition early in the "creation story," where *mauri* is represented as emerging from an original chaos — *Te*

Korekore.[13] The word *mauri* is commonly translated into English as "life force," but our examples suggest that, in the context of environmental virtue ethics, it is perhaps better thought of as "character" or "nature." However it is translated, the central idea here is that *all* things have a *mauri* — a life or nature or character of their own — which must be respected. This respect applies not only to obviously living things — humans, animals, plants — but also to such things as houses, villages, meetings, and rivers. Because everything has a *mauri*, which must be respected, nothing is to be regarded as a mere means to our ends. Use of a material, for example, must be justified — the product must be worthy of the material.

We should not, however, be coldly analytical here. Although on the account that we have so far, *mauri* and *tapu* seem to be distinct, no less an authority than John Rangihau considers that the words may be interchangeable.[14] We may, therefore, be wise to consider the messages relating to *mauri* and *tapu* as a whole. Personally, I tend to associate the idea of *tapu* with the negative or restrictive aspect — that other items in the world have not been put there for my benefit. Moreover, I associate the idea of *mauri* with the positive or permissive aspect — that my relations and interactions with other items in the world should be understanding, sympathetic, and creative — understanding of and sympathetic toward the nature or special character of each item, and dealing with it creatively.

Whanaungatanga

Another Maori ethical concept that features in an explanation of the traditional narratives is *whanaungatanga.* The term derives from *whanaunga*, meaning "relative" or "blood relation," and is now used to refer to the way in which kin should interact with each other.[15] As an environmental virtue, *whanaungatanga* highlights the point that to be destructive of the environment is inappropriate for environmental kin. And failure to provide necessary *protection* is environmentally hostile.

The other side of that coin is that kin should interact *creatively*, as illustrated by Tane decorating his parents. Of course, kin should not be destructive of one another; in addition, however, they should actively promote each other's interests. Thus, in relation to the environment, *whanaungatanga* reminds Maori to seek and implement ways of enhancing the welfare of the whole environment and all its members, rather than simply abstaining from harming them. Of course, destructiveness and wastefulness are environmental vices; however, simply to refrain from them is not enough. Just as those engaged in the crafts try to make creative use of their materials, all of us in all of our activities should do what we can to make the whole environment better, and in particular, do what we can to heal environmental injuries, whoever caused them.

Another Maori concept that features in the explanation of such narratives as Tane protecting and decorating his separated parents is *aroha.* Commonly translated as "love," this word expresses the ways in which kin should act and feel toward each other. If humans really are to see themselves as kin to the whole natural world, we should show the appropriate forms and degrees of *aroha* toward all natural items.

At this point, the skeptic is likely, and entitled, to recall some rather insipid or woolly ideas of "loving nature." There is, however, quite a range of concepts of love available here, not all of them woolly or insipid. For example, there is the hard-headed view that real love entails a willingness to sacrifice one's personal interests, even one's life, and this willingness is certainly a requirement of *aroha*, at least among close kin. Another quality that distinguishes *aroha* from the woollier varieties of "love of nature" is the fact that, traditionally, *aroha* is not a universal "right." There is a proverb to the effect that it has to be earned and reciprocated: "*Aroha mai, aroha atu*" — "Love toward us, love going out from us."[16] Although many Maori nowadays accept Christian ideas of universal love, and express it in terms of *aroha*, the idea that *aroha* has to be earned and repaid is also alive and well.[17]

This reciprocity and balance of *aroha* is prominent in the idea of Papa or Mother Earth. The idea of a two-way love between earth and humans forms a natural basis for an environmental philosophy. Our obligation to show *aroha* to Papa is based upon the *aroha* she shows to us, in feeding and sheltering us.[18]

Manaakitanga

When the children of Tangaroa seek refuge in Tane's forests, he is hospitable and generous toward them. These virtues are implicit in the Maori concept of *manaakitanga*.[19] The question of whether the children deserve or have a right to this generosity does not arise (although they will be expected to repay it if the occasion arises). The forests are under the *mana* of Tane; those who enter them are, therefore, under his *mana* and can expect to be treated well. If they are not received with the best of hospitality, that *mana* would immediately suffer.[20]

Just as Tane's *mana* over the forests requires him to *manaaki* or care for anyone who enters, or at least anyone who enters peacefully, without challenging his *mana*, if I am to claim *mana* over the environment in which I live, I am seen from a Maori point of view as responsible for the welfare of all creatures within that environment, within the sphere of my *mana*. A central theme of environmental ethics is the move away from the ridiculous and dangerous idea that "I" am the center of the universe. By exhibiting the virtue of *manaakitanga* in my dealings with my environment, I accept that others also have their place right here where I am, that my *mana* does not exclude theirs. Thus, environmental *manaakitanga* involves the idea that we should identify with our environmental kin, as parts of a larger whole and as children of common ancestors.

The important concept of *mana*, which underlies *manaaki*, features prominently in the narratives. The *mana* of an ancestor passes on to the descendants, other things being equal. To treat descendants with disrespect is, therefore, to trample on their *mana*, which is their ancestors' *mana*. Respect for *mana* is especially important when it is the *mana* of an *atua*, such as Tane,

because such *mana* amounts to *tapu*.[21] The behavior of the forest *kaitiaki* in the Rata narrative illustrates the place of *mana* in a Maori concept of environmental responsibility. All of us are responsible for the areas that come under our *mana* individually or collectively. To the Maori, that includes the lands and waters with which we are associated, and all their inhabitants and natural features.

Kaitiankitanga

I started with a narrative about *kaitiaki* or guardians. Traditionally, the *kaitiaki* of a place or resource are seen as having been appointed by whatever person, tribe, or being has the appropriate *mana*. Because forests come under the *mana* of Tane, he appoints the forest *kaitiaki*. Likewise, Tangaroa appoints *kaitiaki* for the seas. However, there will also be more local and often human *kaitiaki*: a particular fishing ground, for example, will have *kaitiaki* appointed from among the people who have traditional fishing rights. In all cases, the *mana* of the *kaitiaki* is, as it were, delegated. While to democratized Europeans the concept of a guardian might suggest a sort of authority and authoritarianism that is perhaps out of place in Western environmental philosophy, in Maori terms, environmental guardians both have and need to have *mana*. Without such *mana,* the forest *kaitiaki* would have been powerless against Rata. However, this *mana* does not have to be seen as an authority over a part of the environment so much as an authority over other beings in relation to that part of the environment.

Thus, although from a traditional Maori perspective, *kaitiakitanga* over the environment may not be open to outsiders, there is another sense in which all of us can be *kaitiaki* of the systems in which we live, work, and play. Rather than traditionally appointed guardians, we can be voluntary caretakers, individually and collectively. In this sense, *kaitiakitanga* is an environmental virtue that any of us can practice, daily. Indeed, it is a virtue that many do practice: all who take it upon themselves to care for ecosystems are practicing the environmental virtue of *kaitiakitanga*.[22]

Balance as an Environmental Virtue

If we attend only to distinctively Maori concepts such as *tapu, mana, manaakitanga, whanaungatanga*, and *kaitiakitanga*, we might overlook an important aspect of Maori environmental virtues — *balance*. Although there is no "important" Maori word for balance, the concept is central in Maori ethics and metaphysics (as in Chinese), and a concept of balance is built into the very structure of the Maori language.[23]

The idea of environmental balance is incorporated in many of the traditional narratives. At the beginning, there is a state of balance (e.g., Rangi and Papa united), but then something happens that upsets the balance (Tane separates them), which requires some new balancing action (Tane protects and decorates them). Thus, balance is presented, if only implicitly, as an environmental virtue in the interactions between Rangi and Papa and their children, and among the children. Seeking balance from a different point of view: rather than kill the parents, or leave them close together, Tane achieves a new balance in their separation. The children can thus grow and flourish, and the parents can continue to express their love for one another and for their children, although not in the way they used to. Among the children, balance is achieved, for example, each time the human children of Tu continue to overcome those of Tane, etc. (the plants and animals), but subject to balancing constraints of respect for the *tapu* of the descendants of the original children of earth and sky. It is always important in Maori thought and practice to recognize conflicting demands, and to devise procedures that restore balance when there is trouble. Of course, "restoring balance" is rarely a matter of returning precisely to the initial state; environmental balance is typically dynamic rather than static.

This emphasis on balance reflects a fundamental aspect of a Maori world view: the universe is seen as consisting of polar pairs — male and female, *tapu* and *noa* (common, available) light and dark, life and death, and so on. These pairs in themselves are neither good nor evil. There is no unattainable ideal state; the ideal in Maori ethics is not to stamp out one member of a polar pair and foster the other, but to seek an appropriate *balance* between the polar pairs.[24] Although there is no unconditional dualism in such a world, from any perspective there are likely to be items that are friendly and items that are hostile (as well as vast indifference). This situation is to be expected in terms of the natural properties of the items concerned, and is a contingent matter, perhaps even changeable.

This contingency influences the way I conceive of myself in relation to the environment. Mine is not the only valid perspective. While I am entitled through precedent and ritual to satisfy my needs, so too are others. Environmentally, this polar-complementary perspective encourages me to distinguish my needs from mere wants, and thus adopt an ecocentric view of the world. It contrasts with a dualistic perspective that divides the world into the good and the evil, and views hostile items as items to be eliminated. Maori environmental philosophy neatly avoids this unfounded and environmentally unfriendly idea.

Conclusions

The environment is seen in Maori tradition not simply as resources to be explored, but as a community of kin, other members of which are normally *tapu*, but which can be made available for justified use. This kinship between humans and the environment, as it is expressed in Maori traditions, has familiar parallels in science; the Maori traditions can thus be presented and interpreted as symbolic representations of ecological principles — the trees, for example, separate earth and sky and thus foster the proper development of all organisms, including humans.

The narratives also express a tension between the demands of kinship and the need for survival and growth. Our place in the world is a matter of *mana*. If we are to claim any *mana* over our environment — without which we have no place in it, and no access to "resources" — we must accept the associated strict or unconditional responsibilities of care and protection: we must respect the

environment positively or creatively. Non-tech-
nological peoples have always depended for their
survival on a detailed understanding (and
enforcement) of ecology. Maori environmental
ethics serves to remind us of this requirement, in
principle and in detail. Of course, for a short
period in Western history, technology seemed to
change all that, seemingly making us independent of our "environment," and permitting many
of us forgot the principles of ecology. We now
know that we must learn once more to live in
harmony with the whole natural world. The
Maori give us one insight (among many) of what
is needed, showing us a successful environmental
virtue ethic, alive and working in a contemporary
technological world.

If I were a Maori speaker and this paper were
a Maori *korero* or speech, I would be expected to
conclude with a *waiata* or song, that captures the
essence of what I have been saying. As it
happens, I am not and this conclusion is not.
Instead, I leave you with an image that recalls
Rata and his environmental significance. If you
are lucky enough to be in the right place at the
right time, in the remaining New Zealand forests,
you will be greeted by a mass of brilliant red
flowers lighting up the forest. These are the
flowers of Rata, in his present form as a forest
tree.[25] Knowing as we do the narrative about
Rata and his canoe, and understanding as we do
its environmental significance, these flowers
remind us of the ways in which, according to
Maori tradition and practice, we should relate to
the other creatures in the world in which we live.

Glossary[26]

aroha: love, pity
Atu: away from the speaker
Atua: god, supernatural
Hine-ahu-one: Earth-formed maid
Hine-nui-te-po: Great daughter of darkness
Hine-titama: daughter of Tane and Hine-ahu-one
kaitiaki: guardian
kaitiakitanga: guardianship
karakia: prayer, incantation
korero: speech

mai: toward the speaker
mana: influence, power
manaaki: entertain, befriend
manaakitanga: hospitality
mauri: life force, character
noa: free from tapu
Papa-tuanuku: Earth Mother
raahui: ban, reserve
rangatira: chief, leader
rangatiratanga: sovereignty
Rangi: Sky Father
Rata: the canoe builder, a forest tree
Tane-mahuta: god of trees and birds
Tangaroa: god of fishes
tapu: sacred, forbidden
Tawhiri-matea: god of winds and rain
Te Korekore: original void or chaos
Tu-mata-uenga: warlike ancestor of Maori
waiata: song
whanaungatanga: kinship solidarity

NOTES

1. The traditional narratives that feature in this
   paper, though, are all freely available in a number
   of published sources, the most convenient for the
   English reader being Antony Alpers, *Maori Myths
   and Tribal Legends* (Auckland: Longman Paul,
   1964). Maori language texts of the narratives presented below may be found in George Grey, *Nga
   Mahi a nga Tuupuna* (Wellington: A.H. & A.W.
   Reed, 1971), pp. 1-2 (Separation); pp. 2-4 (Tangaroa); pp. 4-5 (Tu); pp. 46-49 (Rata) and in John
   White, *The Ancient History of the Maori*
   (Wellingon: Government Printer, 1887), vol. 1,
   pp. 117-78 (Tane and Hine). The versions that
   appear in this paper are in the author's words. For
   translations of key terms, see the glossary at the
   end of his paper.
2. The view that Maori ethics is best thought of as a
   virtue ethics is defended in Roy Perrett and John
   Patterson, "Virtue Ethics and Maori Ethics," *Philosophy East and West* 41 (1991): 185-202.
3. This relationship is reflected, for example, in the
   concept of *tika*, which translates into English variously as customary, correct, or lawful. Where tradition is the primary source of ethics, a distinction

between the customary and the lawful is not so obvious as it is elsewhere.

4. Ranginui Walker, "The Relevance of Maori Myths and Tradition," Michael King, ed., *Tihe Mauri Ora: Aspects of Maoritanga* (New Zealand: Methuen, 1978), p. 29.

5. Te Rangi Hiroa (Peter Buck), *The Coming of Maori* (Wellington: Maori Purposes Fund Board, 1950), p. 455.

6. John Patterson, "A Maori Concept of Collective Responsibility," in Graham Oddie and Roy Perrett, eds., *Justice, Ethics and New Zealand Society* (Auckland: Oxford University Press, 1992), pp. 20-22.

7. Indeed, *tapu* is the standard word for "sacred" in Maori Christianity.

8. Compare a familiar (if challenged) interpretation of Hebrew and Christian traditions, where the world can be seen as being under our dominion, to use as we see fit.

9. And the associated concept and practice of *raahui*.

10. Detailed examples of ethical interpretation of one Maori "metaphysical" concept are provided in John Patterson, *Exploring Maori Values* (Palmerston North: Dunmore Press, 1992), pp. 28-33.

11. Erenora Puketapu-Hetet, *Maori Weaving* (Auckland; Pitman, 1989).

12. Rangi Hetet, interview in Darcy Nicholas, ed., *Seven Maori Artists* (Wellington: Government Printer, 1986), p. 29.

13. Maori Marsden, "God, Man and Universe: A Maori View," in Michael King, ed., *Te Ao Hurihuri: The World Moves On* (New Zealand: Hicks Smith and Methuen, 1977), p. 147.

14. John Rangihau, "Learning and *Tapu*" in King, *Te Ao Hurihuri*, p. 11.

15. Perhaps *whanaungatanga* is a rather recent term, as it does not appear in some dictionaries. Nevertheless, it is given a central place by contemporary writers such as Rangimarie Rose Pere, *Ako, Concepts and Learning in the Maori Tradition* (Hamilton: Department of Sociology, University of Waikato, 1982). See also Joan Metge, "*Te Rito o te Harakeke*: Conceptions of the *Whaanau*," *Journal of the Polynesian Society* 99 (1990): 55-92.

16. T.S. Karetu, A.E. Brougham, and A.W. Reed, *Maori Proverbs* (Auckland: Reed Methuen, 1987), p. 61.

17. Tilly Te Koingo Reedy, "The Maori in the Future: A Woman's View," in *He Maataapuna: Some Maori Perspectives* (Wellington: New Zealand Planning Council, 1979), p. 47.

18. Again we do not have to take the narratives as literal and metaphysical — they can be taken as symbolic expressions of ethical messages. As in the case of the Gaia hypothesis, we do not literally have to believe that Papa has *feelings* of *aroha* towards us; only that she (or "she") behaves (or "behaves") in an appropriate way.

19. They are also implicit in the idea of *rangatiratanga*, the qualities shown by a *rangatira* or leader.

20. Lao Tzu: "Those who are good I treat as good. Those who are not good I also treat as good. In so doing I gain in goodness" — D.C. Lau, trans., *Lao Tzu: Tao Te Ching* (London; Penguin, 1963), chap. 49. A Maori parallel might run: "Those who have *mana* I *manaaki*; those who do not have *mana* I also *manaaki*; in so doing I gain in *mana*."

21. A proverb: "*Ko te tapu te mana o nga atua* — Tapu is the *mana* of the spiritual powers" — Moana Jackson, *The Maori and the Criminal Justice System: He Whaipanga Hou — A New Perspective* (Wellington: Department of Justice, 1988), p. 43.

22. In these days of catastrophic human overpopulation we might adopt environmental *kaitiakitanga* as a substitute for *reproducing*. Rather than trying to gain fulfillment through bringing up human offspring, we might chose to become foster parents of *nonhumans,* taking responsibility for the well-being of parts of the ecosystems which sustain us.

23. A proverb we have already met — *Aroha mai, aroha atu* — illustrates this feature of balanced sentence construction in Maori. For an extended example of the place of balance in Maori ethics, see John Patterson, "*Utu*, Revenge and *Mana*," *British Review of New Zealand Studies* 2 (1989): 51-61.

24. Roughly, an Aristotelian rather than a Platonic ethics, a Chinese rather than a European one.

25. *Metrosideros umbellata*, the southern rata, and *M. Robusta*, the northern rata.

26. These glosses are a rough guide only. Many of these words do not translate at all accurately into simple English phrases, and some of them are used rather differently by different speakers.

ON ENVIRONMENTAL LAW

Michael Traynor

Michael Traynor is a senior counsel in the Cooley Godward Litigation Department in San Francisco. He specializes in and has written numerous articles in law journals on intellectual property, internal corporate investigations, and product liability and risk management. Traynor is a past president of the American Law Institute and a member of the board of directors of the Environmental Law Institute. He is also past chair and president of the Sierra Club Legal Defense Fund (now called Earthjustice).

Traynor draws attention to widespread commitments by countries at the United Nations World Summit on Sustainable Development, held in Johannesburg in 2002, to develop policies for strengthening and enforcing environmental laws, for expanding public participation in decision-making, and for sketching a role for the judiciary in connecting environmental law and human rights. Traynor notes, however, that the U.S. refused to join most of the rest of the world in supporting many of the provisions that emerged from the summit. Traynor expresses optimism about the widely shared commitments of people throughout the world, including many Americans, to improving, sustaining, and saving the environment for future generations. But he also points to the difficulty of change when a powerful country such as the U.S. defies and rejects national and international movements to shape and implement policies for addressing serious problems such as global warming.

Many countries as well as some U.S. states recognize a constitutional human right to a healthful environment. But the federal government of the United States does not. Given restrictive trends in the federal courts, an anti-environmental president, and an unsympathetic Congress, it is barely conceivable that any branch of the U.S. federal government will soon recognize such a human right, or even a rudimentary constitutional right not to be poisoned.

By welcome contrast, judges from across the globe have affirmed their commitment "to spare no effort to free all of humanity, and above all our children and grandchildren, from the threat of living on a planet irredeemably spoilt by human activities." These forward-thinking judges convened in Johannesburg, South Africa, in August of 2002 at the Global Judges Symposium on

Sustainable Development and the Rule of Law. Their symposium preceded the United Nations World Summit on Sustainable Development in Johannesburg, which I attended as a representative of the Environmental Law Institute (ELI).

In many ways, the conceptual leadership demonstrated by the Global Judges outstripped the thinking at the summit. The judges readily acknowledged the connection between human rights and sustainable development and affirmed the need for an independent judiciary and judicial process to decide environmental disputes. They pointedly observed that it is the poor who suffer most from environmental deterioration and that there is a pressing need to strengthen the public's rights to enforce environmental laws. They called for expanded public participation in decision-making, help from the judicial system in environmental disputes, and open access to information.

As an American lawyer who has been an environmental advocate for more than forty years, I was inspired by the courageous, forthright, and innovative ideas of the Global Judges and by the possibility that they may lead to effective implementation in concrete cases. Judges from elsewhere in the world seemed surprisingly willing to envision a vital role for the judiciary in forging the link between environmental law and human rights. It seems the courts of the world may go well beyond what is achievable presently in the United States.

Had the delegates to the UN meeting been listening to the judges and acting in concert with them, the summit would have been a far more valuable exercise. Although the delegates achieved modest (and nonbinding) consensus on items such as controlling harmful chemicals, restoring depleted fish stocks, and protecting biodiversity, they failed to match the principled leadership of the Global Judges.

Most of the government leaders who attended the summit seemed to share a progressive spirit — with the notable exception of those representing the United States. President Bush elected not to attend the summit and conveyed the impression to many that he disdained it; the delegation he sent instead, led by Secretary of State Colin Powell, concentrated on protecting oil interests while undermining human rights.

For example, the United States refused to join Europe and most of the rest of the world in key proposed provisions of the consensus document, known as the Plan of Implementation. Instead, allying itself with China, Iran, Saudi Arabia, and a few other notable polluters, the U.S. delegation worked to defeat a specific target to increase the global share of renewable energy sources to at least 15 percent of the total by 2010. It only grudgingly agreed to a commitment to halve the number of people without safe drinking water and adequate sanitation by 2015 and linked that concession to its demands on energy policy. On such a basic issue as decent water and sanitation, the U.S. delegation thus used the prospect of alleviating continuing human misery and disease as a bargaining chip to sustain American consumption of oil and other nonrenewable fossil fuels.

The U.S. delegation did not stop there. It lobbied to delete a proposed statement calling for "public access to information, public participation in decision-making and access to justice." It also succeeded in diluting a proposed statement that would have acknowledged "the importance of the interrelationship between human rights promotion and protection and environmental protection for sustainable development." Instead, the Plan of Implementation now merely acknowledges "the consideration being given to the possible relationship between environment and human rights, including the right to development." The policymakers thus left access to information, public participation, citizen enforcement, and the development of an environmental human right primarily to judges and environmental advocates. Sadly, the Johannesburg summit took a backward step from the 1972 Stockholm Declaration that affirmed the fundamental right to "adequate conditions of life, in an environment of a quality that permits a life of dignity and well-being" and the 1992 Rio Declaration on Environment and Development that reaffirmed it.

The world leaders and official government delegations assembled at Sandton, an upscale suburb of Johannesburg that contains a convention center, office towers, and many elegant shops and restaurants. It might well have passed for a wealthy part of Houston, another city built on the extraction of riches from the earth. Under the rules of the assembly, each leader spoke for only a few minutes. Most followed the harmless formula of thanking South Africa for being a splendid host, agreeing that the world's environmental problems deserve serious attention, and expressing his country's dedication to resolving them. Although many speakers struck bland notes individually, together these became a crescendo of shared concern. Meanwhile, as the U.S. delegation maneuvered to defeat strong environmental commitments, including renewable energy sources and the reduction of agricultural subsidies, another malevolent force rumbled from a different direction through the booming voice of Zimbabwe President R.G. Mugabe.

A powerful speaker — adept at manipulating world opinion while advancing a repressive and violent regime — Mugabe spoke in no uncertain terms: "The multilateral programme of action we set for ourselves at Rio has not only been unfulfilled but it has also been ignored, sidelined and replaced by a half-baked unilateral agenda of globalisation in the service of big corporate interests of the North. The focus is profit, not the poor, the process is globalisation, not sustainable development, while the objective is exploitation, not liberation." He justified the "agrarian reform" ruthlessly underway in his country and said that "this fundamental question has pitted the black majority who are the right-holders, and, therefore, primary stakeholders, to our land against an obdurate and internationally well-connected racial minority, largely of British descent and brought in and sustained by British colonialism." Departing from his prepared text, he adlibbed with a message for Tony Blair: "Keep your England and let me keep my Zimbabwe." Mugabe's remarks received greater and more sustained applause from the official delegations and their guests than the remarks made by any other world leader.

The United States picked Secretary of State Colin Powell for the unenviable task of responding to Mugabe's challenge. Good soldier and decent man that he is, he did his duty. He pointedly noted that "In one country in this region, Zimbabwe, the lack of respect for human rights and rule of law has exacerbated" poverty, AIDS and other infectious diseases, drought, wasteful land use, and economic mismanagement, "to push millions of people toward the brink of starvation." He called for "sound economic policies that encourage entrepreneurs and that spur growth" and for "effective partnerships to unleash the talents and resources of developed and developing countries, civil society and the private sector." He referred specifically to the South African Housing Initiative "to help private contractors build 90,000 houses for a half million people in over the next five years" and to four

new "'signature' partnerships in water, energy, agriculture, and forests," including sustainable forestry in the Congo basin.

Secretary Powell identified a few constructive approaches that the United States is taking, and he and his key staff seemed to be the most open and helpful among the U.S. delegation. However, the delegation's overall retrograde tactics overshadowed its few good ideas for public/private partnerships and foreign aid. It is no surprise that in contrast to the thunderous applause for Mugabe, Powell had to endure the sustained jeers of both official representatives and unofficial guests from the rest of the world. The U.S. delegation's promotion of its nonrenewable energy agenda and its suppression of environmental values, together with the consequent hostility among people from other countries, enhanced Mugabe's strategy of playing the cards of race and colonial imperialism.

During one of the summit's NGO programs, which were held a long bus ride away from the main conference, environmental advocates invited by the ELI from various countries in Africa gave compelling reports on their efforts to address severe challenges. An advocate from Nigeria described his tribe's effort to withstand and confront one company's venture to exploit oil located under a reservoir of natural gas. Instead of using available technology to preserve the natural gas before reaching the oil, he reported, the company simply lit it on fire, thereby wasting the resource, polluting the air, and poisoning the lungs of nearby residents. Without the laws and enforcement we have in the United States — even though they are being undermined by our own government — the struggles that environmental advocates undergo in places such as Nigeria are comparatively fierce and extraordinarily difficult, and they require countervailing intelligence, spirit, and community action, as well as help from the courts.

What did the summit mean for business interests? They were visibly present, particularly at a concurrent meeting of the World Business Council on Sustainable Development that was attended by representatives of the oil, chemical,

utility, mining, and automobile industries. Green-
peace and an organization called Business Action
for Sustainable Development (created by the
World Business Council and the International
Chamber of Commerce) made an important
announcement about a novel collaboration on
climate protection. My impression is that many
business leaders and plant managers want to
achieve sound environmental results under intelligent laws that provide attainable and sustainable goals without undue governmental intrusion
and control. However, the lack of vision and
leadership from our own government and its
overall anti-environmental strategy make positive business action difficult. Without the impetus
of effective laws and enforcement, businesses
may find it difficult, particularly in today's
economy, to justify the investments and long-
range planning that could result in important
future gains but that do not result in an immediate profit reportable in a quarterly or an annual
report. Without leadership that helps people and
countries pull together and that improves and
unifies our own laws, the loose concept of "sustainable development" may simply become a
cover for free riders or a recipe for exploitation
cloaked by deceptive advertising.

Overall, my impressions were mixed. I came
away from Johannesburg feeling positively about
the widely shared commitment of people

throughout the world, including many judges,
lawyers, and business leaders, and many Americans, to improving, sustaining, and saving the
environment for our children and future generations. But I also came away more concerned than
ever about the harm to our environment as well as
to our security and economy that may occur from
the convergence of three powerful forces: first,
the current administration's misguided dedication
to nonrenewable resources and heavy agricultural
subsidies, and its arrogant disregard of environmental interests and human rights; second, the
increasing poverty and environmental distress
and, consequently, the increasing rage of much of
the rest of the world, as exemplified by dema-
gogues like Mugabe; and, third, the possibility
that as her temperature rises, Mother Earth will
go beyond floods and drought to demonstrate
how angry she is at being developed rapaciously
but not sustained.

With its unrivaled power and prosperity, the
United States is in a unique position to counter
these forces. It could provide global leadership
by setting an inspiring environmental example,
instead of undermining environmental protections. But until the Bush administration modifies
its approach, I am afraid that sustainable development, together with a universal right to a
healthful environment, will remain an elusive
goal.

STUDY QUESTIONS

1 According to Ramachandra Guha, what is deep ecology? What, if any, similarities and differences are there between deep ecology and the land ethic or ethical holism as described by Callicott in the previous chapter?

2 What objections does Guha raise to the version of deep ecology defended by American environmentalists? How does this differ from the versions of radical environmentalism in other cultural contexts such as Germany and India?

3 According to Guha, why has deep ecology become rooted in the specific context of American environmentalism? Why is it an inappropriate model to apply to the Third World? Do you agree? Why or why not?

4 Guha takes the debate between anthropocentrism and non-anthropocentrism to be too theoretical and to have little or no application in Third World countries. What is the basis for the disagreement that Eric Katz and Lauren Oechsli have with Guha on this issue?

5 According to Katz and Oecshli, what is problematic about anthropocentric approaches to the environment? Why are these problems particularly acute with respect to policies on the environment in Third World countries?

6 What do Katz and Oecshli mean when they claim that charges by Third World countries of imperialism on environmental policy are legitimate? What are their arguments for holding that non-anthropocentric approaches can avoid these charges and result in the formulation of effective policies?

7 How do Katz and Oecshli use their approach to answer what they take to be legitimate concerns raised by Guha about non-anthropocentrism? Is their answer convincing? Why or why not?

8 According to Robin Attfield, what are the areas of disagreement between environmentalists and developmentalists that tend to position them as opponents?

9 How does Attfield attempt to reconcile the tension between environmental ethicists and development theorists and policy-makers? Is he successful? Why or why not?

10 Could Attfield's bringing together of environmentalists and developmentalists result in formulating policies that both would support? How does Attfield answer this question? How would you? Defend your answers.

11 From what you learned through Maori traditional narratives in John Patterson's account, in what ways do Maori environmental virtues differ from Western values? Does Patterson's account lend support to Guha's claim that it is problematic to romanticize non-Western approaches and think of them as the same?

12 What is Patterson's argument for the claim that the Maori have successfully incorporated Maori environmental virtues in adapting to their increasingly technological world? Can we apply lessons about Maori environmental philosophy to environmental issues in other parts of the world? Why or why not?

13 Is Michael Traynor's approach to environmental issues anthropocentric or non-anthropocentric? Provide reasons for your answer.

14 What happened at the United Nations World Summit on Sustainable Development, held in Johannesburg in 2002, to make Traynor both optimistic and pessimistic with respect to progress on legislation to protect the environment?

15 Do you think that environmental policy needs to be shaped and implemented at the international level? What barriers stand in the way of this possibility? Are there arguments used by authors in this chapter that might be effective with respect to reaching consensus and achieving cooperation on environmental law? Defend your answer.

SUGGESTED READINGS

Barry, Brian. "Intergenerational Justice in Energy Policy." In *Energy and the Future*, edited by Douglas MacLean and Peter Brown. Lanham, MD: Rowman & Littlefield, 1983.

Castro, Fidel. *Tomorrow is Too Late: Development and the Environmental Crisis of the Third World.* Melbourne, AU: Ocean Press, 1993.

Crocker, David, and Toby Linden (editors). *The Ethics of Consumption: The Good Life, Justice, and Global Stewardship*. Lanham, MD: Rowman & Littlefield, 1998.

Douglas, Mary, Michael Thompson, and Marco Verwiij. "Is Time Running Out? The Case of Global Warming." *Daedalus*, v. 132, no. 2 (Spring 2003): 98-107.

Elliot, Robert (editor). *Environmental Ethics*. Oxford: Oxford University Press, 1995.

Grossman, Karl. "Environmental Racism." In *The "Racial" Economy of Science: Toward a Democratic Future*, edited by Sandra Harding. Bloomington, IN: Indiana University Press, 1993.

Hargrove, Eugene C. *Foundations of Environmental Ethics*. Englewood Cliffs, NJ: Prentice Hall, 1999.

Lahar, Stephanie. "Ecofeminist Theory and Grassroots Politics." *Hypatia*, v. 6, no. 1 (Spring 1991): 28-45.

Leopold, Aldo. "The Land Ethic." In *A Sand County Almanac: And Sketches Here and There*. New York, NY: Oxford University Press, 1949.

Nickel, James W., and Eduardo Viola. "Integrating Environmentalism and Human Rights." *Environmental Ethics*, v. 16 (1994): 265-73.

Schrader-Frechette, Kristin. "Practical Ecology and Foundations for Environmental Ethics." *The Journal of Philosophy*, XCII 9 (December 1995): 621-35.

Shiva, Vandana. "Colonialism and the Evolution of Masculinist Forestry." In *The "Racial" Economy of Science: Toward a Democratic Future*, edited by Sandra Harding. Bloomington, IN: Indiana University Press, 1993: 303-314.

——. "Development, Ecology and Women." In *Staying Alive: Women, Ecology and Development*. New York, NY: Zed Books, 1988.

Warren, Karen. "The Power and the Promise of Ecological Feminism." *Environmental Ethics*, v. 12 (1990): 125-46.

Westra, Laura. *Living in Integrity: A Global Ethic to Restore a Fragmented Earth*. Lanham, MD: Rowman & Littlefield, 1998.

ACKNOWLEDGEMENTS

"Why Abortion is Immoral" by Don Marquis in *The Journal of Philosophy*, v. 86, no. 4, April 1989: 183-202. Reprinted with permission of the publisher and Don Marquis.

"Sensationalized Philosophy: A Reply to Marquis's 'Why Abortion is Immoral'" by Ann E. Cudd in *The Journal of Philosophy*, v. 87, no. 5, 1990: 262-264. Reprinted with permission of the publisher and Ann E. Cudd.

"The Importance of Ontology for Feminist Policy Making in the Realm of Reproductive Technology" by Susan Sherwin in *Canadian Journal of Philosophy*, Supplementary Volume 28, 2003: 273-295. Reprinted with permission of the publisher.

"In New Tests for Fetal Defects, Agonizing Choices" by Amy Harmon, *The New York Times*, June 20, 2004, Section 1, Column 1, p. 1 (Sunday Late Edition). Reprinted with permission of the publisher.

"A History of Governmentally Coerced Sterilization: The Plight of Native American Woman" by Michael Sullivan DeFine in *Native American Political Issues* (May 1, 1997), <http://www.geocities.com/CapitolHill/9118/mike2.html>.

"Reproductive Health and Research Ethics: Hot Issues in Argentina" by Florencia Luna in *Cambridge Quarterly of Healthcare Ethics*, v. 13, 2004: 267-274. Reprinted with permission of the publisher.

"Equality and Efficiency as Basic Social Values" by Michael Stingl in *Efficiency Versus Equality: Health Reform in Canada*. Edited by Michael Stingl and Donna Wilson. Halifax: Fernwood, 1996:7-19. Reprinted with permission of the author.

"Euthanasia: The Way We Do It, the Way They Do It" by Margaret Battin in *Journal of Pain and Symptom Management*, v. 6, no. 5, 1991: 298-305. Copyright © 1991 by the US Cancer Pain Relief Committee. Reprinted with permission of Elsevier Science.

"The Instability of the Standard Justification for Physician-assisted Suicide" by Thomas A. Cavanaugh in *Cambridge Quarterly of Healthcare Ethics*, v. 10, no. 1, Winter 2001:103-109. Reprinted with permission of the publisher.

"Unspeakable Conversations" by Harriet McBryde Johnson, New York Times, Sunday, February 16, 2003, Sunday: Late edition, Final, Section 6, p. 50, Column 1. Reprinted with permission of the publisher.

"Dementia, Critical Interests, and Euthanasia" by Nathan Brett. Reprinted with permission of the author.

"Women and Pornography" by Ronald Dworkin in *New York Review of Books*, October 21, 1993: 36-42. Copyright © 1998 NYREV, Inc. Reprinted with permission of the publisher.

"Feminist Anti-Pornography Struggles: Not the Church, But Maybe the State" by Marvin Glass. Reprinted with permission of the author.

"Morality, Censorship, and Discrimination" by Heather MacRae in *Social Politics*, v. 10, no. 3, Fall 2003: 314-345. Reprinted with permission of the publisher.

"A Relational Critique of the Right to Privacy: The Case of Pornography and the Internet" by Alison Minea and Christine Koggel. Reprinted with permission of the authors.

"Public Response to Racist Speech: Considering the Victim's Story" by Mari J. Matsuda in *Words that Wound: Critical Race Theory, Assaultive Speech, and the First Amendment* by Mari J. Matsuda, Charles R. Lawrence III, Richard Delgrado and Kimberle W. Crenshaw. Boulder: Westview, 1993: 17-51.

"All Animals Are Equal" by Peter Singer in *Animal Liberation*. New York: Random House, 1990: 1-9, 17-21, 159-164. Reprinted with permission of the author.

"The Case for Animal Rights" by Tom Regan from *The Case for Animal Rights*. University of California Press, 1985 (excerpts as printed in Singer's *In Defence of Animals*. Blackwell, 1985). Reprinted with permission of the publisher and Peter Singer.

"Vegetarianism and Virtue: Does Consequentialism Demand Too Little?" by Nathan Nobis in *Social Theory and Practice*, v. 28, no. 1, January 2002: 135-156. Reprinted with permission of the publisher and Nathan Nobis.

"Your Daughter or Your Dog? A Feminist Assessment of the Animal Research Issue" by Deborah Slicer in *Hypatia*, v. 6, no. 1, Spring 1991: 108-124. Reprinted with permission of the publisher.

"The Conceptual Foundations of the Land Ethic" by J. Baird Callicot from *Companion to A Sand County Almanac*, 1987. Reprinted by permission of The University of Wisconsin Press and J. Baird Callicot.

"Radical American Environmentalism and Wilderness Preservation: A Third World Critique" by Ramachandra Guha in *Environmental Ethics*, v. 11, Spring 1989: 71-83. Reprinted with permission of the author.

"Moving Beyond Anthropocentrism: Environmental Ethics, Development, and the Amazon" by Eric Katz and Lauren Oeshsli in *Environmental Ethics*, v. 15, Spring 1993: 49-59. Reprinted with permission of the author.

"Development and Environmentalism" by Robin Attfield in *International Justice and the Third World*. Edited by Robin Attfield and Barry Wilkins. London: Routledge, 1992: 151-168. Reprinted with permission of the publisher.

"Maori Environmental Virtues" by John Patterson in *Environmental Ethics*, v. 16, Winter 1994: 397-409. Reprinted with permission of the publisher and John Patterson.

"On Environmental Law" by Michael Traynor in *Daedalus*, v. 132, no. 3,Summer 2003: 116- 119. Reprinted with permission of the publisher.

The editor of the book and the publisher have made every attempt to locate the authors of copyrighted materials or their heirs and assigns, and would be grateful for information that would allow them to correct any errors or omissions in a subsequent edition of the work.